Texas Women

Texas Women

THEIR HISTORIES, THEIR LIVES

EDITED BY

Elizabeth Hayes Turner

Stephanie Cole

Rebecca Sharpless

❀   ❀   ❀

The University of Georgia Press   *Athens and London*

© 2015 by the University of Georgia Press
Athens, Georgia 30602
www.ugapress.org
Set in Minion Pro by Graphic Composition, Inc., Bogart, Georgia
Printed and bound by Sheridan Books, Inc.
The paper in this book meets the guidelines for
permanence and durability of the Committee on
Production Guidelines for Book Longevity of the
Council on Library Resources.

Most University of Georgia Press titles are
available from popular e-book vendors.

Printed in the United States of America
15 16 17 18 P 5 4 3

Library of Congress Cataloging-in-Publication Data
Texas women : their histories, their lives / [edited by]
Elizabeth Hayes Turner, Stephanie Cole, Rebecca Sharpless.
pages cm
Includes bibliographical references and index.
ISBN 978-0-8203-3744-9 (hardback : alkaline paper) —
ISBN 0-8203-3744-7 (hardcover : alkaline paper) —
ISBN 978-0-8203-4720-2 (paperback : alkaline paper) —
ISBN 0-8203-4720-5 (paperback : alkaline paper)
1. Women—Texas—History. 2. Women—Texas—Social conditions.
3. Women—Texas—Biography. I. Turner, Elizabeth Hayes. II. Cole, Stephanie, 1962–
III. Sharpless, Rebecca.
HQ1438.T4T58 2015 305.409764—dc23
2014015923

British Library Cataloging-in-Publication Data available

We dedicate this volume to those
who pioneered and promoted the field of Texas women's history:

To Annie Doom Pickrell, who wrote Pioneer Women in Texas *(1929)*

To Ruthe Winegarten and Governor Ann Richards,
who spearheaded the first expansion of Texas women's history

To Nancy Grayson, who brought Texas into the series,
Southern Women: Their Lives and Times,
at the University of Georgia Press

Contents

Part Two: 1880–1925

Part Three: 1925–2000

Preface

ELIZABETH HAYES TURNER, STEPHANIE COLE,

AND REBECCA SHARPLESS

❀ ❀ ❀

Texas Women: Their Histories, Their Lives offers a collection of biographies and composite essays of Texas women, contextualized to include subjects that reflect the enormous racial, class, and religious diversity of the state. Taken as a whole, this volume offers significant insights into the complex ways that Texas's position on the margins of the United States has shaped a particular kind of gendered experience there. These essays also demonstrate how the larger questions in U.S. women's history are answered or reconceived in the Lone Star State. The book yokes Texas to its neighbor states to the east, placing it firmly in the South as well as the Southwest. As members of the Southern Association for Women Historians, we freely acknowledge the ongoing debate over whether Texas is southern or western and believe that the answer is simply that Texas is both. At times, it is also midwestern, Mexican, western, and American. The essays in this volume show the complexity of Texas women's experiences, heavily influenced by Spanish law as well as by the immigration of Anglo and African American people, mostly from the southern United States.

Beginning with the Spanish colonial era, the essays examine the ways that women used the contours of their time and place and the relationships they established to stretch the boundaries of their lives. Colonial Texas established the region's multicultural character, as European and African women joined Native Americans in populating the northern reaches of the Spanish empire. During the eighteenth and nineteenth centuries, shifts in government provided opportunities for some (but not all) women to resist oppression yet caused others, especially Indian and slave women, to lose ground. As the twentieth century brought greater access to education and civil rights, the number of women who claimed access to power grew, even as membership in the influential group diversified.

In uncovering Texas women's histories, many of the essays make creative use of the sources to explore topics for which there are few records. Others probe issues that have received scant attention in the past, such as businesswomen at the turn of the century or female rodeo contestants who used gender stereotypes to shape their roles as cowgirls. Still other essays offer new insights into oft-studied topics in women's history but include divergent approaches: the origins of the women's rights movement; the ambiguous messages that elite nineteenth-century women received in college; the courageous ambitions of those who at the turn of the twentieth century found paths to politics, medicine, literature, art, and history. Early twentieth-century topics receive fresh interpretations and new histories, including the struggle by women to control the implementation of the Sheppard-Towner Act or the influence of Latinas in communities such as Laredo, San Antonio, and Dallas. Mid- to late-twentieth-century subjects include well-known figures such as Oveta Culp Hobby, Casey Hayden, Barbara Jordan, Hermine Tobolowsky, and Mae Jemison, but the biographies offered here provide unique analyses. The volume closes with a personal reminiscence by noted historian Paula Mitchell Marks, whose views of the changing history of Texas women offer a retrospective as well as an invitation toward future explorations.

This collection had its intellectual beginnings in 2006 at the Southern Conference on Women's History sponsored by the Southern Association for Women Historians at the University of Maryland, Baltimore County. The intellectual atmosphere of that meeting sharpened our senses and honed our desire to create a volume of essays on Texas women. Over breakfast in the cafeteria, the three of us put our heads together and realized that well-known historians of the Lone Star State had produced enough new scholarship to create a substantial volume. Moreover, graduate students and independent scholars were working on additional projects detailing the lives of Texas women. It seemed a propitious time to approach the University of Georgia Press to suggest a volume for what would become their series on Southern Women: Their Lives and Times. We spoke at length with Professor Elizabeth Anne Payne of the University of Mississippi, who along with her coeditors, Martha Swain and Marjorie Julian Spruill, had shepherded to completion the press's two volumes on Mississippi women. Payne encouraged us to pursue a Texas volume and urged us to speak with editor in chief Nancy Grayson, who heartily agreed that it would be a welcome addition to the growing collection of women's histories in the southern states.

With that endorsement, we sallied forth in pursuit of a collection of essays on Texas women's history. In February 2009, Rebecca Sharpless organized our conference, Texas Women/American Women, at Texas Christian University.

A wide array of scholars attended, including many of the contributors to this volume. Elizabeth Hayes Turner gave the keynote address, and Juliana Barr of the University of Florida, Laura Edwards of Duke University, and Marjorie Julian Spruill of the University of South Carolina discussed historiographic trends, contextualizing Texas women's history in the larger scope of southern and American history. Under the guidance of Stephanie Cole, conferees then divided into working groups to brainstorm topics and develop large working lists that ultimately shaped this book. The essays here are designed to speak to those trends while spanning time, space, and ethnicity.

From this wide-angled beginning, we sought contributions that were mostly biographical in nature, at least in the era after women's activism made such biographies possible. We prioritized an analytical approach. Grounded in primary sources, these essays look at individual women not only for what they did but also to explain why their actions mattered to the larger society. In some cases, groups of women acted in concert rather than as individuals, and those essays focus on the larger gatherings. Although not every group could be represented as extensively as one might hope, the women herein comprise a cross-section of Texas society. The essays are arranged chronologically in three sections, with breaks at 1880 and 1925.

As historians, we owe a large debt to previous scholarship. But because of that scholarship, this volume differs from others in the Southern Women: Their Lives and Times series that sought to recover a women's past that had long been ignored. Some volumes in the series stand as the first published collections of essays on women's history for their states. Such was not the case here: Texans' long-standing enthusiasm for their history meant that the state found early supporters for women's history, and the first academic collection of essays on Texas women's history was published more than two decades ago. At the same time, theoretical changes in U.S. women's history have stimulated historians of Texas women to expand their arguments, sources, and perspectives. Dozens of books and articles, on subjects as wide-ranging as early Indian diplomatic relations and the politics of the Equal Rights Amendment, reflect that influence. As a result of both threads—the state's appetite for its own history and the dramatic developments in professional women's history—Texas women's history now stands at an important threshold. Although much remains to be done, there is a need to acknowledge the research and writing that Texas women's historians have produced as well as how much the written record owes to national scholarship on women and gender and to Texas's distinctive history.

A unique context thus shapes this volume. On one hand, the authors have uncovered or reinterpreted the lives of some of the most important Texas women and some of the women least well-known in the Lone Star State—until now. On the other hand, some of the state's better-known women do not appear. Readers should not construe the absence of Emma Tenayuca, Ann Richards, and Lady Bird Johnson as either a political statement or a lapse in knowledge on the part of the editors. Rather, the focus on current scholarship meant that when desirable subjects had solid interpretations published elsewhere, those subjects were omitted on the grounds that there was no need for repetitive portrayals. The goal was to offer a useful source for those readers seeking the roots of women's history in the Southwest. We hope that both the content and the silences in this volume will provide an imaginative impetus for scholars embarking on future research in Texas women's history.

Acknowledgments

Texas Christian University generously provided facilities and underwriting for our conference, and Erma and Ralph Lowe Professor of History Gregg Cantrell was instrumental in getting it off the ground. TCU and the Department of History at the University of Texas at Arlington underwrote printing and mailing expenses. The Department of History at the University of North Texas provided release time to enable us to work on the book. At the University of Georgia Press, former editor in chief Nancy Grayson; her successor, Mick Gusinde-Duffy; director Lisa Bayer; and assistant acquisitions editor Beth Snead guided the book through the travails of editing and proofreading. Two anonymous readers reviewed the entire manuscript and saved us from multiple infelicities. To all of these editorial midwives, we give thanks. Last, we thank Gregg Cantrell, Tom Charlton, and Al Turner for their indulgence and understanding while we spent hours emailing, editing, correcting, proofreading, and indexing—in other words, birthing this collaborative endeavor. To all, we give our heartiest appreciation.

COUNTIES

1. Brazoria
2. Colorado
3. Fort Bend
4. Gonzales
5. Grimes
6. Harris
7. Harrison
8. Lavaca
9. Liberty
10. Rusk
11. Tyler

0   50   100   200 Miles

Texas Women

Part One

1600–1880

STEPHANIE COLE

In 1690, an expedition of Spanish soldiers and Franciscan missionaries crossed the Rio Grande for the first time, intent on establishing a settlement. Over the course of the next three centuries in the territory that would eventually become known as Texas, thousands followed them, sometimes on military quests to subdue the territory or plunder its assets but increasingly often to settle. The shifts in governing authority that accompanied these migrations, along with economic development and an unsettled social order, occasionally brought women in Texas a measure of autonomy uncommon in the eighteenth and nineteenth centuries. But such opportunities were unevenly distributed and declined over time. Once Anglo-American control supplanted Mexican hegemony and most Indians were pushed out or killed, signs of women's independence were harder to find, even for those of wealth and privilege. Frontier conditions prompted the exploitation of all women's labor and especially that of enslaved women. Whereas once women in Texas enjoyed a measure of independence, by the late antebellum period, most lived lives as circumscribed as those of other southern women, and the Civil War and emancipation did little to change that. Some women continued to play important economic roles throughout the nineteenth century, but their influence in the public sphere narrowed.

Women who lived in Texas during the initial years of Spanish colonization enjoyed perhaps higher status than at any later period. Between 1690 and 1780, Spain's footprint in Texas was light, both because of its own hedged commitment—other parts of the empire commanded more resources than did its northernmost province—and as a consequence of the powerful and persistent resistance of the native inhabitants. As one governor put it in the late 1770s, in an "immense desert country," there were only San Antonio, a "villa without order," and "two presidios, seven missions and an errant population of scarcely 4,000 of both sexes." Indians were far more numerous, including Caddos in the eastern part of the territory, Apaches in the western half, and newly arrived Comanches and Wichitas in the north. Though no native group in Texas offered women a political voice, native military dominance meant that Indian women who did not live in missions had more freedom of movement than did women in Spanish settlements and were recognized for both economic and diplomatic contributions. For women within the confines of San Antonio, however, the Spanish legal code, Las Sieta Partidas, offered significant protection. Unlike their English counterparts, courts in New Spain guarded free women's property rights and helped enslaved women purchase their freedom.

The multiple shifts in political and military power that marked the region between 1820 and 1865 were seldom good for women regardless of race or status, though a few found maneuvering room in the frequent periods of uncertainty. In the 1820s, having recognized the shortcomings of the mission system for securing control of the region and fearing American encroachment, the Spanish contracted with several *empresarios* to organize settlers from the United States and Europe. These settlers found themselves with a new government after Mexico won its independence from Spain in 1821, and their numbers grew steadily, reaching 21,000 by 1834. After Texans had their own revolution and created the Republic of Texas in 1836, the number of American residents increased to 30,000 Anglos and 5,000 slaves. Annexation to the United States in 1845 brought a veritable onslaught of settlers, and the white population reached 102,000, with an additional 38,000 slaves by 1847. Not surprisingly, men dominated among those who came by choice, as the appeal of new economic opportunities or of the escape from a bad marriage were often irresistible. The resulting shortage of women offered less advantage than we might assume, however, as women needed men to survive, and abandonment and abuse were a fact of many women's lives. Still, both the republic and state constitutions retained much of the Spanish civil law that governed property rights. In South Texas, women played an important role in bridging the divide between Mexican and Anglo cultures. As the ranching economy expanded there, so, too, did women's influence.

For African American women, these shifts in power were less positive. Though southern migrants to Texas had initially promised the Mexican government that they would convert to Catholicism and obey Mexican laws restricting slavery, they repudiated such promises in favor of pursuing cotton profits. As early as 1820, enslaved women—including Tivi, a runaway who believed that crossing the Sabine River into Spanish Texas rendered her free—eventually secured freedom by escaping into Mexico. But the vast majority of enslaved women could not run away and thus found themselves the reproductive building blocks of a cotton empire. For this group, statehood—and its corollary, increased migration—only made matters worse. When Texas seceded in 1861, one-third of Texans were enslaved, half of them women.

The economic expansion financed by enslaved women's labor benefited women in slaveholding families, though not as much as slaveholding men. Antebellum Texas law mirrored that of other southern states, with only vestiges of Spanish property rights remaining in the protection of wives' claim to community property. Wealthy white women may have experienced less abandonment and more comfort, but their lives were something of a gilded cage. A strict patriarchal social order dictated marriage, children, and a decorative life that gave witness to elite men's honor and virility. Extraordinary wealth and a secure social position meant that Sallie McNeill, granddaughter of Levi Jordan, one of the largest slaveholders in the state, could circumvent part but not all of that equation. Still, elite privilege and white supremacy benefited slaveholding women, and thus most women upheld the gender roles that underwrote class and racial hierarchies. Although secession led directly to a long and costly war, they did not repudiate Texas's decision to leave the Union, perhaps because they acknowledged that the reason given publicly—defense of the institution of slavery—served them as well. In any event, white women in antebellum Texas seldom denied men's right to make such decisions. Harriet Perry, whose husband joined the Confederate Army in 1862, sought to leave decisions in his hands even as his absence and the necessities of war forced her to expand her sphere of action. She was not alone, as perhaps half of Texas men of military age served in either the Confederate Army or state militia troops, and the war made "widows by the thousands."

When the reality of Confederate defeat finally reached Texas in June 1865, enslaved women were freed, but they then confronted a sometimes indifferent, sometimes hostile government in charge of the process of establishing just what that meant. Women were excluded from the turbulent politics of the era, and disorder and lawlessness throughout the state further limited women's public participation. Until 1875, Comanches controlled the western part of the state. But with the final defeat of Indians, women, especially in more settled parts of the state, once again became important economic actors. As capitalists, producers, and boosters in towns such as Waco, women both black and white sought to restore family fortunes as they worked to expand the local economy. In this capacity, they helped to promote the process of urbanization, which ultimately created yet another new role for women in Texas, one that for the first time brought with it a public voice.

Indian Women Who "Carry Gallantry Still Further Than the Men"

A Barometer of Power in Eighteenth-Century Texas

JULIANA BARR

In the August heat of 1749, a solemn procession of visiting dignitaries entered the town of San Antonio de Béxar. For the Spaniards waiting to greet them, few visitors could come close to capturing the power and fear associated with this group. The dignitaries came as representatives of multiple Lipan Apache nations, long a source of Spanish intimidation and dread in response to the raids they had launched against the small villa (town). They had "harassed the province with injuries, ravages, incursions, and attacks," bemoaned one Spaniard, "so that no one dared to leave his house without evident danger of losing his life." Indeed, the Apaches had signaled their approach with agreed-upon smoke signals, ostensibly so that the presidial (military) and state officers awaiting them could arrange the proper rituals with which to receive them. More likely, the signals gave fair warning of their coming to assuage Spanish misgivings and assure a peaceful reception. For Clemencia, an Apache woman held captive within the walls of Mission San Antonio de Valero, the columns of smoke must have elicited both hope and apprehension. Her fate hinged on the outcome of the meetings. The Apache delegation might agree to treaty negotiations, bringing peace to their two peoples for the first time, and through their efforts she might regain her freedom and return to her family. Hearts beat equally fast in the chests of the arriving Apaches. They did not come simply for diplomacy but also to retrieve wives, sisters, sons, and daughters who, like Clemencia, had been captured by Spanish soldiers. San Antonio did not represent simply the base of their former enemies; it was the prison of lost loved ones.[1]

APACHE WOMAN AND CHILD ON MULEBACK
IN CENTRAL TEXAS

Painting by Friedrich Richard Petri, ca. 1850.
Petri (Friedrich Richard) Collection, di_04091.
Courtesy of the Dolph Briscoe Center for American
History, University of Texas at Austin.

One might imagine that this diplomatic entourage was made up entirely of men—who else would Apaches send into the enemy camp to hammer out a military truce? However, such an assumption would be wrong. Indeed, neither Apaches nor Spaniards would have reached this moment if not for the labors and the suffering of Apache women. Over the preceding three decades, streams of Apache women, primarily those captured by Spanish forces, had beaten paths between the Spanish town and Apache villages as emissaries of peace. The stream was made up of either captive women sent home by Spanish officials with diplomatic overtures or free women chosen by Apache leaders to carry similar messages to their Spanish foes. That it had taken thirty years to reach this moment spoke volumes about the enmity between the two peoples. That women stood at the fore of such negotiations tells much about both customary Native diplomacy in the region and the state of relations with Spaniards. Apache men alone could not approach this town—hostile intent would be assumed, and Spaniards would take them to be a war party.

Over the five days that followed the Apache dignitaries' arrival, Spanish and Apache women and men came together for meetings, ceremonies, and ultimately celebration. The men—warriors, soldiers, missionaries, citizens, chiefs, and officials—ratified the treaty in the town plaza by ritually burying past weapons of war. Spanish women provided a "feast of beef, corn, squashes, and fruit," and Apache women, many newly freed from captivity, joined their families (and those of the Spaniards) in the entertainments that followed. More important, Apache women emerged as the centerpiece of Apache and Spanish pledges of alliance. Spaniards initially freed only the most recently captured female prisoners; others had been sold away to distant towns, and months would pass before Spanish officials' orders could bring about their return, if it could be achieved at all. Meanwhile, Apache leaders brokered marriages for some of the former and current captives, some of whom were the leaders' daughters and sisters, seeking spouses for them from among San Antonio residents. "With these ties, peace would be assured," for these "maidens" represented the Apaches' commitment to a long-lasting peace. The Apache men sought the unions as a means of creating kinship ties and a measure of identity and security for the Apache women still in Spanish settlements.[2]

These gestures represented an unusual amelioration of Apache-Spanish captive diplomacy, since many of the young women chosen for these political unions had for years been held hostage in the San Antonio missions. In that time, they had been baptized and so by Spanish custom could not be returned to live in what the Spaniards would view as apostasy, given their assumption that Indian converts who lived outside a Christian community would renounce the faith. Combined with the Spaniards' refusal or inability to return captives who had been enslaved, deported, or sold long distances away, the Apache men's efforts likely reflected their worry that the women might never be freed to return to them; thus, their futures had to be secured by other means. Mission records confirm twenty-three baptisms and at least ten marriages of Apache women to Indian residents at Mission San Antonio de Valero (now known as the Alamo) between 1749 and 1753. Adding even greater import to the marriages, one of the girls was the niece of Apache chief Boca Comida.[3]

On the other side of the equation, Indian officials and families in the missions invested the unions with great political significance. Thus, Clemencia (her baptismal name) married Roque de los Santos, a Xarame Indian who served as governor of Mission Valero for nine years, and another woman, Barbara, married the grandson of Xarame Miguel de Aldana and his Payaya wife, Marzela, one of the first families of San Antonio de Valero whose members had long held governing positions as *fiscals* (officials in charge of maintaining mission lands). Yet another woman, Angela, married Melchor Medina, the son of a Valero *alcalde* (magistrate). Rosa María became the wife of Joseph Miguel Puente, the founder of the leading Papanac family at the mission. Years later, the children of such unions, including María de la Candelaria, María Dolores Cuevas, Feliciana de Villegas, María de los Dolores, and María de Silva, continued their mothers' legacy by integrating Apaches into Valero's leading Indian families through marriage. During this period, Franciscan missionary Mariano de los Dolores y Viana reported that he baptized and married several Apache women to Native men of the Valero pueblo, while other mission residents had traveled to the Apache encampments outside of town and returned happy with the results of their visits and perhaps the courtships they had pursued while there. He concluded that Apache headmen "demonstrated their stability and firmness, significant of the union they desire in having agreed that some Indian women marry those of Mission San Antonio [de Valero]." The marriages of Apache women thereby solidified Spanish and Apache male leaders' political investments in the alliance.[4]

The emancipation of Apache women captives or their marriages to San Antonio residents signaled the beginning of Apache-Spanish ties in and around San Antonio de Béxar. With the permission of Apache leaders, Spaniards also later built small settlements, the San Sabá and El Cañón mission-presidio complexes, in the heart of Apachería (the Apache nation and its lands) to broaden and strengthen these bonds. Yet these treaty efforts did not pave the way for peace in the region. Watching from a distance, Comanches, Wichitas, and their allies (known collectively to the Spaniards as Norteños [Nations of the North]) saw the pact as a potential threat to their own expanding power in the borderlands. Their escalating raids against Spaniards and Apaches plunged both into a new era of unbridled fear and hostility. Spanish and Apache efforts to contain Norteño wrath kept women at the forefront of the military struggles. Indeed, the contrasting statuses and experiences of Spanish, Apache, Comanche, and Wichita women tell us a good deal about power relations in the eighteenth-century borderlands. Just as Apache women such as Clemencia had borne many of the burdens of the 1749 Apache-Spanish treaty agreement, the costs of the failure of that peace and the ensuing two decades of warfare fell disproportionately on the backs of the women involved.[5]

This essay explains the significance of women in these intercultural power relations by retelling the dramatic events that quickly unfolded as a result of the Spanish-Apache alliance, most prominently the 1758 Norteño annihilation of the San Sabá Mission. That story, however, must be told from three different perspectives—those of the Spaniards, the Apaches, and the Norteños—to see fully how the Spanish mission-presidio complex in Apachería became not only a lightning rod for Norteño fury but also a divining rod for the shifting fates of Indian women for the remainder of the century. Political and military sovereignty in eighteenth-century Texas determined who lived in fear and who did not. Thus, when Comanche, Wichita, Spanish, and Apache men expressed fears for their women in the midst of these imperial struggles, those expressions served as a medium of communication, an inspiration for alliance, a call to arms, and a gauge of power (or powerlessness). Apache, Wichita, and Comanche women often acted as the go-betweens and diplomatic agents as those struggles were negotiated. Put simply, women marked the lines of dominion among Spanish and Indian nations in Texas.

Understanding the San Sabá episode is not possible, however, without a basic understanding of the position of Texas Spaniards in the borderlands at midcentury. The Spaniards' standing in the region was a far cry from what they hoped it to be: that of representatives of the wealthiest and most expansive European empire in the Americas. That expansion had stopped cold in this region of North America where Native peoples could be neither conquered nor subordinated. In fact, during the first half of the eighteenth century, the Spaniards' presence was so insubstantial that they had gone largely unnoticed by Comanches, Wichitas, and many other Indian nations. That changed when the Spaniards united with the Lipan Apaches.

The only part of the region in which Spaniards could legitimately claim to exercise control (though their territorial ambitions certainly looked beyond these boundaries) consisted of the south-central areas of San Antonio de Béxar and La Bahía. There, Coahuilteco- and Karankawa-speakers had allowed Spaniards to establish small fortified settlements focused on mission-presidio complexes where both Spanish and Indian families united in defense against raids executed first by Apaches and later by Comanches and Wichitas. To the east, where Los Adaes had been established, the Spanish government maintained a presidio and missions at the sufferance of Caddos, whose lands surrounded the tiny pocket occupied by Spaniards. Beyond these three towns and their immediate environs, the region's Indian populace had no reason to identify the remainder (and majority) of present-day Texas as anything but Apachería, Comanchería, Wichita, and Caddo territory. In turn, as long as the dominant Caddo, Wichita, and Comanche nations could rely on French markets in Louisiana to supply guns, ammunition, and material goods in exchange for horses and hides, they had little need to pay attention to Spaniards—except, that is, for targeting the horse herds that aided hunting, defense, and market exchanges with Frenchmen. The power of these Indian nations ensured that Spaniards never broadened their reach beyond South Texas. The one time they attempted it, their efforts resulted in the 1758 debacle at San Sabá. The denouement made clear that Indians were not living in a Spanish borderland; rather, Spaniards were living along Indian borders that could be trespassed only at great peril.

Fear had defined the Spanish experience in Texas from the first attempts at settlement. Spaniards unknowingly established the missions and villa of San Antonio de Béxar on the border of the "great nation" of Apaches, who had extended their domain more than eight hundred miles from New Mexico to the land of the Tejas (Caddo Indians) and north to the southern Plains. In 1721, Apache warriors immediately issued a warning against the Spanish encroachment by planting arrow shafts with red cloths flying from their tops in a line along the presidio (fort) walls. For the next thirty years, Spaniards knew Lipan Apaches only as enemies who used Spanish settlements and ranches in south-central Texas as supply depots for horses. Throughout the 1720s, 1730s, and 1740s, as Apaches mounted raids on San Antonio, fear and frustration escalated among Spanish settlers, soldiers, and officials. The inability of presidial forces to stop the warriors' attacks transformed horse raids into what many Spaniards believed to be signs of a supposed war of extermination against them. Thus, the Apache strategists who took hundreds of horses became, in Spanish telling, "enemies of humanity," terrorizing civilian populations of women and children. Through such constructions, Spaniards transformed their soldiers and officers into chivalrous defenders of "civilization" while reducing Apache war-riors to barbarous savages preying on the "most defenseless of innocents." Their rhetoric thereby used women to define both extremes of male honor.[6]

It was no coincidence that the Indian bands that posed the greatest threat to the authority Spaniards wished to extend to the region figured prominently in images of Indian warriors as savages so cruel they "killed regardless of sex and age." The real danger of attack, however, remained distant from the arenas and activities of women and children. Apaches targeted horses, not women, and their raids focused on the herds on nearby ranches outside civilian settlements. Fray Benito Fernández de Santa Ana carefully noted that though enemy Apaches "can travel through the land as they please," only the "shepherd Indians" in charge of the herds were endangered by the raids. In instances when Span-ish officials had deaths to back up their rhetoric about the murder of women by hostile Apaches, those women were mission Indians rather than Spaniards. It seems likely that the location of the women's labor—in agricultural fields outside of mission and villa walls—put them in the path of raiders and thus in the line of fire. Yet even these deaths remained few and far between. The burial records of Mission Valero, for example, indicate that out of 1,088 deaths recorded between 1718 and 1782, only 15 were at the hands of hostile Apache, Comanche, and Coco raiders—and Apaches clearly did not bear sole respon-sibility for such deaths.[7]

Nevertheless, from the Spanish perspective in the 1730s and 1740s, Apache "depredations" had to be stopped, and the Spaniards sought to do so by launch-ing multiple campaigns against Apache *rancherías* (villages), taking numerous women and children captive. Fray Benito Fernández argued that the raids ac-complished nothing except increasing Apache hatred and that it was "ridicu-lous" that soldiers and citizens who pledged their service to the king sought only their own gain through the "capture of horses, hides, and Indian men and women to serve them." Such vile intentions would result in an equally vile out-come, he concluded. Fray Juan Domingo Arricivita agreed, arguing that the campaigns supposedly intended to bring a "cessation of strife" had instead "en-livened the war," because "in proportion as the Apache suffered harm, so did their hatred and the revenge they took increase." Even presidial commander Toribio de Urrutia admitted his trepidation, reporting to the viceroy that by 1740, no one traveled along the roads out of fear of Apaches; in addition to the sentinels stationed along the routes, he and his forces maintained constant vigi-lance at all hours of the night because "no moon passes without [Apache] tracks being found near the presidio." If things continued in this way, he worried, all respect for the presidios and settlements would be lost.[8]

Having cast Apache men as beyond redemption, Spanish officials also removed Apache women from a category of womanhood meriting chivalric
consideration as noncombatants. Spanish military policies—such as daybreak
attacks on Apache family villages—regularly involved the indiscriminate killing of women, children, and the elderly. Thus, one finds opinions like that of
military officer José Castillo y Terán, who believed that Apache women's lives
should not be spared because only by "shedding their blood by means of firearms—pardoning only the children or those who voluntarily surrender—will
[Apache] pride be punished." Apache warfare and raiding did not customarily
involve women, but Spanish *juntas de guerras* (councils of war) argued that
combat decisions had to take Apache women into consideration because "even
if perhaps they do not wage war in the same manner as the men, they do help
with it." Spanish leaders contended that Apache women represented an equivalent to "reserve corps." Even if women were present at battles only to hold horses
while men fought or to swell Apache numbers and an appearance of force,
Spaniards cast their duties in the same category as those of Apache warriors,
thereby desexing them. Such constructions resulted in the belief that if Indian
women were not "women" by Spanish standards, then perhaps their deaths at
Spanish hands did not violate Spanish codes of male honor. If women's lives
were sometimes spared, it reflected the fact that their capture and enslavement
could be used for political or economic profit.[9]

One can imagine the inversion of gendered standards of honor—an inversion bred of fear—that drove Spanish officials to manipulate captive Apache
women in efforts to coerce the peace eked out in 1749. But how could the Spaniards persuade the powerful Apaches to maintain the peace? After the agreements forged at San Antonio de Béxar, missionaries next proposed to offer the
Lipans missions to cement the alliance; religious conversion seemed a sure way
to "pacify" the Apaches. And it soon looked like the Franciscans might realize
that goal, as Apache families began to express interest in a mission in the 1750s,
asking only that it be a mission-presidio complex and that it be built in their
lands northwest of San Antonio. Many Spaniards doubted the Apaches' commitment to Christianity, but the gamble seemed worthwhile. Spanish officials
vested multiple hopes in this new establishment: that it might be the first in a
series of mission-presidio complexes to neutralize Apaches across the northern
provinces, that it might expand Spanish territorial boundaries, that it might
open the way for discovery of mineral wealth believed to be in those northern
regions, and that it might become a jumping-off point for an overland trade and
communication route to Santa Fe, New Mexico.[10]

Eight years after the peace accord, then, Spaniards traveled into Apachería for the first time in peace. They built the Mission Santa Cruz de San Sabá, northwest of San Antonio in present-day Menard County, and planned two more missions along the San Sabá River within Apache territorial borders. The Spaniards also built a presidio, San Luis de las Amarillas, with room enough for three to four hundred soldiers and their families. At the Franciscans' request, the presidio was constructed across the river and three miles away from the mission so that soldiers could not harass Indian women. At the same time, the soldiers needed to be nearby, as the religious fathers believed that an "authority of arms" would be essential to maintaining warriors' respect.[11]

Spanish plans recognized women as just as essential as men to the success of this institution of alliance. Balancing the hope of military intimidation was the clear desire to attract Apache families to the missions. Full conversion would not succeed without them, and equally important, Franciscans believed that the presence of women and children guaranteed the Apache men's peaceful intent. Thus, while one storeroom at the mission held saddles, horse bits, and horse blankets (the usual gifts for men), supply lists of blouses, skirts, earrings, necklaces, rings, and flannels made clear the Spanish desire to attract women into permanent residence. Spanish officials even set aside funds to have clothes made for the women by tradesmen in San Antonio. With care, Spanish officials sought to recognize hierarchies among Apache men and women, specifying certain blouses and skirts for head women, certain coats and trousers for chiefs, and rings for "princes." Perhaps as a mutual gesture of trust (or bravado), Spanish forces brought their own families, filling the presidio with 237 women and children. The soldiers stationed as guards at the mission also brought their wives, as did three Tlaxcalteco Indians sent to help guide conversion efforts: Apache and Spanish families would live together within the mission walls.[12]

Despite the best-laid Spanish plans, "no Apaches were to be seen" as the complex went up during the spring of 1757. Fray Benito Varela was sent by superiors in search of the "wayward" Apaches, but he had no success in drawing them to the mission. By the summer and fall of that year, church and state officials increasingly lamented that the Apaches were proving themselves "fickle" and "faithless." At no time did the Apaches take up residence, but family bands occasionally dropped by the mission during bison hunts. Because missionaries gave them food and horses as inducements to stay, the mission quickly came to function as a supply depot for the Apaches. What was not immediately apparent to the Spaniards was that the Apache parties were also heading north to engage in sorties against Comanches and Wichitas.[13]

Spanish officers and missionaries repeatedly chose to disregard hints of brewing trouble. Several small groups of Lipan warriors passed through in the fall of 1757, stopping only overnight at the mission before hurrying to the south. Over the winter, the Spaniards at San Sabá began to hear rumors that Norteños were massing to destroy the Apaches, but since no Apaches could be found at the mission-presidio complex, the Spaniards turned a deaf ear to suggestions that the complex might be a target. The growing number of Norteños in the region soon became undeniable, and at midnight on February 25, 1758, warriors later identified as Comanches and Wichitas stampeded the presidio horse herd and drove off sixty animals. Though commanding officers sent fourteen soldiers in pursuit, twelve days of tracking the raiding party brought no recovery of the animals or punishment for the raiders. Several days later, another squad sent to escort a supply train as it approached the complex came under attack by twenty-six warriors.[14]

Nevertheless, Spaniards could not anticipate the scale of force that was approaching. On March 16, a united band of two thousand Comanches, Wichitas, Caddos, Bidais, Tonkawas, Yojuanes, and others (twelve different Indian nations in all) surrounded the mission at dawn. As soldiers reported, the echoes of shouts, the nearby firing of guns, the puffs of powder smoke, and the pounding of horse hooves made clear the vast number of approaching Indians, "until the country was covered with them as far as the eye could reach." During the attack, they pillaged mission stores and herds, burned mission buildings to the ground, and killed eight Spanish men, including two missionaries who would go down in record books as having been martyred in the cause of saving Apache souls. During the attack, Spaniards took pointed note of the fact that the attacking Indians rode Spanish horses and carried European arms and ammunition, which they could only assume represented the profits of raids on Spanish settlements in New Mexico and trade in the French markets of Louisiana.[15]

The appearance of this virtual army of Indians—unprecedented in both numbers and diversity—sent shock waves all the way down to Mexico City. It was one thing for leather-armored soldiers to fight Indians armed with bows and arrows; it was quite another to face a force armed with guns as good if not better than those of Spanish soldiers. "Never before" had one of the mission guards "seen so many barbarians together, armed with guns and handling them so skillfully." Colonel Parrilla, the commander of Presidio San Luis de las Amarillas, summed up the military reaction: Spaniards in Texas were facing a fearful new Native challenge. "The heathen of the north are innumerable and rich," he argued; "they enjoy the protection and commerce of the French; they dress well, breed horses, handle firearms with the greatest skill, and obtain ample supplies of meat from the animals they call *cíbolos* [bison]. From their intercourse with the French and with some of our people they have picked up a great deal of knowledge and understanding, and in these respects they are far superior to the Indians of other parts of these Kingdoms."[16]

The responses of intimidated soldiers and officers fixed on the fate of Spanish women, with cries that the Norteños intended to "catch the Presidio off guard, capture it, and murder us all, including our wives and children." After the San Sabá attack, one soldier declared falsely, "Our forces had endured much suffering and many deaths at the hands of the savage barbarians, who did not spare the lives of the religious, or those of the women and children." If "wild hordes" who were armed with European weapons and who "wanted to kill" all the Spaniards stood poised to descend and savagely slaughter women and children, the rumors were all the more ominous. The Norteños' overwhelming victory at San Sabá, Parrilla warned the viceroy, "will encourage the barbarians to still greater boldness and audacity, for they will consider themselves capable of scattering our settlements and blocking our troops from advancing." Such a force might well be capable of a hitherto unthinkable feat: the invasion and conquest of Spanish lands and the confounding of Spanish imperial power. "It is also quite probable," Parrilla concluded miserably, that the Natives "might undertake the occupation of more territory, thus doing great harm to our settlements." Alarm rapidly spread from San Sabá to San Antonio and from there to Coahuila, Nuevo León, and ultimately Mexico City. Spanish women and children everywhere were imperiled.[17]

At the San Sabá presidio, now on the front lines of the Spanish defense, soldiers demanded that the fort be moved southward, to safer (Spanish) territory, casting their fears in terms of concern for their wives and children. Deposition after deposition stressed that the soldiers were merely responding to the "continual outcries of women and children" and that the "helpless condition of the women" drove their pleas. The soldiers rationalized their unprecedented insubordination in demanding a retreat despite orders to hold their position at the presidio as praiseworthy service, not cowardice, because they merely sought to protect women and children who should not be reduced to "bait for the cruel and bloodthirsty heathen." Their desperation became so great that Colonel Parrilla faced imminent mutiny and desertion, and he feared that men would run off while tending the horse herds outside presidial walls, leaving their women and families behind in their terror. Provincial and viceregal authorities stood firm, however, asserting that Spanish honor forbade the abandonment of San Sabá as "ignominious and shameful." If Norteño "insolence" went unanswered, "it would be natural that the offending Indians would assume that the fear among the Spaniards of another attack was what had occasioned the change and this very notion might encourage them to start it." Moreover, the Apaches could not be given the impression of Spanish fear or the inability of Spanish arms to protect their families lest the alliance fail. In the end, Spaniards commemorated the series of catastrophes in their records and history as the "massacre" at San Sabá. More important for the immediate future, they put rhetorical spin to very real fears of powerlessness and transformed the endangerment of Spanish women into a call to arms for Spanish men.[18]

It is difficult to know exactly how Lipan Apaches would have told the story of San Sabá, since they left no accounts. Hypotheses must be based on their actions, and Apache actions made clear that they, too, came to San Sabá out of fear for their families, children, and elderly.

Beginning in the 1720s, Apaches in Texas had begun to experience new pressures from expansive Comanche and Wichita bands that were moving steadily south into lands long held by the Apaches. The Apaches' need for horses increased with these growing challenges to their territorial claims. As their safety and defensive capabilities became more and more tied to the ability to move quickly, a regular supply of horses became critical to their survival. In answer to this need, raids on the mission and presidial herds of Spanish settlements had offered a regular supply of horses for the thirty years prior to the 1749 Spanish truce. What Spaniards often viewed as wars of extermination in actuality represented the strategic decision by warriors to make San Antonio and Bahía gathering sites from which to acquire horses needed for hunting to feed women and children and for riding to battle to defend communities. Economic and geopolitical considerations, not "bloodthirst," explained Apache men's raiding.

At the same time, Apache women faced increasing dangers. As raiding and hunting parties became larger, women and children traveled with warriors, assisting men in maintaining camps, processing hides, and even making arrows. In turn, the presence of women in these parties put them in the line of fire when hostilities arose. In addition to a growing number of epidemics that swept through Lipan settlements, the capture of women and children by enemy Indian and Spanish groups, who preferred to sell them as slaves rather than return them to their families via negotiations, meant devastating demographic loss. Apache codes defined warfare as a male profession and the battlefield as a site of male activity—there was no place for women as victors or victims. Women might accompany raiding parties to supervise the removal of horses back to villages, for example, but they remained far from the sites of battle. Indeed, men put much thought and care into removing noncombatants to places of safety when they anticipated war, so much so that Spaniards learned to interpret the placement of women, children, and elderly in areas that lent themselves to safety and defense as a preparatory sign of hostility by Apache men. Governor Domingo Cabello wrote with assurance that the evidence that Lipan Apaches were "planning the most terrible revenge" for a Spanish attack that had killed men and women lay in the fact that "they are thus moving all their women and children to the canyon of San Sabá preparatory to falling upon the afore-mentioned places."[19]

By the 1750s, Apache leaders decided to seek European arms, military aid, and safety for their women and children by a new means, leading to the official peace with Spaniards. The treaty not only ended hostilities but also, in the eyes of the Apaches, created a military alliance. With treaty in hand, the next step was to make the Spaniards act on the alliance. To that end, the Lipans requested a mission-presidio complex for their people, seeking to mollify Spanish demands for conversion and to gain the service of presidial soldiers whom the Apaches knew would be assigned to protect the mission. More difficult was the task of persuading Spaniards to build the complex in Apache territory, as their defensive needs required, but several years of lobbying in San Antonio by Apache men and women finally led to the erection of the San Sabá complex in the "lands of the Apaches." Apache chiefs welcomed the news from Fray Mariano de los Dolores that the Spanish government had committed "to provide them with a presidio with one hundred men, who would defend them against all their enemies." Spaniards chose to concentrate on the mission element of the complex, believing the presidio to represent merely enforcement of the pacification and conversion process. Apaches focused on the military aspect of the complex, viewing the presidio as a practical means of obtaining allies with guns against their Comanche and Wichita rivals.[20]

By the time the complex had been completed in 1757, however, the Apaches had begun to doubt the structure's promises of protection. An encounter not even registered by the Spaniards was a key element to Apache decision making. An Apache woman attempted to explain the situation to Fray Benito Varela when he came looking for the missing Apache "flock." She told him that she had just escaped capture by a raiding party of Caddos and four apostate warriors from the San Antonio missions. She was a member of the family band of Apache chief Casa Blanca's brother, and while they were camped on the Colorado River, the raiders had killed him, his wife, and their two children before taking two women and two children captive. She had later escaped, bringing with her one of the little girls, who had been wounded by a bullet.[21]

The woman refused to accompany Fray Varela to San Sabá, but other relatives traveled there in May 1757 to warn of the region's growing perils. The family bands set up encampments near the mission, and in negotiations that followed,

Apache leaders tried to explain why their visit would be only temporary. Two chiefs, Chico and Casa Blanca, alternately pledged their continued friendship and hedged on the arrival date of all their peoples. They struggled to settle on an explanation that would satisfy and avoid alienating the Spanish missionaries and officers. Casa Blanca expressed his rejection of settlement at the complex outright, angered by the recent death of his brother and the capture of his female relatives. He explained that with only seven hundred warriors to defend the two thousand women, children, and elderly under his protection, the one hundred soldiers at the San Sabá presidio were insufficient to dissuade him from moving his people south to mountains his enemies could not penetrate. Despite Spanish gifts of tobacco and three head of cattle to "soothe his wrath" and "comfort" his grief, the chief brusquely concluded that "neither he nor his people would settle in a mission because that was not their choice." More important, the "lives and liberty of all his followers" came first. In addition, his people needed to leave immediately if his men were to join other Apaches in a war against the Norteños. Vengeance and the recovery of lost family members demanded this action.[22]

Chief Chico tried to be more conciliatory, explaining his inability to settle at the mission as a consequence of his responsibilities to family and to his people—his inability "to deny his people what they asked of him on account of the love he felt for them." Chico explained that more time was needed for their bison hunts and that during those hunts, families had to be kept together for fear of Norteño attack. If Spanish soldiers would join the Apache groups in a campaign against these enemies, he implied, their congregation at the mission would take place all the sooner.[23]

Further ill fortune—the deaths of Chico's brother and sister, who fell gravely ill while at San Sabá—cemented the Apaches' departure. Apache custom regarding the proper rituals of mourning required that family members and their community immediately leave the area of death. Spanish missionaries noted that the deaths "stunned the mind and spirit of Chief Chico," though he did not share his grief with them. In speaking to Fray Jiménez, Chico said simply that obligations of honor demanded that he aid the other Apache leaders, who "had asked him with tears in their eyes not to abandon them at a time when they had decided on a campaign against the Comanches."[24]

By the winter of 1757, the Apaches' outlook had grown even more grim as they had come to realize that the mission-presidio complex might prove a trap in which their women and children would be sitting ducks for their enemies. Tracks all over the region indicated that the Norteños were massing. Apache leaders tried to make clear to the inattentive Spaniards the danger of remaining in the area. To bring that point home, Apache men cast their fears in terms of the safety of their women and children. But the missionaries and officers realized the Apaches' dilemma only in hindsight. Years after the San Sabá attack, in a Franciscan history of the region, Fray Juan Domingo Arricivita wrote that because Chief Casa Blanca "had only seven hundred warriors to protect over two thousand, including women, children, and old men, and two thousand seven hundred head of stock, if he waited for his enemies [at San Sabá], who were more numerous and had the advantage of firearms, the slaughter this would inflict would be frightful and would exterminate them completely."[25]

In March 1758, Apache men passed through the region and again tried to warn the Spaniards of approaching danger, but they failed to comprehend the seriousness of these fears. In frustration, Apache warriors moved south to safer ground, far from their Spanish allies. Therefore, when the attack came, Apache warriors had sequestered their families, ensuring that no women and children fell victim to the Norteño raiders. Yet two Apache men who had remained behind aided the escape of a Spanish woman and children from the mission. Providing "support and comfort," they helped the wife of one of the mission guards, Corporal Ascensio Cadena, and two soldiers' sons travel more than 130 miles on foot along hidden pathways to San Antonio, carrying the children on their backs the entire way.[26]

From the Apache vantage point, the events at San Sabá suggested that the Spaniards were ineffective allies. They neither provided the military aid the Apaches needed to defend their families nor held the Apaches in sufficient esteem to listen to them as equals or consider Apache women's safety on par with that of Spanish women. Yet new rounds of commitment encouraged a continued alliance. The renewed agreement to joint settlement at a mission complex had a propitious beginning as a result of concerted Spanish efforts to rescue the daughter of a principal chief who had been captured and sold off to Nuevo León. Again, the security of women inspired Apache loyalty to their allies. Between 1758 and 1767, Spaniards fortified the presidio at San Sabá, transforming it from a wooden to stone fort, and built two new missions for Apache settlement, San Lorenzo de la Santa Cruz and Nuestra Señora de la Candelaria del Cañón, along the Nueces River at a site long proven to provide shelter for Apaches. From this new base farther south in Apache lands, tribal leaders felt confident leaving their women and children within the mission walls for safekeeping while raiding northern foes and hunting bison—accompanied by Spanish soldiers—on lands they still sought to defend against Comanche and Wichita incursions.[27]

Norteño violence and European disease soon spelled the end, however. The Norteños' refocused ire resulted in a steady barrage of attacks in the 1760s. Heightened tensions led one chief, El Lumen, to fall into nightmares while away on a hunt in 1763, dreaming that Spanish forces had taken advantage of the men's absence to kidnap Apache women and children and sell them into slavery. The members of the hunting party hastily returned to move their families to a safer location, far from Norteño rivals and Spanish allies alike. In 1764, the Apache women and children among the remaining population suffered a devastating smallpox epidemic that hit while their husbands and fathers were away. Dwindling hope of safety from the ravages of disease and warfare inspired the mystical apparitions of a spirit who took male and female form, preaching to men and women, respectively, to both resist Franciscan baptism and reject Spanish alliance. The denouement came in November 1766. At the orders of the desperate officer in charge, Lieutenant Váldez, Apache women dressed in soldiers' overcoats and hats and took up arms to stand guard along the mission walls, in clear contradiction to the Apaches' gendered rules of war. From the Natives' perspective, if Spanish men were unable to mount adequate defenses, Apache men could not rely on them as fellow protectors of Apache women and children. Within a month, all Lipans who had sought shelter at the missions had fled.[28]

So what did the conflicts focused on San Sabá look like from the other side of the battle lines? Documentary records explain even less about the Comanche and allied Norteño perspectives than about those of the Apaches. Perhaps most critical for their viewpoints, Comanche, Wichita, and Caddo women remained far from these scenes of violence, safely ensconced deep within their own sovereign borders. And their borders, unlike those of Apaches and Spaniards, remained inviolate. But for Comanche, Wichita, and Caddo men, political economies related to defending or expanding the resources required by their family bands still determined their actions. The bounty of raids against Apaches— Spanish horses and Apache women captives—as well as expanded hunting territories carved out of Apachería had helped all three nations to underwrite lucrative trade alliances with the French in Louisiana. Comanches and Wichitas had not previously given Spaniards in Texas much attention, but by midcentury, hostilities with the Lipans eventually attracted their gaze. In the 1740s, the Comanches' pursuit of Apache raiders led them to the San Antonio area and alerted them to the association between the Lipans and the Spaniards. In the 1750s, the San Sabá mission-presidio complex confirmed the possibility of an economic, military, and civil alliance. To Norteño eyes, the presidio conveyed a Spanish commitment to protect the Apaches, while the mission represented material succor and bounty, with its herds of domesticated animals, its agricultural fields, and a regular supply of goods. The large number of Spanish women and children at the presidio signaled the coming together of Apache and Spanish families in a long-term plan of joint settlement in the heart of Apachería.

The complex was not merely a supply depot for Apache settlers but also a base for Apache raiders, which added to Norteño suspicions of Spanish collusion in attacks on Comanche and Wichita *rancherías* (settlements). Thus, the same presidio-mission complex that Spaniards and Apaches hoped would spell safety and peace looked like an indication of escalating enmity to the Norteño allies who watched its construction from a distance. By Native rules of alliance and enmity, Spanish alliance with the Lipans put Norteño blood on Spanish hands, and Texas Spaniards became targets for the animosity previously directed only at Apaches. The 1758 destruction of San Sabá mission was the concerted Norteño response.[29]

So how does one analyze the Norteño attack at San Sabá? The most important thing about the attack is that despite their clear numerical advantage, the Norteño allies never sought to engage the presidial forces in battle. The reputed two thousand warriors never approached the presidio, though it was located only three miles from the mission. As a result, despite Spanish rhetoric that the attackers sought to kill women and children, all 237 of those women and children remained unharmed within the presidio walls. During the three days it took to plunder and destroy the mission, Norteño warriors kept watch on the presidio, because "several Indians were seen in the tree tops and on hillsides": they clearly wanted their presence known, "let[ting] themselves be seen." Such watch would have alerted the Norteños to the fact that forty-one of the one hundred soldiers assigned to the presidio were absent and that the women and children there were consequently vulnerable. The women did not attract the attention of the raiders, however. Indeed, the warriors not only chose not to attack but allowed presidial forces to bring their herds into the presidio stockade, to send a squad of fourteen soldiers and three Indians to reconnoiter the "state of affairs" at the mission, and then, after reporting back to Colonel Parrilla, to continue along the road toward San Antonio to meet a supply train. In fact, the Norteños allowed the supply train to enter the presidio walls. Tellingly as well, twenty-six escapees from the mission—seven soldiers, one missionary, two soldiers' wives, eight soldiers' sons, three mission Indians, an Indian interpreter and his wife, an unnamed "youth," and two Apache men—safely traversed the ground between mission and presidio under the watchful gaze of Norteño lookouts and gained the sanctuary of the presidio unchallenged. For three days, the Norteños kept the presidio waiting for an attack that never came.[30]

Meanwhile, at the mission, Norteños persuaded the naive missionaries to allow them entry. Once inside, the evidence of their eyes and the Franciscans' statements told the Norteño warriors that Apaches were not present. (The few still there were hidden.) Yet they saw plenty to enrage them. The mission, with its buildings, cattle, provisions, and nearby protective presidio, offered proof positive of the Spanish alliance with the Apaches. Adding insult to injury, the fathers sought to mollify the visitors with gifts, which surely told the warriors the source of the goods that provisioned Apache raiding parties against Comanche and Wichita villages. Norteño warriors promptly set about destroying all objects and structures signaling Spanish-Apache alliance. Strikingly, though, they took very little for themselves, leaving the smoldering remains to be found by Spaniards, including "bales of tobacco, boxes of chocolate, barrels of flour, and boxes of soap, broken apart and burning."[31]

Only eight people died during the three days of ransacking and demolition that followed. In all that time, the Norteños made no effort to locate, much less kill, the Spaniards and Apaches who had hidden in one of the buildings (and who later escaped under the watchful eyes of the Norteño lookouts). That building was not even set afire. Moreover, all eight killed were men. Half of the dead, including one of the missionaries, Fray Alonso Giraldo de Terreros, fell in an initial volley that cleared the mission grounds and allowed the attackers access to mission stores and supplies. One woman, the wife of mission servant Juan Antonio Gutiérrez, fell prey to one attacker's attention: he robbed her of her clothes (which perhaps reflected a desire for plunder as much as humiliation) but did not injure her bodily. The raiders saw no value in harming or capturing Gutiérrez's wife or any of the other women present.[32]

The only individuals violently attacked after the first shooting were men who foolishly interrupted the raiders in their ransacking. More interesting still, despite the arsenal of French guns that so exercised Spanish imaginations, Norteño warriors primarily chose beating as their means of attack. Why? According to Comanche, Wichita, and Caddo protocols of warfare, opponents had to be equally matched for a contest to be meaningful. Victories were measured not by the number of dead but rather by "grades" of martial deeds demonstrative of a warrior's valor and prowess. In a warrior's manner of attack might be read his estimation of the enemy he struck down, and the judgment of Spanish manhood seems clear. In sum, the Norteños never sought a fight with presidial soldiers; when forced to fight, they chose fisticuffs over armed combat and rejected possible battle trophies, and upon leaving the area, they taunted the soldiers at the presidio who never came out to fight. Combined with the number of people allowed to escape, the treatment meted out indicates that the raiders did not view the Spaniards as worthy of combat, much less honorable warrior deaths. Except for nine soldiers sent over by the presidio, the presidial forces mounted no defense of the complex or the women and children within it. If the Spanish soldiers could not fulfill the part of warrior, they would not be treated as such.[33]

Norteño fearlessness in the face of their new Spanish foes became even clearer when Spanish forces sought to redeem their honor through a direct assault on a Wichita village five months after the San Sabá debacle. Their mission of vengeance collapsed at the hands of Comanche and Wichita men—and, even worse, Wichita women. In August 1758, a punitive expedition of 600 men—380 presidial soldiers and militiamen from Coahuila, Nuevo León, and Saltillo (with only 30 from Texas itself), 120 mission Indians called up as auxiliaries, and 134 Apache warriors—set out for the Red River, where the Norteño foes were massed. Along the way, the Spanish forces attacked a Yojuane village; killed 55 people, including women and children; and took captive 149 other women and children, who were then sold into slavery. They surely hoped to subject the Comanches and Wichitas to the same fate.[34]

In settlements along the Red River, Norteño forces awaited the Spanish expedition at a fortified Wichita village while allies continued to pour in "without ceasing." They did not simply outnumber the Spanish forces arrayed against them—they outnumbered the entire Spanish population in Texas. At the end of a road "skillfully cleared by hand for great smoothness," the Norteños greeted the foreign intruders from within a village surrounded by a stockade and moat as well as extensive agricultural fields of corn, beans, pumpkins, and watermelons, "all in bloom" and enclosed by a palisade. Warriors armed with French muskets lined the walls. All in all, it was a far more imposing fortification than any offered by Spaniards in defense of their families. Wichita women evidently felt safe within those walls. In clear sight of Spanish soldiers, "many Indian women and children entertain[ed] themselves, it seems, by watching the action." As Wichita and Comanche men "fought dexterously outside," the women inside cheered them on, "secure in their fortress," adding their voices to those of their husbands, fathers, and sons and "mock[ing] the accuracy of Spanish swivel guns." With great "bearing," "boldness," and "well-ordered valor," the Norteños drove the intruders away from the village. In the end, fifty-two soldiers died, militiamen quickly began to desert, and the Norteños captured two cannons. Finally, after the expedition deemed retreat the only option, the unrelenting Norteño warriors pursued Spanish forces all the way back to San Sabá. While the Wichitas and Comanches "exerted great effort in their defense and protection of their territory" (and their women), Spanish officials lamented the humiliating rout as "the very disgraceful campaign" that brought "such shame to the nation" and "disgrace to our arms."[35]

In the months and years that followed their victory at San Sabá, the dominant position of Norteños (and especially Comanches) in the Texas borderlands became clearer still. They never again allowed the Spaniards to advance northward, and by 1771, viceregal authorities ordered that the San Sabá presidio be abandoned and that diplomacy with the feared Comanches and Wichitas be pursued with great vigor. As new contacts and ultimately peace agreements unfolded, Comanche and Wichita women assumed unprecedented roles in Spanish diplomacy. Thus, the routes blazed by Apache women back and forth to San Antonio in the 1730s and 1740s continued to be traversed by Comanche and Wichita women, who went to the Spanish villa to command the respect and obligation of their Spanish neighbors. Yet unlike Apaches, these women rarely traveled as captives. Their diplomatic service reflected the dominant position from which their nations negotiated with Spaniards.[36]

Proof of the women's authority became even more apparent when Spaniards next visited the principal Wichita village on the Red River in 1778. Wichita leaders called on their women and children to greet the visitors, who arrived in hopes of solidifying peace agreements. All day long, women "from all the houses" assumed their customary roles at the center of Wichita hospitality rituals, coming forward to offer feasts for the dignitaries. In return, Spaniards honored the women with diplomatic ritual and presents. Only after entering the Wichita palisades did the Spaniards understand the economic power that gained Wichita women such status—they "tan, sew, and paint the skins, fence in the fields, care for the cornfields, harvest the crops, cut and fetch the firewood, prepare the food, build the houses, and rear the children, their constant care stopping at nothing that contributed to the comfort and pleasure of their husbands." So prominent were women's labors that one of the Spanish officials could only conclude in a report to his superiors that the Wichita "government is democratic, not even excluding the women, in consideration of what they contribute to the welfare of the republic." In this land, women "carry gallantry still further than the men." No wonder Wichita men evidenced such determination to protect them from any threat from outside those walls; no wonder Wichita women displayed so little fear from within them.[37]

Comanche women operated from an even greater base of power and traveled the roads of Texas without worry or trepidation. In the wake of the first Spanish-Comanche treaty in 1785, Spaniards in San Antonio de Béxar gawked at the seeming boldness of the Comanche women, who arrived with little guard and few defensive pretensions. Governor Cabello tried to warn them about such "strange" behavior, little conceiving the power of the Comanche nation that made possible the security and impunity of its women as they moved between their *rancherías* and his town. Roads on which no Spanish woman dared to venture, even with a well-armed expedition, held little danger for their Comanche counterparts. The Comanche women went to San Antonio as delegates and emissaries of leading chiefs, delivering messages and receiving diplomatic gifts just as would their fellow men. As officials amended their gift lists to include items chosen specially for leading women, townspeople organized services that befit such important visitors—providing repair to Comanche women's cookware alongside the rifles of Comanche men. Even the embassy built to house the multiple delegations now calling on the Spanish governor included servants and cooks to relieve Comanche women of any domestic duties during their stay. Women, like María, the wife of Chief Soquina, found their names recorded in diplomatic guest books and recognized on the tongues of Spaniards who could have never imagined treating women on terms equal to that of men. María and other Norteño women would be heralded for the remainder of the century whenever they visited Spanish settlements as part of their peoples' "practices of peace."[38]

Where, then, one might ask, was the fear from a Norteño perspective? In the actions surrounding San Sabá, Comanches and Wichitas indicated clearly their fearlessness when it came to Spanish opponents. And that fearlessness was made manifest by their women.

If the stories of Clemencia (the liberated Apache captive of Spaniards) and María (the venerated Comanche wife of Soquina and diplomat to Spaniards) tell readers anything, it is that one must discard any assumption that Spaniards dominated and Indians cowered in the colonial worlds of eighteenth-century Texas. That image was a mirage produced by Spanish fantasy and presumption. For eighteenth-century Spaniards, presidios were protective garrisons for civilians and families on Spanish frontiers rather than bastions of force through which Spaniards conquered Indian populations on those frontiers. A more accurate view, one illustrated by the comparable experiences of women caught up in the forces surrounding San Sabá, reveals that Norteño women were the most secure, as they thrived behind the impenetrable palisades of Wichita villages or traveled along well-worn Texas highways. In contrast to Spanish illusions of grandeur, the geopolitics of rival Apache, Comanche, Wichita, and Caddo nations entangled Spaniards in networks of alliance and enmity they knew little how to navigate, much less master. The resulting fear for the safety of their own women and children offered a clear barometer of asymmetrical power relations in which Spaniards were the losers.

NOTES

This essay comes from parts of the author's book, *Peace Came in the Form of a Woman: Indians and Spaniards in the Texas Borderlands* (Chapel Hill: University of North Carolina Press, 2007), esp. chaps. 4, 6.

1. Lipans and other eastern Apaches—Faraones (a division of the Jicarillas), Mescaleros, and Natagés (a division of the Mescaleros)—had moved into Texas by the seventeenth century and were increasingly pressing on the homelands of Coahuilteco speakers and others who lived in the San Antonio area. For discussion of their territorial boundaries, see Juliana Barr, "Geographies of Power: Mapping Indian Borders in the 'Borderlands' of the Early Southwest," *William and Mary Quarterly*, 3rd ser., 68 (January 2011): 5–46; *Apostolic Chronicle of Juan Domingo Arricivita: The Franciscan Mission Frontier in the Eighteenth Century in Arizona, Texas, and the Californias*, trans. George P. Hammond and Agapito Rey, rev. Vivian D. Fisher (Berkeley, Calif.: Academy of American Franciscan History, 1996), 2:31 (for "harassed").

2. William E. Dunn, "Apache Relations in Texas, 1718–1750," *Quarterly of the Texas State Historical Association* 14 (January 1911): 260–62 (for "feast"); *Apostolic Chronicle*, 2:41; Fray Benito Fernández de Santa Ana to Viceroy Conde de Revilla Gigedo, February 23, 1750, in *The Presidio and Militia on the Northern Frontier of New Spain: A Documentary History*, vol. 2, pt. 2, *The Central Corridor and the Texas Corridor, 1700–1765*, ed. Diana Hadley, Thomas H. Naylor, and Mardith K. Schuetz-Miller (Tucson: University of Arizona Press, 1997), 485 (for "With these ties").

3. Fray Mariano de los Dolores y Viana to Captain Toribio Urrutia and Lieutenant Joseph Eca y Músquiz, September 17, 1750, and Fray Mariano de los Dolores y Viana to Viceroy Conde de Revilla Gigedo, October 8, 1750, in *Letters and Memorials of the Fray Mariano de los Dolores y Viana: Documents on the Missions of Texas from the Archives of the College of Querétaro*, ed. Marion A. Habig, trans. Benedict Leutenegger (San Antonio: Old Spanish Missions Historical Research Library at Our Lady of the Lake University, 1985), 120, 123–24.

4. Xarames, Payayas, and Papanacs were among the many Indian groups that lived in the San Antonio region and had earlier formed alliances with Spaniards who moved there. The joint settlement of Indians and Spaniards at San Antonio represented their alliance in the form of a mission-presidio complex. *Fiscal* and *alcalde* were titles of office given to Indian leaders in recognition of their authority within the mission communities. Mardith Keithly Schuetz, "The Indians of the San Antonio Missions, 1718–1821" (PhD diss., University of Texas at Austin, 1980), 336–55 (for list of marriages); Fray Mariano de los Dolores y Viana to Captain Toribio Urrutia and Lieutenant Joseph Eca y Músquiz, September 17, 1750, and Fray Mariano de los Dolores y Viana to Viceroy Conde de Revilla Gigedo, October 8, 1750, in *Letters and Memorials of the Fray Mariano de los Dolores y Viana*, ed. Habig, 132–33 (for "demonstrated").

5. Eastern Comanches (primarily Kotsoteka bands) and Wichitas (Taovayas, Tawakonis, Iscanis, Kichais, Flechazos, and Wichitas proper) moved southward from the southern Plains into the region of present-day Texas by the mid-eighteenth century, and the borders of Comanche territory expanded to enclose the San Antonio community almost completely by the 1770s. Wichita settlements remained to the north, closer to their Caddo and French trading partners.

6. "Peña's Account of the 1720–1722 Entrada," in *Presidio and Militia*, ed. Hadley, Naylor, and Schuetz-Miller, 411; Dunn, "Apache Relations in Texas"; Bernardo de Gálvez, "Notes and Reflections on the War with the Apache Indians in the Provinces of New Spain," in Elizabeth A. H. John, "A Cautionary Exercise in Apache Historiography," *Journal of Arizona History* 25 (Autumn 1984): 304; Elizabeth A. H. John, "Bernardo de Gálvez on the Apache Frontier: A Cautionary Note for Gringo Historians," *Journal of Arizona History* 29 (Winter 1988): 427–30.

7. Fray Benito Fernández de Santa Ana to Viceroy Archbishop Juan Antonio de Vizarron, June 30, 1737, in *Letters and Memorials of the Father Presidente Fray Benito Fernández de Santa Ana, 1736–1754: Documents on the Missions of Texas from the Archives of the College of Querétaro*, ed. Benedict Leutenegger (San Antonio: Old Spanish Missions Historical Research Library at Our Lady of the Lake University, 1981), 26–27 (for "can travel"); Dunn, "Apache Relations in Texas"; "List of the Men and Women Killed by Indians, from 1813 to 1820, San Fernando Church Listings, Béxar County Archives, microfilm roll 63, #821, transcription in Adolph Casias Herrera Papers, Daughters of the Republic of Texas Library at the Alamo; Schuetz, "Indians of the San Antonio Missions," 160.

8. Fray Benito Fernández de Santa Ana to Fray Guardian Pedro del Barco, February 20, 1740, in *The San José Papers: The Primary Sources for the History of Mission San José y San Miguel de Aguayo from Its Founding in 1720 to the Present*, pt. 1, 1719–91, trans. Benedict Leutenegger, ed. Marion A. Habig (San Antonio: Old Spanish Missions Historical Research Library at San José Mission, 1978), 64 (for "ridiculous"); *Apostolic Chronicle*, 2:32 (for "cession"); Captain Toribio de Urrutia to the Viceroy, December 17, 1740, in *San José Papers*, ed. Habig, 86 (for "no moon").

9. Joseph de Castillo y Terán, "Description of Coahuila, 1767," trans. Ned F. Brierley, in *Imaginary Kingdom: Texas as Seen by the Rivera and Rubí Military Expeditions, 1727 and 1767*, ed. Jack Jackson (Austin: Texas State Historical Association, 1995), 168 (for "shedding"); Minutes and Resolutions of the Third Junta de Guerra Held in Chihuahua, June 9–15, 1778, Béxar Archives, Dolph Briscoe Center for American History, University of Texas at Austin (for "even if perhaps" and "reserve corps"); Antonio Cordero, "Cordero's Description of the Apache—1796," trans. Daniel S. Matson and Albert H. Schroeder, *New Mexico Historical Review* 32 (October 1957): 340–41.

10. William E. Dunn, "The Apache Mission on the San Sabá River: Its Founding and Failure," *Southwestern Historical Quarterly* 17 (April 1914): 379–414.

11. Dunn, "Apache Mission"; Robert S. Weddle, *The San Sabá Mission: Spanish Pivot in Texas* (Austin: University of Texas Press, 1964); *Apostolic Chronicle*, 2:23–87, 48 (for "authority of arms"); Fray Benito Fernández de Santa Ana to Viceroy Conde de Revilla Gigedo, February 23, 1750, in *Letters and Memorials of the Father Presidente Fray Benito Fernández de Santa Ana*, 170.

12. Fray Francisco Manuel Arroyo, "Relación de los Sacrilegos . . . en los Confines de los Texas en el Rio de San Sabá, c. 1758," and Fray Alonso Giraldo Terreros, "Inventory of Supplies Purchased in Mexico for the Mission Santa Cruz de San Sabá," November 1757, in V. Kay Hindes, Mark R. Wolf, Grant D. Hall, and Kathleen Kirk Gilmore, *The Rediscovery of Santa Cruz de San Sabá: A Mission for the Apache in Spanish Texas*, Spanish document translations by Philip A. Dennis, San Sabá Regional Survey Report no. 1, Archaeology Laboratory, Texas Tech University (Lubbock: Texas Historical Foundation and Texas Tech University, 1995), 12, 72–77 (for gifts); Deposition of Sergeant Joseph Antonio Flores, March 21, 1758, in *The San Sabá Papers: A Documentary Account of the Founding and Destruction of San Sabá Mission*, ed. Lesley Byrd Simpson, trans. Paul D. Nathan (1959; Dallas: Southern Methodist University Press, 2000), 50; Weddle, *San Sabá Mission*, 82.

13. *Apostolic Chronicle*, 2:59.

14. Deposition of Sergeant Joseph Antonio Flores, March 11, 1758, in *San Sabá Papers*, ed. Simpson, 58.

15. Deposition of Andrés de Villareal, March 22, 1758, Deposition of Juan Leal, March 11, 1758, both in ibid., 73, 68.

16. Deposition of Juan Leal, Deposition of Ensign Don Juan Cotinas, March 27, 1758, Deposition of Colonel Parrilla to Marqués de las Amarillas, April 8, 1758, all in ibid., 76 (for "never before"), 137–38 (for "the heathen").

17. Petition Presented to Colonel Parrilla by Members of the Garrison, San Luis de las Amarillas, April 2, 1758, Deposition of Sergeant Joseph Antonio Flores, Deposition of Mission Guard Andrés de Villareal, Deposition of Colonel Parrilla to Viceroy Marqués de las Amarillas, all in *San Sabá Papers*, ed. Simpson, 53 (for "our forces"), 71 (for "wanted"), 107 (for "catch the Presidio"), 145 (for "will encourage" and "it is also quite probable").

18. Petition Presented to Colonel Parrilla by Members of the Garrison, San Luis de las Amarillas, April 2, 1758, Deposition of Sergeant Tomás de Ogeda, Deposition of Sergeant Domingo Castelo, Deposition of Colonel Parrilla to Marqués de las Amarillas, all in *San Sabá Papers*, ed. Simpson, 107–9, 110, 112 (for "bait"), 114 (for "helpless"), 115 (for "continual"), 136; *Apostolic Chronicle*, 2:71 (for "ignominious"), 72 (for "it would be natural").

19. Governor of Texas Domingo Cabello to Commandant General Teodoro de Croix, October 20, 1780, Béxar Archives; Cordero, "Cordero's Description of the Apache," 345; Hugo O'Conor, *The Defenses of Northern New Spain: Hugo O'Conor's Report to Teodoro de Croix, July 22, 1777*, trans. Donald C. Cutter (Dallas: Southern Methodist University Press for the DeGolyer Library, 1994), 71–72. See also Morris Edward Opler, *Myths and Legends of the Lipan Apache Indians* (New York: American Folk-Lore Society, 1940), 223; Governor of Texas Domingo Cabello to Commandant General Jacobo Ugarte y Loyola, June 12, 1786, Béxar Archives.

20. *Apostolic Chronicle*, 2:57.

21. Ibid., 60.

22. Ibid., 60–65.

23. Ibid., 61–63 (63 for "to deny").

24. Ibid., 60–63 (62 for "stunned," 63 for "had asked"); Morris Edward Opler, *Lipan and Mescalero Apache in Texas* (New York: Garland, 1974); Morris Edward Opler, "The Lipan Apache Death Complex and Its Extensions," *Southwestern Journal of Anthropology* 1 (Spring 1945): 122–41; Thomas F. Schilz, *Lipan Apaches in Texas* (El Paso: Texas Western Press, University of Texas at El Paso, 1987); Andreé F. Sjoberg, "Lipan Apache Culture in Historical Perspective," *Southwestern Journal of Anthropology* 9 (Spring 1953): 76–98.

25. *Apostolic Chronicle*, 2:65.

26. Fray Miguel de Molina quoted in ibid., 2:70.

27. Felipe Rábago y Terán, Autos, December 31, 1761, A.G.M. Historia, vol. 84, pt. 1, cited in Curtis D. Tunnell and W. W. Newcomb, *A Lipan Apache Mission: San Lorenzo de la Santa Cruz, 1762–1771* (Austin: Texas Memorial Museum, 1969): 163; *Apostolic Chronicle*, 2:76.

28. Fray Diego Jiménez and Fray Manuel Antonio de Cuevas, "Consultation and Advice to the Señor Auditor of the Viceroy," February 25, 1763, A.G.I., Audiencia de Mexico, Dunn Transcripts, 1748–1763, Briscoe Center for American History; Fray Diego Jiménez, State of the Missions in the Presidency of the Northern Rio Grande from October 1758 to December 1767, A.G.M. Historia, vol. 20, Briscoe Center for American History; *Apostolic Chronicle*, 2:81–82, 86; Felipe Rábago y Terán, Autos, February 28, 1767, A.G.M. Historia, vol. 94, pt. 1, cited in Tunnell and Newcomb, *Lipan Apache Mission*, 172.

29. Deposition of Juan Leal, Deposition of Father Miguel de Molina, March 21, 1758, both in *San Sabá Papers*, ed. Simpson, 74, 87.

30. Petition Presented to Colonel Parrilla by Members of the Garrison, San Luis de las Amarillas, April 2, 1758, in Deposition of Sergeant Joseph Antonio Flores; Minutes of Colonel Parrilla's Interrogation of Lieutenant Juan Galván and Various Noncommissioned Officers and Soldiers, March 22, 1758, Deposition of Sergeant Joseph Antonio Flores, Deposition of Andrés de Villareal, all in *San Sabá Papers*, ed. Simpson, 107, 48–50, 53–54, 64, 71.

31. Deposition of Sergeant Joseph Antonio Flores, in ibid., 56.

32. *San Sabá Papers*, ed. Simpson, 107, 53, 69, 74.

33. Deposition of Father Miguel de Molina in ibid., 89; Fray Agustín de Morfi, *History of Texas, 1673–1779*, 2 vols., trans. Carlos E. Castañeda, (Albuquerque: Quivira, 1935), 384; *Apostolic Chronicle*, 2:68; George A. Dorsey, *The Mythology of the Wichita* (Washington, D.C.: Carnegie Institution, 1904), 7; E. Adamson Hoebel, *The Political Organization and Law-Ways of the Comanche Indians* (Menasha, Wis.: American Anthropological Association, 1940), 21.

34. Robert S. Weddle, *After the Massacre: The Violent Legacy of the San Sabá Mission*, with the original diary of the 1759 Red River Campaign, trans. Carol Lipscomb (Lubbock: Texas Tech University Press, 2007), 26–28.

35. Weddle, *After the Massacre*, 123 (for "skillfully"), 124 (for "secure in their fortress" and "fought dexterously"), 125 (for "mock[ing] the accuracy"), 126 (for "all in bloom," "many women and children," and "exerted great effort"), 127 (for "without ceasing"); *Apostolic Chronicle*, 2:74; Athanase de Mézières to Governor of Louisiana Luis Unzaga y Amezaga, February 1, May 20, 1770, both in *Athanase de Mézières and the Louisiana-Texas Frontier, 1768–1780: Documents Published for the First Time, from the Original Spanish and French Manuscripts, Chiefly in the Archives of Mexico and Spain*, ed. Herbert E. Bolton, 2 vols. (Cleveland: Clark, 1914), 1:141 (for "disgraceful" and "shame"), 200 (for "disgrace to our arms"); Henry Easton Allen, "The Parrilla Expedition to the Red River in 1759," *Southwestern Historical Quarterly* 43 (July 1939): 53–71.

36. Marqués de Rubí, Dictamen of April 10, 1768, in *Imaginary Kingdom*, ed. Jackson, 181–82.

37. Athanase de Mézières to Teodoro de Croix, April 7, 18, 19, 1778, all in *Athanase de Mézières*, ed. Bolton, 2:203 (for "tan, sew" and "their government"), 205 (for "from all the houses"); "Account of the Journey of Bénard de la Harpe; Discovery Made by Him of Several Nations Situated in the West," trans. Ralph A. Smith, *Southwestern Historical Quarterly* 62 (April 1959): 532–33 ("carry gallantry").

38. Domingo Cabello to José Antonio Renjel, December 24, 1785, April 24, 1786, Rafael Martínez Pacheco to Jacobo Ugarte y Loyola, October 12, 27, 1787, January 7, 1788, A Report on the Gifts and Food Offered Visitors from the Comanche Nation, January 31, March 31, April 11, June 5, October 21, November 5, December 14, 26, 1787, Dionisio Valle, Diary of Events at Nacogdoches for June 1805, July 1, 1805, all in Béxar Archives.

Spanish Law and Women
in Colonial Texas, 1719–1821

"I Wish to Make Use of All the Laws in My Favor"

JEAN A. STUNTZ

In August 1735, Señora Antonia Lusgardia Hernández filed a petition with Governor and Captain General Don Miguel de Sandoval for the return of her son. She had been working for eight or nine years as a servant for Don Miguel Nuñes Morillo. She left because he did not pay her, did not give her clothes to wear, and overall treated her badly. She already had a daughter when she began working for him, and she had a son while there. Though the record does not say, the father of her son was probably Don Miguel. In her petition, she stated that Don Miguel had taken away her son, "the only man I have and the one who I hope will eventually support me." She ended her petition with a plea for justice: "I being but a poor, helpless woman whose only protection is a good administration and a good legal system . . . I wish to make use of all laws in my favor."[1]

Don Miguel de Sandoval ordered Don Miguel Nuñes Morillo to return the son to Antonia Lusgardia. Don Miguel announced that he would comply with this order but thought it was a bad idea. The boy, Ignacio, had formed "a good, spiritual relationship" with his godmother, Doña Josepha Flores, the wife of Don Miguel, and wanted to stay with her. Don Miguel claimed that he wanted to protect the boy and that giving him to his natural mother was not in the best interest of the child. He said that Antonia had renounced all her rights to the boy and so should not get him back.[2]

This case brings to light several things about Hispanic culture in colonial Texas. First, family was important in ways dissimilar to the English tradition. Spanish fathers took care of their children whether or not they had been born to a legal wife. Illegitimate children could inherit from their fathers if recognized, and most fathers did recognize and legitimate their offspring. Having the father's legal wife serve as godmother was a way to give such children good standing in the town. Godparent relationships were very close and in some ways more important than parenthood in establishing social status. Bastardy was not the lifelong shame that it was in England. The rights of natural children were written into the law, and most bastards were either included in the father's family, as attempted here, or otherwise provided for. Though Spanish culture did value women's sexual purity, this acceptance of illegitimacy in legal terms offered some unmarried mothers a measure of tolerance that was lacking among their English counterparts. As long as the father recognized and provided for the child, both mother and child held a recognized status within the community.

Second, Spanish women did not take their husbands' names upon marriage. Don Miguel's wife did not share his last name. Each person had a baptismal name (generally not used outside of church), a first name, and sometimes a second name, followed by the father's last name and then the mother's last name. Sometimes (but not always), *y*, (and) separated the father's last name and the mother's last name. Antonia's father's last name was *Lusgardia*, and her mother's last name was *Hernandez*. Most often, only the father's name was used for everyday purposes, but if the mother's family was more important, her last name would be used instead. Naming patterns hint at the differences between Spanish women's status and that traditionally found under English common law and other legal systems. A woman's name and her legal identity did not disappear upon marriage, as they did in Anglo America.

Antonia Lusgardia's case illustrates a third nuance—Spanish women had rights. Indeed, even a poor servant woman had the right to file suit. Her marital status was not mentioned because it was not important here: married women as well as single women and widows had the right to file suits in their own names. The Spanish legal system had developed many laws and traditions protecting the rights of women, and these provisions remained in force in colonial Texas.

Antonia Lusgardia was not an important woman by any traditional measure. She was neither wealthy nor philanthropic; she did not help to win any new political rights for women or otherwise provide much-needed leadership for Spanish colonists in eighteenth-century Texas. And her case—our only means of knowing about her existence—did not set any significant legal precedents. And yet Lusgardia's petition can provide an important illustration of how the confluence of several factors—Spanish laws and culture as well as the political and diplomatic context for their expansion into New Spain—created an inter-

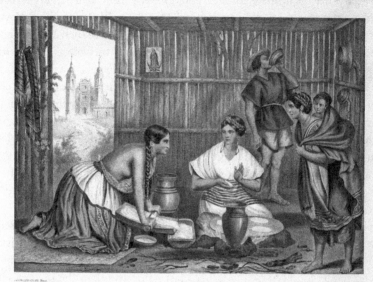

MEXICAN WOMEN MAKING TORTILLAS, 1850

Las Tortilleras, lithograph by Pierre Frederic Lehnert.

Courtesy of the DeGolyer Library, Southern Methodist University,

Dallas, Texas, Ag2000.1297; Vault Folio-2 F1213.L45.

stice for all women, regardless of their economic status. The petitions, wills, and other legal documents in which Antonia Lusgardia's contemporaries appear reveal that Spanish laws, as enacted in northern New Spain, made Spanish women's lives quite different from the lives of their British counterparts. Women in colonial Texas had a legal right to claim the assistance of the state, even against powerful men, while the state acknowledged their right to own land and engage in business. In essence, they had room to negotiate some autonomy, even if those negotiations sometimes failed.

To understand why these differences in legal rights developed for women in colonial Texas requires looking far back in time. The origins of Spanish law are intertwined with medieval Spain's religious and military history, just as the continuation of those laws in early Texas (or northern New Spain) involved extending and protecting the Spanish New World empire. The evolution of the extraordinary rights for Spanish women began at the end of the Roman empire, when Visigoths overtook the Iberian Peninsula. These Germanic peoples believed that women and men had approximately the same property rights. Under the Visigothic code, the Forum Judicum, daughters inherited equally with sons, and female relatives inherited equally with male relatives.[3] Then, in 711 CE, Moorish Muslims invaded Spain, quickly conquering the entire peninsula except for the tiny kingdom of Navarre. The advance was finally stopped in France at the Battle of Tours in 732, where Charles Martel defeated the Moors and pushed them back south of the Pyrenees two years later. For the next seven centuries, the force that shaped the character of Spanish society and the Spanish legal system was the Reconquest: the Spanish effort to retake the Iberian Peninsula from the Moors. The kingdom of Castile, at first a small kingdom in southern Spain, benefited the most from the Reconquest. Through the centuries of skirmishes, it grew in both power and size to become the largest and most powerful of all the Spanish kingdoms. Towns also grew in power and autonomy during this time. The nobility who ruled the towns served on the parliamentary body known as the *cortes*, giving them a great deal of influence over the king. The nobles used their power to safeguard their own rights and thereby also safeguarded the rights of the towns.[4]

The battles of the Reconquest generally centered on the taking of towns from opponents. As Christian forces conquered each town, they needed to bring in respectable women to settle it. Women had the responsibility of passing societal expectations and tradition to the next generation. However, most respectable women did not want to move to the parts of the frontier where the fighting was ongoing and had to be bribed to move there. These individual bribes might occasionally be monetary, but large groups of women could be bribed with expanded legal rights. As the frontier moved southward, women kept all the rights given them in one town and added to them in the next.[5]

In Castile, these rights were compiled in Las Siete Partidas (the Seven Divisions of Law). Under the order of King Alphonso X, experts drew on canon law, the Visigothic Code, maritime rules, and the customs of the various Spanish cities. They included every known aspect of law. But since the Partidas were written to give power to the king, the nobles deposed Alphonso X. The laws were never put into effect as the actual legal system of Castile, but they became known as official tradition, and judges throughout the land referred to them to settle cases. The rights of women were included in this compilation. When Isabel of Castile married Ferdinand of Aragon in 1469, she specified that the laws of Castile would control their joined kingdoms. Thus, when Columbus discovered the New World, Castilian law controlled it as well. The legal system that gave so many rights to women during the Reconquest of Spain itself remained unchanged during the conquest of New Spain. When the Spanish settled Texas, civil authorities used Castilian laws as set down in the Partidas (plus the rulings of the Council of the Indies) as their legal system. As was their tradition, Spanish colonists preferred to settle their disputes in court, and Spanish authorities kept extensive records of all proceedings.[6]

That unique legal system became particularly important because of the nature of Spanish colonization. Spain settled Texas for two main reasons: to convert the Indians into Catholic, Spanish subjects and to prevent first France, then Great Britain, and finally the United States from getting any closer to the rich silver mines in northern Mexico. Spain's settlement patterns differed from British patterns. Because a main reason to send Spanish people into this area was to convert the Indians, missionaries, mostly Franciscans, went first. The missions they established, however, had to be approved by the Spanish Crown before they could be built. Their objectives included religious conversions of Natives, accompanied by lessons in how to be Spanish. In these missions, Indians learned Spanish trades, wore Spanish clothes, and learned to speak Spanish as well as memorized the basics of a Roman Catholic catechism. They received Spanish names at baptism as a sign of both their religious and cultural conversion. As they became Hispanicized, they assimilated into the Spanish settlements. Not all Indians wanted to convert, so the missions needed protection, especially in the early years, from hostile Indians. For this reason, Spanish military officials built a presidio (fort) near each mission. Even after a mission had been in existence for several years, the surrounding area still had numerous Native Americans who kept their traditional ways. Towns often grew near missions and presidios, filled with civilian support personnel and their families. The Spanish also planned villas (towns), near the mission/presidio complex to encourage civilian settlement. Their logic was that with more Spaniards in Texas, the French or British would be less likely to take it over.[7]

In the 1690s, Spain, worried in part by threats of French incursions, attempted to establish missions and presidios in eastern Texas, among the Caddoan Indians. But these efforts proved unsuccessful, and Spanish officials ordered that the missions be moved to the San Antonio area. The mission San Antonio de Valero and the presidio San Antonio de Valero were established in 1718 along the San Antonio River. Mission San José y San Miguel de Aguayo moved there in 1720, San Francisco Xavier de Nájera in 1722, and Nuestra Señora de la Purísima Concepción de Acuña, San Juan Capistrano, and San Francisco de la Espada in 1731. The same year, settlers arrived from the Canary Islands as part of the Crown's plan to populate the area. At that time, the villa of San Fernando de Béxar was established and the town drawn up somewhat according to the official procedure. With all these missionaries, neophytes, and settlers added to the existing population, resources became strained and tempers flared. In the 1730s and 1740s, missionaries battled (in court) the townspeople and presidio for Indian labor, townspeople complained about presidio and mission livestock ruining their crops, and presidial soldiers grumbled about the lack of pay and proper equipment. After a generation or two of intermarrying and the intermingling of kinship groups through godparenting, these rivalries subsided, leaving San Fernando de Béxar as a cohesive community.[8]

By 1768, the missions around San Antonio were self-sufficient as far as food supplies went, a condition that allowed significant elements of Spanish culture to remain in the colony. The neophytes grew both native foods such as corn and beans and Spanish imports of melons, potatoes, and sugarcane. They had orchards of fruit trees, especially peach trees. They raised livestock—horses, mules, cattle, sheep, and goats—and used oxen to plow the fields. The Indians in the missions spoke Spanish and had mostly acculturated to a Spanish lifestyle. As in Spain, women worked primarily in and around the house. They took care of the gardens and smaller animals such as chickens, goats, and milk cows while the men went outside the village proper to take care of beef cattle and other larger livestock. Men now did the farming, a major sign of how much area Indians had adopted Spanish ways. They even played guitars and lived in houses, as Europeans did.[9]

In these new communities, Spanish settlers also went to court, a tendency much appreciated by historians. Rather than resorting to fisticuffs or duels, they preferred to take disputes to justices and governors. Disputes involved women as well as men, so women appear frequently in these documents as plaintiffs, defendants, and witnesses. Since most women could not read or write and thus did not leave other written records, court documents remain one of the few primary sources available to historians.[10]

Testimony from lawsuits in the Spanish settlements reveal the way hard work shaped women's lives. Civilians who lived in the villa proper also grew crops on irrigated farmland and pastured livestock on common lands outside the city limits. While women did the work in town, men rode out to the fields every day. Digging *acequias* (irrigation ditches) and building fences for common land was one of the first municipal tasks, so essential that both men and women did this manual labor. Settlers bought water rights in units of an hour—that is, they had the right to irrigate their land from the common *acequia* for one hour each day or week. Women often had the responsibility of opening and closing the irrigation gates, a process that involved lifting heavy boards to start the water flow and then reinserting them to stop the water when their time was up. Gardening took a considerable amount of time for nearly all of San Antonio's women, who had to raise their own food.[11]

Even though Spanish women did not write down anything about their daily lives, information can be gleaned from official records. Like most women everywhere at all times, Spanish women in Texas spent time on their families. Grinding corn and cooking took hours each day, as did cleaning the household goods, making and repairing clothes, tending livestock, and healing the sick and injured. Taking care of children was an ongoing task. Women worked every day in their gardens and orchards. Since they lived in small towns, they often visited with neighbors. As Catholics, they went to Mass almost every day as well. These daily routines were punctuated by occasional fiestas: religious holidays, fandangos, horse races, *quinceañeras* (celebrations of a girl turning fifteen and becoming a woman), weddings, funerals, christenings, and more. Woman had constant interaction with other townsfolk; unlike many frontier women in antebellum Anglo Texas, they did not suffer from loneliness. While a woman's main purpose in life was to marry and raise a family, Spanish women in Texas could also run businesses, own property, and protect their rights in court.[12]

Women participated actively in court cases as accusers, accused, and witnesses. One especially colorful set of cases illustrates that even with a certain amount of gender equality, race and class continued to matter a great deal to the honor-conscious colonists. Moreover, these incidents suggest that women played a significant role in defining and defending honor. In 1783, Don Francisco Rodriquez filed suit in court against Juan Manuel Padrón for beating and insulting the don's wife, calling her a worthless, meddling pig and a mulatta. Don Francisco also filed a second suit against Padrón's mother and sister for inciting the fight and name-calling. Doña Antonia de Armas, Padrón's mother, responded that witnesses to the fight affirmed the principal role of Don Francisco's wife, Juana Travieso, who allegedly had a history of fighting and name-calling. Doña Antonia added that Travieso had started the fight and the name-calling, but that no one called Travieso a mulatta. Thus, according to Doña Antonia's testimony, the original accusation that Don Francisco's wife had been publicly called a mulatta was a lie.[13]

Don Francisco's next action was to file criminal charges against Padrón for offending the don's honor by the disrespect shown his wife. Yet however much he wanted to defend his wife's honor (and by extension, his own), he indicated that he was unwilling to do so if his wife's racial purity was in doubt. If, in fact, his wife was a mulatta, then their marriage was based on fraud because she had represented herself as Spanish, and he was entitled to an annulment. Further, if she was having an affair with the Indian she was protecting in the fight, then he wanted a legal separation of bed and board. Regardless of his uncertainties about his marital situation, he was unwilling to ignore an opportunity to correct his social inferiors, noting that Doña Antonia's answer showed her ill breeding and lack of civility.[14]

The facts of the case are not obvious, but it appears that a Hispanicized Indian named Montes threatened Juan Padrón in the presence of the don's wife, Travieso. The two men started fighting, and she intervened, insulting Padrón in the process. (Travieso's defense of the Indian evidently led Don Francisco to assume that his wife and Montes were lovers.) Padrón responded by insulting Travieso and hitting her as she got between the two men. Padrón's mother and sister were present. They did not attempt to stop the fight physically but did engage verbally with the belligerents. Other people gathered to watch the fight but did not interfere. The result of the suits was that Padrón served twelve days in jail for the fight and Don Francisco was ordered to pay court costs for dragging the whole mess into court. The don refused to pay these costs until after appeal, though no records of an appeal have been located.[15]

The gender disparities are obvious: a woman stepped in to stop a fight between two men. By stepping outside the traditional female role, Travieso opened herself to insults from participants and their families as well as her husband, who suspected that she was having an affair with one of the men. Honor was incredibly important to the Spanish, and any insult had to be dealt with immediately lest the family's honor suffer. Women's actions could easily cause a family to lose honor.[16] Race and class differences played a role here, too. The original fight was between an Indian and a Spaniard. As a Spaniard, Padrón had a higher status than the Indian, but he was not a don. Only Don Francisco and Doña Antonia received that honorific. Travieso, as the wife of a don, and Padrón, the son of a doña, had relatively equal status, but she lacked the title. Her family might have been less wealthy. Still, no "decent" Spanish woman would have physically attacked a man. Spanish women had to conform to society's ideals of female behavior to reap the benefits of the system. Once a woman lost her reputation as lady, she would find have difficulty winning acceptance in her community.

Striking also is Don Francisco's fear that he might have unintentionally married a mulatta, a fear apparently caused only by the accusation in the midst of a violent confrontation. Claiming to be Spanish when one was in fact a mulatta was so great a fraud that it could be grounds for an annulment. Spaniards took marriage seriously. No divorce was possible, and it was most difficult even to get a legal separation. A willingness to consider an annulment in this situation shows just how deeply race mattered.[17] Finally, even though the physical fight took place between two men, the case was between and about women. Women's actions had legal consequences. Don Francisco brought suit on behalf of his family honor, while Doña Antonia filed papers on her own behalf.[18] Women gave their testimony, and their words had the same weight as those of men. Legal, economic, and religious roles granted Spanish women a good bit of public visibility. In turn, some were feisty, independent, and sure of their legal rights.

A similar incident two years later shows that women commonly acted on their own behalf both in economic situations and as parties to lawsuits. Autonomy had a few social limits in theory, but in practice, women felt capable of acting on their own behalf, in part because the two roles were related. That is, as economic actors, they could find themselves parties to lawsuits. In this suit, two merchants in town, Don Fernando Veramendi and Luiz Mariano Menchaca, competed for customers. One day, Fernando de Arocha, a private stationed at the presidio, went to Menchaca's store to close out his account and transfer his business to Veramendi. Displeased with the loss of business, Menchaca argued with Arocha and then started calling him names, including "worthless mulatto." Menchaca's wife, who helped him run the business, got into the fray. She called Arocha and all his family members names and began beating him with a measuring stick.[19]

Arocha escaped with his life and promptly sued both for slander and for physical assault. As a descendant of one of the Canary Island migrants, Arocha held privileges based on his status as *hidalgo* (Spanish nobility) and as original settlers of the villa as well as on birthplace. (People born in Spain itself, called *peninsulares*, had a much higher standing than even pure-blood Spaniards born in the Americas, known as *criollos*). As a result, Arocha was very conscious of his family's high standing in the community. One of the witnesses was Efigenia

Leal, wife of Joaquín de la Garza, who was in the store at the time. Her testimony carried the same weight as that of a man or an unmarried woman. The court ruled in favor of Arocha and ordered Menchaca imprisoned both for his actions and for his wife's words and deeds. The judge held the husband responsible for his wife's actions in part because there was no place to incarcerate a woman. But the case also reminds us that wives took an active role in the family business. Though the judge seemed to chide Menchaca for failing to control his wife, it is plain that Spanish women felt free to take matters into their own hands when needed. In the end, Menchaca apologized and was set free, though he was responsible for court costs. Menchaca's release suggests that many residents were unhappy with the monetary cost Menchaca would have had to pay for his wife's actions. As was common in the Spanish system, community welfare outweighed personal vengeance. It was more important to uphold Spanish traditions concerning proper behavior than to punish any individual.[20]

Women's public roles were filtered not only through their connections as wives but also through their roles as businesswomen. In 1771, Ygnacia de Castro filed suit to void a contract she had made to sell property to her brother, Marcos. There was no written deed of sale, and he had never paid more than a down payment of a length of cloth, so the contract was voided. Marcos tried to argue that she could not sue without her husband, but the judge said that Ygnacia's marital status was irrelevant because Marcos had acted maliciously. Husbands usually filed suit for their wives, but doing so was not necessary. Women could and did go to court on their own behalf.[21]

Spanish settlements were few and far between in northern New Spain, a fact that inconvenienced both male and female business owners. Women as well as men who wished to carry out business and legal transactions had to give powers of attorney to people, usually men, in distant places to complete transactions on their behalf. In March 1744, Don Francisco Javiela Maldonado, Doña María Maldonado, Luís Maldonado, and Juana Francisca Tribiño all gave powers of attorney to their uncle, who lived in Saltillo, so that he could settle their grandfather's estate. In the document, "the said women grantors renounce[d] the laws relative to and in favor of women in order that they may be compelled to comply" with the court's orders.[22] In contrast, under British law, a married woman could not have granted power of attorney to anyone, as she had no legal identity herself. Once again, the Spanish legal system allowed women much higher status than did English common law.

From early in the colonial period, Spanish law required that women formally renounce the laws that protected women from any bad decisions. On the one hand, the law categorized women as incompetent and included them with children and other noncompetent people who could cancel contracts that turned out not to benefit them. Such laws were intended to reduce the impact of poor decisions, but they did not work well with Spanish law that also allowed women to convey property and conduct business. Thus, in contrast to the presumed incompetence, women were often permitted to engage in legal transactions. Women who engaged in these legal transactions had to formally renounce the protective laws so that their contracts could be enforced. In 1743, Doña Rosa Flores y Valdés, widow of Captain Don Joseph de Urruttia, gave power of attorney to Don Juan de Angulo of Mexico City to settle her husband's estate there. Two years later, she revoked that power and gave it to Don Joseph de Plazas of the city of San Pedro de Voca de Leones. In both cases, she stated that she renounced the laws that protected women, because the laws governing legal engagement required that women who moved into this realm relinquish those protections. Doña Josepha Flores y Valdés had been widowed twice, and in 1744, she gave power of attorney to Don Francisco de Liñan to settle both husbands' estates. She also renounced the laws in favor of women. Perhaps most astonishing for those familiar with English common law, in 1772, Raphaela de la Garza gave power of attorney to her husband, Francisco Flores de Abrego. As the form required, she swore that he had not forced, persuaded, or compelled her to do so.[23]

This last grant, too, would have been impossible under English common law, in which marriage meant that a husband automatically assumed all of his wife's legal rights and obligations. A married woman had no legal existence outside that of her husband, so she could never have granted anyone a power of attorney. She did not have the power to conduct business on her own behalf and thus could not give such power to someone else.[24]

Under Spanish law, wives could also represent their husbands in legal matters, which rarely happened under English common law.[25] In 1745, Tomasa de la Garza, a new resident of the villa, represented her husband, Gabriel de los Ríos, in asking the city government for a lot for them to live on. She, not her husband, received title to the lot. She "dug in the ground, threw earth, pulled up stakes, marked the boundaries, and performed all the other ceremonies necessary according to law, as the legitimate owner, holder, and possessor of the said town lot."[26] Four years later, Gertrudes de la Garza, widow of Martín Saucedo, sold a city lot with fruit trees on it to Don Alberto Lopez. This transaction may have been part of an estate settlement, as the documents showed that Saucedo had contracted to sell the lot but had died before the sale went through. In selling land to settle this estate, Garza was acting in her late husband's name, but doing so nevertheless required her to renounce all laws that protected women.[27]

As the ability to own land is generally regarded as a marker of citizen status, it is significant that Spanish law had no barriers to women's ownership, purchase, or sale of land. In 1748, Don Manuel de Niz, with the express permission of his wife, Doña Sebastiana de la Peña, sold land to Don Thoribio de Urrutia. The document repeatedly used *we* to indicate joint ownership of that land. Doña Sebastiana also renounced all laws in favor of women and had to aver that she had not been intimidated by her husband.[28]

The same year, Joseph Montemayor sold to Doña Josepha Flores y Valdés some land near the presidio for fifty pesos. The only structure on it was a very old *jacal* (hut). In 1749, Jabiela de los Ríos sold a fenced town lot on the *acequia* to Juan Joseph Villegas for one hundred pesos. Marital status occasionally did not matter. Widows sometimes signed documents renouncing all laws in favor of women even though they should not have had to do so under Spanish law. For example, in 1746, Doña Juana de Urruttia, identified as the widow of Don Ygnacio Gonsales de Ynclán, received five hundred pesos from Don Diego Ramón in exchange for a plot of land partially surrounded by a board fence and with sixteen peach trees and a solid house. As part of the sale, Doña Juana renounced all laws in favor of women.[29]

The pattern of married women claiming, buying, and selling land on their own was not restricted to the early period of settlement, which ended in 1773, when San Antonio became the provincial capital. In 1787, Rosalinda Rodriguez, wife of Juan José Sanchez, requested an unclaimed piece of land. She stated that none of her three husbands had received any land since they were all soldiers stationed at the presidio. She, however, was a Canary Islander descendant and deserved land of her own. The authorities agreed but said that the specific piece she requested had already been assigned to someone else. In 1782, "with the permission of her husband," Doña Juana Delgado sold two plots of land that she owned and one day of water rights that belonged to him.[30] These cases show that women could receive land from the government in their own names. Married women could buy and sell land and personal property belonging to their husbands as long as they had his permission. In the early national period of the United States, married women did not have these rights.

A more complicated court case reflecting women's centrality to legal disputes involving landownership began in 1779, somewhat conventionally, with a husband, Don Francisco Prov, acting on behalf of his wife, Doña María Caravajal. Don Prov claimed that the land in question had been granted by the Crown to Mateo de Caravajal, Doña María's grandfather. He had built a house on the land and had lived there. The suit then acknowledged that a city official had granted that same land again, this time to brothers Andres and Francisco Hernandez,

Doña María's uncles. Francisco eventually sold his share to Joseph Caravajal (Mateo's son and Doña María's father), who, the plaintiffs claimed, already owned the land through inheritance. The first suit asked for the return of the land and the purchase money that Joseph had paid for land that was really his, plus any damages and court costs.[31]

The suit then took a turn that would have been unanticipated in the British colonies but was to be expected in this context: another woman in the family, Josepha Hernandez, entered the suit in her own name. As heir to Andres Hernandez, she claimed that the land was hers, citing a title in the city archives. But when the city officials called witnesses, they verified that the land belonged to Mateo, not Hernandez. The city officials decided in favor of Doña María Caravajal. Hernandez appealed to the governor, to no avail. The decision stood in favor of Don Francisco Prov, "husband and conjoint person of" María de Caravajal.[32]

While the case was being heard, Doña Josepha Hernandez started building a fence around what she considered her property. City officials ordered her to stop until the case was finalized, but she refused. She entered a new petition in her own name asking that the original suit be suspended because the lot was hers. At this point, Doña María de Caravajal, without her husband's joinder, asked the court for damages accrued from the defendant's use and abuse of the land. The governor finally declared an end to the battle between these two women. He extended the boundaries of his previous decision to give Doña María more of the land and ordered that Doña María take possession in the presence of Josepha and walk the boundaries so that Josepha would know what they were.[33] These actions are unremarkable within the Spanish system but contrast dramatically with English common law, where married women would not have been able to own, buy, or sell land in their own names.

Women's property rights extended to buying and selling slaves, though there were few slaves in the region. Most slaves had some African ancestry, since it was against the law to make slaves of the Indians. In October 1743, Doña Josepha Flores y Valdes traded slaves with Lieutenant Colonel Don Justto Voneo y Morales, the governor and captain general of Texas. She sold him Luís for 200 pesos, and he sold her Francisco Joseph for 270 pesos. Francisco Joseph had been purchased from Doña María Eugenia de Oliva, wife of Don Sebastión de Benghechea of Mexico City. In 1770, María Fernandez de Castro sold her slave, María de los Dolores.[34] These deeds show that married women could own personal property in their own name and buy or sell this property without their husbands being party to the sale. In contrast, English common law did not usually allow married women to own or control property. Women under Spanish law had almost equal status to men.

Women in Spanish Texas frequently acted as executors of their husbands' estates, only one of the ways inheritance laws affected women there. Under Spanish tradition, all property accumulated during a marriage was considered community property—that is, equally owned by husband and wife. Each spouse could also have separate property either brought into the marriage or acquired by gift or inheritance during the marriage. When a spouse died without a written will, the separate property owned by that spouse was taken out and the surviving spouse kept his or her share of the community property, which was not part of the estate. The half of the community property that was owned by the deceased plus his or her separate property was divided in half, with half going to the surviving spouse and half divided equally among the deceased's children. Widows, therefore, kept all of their separate property and their half of the community property as well as inherited half of the husband's separate and community property. In Spanish Texas, this allotment procedure usually did not amount to large inheritances, since no one was extremely wealthy. But it did keep widows from the kind of economic indignities sometimes suffered by widows under other European legal systems.[35]

Women could write wills, of course, and like all wills in the colony, those written by women took precedent over the laws of succession for those who died without making wills. The earliest will by a woman in the Béxar Archives is that of María Melián, and it offers a good example of common practices of women in New Spain. Her first directive designated the gift of two reals to the Holy Church of Jerusalem to ransom captives and to help orphaned girls. She then described her estate. Her only separate property, brought with her into her second marriage, was one cow. That cow had four calves, two of which were her half of the community property. She directed that one of these calves was to go to her youngest daughter and the other was to go to her son from her first marriage. The other two calves belonged to her husband as his share of the community property. She also owned as separate property five cows that she received for being an original settler of the villa: they went to her other children. All other property was to be divided equally among all her children.[36] By providing for her children, her directives thus closely followed the rules for intestate succession and thus reflected community expectations.

The will of Mateo Peres, a merchant who died in 1746 or 1747, offers insight into both inheritance patterns and the ways in which Spanish social structure offered women a central place and respected family without regard to the questions of legitimacy that often restricted women's sexual autonomy. Peres's will listed debts owed to his estate. Gertrudes de la Cruz, wife of Joseph Lisardo, owed him sixteen pesos for material. An otherwise unidentified woman named

Dominga owed him eight pesos, four reals. Gertrudes, widow of Joseph de Sosa, owed him twelve pesos. Ana Garzía owed him six pesos worth of corn. Peres then listed his special bequests. Each of his sons had already received a horse, so his daughter, María Antonia, would receive the value of a horse in cash. Rosa Peres, a mestiza who had been born in his house and raised as his daughter, received six breeding cows. Her son, Joseph María, got two breeding cows, two horses, and a saddle. María de Saragoza, his servant, got six cows and one bull. The bulk of his remaining estate would then be divided equally among his legitimate children.[37]

All of the debtors Peres named were women. Whether this was because women did all the shopping or because he did not extend credit to men is unknown. Whatever the reason, married women could incur debts of their own. Gertrudes's husband's name appeared only to identify her, not to imply that he was responsible for the debt. One of the debts was to be paid in corn, because there was little cash in the Spanish settlement. Most important, the will highlights the importance of family. Peres's illegitimate daughter, Rosa, and her son both got enough livestock to support them. Even the servant received livestock so that she could be independent. The legitimate sons and daughter inherited equally, showing that they had equal status. This type of estate division was normal, though not everyone left property to their servants.

Spanish law did allow wills that did not follow the rules of intestate succession. A will filed in 1770 gave all property to the deceased man's widow and provided that their children would inherit only after her death. The children objected, demanding what they considered their fair share of the estate, but the widow filed suit to be declared sole heir, and the will was upheld. Estates could be divided amicably even in cases without a will and without following the rules of intestate succession. When Cayetano Guerra died, his children divided his belongings. The legitimate children, three sons and two daughters, split most of the estate equally, while two women—apparently Guerra's illegitimate daughters—each received a silk shirt, an arrangement that pleased everyone involved.[38] Most Spanish laws governing property rights preserved the happiness and welfare of the community instead of one individual, a requirement that could work in women's interest. Judges acted as needed for the benefit of the family as a whole or for the larger community. Stopping and preventing conflicts held high priority in the courts. Here, as in so many other cases, all parties to the dispute—men and women, legitimate and illegitimate children—had to declare that they were satisfied with the results.

When Don Fernando de Veramendi, one of San Fernando de Béxar's richest residents, was killed by raiding Apaches, his will showed both the extent of his property and his familiarity with Spanish legal tradition. He stated that he had brought twenty-six hundred pesos to his marriage and that his wife had brought no cash, but he also stipulated that her jewelry, clothing, and kitchen utensils were her separate property and were not to be counted with his estate. He directed his executors to inventory all his property, deduct twenty-six hundred pesos (to account for his separate property), and give half of the remainder to his wife as her share of the community property. Twenty-six hundred pesos plus the remaining half of the community property constituted his estate. He directed that after his debts were paid and expenses were deducted, the remainder of his estate was to be divided equally among his heirs.[39]

Doña Josepha Grandos, the widow of Don Fernando Veramendi, was one of his executors and had an equal role with his business partners. The listing of his assets showed extensive debts owed to him (by both men and women) as well as the inventory from his store. The fine fabrics mentioned show that by 1783, elite women in San Fernando could dress in silks, lace, and brocade. Doña Josepha was pregnant when Don Fernando died, but the document stated that since she was known to be honorable and virtuous, the child would be assumed to be his and would share in the estate. Women without such a reputation would be watched carefully to assure that they did not become pregnant after their husbands' deaths. The widow eventually received more than 4,000 pesos as her share of the community property, and the children split the remaining 6,734 pesos equitably.[40]

On occasion wills, like other legal deeds, revealed that family relations were not always amicable, but even then, women had the right to inherit property. Raphaela de la Garza brought suit against her son, Joseph Antonio Curbelo, claiming that he had entered the house she shared with her second husband, demanded that he provide her with a house so that Curbelo could have the one that had been his father's, and then tried to kill his mother's new husband with a sword. Joseph countersued, saying that he had only become violent after his new stepfather had thrown him out of the house. Curbelo asked that his father's estate be probated so the new husband would not spend all of Joseph's inheritance. The outcome of this case was not recorded, but the case demonstrates the social and legal bulwark that protected widows' property rights.[41]

In the legal cases that involved marriages, extramarital affairs, and engagements, evidence of women's subordinate status moderates the stories of their independence. On the whole, women could make choices about their personal relations, but those choices were limited by their husbands' privileged access to their body: the law sided with the husband's rights over the wife's choices. In 1783, Antonio de el Toro brought charges against his employer, Felipe Flores, for having an affair with de el Toro's wife, who was also Flores's servant. Flores was fined fifty silver pesos and warned against further dealings with either of them. Another such incident would result in a fine of five hundred pesos and banishment for five years. Flores also had to pay court costs of ninety-five pesos. This case, in combination with that of Antonia Lusgardia Hernandez, suggests that community standards allowed men to have an affairs with unmarried servants but not with married ones.[42]

Diego Menchaca engaged in illicit relations with Gertrudis Barron, wife of Juan de Sosa. When de Sosa found out, he killed Menchaca. The affair apparently was consensual, for the judge ordered Barron shackled and imprisoned because her actions had led to the affair and thus to the murder. De Sosa was also imprisoned for the murder, but he was freed after arguing that it was legal for him to defend his wife's honor by killing the adulterer. Again, the husband had the right to secure access to his wife's body even through lethal means. At de Sosa's request, Barron, too, was later freed.[43]

Pedro Joseph Texada petitioned for a legal separation from his wife after he found her in bed with Francisco Seguro on two occasions. Seguro, an Indian, had a reputation for having affairs with married women. At first, Seguro was imprisoned and the wife was held in custody in the house of a city official, but Texada changed his petition to ask that his wife return to him; however, he remained adamant that Seguro be punished for his actions. The court found that Seguro was indeed a threat to domestic bliss and exiled him for two years.[44] Society expected not only that married women would uphold the family honor but also that men who had sex with married women would be punished.

In another instance where societal expectations for women's purity led to violence, Joseph Antonio Ballejo was shot to death while walking from the villa to the presidio with his wife, María Refugio de Jesús de Santa María, an Indian. She was immediately arrested and charged with his murder. In her defense, she claimed that an Indian male named Arocha had paid her husband two pesos to have sex with her. She refused to go along with the deal and suspected that Arocha had shot Ballejo in revenge. When she told the judge that she had not seen the actual shooting, he did not believe her. After extensive questioning, she confessed to having asked Arocha to kill her husband and received a sentence of seven years of "labor suitable for women."[45]

María Caravajal provides further insight into how the Spanish system punished adulteresses. Caravajal's husband, a soldier, had been absent for twelve years. During that time, she lived with another man, Juan José Vergara, and they had children. When news came that her husband was about to return, Vergara was imprisoned and then exiled for two years. He returned before the end of the allotted time and was reimprisoned. Caravajal was warned to avoid Vergara and live properly with her husband.[46] Here again, the judgment prioritized community peace over severe punishment. The law demanded that women behave properly—that is, be faithful and live with their husbands as recognized by the church. But here the judge did not order any other punishment for the adulteress. Such a decision echoed the wills that recognized servant-mistresses and their illegitimate offspring and reflected an inclination within New Spain to acknowledge that controlling women's bodies was at least a complicated if not impossible enterprise for men.

Through the lens of these public affairs, it can be seen that women had more latitude in their private lives than might be expected. However, a husband did have the legal right to control his wife's sexual actions, which often brought dishonor onto the family. He could even kill a man who committed adultery with his wife. The husband had the authority to punish his wife for sexual infidelity, but the courts apparently did not, for women did not face severe physical punishment or fines from Spanish officials for having extramarital affairs.

Marriages among Spanish and Hispanicized families brought them together in ties of kinship, so prospective marriages concerned everyone in the families. Women had the legal right to choose whom they would marry or at least to veto their families' selections. Cases involving marriages also indicate that men could use their female relatives, especially younger women, to advance social status and show the antagonism between the mission and the villa. In 1779, Francisco Menchaca, a Hispanicized mission Indian, had promised to marry Francisca Uriega, who appears to be another Indian. The vicar of the mission favored the union, as Catholic marriages tended to keep Indians at the mission. After Menchaca changed his mind, Uriega complained to the vicar, who ordered Menchaca arrested and imprisoned by the secular authorities. Governor Domingo Cabello y Robles subsequently ordered Menchaca freed on the grounds that the vicar lacked the authority to order such an arrest. Undaunted, the vicar again ordered Menchaca arrested; Cabello again had him freed because the vicar had not followed proper procedure. At this point, Menchaca fled the mission. The vicar complained about the governor's interference, blaming him for Menchaca's departure.[47]

Urbano Hinojosa, another mission Indian, promised to marry María de la Trinidad Hernández, a young Indian girl. Fray José de Salas promoted this marriage, giving gifts to María's mother to secure her consent. However, María's brothers, Carlos and Pedro Hernández, and her uncles, José Miguel and Francisco de Salas Games, protested. Her brothers, who were soldiers at the presidio, wanted to marry her off to a soldier friend of theirs. When this case first came to trial, Spanish officials said that because the girl was only twelve years old, the proposed marriage was an offense against God. Authorities ordered the girl placed with a Spanish family so that she could learn true Christian values. The friar answered that the girl's father was dead, so the mother's wishes should control her; moreover, because she was thirteen and a half, she was old enough to marry. The brothers argued that the mother was lazy and a spendthrift and had agreed to the marriage only to receive gifts. Because their mother had such a bad reputation, the brothers contended, they should be able to choose their sister's husband. The litigation might have continued for a long time, but Hinojosa asked to be released from his contract so that he could marry another woman. María then released him from his pledge.[48]

In both of these cases, women had agency to choose whom they would marry and had the force of Spanish law to enforce marital promises. Only the hostility between the mission and government officials prevented the first marriage, and only Hinojosa's change of heart stopped the second. Spanish women, including Hispanicized Indians, had the legal authority to choose their husbands, though families had some power to prevent unscrupulous men from taking advantage of innocent young women. One Spanish official commented in 1783 that children under the age of twenty-five needed parental consent to marry, and mothers could not provide that consent unless fathers agreed.[49]

Some older women had different motives for marrying. A widow could collect the pension of a soldier who died in service, a profit motive that apparently led to several marriages to presidial solders. In 1780, the captain of the presidio ordered that army officers' widows receive their husbands' pensions only if the men had died in battle. It seems that some women were marrying older soldiers, letting them die of disease or old age, inheriting their pensions, and then immediately marrying again, a crass approach to which the Spanish officials objected.[50]

In a case reminiscent of that of Antonia Lusgardia, María Gertrudis de la Peña, a native of Camargo, was a slave in San Fernando. She had been sold by José de Bocanegro to Don Pedro José de la Peña, who was supposed to treat her like a daughter. However, after he got her pregnant, he transferred her to Don Antonio Toledo y Oquilla, who was supposed to treat her as a daughter and servant, not as a slave. But Oquilla grew angry with her and took away all her clothes so that she could not leave the house. He then sold her to Don Antonio Navarro, who was supposed to free her after three years. She petitioned for her freedom early because he treated her so badly. The court found out that she was an Indian and thus could not be enslaved under Spanish law. The judge declared her free and told her to go back to her own people so that other Spanish men could not abuse her. As in Lusgardia's case, the Spanish court acted to protect a poor, helpless woman.[51]

Finally, the experience of women in mission towns was replicated in other New Spain settlements. South Texas was settled in a different manner than the rest of Texas. The area between the Rio Grande and the Nueces River was part of Nuevo Santander, now northern Mexico. José de Escandon, a military officer who had earned the title of Count of Sierra Gorda, held political and military control over this area as governor and captain general and laid out townships along the lower Río Grande beginning in 1747. Each town was to be self-sufficient and contain a mission and a small presidio. Settlers received free land, money to buy farming tools and supplies, and a ten-year tax exemption. Lots were distributed according to the relative merits of the individuals and their service to the Crown. Presidial captains, for example, received better lots than common soldiers, who got better lots than civilian settlers. Captains' widows also received preferential treatment.[52] Land grants for towns in this region make it clear that women, mostly but not all widows, bought, sold, and traded land.

In the founding of Laredo, Francisca de Oribe, a widow, and María de Jesús Sánchez, whose marital status was not listed in the original documents, received lots. Francisca received a town lot with river frontage, while María's lot was just off the town plaza. In Revilla, women received eight lots. Isabel María Sánchez, a widow, immediately traded hers for one belonging to José Santiago Gutierres. Isabel Gonzales was listed as a widow, but no marital status was mentioned for the other women. Macela de la Garza's son, Nicolás Guerra, took possession for her, but the other women apparently took possession for themselves. From the map, these *porciones* (plots of land) seem at least as good as the ones given to men, with good riverfront access for irrigation.[53]

In the establishment of Mier, three women received lots. Rosa Garcia, formerly a resident of the neighboring town of Camargo, had an improved *estancia* (a large farm suitable for raising livestock). María Bartola had a farm of her own. The land given to Ana María Guajardo fronted the river. In large and prosperous Camargo, women received eight land grants. One of the best lots went to María Quitería Villareal, a widow who had remarried a soldier, was the daughter of an original settler, and already owned a rancho. Her brother, Venacio Villarreal, took possession for her. Rosa Zamora was a widow of an original settler and so received a lot, but she left the area so the land went instead to a former soldier. Petra Rodriguez, María Marcela Marinez, Josefa Benavides, Margarita Gonsales, Ana Guerra, and Josefa de los Santos are all listed as widows or original settlers, but Baptista López was just listed as *antiguo agregado*—someone who had not been an original settler but who had lived there for at least six years. Nine women, all of them widows, received land in the town of Reynosa.[54]

These assignments of land show that Spanish women held a certain amount of power in their communities. Women, usually widows but not always, claimed land and the rights of settlers equally with men. Spanish settlers saw it as normal that a woman would own and run ranches, farms, or businesses. Because widows could inherit full title to land from their husbands instead of merely having life estates, they could ensure future prosperity for themselves and their children. While widows often remarried, they did so by choice, not out of economic necessity, precisely because they had legal status.[55]

Antonia Lusgardia Hernández, the wronged servant, was right to put her faith in Spain's legal system. It not only protected women from the vagaries of men but also gave them the freedom to shape their lives as they saw fit. Women in Spanish Texas held almost equal status with men. They had the most important right, the right to own land, which could make them self-sufficient. They could buy or sell that land as they wished, sue in court to protect their rights, and were trusted as witnesses. Most women, of course, never went to court or exercised any of these legal rights. But the ones who did left an indelible message about the strength and character of women in Spanish Texas and how they could use the law for their benefit.

NOTES

1. Béxar Archives Translations, reel 2, vol. 7, 117–18. Spanish spelling of names was creative and inconsistent. For example, *Antonia* was sometimes spelled *Anttonia*, and *Hernándes* was sometimes spelled *Ernandes*.

2. Ibid., 119–21.

3. S. P. Scott, ed. and trans., *The Visigothic Code (Forum Judicum)* (Littleton, Colo.: Rothman, 1982), 10–24.

4. Joseph F. O'Callaghan, *A History of Medieval Spain* (Ithaca: Cornell University Press, 1975), 26–67, 116–427, 435–45; Derek W. Lomax, *The Reconquest of Spain* (London: Longman, 1978), 10–467.

5. For a detailed discussion of this acquisition of rights, see Heath Dillard, *Daughters of the Reconquest: Women in Castilian Town Society, 1100–1300* (New York: Cambridge University Press, 1984).

6. Evelyn S. Proctor, *Alfonso X of Castile: Patron of Literature and Learning* (Oxford: Clarendon, 1951), 49–64; Samuel Parsons Scott, ed. and trans., *Las Siete Partidas* (New York: Commerce Clearing House, 1931).

7. For a more detailed explanation of the early settlement of Texas, see Donald E. Chipman and Harriet Denise Joseph, *Spanish Texas, 1519–1821* (Austin: University of Texas Press, 2010), esp. chaps. 5–7; Robert S. Weddle, *The French Thorn: Rival Explorers in the Spanish Sea, 1682–1762* (College Station: Texas A&M University Press, 1991).

8. Chipman and Joseph, *Spanish Texas*, 128–73. See also Jesús F. de la Teja, *San Antonio de Béxar: A Community on New Spain's Northern Frontier* (Albuquerque: University of New Mexico Press, 1995).

9. William C. Foster, *Spanish Expeditions into Texas, 1689–1768* (Austin: University of Texas Press, 1995), 204–5.

10. There are large archives of material pertaining to Spanish Texas. Spanish officials carefully recorded all disputes, testimony, and pleadings as well as the usual government documents. Many of these documents are housed in the Dolph Briscoe Center for American History, University of Texas at Austin, and are available on the web as well as in microfilm. Much of the material in the Béxar Archives has even been translated into English.

11. Gilbert R. Cruz, *Let There Be Towns: Spanish Municipal Origins in the American Southwest, 1610–1810* (College Station: Texas A&M University Press, 1988), 52–80; David Weber, *The Spanish Frontier in North America*, brief ed. (New Haven: Yale University Press, 2009), 144–45; Chipman and Joseph, *Spanish Texas*, 128–73.

12. While most of the material on this chapter comes from the Béxar Archives, other archives confirm that Spanish women in colonial Texas owned land, wrote wills, and otherwise took advantage of their legal rights. In *A Report on the Spanish Archives in San Antonio, Texas*, Carlos E. Castañeda describes documents found in churches and local government offices but not collected in the Béxar Archives. Women, mostly widows, petitioned the villa for lots to live on. For example, the governor granted requests from Janiera Cantu in 1736 and from Nicolasa Ximenes in 1737 for lots on which to build homes. Four women's wills appear on a single page that covers 1767 to 1779: only one of the women is described as a widow. A page from 1807–8 lists two suits to settle estates and four deeds of sale involving women. In one of these cases, María Antonia Navarro is listed as the wife of Ygnacio Perez. See Carlos E. Castañeda, *A Report on the Spanish Archives in San Antonio, Texas* (San Antonio: Yanaguana Society, 1937), 28, 78, 56.

13. Béxar Archives Translations, reel 14, vol. 120, 26–41.

14. Ibid, 37–46.

15. Ibid., 26–41.

16. Charles R. Cutter, *The Legal Culture of Northern New Spain, 1700–1810* (Albuquerque: University of New Mexico Press, 1995), 135.

17. For more about marriages in Spain, see Dillard, *Daughters of the Reconquest*; Thomas Glick, *From Muslim Fortress to Christian Castle: Social and Cultural Changes in Medieval Spain* (New York: Manchester University Press, 1995). On how these Spanish norms transferred to New Spain, see Jean A. Stuntz, *Hers, His, and Theirs: Community Property Law in Spain and Early Texas* (Lubbock: Texas Tech University Press, 2005).

18. Doña Antonia may have been a widow, which would explain why no husband filed on her behalf, but her marital condition is not noted in the legal records. Marital status usually was noted for both men and women, but as identification, not as a limitation on their legal rights.

19. Béxar Archives Translations, reel 16, vol. 135, 12.

20. Ibid, 30.

21. Ibid., reel 7, vol. 50, 15–21.

22. Ibid., reel 2, vol. 10, 114–16.

23. Ibid., reel 2, vol. 10, 95–99, 169–74, 117–19, reel 7, vol. 48, 76.

24. For more on women's rights and the lack thereof under English common law, see Marylynn Salmon, *Women and the Law of Property in Early America* (Chapel Hill: University of North Carolina Press, 1986); Stuntz, *Hers, His, and Theirs*, 87–108.

25. English common law allowed the courts to name women as "deputy husbands," this procedure was extremely rare.

26. Béxar Archives Translations, reel 3, vol. 17, 1–6.

27. Ibid., vol. 18, 153–56.

28. Ibid., 72–77.

29. Ibid., 68–71, 145–48, reel 2, vol. 10, 198–201.

30. Ibid., reel 9, vol. 67, 67–70, reel 13, vol. 112, 34.

31. Ibid., reel 7, vol. 48, 16–23.

32. Ibid., 27–39.

33. Ibid., 43–65.

34. Ibid., reel 2, vol. 10, 100–105, reel 7, vol. 48, 86.

35. Joseph McKnight, "Spanish Law for the Protection of the Surviving Spouse," *Anuario de Historia del Derecho Español* 57 (1987): 373–95. See also Salmon, *Women and the Law of Property*.

36. Béxar Archives Translations, reel 2, vol. 10, 51–55.

37. Ibid., vol. 18, 104–11.

38. Ibid., reel 7, vol. 48, 74, vol. 49, 101.

39. Ibid., reel 14, vol. 118, 2.

40. Ibid., 12, 74–83.

41. Ibid., reel 7, vol. 48, 73–78.

42. Ibid., reel 14, vol. 117, 1–54.

43. Ibid., reel 7, vol. 52, 41–116.

44. Ibid., reel 13, vol. 109, 11–26.

45. Ibid., reel 8, vol. 62, 57–105.

46. Ibid., reel 13, vol. 109, 55–65.

47. Ibid., reel 11, vol. 91, 47–53.

48. Ibid., reel 13, vol. 108, 1–44.

49. Ibid., reel 9, vol. 68, 115–18.

50. Ibid., reel 12, vol. 93, 7.

51. Ibid., reel 6, vol. 45, 85–88.

52. Galen D. Greaser, *New Guide to Spanish and Mexican Land Grants in South Texas* (Austin: Texas General Land Office, 2009), 6–7. The guide explains the method by which the various plots of land were disbursed as well as maps of each area.

53. Ibid., 29, 33–34, 39, 43–46.

54. Ibid., 49, 52–55, 57–66, 69–79.

55. See Salmon, *Women and the Law of Property*; Carol Berkin, *First Generations: Women in Colonial America* (New York: Hill and Wang, 1996); Mary Beth Norton, "The White Woman's Experience in Early America," *American Historical Review* 89 (June 1984): 593–619.

The Lives of Enslaved Women in Texas

Changing Borders and Challenging Boundaries

ERIC WALTHER

Traveling through Texas in the 1850s, northerner Frederick Law Olmsted observed that "elsewhere slavery is settled and accepted but in Texas it is a state of war and brutal." In 1910, a former slave known as Aunt Kitty marveled at the relatively light fieldwork she had done in North Carolina before her sale to the Lone Star State: "Dey work you hard in Texas, most till midnight."[1] Olmsted and Aunt Kitty were among many who have seen Texas as exceptional, in this instance because of brutal conditions for the enslaved. But while the evidence cannot confirm that Texas was unique in this way—indeed, enslaved women in Texas faced obstacles similar to those faced by their counterparts elsewhere in the South—it does suggest that Texas's unique history as a Spanish colony and its place in the expansion of the cotton economy at that industry's high point had a pronounced impact on slaves there. Historians recently have focused on the role of gender and the central role of economic profitability in the development of slavery. These concepts help us to understand enslaved women's lives in Texas, certainly. But concurrent with these two concerns is the role of governmental regulations. As the Spanish, Mexican, Texan, and U.S. governments swapped control, they brought new rules, and conflict among the differing governments created places for slaves to resist slaveholders' control. Throughout these changes, slaveholders' pursuit of profits meant that control of women's productive and reproductive labor lay at the heart of slavery in Texas. Slaves, however, did not define themselves in terms of capitalist endeavor, and that resistance challenged white supremacy.

As the preceding essays suggest, the frontier era of slavery in Texas lasted for centuries yet involved few people.[2] Without large cities or gold or silver, the northeasternmost part of New Spain languished. Even though African slavery

MANDY HADNOT, FORMER SLAVE
Woodville, Texas, 1937.
Federal Writers Project, Former Slave Narratives,
Library of Congress, Washington, D.C.

had made its mark in Mexico proper, the institution existed in Texas on a scale smaller than the general population. The first reliable census of slaves in Spanish Texas revealed that in 1777, San Antonio de Béxar, Nacogdoches, and La Bahía had but 3,103 people, only 20 of whom were Negroes, most likely slaves. Eight years later, the total population had dropped to 2,919, but 43 were counted as slaves (24 in San Antonio, 16 in Nacogdoches, 3 in La Bahía). By 1790, 37 slaves resided among the total population, which had dwindled to 2,417. In these three settlements, female slaves outnumbered male slaves by 26 to 17 in 1783 and by 22 to 18 the next year.[3] Clearly, then, eighteenth-century Texas was a small society with a few slaves rather than a slave society in which the institution character- ized the entire region. Because of the sparse population, Spaniards had little influence in Texas. Instead, Caddos, Wichitas, Comanches, Osage, and other Native Americans dominated. The vastness of the territory, its many indige- nous peoples, and international competition over the area left their marks as the experiences of enslaved Texans changed dramatically between 1820 and 1865.[4]

Of course, for those who were enslaved, the scope of the institution mattered very little, above all when it came to buying and selling of human beings, a pro- cess that often broke up families. Especially in light of the meager population, masters bought and sold slaves frequently. On May 16, 1772, Joseph Dickison of San Antonio sold Mary Cook to the governor of the province of Texas, Barón de Juan María Vicencio Ripperdá, for seventy-five dollars. On March 20, 1797, two Spanish soldiers stationed at Nacogdoches sold María Isabel; her daugh- ter, Manuela; and son, Manuel, for 350, 200, and 150 pesos respectively.[5] Fran- çois Morvan of Nacogdoches, a sixty-two-year-old farmer, lived with his three nephews, one niece, and one black slave and one Apache slave, neither of whom were identified by sex. In 1806, Nacogdoches farmer Don Jose María Mora and his wife lived with their four children as well as a thirty-five-year-old slave, Luisa, who had been separated from her husband and their nine-year-old son.[6]

The separation of Luisa from her family may have violated Spanish laws regarding slave marriages and families. Although slave marriage as a legal arrangement never existed in Anglo-American slave law, it did in Spanish law, the Siete Partidas. In many ways, the Spanish slave code stood in sharp contrast to English and American laws as well as to basic assumptions of the human con- dition. The Anglo-Saxon tradition defined slaves as chattel property; the Siete Partidas viewed slavery as an "accident of fate and against the laws of nature." It defined both rights and obligations of slaves, including the right to a mea- sure of personal security and legal relief from a cruel master, conjugal rights, the right not to be separated from children, and the rights to hold property and initiate lawsuits. It allowed slaves to buy family members and to purchase and free themselves. Slave women could obtain freedom for themselves and for their children through uncompensated manumission, which often involved sexual relationships with their masters. And Spanish law more generally required generosity by male heads of households toward all dependents, both their own families and others living in their homes.[7] In 1793 in San Antonio, a slave, José Tomás Blas, approached local authorities to seek permission to visit his wife, María Luisa, and their children in far-off Nacogdoches. Because María Luisa's master refused to allow a visit, the provincial government forced him to release María so that she could live with her husband. In 1823, Tejano Mariano Lopez emancipated his twenty-one-year-old slave, María Rosa de la Rosa, who received not only her freedom but also cash and the right to own property. Near the end of the Mexican possession of Texas, in 1832, a member of Stephen F. Austin's colony manumitted his slave, Celia, and her children, an act nearly impossible to replicate after Texas revolted against Mexico.[8]

Few slaves were docile, and many sought to liberate themselves. Spain's vast domain in North America grew even larger after the 1763 Treaty of Paris transferred the expansive Louisiana Territory from France to Spain. Bernardo de Gálvez, governor of Spanish Louisiana, wrote frequently to his counterparts in Mexico, seeking their help in finding and returning runaways. The border between Louisiana and Texas was quite porous.[9] After the U.S. acquisition of Louisiana in 1803, the changing border added an international dimension to the apprehension of runaways. In 1805, Spanish authorities bolstered their presence in East Texas by creating the Trinidad de Salcedo settlement to curb smuggling and illegal American immigration into Texas. But western Louisiana's ever-increasing population undermined those efforts, as did the persistence of trade and kinship ties, especially between Natchitoches, Louisiana, and Nacogdoches, Texas.[10]

The Texas border situation changed yet again with the Adams-Onís Treaty of 1819. The United States had claimed much of eastern Texas as part of the Louisiana Purchase of 1803 but sixteen years later formally ceded to Spain all land south of the Red River and west of the Sabine. This move did not sit well with many Americans. James Long of Mississippi led a filibustering expedition from Natchez to conquer Texas. He spent the winter of 1821–22 near Galveston, on the Bolivar Peninsula, with his wife, two children, and Kiamatia, a twelve-year-old slave girl. The expedition proved disastrous for the Americans: Long was captured, imprisoned, and finally shot and killed by a guard in 1822. Kiamatia remained with Jane Long at Bolivar Point, helping her give birth, and later accompanied her mistress to Richmond, Texas, near Houston.[11]

The fluctuating situation along the border between the United States and Spanish Texas also opened the door for daring souls who saw an opportunity to flee from slavery in the United States. A female slave named Tivi was born on a North Carolina plantation in 1796 and later toiled there as a house servant. Tivi recalled her first master as kind, despite the fact that he sold her to James Kirkham for one thousand dollars. Kirkham moved to a cotton plantation in Natchitoches, taking Tivi with him. She and three male slaves subsequently stole a pair of horses and a mule and ran away from Kirkham and headed toward Mexican Texas, hoping that American laws that defined them as slaves would not follow them into New Spain. Once they crossed the Sabine River, they thought that they were free. When the runaways saw Spanish troops camped near Nacogdoches, they surrendered. The soldiers took them to town, where civil authorities sent them to Monterrey. They arrived there in April 1820 and were interrogated. Tivi justified her actions by complaining about the harsh treatment she had received from Kirkham and his wife. Tivi thought Spaniards would treat her better. When asked if she understood that running away hurt her master financially, Tivi replied that she had been mistreated and she had a right to flee from brutality. Kirkham worked strenuously to retrieve his valuable human property, eventually convincing the viceroy of New Spain to order the return of Tivi and the others, but the Mexican Revolution against Spain that started in 1810 reached fruition with Mexican independence in 1821, and Tivi and the three men remained free.[12]

The steady decline of population in Texas and the Mexican Revolution resulted in changes for slaves and the institutional support for slavery. The population of Texas's largest town, San Antonio, dropped to sixteen hundred in 1820, a decrease of two hundred since 1783. Most of the area's missions had been abandoned, and poverty characterized the town. But many Béxariños supported the growing connections between Tejanos and Anglo-American immigrants, an arrangement formalized by Stephen F. Austin's successful efforts to plant a colony of American immigrants in Texas. Spanish and Mexican authorities, in turn, concluded that the only way to solidify their hold on Texas was through Americans—particularly Austin and his father, Moses—and the thriving cotton culture of the southern United States.[13]

With the arrival of Americans came a clash of cultures with newly independent Mexico. Many of the leaders of the revolution opposed slavery. Although Stephen F. Austin and other Americans brought some slaves into Texas, Mexican authorities chafed at the practice. The Mexican Congress outlawed the slave trade in 1824 and three years later forbade slavery altogether; further statutes for enforcement followed. Austin and others quickly found a way around these legal restrictions: indentured servitude. Prospective migrant masters took slaves to notary publics or other government officials, either in the United States or in Texas, and set free the slaves, who were then forced to make their marks on indentures that stated working conditions and terms of service. Marmaduke D. Sandifer, for example, took his slave, Clarissa, to an alcalde at San Felipe de Austin on Christmas Day 1833 and forced her to sign a ninety-nine-year indenture. On September 24, 1831 a notary public in New Orleans, William Young Lewis, issued indentures for a total of forty-five bondspeople—twenty-two females, eighteen males, and five children. The group included a woman, Kit, and her son, Simon; Betty and her daughter, Julia-Ann; an entire family consisting of Nancy, her husband, Jim, and their three mulatto children; and Esther and her two children.[14]

The story of Hendrick Arnold provides a complex example of the crossing of both international borders and racial boundaries during the Mexican period. Arnold, who later served as a spy during the Texas Revolution, moved to Texas in 1826 from Mississippi with his parents, Daniel Arnold, a white man, and Rachel Arnold, apparently a black woman. They settled on the Brazos River. Although most people considered Hendrick black, his brother was referred to as white, and both were free, even though there is no record of their manumission. In 1827, Hendrick and an Arnold slave, Dolly, had a daughter, whom Hendrick kept as a slave.[15]

Forced across the Texas border by the original 297 white families organized by Stephen F. Austin between 1821 and 1825, African American slaves began to appear in the region in significant numbers. By 1825, sixty-nine of those families owned a total of 443 slaves, representing almost 25 percent of the colony's population along the Lower Brazos River.[16] With productive, abundant land and settlers intent on finding the cheapest sources of labor, many whites in Mexican Texas (as well as during the period of Texas independence) looked overseas. In the early 1830s, slaves from the west coast of Africa could be purchased for less than forty dollars each, while those from Cuba cost less than three hundred dollars apiece. Although the United States outlawed the Atlantic slave trade by 1808 and Spain followed suit in 1820, the illicit nature of the trade, combined with great demand in Texas and elsewhere, brought tremendous profits for smugglers. Between 1833 and 1843, slaves from overseas sold in Texas for between five hundred and fifteen hundred dollars. Between 1831 and 1835, Cuba imported eighty-five thousand slaves from Africa, and Havana was only a few days' journey from Galveston. More than five hundred African-born slaves were forced to Texas, and many of them ended up in settlements along the Brazos River. James W. Fannin, an early Texas settler, smuggled more than 150 African slaves from Cuba during one August 1835 trip. The most infamous Texas slave smuggler, Monroe Edwards, landed a cargo of 170 Africans, via Cuba, at the mouth of the Brazos on February 28, 1836.[17]

Once these men and women arrived in Texas, they had to change the way they communicated and behaved; they, in turn, changed the slave communities of Texas. Whether produced by Africans or by their descendants, by men or by women, archeological artifacts from the Levi Jordan Plantation in Brazoria County reveal that African culture, especially spiritual expressions, persisted in Texas beyond the Civil War. Some of the objects found may be the remains of anthropomorphic wooden figures called Nkisi, part of a general ritual tool kit originally from the Kongo. Nkisi also helped to treat the ill, protected people and communities, and initiated others into the common rituals.[18]

Henry Jones, an early settler, planter, and rancher in what would become Fort Bend County near Houston, purchased several of the young African males landed by Edwards in 1836: Colly, Shepherd, Firmna (later Firema), and Hiram ranged from ten to fifteen years old at the time of their purchase. Firema formed a relationship with Jones's slave, Celia, who was born in Texas in 1830. Firema later took the surname Edwards, a reminder of his original captor. The couple had two children, Cain and "Little Mary." Colly joined Jones's slave, Caroline, born in Texas in 1835; Shepherd formed a bond with Diana Jones, born in South Carolina in 1830; and Hiram joined with Margaret Ryon, a Jones slave born in Virginia in 1835. Though no documents exist about their private lives, these couples and their families must have undergone the creolization of African and African American ways that has characterized much of the history of slavery in the United States.[19] Harriet Barrett, born a slave in Texas about 1851, recalled that while her mother was born in Virginia, her father was born in Africa. "I's heered my grandpa was wild and dey didn't know 'bout marryin' in Africy." Josephine Howard remembered that both her mother and grandmother were born in Africa. One day, while the men from their community were hunting, "de man come in a little boat to de sho' and tell dem he got presents on de big boat . . . locked in a black hole." Andrew Simms recalled that slave hunters caught both his mother and father in Africa. Their master moved them all to Texas during the Civil War.[20]

The Mims Plantation on the San Bernard River provides a glimpse into the private lives of African and African American slaves in Texas. In 1845, that plantation had thirteen slave households, at least seven of which included at least one African-born person; five of the households persisted until 1870. None of the African-born women formed unions with African American men, and of the eight African men with families, three married African women and three married African-American women, one of whom had African-born parents. (The nativities of the wives of the other two men remain unknown.) After slavery, as many as twenty-eight of the thirty-three African-born women of

Brazoria County married African-born men. In 1840 in Houston, a slave couple, Amanda and Frank, were offered for sale in a newspaper ad that described them as Africans who knew little to no English.[21]

As Mexico moved away from slavery, the few protections for slaves and their families in Texas vanished along with the enforcement of the Siete Partidas, as Mexican authorities took no significant action to meddle with the small but growing slave population. Out of this legal vacuum, American legal and customary standards for slavery prevailed, outlawing slave marriages on the grounds that property (human or otherwise) could not marry property. But the intimate bonds between slaves—married, if only in their own minds—occasionally challenged masters' power. In 1835, William Russell of Brazoria County hired eight male slaves from Ashmore Edwards, brother and partner to smuggler Monroe Edwards. Russell had to fool the men to get them to leave their wives, and all fled his plantation to return to their spouses. A vexed Russell complained to Edwards, "If their wife are taken from them again, unless they are kept in chains they will follow there, and take them with them in the woods, fully determined to live there and not serve either yourself or me."[22]

Although slavery remained small in scale under Mexican rule and the demand for labor—usually the province of young male slaves—was immense, a surprisingly balanced sex ratio existed at this time that resulted in cohesive family units. Texas's largest slaveholder in 1831, Jared Groce, owned 117 slaves at his Bernardo Plantation. His slave quarters contained twenty-six households, seventeen of which included two parents and children; eight more included a single mother with at least one child. Only one man lived alone. However rare or surprising this might have been, from the start of European exploitation of African slave labor, many masters recognized a distinct advantage in acquiring female slaves instead of men: they were simultaneously productive and reproductive. That is, they could both toil and produce children who would add to a master's wealth and supply more labor over time.[23]

Tensions between Texans and Mexico City over the expansion of slavery contributed to the Texas Revolution and independence in 1836. By August of that year, an American envoy to the Republic of Texas estimated that 30,000 Anglo-Americans lived there, along with 5,000 African Americans, 3,470 Mexicans, and 14,500 Native Americans.[24] Despite the preponderance of Anglo-Americans in the revolution, many Mexicans who owned or supported slavery joined the fight, most notably Erasmo Seguin of San Antonio, a friend and supporter of Austin and owner of a mulatto slave, María Juliana Cureste.[25]

Independence achieved two paradoxical results for slaves in Texas. First, slaveholders ensured that the institution of slavery would be protected absolutely, resulting in a massive new wave of American migration. Second, the Rio Grande now represented an international border, with slavery to the north and freedom to the south, and Texas slaves by and large knew it. One recalled many years later that he laughed when he heard others speak of running to freedom in the North. "There wasn't no reason to *run* up North. All we had to do was to *walk*, but walk *South*, and we'd be free as soon as we crossed the Rio Grande." More than five thousand slaves crossed that southern border to freedom, including at least one group that crossed both racial boundaries and multiple borders to get to Mexico. In 1835, the U.S. government forcibly relocated a group of African American Seminole Indians, descendants of runaway slaves in southern Florida, to Indian Territory (Oklahoma). Fearing recapture by white slave traders, many of them took the tremendous risk of fleeing through Texas to Coahuila, Mexico. By 1861, they returned to Indian Territory, and many later headed back to Texas, settling near Brackettville, 130 miles south of San Antonio. As late as the 1990s, some of the Brackettville Seminoles could still speak a few words of the African American Gullah dialect.[26]

Tremendous fluidity occurred across the Red River border between Texas and Indian Territory. Mary Lindsay, the child of an enslaved black mother and a "Chickasaw part-breed name Sobe Love," was a member of the large Love family that moved from Mississippi to Indian Territory, settling near the Red River by Fort Washita, where Mary was born. Love married off Mary's mother to a slave, William, who was "believed to be a full-blood Chickasaw man named Chick-a-lathe." Mary's master, Bill Merrick, called her Mary-Ka-Chubbe. Her master took Mary from her parents and gave her to a young mistress who then moved to Texas, between Bonham and Honey Grove. Another crosser of the Red River border was Sarah Wilson, born in Arkansas as "a Cherokee slave." Her master, Ben Johnson, had moved Sarah's grandmother from the Sequoyah District, a Cherokee settlement in Indian Territory. His son, Ned Johnson, was Sarah's father. During the Civil War, Johnson moved them all to Texas and hired out all his slaves, including Sarah.[27]

As independent Texas settled into the U.S. cotton economy, enslaved women there lost most of their pathways to autonomy and found, like enslaved women elsewhere in the South, that their lives were often shaped by their capacity to reproduce, their life-cycle stages, and their value as workers. Even while they suffered enormous dislocation, many worked endlessly to hold onto their own identities. Their resistance became more subterranean, though it never disappeared.

The steady rise of abolitionism and the Panic of 1837 convinced many U.S. slaveholders to move to the Republic of Texas. A British minister to the United

States predicted correctly that Texas would "afford an immense opening of the domestic slave trade." The growing use of steamboats facilitated the rush to Texas. Connecticut-born Charles Morgan started the first regular steamship service to Texas from New Orleans in 1837 and steadily expanded that service and his shipping fleet, serving Galveston, Matagorda Bay, and Brazos de Santiago. Whereas the journey from New Orleans to the Texas Gulf Coast had previously taken up to two weeks, steamers took only thirty-six to fifty-four hours and cost only about two dollars more per person than it did to force slaves over land, with less chance for slaves to escape. Moreover, the slaves could easily be sold in Texas, providing a quick profit for slave traders. Ships carried up to 135 slaves, plus free passengers and cargo. By 1845, Texas had more than 27,555 slaves, an increase of more than 450 percent in the nine years since independence. Five years later, the enslaved population had grown another 211 percent to 58,161, and by 1860, it had reached 182,566. The number of slaves had more than tripled over the preceding decade, the most rapid increase of slavery across the South during that period. The balanced sex ratio that existed in Texas before independence continued until the eve of the Civil War: in 1850, 50.65 percent of Texas's slaves were female, and that number had dropped only a tiny bit, to 50.05 percent, by 1860.[28] Slaveholder Alva Fitzpatrick spoke for many Texans in 1849 when he encouraged his nephew to come and to "get as many young negro women as you can. Get as many cows as you can. . . . It is the greatest country for an increase that I have ever saw in my life. I have been here six years and I have had fifteen negro children born and last year three more young women commenced breeding which added seven born last year and five of them is living and doing well."[29]

Interviewed fifty-five years after freedom came, Aunt Kitty recalled that the hardest part of slave life was being taken from her mother and siblings in Alabama. The voyage from Mobile to New Orleans "were dark an' I were feared an' homesick an' seasick." Sally Chambers Banks recollected, "When old massa come to Texas he brung us over first by wagon, a mule wagon with a cover over de top." As a child, Mintie Miller endured a three-month journey from her birthplace in Tuscaloosa, Alabama, to Texas "by wagon, a mule wagon with a cover over de top." Kentucky-born Anna Miller was sold with her parents to a master in Missouri who later sold her mother. When Miller was eight, her master moved to Palo Pinto, west of Fort Worth, with Miller riding in a covered wagon pulled by oxen.[30]

The slaves of Sam Houston illustrate the influx of slaves to Texas, the expectations for enslaved women, and the pressures under which they lived. When Margaret Lea of Alabama, married Houston in 1840, he became the owner of her slaves, Dinan, Polly, Eliza, Charlotte, Vianna, Jet, Bingley, and Joshua. Margaret's father had purchased Eliza to serve his daughter as a cook and Charlotte as a house servant. But in the still-sparse population of the Republic of Texas, Eliza also served as a makeshift nurse when Margaret became ill in 1841, tending her mistress with herbal medicines. Early the next year, Margaret contracted malaria, and Sam Houston sent her back to Alabama for treatment, accompanied by Eliza. After Margaret Houston recovered her health and returned to Texas, she bore a son, Sam Houston Jr. Eliza's jobs now included tending her owners' baby. With her politician-husband away from home so often, Margaret Houston took charge of their slaves. In 1848, Vianna, one of the house servants, died from pneumonia. Only a few months later, Eliza contracted tuberculosis. Greatly upset, Margaret Houston sent Eliza to a local doctor. Charlotte, another house servant, might have been tempted to take advantage of Sam's absences by defying her mistress, and in 1849, Margaret Houston felt compelled to sell Charlotte: "I bore with every kind of insolence until a mixture of some kind was discovered in one of our dishes, and circumstances fixed it on her as the guilty one." Eliza, in contrast, remained a family favorite. The Houstons allowed her and some other slaves to join the same local Baptist church that their owners attended, going to services with their masters but sitting upstairs with other slaves. Eliza also accompanied Sam and Margaret Houston to the governor's mansion in 1860.[31]

Another prominent Texas slaveholder, Philip Minor Cuney, left a legacy, common enough among slaveholders, by violating the sexual boundary that supposedly separated the races. He developed one of the larger slaveholdings in Texas at Sunnyside Plantation, near Hempstead, which recorded 105 slaves in 1850. Adeline Stuart, one of his house slaves who was born in 1818, had a light complexion, reflecting her African American, white, and Potomac Indian heritage. After the death of his first wife, Eliza Cuney, Philip began a sexual relationship with Stuart that continued through his second and third marriages. It is unlikely that Adeline Stuart—or most enslaved women, for that matter—could have consented to these arrangements: they were raped. Adeline bore eight of Philip Cuney's children. One daughter, Jennie Barbour, had her father's blue eyes and blond hair. The Cuneys moved to Houston in 1853, and Philip soon started to manumit his mixed-race children, possibly as a result of his third marriage, to Adeline Spurlock. Adeline Stuart and the last of the children were freed in 1859. He sent most of the children away for their education: Jennie and her future sister-in-law, Josephine, went to a private school for girls in Mannheim, Germany, while the fourth child, Norris Wright Cuney, born in 1848, went to school in Pittsburgh. When he returned after the Civil War, he settled in Galveston and quickly became active in Texas politics during Reconstruction.[32]

Perhaps the longest illicit interracial relationship in antebellum Texas began in the late 1820s and involved Columbus R. "Kit" Patton, who left Kentucky for Mexican Texas. He settled in what became Brazoria County, establishing a sugarcane and cotton farm that grew steadily into a large plantation. Patton became involved sexually with a mixed-race slave named Rachel, who also became his confidante. Everyone in the neighborhood—black and white alike—recognized Rachel as the de facto plantation mistress. This infuriated Patton's mother; his young nephew, Matt; and even his younger and unwed brother, Charles, who lived nearby with his own slave mistress. By 1853, Kit Patton's relationship and odd religious ideas convinced his family that he had become "eccentric." In 1854, Charles and Matt Patton had Kit declared non compos mentis and sent to an insane asylum in South Carolina. Sarah Ford, a slave born on the Patton plantation in 1850, recalled that Charles put Rachel to work in the fields with the other hands.[33]

Several former slaves recalled instances and consequences of concubinage. As a child, Adeline Marshall knew that her master, Captain Brevard of Oyster Creek in Fort Bend County, had no wife "but a black woman what stays at de house." Auntie Thomas Johns remembered her mother's stories of their master, Major Odom of Burleson County. Odom never married but had a mixed-race slave mistress, Aunt Phyllis. Auntie Johns remembered them and their five sons, who, like many children of racially different parents, varied in skin color from nearly white to "nigger dark." That boy's father was a slave. Even though Odom never whipped anyone, he treated all his children as slaves, and when his sons were old enough, he sent them to live in the slave quarters. Francis Bridges of Red River County recalled hearing talk of a white man who was married and had a black mistress who had said that "she didn't want no Negro man smutting her sheets up."[34]

Although slaves lost the legal right to marry after the revolution, most took seriously their relationships with others. Will Adams of Harrison County recalled that his master did not like his slaves to marry "off the place, but sometimes they'd do it, and massa say, 'My nigger am comin' to you place. Make him behave.'" Galveston attorney William Pitt Ballinger gave his slave, Josey, permission to visit his wife whenever he wanted but refused to purchase her because he had no need for another house servant. Rural slaves faced similar problems, with the success or failure of uniting couples wholly dependent on masters. Jeff Calhoun of Austin explained, "You picks out a girl and tell your boss." If she lived at another plantation, her master's permission was required. If it was granted, "they says to de girl, 'You's love dis man?' Dey says to de man, 'You loves dis girl?' If you say you don't know, it's all off, but if you say yes, dey brings in de broom and holds it 'bout a foot off de floor and say to you to jump over. Den he says you's married." Nancy King fondly remembered her wedding day during the Civil War: her mistress gave her cloth and dye for a wedding dress, and she married at a church with a preacher. "After the weddin' massa gave us a big dinner and we had a time."[35]

Of course, like people everywhere, many enslaved women and men in Texas had sexual encounters outside the bonds of matrimony, a situation created in part by the division of enslaved couples by their masters, the frequent lack of options for partners, women's difficulty in fending off men's sexual advances, and the retention of African sexual mores. John White, a cook on a Texas plantation, recalled, "Sometimes I'd slip some things out from the kitchen. The single womenfolks was bad that way. I favors them with something extra from the kitchen. Then they favors me—at night." Former slave Julia Malone's father had died before she was born, but she was proud that "he was make de husband to lots of women on de place, 'cause he de big man."[36]

Many female slaves did not care for marriage, arranged or otherwise. Louis Love's first wife, Celeste, refused to come to Texas with him during the Civil War, "and dat 'solve de marriage." Sarah Ford of Brazoria County explained that her master used to put a man together with a "breedin' woman"—like mules rather than a real marriage. Aunt Pinkie Kelly of Brazoria County held interesting views of marriage, either because she had grown up in a slave society or as a consequence of her own personality. She married Allen Kelley on January 30, 1870, and recalled that he "was de first husban' what I owned and he die. Houston Edmond, he was the las' husban' I ever owned and he die, too."[37]

Rose Williams hated her master because when she was sixteen, he forced her to live with Rufus, a bully, big and bossy. Once night, Rufus climbed into Rose's bunk with her: "I says, 'What you means, you fool nigger?'" When he told her that it was his bunk, too, she responded, "Git out" and shoved him to the floor with her feet. He became enraged and tried to get back in, whereupon "I jumps for de poker. It am 'bout three foot long and when he come at me I lets him have it over the head." He told her, "Jus' wait. You thinks it am smart, but you's foolish in de head. Dey's gwine larn you somethin.'" Two days later, the master told Rose that he had paid a lot of money for her because he wanted her to bear children. He said, "I's put yous to live with Rufus for dat purpose. Now, if you doesn't want whippin' at de stake, yous do what I wants." Rose thought about her options. "Dere it am. What am I's to do? So I 'cides to do as de massa wish and so I yields." The experience soured Rose, and she never married: "After what I does for de massa, I's never wants no truck with any man."[38]

Perhaps no other aspect of the slave life dramatized the range of experiences as did childhood for enslaved girls. Some formerly enslaved women recalled their youth with fondness. During Rosanna Frazier's formative years in Tyler County, all the children at her farm played together, and "white folks calls us 'free niggers.'" A white mistress in southeast Texas wrote to her husband that her daughter was "playing with the little negroes." Mollie Watson loved playing with her master's children, and when they got into fights, her master would punish his children if they were responsible. Mandy Hadnot had a sandpile in which to play but lamented that there were no other children to join her, black or white. Hadnot had happier memories of her mistress, who never lost temper and let the girl "bump on her pianny and didn' say nothin'." Hadnot and her mother remained with that mistress after slavery. In contrast, Emma Taylor was never allowed to play with white children, and "de worstest whippin' I ever got was for playin' with a doll what belonged to one marse's children. I 'members it yet and I ain't never seed a doll purty as dat doll was to me."[39]

But enslaved children were also commoditized and utilized at the whim of their masters, just like older girls and women. Ellen Polk had to feed other children while their mothers worked the fields. "Missy Hannah would have de cooks fix de grub in a big pan and I would take it to de cullud quarters and feed 'em." Adeline Cunningham and Rosina Hoard recalled that all children had to work in the fields as soon as they were old enough to do so. Child labor has always been fraught with danger for free and slave alike. A Houston newspaper reported grimly that an eight-year-old slave girl was missing after she had gone to Buffalo Bayou to fetch a pail of water but lost her footing on a plank over the water and fell in.[40]

As girls grew older and became mothers—often in their mid-teens—their lives grew more complex. They had to work longer and harder, tending to their children as well as they could while preparing food and clothing for their husbands and elderly relatives. As a child, Katie Darling had to be up by five in the morning with her sister, Violate, to milk cows. As Darling grew older, she became a house servant, nursing seven white children "in them bullwhip days." Julia Francis Daniels's mother served as the cook for her master's family, her own family, and her Uncle Joe's family. Julia recalled that her mother "didn't have much time for anythin' but cookin' all the time." Julia bore her first child at age fourteen. In addition to all parents' responsibility to discipline their children, enslaved mothers had to make certain that their children did not incur the wrath of masters and mistresses. Sarah Ford received a beating from her mother for lying; she could have been punished more severely by her owners.[41]

Cotton dominated the economy of antebellum Texas, so women also worked along with men in the fields. Emma Thomas's earliest memory was of "following my maw in the cotton patch"; at the end of each grueling day, she would come home to cook for her family. Harrison Beckett's sisters, Ellen, Sani, Georgy-

Ann, and Cindy, and their mother worked the fields. When they returned to their cabin at nine or ten at night, their mother would be worn out, but she usually found the energy to provide her children with a "feast. But lots of times she's so tired she go to bed without eatin' nothing herself." Mary Kincheon Edwards noted that mothers brought oilcloths to the fields to make shade for their children. As a young woman, Kincheon served as a wet nurse for her master's son, knitted socks, washed clothes, and sometimes worked the fields. She related proudly that she could pick three or four hundred pounds of cotton a day without ever harming her back. For her productivity, her master often rewarded her with a cake or clothes—on one occasion, a dress and shoes.[42]

As enslaved women aged, their owners often assigned them to less grueling tasks. Ann Hawthorne's aunt served as a weaver for both their masters and the slaves. The mother of Sally Banks Chambers milked cows and made and washed clothing. Harriet Barrett's aunt was a weaver for her master and her fellow slaves, while her grandmother was a house servant. At Ellen Polk's plantation on the Guadalupe River in Gonzales County, older women spun yarn, made cloth on looms, and gathered bark, vegetables, and copper into a boiling pot to dye clothing. At his plantation near Henderson, Texas, Jeptha Choice noted that "when babies was born old nigger grannies handled them cases."[43]

Enslaved women often served as medical practitioners. Many of their remedies represented their African heritage, either learned in Africa or passed down from earlier arrivals, as well as Native American influences. Harriet Barrett recalled, "Charcoal and onions and honey for de li'l baby am good, and camphor for de chills and fever and teeth cutting." She boiled red oak bark to make a tea for fever and used cactus weed root to treat fever, chills, and colic. Native Americans used red oak bark as a medicine for heart maladies and bronchial infections and as a disinfectant or astringent. But Barrett's preferred remedy for chills and fever was "to git a rabbit foot tie on string 'round de neck."[44]

Masters, mistresses, or overseers controlled food distribution, and although some were generous, others were quite stingy. Ann Hawthorne's master "fed us good back in slavery. Give us plenty of meat and [corn]bread and greens and t'ings." She often got watermelon, sugarcane, and sweet potatoes, and her grandmother was permitted free access to a smokehouse full of hog meat. Nevertheless, her owner asserted his mastery. "We better eat and shut our mouf. We dassant raise no squall." Silvia King remembered working hard but receiving plenty of food. She and other slaves could help themselves to a smokehouse full of bacon and ham and could drink as much cider and beer as they wanted as long as they did not get drunk—"Marse sho' cut us up if we do." Emma Taylor's master gave his slaves a ration of food for one week; if they finished it before week's end, they received no more. As a girl, she snuck out to a potato patch at night to steal food and never got caught, though on one occasion, a dog came after her. The daring girl "put pepper in dey eyes and dey stopped." Anna Miller grew up on a diet of beans, cornmeal, and molasses. She seldom got meat, never tasted wheat flour, and complained, "Dere was a trough for de niggers and one for de hawgs." As a child, Lou Smith had little to eat. Her mistress, Miss Jo, "wouldn't feed us niggers. She'd make me set in a corner like a dog. I was so hungry and howled so loud they had to feed me." When freedom came to Smith, she ran to an orchard and repeated over and over, "I'se free, I's free; I ain't never going back to Miss Jo."[45]

With few exceptions, women and girls enslaved in Texas had meager clothing. Miss Jo was as stingy with clothing as with food, leading Lou Smith to recall, "I was jest a little child but I knowed I' should not go without any clothes. When Miss Jo forced her to remove all her clothing, Smith "jest crept off and cried." As a child, Julia Francis Daniels wore only a simple, one-piece garment made from sacking: "I ain't wore no underwear then," she lamented. Ann Hawthorne remembered that girls wore only plain, long-waisted dresses, cut straight and with buttons down the back. Her leather shoes were so hard they often blistered her feet, and she always looked forward to summer, when she could go barefoot. Anna Miller's chores included weaving cloth, but she was not allowed to wear anything she produced and shivered through winters.[46]

Tremendous variety characterized slave quarters. Mandy Morrow's accommodations in Georgetown, Texas, were rare: cabins with real windows and a solid wood floor. Adeline Cunningham's quarters in Lavaca County were more typical: she and her family were crammed together with another family on bunk beds in a one-room cabin with dirt floors. Rose Williams's second master, Hall Hawkins, had about fifty adult slaves and many enslaved children. Hawkins provided twelve cabins, all made from logs and equipped with tables and benches, bunk beds, and a fireplace for cooking and heat, though the floor was dirt. Harriet Barrett lived in a log cabin; she slept on deerskins stretched over the floor, with moss on top of the skins. Her master locked the slaves into their cabins every night and had someone patrol the quarters. Millie Williams often sang a lament:

> Massa Sleeps in de feather bed
> Nigger sleeps on de floor
> When we gits to Heaven
> Dey'll be no slaves no mo.[47]

Faith in a loving God clearly helped slaves grapple with their earthly condition, yet often they were so worn down by the dehumanization of slavery that expressing that faith proved trying and sometimes resulted in additional problems. Mandy Hadnot's mistress held prayer meetings every day, and when Hadnot turned nine years old, her mistress bought her a white dress and took her to church for the first time. One Easter, Hadnot's mistress bought her a hat as a gift. Hadnot's experiences were far from typical. Josie Brown was happy that her master did not force her to toil on Sundays and looked forward to church meetings, "But dey has to have it in de ya'd, so de white folks could see de kin' of religion 'spounded." As a girl, Millie Ann Smith slipped away with other slaves for prayer meetings, "but daren't 'low the white folks know it and sometimes we hums 'ligious songs low like when we's workin'. It was our way of prayin' to be free, but the white folks didn't know it." Susan Merritt's owner had a church built for his slaves on his property, but sometimes "at night us gather 'round the fireplace and pray and sing and cry, but us daren't 'low our white folks know it." The consequences of getting caught praying without a master's consent could be horrifying. Ida Edwards's mistress read the Bible to her slaves every Sunday and allowed them to attend church, but patrollers allowed no evening worship in the slave quarters. Once a patroller caught Edwards's mother praying aloud. "Dey strip her naked and tied her hands together and wid a rope tied to de hand cuffs and threw one end of de rope over a limb and tied de other end to de pommel of a saddle on a horse. . . . [D]ey pulled her up so dat her toes could barely touch de ground and whipped her."[48]

Occasionally masters allowed slaves a welcome break from their rigorous routines. Many masters allowed slaves to have parties and dances after crops were laid and after fall harvests. Julia Francis Daniels fondly remembered singing, playing games, and dancing. "I used to cut a step or two," she boasted in the 1930s. The masters of Ann Hawthorne and Susan Merritt gave their slaves half of each Saturday off, although, like many other masters, time "off" offered women their only opportunity to wash clothes and clean themselves. Every Saturday night Harriet Barrett's master allowed slaves to "go to nigger dance if it on 'nother plantation."[49]

Of course, not every slave in Texas lived and labored on plantations or farms. Although few cities in Texas in 1860 were worthy of the name (San Antonio had a population of 3,436 people that year), approximately 20 percent of the populations of Austin, Galveston, and Houston were slaves. Urban slaves were generally spared the dawn-to-dusk work typical of rural slaves, and because most toiled as house servants, they lived under the same roofs as their masters and ran errands for their masters in town, meaning that they tended to have far better clothing and food as well. The apparel of urban female slaves shocked an English observer during his visit to the cotton-boom town of Houston at the outbreak of the Civil War. "I saw innumerable . . . Negresses parading about the streets in most outrageously grand costumes—silks, satins, crinolines, hats with feathers, lace mantles, &c., forming an absurd contrast to the simple dresses of their mistresses." Catherine Hulbed owned the Rusk House Hotel in Houston and staffed it with one male slave and two females, thirty-year-old Amanda and twelve-year-old Mary. Masters offered slaves for hire in both agricultural and urban settings, but both those seeking slaves for hire and those wishing to hire them out often placed advertisements in town newspapers. John E. Garey and Sons advertised "For Hire. For Six months. Four or Five Negro Women, good House Servants." Houston merchants Dart and Masterson listed a girl for hire "of eight or ten years suitable for a nurse." Two female slaves, Mahala and Lilly, were hired out to the highest bidder in Houston for a year to settle part of the estate of their deceased owner, Pamela Brown.[50]

In urban and rural areas alike, the domestic slave trade provided the engine of slave expansion. The *Austin Gazette* advertised the sale of a twenty-five-year-old mulatto woman as house servant, cook, ironer, and washer. In Austin County, G. F. Shelburn placed an ad in the *Bellville Countryman* to announce the auctioning off of a thirty-year-old black woman, Charlotte, along with her two young children, Sarah and Lewis. Slave traders Darragh and Sims of Galveston offered for sale a twenty-three-year-old female as a cook, washer and ironer, or field hand, along with her son and daughter.[51]

The trauma of slave sales left indelible scars on the victims. Sarah Ashley was born in Mississippi and sold at auction in New Orleans as a child. "I was scairt and cry, but dey put me up dere anyway." Her sisters and father were sold to one man, but Ashley's new master, Henry Thomas, a slave trader, took her to Georgia, where he sold her to Mose Davis of Texas, who "was buyin' up little chillen for he chillen." Josie Brown of Woodville, near Beaumont, remembered seeing children too little to walk sold away from their mothers "jus' like calfs." Green Cumby of Henderson, Texas, recalled watching speculators on horseback driving large groups of slaves from place to place. Women carried their small children in their arms, and at night mothers and children would "bed 'em down jus' like cattle right on the ground." The only childhood memory of William Hamilton from Village Creek, about thirty miles northwest of Houston, was "dere was lots of cryin' when de tooks me 'way from my mammy. Dat something I never forgets."[52]

Some whites enjoyed the buying and selling of human beings and the emotional damage it caused. After Julia Francis Daniels's master was killed during the Civil War, the dead man's father decided to sell her and her two sisters at auction, telling her "not to fret." During the bidding, a friend of "old man Denman" shouted out that he was there to buy slaves for William Blackstone. Julia and her sisters came back home with the elder Denman, who laughed and said, "My name allus been William Blackstone Denman." The whole affair was a sick joke by their new master.[53]

As in all aspects of slavery, the enslaved often fought for themselves and others as best they could at sales—always, of course, at great risk to themselves and those they loved. When the master of Emma Taylor and her mother decided to sell the pair, a trader brought them to a large platform, removed most of their clothes, and started hollering out for bidders. Emma "was scart and thunk I was to leave maw, so I 'gins hollerin' jist as loud as he does. He turn 'round and say, 'Shut up, you li'l coon, you. I can't hear nothin'." Taylor hid her face in her mother's apron, so traumatized that she remembered nothing else until she and her mother were loaded into a wagon to travel to their new home. Lou Smith heard from her mother the story of a master who owned a woman who produced three children, each of whom he sold within two years. At the birth of her fourth child, the mother poisoned the infant, preferring to kill her baby over allowing the child to be sold.[54]

Physical cruelty accompanied the psychological cruelty faced by enslaved women in Texas. Although violence, or at least the specter of violence, was a part of every slave society to control the enslaved population, the level of violence in Texas—torture, in fact—may have exceeded the levels elsewhere in the American South, as Olmsted observed in the 1850s. This high level of cruelty may have been a legacy of the process by which Americans foisted slavery into Mexican Texas in violation of local law and their determination to expand the institution as quickly as possible. The concept of "mastery" and the nearly total power over other human beings endemic in African American slavery, including legal dismemberment of slaves (toes, fingers, and castration), was manifest in Texas. Eva Strayhorn, who was born and raised in Arkansas, did not recall ever seeing slaves punished until she came to Texas during the Civil War. There, she once saw a woman tied down to the ground and whipped: "Dey say dat de people in Texas was a lot harder on dere slaves during the war dan dey ever had before."[55]

The master of Susan Merritt of Rusk County, a man named Watt, assigned a slave driver to mete out punishment. Merritt recalled seeing him "tie niggers to a tree and cowhide 'em till the blood ran down onto the ground." For women, the driver dug a hole "'bout body deep, and makes them women lie face down in it and beats 'em nearly to death." Somehow divorcing the driver from her master, Merritt had good memories of him, but as was the case with many enslaved women, she had nothing but horrible memories of her mistress, who often tied Merritt to a stub in the yard and whipped her "till she gave out, then she go get some rest and come back and beat me some more. She stomp and beat me nearly to death," leaving Merritt sick with fever from infections for a week. That same mistress once saw Merritt allow some chickens to get too close to a fire, decided that Merritt let the chicks do it, "and made me walk barefoot through that bed of coals sev'ral times." The mother of Van Moore once told him that she knew of a weary slave woman nearing the end of her pregnancy who briefly sat down to rest. The master had another slave dig a pit for her stomach and had her lay in it face down "and flog her till she lose her mind." The mistress of Ida Henry once decided that a slave had not fully cooked a baked potato and screamed to the female cook, "What you bring these raw potatoes out here for?" She then grabbed a fork and used it to pull out one of the cook's eyes.[56]

Many female slaves challenged the slave system by running away, despite the risk that they might lose their children or that family members left behind might be punished. Most of Texas's fugitive slaves were likely among the five thousand or so who fled to freedom in Mexico. But like many slaves throughout the South, some in Texas bolted from their masters for a brief respite from brutality. Auntie Pinkie Kelly recalled, "Sometimes we'd run away and hide in de woods for a spell," even though they knew that they would get tied down and whipped when captured. Peggy and Jim, an enslaved couple in Austin, together fled from their master. Emily, a resourceful and brave twenty-five-year-old slave, not only ran away from Houston in 1842 but also stole two horses to aid in her escape. Another audacious escapee, Charlotte, ran to Houston in 1857 and made no effort to hide there or to blend in with urban slaves; a local newspaper complained that she could be seen in "broad daylight," a common situation in urban slavery.[57]

A slave named Susan devised a novel way to challenge slavery without running away. After her master, James M. Robinet of Houston, died in 1855, Susan immediately assumed the surname *Jordan* and simply told anyone who inquired that Robinet had set her free. But her plan fell apart soon after Robinet's estate went to probate court, where officials concluded that Susan Jordan was "a negro woman who is now going at large without the proper control of any person." Susan's ruse was not helped by the fact that Texas law permitted manumission only by the state assembly. Authorities quickly apprehended her and sold her at auction for one thousand dollars to Sam B. Ewing, a farmer on the Brazos River.[58]

Great peril and upheaval stirred the cauldron of slavery in Texas with the coming of the Civil War. In the aftermath of John Brown's failed 1859 raid on Harpers Ferry, panic spread throughout the South as whites feared that slaves might rise up against them. Terrified white southerners imagined diabolical plots against them, but nowhere did these fears jeopardize the safety and lives of slaves more than in Texas. In the summer of 1860, "Texas Troubles" broke out across the state after a series of mysterious fires damaged or destroyed the towns of Denton, Dallas, Pilot Point, Ladonia, Honey Grove, and Milford. The most likely cause was highly combustible phosphorous matches, which were known to burst into flames on store shelves. But rumors quickly spread that abolitionists had instigated slaves to turn to arson, and some whites even believed that an abolitionist army would swoop down from Kansas to finish the job. In Dallas County, some whites called for the hanging of all slaves suspected of participating in the alleged conspiracy. On July 23, vigilantes voted to hang 3 male slaves, but the crowd that gathered decided that every African American in the county—all 1,074 of them, including 561 women—should be whipped.[59]

Although the Civil War devastated much of the South, Union forces barely had a presence in Texas until the war ended. Nevertheless, the war affected slaves in many ways. Ida Edwards remembered that after her master headed east to fight, his overseer "tried himself in meanness over de slaves as seemingly he tried to be important." He worked them night and day, locked them in jail overnight without food, whipped them in morning, and provided only bread and water. Slaves who tried to escape and were caught found themselves attached to balls and chains. One day, other slaves caught the overseer and killed him with a blow to the head.[60]

The war's greatest effect in Texas was felt as masters from other southern states sent their slaves to the Lone Star State in a futile attempt to prevent them from reaching Union troops and thus freedom. The long, frantic trek often proved perilous. Mattie Gilmore's master, Thomas Barrow, moved his slaves from Mobile late in the war. They traveled only at night, afraid to build fires that would expose them, and slept during the day. Along the way, Mattie recalled seeing many dead men, white as well as black. Cannons boomed as they crossed the Mississippi River, and the small boat that carried them west was tossed around so much that Mattie vowed never again to deal with wars or boats. The Barrow slaves finally settled in Athens, Texas, just before the war's end. When Yankees approached the home in Mississippi where Elvira Boles's master lived, he decided it was time to flee. On the journey to Texas, she "lost my baby, its buried somewhere on dat road. . . . Dey say we'd never be free iffen day could git to Texas wid us." Ben Simpson could not forget his family's journey from Georgia to Texas. His master chained together his slaves including Simpson's mother and his sister, Emma, by their necks, fastened those chains to horses and forced them to walk. Any slave who fell behind received a whipping. "Mother, she gave out on the way, 'bout the line of Texas. Her feet got raw and bleedin' and her legs swoll plumb out of shape. Then massa, he ju' take out he gun and shot her, and whilst she lay dyin' he kicks her two, three times and say, 'Damn a nigger what can't stand nothing.' . . . [H]e wouldn't bury mother, jus' leave her layin' where he shot her at."[61]

On June 19, 1865, Union General Gordon Granger arrived in Galveston and informed Texans that the war was over and that he and his soldiers would enforce emancipation. Yet the joy of freedom often intermingled with confusion and despair. Millie Williams recalled, "Dere sho' was a mighty party sight when de slaves knows de free. Dey hug one 'nother and almos' tear dere clothes off. Some cryin' for de husban', and some cryin' for de chillen." Aunt Pinkie Kelly's master, Greenville McNeel, one of the Old 300 families settled long ago by Stephen F. Austin, never told his slaves that they were free. One day a stranger—presumably a Freedmen's Bureau official or Union soldier—rode up and confronted McNeel: "You can't work these people, without no pay, 'cause they's as free as you is." Kelly remembered her deliverance, "Law, we sho' shout, young folks and old folks too," but they had to stay where they were because they had no money and nowhere to go. Ann Hawthorne's mother had married a man in Georgia whose owner refused to sell him when her master moved with her to Texas. After freedom came, her former master went to Georgia to try to reunite the couple, but her husband was "raisin' up anudder family dere and won't come. Li'l befo' she die her husban' come. When he 'bout wo' out and ready to die, den he come."[62]

Many masters had trouble facing the reality of slavery's demise. When Anna Miller's master told his slaves that they were free, he told them they could all go but offered them nothing—no clothes, food, or provisions. Her father and most others left; she stayed. Her master's disposition grew worse over time. According to Miller, he said "he don' want to live in a country where de niggers am free" and committed suicide about a year later. The most mundane assertions of freedom by former slaves often resulted in horrific reprisals by whites who refused to accept emancipation. In July 1865 in Brazoria County, a white man named Spencer pulled down to the waist the clothes of a freedwoman called Adelaide and inflicted about two hundred lashes, alleging that she "had made an insulting noise when his wife passed." In Liberty County, Michael Linney learned that one of his former slaves, Selina Parker, was going to leave his daughter's house and head to nearby Houston; he kicked Parker, stole her money, and took away her clothes and her child. In July 1866, more than a year after freedom came to Texas, Harris County's James Cotton beat a freedwoman over the head with a club and threatened to kill her husband because the couple planned to leave him.[63]

But many former slaves left their former masters and asserted themselves despite the peril. Some danced "the dance of freedom." For many, among their first acts of freedom was to obtain a legal marriage license and give themselves surnames. During the first year after emancipation, 108 validated their relationships in Harris County; another 180 couples did so over the next year. Of the 144 brides, 4 went by a first name only, and 12 registered with the same surname as their husbands. The other 128 women asserted themselves by selecting their own last names. With the help of the Freedmen's Bureau, many black women successfully sued their husbands or lovers for nonsupport of themselves and their children. And when the right to vote and run for public office came to African American men in 1867, a handful of black women formed the Thaddeus Stevens Republican Club, naming their group after a leading antislavery senator from Pennsylvania and proponent of rights for former slaves. The organization sought "to uphold and strengthen the hands of their brethren." Having learned to maneuver through their lives as slaves, these women now tested the boundaries of American politics through grassroots involvement and asserting their rights as free people.[64]

NOTES

1. Frederick Law Olmsted, *A Journey through Texas; or, A Saddle-Trip on the Southwestern Frontier: With a Statistical Appendix* (New York: Dix, Edwards, 1857), 123 (quote), 242–43, 256–58, 362–63; Aunt Kitty in John W. Blassingame, ed., *Slave Testimony: Two Centuries of Letters, Speeches, Interviews, and Autobiographies* (Baton Rouge: Louisiana State University Press, 1977), 533.

2. Randolph B. Campbell, *An Empire for Slavery: The Peculiar Institution in Texas, 1821–1865* (Baton Rouge: Louisiana State University Press, 1989), 10–11; Douglas W. Richmond, "Africa's Initial Encounter with Texas: The Significance of Afro-Tejanos in Colonial Tejas, 1528–1821," *Bulletin of Latin American Research* 22 (April 2007): 200–221. For a broad range of literature on enslaved women in Texas, see Angela Boswell, "Black Women during Slavery to 1865," in *Black Texas Women*, ed. Bruce A. Glasrud and Merline Pitre (College Station: Texas A&M University Press, 2008), 30–31, nn. 1–4.

3. Colin A. Palmer, *Slaves of White Gods: Blacks in Mexico, 1570–1650* (Cambridge: Cambridge University Press, 1976); Campbell, *Empire for Slavery*, 11; Carmela Leal, ed., "Translations of Statistical and Census Reports of Texas, 1782–1836, and Sources Documenting Blacks in Texas, 1603–1803" (San Antonio: Institute of Texan Cultures, 1979), reel 1, 2, 8, unnumbered page dated December 31, 1784.

4. Juliana Barr, *Peace Came in the Form of a Woman: Indians and Spaniards in the Texas Borderlands* (Chapel Hill: University of North Carolina Press, 2007), 1–4, 7; Francis X. Galán, "Lost in Translation: Tejano Roots on the Louisiana-Texas Borderlands, 1716–1821," in *Recovering the Hispanic History of Texas*, ed. Monica Perales and Raúl Ramos (Houston: Arte Público, 2010), 3–6; Andrew Jonathan Torget, "Cotton Empire: Slavery and the Texas Borderlands, 1820–1837" (PhD diss., University of Virginia, 2009), 39–40; David J. Weber, *The Spanish Frontier in North America* (New Haven: Yale University Press, 1992).

5. Leal, "Translations," reel 3, unnumbered pages.

6. Ibid., reel 1, 107–8 (slaves of Prudhomme and Morvan); unnumbered page, January 1, 1806 (slave Luisa). For the use of Indian slaves, see Jesús F. de la Teja, *San Antonio de Béxar: A Community on New Spain's Northern Frontier* (Albuquerque: University of New Mexico Press, 1996).

7. Jane Landers, "'In Consideration of Her Enormous Crime': Rape and Infanticide in Spanish St. Augustine," in *The Devil's Lane: Sex and Race in the Early South*, ed. Catherine Clinton and Michelle Gillespie (New York: Oxford University Press, 1997), 206.

8. Torget, "Cotton Empire," 57 (María Lusia); Raúl A. Ramos, *Beyond the Alamo: Forging Mexican Ethnicity in San Antonio, 1821–1861* (Chapel Hill: University of North Carolina Press, 2008), 92 (María Rosa de la Rosa); *Texas: Being a Collection of Rare and Important Books and Manuscripts Relating to the Lone Star State*, intro. Archibald Hanna (New York: Eherstadt, n.d.), item no. 149, "Negro Emancipation in Texas"), photocopy in author's possession, with thanks to Michael Parrish.

9. See Leal, "Translations," reel 3, January–March 27, 1778, for correspondence by Governor Galvez, esp. Galvez to Don Antonio María Bucarely y Ursa, November 3, 1777.

10. Galán, "Lost in Translation," 12–13; Gwendolyn Midlo Hall, *Africans in Colonial Louisiana: The Development of Afro-Creole Culture in the Eighteenth Century* (Baton Rouge: Louisiana State University Press, 1992), 148; Helen Sophie Burton, "Family and Economy in Frontier Louisiana: Colonial Natchitoches, 1714–1803" (PhD diss., Texas Christian University, 2002), 142.

11. Campbell, *Empire for Slavery*, 12–13; David A. Williams, *Bricks without Straw: A Comprehensive History of African Americans in Texas* (Austin: Eakin, 1997), 4–5.

12. Torget, "Cotton Empire," 22–25, 30–33, 37, 47, 53–55, 57–71. Special thanks to Andrew Torget, who discovered this story while conducting archival research in Mexico.

13. Ibid., 28, 43; Ramos, *Beyond the Alamo*, 92; Gregg Cantrell, *Stephen F. Austin: Empresario of Texas* (New Haven: Yale University Press, 1999), esp. chaps. 4, 5.

14. Campbell, *Empire for Slavery*, 14–25, 27, 29–32, 34 (Clarissa on 24); *Western Americana* (New Haven, Conn.: Reese, 2000), item no. 129, with thanks to Michael Parrish. On slave rape, see Debra Gray White, *Ar'n't I a Woman?: Female Slaves in the Plantation South* (New York: Norton, 1985), 152–53, 164–65; Anthony E. Kaye, *Joining Places: Slave Neighborhoods in the Old South* (Chapel Hill: University of North Carolina Press, 2007), 53, 59–63, 66–69, 75, 78–81, 89, 126–27, 142; Angela Boswell, *Her Act and Her Deed: Women's Lives in a Rural Southern County, 1837–1873* (College Station: Texas A&M University Press, 2001), 86.

15. Nolan Thompson, "Arnold, Hendrick," *Handbook of Texas Online*, http://www.tshaonline.org/handbook/online/articles/far15 (accessed October 23, 2010).

16. Christopher Long, "Old Three Hundred," *Handbook of Texas Online*, http://www.tshaonline.org/handbook/online/articles/umo01 (accessed February 3, 2011).

17. Sean M. Kelly, *Los Brazos de Dios: A Plantation Society in the Texas Borderlands, 1821–1865* (Baton Rouge: Louisiana State University Press, 2010), 1, 50–53; Michael R. Moore, "Settlers, Sharecroppers, and Stockhands: A Texas Plantation-Ranch, 1824–1896" (master's thesis, University of Houston, 2001), 85–87.

18. Nancy Ann Phaup, "Cultural Modification of Buttons at the Levi Jordan Plantation, Brazoria County, Texas" (master's thesis, University of Houston, 2001); Kenneth L. Brown and Doreen C. Cooper, "African Retentions and Symbolism," 1998, http://www.webarchaeology.com/html/african.htm (accessed December 13, 2010).

19. Moore, "Settlers, Slaves, Sharecroppers, and Stockhands," 85–87, 110–12; for Moore's careful reconstruction of slave families at the Jones Ranch, see 112–15. Since renamed the George Ranch, it is still a working ranch near Houston. The best study of "cultural creolization" is Charles Joyner,

Down by the Riverside: A South Carolina Slave Community, 2nd ed. (Urbana: University of Illinois Press, 2009).

20. Harriet Barrett, Texas Narratives, vol. 16, pt. 1, 49, Josephine Howard, Texas Narratives, vol. 16, pt. 2, 49, Andrew Simms, Oklahoma Narratives, vol. 13, 295, all in *Born in Slavery: Slave Narratives from the Federal Writers' Project, 1936-1938*, 2001, http://memory.loc.gov/ammem/snhtml/ (accessed January 19, 2014) (hereafter cited as [State] Narratives).

21. Kelly, *Brazos de Dios*, 77-78; *Houston Morning Star*, December 23, 1840.

22. Kelly, *Brazos de Dios*, 72; on slave "marriages," see Emily West, *Chains of Love: Slave Couples in Antebellum South Carolina* (Urbana: University of Illinois Press, 2004), 19-43.

23. Kelly, *Brazos de Dios*, 74; Jennifer L. Morgan, "'Some Could Suckle over Their Shoulder': Male Travelers, Female Bodies, and the Gendering of Racial Ideology, 1500-1770," *William and Mary Quarterly*, 3rd ser., 54 (January 1997): 167-92; James Oakes, *The Ruling Race: A History of American Slaveholders* (New York: Knopf, 1982), 26, 172-73; Steven Deyle, *Carry Me Back: The Domestic Slave Trade in American Life* (New York: Oxford University Press, 2005), 47. For labor of enslaved children, see Wilma King, *Stolen Childhood: Slave Youth in Nineteenth-Century America* (Bloomington: Indiana University Press, 1995); Marie Jenkins Schwartz, *Born in Bondage: Growing Up Enslaved in the Antebellum South* (Cambridge: Harvard University Press, 2001).

24. Campbell, *Empire for Slavery*, 48-49, 54-55.

25. Jesús F. de la Teja, "Seguin, Juan Jose Maria Erasmo de Jesus," *Handbook of Texas Online*, http://www.tshaonline.org/handbook/online/articles/fse07 (accessed January 28, 2011); Ramos, *Beyond the Alamo*, 92.

26. Felix Haywood, Texas Narratives, vol. 16, pt. 2, 132. See Ronnie C. Tyler, "Fugitive Slaves in Mexico," *Journal of Negro History* 57 (January 1972): 1-12; William Dean Carrigan, "Slavery on the Frontier: The Peculiar Institution in Central Texas," *Slavery and Abolition* 20, no. 2 (1999): 63-96; B. Ann Rodgers and Linda Schott, "'My Mother Was a Mover': African American Seminole Women in Brackettville, Texas, 1914-1964," in *Writing the Range: Race, Class, and Culture in the Woman's West*, ed. Elizabeth Jameson and Susan Armitage (Norman: University of Oklahoma Press, 1997), 585-87.

27. Mary Lindsay and Sarah Wilson in T. Lindsay Baker and Julie P. Baker, eds., *The WPA Oklahoma Slave Narratives* (Norman: University of Oklahoma Press, 1996), 246-48, 492-93, 497.

28. Deyle, *Carry Me Back*, 64, 66 (quote), 98-100; James P. Baughman, *Charles Morgan and the Development of Southern Transportation* (Nashville: Vanderbilt University Press, 1968), 24-27, 37, 45-47; Walter Johnson, *Soul by Soul: Life inside the Antebellum Slave Market* (Cambridge: Harvard University Press, 1999), 61-62. For the number of those enslaved, see Campbell, *Empire for Slavery*, 55. Census information is drawn from *University of Virginia Library Historical Census Browser*, http://mapserver.lib.virginia.edu/index.html (accessed November 26, 2010).

29. Oakes, *Ruling Race*, 74. See Randolph B. Campbell and Richard Lowe, "The Slave-Breeding Hypothesis: A Demographic Comment on the 'Buying' and 'Selling' States," *Journal of Southern History* 42 (August 1976): 401-12.

30. Aunt Kitty in *Slave Testimony*, ed. Blassingame, 533; Sally Banks Chambers, Texas Narratives, vol. 16, pt. 1, 214; Mintie Maria Miller, Texas Narratives, vol. 16, pt. 3, 85; Anna Miller, Texas Narratives, vol. 16, pt. 3, 82. For fear of separation from families through the slave trade, see Johnson, *Soul by Soul*, 16, 19, 34-37, 39-40, 64-65.

31. Patricia Prather Smith and Jane Clements Monday, *From Slave to Statesman: The Legacy of Joshua Houston, Servant to Sam Houston* (Denton: University of North Texas Press, 1993), 6, 8, 9, 10, 18, 20-21, 37, 39, 42-43 ("insolence"), 51, 53. See Charles Israel, "From Biracial to Segregated

Churches: Black and White Protestants in Houston, Texas, 1840–1870," *Southwestern Historical Quarterly* 101 (April 1998): 428–58.

32. Douglas Hales, *A Southern Family in Black and White: The Cuneys of Texas* (College Station: Texas A&M University Press, 2003), 4–6, 10–12; Thomas W. Cutrer, "Cuney, Philip Minor," *Handbook of Texas Online*, http://www.tshaonline.org/handbook/online/articles/fcu21 (accessed January 4, 2011); Merline Pitre, "Cuney, Norris Wright," *Handbook of Texas Online*, http://www.tshaonline.org/handbook/online/articles/fcu20 (accessed January 4, 2011). For concubinage, see White, *Ar'n't I a Woman?*, 35–37; Ann Patton Malone, *Women on the Texas Frontier: A Cross-Cultural Perspective* (El Paso: Texas Western Press, University of Texas at El Paso, 1983), 28, 42; Sally G. McMillan, *Southern Women: Black and White in the Old South* (Wheeling, Ill.: Harlan Davidson, 1992), 119–24. For more on slave rape, see White, *Ar'n't I a Woman?*, 152–53, 164–65; Stephanie M. H. Camp, *Closer to Freedom: Enslaved Women and Everyday Resistance in the Plantation South* (Chapel Hill: University of North Carolina Press, 2004), 64–65; Kaye, *Joining Places*, 53, 59–63, 66–67, 75, 78–81, 89, 126–27, 142.

33. Mark M. Carroll, *Homesteads Ungovernable: Families, Sex, Race, and the Law in Frontier Texas, 1823–1860* (Austin: University of Texas Press, 2001), 51–53; Sarah Ford, Texas Narratives, vol. 16, pt. 2, 42.

34. Adeline Marshall, Texas Narratives, vol. 16, pt. 3, 46; Auntie Thomas Johns, Texas Narratives, vol. 16, pt. 2, 205; Francis Bridges in Baker and Baker, *WPA Oklahoma Slave Narratives*, 63, 65–66 (quote); Clinton and Gillespie, *Devil's Lane*; on miscegenation, see McMillan, *Southern Women*, 21–28; West, *Chains of Love*, 116–43.

35. Will Adams, Texas Narratives, vol. 16, pt. 1, 3; John Anthony Moretta, *William Pitt Ballinger: Texas Lawyer, Southern Statesman, 1825–1888* (Austin: Texas State Historical Association, 2000), 112; Jeff Calhoun, Texas Narratives, vol. 16, pt. 1, 189; Nancy King, Texas Narratives, vol. 16, pt. 2, 288.

36. Eugene D. Genovese, *Roll, Jordan, Roll: The World the Slaves Made* (New York: Random House, 1974), 461–75 (quote on 465); Julia Malone, Texas Narratives, vol. 16, pt. 3, 44. See also McMillan, *Southern Women*, 16, 30; Kaye, *Joining Places*, 7–8, 52–65, 69.

37. Louise Love, Texas Narratives, vol. 16, pt. 3, 31; Sarah Ford, Texas Narratives, vol. 16, pt. 2, 42; Eliza Elsey in Baker and Baker, *WPA Oklahoma Slave Narratives*, 140; Aunt Pinkie Kelly, Texas Narratives, vol. 16, pt. 2, 254; Brazoria County, Texas, Marriage Book 1, 1852–70, January 30, 1870, Clayton Genealogical Library, Houston.

38. Rose Williams, Texas Narratives, vol. 16, pt. 4, 176–77, 178–79; Camp, *Closer to Freedom*, 43.

39. Rosanna Frazier, Texas Narratives, vol. 16, pt. 2, 63; Celima Duncan to William B. Duncan, January 2, 1863, William B. Duncan Papers, Sam Houston Regional Library and Research Center, Liberty, Texas; Mollie Watson in Baker and Baker, *WPA Oklahoma Slave Narratives*, 45; Mary Hadnot, Texas Narratives, vol. 16, pt. 2, 103–4. See King, *Stolen Childhood*, 45–56, 160.

40. Gavin Wright, *Slavery and American Economic Development* (Baton Rouge: Louisiana State University Press, 2006), 117–19; Ellen Polk, Texas Narratives, vol. 16, pt. 1, 189; Adeline Cunningham, Texas Narratives, vol. 16, pt. 1, 267; Rosina Hoard, Texas Narratives, vol. 16, pt. 2, 142; *Houston Tri-Weekly Telegraph*, August 29, 1862.

41. Katie Darling, Texas Narratives, vol. 16, pt. 1, 278; Julia Francis Daniels, Texas Narratives, vol. 16, pt. 1, 274 (quote), 277; Sarah Ford, Texas Narratives, vol. 16, pt. 2, 41.

42. Emma Thomas, Texas Narratives, vol. 16, pt. 4, 73; Harrison Beckett, Texas Narratives, vol. 16, pt. 1, 54; Mary Kincheon Edwards, Texas Narratives, vol. 16, pt. 2, 15–16; Sarah Ashley, Texas Narratives, vol. 16, pt. 1, 35.

43. Sally Banks Chambers, Texas Narratives, vol. 16, pt. 1, 214; Ann Hawthorne, Texas Narratives, vol. 16, pt. 2, 119; Ellen Polk, Texas Narratives, vol. 16, pt. 1, 188; Jeptha Choice, Texas Narratives, vol. 16, pt. 1, 218.

44. Harriet Barrett, Texas Narratives, vol. 16, pt. 1, 50; Maisah B. Robinson and Frank H. Robinson Sr., "Slave Medicine: Herbal Lessons from American History," *Mother Earth Living*, July–August 1998, http://www.herbcompanion.com/health/Slave-medicine.aspx (accessed March 5, 2011). See also Todd L. Savitt, *Medicine and Slavery: The Diseases and Health Care of Blacks in Antebellum Virginia* (Urbana: University of Illinois Press, 1981).

45. Ann Hawthorne, Texas Narratives, vol. 16, pt. 2, 120; Silvia King, Texas Narratives, vol. 16, pt. 2, 290; Ann Miller, Texas Narratives, vol. 16, pt. 3, 83; Lou Smith in Baker and Baker, *WPA Oklahoma Slave Narratives*, 391.

46. Lou Smith in Baker and Baker, *WPA Oklahoma Slave Narratives*, 391; Julia Francis Daniels, Texas Narratives, vol. 16, pt. 1, 277; Ann Hawthorne, Texas Narratives, vol. 16, pt. 2, 121; Anna Miller, Texas Narratives, vol. 16, pt. 3, 82.

47. Adeline Cunningham, Texas Narratives, vol. 16, pt. 4, 139; Mandy Morrow, Texas Narratives, vol. 16, pt. 3, 139; Rose Williams, Texas Narratives, vol. 16, pt. 4, 175–76; Susan Merritt, Texas Narratives, vol. 16, pt. 3, 75; Ellen Polk, Texas Narratives, vol. 16, pt. 1, 189; Harriet Barrett, Texas Narratives, vol. 16, pt. 1, 49; Millie Williams, Texas Narratives, vol. 16, pt. 4, 172.

48. Mandy Hadnot, Texas Narratives, vol. 16, pt. 2, 103–4; Josie Brown, Texas Narratives, vol. 16, pt. 1, 164; Millie Ann Smith, Texas Narratives, vol. 16, pt. 4, 43; Susan Merritt, Texas Narratives, vol. 16, pt. 3, 77; Ida Henry, Oklahoma Narratives, vol. 13, 135; Kaye, *Joining Places*, 40–41.

49. Julia Francis Daniels, Texas Narratives, vol. 16, pt. 1, 274; Ann Hawthorne, Texas Narratives, vol. 16, pt. 2, 122; Susan Merritt, Texas Narratives, vol. 16, pt. 3, 76; Harriet Barrett, Texas Narratives, vol. 16, pt. 1, 50; on holidays and celebrations, see Kaye, *Joining Places*, 39, 46.

50. Paul D. Lack, "Slavery, Urban," *Handbook of Texas Online*, http://www.tshaonline.org/handbook/online/articles/yps02 (accessed March 8, 2011); Arthur James Lyon Fremantle, *The Fremantle Diary: Being the Journal of Lieutenant Colonel Arthur James Lyon Fremantle, Coldstream Guards, on His Three Months in the Southern States*, ed. Walter Lord (Short Hills, N.J.: Burford, 1954), 58; *Indianola Bulletin*, October 27, 1860; *Houston Tri-Weekly Telegraph*, April 19, 1862; *Houston Morning Star*, December 17, 1840; for urban slaves, see Boswell, "Black Women during Slavery," 24; on hiring out, see Randolph B. Campbell, "Research Note: Slave Hiring in Texas," *American Historical Review* 93 (February 1988): 107–14; Jonathan Martin, *Divided Mastery: Slave Hiring in the American South* (Cambridge: Harvard University Press, 2004).

51. *Austin Gazette*, December 8, 1840; *Bellville Countryman*, September 22, 1860; *Galveston Tri-Weekly News*, February 1, 1856.

52. Sarah Ashley, Texas Narratives, vol. 16, pt. 1, 34; Josie Brown, Texas Narratives, vol. 16, pt. 1, 164; Green Cumby, Texas Narratives, vol. 16, pt. 1, 260; William Hamilton, Texas Narratives, vol. 16, pt. 2, 106.

53. Julia Francis Daniels, Texas Narratives, vol. 16, pt. 1, 276.

54. Mintie Maria Miller, Texas Narratives, vol. 16, pt. 3, 86; Emma Taylor, Texas Narratives, vol. 16, pt. 4, 74; Millie Williams, Texas Narratives, vol. 16, pt. 4, 174–75; Lou Smith in Baker and Baker, *WPA Oklahoma Slave Narratives*, 392; on infanticide, see McMillan, *Southern Women*, 51–52.

55. On the role of slavery in the Texas Revolution, see Campbell, *Empire for Slavery*, 48–49; for the pervasiveness of violence in slave societies, see Orlando Patterson, *Slavery and Social Death: A Comparative Study* (Cambridge: Harvard University Press, 1982), esp. 59, 206 (branding and ear

cropping); Thomas D. Morris, *Southern Slavery and the Law, 1619–1860* (Chapel Hill: University of North Carolina Press, 1999), chap. 8, 178–79, 238, 281, 342; William S. Pugsley and Marilyn P. Duncan, comps., *The Laws of Slavery in Texas: Historical Documents and Essays*, ed. Randolph Campbell (Austin: University of Texas Press, 2010); Eva Strayhorn in Baker and Baker, *WPA Oklahoma Slave Narratives*, 411.

56. Susan Merritt, Texas Narratives, vol. 16, pt. 3, 76–78; Van Moore, Texas Narratives, vol. 16, pt. 3, 129–30; Ida Henry in Baker and Baker, *WPA Oklahoma Slave Narratives*, 135. For the viciousness of slave mistresses, see Thavolia Glymph, *Out of the House of Bondage: The Transformation of the Plantation Household* (New York: Cambridge University Press, 2008), esp. 5–7, 17, 25, 30–31, chap. 2, "'Beyond the Limits of Decency': Women in Slavery"; Camp, *Closer to Freedom*, 36–40, 132; Elizabeth Fox-Genovese, *Within the Plantation Household: Black and White Women of the Old South* (Chapel Hill: University of North Carolina Press, 1993), 132; Jacqueline Jones, *Labor of Love, Labor of Sorrow: Black Women, Work, and the Family from Slavery to the Present* (New York: Vintage, 1995), 26–27; Wilma King, "The Mistress and Her Maids: White and Black Women in a Louisiana Household, 1858–1868," in *Discovering the Women in Slavery: Emancipating Perspectives on the American Past*, ed. Patricia Morton (Athens: University of Georgia Press, 1996), 82–106.

57. See John Hope Franklin and Loren Schweninger, *Runaway Slaves: Rebels on the Plantation* (New York: Oxford University Press, 2000); Aunt Pinkie Kelly, Texas Narratives, vol. 16, pt. 2, 254; *Austin Gazette*, November 18, 1839; *Houston Morning Star*, September 16, 1842; *Houston Telegraph*, April 23, 1857.

58. Harris County Probate Records, vol. M, microfilm roll 1314027, 512, 518, Clayton Library for Genealogical Research. I thank Kelly Ray.

59. Campbell, *Empire for Slavery*, 224–25; Donald E. Reynolds, *Texas Terror: The Slave Insurrection Panic of 1860 and the Secession of the Lower South* (Baton Rouge: Louisiana State University Press, 2007), 80–81; *University of Virginia Library Historical Census Browser*, http://mapserver.lib .virginia.edu/php/county.php (accessed March 9, 2011).

60. Campbell, *Empire for Slavery*, 231–51; Ida Edwards, Oklahoma Narratives, vol. 13, 135.

61. Campbell, *Empire for Slavery*, 233–46; Dale Baum, "Slaves Taken to Texas for Safekeeping during the Civil War," in *The Fate of Texas: The Civil War and the Lone Star State*, ed. Charles D. Grear (Fayetteville: University of Arkansas Press, 2008), 83–103; Mattie Gilmore, Texas Narratives, vol. 16, pt. 2, 71–73; Elvira Boles, Texas Narratives, vol. 16, pt. 1, 108; Ben Simpson, Texas Narratives, vol. 16, pt. 4, 27.

62. Campbell, *Empire for Slavery*, 249–51; Millie Williams, Texas Narratives, vol. 16, pt. 4, 172–73; Aunt Pinkie Kelly, Texas Narratives, vol. 16, pt. 2, 254; "McNeel, John Greenville," *Handbook of Texas Online*, http://www.tshaonline.org/handbook/online/articles/fmcac (accessed March 25, 2011); Anne Hawthorne, Texas Narratives, vol. 16, pt. 2, 123–24.

63. Anna Miller, Texas Narratives, vol. 16, pt. 3, 83–84; Barry A. Crouch, *The Dance of Freedom: Texas African Americans during Reconstruction*, ed. Larry Madaras (Austin: University of Texas Press, 2007); Records of the Assistant Commissioner for the State of Texas Bureau of Refugees, Freedmen, and Abandoned Lands, 1865–69, National Archives Microfilm Publication M821, Roll 32, "Miscellaneous Records Relating to Murders and Other Criminal Offenses Committed in Texas, 1865–1868," July 26, 1865, September 1865, July 11, 1866; Gregg Cantrell, "Racial Violence and Reconstruction Politics in Texas, 1867–1868," *Southwestern Historical Quarterly* 93 (January 1990): 333–55.

64. Crouch, *Dance of Freedom*; Barry A. Crouch, "The 'Chords of Love': Legalizing Black Marital and Family Rights in Postwar Texas," *Journal of Negro History* 79 (Fall 1994): 334–51; Marie Rus-

sell, comp., *Marriage Records Harris County, Texas*, vol. 2, 1865–81 (La Porte, Tex.: Russell, 1985); Barry A. Crouch and Larry Madaras, "Reconstructing Black Families: Perspectives from the Texas Freedmen's Bureau Records," in *Our Family, Our Town: Essays on Family and Local History Sources in the National Archives*, comp. Timothy Walch (Washington, D.C.: National Archives and Records Administration, 1987), 155–67; *Houston Union*, September 2, 1868, with thanks to Ty Wellborn; Hans L. Trefousse, *Thaddeus Stevens: Nineteenth-Century Egalitarian* (Chapel Hill: University of North Carolina Press, 1997); James Smallwood, "Black Freedwomen after Emancipation: The Texas Experience," *Prologue* 27 (Winter 1995): 303–17.

Sallie McNeill

A Woman's Higher Education in Antebellum Texas

REBECCA SHARPLESS

In December 1858, eighteen-year-old Sallie McNeill and her thirteen classmates received diplomas from Baylor University. The flowers of plantation society, these young graduates were about to scatter from Baylor's hilltop campus in the hamlet of Independence, in Washington County, to their homes across Texas. Almost all would soon become wives and mothers; none would put her education to use in the public sector. Yet Baylor was much more than a finishing school for the wealthy. McNeill and the other young women had studied mathematics, natural sciences, literature, and languages; had published their words in the college newspaper; and had defended their learning in a series of oral examinations before panels of distinguished men and the interested public. At graduation, each student read aloud her commencement address. McNeill's experience at Baylor suggests that this rigorous education was something more than a frivolous indulgence for wealthy southern belles.

McNeill, bookish and introspective, recorded in her diary her impressions of her two years at Baylor and the nine years following, until her death in 1867 at the age of twenty-seven. Her entries give insight into the dilemma of education for women in antebellum America, particularly in the South: What should women be taught, and how should they use what they learned? McNeill was the granddaughter of Levi Jordan, a very wealthy sugar planter in Brazoria County, and she represented a class of women whose lives of privilege were built on slavery. But she was also a voracious reader who loved the life of the mind, and her college education fed and encouraged her intellectual enterprises.

Like universities today, Baylor in the 1850s formed young women not only through its curriculum but also through the social experiences it afforded them.

The university was a safe space in which young people could live away from home, amid their social peers, and sometimes seek suitable mates. Some of the students took their intellectual development more seriously than others, but most—perhaps all—formed relationships that would last lifetimes. Sallie McNeill's time at Baylor mattered deeply to her as an individual, influencing her friendships with other women for the rest of her brief life. She and her classmates were integrally enmeshed in the "female world of love and ritual" that Carroll Smith-Rosenberg aptly described for many nineteenth-century women in comfortable circumstances.[1] McNeill did not follow the traditional path of elite Texas women into marriage and children after her time at Baylor, in part as a consequence of her own nature. But her decision was also the product of an educational process that encouraged her intellectual interests. McNeill's life, Baylor University's beginnings, and the links between the two provide a window into the contradictions that elite women in Texas faced in the middle of the nineteenth century.

The existence of a cadre of educated women also mattered for Texas society in subtle and indirect ways. Almost all of the Baylor class of '58 married, many within three years of their graduation, becoming the wives of men of wealth and influence. Their general classical educations helped to shape their lives as mothers, wives, and mistresses of some of the most elegant households in the state. By 1856, Baylor Female Department principal Horace Clark could eloquently proclaim the right of women to receive an education equal with men's, declaring in his commencement address, "The education of woman is as much her birthright, as is the air she breathes, the food she eats, or apparel she wears." But Clark clearly realized that most of his students were destined for lives of domesticity: "Whatever course of intellectual and moral cultivation will enable her to discharge with the greatest efficiency the responsible duties of daughter, wife, mother, and member of society, is hers of right." Even as he called for equal education for women, Clark could not countenance roles outside the family sphere. As historian Margaret Nash observes, such limitations formed the central paradox of women's higher education in the early nineteenth century: support for women's education "did not imply a concomitant belief in legal, political, or economic equality."[2]

The men who founded Baylor in 1845 almost surely had in mind the production of cultivated, poised young women, a vision shared by numerous other college founders in the early nineteenth century. In the early American republic, formal education for white women increased dramatically. Reformers and writers such as Judith Sargent Murray called for women's schooling both as an individual good for the women and as a necessity for a civilized society. By

MAIN BUILDING OF BAYLOR UNIVERSITY FEMALE CAMPUS

Independence, Texas, ca. 1865.

Courtesy of the Texas Collection, Baylor University, Waco.

1840, hundreds of academies and seminaries for women, both coeducational and single-sex, had been established throughout the United States. The South was an integral part of this trend. The Ursuline sisters in New Orleans set up their academy in 1727, and prestigious schools of the early republic included Salem Academy in North Carolina, founded in 1802, and Ann Smith Academy in Virginia, established in 1807. In Georgia, most of the academies were coeducational, while in Alabama, about half were.[3]

In Texas as in the rest of the South, elites apparently assumed that the education of socially prominent women was an essential part of a civil society. After the creation of the Republic of Texas in 1836, Texans began establishing educational institutions at all levels, from preparatory to college. By any measure, women's education was a high priority for antebellum Texans, who founded at least thirty-seven schools between 1836 and 1860. At least twenty-seven of these institutions enrolled women, and fourteen were exclusively for women.[4]

Thousands of young people in antebellum Texas attended schools labeled "male and female institutes," and in a few cases the women and men may have taken classes together and had identical curriculums. For the most part, however, even schools with "male and female" in their titles kept sex-segregated facilities. San Augustine College advertised in 1843, "In one part of the building is a Female Academy, where young ladies will be taught the solid as well as the polite branches of education." Nacogdoches University maintained a two-story adobe structure with the male department on the lower floor and the female department above.[5]

Early Texas schools frequently shifted their enrollments, seeking the right mix of sexes, and at least four of them began with females and males attending together but then separated into single-sex institutions. Such was the case at Baylor University, where the split into female and male departments was notably acrimonious. The most direct evidence to support the probability that men and women attended classes together at Baylor came from J. M. Carroll, who attended the university in the 1870s and began collecting historical materials while a student. In 1923, he wrote, "Baylor University and Baylor College, now two schools, began originally as one, and for five years were taught co-educationally, but gradually drifted, or developed, or evolved, or was rent into two. Originally, it had but one name, and for about five years was carried on in one small building and was taught by the same faculty." When Rufus C. Burleson became president of the struggling university in 1851, he laid down five conditions for accepting the position, one of which was "that the male and female pupils were to be separated, and the two departments to be conducted separately." Burleson's reasons for demanding the separation have not survived, but the board of trustees agreed and moved the male campus three-quarters of a mile across Independence Creek from the original site, where the females and the children in the academy remained. The separation of the campuses set in motion a schism that resulted in a split of the schools into completely separate institutions in 1866, moves to separate towns in 1886, and decades of ill will between them.[6]

When Sallie McNeill arrived about 1856, the newly divided university was only a decade old, but local residents had already supported women's education for a generation. Baylor had opened its doors in 1846 as the creation of the Texas Baptist Education Society, which apparently assumed from the beginning that the school would educate women. The founders chose to locate in the flourishing village of Independence because of generous financial backing from local citizens. The townspeople were accustomed to the idea of female education, for three short-lived girls' schools had already come and gone. Parents' efforts to create schools and keep the young women close to home rather than sending them away to school probably emerged from contemporary sensibilities about gender. Dispatching a son to a school far away was likely much easier both logistically and emotionally, as women seldom traveled alone and often remained more closely tied to their families than did their brothers. By 1845, the teachers in the earlier institutions had moved on, leaving an empty two-story frame building available to Texas Baptists and their new Baylor University. After the male-female split, the trustees funded a splendid three-story stone classroom building for the women on the original campus, and it was there that Sallie McNeill took her classes. Horace Clark, the principal of the Female Department that McNeill attended, nominally answered to the president of the university, Rufus Burleson, who also served as principal of the Male Department.[7]

Although they separated men and women, the founders readily included women as a part of Baylor University and in so doing joined a wave of Baptist education following the Second Great Awakening. Religion certainly motivated many of the founders of antebellum Texas colleges, as elsewhere, but religious motivations were not all-encompassing. According to historian Frederick Eby, all of the early Texas schools were "broadly Christian" but "disavowed sectarianism. . . . No courses of a sectarian nature were offered in any school, nor was the Bible a text book except in rare cases." Baylor trustees expected students to attend church services on Sundays but did not force them to do so. Though chapel attendance was required each morning before classes, for these early Baptists, the foremost goal was education, not indoctrination.[8]

Like other wealthy Americans, the parents of Baylor students likely viewed the education of their daughters as markers of their social status. Only the financially elite enrolled their daughters at Baylor. In 1859, a semester's tuition was fifty dollars, and elective courses in modern languages, music, and "ornamental" courses in painting and embroidery could easily triple the cost. The female students represented the cream of early Texas society. Julia A. Robertson, class of 1858, was the daughter of Jerome B. Robertson and the sister of Felix Robertson, soon to be generals in the Confederate Army, and Sallie McNeill was the granddaughter of one of the wealthiest men in Texas.[9]

But Baylor was first and foremost a school, and the curriculum that the Baylor trustees and faculty members set up resembled that of women's institutions elsewhere in the United States. Before 1851, Baylor appears to have had a unified curriculum for females and males that included English, geography, arithmetic, ancient languages, natural science and mathematical science, moral and intellectual philosophy, French and German as modern languages, piano and guitar for music, and painting and embroidery in the fine arts, probably as electives open only to women. Both males and females attended four one-hour classes per day. The earliest female students received only diplomas, not bachelor's degrees, but in 1851, the trustees elected to create a "regular course of study" that would lead to a bachelor's degree. The 1857 catalog for the Female Department laid out a four-year plan designed to culminate in a bachelor's of arts degree: arithmetic, algebra, geometry, and trigonometry; grammar and composition; anatomy and physiology, chemistry, meteorology, and astronomy; logic; rhetoric; intellectual and moral philosophy; "evidences of Christianity"; and four years of elocution and vocal music. Such emphasis on the sciences mirrored changes in education for women across the United States in the middle of the nineteenth century. An optional curriculum included language, music, and art. As elsewhere in the country, the ornamental departments were very much outside the core curriculum, and Baylor, like other schools, charged a premium for such courses. A harp class, for example, cost half again as much as the full academic curriculum. Piano tuition equaled the academic cost, and oil painting was 80 percent of the total (forty dollars). The trustees plainly intended to give their women students a firm grounding in a classical education. The ornamental subjects were not necessarily in opposition to the academic subjects but were complementary, showing taste and refinement and signifying the young women's privilege.[10]

Faculty members did not hesitate to push their pupils when necessary. They persisted in instilling both knowledge and poise under pressure in their graduates, and students recalled high expectations for their performances. Fannie Rogers Harris, class of 1858, remembered, "Dr. Clark taught reading to the advanced pupils. I have known one whole division [class period] given to one paragraph or verse until it was properly rendered." McNeill dreaded a different class, writing in her diary, "I do not like Geometry, and I can't learn it without [constant] application, and this I am not willing to give." Neither McNeill nor the faculty would yield; they did not ease the class for her, and she did not work hard for them.[11]

The Baylor curriculum, like that in similar institutions elsewhere in the United States, taught young women to speak in public even though they would have only limited opportunities to do so after graduation. One venue for public speaking was the so-called regular program. Fannie Rogers Harris recalled, "We had semi-monthly open exercises when a program was rendered consisting of music, compositions, and the reading of our school paper, 'The Prairie Flower.' The students from the male department could come if they had the courage to face Dr. Clark." For trustees' visits, said Rogers, "the best was put forward." Rather than being encouraged to be shy or retiring, women spoke regularly in front of both young men and those who controlled their school. At graduation, furthermore, each young woman read an original composition. In 1858, the subjects ranged from specific topics—Julia Robertson's oration on the trans-Atlantic telegraph—to glorious abstractions such as Mary A. Whiteside's discussion of "The Mission of Liberty." McNeill's address, "Footprints on the Sands of Time," fell into the latter category. She saved the text of her address, which was about four hundred words long and probably took about five minutes to read. McNeill began with comments on the nature of time, discussed how the world would remember good deeds despite the fleeting nature of existence, and concluded with praise for the selfless actions of George Washington, "La Fayette," Sir Isaac Newton, and English philanthropist John Howard, which rendered their "footsteps indelibly stamped upon the shores of time." Although McNeill used men as exemplars, her message took on a personal tone when she addressed her peers: "Man is not destined to live for himself alone, but to labor for his fellow-man. And the influence he exerts will either be for good or evil. Oh! what a fearful weight of responsibility rests on *our* conduct!" While McNeill sought to inculcate virtue in her listeners, she pointed to recognition and notice as possible rewards for doing good, a distinctly unfeminine goal for a young woman from Brazoria County.[12]

As in other schools in the South, each term at Baylor ended with oral examinations before a panel of outside questioners, and the examinations were open to the public. The panel for 1858–59 consisted of twelve men from throughout Texas, including three ministers, two medical doctors, and three attorneys. Thus, young women performed in public, judged by adult men. Harris remembered, "How we trembled in our shoes as we took our seats in front of them."

Some parents, fearing the stress of the examinations, apparently withdrew their daughters before the pressure built, prompting a sharp order in the 1857 catalog: "The practice of indulgent parents in removing pupils from the Institution before the close of the session to avoid these exercises cannot be too [earnestly?] reprehended. . . . In future no young lady can thus leave without the consent of the Principal; nor can she resume the position in her class." Perhaps parents withdrew their daughters because of fear that the stress would prove harmful, or perhaps they simply had low expectations for their daughters' attainments. The women's instructors clearly clashed with the parents in either case.[13]

Two months after her senior exams, McNeill described them in her diary: "Well, the long expected and anxiously looked for, yet dreaded day arrived, on the whole our school acquitted themselves creditably, Mr. Kemble (one of the board of Examiners) came with the expressed determination to tease & make us miss as he did the boys, especially in Latin. He succeeded in puzzling —— and [all] afternoon worried us with his simple questions. Becca missed, Rach & myself guessed through. He is very ungallant to Ladies."[14] McNeill was acutely aware of the gendered nature of a man quizzing young women, giving them equal treatment as their male peers. She seemed to believe that Kemble should ease his questioning of the females.

Yet the exams, as terrifying as they might be, also had a social side. McNeill got a new dress for the occasion of her senior exams, "blue with flounces," wanting to look her best for the day of her disquisition. Family members, townspeople, and alumnae from near and far attended the examinations. Margaret Lea Houston, who lived across the road from the women's college, wrote to her husband, U.S. Senator Sam Houston, in December 1853, "The examination came off last week, and although we have had bad weather a part of the time, it was really a grand affair. We had a house full of visitors all the time, and every body else who entertained company seemed to have quite as many, and all seemed greatly delighted with the attainments of the students, both of the male and female department." Sallie McNeill returned as an alumna in 1860. Well pleased with the proceedings and nostalgic for her school days, she wrote in her journal, "I never witnessed an examination conducted so well. I seemed carried back through two years, to my own classes & exercises." Young women entertained with their intellectual achievements on the same basis as men.[15]

Women vied for academic honors, competing against one another and receiving public recognition. Although she did not graduate as a result of ill health, Mary Jane Haynes read the first valedictory address, in 1857, and received a silver medal for achievement. Criteria for academic honors were less than clear, and the unhappiness created by the vagueness speaks to the competitive nature of these young women. Horace Clark, principal of the Female Department, selected Fannie Rogers as the valedictorian for the class of 1858. McNeill discussed his choice at length in her diary. Clark told the class that people might disagree with him, and McNeill observed that "no one opposed it then, but several are dissatisfied." McNeill named three possibilities for the position and discounted Mary Louise McKellar, who had been at Baylor for eight years but "had not attended regularly, nor is she as good a scholar as Fannie." Rogers had been at Baylor for six years and was "noted for good scholarship and conduct." She was not popular with her peers, however: "She does not associate freely with the girls, and they think her proud and exclusive." McNeill favored her good friend, Mary Whiteside, who had been at Baylor only two years but "is the best scholar in the school." McNeill questioned Clark's decision: "If this honor had been bestowed on merit, [Whiteside] would have gained it, or if it had been left to the vote of the class." Rogers declared that "rather than be the object of envy to any she will resign; but Mr. C will not permit this, I am certain." Rogers remained the valedictorian and delivered an address on "The Responsibilities of Genius." The selection of the valedictorian was clearly a subject of great interest to the young women in the class. McNeill seems to have viewed the decision somewhat as a popularity contest, complaining about Rogers's perceived haughtiness, but she also believed in merit, favoring Whiteside as the "best scholar."[16]

For the first five years of Baylor's existence, the male and female departments shared a faculty, which in 1850 consisted of five men and Louisa Buttlar, who taught music and embroidery. In June 1851, however, as Rufus Burleson's decree divided the male and female campuses, two separate faculties arose. Over the next ten years, faculty members came and went, including two family groups. Horace and Martha Davis Clark arrived from La Grange, Texas, to lead the Female Department, bringing with them Harriet Davis, Martha Clark's sister. (A third sister, Mary Russell Davis, arrived in 1857, having recently completed missionary work among Native Americans.) Harriet Davis married B. S. Fitzgerald, who became a faculty member, and two of his female relatives joined the boardinghouse staff. In 1859, four members of the Chase family arrived to teach music and drawing.[17]

While instructors influenced their pupils through the formal curriculum, in many ways female faculty members held even greater sway outside the classroom. The students plainly adored Principal Horace Clark, but his wife and sisters-in-law had closer affinity with them. As the chief disciplinarian, Clark had to maintain a stern visage toward his pupils, while the women could have more intimate contact with them, sometimes acting as foster mothers or sisters. When more than twenty of the students fell ill with a fever, a Miss Morrill took the lead as nurse, visiting the young women "several times" each day.[18]

Keeping young women amused and safe in Independence constantly challenged the faculty members, who went to great pains to create single-sex di-
versions. In May 1858, Liane DeLassaulx, instructor of modern language and
embroidery, gathered the young women for a "dialogue," or skit. The characters
included "fashionably dressed ladies," a grandmother, and an Irish servant. The
performance was, McNeill reported, "very good, considering the short time for
preparation." DeLassaulx then proposed "tableaux" (living pictures) for the next
Friday night, including a procession of nuns. McNeill objected, saying that she
had "a perfect horror of Catholics and Catholicism," only to be met with gales
of laughter from her classmates, for DeLassaulx was Roman Catholic. A week
later, McNeill wrote, "Our tableaux party passed off pleasantly, Miss De L. asked
me to be a nun and I consented." Other characters played by students included
a "bride nun," a "Mother Abbess," a "high priest," and "the Count."[19] DeLassaulx
gave of her time to organize the young women into amusements, and McNeill's
anti-Catholic sentiments crumbled before the admirable example of the young
faculty member.

Although Baylor rules did not push religious conformity on its students, religious revivals provided both entertainment and spiritual nurturance. McNeill
and several of her classmates had religious awakenings, which some observers
might call conversion experiences, during a revival held at Baylor. She wrote,
"A few weeks before the Examination Fannie Rogers, C. Woodruff, S[usan].
Rhem and myself were received into the Church and baptized. . . . I hope and
pray, that I may not be a 'cumberer of the ground' but may 'bring forth fruit' to
the honor and glory of God. But without his help, how weak and sinful are we?
O God may I feel my dependence on Thee and ever look upward for Thy aid."
Instructor Mary Davis helped assuage McNeill's fears about the depth of her
religious experience: "She told me she did not think I ought to determine the
degree of sorry that I should feel, that God often ordered things in a way directly
opposite to that which we expected. And that I must take hold of the promises of God by faith. And believe that through the merit of Jesus alone we can
be saved." McNeill took seriously her religious commitment for the rest of her
life, despite her infrequent church attendance. Her last journal entry before her
death contained a meditation on the metaphor of Christ as the good shepherd.
Some religious conversions were more lasting than others. McNeill told of her
friend and fellow student Josephine Mims, who decided that she wanted to
dance, an activity considered unacceptable by Baptists, and therefore intended
to withdraw her church membership.[20]

Late-adolescent women such as McNeill and Mims sought to determine how
to act and think for themselves. Many a young woman, away from the supervision of family members for perhaps the only time in her life, developed a new

sense of herself. Students created community with each other, particularly those who shared their living quarters. At Baylor, most of the female students lived in a boardinghouse maintained by Martha Clark, with as many as four to a room. The college administration devised rules to attempt to keep order, while the young women strove to make their living space as flexible as possible. They were constrained to "occupy the Rooms assigned them" and forbidden to leave the college grounds without permission. Sallie McNeill observed that Martha Clark wanted the boarders up in time for breakfast on Saturdays, but not all of the women chose to abide by her rules. They had no fear of Clark, McNeill commented: "The girls do not consider her laws like that of the Medes & Persians, which changeth not."[21]

The young women paid as much attention to their appearance as school rules would allow. Mary Kavanaugh recalled that the students created homemade cosmetics, including a mask made of honey and flour that hardened like plaster and had to be cracked off. The arrival of new hoop petticoats was noteworthy, and students arranged each others' hair. Horace Clark decried his students' love of finery. He limited their access to charge accounts with local merchants and specified that they wear plain dresses "without flounces or tucks" and that bonnets could only be white with solid pink ribbons. "Gay and expensive ribbons are not allowed, nor extreme fashions indulged," he wrote in 1859. Sallie McNeill noted one incident in which Clark "only let those go to church, who wore or tried to get Solid pink color." Yet McNeill observed that Martha Clark and two of her classmates had new bonnets. Students also apparently tried swapping clothes, given that the rules soon forbade "wearing each other's clothes." Clark might try to keep the clothing simple, but he could not stop the young women from caring about who wore what.[22]

Once the male students moved to the new campus a mile away, administrators of the female campus expected their students to keep completely separate from the men, socially as well as academically. The 1859 catalog stipulated that students were prohibited "from communicating with gentlemen, or receiving their attentions." As principal of the Female Department, Clark was particularly adamant, claiming that "boys and books don't go together." Clark earned his students' derision with such rules; when Bettie Allen, a student from Chappell Hill, invited McNeill to visit her at home, she wrote, "You can see a great deal more of pleasure here than you can see under Clark's eye."[23]

Stern rules, often blithely ignored, governed contact between males and females. Fannie Rogers Harris noted, "We never associated with the boys except on holidays or at occasional social functions. . . . Our holidays were April 21, when we had a patriotic program at the church. The ladies of the town served dinner in a live-oak grove in front of the church. After dinner we were permitted to talk to 'the boys' until time to leave. May 1 we crowned a queen. We had a dinner and could 'talk to the boys.'" Harris also recalled that brothers and first cousins could visit their female relatives on Saturday afternoons.[24] Contact between young people fostered ties between their families and brought together potentially suitable mates.

As the disagreements between the leaders of Baylor became increasingly bitter, the men in charge used the male-female split to further their political ends. Although he had initiated the division of the male and female campuses, President Rufus Burleson and his wife, Georgia Burleson, sought to bring men and women together socially by hosting exclusive gatherings of selected young people at their home. Clark opposed the gatherings so vehemently that when the two men presented written charges against each other to the trustees in 1860, Burleson alleged that "he has treated my wife and myself with disrespect, in not allowing the daughters of my friends and brethren to meet a few select friends at my house." Harris, one of the chosen number, recalled that

> our social gatherings were few and far between and only for a favored few. They were always held at Dr. Burleson's residence, an octagonal two-story building with a porch all around the second floor where the parlors were located. The principal amusement was promenading, that was walking around with a chosen companion. Our hearts quickened as we watched for our companion. Would it be the boy—all girls have sweethearts. If it was, we accepted his escort, our fingers resting lightly on the coat sleeve of the left arm, as we approached the door. We went home with the teachers. There were no dates made.

Burleson obviously lacked Clark's reservations about students mingling socially under diligent supervision, choosing to create situations in which courting rituals could occur. Perhaps Burleson's encouragement of social activities indicated his opinion that women belonged in courting situations rather than in the classroom, pursuing their only suitable role—as mates for his male students.[25]

As the tension increased between the female and male departments, visits between campuses became fraught, centered on the inability of male scholars to take seriously female scholars. In August 1858, Sallie McNeill and her classmates attended an evening at the men's campus "at an especial invitation." McNeill had a terrible time, and she criticized the men's performance, which she believed belittled the women's department: "Some of the pieces were good, others contemptible, full of nonsense and love-sick speeches; And moreover they insulted us to our face, in a rhyme, calling us Mr. Clark's fair and happy cavalcade or yard. They all shouted and stomped, but Mr. C. looked indignant, & I am sure those of us who possessed any pride, felt highly insulted. I never want to go again, never. If they cannot write about anything but abuse and ridicule, I hope

Mr. C. will not patronize them at all." Sure enough, Clark later refused to let the female students attend the "public monthly exercise of the senior class or the commencement party." The female students defended Clark in his feud with Burleson, circulating a petition in which each signer signaled her refusal to go to the boys' party. The young men seemed unable to accept their female cohorts as peers, and the young women reacted sharply to such disparagement.[26]

Even as the older generation disagreed about the content of the rules, teenagers found myriad ways around the strictures set by the schools, with young women just as inventive as their male counterparts. Mary Gentry Kavanaugh remembered young women sneaking away from the campus to race horses against the men: "Parents of students stabled horses near the school. The caretaker loaned the horses to young men students. Then by prior arrangement the girls would arrive at a designated spot where they would indulge in races against the boys. Girls dressed in riding habits with long skirts and rode sidesaddle. How they escaped from the dormitory unseen is still a mystery."[27] The concept of young women both sneaking out and racing young men would likely have caused considerable consternation among parents trying to rear ladylike daughters. Kavanaugh did not note the impact of riding sidesaddle on the girls' competitive ability.

As testimony to the matchmaking possibilities of the Sunday visiting policy, Fannie Rogers Harris told of the attention given to her male first cousin. Six young women claimed to be his kin to assert visiting rights: "By some strategy he was accredited with six cousins who greeted him on his visits. Suddenly it dawned on the teachers that the girls claimed no kinship with each other. After investigation only one cousin remained." Sisters and cousins also passed written communications between would-be couples.[28]

The exchange of letters and photographs between students in the Male and Female Departments led to high drama in May 1858. Sallie McNeill wrote in her diary,

> Oh! such stormy and distressing scenes we have had this week, very different from last. Poor Mat. [possibly Matilda Calloway of Wharton] is Suspended for a week, for What? Writing to that low fellow, as Mr. C[lark]. calls, White Smith [Whiteford L. Smith of Daingerfield]. She confessed having written about ten, besides possessing his ambrotype and he hers. He refused to deliver up her letters and said she would not even before a can[n]on, right I think. Mattie talked of killing herself, even asked for Laudnum, I offered her Paregoric but she did not want that, I locked my Laudnum up, though I had not the most distant idea, that she would drink it.

As numerous female students cried vigorously in distress over "Mat's" situation, more offenses came to light. Fannie Rogers "owned that she wrote two letters to Thomas, but [denied] that they were love letters. But Bettie Carter [denied]

writing any to C[icero]. Jenkins, as Mr. C. proved. . . . —— & Emeline are suspected of the same offense, as also —— Gresham." The drama of the situation
was heightened because most of the offenders were in their last year of school
and "it [would] have been awful to expel or Suspend a Senior." In the end, Clark
relented, and no suspensions occurred.[29] Still, the entire episode, including the
possibility of Mat's suicide, indicates how seriously the young people took both
their relationships with one another and the chastisement by their elders.

When the class of 1858 dispersed, McNeill returned home to the plantation,
about a hundred miles and a day's journey from Independence by rail and
stagecoach. With a widowed mother and a domineering grandfather in the person of Levi Jordan, she felt she had little choice. Two months after her departure,
she questioned her years at the university, despite sprinkling the French she had
learned there in her musings:

> Two years have I spent at Baylor University and now with a Diploma, testifying my
> education to be completed, I am again *a la maison*, quietly endeavoring to instruct
> my little school, composed of three boys and two girls. Whether my efforts will
> prove satisfactory to them or myself, the future alone will reveal. How little good
> have I done in the world. My friends do not say so, but I feel my deficiencies. Kept
> at school all my life, and treated as a child, with nothing but books to employ my
> thoughts, it is not strange that I should be indolent and idle. I am a child still,
> dependent on others.[30]

But while the return to the family household left McNeill feeling infantilized,
the education she earned at Baylor shored up her apparent resolution to follow
a different path.

Sallie McNeill experienced what reformer Jane Addams referred to as "the
family claim," in which young women's families insist that daughters with aspirations beyond the family instead meet familial expectations. Young women
could change, but they could not change too much. Baylor student Nancy Has-
sletine Anderson reassured her parents in 1859, "Tell Aunt Polly that I haven't
forgotten her if I am going to Baylor University, I am the same old Nannie."
Two years after graduation, McNeill wrote of her mother's dominance during a
visit to Independence: "I wanted to stay longer, oh! so much. . . . But Ma would
not consent & I was not willing to leave her in such poor health." As a young
woman of privilege in the South, McNeill had no choice but to return to the
family fold.[31]

Yet McNeill, like many of her peers, continued her important attachments
to women her own age. After McNeill returned to the plantation, she clung to
the connections with her Baylor classmates even as they embarked on marriage
and motherhood. She wrote letters and grumbled when her classmates did not

respond according to her expectations: "All my correspondents are forsaking me, and I will soon have nothing left but the memory of *auld lang syne* far away at our old Alma Mater. *Eh bien,* such is nature and human fallibility, and I must submit, patiently." She was particularly bothered by Mary Whiteside's failure to keep up her side of the correspondence after Whiteside returned to Navarro County following graduation and became engaged:

> Ah! Mary, how unjust to forget the friend of "Auld Lang Syne." Sometimes tempted to make a third effort to obtain her correspondence. But pride opposes. I can't believe both of my letters miscarried. Of all my fourteen or rather thirteen classmates, she was one of two most beloved. Yet she never showed the same preference for me, and now my affectionate letters are unanswered. . . . In the new & responsible relation, she is said to be about, to assume, my hopes & wishes are for her happiness.

McNeill was jealous of Whiteside on two accounts. She was particularly aggravated when she discovered that Whiteside, a gifted student who had contended to be class valedictorian, had published a school composition on Hungary in "a Southern College Magazine from Florence, Ala." McNeill lamented, "So Mary is turning authoress. Success to her efforts. . . . And Mary has forgotten me—no, such as being as she never forgets, there must be some other reason." Then, as Whiteside approached marriage, McNeill chafed at her alleged infidelity to Rachel Barry: "She has neglected Rachel lately. I wonder if happiness renders everyone deaf to the claims of friendship. . . . All, nearly all, have forgotten each other in one year—oh! human nature, how fallible & weak." Despite her whining, however, McNeill recorded letters from at least four of her Baylor classmates through the start of the Civil War.[32]

In many ways, McNeill's ties with unmarried female faculty members remained as strong as those with her peers. Mary Russell Davis in particular stayed close to her pupil. In June 1860, Davis wrote "begging earnestly" for McNeill "to come at least a week" to witness the examinations at the end of the spring 1860 term. "It is strange," McNeill mused; "She takes so much interest in such a poor body as I!" McNeill had a lovely visit to Independence in early July 1860, marked by particular attention from Davis: "My reception would flatter my vanity if anything would. . . . Miss Mary took entire possession of me letting me go out to dinner and tea a few times, though she grumbled at the necessity and brought me back every night. We had one good long talk Sat. while she was putting the Reading-room in order & I assisting a little." McNeill and Davis stayed in touch despite the outbreak of the Civil War; in February 1862, McNeill wrote, "Dear Miss M. wrote me such an encouraging letter, who else ever praises me as she does. I have at last tried to deserve her good opinion."[33]

When Davis died in November 1865, McNeill was devastated: "My almost best friend—I do not realize, that I will never behold her again. . . . Dear dear Miss Mary! who will hear and sympathize with my troubles now? No one appreciates me, as did Miss Mary! . . . I have lost my friend—an unselfish, devoted friend. I have so few, ill can I spare one." Although McNeill was no stranger to death, losing two of her younger sisters in 1861, the loss of her mentor hit hard. During a visit to Independence seven months after Davis's death, she continued to grieve.

McNeill's unwed state set her apart from most of her classmates, many of whom married shortly after graduating from Baylor. McNeill, disinterested in marriage for herself, cataloged the marriages of her classmates, along with her disapproval. On May 28, 1860, eighteen months after graduation, she recorded in her diary the fourteen members of her class and the married names of the five who had already wed. A week earlier, she had copied an entire letter in which Rachel Barry described her sudden engagement to attorney Charles Stewart: "Mr. S. is a lawyer, about 6 ft 6 inch high, fair skin, light hair, & rather (of) a commanding appearance. . . . Of course I think, that he is all that is noble & good. He is 24 years old & I am the first lady he ever visited or shewed any attention whatever." Barry invited McNeill to the wedding and swore her to secrecy: "Sallie I want you to come if possible. You are the only one of my schoolmates, that I have mentioned it to, & the only one I intend to." McNeill declined the invitation and quoted Byron in her diary: "I answered her, considering it almost a final farewell. I always thought she would marry early, but hope she is suitably matched. 'Farewell & if forever still forever fare thee well'!" Despite McNeill's doubts, Barry did keep in touch after her marriage; six months after the wedding, she wrote, in McNeill's words, "still in raptures about her husband and housekeeping!" Barry's marriage, apparently for love, also proved socially advantageous. The Stewart family eventually moved to Houston, where Charles Stewart held numerous elected offices and served five terms in the U.S. House of Representatives. Before she was forty, Rachel Barry Stewart was keeping a fine household with multiple servants on Rusk Street in central Houston.[34]

Eventually at least twelve of McNeill's thirteen classmates married, a much higher ratio than in the rest of the South, possibly as a result of the fact that white males outnumbered white females in Texas in 1860 by a ratio of about seven to six. The young women tended to marry well, sometimes to other Baylor alumni. Caroline Mooney, class of 1856, wed Confederate commander Leonidas Willis. Like Rachel Barry, Mary Louise McKellar married a future congressman, William S. Herndon, in November 1860. Eudora Pettus married future judge and state senator Edwin Hobby in 1866; their son, William Pettus

Hobby, became governor of Texas in 1917. For this group of women, mother-hood quickly followed marriage; McNeill noted in April 1860 that her class-mate Sarah Chambers Kavanaugh had "a little daughter." For herself, McNeill rejected such a role. In May 1860, she coolly appraised herself: "Have what is called a good education; possessed of no accomplishments. And am generally considered a plain, matter-of-fact young lady, already looked for an old maid; that despised title, to so many." At twenty, she thought that society had decreed her too old for marriage.[35]

Despite the growing numbers of American females who worked as teachers in the middle of the nineteenth century, Baylor women eschewed the classroom. Teaching attracted primarily middle-class women, and Baylor alumnae came from the upper echelons of Texas society.[36] McNeill was the only one of her peers who became a teacher during the antebellum period, and she taught only on her home plantation, with her younger siblings as her pupils.

With no prospects off the plantation, McNeill turned instead to the life of the mind. Isolated and sheltered from domestic duties by slave labor, she made books her best company. She never had as much reading material as she wanted and complained vigorously about her grandfather's stinginess with regard to her buying books. In September 1859, she wrote, "If only I could get new books occasionally, I would be happy while reading"; six months later, she observed, "I think it is somewhat hard, that I cannot have many books or society either. Grandpa says I may have all I need, but he has no idea of allowing that I do *need* many. Sometimes I know I too easily submit to deprivations & Ma always." Without money of her own, McNeill chafed at her grandfather's restrictions, which she believed limited her intellectual life.[37]

McNeill absorbed what she read, perusing certain works multiple times. She apparently memorized many lines of both Scripture and poetry, able to summon them as the moment seemed to warrant, and she peppered her diary entries with quotations from the Hebrew and Christian Bibles and from British and American poets. Most of the poetry that she cited was from the eighteenth and nineteenth centuries. She particularly loved the poets of the Romantic school, regularly adding lines from Burns, Byron, and Shelley to her diary. Longfellow appears to have been her favorite American poet.[38]

McNeill read voraciously from what she could buy, borrow, or swap with neighbors. In March 1860, she extended both books and periodicals to neigh-bors "Mrs. H." and Eliza Adams, a widow. Mrs. H. told McNeill that she was "lonesome, begging books." For all of these women, the printed words may have served numerous purposes. The publications not only provided information but also gave the women occasion to interact with one another and form bonds of shared experience as they compared what they had read.[39]

Yet even as books tied McNeill closer to other women in Brazoria County, they also sent her mind spinning far beyond the fences of the plantation. McNeill read English classics, both fiction and nonfiction from the sixteenth, seventeenth, and eighteenth centuries: William Shakespeare, Daniel Defoe, John Milton, Joseph Addison, Oliver Goldsmith, John Bunyan. She extended her circle into the nineteenth century through nonfiction works such as John L. Stephen's *Travels in Greece, Turkey, Russia, and Poland* and British fiction by Sir Walter Scott and Charles Dickens. Indeed, with her absorption in Scott's poetry and prose, she joined the mass of educated Americans who made him the most widely read author in antebellum America. McNeill also kept abreast of popular fiction of the 1850s and 1860s, finding *The Mill on the Floss* by British female author George Eliot extremely depressing: "There are some truths in the book, but the whole has left a bad impression on my mind. I suppose chiefly because I would fain believe better of 'human nature.'" She "enjoyed immensely" *Beulah* (1859), the second work by popular southern novelist Augusta Jane Evans. *Beulah*, which sold twenty-two thousand copies in its first year of publication, told the story of an orphaned young woman who struggled to be independent and come to grips with important intellectual and philosophical questions. McNeill also recorded pleasure at the novels of Marion Harland (pen name of Virginia Terhune), particularly *The Hidden Path* (1855). In addition to Bunyan, McNeill read popular theology from the nineteenth century, including *Thoughts on Religious Experience* by Presbyterian minister Archibald Alexander (1841) and *The Way to Do Good* (1836) by Congregational minister and children's author Jacob Abbott.[40]

Periodical literature played a major role in shaping antebellum American opinion and thought, and educated Americans in the South enthusiastically read publications issued in the North. McNeill read or was exposed to numerous national periodicals. In May 1858, the female students at Baylor created a tableau that likely was based on Virginia de Forrest's story, "Mrs. Daffodil's Interview with a Count," which had appeared in *Godey's Lady's Book* only a month earlier. The women of Baylor evidently enjoyed the fiction, poetry, and illustrated fashions in *Godey's*, the most popular U.S. periodical of its time. The Jordan-McNeill household also received multiple periodicals, several published in the North. Sallie McNeill took pleasure in *Arthur's Home Magazine*, published in Philadelphia, although she sniffed that it consisted "principally of light reading." McNeill was well aware of the northern origins of these periodicals. As

Texas prepared to secede from the Union, she mourned, "We can have no more Northern magazines till the impending political crisis is past. I shall,—all the children will miss the pleasant stories, with an instructive moral to each and the life-like engravings, as well as patterns, embroideries, etc., so useful to country folks." By 1867, however, McNeill had resumed reading *Frank Leslie's Weekly*, a New York–based magazine with widespread national distribution. The disruptions of the war were only temporary.[41]

McNeill's life came to an abrupt end, likely from yellow fever, on October 28, 1867. She was twenty-seven years old. During her short lifetime, she enjoyed many of the privileges of being a young woman in an elite southern family, including the best education that the region afforded. Though the founders of Baylor thought that perhaps her sojourn there would integrate her socially into elite Texas society, McNeill was not interested in marriage and resented the claim it made on her friends. Instead, she more fully absorbed other lessons Baylor offered, including a spiritual outlook, a love of knowledge for its own sake, and confidence in intellectual pursuits as a right. She sought to extend her education through her teaching, her reading, and her continued ties with teachers and classmates from Baylor. Although her physical life was generally constrained to Brazoria County, her imagination roamed the globe. Sallie McNeill was as free a spirit as she could be in nineteenth-century Texas.

NOTES

1. Carroll Smith-Rosenberg, "The Female World of Love and Ritual: Relations between Women in Nineteenth-Century America," *Signs* 1 (Autumn 1975): 1–29.

2. *Catalogue of the Trustees, Officers, and Students of Baylor University, Female Department, 1857*, 24–25 (quotations), Texas Collection, Baylor University, Waco; Margaret Nash, *Women's Education in the United States, 1780–1840* (New York: Palgrave Macmillan, 2005), 1.

3. Barbara Miller Solomon, *In the Company of Educated Women: A History of Women and Higher Education in America* (New Haven: Yale University Press, 1985), 14; Mary Kelley, *Learning to Stand and Speak: Women, Education, and Public Life in America's Republic* (Chapel Hill: University of North Carolina Press, 2006), 43; Nash, *Women's Education*, 3, 5; Fletcher Melvin Green, "Higher Education of Women in the South Prior to 1860," in *Democracy in the Old South and Other Essays by Fletcher Melvin Green*, edited by J. Isaac Copeland (Nashville, Tenn.: Vanderbilt University Press, 1969), 201. Unraveling the nomenclature of "institute," "seminary," "academy," and "college" is, according to educational historian Margaret Nash, "perhaps impossible" (*Women's Education*, 5). No clear definitions existed at the time, and the name of a school indicated very little about its curriculum or its intellectual rigor. While colleges generally were designed to prepare men for the ministry, law, or medicine, the curriculum of the academy was often indistinguishable from that of the college. See also Anne Firor Scott, "The Ever Widening Circle: The Diffusion of Feminist Values from the Troy Female Seminary, 1822–1872," *History of Education Quarterly* 19 (Spring 1979): 3–25.

4. Lois Smith Murray, *Baylor at Independence* (Waco: Baylor University Press, 1972), 4, 84, 130; Angela Boswell, *Her Act and Deed: Women's Lives in a Rural Southern County, 1837–1873* (College Station: Texas A&M University Press, 2001), 59; Donald W. Whisenhunt, *The Encyclopedia of Texas Colleges and Universities: An Historical Profile* (Austin: Eakin, 1986).

5. Wreathy Aiken, *Education of Women in Texas* (San Antonio: Naylor, 1957), 32, 33.

6. Whisenhunt, *Encyclopedia*. Three of the schools are Chappell Hill Male and Female Institute, which became Soule University and Chappell Hill Female Institute; Tyler University, where the male department closed after a fire and the female department continued as Eastern Texas Female College; and Marshall University, whose female department separated and became the Masonic Female Institute. See also Arthur A. Grusendorf, *A Century of Education in Washington County, Texas: A Revision of the Author's Doctoral Dissertation Entitled "The Social and Philosophical Determinants of Education in Washington County, Texas, since 1835, the University of Texas, June 1838* (n.p., n.d.), 120, 123; J. M. Carroll, *A History of Texas Baptists* (Dallas: Baptist Standard, 1923), ix, 226 (first quotation); Harry Haynes, "Biography of Dr. Burleson," in *The Life and Writings of Rufus C. Burleson*, comp. Georgia Jenkins Burleson (Waco: Burleson, 1901), 115 (second quotation). Baylor historian Lois Smith Murray writes, "During the Graves administration, actual coeducation was the policy" but does not cite any evidence to back up her claim (*Baylor at Independence*, 153). Such physical separation of males and females apparently was not unusual. At Rutersville College, in Fayette County, the two campuses were an estimated eight hundred yards apart (Ralph W. Jones, *Southwestern University, 1840–1861* [Austin: Jenkins, 1973], 58). In 1866, the female department became Baylor Female College, with its own board of trustees. In 1886, the women's college moved to Belton and the men's to Waco, where it merged with the coeducational Waco University and became coeducational. The women's college was renamed Mary Hardin-Baylor College after a generous gift from the Hardin family in 1934 and became coeducational in 1971.

7. In 1835, John P. Coles and other settlers had funded the establishment of Trask Academy, taught by Massachusetts emigrant Frances Soames Trask, to educate their daughters. When Trask Academy closed, area residents soon supported another school, Independence Academy, also called Independence Female Academy, taught by a Miss McGuffin. A pair of sisters named Simms also taught fine arts in the academy building. See Grusendorf, *Century of Education*, 48–54, 70–74; Murray, *Baylor at Independence*, 2–3, 6–7, 113–14, 118, 125, 132, 148, 153–55; Frederick Eby, "Education and Educators," in *Centennial Story of Texas Baptists* (Dallas: Baptist General Convention of Texas, 1936), 128; Green, "Higher Education," 215; Michael A. White, *History of Baylor University, 1845–1861* (Waco: Texian, 1968), 14, 18–19, 54, 57.

8. Eby, "Education and Educators," 127, 139 (quotation); White, *History of Baylor University*, 8; Catherine Clinton, "Equally Their Due: The Education of the Planter Daughter in the Early Republic," *Journal of the Early Republic* 2 (Spring 1982): 45–46; Solomon, *In the Company*, 16; Nash, *Women's Education*, 55; *Catalogue of the Trustees, Officers, and Students of Baylor University, Female Department, 1859*, Texas Collection, Baylor University, 27. McKenzie College began with prayer at four o'clock each morning (Macum Phelan, *A History of Early Methodism in Texas, 1817–1866* [Nashville: Cokesbury, 1924], 406).

9. Clinton, "Equally Their Due," 41, 55; Christie Ann Farnham, *The Education of the Southern Belle: Higher Education and Student Socialization in the Antebellum South* (New York: New York University Press, 1994), 2–3; Murray, *Baylor at Independence*, 34, 106; Randolph B. Campbell, *An Empire for Slavery: The Peculiar Institution in Texas, 1821–1865* (Baton Rouge: Louisiana State University Press, 1989), 274. Tuition for collegiate studies with English, Latin, and Greek was fifty dollars; French and German were twenty dollars each; harp, seventy-five dollars; piano, fifty dollars; guitar, fifty dollars;

oil painting, forty dollars; oriental painting, thirty dollars; watercolors, twenty dollars; pastels, twenty dollars; "Grecian painting," ten dollars; "antique painting on glass," ten dollars; embroidery, twenty dollars; and wax work, twenty dollars (*Baylor University Female Department Catalogue, 1859*, 18–19). Fifty dollars in 1860 would have been worth approximately fifteen hundred dollars in 2012 (http://www.measuringworth.com/uscompare/relativevalue.php [3 February 2014]).

10. Murray, *Baylor at Independence*, 94, 109; White, *History of Baylor University*, 63; Kim Tolley, "Science for Ladies, Classics for Gentlemen: A Comparative Analysis of Scientific Subjects in the Curricula of Boys' and Girls' Secondary Schools in the United States, 1794–1850," *History of Education Quarterly* 36 (Summer 1996): 130, 136; Clinton, "Equally Their Due," 42; Laura F. Edwards, *Scarlett Doesn't Live Here Anymore: Southern Women in the Civil War Era* (Urbana: University of Illinois Press, 2000), 18; *Baylor University Female Department Catalogue, 1859*, 16–18, 19; Kelley, *Learning to Stand*, 69. Between 1855, when the first woman finished her course of study, and 1862, women finishing their educations at Baylor received diplomas or certificates, not bachelor's degrees. The principal of the Female Department, rather than the president of the university, signed the certificates (Murray, *Baylor at Independence*, 128, 133, 209–10). Baylor awarded the first bachelor's of arts degrees to women in 1862. The first institution in the South to offer a bachelor's of arts degrees to women was Georgia Female College in 1840 (Green, "Higher Education," 217). In 1859, the core curriculum had shifted slightly to encompass geography, history, botany, and mythology, four years of penmanship, and the Bible. Options included German and French language, music (harp, piano, guitar), and the "ornamental departments," including four types of painting, embroidery, and wax work. The music department possessed eight pianos and a harp, indicating a considerable capital investment in the music program (*Baylor University Female Department Catalogue, 1859*, 25–26). Texas's McKenzie College, San Augustine College, and Nacogdoches University had similar curriculums for their women students, including the extra tuition for music and drawing (Jones, *Southwestern University*, 80; Aiken, *Education*, 32, 33). The Men's Department had far more emphasis on Greek and Roman classics and took mathematics through calculus (*Catalogue of the Trustees, Officers, and Students of Baylor University [Male Department], 1859*, Texas Collection, Baylor University, 18).

11. Fannie Rogers Harris, "Baylor at Old Independence," *Baylor Monthly* 3 (March 1928): 6 (first quotation); Sallie McNeill, *The Uncompromising Diary of Sallie McNeill*, ed. Ginnie McNeill Raska and Mary Lynn Gasaway Hill (College Station: Texas A&M University Press, 2009), 26 (second quotation).

12. Anya Jabour, *Scarlett's Sisters: Young Women in the Old South* (Chapel Hill: University of North Carolina Press, 2007), 57; Harris, "Baylor at Old Independence," 6 (first quotation); *Baylor University Female Department Catalogue, 1859*, 34–35; McNeill, *Uncompromising Diary*, 35–36 (second quotation; emphasis added).

13. Clinton, "Equally Their Due," 54; Anya Jabour, "'College Girls': The Female Academy and Female Identity in the Old South," in *"Lives Full of Struggle and Triumph": Southern Women, Their Institutions, and Their Communities*, edited by Bruce L. Clayton and John A. Salmond (Gainesville: University Press of Florida, 2003), 83; Jabour, *Scarlett's Sisters*, 58; Kelley, *Learning to Stand*, 97; Murray, *Baylor at Independence*, 155 (second quotation), 378; Harris, "Baylor at Old Independence," 6 (first quotation).

14. McNeill, *Uncompromising Diary*, 32–33. Kemble, who is not further identified, did not return as an examiner in 1859 (*Baylor University Female Department Catalogue, 1859*, 3), perhaps because of his behavior toward the young women.

15. McNeill, *Uncompromising Diary*, 29 (first quotation), 79 (third quotation); Sam Houston, *The Personal Correspondence of Sam Houston, 1852–63*, ed. Madge Thornall Roberts (Denton: University of North Texas Press, 2001), 82 (second quotation); Grusendorf, *Century of Education*, 133.

16. Laura Simmons, *"Out of Our Past": Texas History Stories* (Waco: Texian, 1967), 34; Murray, *Baylor at Independence*, 151, 165; McNeill, *Uncompromising Diary*, 31 (quotation).

17. The Davis sisters came from a family that valued education; their father, Abner Davis, was an early educator at Shurtleff College, a Baptist college for men in Alton, Illinois, and Martha Clark was a graduate of Monticello Seminary, a women's school located in Alton. See *Catalogue of the Trustees, Officers, and Students of Baylor University, Independence, Washington County, Texas, 1851–52*, 24–25, Texas Collection, Baylor University; Murray, *Baylor at Independence*, 77, 104–5, 155; Texas Historical Marker, Independence, Texas, http://atlas.thc.state.tx.us/shell-county.htm (accessed September 3, 2010); *Baylor University Female Department Catalogue, 1859*, 4–5; White, *History of Baylor University*, 75.

18. Jabour, "'College Girls,'" 77; Jabour, *Scarlett's Sisters*, 62; McNeill, *Uncompromising Diary*, 26, 29, 32.

19. McNeill, *Uncompromising Diary*, 25.

20. Ibid., 31–32 (second quotation), 34–35 (first quotation), 84, 154.

21. Clinton, "Equally Their Due," 57; Jabour, "'College Girls,'" 74, 76, 78, 80, 87; Jabour, *Scarlett's Sisters*, 64; *Baylor University Female Department Catalogue, 1859*, 30; Murray, *Baylor at Independence*, 133; McNeill, *Uncompromising Diary*, 24 (quotation).

22. Murray, *Baylor at Independence*, 134; McNeill, *Uncompromising Diary*, 27, 29; *Baylor University Female Department Catalogue, 1859*, 27, 30.

23. *Baylor University Female Department Catalogue, 1859*, 30; Murray, *Baylor at Independence*, 116 (first quotation); McNeill, *Uncompromising Diary*, 28 (second quotation). Baylor had ample company in its attempt to keep the sexes separated. A school in Chappell Hill assured its readers that "the two Departments of the College, (male and female), are kept distinct and apart, with no intercommunication, save through the officers of the Institution" (Phelan, *Early Methodism*, 358).

24. Harris, "Baylor at Old Independence," 6. April 21 is San Jacinto Day, the day of the Texas victory over Mexico in its 1836 war for independence. Student Florence Davis wrote to her father on April 29, 1859, of a "jubilee" held to commemorate San Jacinto Day. Sam Houston, whose children were attending Baylor, addressed the celebration (Murray, *Baylor at Independence*, 173).

25. Haynes, "Biography," 215 (first quotation); Harris, "Baylor at Old Independence," 6 (second quotation).

26. McNeill, *Uncompromising Diary*, 28–29 (quotation); White, *History of Baylor University*, 46.

27. White, *History of Baylor University*, 134.

28. Harris, "Baylor at Old Independence," 6 (quotation); Murray, *Baylor at Independence*, 159.

29. McNeill, *Uncompromising Diary*, 26.

30. Ibid., 43–44.

31. Joyce Antler, "'After College, What?': New Graduates and the Family Claim," *American Quarterly* 32 (Fall 1980): 409–34; Jane Addams, *Democracy and Social Ethics* (New York: Macmillan, 1915), 85–86; Jabour, "'College Girls,'" 74; Simmons, *"Out of Our Past,"* 33 (first quotation); McNeill, *Uncompromising Diary*, 79 (second quotation).

32. Jabour, "'College Girls,'" 78; McNeill, *Uncompromising Diary*, 44 (first quotation), 49 (second quotation), 56 (third quotation), 58 (fourth quotation), 106, 112.

33. McNeill, *Uncompromising Diary*, 77 (first quotation), 78 (second quotation), 91, 114 (third quotation).

34. Ibid., 161, 73–74 (quotation), 91; U.S. Census, 1880; Anne W. Hooker, "Stewart, Charles," *Handbook of Texas Online*, http://www.tshaonline.org/handbook/online/articles/fst52 (accessed November 8, 2010); "Stewart, Charles," *Biographical Directory of the U.S. Congress, 1774 to the Present*, http://bioguide.congress.gov/scripts/biodisplay.pl?index=S000904 (accessed November 8, 2010).

35. *Baylor Bulletin* 17 (August 1914): Alumni Directory, 1854–1914; McNeill, *Uncompromising Diary*, 68 (first quotation), 75–76 (second quotation). The only classmate besides McNeill with no notation of marriage is Rebecca Skelton. In other regions of the South, the number of never-married women may have reached 20 percent of the female population (Christine Jacobson Carter, *Southern Single Blessedness: Unmarried Women in the Urban South, 1800–1865* [Urbana: University of Illinois Press, 2006], 3). The white population of Texas in 1860 consisted of 228,585 males and 192,306 females (U.S. Census, 1860). McNeill continued grieving over Barry's marriage in the entry she wrote on June 5, 1860, Barry's wedding day (*Uncompromising Diary*, 76). Zilphia Guthrie Fuller, the other member of the class of 1856, married John Calhoun Chew in 1861 and died in 1863, the year after the birth of her son (Lawrance Buckley Thomas, *Pedigrees of Thomas, Chew, and Lawrance: A West River Regester, and Genealogical Notes* [n.p.: Whittaker, 1888], 23).

36. Joel Perlmann and Robert A. Margo, *Women's Work?: American Schoolteachers, 1650–1920* (Chicago: University of Chicago Press, 2001), 22, 44–45.

37. Mary Kelley, "Reading Women/Women Reading: The Making of Learned Women in Antebellum America," *Journal of American History* 83 (September 1996): 402; McNeill, *Uncompromising Diary*, 47, 64, 65 (quotation), 87. The source through which McNeill bought books is not specified.

38. McNeill, *Uncompromising Diary*, 49, 82, 91, 95, 134, 153, 118, 128, 149, 151.

39. Ibid., 64 (quotation), 65, 115.

40. Kelley, *Learning to Stand*, 173–74, 180–81; McNeill, *Uncompromising Diary*, 41, 51, 58, 87, 88, 108, 113 (quotation), 114, 147; Carter, *Southern Single Blessedness*, 58–60.

41. Jonathan Daniel Wells, *The Origins of the Southern Middle Class, 1800–1861* (Chapel Hill: University of North Carolina Press, 2004), 42–43; McNeill, *Uncompromising Diary*, 25, 41, 45 (first quotation), 51, 52, 90–91 (second quotation), 143; Collection Description for the D. H. Hill Papers, University of North Carolina, http://www.lib.unc.edu/mss/inv/h/Hill,D.H.html (3 February 2014).

Harriet Perry

A Woman's Life in Civil War Texas

ANGELA BOSWELL

In 1862, Harriet Perry of Marshall, Texas, wrote to her husband, Theophilus, who was serving in the Confederate Army in Arkansas, "This separation from you is almost insupportable, but should you never come, oh what will become of me."[1] Harriet's words summarized the anxiety women throughout Texas endured as their lives were physically and emotionally altered by the conflict of the American Civil War. As a southern woman in the cotton region of East Texas, Harriet had certain expectations of the roles she played in her family and in her community. Her correspondence with her husband and other family members from May 1862 to March 1864 illustrates how she struggled to fulfill these expectations despite the tremendous strains of the war and the ways in which it ultimately reshaped the lives and roles of Texas women.

Twenty-six-year-old Harriet Perry's husband, Theophilus, joined the Confederate Army in 1862 and served in the 28th Texas Cavalry (Dismounted), Randal's Brigade, Walker's Texas Division, which was headquartered in Arkansas for most of the war. The Perrys were from elite North Carolina families and had moved to Marshall, Texas, in Harrison County after their marriage in 1860 to live near Theophilus's father. While his father owned a large plantation, Theophilus and his new wife bought an eight-acre lot in town, and he practiced law. At the time of Theophilus's enlistment, the couple held eight slaves and had a daughter about one year old, with another child on the way.[2]

As a young mother separated from her husband, Harriet was far from unique in Texas or the South. Most likely, somewhere between sixty thousand and seventy thousand Texas men served in the armies during the Civil War, with some estimates ranging as high as ninety thousand. These figures represent between 60 and 90 percent of Texas men between the ages of eighteen and fifty.[3] While

COTTON COMBS

at the Jefferson Historical Museum, Jefferson, Texas.

Photograph by Barb Boswell.

not all of these men were married, many of them no doubt had families like the Perrys. Many of those who were married had only very recently wed in the excitement as men went off to war, a phenomenon that Harriet abhorred: "I would not marry . . . these war times were I a young girl—It is no time for marrying." Harriet was not disenchanted with the institution of marriage in any way. For her, marital bliss had led to so strong an attachment between husband and wife that she advised women not to marry men likely to go to war because "I would rather grieve for a sweetheart than a husband."[4]

Not only were marriage and motherhood the most sacred callings for women in the antebellum South, they were two of the few avenues of respectable usefulness. Especially within marriages of elites, newer ideals of "companionate marriage" shaped the relationships between husbands and wives as much as older patriarchal ideals where the father commanded obedience and submissiveness from his wife, children, and slaves. Companionate marriage ideals emphasized loving if unequal partnerships based on love and respect. Yet the emotional connections as well as duties owed to spouses were very difficult to maintain when separated by distance for such extended periods of time.[5]

Theophilus's letters to Harriet contained many expressions of anxiety and sadness over their separation: "I shall bear the separation from you with as much philosophy as I have, though I often get low spirited, and feel like dying with loneliness and heart sickness." Yet he always admonished Harriet to "be cheerful and hopeful . . . and look forward for happy and prosperous times."[6] The Confederate government and newspapers urged correspondents not to fill their letters to the soldiers with depressing news but to keep up the spirits of the South's defenders.[7] For the most part, Harriet wrote only positive letters, suppressing any expressions of regret that might sadden her husband. Her emotions occasionally seeped into her writing, but she always apologized for such lapses. "I am dying to see you, but I will not write my feelings, for it will only make you unhappy and will do no good," she wrote in 1862. "There is no pleasure in life to me, having to live separated from you as I do—I don't care to live."[8] And later that year she implored, "I don't mean to complain darling, only please write if you can and come too, oh do come how can I do without you. I don't mean to urge you too much but you know how I feel dear husband. Don't let what I write make you sad."[9]

To ease the pain of separation, Harriet and Theophilus used their correspondence to sustain their emotional bond and to attempt to continue fulfilling their roles within the partnership. Ideally, wives were submissive to their husbands, but antebellum ideology also carved out a place for greater assertiveness by encouraging the benefits of female "influence." Harriet wielded influence in her letters in less-than-subtle ways. Admonishing Theophilus to "take care of your-self. Do what is right in all things," she called on his responsibilities as a husband and father: "Remember your wife and child. You are our all in all."[10]

Her advice carried with it the moral overtones of a nineteenth-century woman urging a man to more charitable, Christian pursuits. Her messages bore strong class privilege and economic overtones as well. Southern elites carefully upheld their positions in society, which could be strengthened by cultivating honor or lost by tarnishing that honor. The rather recent settlement and growth of Texas before the Civil War offered many families the opportunity to estab-lish themselves as leaders in new communities.[11] Harriet's decision to marry Theophilus and move with him to Texas may indicate that she sought the op-portunity to be among the respected as strongly as he. In one of her letters she alluded to the fact that Theophilus "*always* said I was ambitious."[12]

Whether her ambition matched or exceeded his, Harriet felt free to use her letters to advise Theophilus on his career and comportment, and he never chas-tised her for doing so. "I am proud of my husband and nothing is more gratify-ing to me than know[ing] you are promoted and hope you will ever be an honor to your position. I know you can be. Do your *best all* the time in the most trivial matters."[13] Harriet believed it was within her power and prerogative to influence him: "*All depends on yourself my Husband. You* can accomplish any thing any other man can, if you will persevere and not despond, which you are too apt to do." And although the separation caused by the war allowed history to capture her attitudes and encouragement in letters, the letters themselves indicate that her assertiveness was merely a continuation of prewar patterns. Thus in 1863, she called on him to "be encouraged and remember what I have often told you, that wherever you are and at whatever engaged, if you do your duty, you will be content, if not happy"[14]

Harriet's involvement in Theophilus's career, however, went beyond mere words of encouragement. When it appeared that her husband's promotion would only be temporary, she expressed bitter frustration: "I should not like *always* to be filling offices and never getting them—though it is our duty to make ourselves as useful as we are capable of—and I am glad for you to render all the service you can, but I want you to have *some* of the credit and benefit."[15] At another slight her husband suffered, Harriet lashed out "I *never will like* Randall [*sic*] *nor do I thank him for the way he has acted*. If he desired you to have a position why not give it to you instead of keeping you at work always for the honor and credit of some one else."[16] But once Theophilus was promoted, she offered concrete, specific advice about being a good officer: "I hope you . . . will gain the esteem and affection of your men—do not be too familiar with them—keep yourself at a respectful distance. You can do so without seeming to mean it and without offence." In case he might doubt that a woman should advise him on the subject of how to command men in the military, she asserted that "a word of advice from your wife is worth regarding, the intention at least."[17]

Antebellum southern men and women worked closely together on farms and plantations in collective economic and social units in which individual fortunes rose and fell with the whole. For this reason, a clear demarcation of separate spheres of authority was less present than in the urbanizing and industrializing North. Just as she felt comfortable advising her husband on his career and economic choices made primarily among men at home, Harriet also did so while he was away in the army. In the same way, Theophilus also used their correspondence to stay involved in the life of his family.[18]

Theophilus and Harriet's daughter, Mattie, was the light of Theophilus's life, and he constantly sent his wife advice for his little "Sugar Lumpy": "Rise early, let Sugar Lumpy run about in the yard all day in shady places. It makes no matter how dirty she gets."[19] In the winter, he worried "that little Sugar Lumpy will get burned by the fire this cold winter weather. Be extremely careful of her my Dear to keep her from the fire. A spark might catch her thin cotton garments."[20]

Theophilus's love and concern for his daughter were obvious even before his departure. When Harriet gave birth to their second child, a son, on December 24, 1862, she wrote, "Aunt Betsy says, tell you, he would not be good if *you were here, you would spoil him.*"[21] As solicitous as Theophilus was about his daughter's care, he seemed unconcerned about their newborn son. When Harriet noted this, Theophilus answered her honestly: "Indeed my dear if I must speak, my thoughts are occupied with you and Sugar Lumpy much more than they are with little Theophilus. I do not know how to think about him at all." Far away from his family, the elder Theophilus waxed philosophical about the true meaning of fatherhood, highlighting the difficulties of the separation. "There undoubtedly is much in blood," he wrote, "but it is the care and support and daily attention to children that places the strongest feeling in the bosom of a father."[22]

Theophilus used their correspondence to try to continue his active engagement in raising his daughter, while Harriet used their correspondence to participate in the career of her husband and the advancement of the family. As women throughout Texas and the South found, however, letters were poor substitutes for having partners at home to take care of the customary tasks and to provide emotional comfort. Indeed, no amount of letter writing could take the place of a husband at crucial times. As letters of many southern women during the Civil War reveal, husbands' absences were felt most acutely during childbirth. This event was not exclusively a female domain in the South—about half of the elite southern women hired male doctors for childbirth when they could.[23] Harriet expressed her preference for a male doctor, although she knew he was in demand. Husbands, however, were almost never in the birthing room. Yet even Harriet and other women who were trying to be cheerful in their letters to their husbands were surprisingly honest about their fears of childbirth and their disappointment that their husbands would be away. "I experience daily and nightly all the horrors of giving birth to an infant in mind, and the recollection of it is as vivid as the hour of my baby's birth—I dread it much more, for I know now how bad it is—my being alone is worst still. . . . Oh if you were with me, this trying time would be robbed of half its fears and terrors."[24]

Harriet's expressed desire for her husband was couched in a discussion of who would attend her when she went into labor. She debated whether a neighbor would arrive in time and whether she would be able to get a doctor there. Above all, she knew that "no one in this world could supply the place of my husband now."[25] Even after Aunt Betsy came to stay with her, Harriet's letters remained despondent: "I . . . feel so badly I can scarcely live—I have looked and wished for you till I am worn out and heart-sick."[26] Theophilus, like most southern soldiers, was unable to get a furlough to be with his wife. Though missing her husband, Harriet safely delivered the boy with the help of a midwife (whom Harriet professed "can do much better than Dr. Young").[27]

Furloughs were granted to soldiers according to wartime needs and not the needs of childbirth. Yet because soldiers did obtain furloughs, women continued to get pregnant and have children throughout the war, something that Harriet did not want to repeat on her own. "While I was in labor and bemoaning my separation from you Mrs. Marshall said she would tell me *for my encouragement*, that you would come in about a year, just time enough *for me to start again*, she termed it—well I told her if you did come now, I did not want you to come for that."[28] It was not just the height of labor that made her feel that way. Nearly a year later, after her husband had a furlough, Harriet wrote gleefully, "You told me I must write as soon as I found out *about myself*—There is nothing the matter at all. Aint I fortunate?"[29]

Like the thousands of Texas women continuing their productive and reproductive tasks throughout the Civil War without their husbands, brothers, and sons, Harriet's letters were filled with news of caring for infants, including her sleepless nights and their numerous illnesses. When both children were sick, Harriet worried about the negative effects of medicine but had to administer the drugs without the advice of her husband. Theophilus regretted the situation as much as Harriet did: "Children are always very bad off when the time comes for them to take Medicines. . . . It is impossible for me to be with you. How willingly would I share your tasks, and sit watching by the little children."[30]

Although Theophilus might have wished to share his wife's tasks and ease her burdens, women's work only increased during the war. Few Texans faced the scarcity of food that led to rioting in Richmond and some other parts of the Confederacy. Mostly undisturbed by troops of either army stationed in their midst, most Texas farms continued to produce abundant foodstuffs, with less chance of crops being impressed by the Confederate government than in areas east of the Mississippi. Throughout the South, women with few male family members, slaves, or hired help to assist with the farming had to perform manual labor after their husbands or sons were drafted into the army. As difficulties mounted and prices escalated, many of these women struggled and even starved. Many southern states enacted measures to help alleviate the suffering, and most Texas counties attempted to provide relief to widows, parents, and children of soldiers who needed support. The Colorado County Court, for example, paid families between ten and forty dollars a month, but with wartime inflation, the amount was barely enough to ward off starvation.[31]

Harriet's circumstances were straitened by the war, but having slaves and living near a large, wealthy family kept her from suffering from food shortages. In fact, women in her community had not only basic food necessities but "nice things" such as watermelons. Enjoying such treats caused Harriet and her friends to feel guilty about their high living when they knew the men lacked such fare.[32] Harriet did her best to share with her husband some of her family's abundance, sending dried sausages, dried peaches, pears, figs, apples, bacon, and lard and doing so out of love and a desire to keep him healthy. Theophilus wrote to her, "I endeavor to live as well as possible to keep off sickness. Bad diet is the cause of many deaths in the army."[33]

While food was abundant enough in the Perry household and a steady stream of friends and acquaintances carried packages and letters back and forth between Texas and Arkansas, certain items not produced in Texas—coffee, sugar, and whiskey, among others—became difficult to acquire because of the Union blockade. In only one package was Harriet able to send "a little coffee (all I had)."[34] Ironically, in the state that came to be renowned for its cattle, leather was almost impossible to find by 1863. As one historian has noted, "It would seem that all the cobblers in Texas had entered Confederate service."[35] Theophilus asked frequently for shoes, and Harriet apologized, "I do not know when I shall get your shoes made—I cannot get any leather—but I will have them

if I can." Soldiers' need for shoes outpaced that of the civilians, and the entire
Perry family seemed willing to sacrifice to get shoes for the soldiers. As Theophilus's father wrote to him in 1863, "We are all nearly barefooted but cheerful."[36]

The most time-consuming female tasks in the antebellum years also became
the most challenging ones during the Civil War—procurement and preparation of clothing. Harriet took seriously her responsibility to clothe her husband. Early in their correspondence, Harriet implored Theophilus to "note
everything you want and you shall have it if it can be procured—I am willing
to deprive myself of the last thing to add to your comfort and protect you from
the cold."[37] Theophilus at first seemed reluctant to ask for much. Harriet wrote
a berating letter in the cold winter of 1862 asking, "Are your clothes wearing
out? And which ones? . . . I am anxious about it for you never write a word."
Theophilus finally shared with her his gratitude for her provisions: "Nothing
could have been more acceptable than the winter clothing. The Gloves have
lasted me throughout the winter. . . . I think they are the nicest pair I have seen
in the whole Division. I have taken much pride and pleasure in observing that
they have often time attracted the attention of my friends."[38] During the years
of his absence, Harriet sent among other items, shoes, shirts, pants, pantaloons,
drawers, socks, overcoats, suits of clothing, a hat, a cravat, a towel, and a piece
of cloth for washing dishes.[39] As Harriet explained to her sister, "I have prepared
a good many nice things to send Mr. Perry. I want to have him as well fixed as
any one in the army—add all to his comfort I can, for there is little enough in
camp—he is so cold natured I rec[k]on he will freeze this winter—I am always
thinking what I shall do for him."[40]

After his promotion, Harriet's assistance in procuring necessities for his new
rank became even more important, and Theophilus's requests became specific:
"I frequently need nice clothes, and feel a little badly without them. I wish I had
a fine suit. I would send for my Broadcloth coat, but it is not the Pattern of the
Army. I desire a fine uniform but none can be obtained. A uniform Coat and
pants sell for about 175 dollars. This appears to be excessive but officers must
dress well if they seek to command respect."[41] Harriet made and procured all
that she possibly could, but she found that scarcity of materials sometimes made
it impossible to get him everything he needed.[42] She gently warned him, "You
must take as good care as you can of your shirts—it is difficult to get cloth at
any price—I do not know when I shall get more." But she assured him that "all
the money I spend will be for my dear Husband."[43]

Although Harriet almost always answered her husband's requests for provisions, she also exerted control over how his needs were met. Theophilus asked
Harriet to get a particular homespun Confederate cloth that others in his unit

were wearing. Homespun cloth, especially late in the war, was a sign of southern independence and an indication that the South could provide for itself. Harriet did as he asked and inquired about the price, yet she decided not to purchase the cloth because "it is cheaper for you to wear any other kind and I know it looks better than the homespun. . . . Remember your wife has *some* judgment and taste which I think you might rely on." She did promise submissiveness to his wishes if he insisted. And, she wrote, "if Mrs Dukes has the cloth and will sell at a reasonable price, I will buy for you. I want to please you in all things."[44] Theophilus acquiesced, "You advise me about my dress, and advise not to buy homespun. I yield to the sweet influence, and acknowledge your superior judgement." Harriet's stylistic and financial concerns overrode Theophilus's desire to make a political statement with his attire.[45]

Elite whites were accustomed to purchasing and wearing fine manufactured cloth for themselves, but they provided only coarse "negro" cloth for their slaves. The blockade caused both to be in short supply for civilians because the Confederate Army needed cloth for uniforms, blankets, and tents. At Huntsville, the prison became a cloth factory, but as civilians such as Gideon Lincecum discovered, the cloth was reserved for the army only and none was available for purchase. According to Lincecum, "People in this country are complaining mightily, and indeed some of them are really frightened at the thought of approaching nakedness."[46]

Texas women such as Harriet thus worked to clothe their families and soldiers amid great scarcity. Southern women were encouraged and at times even forced to get the spinning wheels and looms out of the attic, but the obstacles to home production were significant. Cotton production in Texas did not fall as much as in other southern states, but it did drop considerably as men went off to war and as the difficulty of exporting cotton through the blockade discouraged many people from growing the crop. Texans, however, could thwart the blockade by taking their cotton crops overland to Mexico, for it was more profitable to send cotton through Brownsville than to turn it into textiles locally. Above all, the shortage of cotton cards prevented most southern families from producing cloth. Cards were necessary to prepare the cotton fibers for spinning, but few were manufactured in southern states. Recognizing this shortage, the military board purchased forty thousand of the cards and distributed them to county governments throughout Texas, but even so, they remained scarce and expensive.[47]

Harriet and her husband's extended family were fortunate to have cards and later to be able to buy more, although Harriet lamented the exorbitant price. In 1862, she complained, "Cards are $15 and 20 dollars and *very* scarce," but by

December 1863, she bought a pair for forty dollars without much remark. Less than two months later, she decided to purchase another pair because they were selling for seventy-five dollars and she thought she should "get a pair before they get any higher."[48] Theophilus's stepmother seemed to be the driving force in stepping up the production of cloth in the Perry family, and the spinning wheel hummed in the background of nearly every letter Harriet sent to her husband. "The spinning machine spins thirteen yards of cloth per day—they have two looms weaving now," and "Your Mother keeps her spinning Machine making 15 yards of cloth a day" were typical lines.[49] Before moving in with Theophilus's family, the pregnant Harriet felt "very lazy *not* keeping time with the rest of the ladies."[50] The coarse "common plain negro cloth" could be made the most quickly, but cloth suitable for the white family took longer and earned special remarks from the Perry women. Theophilus's sister, Louisa, reported that "Aunt Betsy has wove a very pretty piece of Jeans to make Papa, you, bro Hugh and Levin some clothes. Levin has had one suit off of it."[51]

The Perry women's cloth production kept the family from a fear of "approaching nakedness." Their production, however, also proved lucrative. Theophilus's father, Levin, wrote in 1863 that "we are selling cloth at the rate of from one hundred to one hundred and twenty five dollars per week and paying debts with the money." Even though the Perry women were producing the cloth, all labor in a southern home accrued to the benefit of the entire household under the direction of the male head, so Levin had no sense of irony in writing "we," any more than his wife and daughter did when referring to the labor of their enslaved women. Among the women who made various grades of cloth, however, there was a sense of pride and ownership. Later that same year, Harriet perceived the financial arrangements a bit differently than Levin, crediting her mother-in-law with contracting to produce cloth when she wrote to Theophilus, "Your Mother is going to have plain cloth for the Government [and] has engaged to weave 120 yards before Christmas."[52]

Men in the household occasionally used language to obscure the importance of women's contributions to the finances of the household, even paying down debts. Yet women just as often used language to obscure those who provided the most strenuous labor—enslaved women. The white women of the family worked hard, as Harriet noted—"I sew or knit day and night."[53] Yet when Harriet wrote that "Your Mother keeps her spinning Machine making 15 yards of cloth a day," she actually meant that "Willis and two [other slave] women spin from light till dark." It was by these means that "*she* has made nearly two thousand yards of cloth."[54] Owning slaves placed the Perry family in the 27 percent of the South's 1860 population that held bondspeople, and during the war, slave ownership enabled financial gains that were not available to nonslaveholding families. In addition to growing crops for the Perry household, slave women made enough cloth not only to help pay the family's debts but also to purchase the scarce cotton cards to make cloth for themselves. Poorer families that might have made their own cloth were denied that opportunity.[55]

Of course, enslaved women were unable to direct their own labor during the Civil War, yet the war disrupted their lives as surely as it did elite and yeoman white women. Glimpses of the toll of the war on slave women appear in the Perry correspondence. Women worked from light till dark spinning or working in the fields. Then they took care of the white family's needs before their own. Harriet described her industriousness to her husband: "Since the new year came in I rise every morning, dress my baby, make up my bed and clean up my room before breakfast—I do that in order to give Mary Ann more time to spin." Mary Ann only "comes and makes a fire and brings water, then goes to work." Because Harriet dressed herself and her own baby, Mary Ann "spins eight cuts a day that is as much as any woman on the place gets. I am determined she shall not get less."[56] Harriet gave no thought to the fact that Mary Ann had at least one child of her own.[57]

In addition to increased workloads, enslaved women in Texas also faced wartime separations from their husbands and families. Many southern slaves found themselves far away from loved ones when slaveholders moved their slaves to Texas in advance of Union troops. "Refugeeing" was much less likely to disturb slave families in Texas because few Texas families needed to flee. Many enslaved men were pulled from their families to serve the Confederate cause, however. In March 1863, the Confederate Congress authorized military commanders to impress slaves into service to build fortifications and to provide other labor, thus freeing more soldiers to fight the war. These impressments were to last sixty days, but by late 1863, the period of impressment could be substantially longer. In addition, many elite Confederate men took one or more trusted male slaves with them when they joined the army. Both practices separated African American wives from husbands for extended periods of time.[58]

When Theophilus left for the army, he took with him one of his father's slaves, Norflet. Unlike Theophilus and Harriet, who used letters to maintain their emotional ties and learn news about each other, Norflet and his wife, Fanny, were unable to do so frequently, and Fanny could not take the same kind of care of her husband that Harriet took of hers. Fanny did, however, try to do so when she could. In describing the contents of a package, Harriet wrote to Theophilus that Fanny was sending Norflet "two pair of socks and the comforter."[59] Most of the time, however, Harriet determined how Norflet was to be provisioned, and her concern was far less than that of his wife. Harriet advised her husband, "Dont be spending your money on [Norflet], let him rough it and you *save the money. We will need it all and more.*"[60]

Military impressments and service to masters in the army were the most common reasons enslaved women were separated from their husbands. Yet the circumstances of the Civil War exerted other disruptions on slave women's lives, as hundreds of women left alone to manage farms and plantations chose to sell or "hire out" their slaves rather than oversee them. Harriet eventually hired out most of the Perry slaves to other households, but she kept with her at least one personal slave, Mary Ann. The correspondence does not provide any information about Mary Ann's husband, if indeed she had one, but Harriet noted in February 1863 that "Mary Anns baby [was] sick teething," meaning that an infant was likely separated from his father and a wife from her husband.[61]

Women of southern slaveholding families had frequently stepped in for absent husbands before the war and managed plantations and slaves. Their authority and ability to do so were predicated on a social system in which white men could still offer the threat of punishment and discipline. During the Civil War, as entire communities suddenly seemed devoid of white men, the system of slavery began to break down, even in Texas, where it never faced serious threats from the Union Army. With women unable to wield physical punishment, slaves became more difficult to manage. Lizzie Neblett of Grimes County, Texas, struggled with slave management throughout the war, using a series of overseers and then losing even that assistance. In Lizzie's correspondence with her husband, Will, she despaired of ever successfully operating the plantation of slaves in his absence and declared, "I am so sick of trying to do a man's business."[62]

Harriet initially tried to cope by managing the Perry place alone. A little over a month after Theophilus left, she seemed pleased at the prospect of overseeing the slaves herself, reporting, "I kept Jane hauling manure all day," and "I got up early put Sam to bedding the Irish potatoe patch and took the others in the garden." Although she did some manual labor herself, her pregnancy led her to "the palpitation of the heart so much" and complicated her ability to do much physical labor or even stand to oversee slaves' labor. Early on in Theophilus's absence and in her pregnancy, she solved this problem: "I took a chair and staid all the time."[63]

Even her initial confidence, however, contained a tinge of foreboding: "We have got on very well so far, the negroes seem to do as well as when you were here so far. I cant tell how long they will hold out." More than a year into the war, slaves had begun to exert more independence, and she had no doubt heard reports from her community and family in North Carolina about slaves running away to Union lines. With word of the preliminary Emancipation Proclamation, Harriet's foreboding turned to alarm by October 1862: "I have not been afraid to stay here till now—I feel very uneasy indeed."[64]

By February 1863, Harriet had decided to leave her home and move in with her husband's family north of town. "I see no likelihood of the wars ending and I am tired and afraid to stay here alone and I cannot have any thing done at all," she explained. Her fear of being alone with a newborn child and a toddler played a role in her decision, but her inability to make the slaves work figured most prominently. She calculated that the slaves "will hire for a little and if they stay here they will make nothing," but she had "heard of no one buying or selling," so selling the slaves was not an option. Many extended Texas families lived together and pooled resources, so women could rely on the few men who were left behind or have the support of other adult women. Harriet agonized about whether to leave her home and wished her husband could tell her what to do. She decided to move before she could hear from Theophilus. As she explained, "I tried living alone seven months and became so tired and dissatisfied I concluded it would be best to break up." She also informed her husband that she would "hire out the negroes" because "they would not work for me."[65]

Because plantation business often took place within the home, southern women were not completely unacquainted with crops, slave management, and even financial and business transactions. Like slave management, however, women were accustomed to influencing these matters and taking the authority only for temporary periods. The extended absence of husbands during the Civil War, a quickly changing and deteriorating economy, and laws and customs that gave women few rights or experience in monetary transactions made for complex decisions within households and within the community.[66]

Texas laws were unique in the South in allowing married women to own property in their own names and by granting married women half of the interest of property acquired by the couple after marriage. Yet control of a married woman's property was still vested in her husband. Legally, therefore, men controlled the buying, selling, and leasing of real estate, slaves, cattle, and horses; women, who were often, as Lizzie Neblett complained, "tied to the house by a crying young one," were less likely to be able to travel to court and/or market to make such transactions.[67]

A married woman still had to grant permission for the sale of any of her separate real estate and all real estate held jointly by the couple. In addition, most business decisions were made at the farm or plantation, where women could use their influence. Finally, women were not completely barred from market transactions, although their transactions tended to be smaller than men's. Laws allowed women to contract for "necessities," and not only had most women taken advantage of this right, but women on farms and plantations commonly bought and sold certain farm products. When Harriet chose to move in with her in-laws, she sold the fowl she had been raising and considered her own, telling her husband, "I have sold my turkeys and ducks" and "I have been selling butter at thirty cents a pound and eggs at twenty five cents a dozen."[68]

When men left for war, a great responsibility for financial decisions fell to wives, but such duties were not always completely foreign. In Colorado County, the courts eased restrictions against a married woman entering into financial transactions and recognized a married woman's right to hold her husband's power of attorney. Still, the expectation that men would take care of business made for interesting legal and interpersonal relationships. As George Rable and other historians have noted, early in the war, men throughout the South continued to try to direct all the financial and planting arrangements, but as the war stretched on, they gradually yielded to their wives' judgment, since they knew less and less about what was happening on the home front.[69]

Theophilus worried about his financial position and bemoaned the opportunities missed because of his absence, believing that "if I was at home I could make some good arrangements." He often admonished Harriet to "consult Papa in every thing."[70] Yet Harriet's opinion was clearly as important to Theophilus, if not more important. In fact, one of his first directives sounds as if he were responding to a suggestion made by Harriet. "I also believe it would be to our advantage to sell [our house], but I am such condition of mind as to doubt almost every thing."[71] Within a couple of weeks, Theophilus yielded entirely: "You write to me about selling my place . . . and wish to learn my wishes upon the subject. I am willing to do any thing you or Papa may think best." Although he hinted strongly that she should solicit his father's advice, he concluded, "Whatever you do, will meet my approval."[72]

With his explicit approval to make major decisions concerning the buying and selling of real estate came greater responsibilities than Harriet had borne before the war. Theophilus's desire that she consult another man—in this case, his father—was not an indication of a lack of faith in her judgment but a matter of practicality. Had Theophilus been at home, he, too, would have consulted his father on major matters. And Harriet needed Levin's assistance in the sale and leasing of the property. Tied as she was to the house with two very small children and an immense amount of cloth making and food preparation and preservation, she could not get to Marshall to negotiate with potential buyers or renters. "I suppose Mr. Witherspoons has rented our place to Dr. Wilson's son-in-law. . . . Your Father will go to Marshall to-morrow and I shall hear all about it." Even though she learned about the transaction from her father-in-law, she expressed ownership of the deal: "*I* am glad *I* found a tenant so soon."[73]

In matters smaller than the transfer of real estate, Theophilus was explicit in his desire for Harriet to take control. When he decided that it was necessary to get out of debt, he sent her clear instructions on how to pay the debts and to whom and told her, "Do not mention these little things to Papa. It is disagreeable to him to talk about debt."[74] Throughout their two years of separation, finances and household management were the most common topics in their letters. Although he frequently directed her to make arrangements for "him" or "his debt" or "his place," he did it in the best interest of the family, with her advice and consent. She was as eager to get free of debt as he was: "When your Father goes [to Marshall] and pays out this money we will owe no one but Capt Harris, Mr. Dane and Mr Marshall. . . . I begin to breathe better now Husband and feel greatly relieved."[75]

Before long, Harriet was the financial manager, and Theophilus wrote to her to ask, "What do I owe?" By 1864, Theophilus concluded that the war would be ending soon, Confederate money would be worthless, and "the Beginning of the end of African Slavery has come." He directed Harriet to have his father purchase improved land for the couple to live on at the end of the war. Harriet responded, "I did not read that portion of your letter to your Father relating to buying Land." They had no money to purchase land, and she thought it best not to worry his father about it. In a tone not of submissiveness but of seeking the advice of a partner, she asked, "Do you not think I am right?" Without firsthand knowledge of the situation at home, Theophilus expressed either resignation or faith in his wife's abilities: "You have acted right in not buying land. I approve of your judgement."[76]

Harriet and Theophilus were fortunate to have his father available to give advice on and carry out the financial transactions for his son and daughter-in-law. Not all Texas women were as lucky. Those who were not had to find the time and the wherewithal to conduct business at the courthouse themselves. As military fortunes faded in February 1864, the Confederate government expanded the draft to cover all men between the ages of seventeen and fifty. In March, rumors abounded that the age limit would be increased even further, to fifty-five. The members of the Perry family feared the worst. Not only were their husbands and brothers already fighting the war, it now seemed as if their fathers would also be removed. Theophilus wrote that the rumored change "will take Papa into the service. I do not know whether it takes your father or not. I think it does. I am in hopes that both of them will succeed in getting agreeable and easy places, where they will be near home and can pay some attention to their family interest."[77] Theophilus's desire that his father continue to look after the family's interests reflected the younger man's greatest concern—his own neglected family interest.

In addition to the added responsibilities of making cloth, feeding families, running farms and plantations, and overseeing family financial decisions, Texas women during the Civil War also banded together to form soldiers' aid organizations. Before moving her household, Harriet attended the Marshall Ladies' Aid Society, which formed committees to make items for soldiers, such as the box of lint bandages requested by a doctor headed to the army. The society kept constantly busy, answering letters coming from the local units "begging them to send clothing and blankets or covering of some kind to the soldiers for God's sake."[78] Another aid society operated near where Theophilus's father lived, and like many societies, they planned a tableau (living picture) "and have prevailed upon your Father to let them have it at his house."[79] Tableaux raised money for soldiers' supplies and fostered support for the Confederacy. Women dressed to portray the patriotic cause, often with each young woman representing a state in the Confederacy. Although the women moved on the stage, there were few, if any, dramatic lines. Thus, the ladies could participate without being accused of being actresses, an unacceptable activity for respectable women. Some Perry women acted in the tableaux at the Perry household. Harriet hoped they would "do all they can for the soldiers." Harriet missed two opportunities to attend tableaux while in Marshall because she found herself too busy. Even as preparations were undertaken, she could not feel the same "great interest" as others did because "I do not take any pleasure in any thing without you," she wrote to Theophilus.[80] Unlike northern women's sanitation fairs and other fund-raisers and aid societies, southern efforts, like the ones in Harriet's community, remained small and unstructured. They provided assistance with bandages and blankets, but Harriet and many other Texas women were so busy trying to provision their families that the societies never reached northern levels of activity.[81]

Ladies' aid societies were important outlets for women who at least initially bemoaned their inability to do more to support the Confederate cause. War historically was an opportunity to reinforce gender roles, as men went off to war to prove their manhood, while women waited passively at home. Private correspondence and newspaper editorials alike abound with women such as "Helen," who lamented in the Columbus, Texas, newspaper that her sphere did not permit her "to go to the wars" or else she "should have taken delight in going some time ago, and nothing could have prevented [her] from going."[82]

While some women fantasized about fighting or envied the men who did so, most women, including Harriet Perry, were willing to accept the gendered ideals that war reinforced. During the Civil War, however, the war was not far off. Nearly all battles were fought in the South, making the war front and home front one and the same. Corpus Christi resident Maria von Blücher described the hardships caused by nearby battles. When Union ships prepared to bombard the city, residents packed up and left in haste—"For 4–5 miles along the wayside, one saw one household after another loaded up." Her home was unhurt by the bombardment, but the danger was very real, as she reported to her parents: "In our yard the children found a shell 13″ long, a similar one 10″ long weighing 26 pounds, and one of 24 pounds, 9″ long, all of them unexploded."[83]

Harriet Perry's community, like most of Texas, never suffered from invading Union armies. But Texas women at the time could not know whether Union troops would ever arrive, and fear of war, occupation, and advancing armies preoccupied the thoughts of many women left alone to care for homes and family members. Lizzie Neblett wrote how "Last night . . . I found myself sitting bolt upright in bed, listening with terror to what I thought at the moment was the noise and roar of cannon."[84]

With the occupation of New Orleans in May 1863, the threat of a Union invasion felt ever more real. In December 1862, Harriet confessed, "I am much alarmed about them coming up Red River—I shall have to leave home I know—I am saving money for that purpose if they come."[85] In 1864, Union commander Nathaniel Banks did lead troops up the Red River, causing rumors and fear in Marshall. Harriet heard that "a fleet of Gunboats [was] at the mouth of the Red river, some say 40 some 20—no one seems to doubt it." The effect of such news was clear. Harriet's letter apologized for possible repetitiveness and confusion: "My mind is so much harassed my memory is very poor."[86]

Texas women did not have to imagine problems that might arise if Union troops or battles were to come within range of their homes. They heard such stories from people they trusted. Most Texans still had families living in southeastern states, and they received letters or oral accounts of family members who lived in areas occupied by Union or Confederate troops. Many people fled their homes in advance of Union troops and moved slaves to safety. Texas, in fact, was a destination for many fleeing southerners, who brought news of the destruction. Harriet explained to her husband how a mutual friend, Mrs. Sanders, had spent the day with her. The woman and her children had left their home on the Mississippi River to stay with relatives in Marshall. Her husband had remained on the plantation but sent all the slaves westward for safekeeping. The family had also moved all its furniture, although according to Harriet, Mrs. Sanders "said the Federals had been there but troubled nothing at all." Instead of reassuring Harriet that even if the Union troops came, they might not destroy everything, the news made her suspicious of Mr. Sanders: "It has been whispered here that the old man took the oath of allegiance."[87]

The presence of refugees triggered as much fear as did rumors of Union troop movements. On July 20, 1863, the members of the Perry family were preoccupied with the possibility of having to flee, and three people mentioned it in their letters to Theophilus. His sister, Louisa, reported that the family was "very uneasy about the Federals getting here." She believed that she "would be frightened nearly to death if they were to do so."[88] Harriet reported, "Your mother is talking strongly of packing up and moving off to a place of safety—I know not where we will find that. I wish there was such a place."[89] Nothing in the letters explains precisely what triggered such sudden fear and plans for relocation. News of the fall of Vicksburg had no doubt recently reached the Perrys, leading them, as well as others in Texas, to fear an immediate threat. Also in those letters was mention of "a gentleman and lady residing here (refugees from Kentucky)," who probably reminded the family of the problems of advancing Union troops.[90]

Harriet Perry and her family did not have to relocate. Despite repeated rumors, Union troops never invaded East Texas (although battles at Galveston, Corpus Christi, and Sabine Pass brought the war directly to some Texas women). Packing up households and moving slaves were exhausting tasks to contemplate under any circumstances, and the Perrys and their neighbors were missing the strongest, most able men in their families. Even von Blücher's relocation during the Battle of Corpus Christi had to await her husband's return.[91]

Fear of invasion, scarcity of goods, price inflation, runaway and disobedient slaves, loneliness, and the absence of their husbands during both difficult and joyous times were not the greatest hardships southern—or Texan—women faced. The greatest hardship was, of course, the death of husbands and other loved ones.[92]

Harriet's letters constantly expressed her worries about her husband: "I fear [the Federals] will come upon you before you are ready, how I dread the battles for you," she wrote in October 1862.[93] As much as she dreaded the danger to her husband, she tried to be stoic for his sake, as when she told him, "I was very much distressed when I heard you were going to Vicksburg though you seemed glad to go. I must try to bear this in mind, that you must be in battle wherever you are and exposed to the enemy."[94] Nonetheless, she did not always succeed in putting up a brave front: "I get sad when ever I hear of the death of any one in the War—May Heaven smile upon and spare you my dearest love, my sweet Husband."[95] In a letter to her sister, Harriet was painfully blunt, explaining why she would not relocate to North Carolina to be with her family: "I should then be so far from Mr. Perry. I could not hear from him hardly ever. I want to stay as near him as I can while he lives for I have no idea he will ever return to stay. War makes its widows by the thousand."[96]

On April 17, 1864, the war made Harriet a widow. In Louisiana, at the Battle of Pleasant Hill, Theophilus suffered a mortal wound. Like the thousands of other Texas war widows, Harriet had to contend with a changed economy and society without the aid of her husband. Harriet's hopes and dreams for the future died with her husband and with the war. Still in debt, with little property and their investment in slaves forever erased by emancipation, Harriet had to start over again. Shortly after the war ended, her daughter, Mattie, died, too, leaving her with only Theophilus Jr. She returned to live with her family in North Carolina in 1865 and remarried in 1872. Thirteen years later, forty-nine-year-old Harriet died, too.[97]

No other four-year period of time saw more dramatic changes than those that occurred during the American Civil War. Texas women took on new responsibilities, lived in households and communities with few or no men, and struggled to make do in an economy wracked by blockades, inflation, and speculation. For all the changes, elite Texas women still tried to operate during the war with the same gendered social expectations and to maintain the same ideals about marriage and family. Fulfilling the reciprocal roles of husband and wife, however, was extremely difficult through correspondence alone, as women across the South discovered. Many women began to doubt the war and the Confederacy, writing letters to the government begging for men to be released from service to care for the families. Though Harriet Perry lacked the daily protection and guidance of her husband, she was able to move into a family household where a man temporarily fulfilled certain male duties, such as handling financial transactions and overseeing slaves. As a result, Harriet and Theophilus's marriage probably faced fewer challenges to gendered expectations than other southern couples. Like hundreds of thousands of other southern women, however, Harriet found herself a widow at the end of the war, left alone without the protection and companionship of her husband. Harriet and Theophilus's correspondence illustrates that the Civil War affected women in Texas similarly to and as significantly as women elsewhere in the South.[98]

NOTES

1. Harriet Perry to Theophilus Perry, December 23, 1862, in Theophilus Perry and Harriet Perry, *Widows by the Thousand: The Civil War Letters of Theophilus and Harriet Perry, 1862–1864*, ed. M. Jane Johansson (Fayetteville: University of Arkansas Press, 2000), 74 (hereafter cited as *Widows*).

2. Ibid., xvi–xix.

3. Randolph B. Campbell, *Gone to Texas: A History of the Lone Star State* (New York: Oxford University Press, 2000), 261; Ralph A. Wooster, "Civil War," *Handbook of Texas Online*, http://www .tshaonline.org/handbook/online/articles/qdco2 (accessed November 11, 2010).

4. Harriet Perry to Sallie M. Person, February 18, 1863, Harriet Perry to Theophilus Perry, October 26, 1862, both in *Widows*, 101, 49.

5. Christine Jacobson Carter, *Southern Single Blessedness: Unmarried Women in the Urban South, 1800–1865* (Urbana: University of Illinois Press, 2006), 2–3. Scholarship that speaks to the relative companionate or patriarchal nature of southern marriage includes Anya Jabour, *Marriage in the Early Republic: Elizabeth and William Wirt and the Companionate Ideal* (Baltimore: Johns Hopkins University Press, 1998); Elizabeth Fox-Genovese, *Within the Plantation Household: Black and White Women of the Old South* (Chapel Hill: University of North Carolina Press, 1988), 63–70; Brenda E. Stevenson, *Life in Black and White: Family and Community in the Slave South* (New York: Oxford University Press, 1996), 63–94; Catherine Clinton, *The Plantation Mistress: Woman's World in the Old South* (New York: Random House, 1982), 87–109; more recently, V. Lynn Kennedy, *Born Southern: Childbirth, Motherhood, and Social Networks in the Old South* (Baltimore: Johns Hopkins University Press, 2010), 113–36.

6. Theophilus Perry to Harriet Perry, November 22, 1862, in *Widows*, 61.

7. Drew Gilpin Faust, *Mothers of Invention: Women of the Slaveholding South in the American Civil War* (Chapel Hill: University of North Carolina Press, 1996), 118.

8. Harriet Perry to Theophilus Perry, October 26, 1862, in *Widows*, 48.

9. Ibid., December 13, 1862, 69.

10. Ibid., December 3, 1862, 67; George C. Rable, *Civil Wars: Women and the Crisis of Southern Nationalism* (Urbana: University of Illinois Press, 1989), 23; Scott Stephan, *Redeeming the Southern Family: Evangelical Women and Domestic Devotion in the Antebellum South* (Athens: University of Georgia Press, 2008), 95–99; Steven M. Stowe, *Intimacy and Power in the Old South: Ritual in the Lives of the Planters* (Baltimore: Johns Hopkins University Press, 1987), 122–28, esp. 128.

11. For insight into the importance of honor, see Bertram Wyatt-Brown, *Southern Honor: Ethics and Behavior in the Old South* (New York: Oxford University Press, 1982), 117–48, 331–39; Stowe, *Intimacy and Power*, 1–49, 122–59. See also Jane Turner Censer, "Southwestern Migration among North Carolina Planter Families: 'The Disposition to Emigrate,'" *Journal of Southern History* 57 (August 1991): 407–26; Angela Boswell, *Her Act and Deed: Women's Lives in a Rural Southern County, 1837–1873* (College Station: Texas A&M University Press, 2001), 54–78; Randolph B. Campbell, *A Southern Community in Crisis: Harrison County, Texas, 1850–1880* (Austin: Texas State Historical Association, 1983).

12. Harriet Perry to Theophilus Perry, September 24, 1862, in *Widows*, 40.

13. Ibid.

14. Ibid., February 8, 1863, 97.

15. Ibid., October 4, 1862, 43.

16. Ibid., February 8, 1863, 96–97.

17. Ibid., July 20, 1863, 153.

18. Fox-Genovese, *Within the Plantation Household*, 66–68; Jabour, *Marriage in the Early Republic*; Stowe, *Intimacy and Power*, 128. For the ways this phenomenon made the South distinctive from the North in the matter of law, see Peter W. Bardaglio, *Reconstructing the Household: Families, Sex, and the Law in the Nineteenth-Century South* (Chapel Hill: University of North Carolina Press, 1995), 25–36.

19. Theophilus Perry to Harriet Perry, July 8, 1862, in *Widows*, 7.

20. Ibid., February 6, 1863, 93.

21. Harriet Perry to Theophilus Perry, January 18, 1863, in *Widows*, 85.

22. Theophilus Perry to Harriet Perry, March 8, 1863, in ibid., 109. See also Jane Turner Censer, *North Carolina Planters and Their Children, 1800–1860* (Baton Rouge: Louisiana State University Press, 1984), esp. 39. A more patriarchal characterization of fatherhood among elite southerners can be found in Kennedy, *Born Southern*, 113–36.

23. Sally G. McMillen, *Southern Women: Black and White in the Old South* (Arlington Heights, Ill.: Harlan Davidson, 1992), 60.

24. Harriet Perry to Theophilus Perry, October 30, 1862, in *Widows*, 51.

25. Ibid.

26. Ibid., October 30, December 3, 1862, 51, 65.

27. Harriet Perry to Mary Temperance Person, January 6, 1863, in ibid., 77.

28. Harriet Perry to Theophilus Perry, January 18, 1863, in ibid., 88.

29. Ibid., December 18, 1863, 185. See also Elizabeth Scott Neblett, *A Rebel Wife in Texas: The Diary and Letters of Elizabeth Scott Neblett, 1852–1864*, ed. Erika L. Murr (Baton Rouge: Louisiana State University Press, 2001), 20. A different perspective on southern women's attitudes on controlling reproduction can be found in Sally G. McMillen, *Motherhood in the Old South: Pregnancy, Childbirth, and Infant Rearing* (Baton Rouge: Louisiana State University Press, 1990), 35.

30. Theophilus Perry to Harriet Perry, July 29, 1863, in *Widows*, 158.

31. Faust, *Mothers of Invention*, 32; Laura F. Edwards, *Scarlett Doesn't Live Here Anymore: Southern Women in the Civil War Era* (Urbana: University of Illinois Press, 2000), 91–92; Boswell, *Her Act and Deed*, 102.

32. Harriet Perry to Theophilus Perry, August 3, 1862, in *Widows*, 13.

33. Theophilus Perry to Harriet Perry, December 29, 1863, in ibid., 192.

34. Harriet Perry to Theophilus Perry, February 19, 1863, in ibid., 102.

35. Vera Lea Dugas, "A Social and Economic History of Texas in the Civil and Reconstruction Periods" (PhD diss., University of Texas at Austin), 284.

36. Harriet Perry to Theophilus Perry, January 29, 1864, Levin Perry to Theophilus Perry, July 20, 1863, both in *Widows*, 202, 154.

37. Harriet Perry to Theophilus Perry, October 26, 1862, in ibid., 48. See also Faust, *Mothers of Invention*, 45–52.

38. Harriet Perry to Theophilus Perry, December 13, 1862, Theophilus Perry to Harriet Perry, March 8, 1863, both in *Widows*, 70, 107.

39. Harriet Perry to Mary Temperance Person, October 22, 1862, Harriet Perry to Theophilus Perry, December 13, 1862, January 18, February 19, July 28, 1863, January 29, 1864, Theophilus Perry to Harriet Perry, March 8, May 23, December 8, 1863, January 29, February 14, 1864, all in ibid., 45, 70, 84, 102, 157, 202, 107, 134, 174, 205, 212.

40. Harriet Perry to Mary Temperance Person, October 22, 1862, in ibid., 45.

41. Theophilus Perry to Harriet Perry, May 23, 1863, in ibid., 133.

42. Harriet Perry to Theophilus Perry, January 29, 1864, in ibid., 202.

43. Ibid., July 28, 1863, 157.

44. Ibid., February 26, 1864, 218–19; Faust, *Mothers of Invention*, 47–49.

45. Theophilus Perry to Harriet Perry, March 8, 1864, in *Widows*, 225.

46. Gideon Lincecum, *Gideon Lincecum's Sword: Civil War Letters from the Texas Home Front*, ed. Jerry Bryan Lincecum, Edward Hake Phillips, and Peggy A. Redshaw (Denton: University of North Texas Press, 2001), 188, 195, 207.

47. Paula Mitchell Marks, *Hands to the Spindle: Texas Women and Home Textile Production, 1822–1880* (College Station: Texas A&M University Press, 1996), 78–81; Dugas, "Social and Economic History," 263, 284–86; Lincecum, *Gideon Lincecum's Sword*, 207–11; Faust, *Mothers of Invention*, 45–52.

48. Harriet Perry to Theophilus Perry, September 24, 1862, December 6, 1863, January 29, 1864, in *Widows*, 41, 171, 202.

49. Ibid., September 15, 1862, February 19, 1863, 28, 103.

50. Ibid., September 24, 1862, 41.

51. Louisa Perry to Theophilus Perry, November 15, 1862, in ibid., 60.

52. Harriet Perry to Theophilus Perry, December 6, 1863, in ibid., 172.

53. Ibid., December 6, 1863, 171.

54. Harriet Perry to Theophilus Perry, February 19, 1863, in *Widows*, 103; emphasis added.

55. Randolph B. Campbell, *An Empire for Slavery: The Peculiar Institution in Texas, 1821–1865* (Baton Rouge: Louisiana State University Press, 1989), 190–91; Lincecum, *Gideon Lincecum's Sword*, 211–12.

56. Harriet Perry to Theophilus Perry, January 20, 1864, in *Widows*, 200.

57. Ibid., February 8, 1863, 98–99.

58. Campbell, *Empire for Slavery*, 234–38.

59. Harriet Perry to Theophilus Perry, February 19, 1863, in *Widows*, 102. For a discussion of a single letter between Norflet and Fanny, see Randolph B. Campbell and Donald K. Pickens, "Documents: 'My Dear Husband': A Texas Slave's Love Letter, 1862," *Journal of Negro History* 65 (Autumn 1980): 361–64.

60. Ibid., August 4, 1862, 15.

61. Ibid., February 8, 1863, 98–99.

62. Faust, *Mothers of Invention*, 65–70; Rable, *Civil Wars*, 113–15; Neblett, *Rebel Wife in Texas*, 1.

63. Harriet Perry to Theophilus Perry, August 3, 1862, in *Widows*, 11.

64. Ibid., August 4, October 26, 1862, 15, 50.

65. Ibid., February 8–13, 1863, 94–95, 99. Harriet began the letter on February 8 expressing her desire to have Theophilus tell her what to do, but by the time she concluded the letter on February 13, she had already begun the move.

66. Rable, *Civil Wars*, 32, 113–15. See also LeeAnn Whites, *The Civil War as a Crisis in Gender: Augusta, Georgia, 1860–1890* (Athens: University of Georgia Press, 2000).

67. Neblett, *Rebel Wife in Texas*, 1; Boswell, *Her Act and Deed*, 20–24; Jean A. Stuntz, *Hers, His, and Theirs: Community Property Law in Spain and Early Texas* (Lubbock: Texas Tech University Press, 2005), 147–69. See also Stuntz, in this volume.

68. Harriet Perry to Theophilus Perry, February 8, 1863, in *Widows*, 95.

69. Boswell, *Her Act and Deed*, 95–102; Rable, *Civil Wars*, 32, 113–15; Faust, *Mothers of Invention*, 22; Whites, *Civil War as a Crisis*, 31–37.

70. Theophilus Perry to Harriet Perry, January 30, 1863, in *Widows*, 91.

71. Ibid., July 17, 1862, 5.

72. Ibid., September 21, 1862, 34–35. As southern women became more knowledgeable about the household business than their husbands during the war, not all husbands were accepting of their wives' new abilities as Theophilus was. William McLure of South Carolina was never able "to relate to his wife as a person who was in charge of a working plantation." See Joan Cashin, "'Since the War Broke Out': The Marriage of Kate and William McLure," in *Divided Houses: Gender and the Civil War*, ed. Catherine Clinton and Nina Silber (New York: Oxford University Press, 1992), 208–12.

73. Harriet Perry to Theophilus Perry, February 8, 1863, in *Widows*, 99; emphasis added.

74. Theophilus Perry to Harriet Perry, March 8, 1863, in ibid., 110.

75. Harriet Perry to Theophilus Perry, March 24, 1863, in ibid., 114.

76. Theophilus Perry to Harriet Perry, July 9, 1863, January 18, 1864, March 9, 1864, Harriet Perry to Theophilus Perry, January 20, 1864, all in ibid., 146, 198, 226, 199–200.

77. Theophilus Perry to Harriet Perry, March 1, 1864, in ibid., 222–24.

78. Harriet Perry to Theophilus Perry, September 24, December 3, 1862, in ibid., 40, 66.

79. Ibid., February 8, 1863, 94.

80. Harriet Perry to Theophilus Perry, September 24, December 3, 1862, February 8, 19, Harriet Perry to Sallie M. Person, 100, all in ibid., 40, 66, 94, 103, 100.

81. On southern women's lack of ability to organize as much as northern women, see Edwards, *Scarlett Doesn't Live Here Anymore*, 71–99, esp. 76–77; Rable, *Civil Wars*, 136–53; Faust, *Mothers of Invention*, 9–29, 112–13, 234–47. For information on northern women's efforts, see, for example, Judith Ann Giesberg, *Civil War Sisterhood: The U.S. Sanitary Commission and Women's Politics in Transition* (Boston: Northeastern University Press, 2000); Jeanie Attie, *Patriotic Toil: Northern Women and the American Civil War* (Ithaca: Cornell University Press, 1998); Nina Silber, *Daughters of the Union: Northern Women Fight the Civil War* (Cambridge: Harvard University Press, 2005), 162–221; Elizabeth D. Leonard, *Yankee Women: Gender Battles in the Civil War* (New York: Norton, 1994), 51–103.

82. *Colorado Citizen*, September 21, 1861; Faust, *Mothers of Invention*, 20–21.

83. Maria von Blücher, *Maria von Blücher's Corpus Christi: Letters from the South Texas Frontier, 1849–1879*, ed. Bruce S. Cheeseman (College Station: Texas A&M University Press, 2002), 130.

84. Neblett, *Rebel Wife in Texas*, 96.

85. Harriet Perry to Theophilus Perry, December 3, 1862, in *Widows*, 66.

86. Ibid., January 18, 1864, 197.

87. Ibid., April 5, 1863, 119.

88. Louisa Perry to Theophilus Perry, July 20, 1863, in ibid., 154.

89. Harriet Perry to Theophilus Perry, July 20, 1863, in ibid., 155.

90. Louisa Perry to Theophilus Perry, July 20, 1863, in ibid., 154.

91. von Blücher, *Maria von Blücher's Corpus Christi*, 130.

92. Faust, *Mothers of Invention*, 120.

93. Harriet Perry to Theophilus Perry, October 4, 1862, in *Widows*, 44.

94. Ibid., December 23, 1862, 73.

95. Ibid., April 5, 1863, 118.

96. Harriet Perry to Mary Temperance Person, October 22, 1862, in ibid., 45.

97. *Widows*, 244–45.

98. Faust, *Mothers of Invention*, 114–38, 193–94, 238–44; Bardaglio, *Reconstructing the Household*, 130–31.

Capitalist Women in Central Texas, 1865–1880

"A Ready Market"

ROBIN C. SAGER

So lively and bustling was the business environment in Waco, Texas, in the heady 1870s that city residents even revised their notion of what the term *entrepreneur* could mean. Naomi H. Kirkpatrick was just one of many merchants who entered the fray, placing ads in the papers and advancing the interests of a diverse investment portfolio that included the ownership of both groceries and hotels. Promotion was a necessary part of keeping her ventures afloat and prospering. Readers could not have overlooked her advertisement in the September 28, 1873, issue of the *Waco Examiner*, given that it followed her standard style of combining bold print with a large layout. She proclaimed that she expected her share of public patronage as a dealer in family groceries and supplies. Over the following weeks, she waged an all-out promotional campaign, in which this announcement represented only the opening salvo. Kirkpatrick understood the importance of establishing a public name for her various business ventures and never hesitated to use any and all means at her disposal to create that publicity. She knew that she was in direct competition with other businessmen and businesswomen. No one, least of all Kirkpatrick, seemed ready to count her out because she was a woman.[1]

Kirkpatrick's success, or that of a similar female entrepreneur, might have inspired the anonymous author of "The Impoverished South: The Way Out of It," which appeared in a local paper six months after her ad campaign. This economist advised that women should "exchange the *ennui* of listless and objectless lives, for the triumph and enjoyment of the noblest effort possible in life, that of earning by daily toil, the bread that nourishes the body." The author advocated altering traditional gender roles to make way for modernization and the advancement of the South. The link between women business operators and editorial support was not a coincidence. In the years immediately following the Civil War, urban economic growth became the focal point of Waco citizens' hopes and fears. Seeing opportunity alongside destruction, Waco residents looked to establish their city as a prominent Texas commercial center. Their overriding concern was that the town remain an important cattle stop on the way to the more metropolitan locales of Dallas, Fort Worth, Austin, and San Antonio. The process of urbanization meant something unique to each individual in Waco, though particular class, race, ethnic, and gender identities created differences in how they placed themselves within that process. A particular group of women entrepreneurs maintained a public economic presence in the city throughout the Reconstruction period, performing vital functions in the growing town of Waco: they provided capital, fostered competition, employed citizens, and created businesses. In addition, the men and women of Waco encouraged women's capitalist ventures not only by praising them in the press but also by patronizing those businesses.[2]

Learning more about central Texas women adds to an understanding of how women functioned as gendered participants in the market. But perhaps more important, Waco's story necessitates a rethinking of the narrative of urbanization and boosterism in Texas and the South offered by the works of Edward Ayers, Blaine Brownell, and David Goldfield, who placed women as witnesses to but not direct participants in the market. In the 1870s, boosters emerged as a part of the development of an urban consciousness that spread across the South. They promoted their cities in the hopes of attracting both business activity and entrepreneurs. Using whatever methods were necessary to ensure economic vitality, in Waco they turned to women for increased economic participation. The rise of this central Texas community therefore illustrates that postwar southern women not only witnessed but also facilitated and aided the growth of cities through their own labor and capitalistic endeavors.[3]

The story of these Waco female capitalists should be placed within a growing literature on the nature of women's work in the nineteenth-century United States. Following a flurry of historical interest heading into the 1990s, the study of women's economic activities has visibly slowed in recent years, leading to a noticeable gap in the literature. As historian Wilma Dunaway asserts in *Women, Work, and Family in the Antebellum Mountain South*, "It is in the analysis of women's work that U.S. women's history is probably weakest." Fortunately, however, a few cities have been studied well, and they provide a regional and national context for understanding potential linkages between urban develop-

AD FOR WACO BUSINESSWOMAN NAOMI H. KIRKPATRICK

Waco Daily Examiner, January 1, 1874.

ment and women's business activities. Waco's female boosters and business-women followed a trajectory established by women creditors, investors, and business operators from Petersburg, Virginia, to Dallas and from Atlanta to Boston.[4]

Though the postwar era was known for economic downturns in the South, Waco's economic and legal history provided a starting point for women looking for financial investment opportunities. Waco's women had worked as far back as the frontier period, and a vast majority of McLennan County's married women occupied a place in the market, although their place was often hidden. Women were economically aware, though prior to the Civil War, the community did not openly encourage women's engagement in the public sphere of business. However, during the war, married women, many of whom were alone because their husbands were off at war, joined their single counterparts by participating in the market in a variety of ways. They managed plantations, opened businesses, took on wage work, initiated land trades, and advertised publicly. Throughout the war years, women's activities in the economic sphere reached a degree never witnessed before in McLennan County. Although it would have been quite plausible for these women to retire back into the quasi-private sphere at the conclusion of the war, they instead maintained and indeed increased their market presence.[5]

In the immediate postbellum years, the county offered a dynamic demographic environment favoring urban growth. Although the area suffered the loss of a significant percentage of productive male citizens during the conflict, these casualties were somewhat mitigated by an influx of settlers, mostly from the South. The population of the county doubled from 13,488 in 1870 to 26,934 in 1880, and the rate of white population growth was even higher. Many of these new arrivals chose to live in the growing city center of Waco, and even those who settled on the fringes of the county relied on Waco for commercial goods. Mirroring a process that occurred across the South during this period, the growth in the county's population required an increased business presence and provided the labor necessary to build industry within the city.[6]

In the initial throes of commercialization, modernization, and industrialization and faced with serious competition from Galveston and Dallas, the citizens of Waco followed a broad set of strategies to make their city a commercial center. Exploiting ties gained through decades of involvement in the cotton trade and capitalizing on their central location in the state, city leaders made a concerted effort to improve the county's infrastructure. In 1870, Waco completed a suspension bridge across the Brazos River, and one year later, the Tap Railroad reached the county, providing a connection to Houston and Dallas.

Here as elsewhere, the railroad had substantial economic impact. According to one economic historian, "Railroads assumed the status of demigods when it came to urban economic prosperity." Waco's railroad development paid visible dividends in 1873, when the city boasted an economic surplus despite the national depression. While other counties suffered, McLennan County continued to move toward its goal of being an economic superpower in Texas.[7]

This overriding push for economic prosperity in turn influenced understandings of proper gender roles. Whereas women in other postwar southern communities might have been encouraged to boost men's damaged masculinity by emphasizing fragility and ineptness in public activities, this narrative did not play out in central Texas. In contrast, driven by their own economic imperatives, city leaders, local boosters, and average citizens encouraged women to participate in the economy. These men realized that Waco was, for all intents and purposes, an urbanization underdog and that competing with Galveston and Dallas required all available resources, including female investors and businesspeople. According to this logic, if women did not cater to the needs of Waco's citizens, other cities would benefit.[8]

Local newspapers and journalists lauded the efforts of female entrepreneurs, serving as cheerleaders for urban development. By praising women in the papers, local editors both reflected county sentiment and set the tone for how businesswomen were to be treated. An editor might refuse to run an ad for an unproven establishment while highlighting other companies that he deemed worthwhile. After he determined that a Mrs. Morrill was operating a viable hotel, the editor of the *Waco Daily Examiner* seized every opportunity to draw attention to her venture. In successive papers, he commended Morrill's "admirable management" of her "legitimate business." In his words, Morrill's establishment could not be surpassed by any in the state and was crowded nightly with guests from all over the country. This same editor also lavished praise on Mrs. E. Signer, who owned a hairwork business and was an excellent saleswoman who deserved "appreciation." Local citizens also used the press as a mouthpiece for ideas and opinions. The Waco Masonic Lodge, for example, acknowledged women's importance in a front-page newspaper address: "We recognize the power of your influence on the success of any enterprise."[9]

Waco's desire for women participants in the market, however, did not obviate the state's legal restrictions on female economic activity, which meant that women's marital status was important. As a *feme sole*, a single woman could conduct business matters in whatever way she pleased. No gender-specific restrictions limited her activities. Wealthy widows fell into this category and could exercise considerable economic clout in the city. More restricted in their movements, married women operated under specific guidelines for investing or business ownership. Legally, a married woman could use only her separate property for her commercial activities. She could contract without her husband only with respect to this separate property. Any usage of community holdings of the marriage required the consent of her husband and the association with his name. In addition, the status of *feme covert* shielded married women from any legal responsibility stemming from contracts. Some businesspeople might have viewed this implicit protection from lawsuit as a disadvantage, but the record does not indicate that many entrepreneurs shied away from dealing with married women.[10]

To turn Waco from a backwater into a model of modernity, local leaders required capital. This need prompted women to enter the economy as creditors and investors. These women had acquired their caches of capital through a variety of means. One of the most common avenues to wealth was receiving substantial land or property holdings following the death of a husband or relative. Although many women tried to maintain their wealth by avoiding business dealings and hoping, perhaps, for interest to accrue on their properties, others funneled their monetary advantages into various purchasing and investment strategies. Mary A. Blocker, the widow of Richard A. Blocker, continually bought and sold lands and town lots throughout the county during the 1870s. Her sales take up numerous pages in the deed books from the period. In a single transaction, she sold individual lots in Waco to Susan Winn, Cora Raines, Kittie Sinclair, Evaline Crain, Lucy Soloman, and Samira Holder, an African American woman. Although it is difficult to establish an exact pattern, it appears that Blocker preferred to engage in business dealings with other women. By 1875, Blocker was listed in the tax rolls as a property owner claiming more than seven thousand dollars in landholdings.[11]

Some female residents of the area specialized in what we now call flipping properties. They purchased or inherited a piece of land or property and then made minimal improvements to their acquisition, increasing the value and paving the way for a quick and profitable resale. This process was made possible, in part, by the skyrocketing demand for commercial space in Waco proper, which coincided with growth in the percentage of land owned by women. For both 1875 and 1880, women owned 11.5 percent of the county's total acreage, a substantial increase from the 1.8 percent ownership in 1852. This increase was undoubtedly linked, at least in part, to Civil War casualties. The value of property held by women also grew dramatically in the postwar years. In the antebellum period, women-owned property constituted around 1.6 percent of the county's total property value, but by 1880, that figure had climbed to 9.9 percent. In

1880, McLennan County's female residents owned property with an estimated value of $613,504. Julia Ann Clingman, for example, inherited an Austin Street lot valued at $1,000 in 1870. She improved the lot and then sold it for $2,500 to the firm Slyons and Cohn, which wanted space for its business. This process of amassing wealth via property transactions also worked in the county's rural areas, as Hallie Jenkins discovered when she purchased a plot of land valued at $350, built a cottage on it, and sold it for $3,000. The hundreds of settlers descending on central Texas required places to live, and they were willing to pay top dollar for ready-made farms, since the county's soil was some of the state's best.[12]

During this period, a commercial firm such as Slyons and Cohn might well buy a town lot from a woman and then operate using a female investor's deposits of capital. Funneling financial gains from profitable business deals and perhaps inherited wealth, women also became creditors and investors. Of course, the terms of these arrangements varied depending on the parties' needs. In one scenario, a woman might lend hard cash to a businessperson in the hopes of making money off the interest. Ellen S. Hardin, for example, required 20 percent interest on the six hundred dollars in gold that she lent John Scrap Jr. in 1874. These transactions, by their nature, necessitated that the lender undertake a degree of risk. In the highly mobile society that was Texas in the 1870s, a borrower could easily disappear with the money.[13]

Women may have viewed investing operating capital as less risky and more rewarding than providing personal loans, especially if the company appeared to be stable and growing. Throughout the 1870s, J. M. Killough, a Waco businessman, took out numerous bank notes for payments to women. In 1872, he promised to pay Mrs. S. E. Bedwell twenty-two hundred dollars in gold plus 11 percent interest. For nine months straight in 1873, Killough took out promissory notes for the one hundred dollars in interest he owed Mrs. M. L. Johnson on a six-thousand-dollar note. The following year, Killough continued to struggle to pay off the balance, taking out more promissory notes. Mrs. D. C. Luckey, Mrs. H. A. Johnson, and Ellen Renfroe also acted as creditors to Killough. He borrowed these monies to support and expand his business, Killough and Morgan, and the ultimate success of this enterprise showed that female lenders played a vital role in the city's growth. It is not clear whether Killough ever repaid all of his debts to these women, but Bedwell, Johnson, and other women clearly answered the call of the Waco booster who stated, "Are you a capitalist? We want you; your money will net you a good per cent any way you wish to invest it." This booster and the city's business community did not emphasize a gender-specific brand of capitalism.[14]

Not content with simply lending their money to support other people's economic ambitions, many women entered the economic sphere as business owners in the burgeoning commercial districts of Waco. Although most female entrepreneurs came from the wealthier social strata, women with minimal resources also operated businesses, especially for-profit schools. Numerous historians, including Jane Turner Censer in her study of North Carolina and Virginia, have described how teaching became a female-dominated profession by the late nineteenth century. Women often viewed teaching as an extension of their supposedly natural ability to educate and care for the young, and many women in Reconstruction-era Waco created and ran private centers of education. In fact, Waco possessed such a large number of schools during the 1870s that it earned a reputation as the "Athens of Texas." Opening a school required some initial investment in property and materials but was less costly than other business opportunities. A school could be as small or large as the operator wished. In the case of Waco, securing a body of students was made all the easier by the growing population.[15]

Indeed, owning and operating schools provided women with control over their work and placed their fate securely in their own hands. Exploring the business experiences of Francis "Fannie" Leland provides insight into the world of women who operated schools. The Leland Seminary was established in 1868 to cater to "young ladies and children." Student memoirs describe Leland as a highly experienced teacher who wore a thimble on her finger, using it to thump her pupils if they misbehaved. By 1878, the Leland Seminary, located on Second Street, taught one hundred pupils and employed five teachers, two of them women. Two years later, the seminary's faculty grew to eight teachers, six of them female. Throughout the 1870s, Leland advertised her school in the local newspapers in the hopes of attracting more students. She initially announced that her academy would provide an education in "Drawing, Penmanship, Composition, Elocution, and Vocal Music," all included in the two-dollar monthly tuition. One year later, however, she raised the monthly tuition to four dollars and charged extra for language and music instruction. Her school continued to operate throughout the 1870s, and by 1880, the forty-nine-year-old Leland could consider herself a successful businesswoman.[16]

Male-owned and operated schools were not as common, and Leland's primary competition came from another female school proprietor, Sue Lambdin. A veritable advertising war took place throughout the 1870s as the two women struggled to present the largest newspaper ad touting their respective schools' advantages. The stakes were extremely high since the schools supported both Leland and Lambdin: Leland was a widow from out of state, and Lambdin never married. The Lambdin Seminary was located on Austin Avenue and employed a handful of teachers to cater to its upper-class student clientele. The tuition ranged between three and five dollars a month, plus sixteen dollars for board and washing. Lambdin required half of the payment in coin in advance and the other half by the middle of the session. Favored as one of the best schools in the state, Lambdin educated the children of prominent resident General James Edward Harrison, who could apparently afford the hefty tuition.[17]

Women also operated other smaller-scale and less well publicized schools. M. M. Dunnovant opened a school in 1874. The Live Oak Seminary, owned by Lucy B. Gurley, began operation in 1868. Determined to establish a foothold in the industry, Gurley proclaimed in her ads that she expected nothing less than a "liberal share of patronage." Moreover, an undetermined number of women conducted private tutoring that involved teaching pupils in their homes on a daily or weekly basis. While "Professor" F. E. Simeon sold pianos, his wife gave piano lessons. "Madame Simeon" expressed her willingness to travel throughout the county and cited her experiences living in Paris, London, and Hanover to prove her artistic credentials. All of these women owned and operated businesses based on the idea that a superior education could be had for the right price.[18]

The continued success of the Leland and Lambdin Seminaries speaks to the support citizens of the county gave to female-owned schools. Parents sought out the best institutions for their children, and newspaper editors guided this process by highlighting the efforts of particular operators. Even smaller schools could draw the attention of an editor and earn a printed compliment: of Mrs. Edgar's, the *Waco Examiner and Patron* offered, "We bespeak for her the patronage she so richly merits." Inspired by the county's active educational environment, the editor of the *Waco Daily Examiner* published a long statement, "A Noble Example," in which he lauded a pair of female teachers. He concluded, "They are self-sustaining, and like the earnest, noble women they are, they add to, instead of subtract from, the sum of the world's happiness and advantage."[19] While Waco's journalists waxed poetic about female-owned institutions of learning, the more subtle support offered by the city's business directories should not be overlooked. These books or pamphlets provided contact information and advertisements for an area's residents and businesspeople—they constituted a "businessman's guide to other businessmen." Directories generally only appeared in those cities where population growth rendered word-of-mouth advertising less effective. Economic historians consequently have posited that the "appearance of directories seemed to relate directly to urban maturation." All of the late 1870s Waco directories provided detailed descriptions of schools operated by women and thus acknowledged their commercial legitimacy. In addition, the faculty lists for each institution consistently showed the overwhelming presence of women in the teaching profession.[20]

Female entrepreneurs also dominated the market in millinery (hat making) and mantua making (dressmaking). The success of women in these fields has been documented by historians such as Suzanne Lebsock in her study of antebellum Petersburg, Virginia. This occupation did not concern women exclusively but it did provide specialized subfields for them. Seamstresses provided general sewing services for both male and female customers. The start-up costs could be fairly small, depending on the size of the operation, and the range of possibilities meant that even impoverished women could create businesses focusing on clothing production. Women in these businesses had traditionally been among the first to embrace the benefits of publicity, so it is not surprising that the women clothiers of Waco began advertising almost immediately following the war. These initial announcements varied a great deal and could be rather plain or quite elaborate. Ads for Mrs. M. A. Harris, milliner, and Mrs. Chevalier, dressmaker, simply stated their addresses and a brief description of the products they offered. A public proclamation of this nature might prove particularly important if a woman was trying to relocate a business established elsewhere to the city of Waco, as Mrs. J. A. Lane did when she moved to the area from New York City.[21]

The most astute businesswomen made sure that members of the public were kept up to date when businesses changed locations, a frequent occurrence as the county's land market fluctuated and women found it more profitable to set up in the latest commercial districts. In addition to the obvious task of letting a patron know a store's location, ads for milliners and dressmakers used a wide variety of advertising strategies to capture maximum public interest. They touted the proprietors' intentions to go east or overseas to learn the modern styles or to import the most fashionable materials. Mrs. Ludecus, for example, placed an 1874 ad announcing that she was leaving immediately for New York to "lay in her stock of spring goods [and] to bring on a nice stock of millinery." Waco women who shopped at Ludecus's store presumably could dress just as well as big-city fashion plates, an important lure for central Texas women eager to show off their urban sensitivities. Also common were such strategies as appealing to patrons with announcements of close-out sales and low prices.[22]

Assessing the number of women who supported themselves with dressmaking or millinery establishments can be tricky. The directories and censuses from the period seem to offer only conservative estimates, at least compared to evidence provided by advertising. For example, an 1881–82 directory shows twenty-seven women engaged in this occupation. The 1880 Census lists twenty-one women in clothing production, including Fannie Trice, an African American woman who escaped the sharecropping system that dominated the area surrounding the city. Newspapers, however, ran ads for many more establishments, suggesting that the number of female textile merchants was probably more widespread than either the directory or census schedules recorded. Moreover, successful entrepreneurs hired additional laborers, usually female seamstresses, but they were not always identified in the public record. Mrs. E. C. Trewitt, for example, placed a newspaper ad seeking "two ladies of experience to work at dress making; also two young ladies to work as apprentices." No record survives of whether Trewitt found the help she sought.[23]

The perils of expansion represented only one possible stumbling block on the path to success, for female businesses, like all businesses, sometimes failed. When Waco milliners or dressmakers could no longer operate, other women generally bought out the stock to use in an established store or to provide start-up materials for a new shop. Area newspapers announced the terms of these buyouts, often directing attention to the purchaser's commercial potential. When Sallie Truitt sold her stock to Mrs. L. Rawland, the news appeared on page 3 of the *Waco Daily Examiner*. Aside from explaining the terms of the sale, the editor also took the opportunity to praise Rawland's expertise at "pressing and bleaching hats." This transfer of power from one female entrepreneur to the next is relatively unsurprising in light of the fact that the women of Waco possessed an unchallenged monopoly of the millinery and dressmaking trades throughout the 1870s. These businesses satisfied a need in the county that male entrepreneurs were unable or unwilling to meet. Therefore, women took that opportunity to make a living and garnered praise from businesspeople who recognized the inherent necessity of such enterprises in a "modern" town.[24]

Throughout the 1870s, Waco was modernizing and growing, attracting new arrivals to central Texas from all over the United States. Some of these newcomers immediately purchased land and established themselves as farmers. Others did not intend to buy property immediately or even in the long term and needed places to stay while in the city. Accordingly, hotels and boardinghouses sprang up in Waco, as in other frontier areas. These establishments ranged from large-scale buildings to rooms in small shacks. Some proprietors offered clients such amenities as laundry service, while others required boarders to provide their own blankets, pillows, and linens. Some establishments serviced only "day boarders," supplying meals without lodging. Drawn by the work's kinship with housekeeping or simply the potential for high profits, Waco women across all classes provided a home away from home for transplanted residents—for a price.[25]

This pursuit of profit led to the creation of domestic arrangements that often pushed at the boundaries of traditional gender roles. One Waco boardinghouse was operated by Mary Ward, a thirty-eight-year-old woman from Alabama. According to the 1870 Census, sixteen people were staying with Ward, among them a real estate agent, carpenters, a butcher, three physicians, a farm laborer, a stock raiser, a barkeeper, a cook, and a domestic servant (who may well have been an employee). All but four of the boarders were young men, but because she was operating a business, it was socially acceptable for the unmarried Ward to share a house with large numbers of unmarried men. Economic need led to flexibility in gender ideals and proscriptions. Historian Joanne Meyerowitz has found the same phenomenon in Chicago, where "wives or widows who cared for boarders brought in earnings without leaving the often-preferred domestic sphere." And as Ward's example illustrates, successful living establishments allowed proprietors to hire additional women as chambermaids and cooks, further bolstering the local economy.[26]

Despite the influx of fresh arrivals to the city, competition for patrons was intense, and women fought for market position. In some cases, informal arrangements might be made in which the wife of a business owner provided room and board for her husband's employees. In other instances, however, financial success in an accommodation-based industry meant luring in outside customers. Directories served as one way to establish connections with potential lodgers, and female-operated hotels appeared regularly in the listings from the Civil War onward. In 1876, Laura Morrill ran the City Hotel in East Waco, Mrs. Davis operated the Taylor House, and Naomi Kirkpatrick ran an establishment that bore her name, Kirkpatrick House. All of these women hoped to attract a steady stream of customers, including the patronage of Waco employers who might choose to board their employees. Rarely, however, were successful hotels publicized solely by directory listings.[27]

Waco's female hotel operators waged aggressive advertising wars in the local press. Aside from providing the most basic location information, print notices touted establishments' particular qualities. Kirkpatrick, for example, offered both "fresh groceries" and a "good wagon yard." Mrs. A. Hart, whose hotel was located right next to the suspension bridge, asked the traveling public, especially railroad patrons, to visit her hotel. She stood to gain a great deal of business as her rates were comparable to other establishments at $1.50 per day, $4.50 per week, and $25 per month. To maintain a competitive edge, advertisers constantly changed the size of their ads or altered the terms of the boarding arrangements in an effort to keep ahead of the competition. They also employed rhetorical flourishes to make their establishments seem more like palaces than the flimsy buildings they often were in reality. The "large, airy ROOMS

FURNISHED," promised by Laura Morrill at the Calusa House were guaranteed to catch the attention of a cramped traveler. If all else failed or if bravado demanded it, hotel owners might proclaim the superiority of their hotels to all other establishments in Texas. Mrs. Berry thus assured readers that her Waco House offered "fare equal to any Hotel in the interior of Texas." Female boardinghouse and hotel operators could also pick up extra business by perusing the papers for want ads placed by new arrivals trying to find places to stay. These men and women generally described their particular situations and requested accommodations. For example, an 1874 ad in which a man explained that he was looking to board with a private family undoubtedly generated several offers. In fact, only a few days earlier, Mrs. Houston had advertised that she was willing to furnish board and lodging in her home at reasonable rates.[28]

In any event, the newspaper competition that developed in Waco reflected the city's rising importance as a Texas center of trade. Hotels from across the state advertised in Waco newspapers, hoping to entice travelers from afar. Martha McWhirter, the founder of the Belton Woman's Commonwealth, posted ads touting the luxury of her hotel. As the leader of a group of devoutly Christian women who had left their husbands and formed a communal society, McWhirter was a controversial figure who faced intense criticism from Belton residents. However, she counteracted these hostilities by advocating female economic independence. And as a result of her own financial successes, McWhirter became a prominent Belton booster, earning a place on the city's board of trade and recognition as a railroad promoter. The community's displeasure over her controversial religious views waned in the face of her overt contributions to the city's prosperity. Waco was not the only city in Texas experiencing the growing pains of urbanization, and McWhirter's experiences in Belton indicate that female entrepreneurs might have benefited from significant local support in other communities as well.[29]

Hotels of course could run into financial difficulties as a result of such factors as too much competition or poor money management, and these problems often led the establishments to change hands. But, as local journalists pointed out, new ownership was not always bad. When Mrs. Heatherly purchased the McClelland House from Mrs. Skinner, the editor of the *Waco Daily Advance* opined that the McClelland House would continue to prosper because Heatherly possessed "a wide reputation as a hostess." He predicted that she would enjoy a "prosperous career." The transfer of a business might also come when a proprietor died, leaving her relatives in a quandary. After Amanda Smith's death in 1873, the hotel that she had struggled to keep afloat was leased by a man, with the rent going to Smith's children. The lease agreement required that he keep the hotel in a good state of affairs.[30]

Lodging, education, and clothing production were the most common businesses led by Waco's female entrepreneurs, but they also could pursue a wide variety of other career possibilities. According to the 1880 Census, women worked as bankers, horticulturalists, confectioners, authors, and doctors. Newspapers from the period show ads for female-owned and operated laundry businesses, jewelry stores, and portrait galleries. Irene Hamil operated a dairy, producing butter that was described as safe for consumers and free of "potentially deadly contaminants" because she was "a particular dairyman." Waco also was home to female-operated restaurants, coffee stands, and sandwich carts. The editor of the *Waco Daily Examiner*, J. W. Downs, publicly praised "noted colored cook" Martha Downs for "an elegant supper." Martha lived in the alley between South First and Second and Bridge and Franklin Streets and earned quite a reputation in the town for her culinary skills.[31]

During the 1870s and 1880s, the South was engaged in an economic war, and in describing that conflict, southerners employed rhetoric that embraced the efforts of both men and women. An 1878 Waco *Examiner and Patron* article, "What Can Women Do?," argued that the key to economic success was having women understand and enjoy the benefits of financial independence. According to this social critique, every woman who had reached her "middle life" should know at least one thing that she could do well. If a woman had not discovered her particular talent, the author admonished, she had "probably led a useless life, and will hardly succeed in any effort she may make for self-support." A woman of cultivated abilities, by contrast, "can always turn her talent to account if thrown upon her own resources." One such woman supported her entire family through the "liberal consideration" earned by her cooking. Showing little patience for women who might balk at physical labor, the critic mused, "'Unpleasant work' is it? It strikes one that starving is unpleasant work, too." In the end, women must "bravely" advertise their talent, and work would follow.[32]

Coming to terms with the successes and failures of Waco's entrepreneurial women provides scholars with an opportunity to examine the connections between boosterism and women's work, two aspects of southern history heretofore approached separately. Women engaged in financial dealings that shaped the landscape of the developing New South. In an era marked by economic instability, the labor and monetary capital held by women could determine a city's future. Women capitalists in Reconstruction-era Waco served as creditors and investors, encouraged economic competition, stimulated employment, and created businesses. The citizens of Waco responded by praising female-owned businesses in the press and patronizing these establishments. However, it would be a mistake to assume that female entrepreneurs of this period could simply act like men. As *femes coverts*, these women faced unique legal challenges and benefited greatly from the loosening of traditional gender restrictions in response to market forces. As one contemporary observer noted, Waco women did "anything and everything we could to make a living." Although Waco never became the center of Texas commerce that boosters imagined, the city's struggle for economic relevance enabled many Waco women to succeed in business, expanding the concept of "anything and everything" in historically important ways. Nineteenth-century cities served as "repositories of change" for men and women alike.[33]

NOTES

1. *Waco Examiner*, September 28, 1873, 1; W. A. Kirkpatrick to Mrs. N. H. Kirkpatrick, January 28, April 9, 1879, Kirkpatrick Papers, Texas Collection, Baylor University, Waco.

2. *Waco Daily Examiner*, January 4, 1874, 2 (quotation). A version of this argument appeared in Robin Tippett, "The Economic Activities of Women in McLennan County, 1850–1880" (master's thesis, Texas Christian University, 2006).

3. Edward L. Ayers, *The Promise of the New South: Life after Reconstruction* (New York: Oxford University Press, 1992), 20, 28, 64–65; Blaine Brownell and David Goldfield, "Southern Urban History," in *The City in Southern History: The Growth of Urban Civilization in the South*, ed. Blaine Brownell and David Goldfield (London: National University Publications, 1977), 5, 8–10; David Goldfield, "Pursuing the American Urban Dream: Cities in the Old South," in *City in Southern History*, ed. Brownell and Goldfield, 52–91; Lorin Thompson, "Urbanization, Occupational Shift, and Economic Progress," in *The Urban South*, ed. Rupert B. Vance and Nicholas Demerath (Chapel Hill: University of North Carolina Press, 1954), 46; Don Doyle, *New Men, New Cities, New South: Atlanta, Nashville, Charleston, Mobile, 1860–1910* (Chapel Hill: University of North Carolina Press, 1990); Lawrence H. Larsen, *The Urban South: A History* (Louisville: University Press of Kentucky, 1990); Georgina Hickey, *Hope and Danger in the New South City: Working-Class Women and Urban Development in Atlanta, 1890–1940* (Athens: University of Georgia Press, 2003), 28.

4. Wilma A. Dunaway, *Women, Work, and Family in the Antebellum Mountain South* (Cambridge: Cambridge University Press, 2008), 8 (quotation). In their oft-cited edited collection, Susanna Delfino and Michele Gillespie also call for additional scholarship on working women, stating, "Although the past two decades have witnessed an explosion of scholarship on southern women in the nineteenth century, much of this work has focused on the world of the plantation" (*Neither Lady nor Slave: Working Women of the Old South* [Chapel Hill: University of North Carolina Press, 2002], 1). Suzanne Lebsock, *The Free Women of Petersburg: Status and Culture in a Southern Town, 1784–1860* (New York: Norton, 1984); Elizabeth York Enstam, *Women and the Creation of Urban Life: Dallas, Texas, 1843–1920* (College Station: Texas A&M University Press, 1998); Sarah Deutsch, *Women and the City: Gender, Space, and Power in Boston, 1870–1940* (New York: Oxford University Press, 2000); Edith Sparks, *Capital Intentions: Female Proprietors in San Francisco, 1850–1920* (Chapel Hill: University of North Carolina Press, 2006); Hickey, *Hope and Danger*; Joanne Meyerowitz, *Women Adrift: Independent Wage Earners in Chicago, 1880–1930* (Chicago: University of Chicago Press, 1988).

5. For information on women's changing roles during the Civil War period, see Laura Edwards, *Scarlett Doesn't Live Here Anymore: Southern Women in the Civil War Era* (Chicago: University of

Illinois Press, 2000); LeeAnn Whites, *The Civil War as a Crisis in Gender: Augusta, Georgia, 1860–1890* (Athens: University of Georgia Press, 1995); Boswell, in this volume.

6. In 1870, the total McLennan County population was 51 percent male (6,880) and 49 percent female (6,620). In 1880, the total McLennan County population was 52 percent male (14,001) and 48 percent female (12,933). See U.S. Bureau of the Census, *A Compendium of the Ninth Census (June 1, 1870): Compiled from the Original Returns of the Ninth Census* (Washington, D.C.: U.S. Government Printing Office, 1872), 587; U.S. Bureau of the Census, *A Compendium of the Tenth Census (June 1, 1880): Compiled from the Original Returns of the Tenth Census Parts I and II* (Washington, D.C.: U.S. Government Printing Office, 1883), 373, 600.

7. Roger Norman Conger, *Highlights of Waco History* (Waco: Hill, 1945), 48–50; Goldfield, "Pursuing the American Urban Dream," 53 (quotation); Sandra Denise Harvey, "Going Up Bell's Hill: A Social History of a Diverse, Waco, Texas, Community in the Industrial New South, 1885–1955" (master's thesis, Baylor University, 1995), 9.

8. John Sleeper and J. C. Hutchins, comps., *Waco and McLennan County: Containing a City Directory of Waco . . .* (Waco: Golledge, 1876), 19–20, 31.

9. *Waco Daily Advance*, February 18, March 13, 1874; Goldfield, "Pursuing the American Urban Dream," 60–61; *Waco Daily Examiner*, March 8, 1874 (first and second quotations), December 4, 1875 (third quotation), January 4, 1874 (fourth quotation); Lebsock, *Free Women of Petersburg*, 167; Alice Kessler-Harris, *Out to Work: A History of Wage-Earning Women in the United States* (New York: Oxford University Press, 2003), 124–25.

10. Angela Boswell, "Married Women's Property Acts and the Challenge to Patriarchal Order: Colorado County, Texas," in *Negotiating the Boundaries of Southern Womanhood: Dealing with the Powers That Be*, ed. Janet Coryell, Thomas Appleton Jr., Anastasia Sims, and Sandra Gioia Treadway (Columbia: University of Missouri Press, 2000), 92–93; Angela Boswell, *Her Act and Deed: Women's Lives in a Rural Southern County, 1837–1873* (College Station: Texas A&M University Press, 2001), 23; Mark M. Carroll, *Homesteads Ungovernable: Families, Sex, Race, and the Law in Frontier Texas, 1823–1860* (Austin: University of Texas Press, 2001), 28, 80, 88, 100, 129; Kathleen Elizabeth Lazarou, *Concealed under Petticoats: Married Women's Property and the Law of Texas, 1840–1913* (New York: Garland, 1986), 9–11, 45–47, 54–56, 72–73; Enstam, *Women*, 39; Jean A. Stuntz, *Hers, His, and Theirs: Community Property in Spain and Early Texas* (Lubbock: Texas Tech University Press, 2005). See also Stuntz, in this volume.

11. Sonya Salamon, *Prairie Patrimony: Family, Farming, and Community in the Midwest* (Chapel Hill: University of North Carolina Press, 1992), 41; Probate Records, vol. B, April Term 1855, 112, County Clerk's Office, McLennan County Courthouse, Waco (hereafter cco); Deed Records, vol. N, February 14, 22, March 8, 1870, 6, 28, 60–61, 88, cco. The information from the tax rolls is drawn from a database compiled of all female tax claims from 1851–1880. The gender was determined by looking at the name. If the name was questionable then the data was not included in the database. The formal citation for the tax rolls is Records of the Comptroller of Public Accounts, Ad Valorem Tax Division, McLennan County Real and Personal Property Tax Rolls, 1851–1880, Archives Division, Texas State Library, Austin (Microfilm).

12. Lebsock, *Free Women of Petersburg*, 78, 86; Deed Records, vol. N, February 14, 22, March 8, 1870, 6, 28, 60–61, 88, cco; District Court Paper, 1876, Clingman-Stallings Family Collection, Texas Collection, Baylor University, Waco; Lavonia Jenkins Barnes, *Early Homes of Waco and the People Who Lived in Them* (Waco: Texian, 1970), 71; Salamon, *Prairie Patrimony*, 41; Records of the Comptroller of Public Accounts. The census numbers for 1860, 1870, and 1880 were drawn from a database compiled by the author encompassing the information of all of the women fifteen years

and older who were listed in the 1860, 1870, and 1880 census returns for McLennan County. This database provides detailed statistics regarding the numbers of women employed. The cutoff age of fifteen was chosen based on the fact that the 1870 census included people's occupations only if they were over that age.

13. Lebsock, *Free Women of Petersburg*, 128; Deed of Trust Records, vol. L, 1874, CCO.

14. Bank Note, April 3, 1879, Alexander Beville Papers, Texas Collection, Baylor University; Bank Drafts, Killough Papers, Texas Collection, Baylor University; Sleeper and Hutchins, *Waco and McLennan County*, 31 (quotation).

15. Conger, *Highlights of Waco History*, 55 (quotation); Jane Turner Censer, *The Reconstruction of White Southern Womanhood, 1865–1895* (Baton Rouge: Louisiana State University Press, 2003), 7; Sparks, *Capital Intentions*, 65. See also Sharpless, in this volume.

16. Dayton Kelley, ed., *The Handbook of Waco and McLennan County, Texas* (Waco: Texian, 1972), 161; C. D. Morrison, comp., *C. D. Morrison and Co.'s General Directory of the City of Waco for 1878–1879* (Waco: Morrison, 1877), 25; J. Curtis Waldo, comp., *Waldo's City Directory, 1881–1882* (Waco: Southern, 1992), 39; *Waco Examiner and Patron*, December 31, 1875 (quotation); *Waco Register*, December 16, 1876; Census Database 1880; Angel Kwolek-Folland, *Incorporating Women: A History of Women and Business in the United States* (New York: Palgrave, 1998), 67; Ayers, *Promise of the New South*, 212.

17. *Waco Daily Examiner*, January 1, 1874, August 10, 1876; *Waco Examiner and Patron*, July 28, 1876; Henrietta Hardin Carter Harrison, *Transcribed Diary of Henrietta Hardin Carter Harrison: Tehuacana Retreat Plantation near Waco, Texas, 1869–1877*, comp. Emma Harrison Carter Tate (Waco: privately published, 1973), 144. Eliza Earle Harrison was around seven years of age when she attended Lambdin's school.

18. *Waco Daily Advance*, January 1, 6, 1874; *Waco Semi-Weekly Register*, February 12, 1868 (quotation); Barnes, *Early Homes*, 89. None of the advertisements listed specific ages for pupils. However, some highlighted kindergarten or primary programs targeted at young children. Other schools requested "more advanced" students to enroll in preparatory settings. Educational institutions could cater to a single sex, although coeducational facilities had existed in Waco since the late 1850s. See Sharpless, in this volume.

19. *Waco Examiner and Patron*, August 27, 1875 (first quotation); *Waco Daily Examiner*, January 7, 1876 (second quotation).

20. Goldfield, "Pursuing the American Urban Dream," 63 (first and second quotations).

21. *Waco Daily Examiner*, October 11, 1876; Lebsock, *Free Women of Petersburg*, xviii, 180; Timothy Lockley, "Spheres of Influence: Working White and Black Women in Antebellum Savannah," in *Neither Lady nor Slave*, ed. Delfino and Gillespie, 120; Wendy Gamber, *The Female Economy: The Millinery and Dressmaking Trades, 1860–1930* (Urbana: University of Illinois Press, 1997).

22. *Waco Daily Examiner*, July 20, 1875, October 11, 1876; *Waco Daily Advance*, February 3, 1874 (quotation); Barbara Howe, "Patient Laborers: Women at Work in the Formal Economy of West(ern) Virginia," in *Neither Lady nor Slave*, ed. Delfino and Gillespie, 124–30.

23. Waldo, *Waldo's City Directory*, 6–145; Morrison, *C. D. Morrison and Co.'s General Directory*, 25–151; *Waco Advance*, June 8, 1872 (quotation).

24. *Waco Daily Examiner*, December 4, 1875 (quotation).

25. Evelyn Carrington, ed., *Women in Early Texas* (Austin: Texas State Historical Association, 1994), 189; Enstam, *Women*, 41–42; Meyerowitz, *Women Adrift*, 32, 70, 74; Kwolek-Folland, *Incorporating Women*, 27–28; Wendy Gamber, *The Boardinghouse in Nineteenth-Century America* (Baltimore: Johns Hopkins University Press, 2007); Sparks, *Capital Intentions*, 6.

26. Census Database 1870; Waldo, *Waldo's City Directory*, 6–145; Morrison, *C. D. Morrison and Co.'s General Directory*, 25–151; Meyerowitz, *Women Adrift*, 32, 70 (quotation), 74. See also Elizabeth Hayes Turner, *Women, Culture, and Community: Religion and Reform in Galveston, 1880–1920* (New York: Oxford University Press, 1997), 64–65.

27. Sleeper and Hutchins, *Waco and McLennan County*, 153; Waldo, *Waldo's City Directory*, 65, 145.

28. *Waco Daily Reporter*, December 8, 1875 (first quotation); *Waco Semi-Weekly Register*, January 4, 1868 (third quotation); *Waco Examiner and Patron*, August 27, 1875; *Waco Daily Advance*, February 18, March 13, 1874; *Waco Daily Examiner*, February 6, 1874 (second quotation).

29. Carrington, *Women in Early Texas*, 189; Mary Ann Lamanna and Jayme A. Sokolow, "Mc-whirter, Martha White," *Handbook of Texas Online*, http://www.tshaonline.org/handbook/online/articles/fmcax (accessed July 27, 2011); Jayme A. Sokolow and Mary Ann Lamanna, "Women and Utopia: The Woman's Commonwealth of Belton," *Southwestern Historical Quarterly* 87 (April 1984): 371–92.

30. *Waco Daily Advance*, October 19, 1874 (all quotations); Probate Minutes, vol. E, 1873, 304, cco.

31. Census Database 1880; *Waco Daily Advance*, March 14, April 27, July 8, 1874; *Waco Daily Examiner*, May 9, 1876 (first quotation), November 7, 1875 (third quotation), November 2, 1876; Kwolek-Folland, *Incorporating Women*, 61 (second quotation).

32. *Waco Examiner and Patron*, November 8, 1878 (all quotations).

33. Patricia Ward Wallace, *A Spirit So Rare: A History of the Women of Waco* (Austin: Nortex, 1984), 54 (first quotation); Goldfield, "Pursuing the American Urban Dream," 52 (second quotation); Thompson, "Urbanization," 46; Carroll, *Homesteads Ungovernable*.

Part Two

1880–1925

ELIZABETH HAYES TURNER

In the decades following the Civil War, Texas found itself in an advantageous position compared to other states in the Old Confederacy. Few battles had been fought on Texas soil, and the prospects for economic opportunity abounded. Railroads, ranching, cotton farming, shipping and mercantile enterprises, as well as city building consumed the investments and the labor of Texans who were eager to put the disruptions of war behind them. On the horizon stood the prospect of new economic and political agreements within the United States, and Texans sought future growth to parallel that of the northern states. Texas's population increased 36 percent between 1890 and 1900, from 2,235,527 to 3,048,710, and grew another 53 percent between 1900 and 1920, reaching 4,663,228. By 1910, despite its size and its vast spaces, Texas was the most urbanized state in the South, with more people living in towns and cities with populations of more than 2,500 than even Louisiana, with its major metropolis, New Orleans. Five cities claimed important roles in Texas's development—Dallas, Fort Worth, Galveston, Houston, and San Antonio. It is no accident that women's emergence in public life can be attributed in part to the growing sophistication of urban centers in the Lone Star State.

While towns and cities maximized profits and produced megafortunes for the enterprising few, Texas farmers saw a decline in their earnings as overproduction brought the price of cotton, corn, and wheat to new lows in the 1880s and 1890s. The emergence of the Texas Farmers' Alliance brought with it a reform mentality ready to combat what farmers saw as their economic enemies: banks, railroads, and agricultural intermediaries who sold farm equipment and bought cotton and other crops, much to the disadvantage of those who tilled the soil. The agrarian movement affected not only men but also many women, whose participation in the Texas Farmers' Alliance and then the Populist Party can be seen in the life history of Ellen Lawson Dabbs.

Middle-class women were among the first to move from home and domestic life to public activism through their churches and synagogues. Mariana Thompson Folsom, who trained as a Universalist minister, moved to Texas and confounded laypeople who had envisioned only men as ordained ministers. Her public activism supplied an example of leadership for the many public-spirited women who moved from church and community charitable work to even more public roles and organizations. Similarly, Jovita Idar, the product of a Methodist upbringing in Laredo, led her peers in improving the quality of life for Mexican Americans. Many women found voices not only as journalists but also through affiliation with the emerging regional and national women's associations such as the Woman's Christian Temperance Union (WCTU), the General Federation of Women's Clubs (GFWC), the National Association of Colored Women (NACW), and the National American Woman Suffrage Association (NAWSA). The outstanding feature of club work was its grassroots promotion of civic improvement, racial uplift, and gender empowerment. Encouraged by such regional and national organizations, middle- and upper-class Texas women were among the first to capitalize on the momentum toward community projects that often led to political activism.

Members of the WCTU met regularly during the 1880s and 1890s, denouncing the consumption of alcohol in saloons and hotels and leading public demonstrations that sometimes resulted in the closing of taverns and bars. The group also endorsed public kindergartens for children, police matrons for female prisoners, an end to prostitution and corruption in office, and the demise of the convict lease system. These goals catalyzed Texas WCTU members to become politically active, because convincing state legislators to fund kindergartens or pass Prohibition and anti-convict-lease laws required political savvy, organizing, and lobbying. As early as the 1880s, Texas women realized that without the vote, they could exert only limited political pressure on the state legislature; thus, women reformers such as Folsom and Dabbs made suffrage a high priority.

In fact, myriad women moved to become more politicized as Texas entered the Progressive era. While issues such as good roads, business opportunities, and city commission government became the province of men and their desire for Progressive reform, Texas women took on issues related to families, health, education, and equal rights. Dallas women found that the city provided its residents unsafe drinking water; Galveston women discovered that dairymen profited by selling adulterated milk; and Houston women objected to the city's haphazard sanitation. These and other pressing issues regarding health, pure food, and the needs of women and children led them to take their local governments to task or their neighborhood dairymen to court. Texas cities proved the starting points for a Progressive-era revolution among Texas women. From these urban climes came reformers who addressed concerns at the state and national levels. They worked on campaigns for woman suffrage, age-of-consent laws, married women's property rights, and better education, as seen in the election of Annie Webb Blanton to the position of state superintendent of public instruction in 1918. Black Texas women joined the reforming spirit, some by organizing benevolent associations such as orphanages, homes for the aged, and school auxiliaries, others by working for racial equality through local chapters of the National Association for the Advancement of Colored People, founded in 1909. Still others followed the precepts of the NACW and sought racial "uplift." Following in her father's footsteps, Idar became a writer and the publisher of La Crónica. After participating in the Congreso Mexicanisto in 1911, she organized La Liga Feminil Mexicanista to improve schooling for Mexican American children, particularly in South Texas. When the Mexican Revolution spilled over into the Texas borderlands, Idar joined La Cruz Blanca, nursing the wounded and bringing supplies to the war weary of northern Mexico.

These and other revolutionary progressive actions encouraged Texans to think more nationally and internationally, as evidenced by the popular glorification of Texas's historical roots as an independent republic with connections to Mexico and the United States as well as its relative disassociation from the disastrous Confederacy. The Texas State Historical Association, founded in 1897, rediscovered its unique Republic of Texas historical narrative; Adele Briscoe Looscan served as its president between 1915 and 1925. In 1919, Texas became the first state in the South and the ninth in the nation to ratify the Nineteenth Amendment, and a year later, women received the right to vote in national elections. Finally, U.S. senator Morris Sheppard led Texans toward a more national outlook when he cosponsored the Sheppard-Towner Act, which passed in 1921. It provided federal and state funds for maternity and infant health care programs. Led by Professor Mary Gearing, Texas women pressed state politicians to cooperate with the federal law and lobbied hard for the benefits this initiative brought to rural mothers, children, and midwives.

Meaningful change in the form of Progressive activism came to Texas at the turn of the twentieth century. Lone Star State citizens built on postwar economic opportunities and transformed Texas into a twentieth-century powerhouse with the discovery of oil, the success of the cattle industry, and the emergence of national leaders. Cities, which had seen unparalleled growth with few regulations, provided Texas women with a proving ground for their Progressive energies, their social justice activism, and their investment in local, state, and national causes.

Adele Briscoe Looscan

Daughter of the Republic

LAURA LYONS MCLEMORE

In Texas, as elsewhere, some legacies are taken for granted while the individuals who bequeathed them remain virtually unknown. Such is the legacy of Adele Lubbock Briscoe Looscan. Her efforts helped to secure the San Jacinto Battleground and preserve other state historic sites, including the Alamo, old Fort Anahuac, and the grave of Sarah Dodson, designer of the Lone Star flag. Looscan promoted public education, the Houston Public Library, and the creation of the State Library and Archives. As the first woman president of the Texas State Historical Association (TSHA), she served the longest term of any president of the organization at a time when women were just beginning to assume public leadership roles. Yet while her name might be familiar to Houstonians and members of the TSHA, few today know anything of the person memorialized in brick and mortar in Texas's largest city.

Houston is the seat of Harris County, which bears the name of the maternal ancestors of Adele Looscan, the last of a female dynasty in that city established by her grandmother, Jane Birdsall Harris, and carried forward by her mother, Mary Jane Harris Briscoe. Granddaughter of John R. Harris, one of Austin's earliest colonists, and the youngest daughter of Andrew Briscoe, a signer of the Texas Declaration of Independence, Adele Briscoe Looscan was truly a daughter of the Republic of Texas. Her background provides insight into the contributions she and women like her made to the intellectual, social, and cultural fabric of the state and nation. Scholars of women's history have postulated that the collective activity of these women was motivated by a need to band together to promote their own interests, by a hunger for education, and in the South by a desire to vindicate and promote Southern "principles." The causes for which Looscan worked—memorialization, historical preservation and study, education—will

ADELE BRISCOE LOOSCAN, 1867

Courtesy of the San Jacinto Museum of History, Houston, Texas.

be recognized as common to the work of women's clubs all over the country during the Progressive era, but Looscan represents a transitional figure in the history of Texas women as they moved from the nineteenth to the twentieth century. Like southern women elsewhere, she hungered for education and desired to promote causes that interested her.

Looscan's involvement in the women's club movement and historical organizations coincided with the founding of numerous state historical societies around the South. The proliferation of these organizations was part of a well-documented surge of nostalgia as the United States entered the Gilded Age. Historian Michael Kammen has defined nostalgia as a concept that tends to deny the notion that progress or change is necessarily for the better. He has observed that nostalgia is likely to emerge in response to dramatic changes such as revolution or civil war, rapid industrialization, or the crumbling of a venerated value system, all of which were present following the Civil War. At the same time, the professionalization of history was giving rise to a new chapter in American, southern, and Texan historiography. This intersection of the waning of the "revolution generation" and the rise of academic history led to a resurgence of southern patriotism and to Texas's search for its own identity following the Confederacy's defeat.[1] Similarly, Looscan's devotion to the promotion of Texas history signaled her search for her own identity. Unlike many of her peers, she was motivated more by a desire to promote the Texan cause than by her love for the southern cause. Her activities and those of women like her may have had as much to do with the women themselves as with the causes they promoted. The impulse to enshrine the places and persons involved in Texas's independence seems to have stemmed at least in part from the psychological and social needs of the survivors.[2]

Adele Briscoe was born in Harrisburg, Texas, on February 5, 1848, the namesake of Adele Lubbock, wife of Francis R. Lubbock, a neighbor of her family and later governor of Texas. Her father, Captain Andrew Briscoe, was a veteran of the Battle of San Jacinto, judge, rancher, and railroad promoter, but he was in many ways a tragic figure who dreamed of success but repeatedly fell short. A restless man, he moved his family to New Orleans a year after Adele's birth. He died shortly thereafter, leaving his wife financially strapped and alone to rear four children. Mary Jane Briscoe's response set the course for her youngest daughter's life.[3]

Mary Jane buried her husband at his family's home in Claiborne County, Mississippi, and remained there with her children under the protection of her father-in-law, General Parmenas Briscoe. Briscoe was among the earliest American settlers in Mississippi. He had commanded a company in the War of 1812, became a general in the state militia, and served several terms in the Mississippi Legislature. Though supporters urged him to run for Congress, he declined. He had other ambitions, with troublesome consequences for his son's widow and her children.[4]

General Briscoe, like his son, found the lure of the frontier irresistible, and by early 1851, he departed for California. When he died in a storm near Acapulco on the return trip, Mary Jane again found herself and her children with no means of support. She had known that if Briscoe did not return, she and her children would no longer have a home in Mississippi.[5]

In 1852, Mary Jane returned to Texas out of financial necessity and seeking educational opportunities for her children. The prospect of sending her sons to a recently established Episcopal school, combined with the fact that she owned property there, made Anderson, the seat of Grimes County, a sensible location. Moreover, her brother, John, and his family resided there. In 1859, at her mother's urging, Mary Jane returned to Harrisburg, bringing with her a determination to have her children classically educated. In 1860, the citizens of Harrisburg built a schoolhouse and engaged a teacher, but the school folded when Texas seceded.[6]

The outbreak of the Civil War brought changes, but Mary Jane Briscoe's determination to see her daughters educated persisted. Adele's brothers, Parmenas and Birdsall, went off to fight, while Adele went off to Miss Mary B. Browne's School for Young Ladies in Houston, which opened in the fall of 1861 with about fifty pupils of all ages; enrollment soon doubled.[7]

Many daughters of Houston's leading families were educated at Miss Browne's School. While Mary Jane Briscoe had not inherited great wealth, her family background assured her elite standing in the community. Education of children, both male and female, was seen as a mark of gentility, signifying the highest type of refinement. Briscoe valued education not only for its own sake but also as a way to maintain class distinctions. The school's rigorous academic curriculum comprised spelling, penmanship, grammar, geography, and arithmetic. For junior classes, Greek, Roman, and Hebrew biography and history opened the door to more comprehensive courses in ancient geography, history, and mythology. Natural philosophy, chemistry, astronomy, botany, rhetoric, and French completed the senior class studies. Daily, students were inculcated with the principles deemed necessary to form character.[8] Adele's junior address to the senior class in 1864 revealed remarkable sophistication for a girl of sixteen reared on what was still in many respects the frontier. She acknowledged the advantages that she and her classmates enjoyed and the obligation they bore to grow in knowledge and virtue. They had an even more particular obligation, she said, to become a credit to their Texas heritage and to their country. By way of apology for lacking the privileges of those educated in the East or in the capitals of Europe, she emphasized the nobility of "fulfilling the duties of our sphere," referring both to the sphere they occupied as Texans and the sphere they occupied as women.[9]

Two years later, the war over, Adele delivered the valedictory address to her own graduating class. Again, she championed Texas and homegrown education: "My young companions, let us cherish a generous emulation, and show those friends, whose presence lends such sweet encouragement, that the schools of our own loved Texas can develop talent and nourish virtue. Yes: let us endeavor to prove that diligence and care may win science beneath the lowly shingled roof, as well as in the classic structures of distant lands."[10]

This was by no means empty rhetoric. Adele Briscoe followed her own advice. The ideals she expressed as a young graduate marked all she did and how she did it, ironically limiting her in many ways. Her graduation from Miss Browne's marked the end of her formal education and the beginning of a lifelong passion for learning and writing. If Mary Jane Briscoe had always emphasized the importance of education, her other compelling interests were history and securing her family's place in it. She lobbied tirelessly on behalf of Texas veterans and polished their image as heroes, but this dedication may well have involved more than simple patriotism. Her identity was closely associated with that of her pioneering family. Her husband's reputation was linked with the Texas Revolution and Republic. She did all she could to make those males seem eminently successful (or heroic), especially if they were not always thus. Mary Jane passed this mission to her daughters, particularly Adele, who had not known her father. Thus, Adele's mission became the preservation of the glorious history of Texas and its heroes, a mission essential to her self-identity, which she pursued with single-minded purpose during her entire life. This mission cast mother and daughter in the familiar mold of clubwomen yet at the same time distinguished them from typical southern clubwomen of their era.

With her graduation in 1866, a new phase of Adele's education commenced. In the summer of 1870, Adele and her mother embarked on a tour, visiting relatives from coast to coast. The journey allowed Adele to see the country and become acquainted with the extended Harris family. Her uncle, Lewis Birdsall Harris, lived in California, and during the visit there, Adele attracted an admirer who traveled to Texas in 1871 to visit her. Though their affection seemed mutual, her mother's disapproval doomed the relationship, underscoring the influence she wielded.[11]

Another decade passed before Mary Jane Briscoe approved a match for her daughter in the person of Major Michael Looscan, a Civil War veteran ten years Adele's senior who served as county attorney of Harris County between 1870

and 1880. Looscan had been in Houston since the spring of 1865 as inspec-
tor general on the staff of General S. B. Maxey. The exact origin of their acquaintance is unexplained but is undoubtedly linked to his association with
the Confederate veterans. Looscan had immigrated to the United States from
Ireland in 1855, settling in Texas shortly before the outbreak of the Civil War. As
a member of the Texas Second Cavalry, he served in New Mexico and Arizona.
Adele's brothers, Parmenas and Birdsall, also served but were in different brigades. Family correspondence indicates that Looscan had shown some interest
in Adele as early as 1870. In June of that year, while Adele was in California,
her sister, Jessie Briscoe Howe, wrote that Major Looscan had visited twice—
mainly, she thought, to inquire about Adele. The 1880 census showed Mary Jane
Briscoe, Parmenas, and Adele residing with the Howes in Houston. Michael
Looscan was a boarder in the Howe household. During this period, he created
quite a stir. After winning election as Harris County attorney in 1870, he almost
immediately crossed swords with Governor E. J. Davis to such an extent that the
law creating the office was repealed, evidently to get rid of Looscan. The county
commissioners nevertheless retained him, and he brought numerous suits on
behalf of the county against corrupt officeholders. When the office of county
attorney was officially restored in 1876, he was elected by popular vote and held
the office until 1880. In September 1881, he and Adele married.[12]

By that time, Adele Briscoe was a mature woman of thirty-three. For the first
time in her life, she moved into a home of her own, and she fully assumed her
role as a Houston matron. She moved from beneath her mother's shadow as
well. On a wintry Sunday in 1890, Mary Jane mourned in her journal that Adele
and Jessie no longer went to communion with her at Christ Church. Adele remained devoted to her mother, however, an attitude that was understandable.
As a single parent, Mary Jane Briscoe had relied on her children emotionally as
well as for help around the house. In that regard, Adele was typical of American
girls of her generation. The role of dutiful daughter was clearly defined and
urged on girls from their earliest years. She had been expected to help her
mother in tasks recognized as "female," tasks intended to inculcate equally well-
recognized feminine "virtues." The distinction, if one existed, was Mary Jane
Briscoe's inclusion of advanced education among those virtues. In attentiveness
to her mother, Adele epitomized the southern clubwoman, but in many other
ways, as exemplified by her relatively late marriage, she defied all stereotypes.[13]

Adele followed her mother into charity and club work. With no children of
her own, Adele focused her energies outside the home. In 1885, she organized
the Ladies' Reading Club of Houston, which became a model for similar study
clubs around the state. She served as chair of the first Woman's Exchange in

Houston and as the first chair of the Daughters of the Republic of Texas (DRT), which held its organizational meeting in her mother's home.[14] She was a charter member of the Houston Pen Women, the Texas Woman's Press Association (now Texas Press Women), and the TSHA. By her own lights, she was a "pioneer in the up-building of Women's Clubs and Public Libraries and the collection of data for Texas history." She wrote and published articles in the *Gulf Messenger*, the *Texas Messenger*, the *Quarterly of the Texas State Historical Association* (later the *Southwestern Historical Quarterly*), and Dudley Wooten's *Comprehensive History of Texas* (1898). With Katie Shaifer and Carrie Ennis Lombardi, she helped the Houston Lyceum grow into the Houston Public Library, and she became the first president of the City Federation of Women's Clubs.[15]

All of these achievements bore the influence of Adele's Texas heritage and up-bringing, and they hinted that her motivation was more personal than national or sectional. Her mother, who had always been out of the ordinary, had already made a name for herself as a champion for the cause of Texas veterans. Those friends to whom Mary Jane Briscoe looked for business advice and with whom she socialized and grew old shared the same memory places and lived experiences. Associating intimately with the Texas veterans enabled her to relate to the two most important men in her life in a way that elevated her feelings about them and about herself. Like so many women of the nascent club movement, Mary Jane's activism had begun under the auspices of the ladies' association of Christ Church in Houston and through her friendship with Texas veterans such as F. R. Lubbock, a charter member of the Texas Veterans Association. Mary Jane regularly attended the group's meetings, and when it began agitating for the state to purchase the cemetery ground at the San Jacinto battle site, she conducted a lively letter-writing campaign to the governor and legislators. As a result, the legislature appropriated funds for the purchase of the grave site in 1881 and for ten more acres in May 1883. Adele's involvement in club work, like her mother's, was an evolutionary process, but unlike the stereotypical southern clubwomen described by women's historians, her efforts were motivated less by a focus on southern identity than by her focus on Texas identity.[16]

One of Adele's first initiatives, typical of the southern clubwoman movement, drew on the impulse to build a free library for Houston. On the afternoon of February 26, 1885, several women, mostly from the ladies' associations of Christ Church and the First Presbyterian Church, assembled at Mary Jane Briscoe's residence on Crawford Street in Houston to organize a society "having for its object pleasure and improvement." The movement was designed to supply a long-felt need for a common ground on which ladies "having a literary taste might meet." The group named itself the Ladies' History Class, and Adele

Looscan was appointed president pro tempore.[17] Michael Looscan printed up the record of the first year's program in a pamphlet and distributed it to friends all over the state, encouraging the formation of similar study clubs.

The Ladies' History Class represented a milestone not only for Houston women but also for Adele Looscan. It marked her emergence as an individual, not simply the youngest daughter of Mary Jane Briscoe. The Ladies' History Class was one of the earliest women's social organizations in Houston outside of the churches and followed only a few years after the founding of the Houston chapter of the Woman's Christian Temperance Union in 1880. According to Houston historian Betty T. Chapman, one way for women to move "from the parlor to the public" was through women's clubs. Before the Ladies' Reading Club, Houston offered few opportunities for women to gather and voice their opinions except within the church. Like the Woman's Christian Temperance Union, the Ladies' Reading Club had a broad interest in the welfare of women. The charter members of the Ladies' History Class were a mix of married and single women, some of them teachers, and their attitude redefined the "cult of true womanhood." Adele Looscan, as the Houston club's first president, set an example. A woman, she said, should be "one whose mind shall be trained to form her own opinions, to organize her own household, and if need be to make her own living."[18] In an April 1886 address, Looscan revealed her view of the formation of such organizations by women: "That it is easier to drift with the tide of society, doing what others do, perhaps thinking what others think without definite aims for the true advancement of ourselves, or of those who are to come after us, is conceded; but should we not aspire much higher than this? A responsive voice in the heart of every true woman answers that we should; and since all our efforts during the past year have been animated by noble aims, I trust no lady will feel herself less fitted to perform the duties of life, by reason of having devoted some of her time to study, as a member of our Club."[19]

Within two months, the name of the Ladies' History Class was changed to the Ladies' Reading Club, and the ladies wasted no time expanding their reach beyond their own studious circle. Their work to establish Houston's public library illustrates how women's organizations evolved from self-education and social reform into political activism. In this endeavor, the Houston clubs followed the pattern of emerging women's organizations throughout the nation. In her "Address to the Ladies' Reading Club" on its tenth anniversary, Looscan appealed for a "cordial union among all the literary and study clubs" to provide an adequate location for a public library. The various study clubs should be petitioned to gather strength until a public library could be created through their combined efforts.[20] Once the Houston women's clubs united, they immediately realized the need to polish their political skills to achieve their goal. The Houston Lyceum had been exclusively for men until 1887, when lack of revenue moved the group to admit women. Adele Looscan, backed by the members of the Reading Club, told the officers of the Lyceum that all of the women would join the Lyceum at three dollars per year and that the club would give five dollars per month toward the rent provided that the books were moved to a more accessible place. The women's strategy and political instincts demonstrated the nimbleness with which they adapted management of the domestic sphere to the public sphere.[21] Once the members of the Lyceum consented to the move, they needed the city council's financial support. As the *Houston Post-Dispatch* noted in 1928, "At that time women did not go before the council and ask for things; it just wasn't done." So the women decided on "a brave bold plan" to invite the mayor and aldermen to come to them in the library room as invited guests. They wrote to Andrew Carnegie for a grant for a public library, and in October 1899, they were rewarded with the announcement that Carnegie would give them fifty thousand dollars provided that the city would furnish a site and maintain it at a cost of four thousand dollars per year. Not until June 1900 did the city pass an ordinance meeting all the requirements, but thanks to the Ladies' Reading Club, the citizens of Houston had their library.[22] When the Houston Federation of Women's Clubs joined the General Federation of Women's Clubs, Adele Looscan continued to have an active role.

Looscan's talent for organizing and orchestrating may have first received notice with her election as president of the Ladies' Reading Club, but that event was only the beginning of a prodigious career of service. Within five years, Adele had lent her energy and intellect to a new enterprise near and dear to her mother's heart. In the spring of 1891, Galveston's Betty Ballinger and her cousin, Hally Ballinger Bryan, decided to form an organization dedicated to the perpetuation of the memory of the heroes of San Jacinto. Both women traced their lineage to the Texas Republic through their mothers. Hally Bryan was a grandniece of Stephen F. Austin, while Betty Ballinger had gained some experience as a cofounder of the first literary club in Galveston.[23] Their interest in this pursuit was aroused by the recent discovery in an old Galveston cemetery of the neglected graves of David G. Burnet, first president of the Republic of Texas, and Sidney Sherman, a veteran of the Battle of San Jacinto. The cousins solicited support from other Texas women whose husbands or ancestors had helped the republic achieve and maintain its independence. Hally's father, Guy M. Bryan, president of the Texas Veterans Association, introduced her to Mary Jones, widow of Anson Jones, the last president of the Republic of Texas, and to Mary Jane Briscoe.[24] Seventeen women assembled, again in Mary Jane Briscoe's parlor, on November 6, 1891, to form the Daughters of the Lone Star Republic, renamed Daughters of the Republic of Texas at the first annual meeting. Ballinger was chosen for the executive committee that drew up the organization's constitution and by-laws, laying out its purpose in terms of the traditional role of southern women: "The future of Texas is in the hands of her sons[, who,] dazzled by the splendor of the present . . . have forgotten the heroic deeds and sacrifices of the past. But it is not so with woman. . . . Surrounded by the history of the family life, it is her duty to keep alive the sacred fire of tradition. . . . Let us leave the future of Texas to our brothers, and claim as our province the guarding of her holy past." This revealing choice of words echoed the sentiments of many clubwomen across the country, particularly in the South, as they tried to balance traditional roles with their desire to enlarge the scope of womanhood.[25] A difference, however faint, between the DRT and the United Daughters of the Confederacy and similar groups was that the past the DRT venerated was Texas's past, with which these women uniquely identified. They may have been Daughters of the American Revolution and Daughters of the Confederacy, a sisterhood shared by women across the nation and the South, but Texas's holy past was theirs alone.

Adele Looscan immediately threw herself into this cause, raising support for the DRT. She penned dozens of letters urging the daughters of Texas veterans to join. She sometimes met with discouragement, as in the reply of Anna Ehinger of Navasota, who wrote, "I think it impossible to organize *anything* here—even a chapter of the 'Daughters of the Republic.'" Responding to Adele's dedication and determination, some who displayed initial reticence eventually became staunch supporters. Nettie Houston Bringhurst, for example, responded less than enthusiastically to Looscan's initial solicitation: "We are all patriotic and quite willing to work provided it be behind the scenes." Bringhurst exhibited the attitude, typical of many, that although she would contribute moral support, Adele should do the footwork.[26] And she did. One of Looscan's letters found its way to Adina De Zavala, granddaughter of Lorenzo De Zavala, first vice president of the Republic of Texas. She had been active in organizing San Antonio women for patriotic purposes. Her response to Looscan's overture on behalf of the DRT was filled with youthful enthusiasm: "I think it would be a very easy matter to establish here a branch organization. There must be many descendants of heroes and veterans of Texas living here, and if you wish, I will do what I can in the matter."[27] Though Adina was thirteen years Adele's junior, the two seemed to have much in common, particularly the desire to preserve Texas's cultural heritage and memorialize its heroes. Their friendship would withstand much, including the rending of the association that brought them together, and they dedicated themselves to the preservation and promotion of Texas history.

One of their first successful campaigns involved the ongoing effort to acquire the San Jacinto Battleground, a fight that survived both the battles over the Alamo and the DRT. A committee of veterans, including survivors of the battle, had located important sites of the battle events in 1894 and had marked them three years later. The preservation of the battleground as a state historical site became an ongoing joint effort of the Texas Veterans Association and the DRT. By 1912, the Daughters had raised the money to mark the sites with granite boulders.[28] The men approached the governor and legislature; the women, unable to take such a direct route, relentlessly wrote memorials, letters, pamphlets, and circulars to garner state support for the battleground and to raise money to purchase more of it.[29]

Looscan did not confine her writing to letters. Her interest in Texas history and her writing talents led her to submit articles to newspapers and literary magazines in Houston, Austin, San Antonio, and Dallas. When the Texas Woman's Press Association organized in 1893, she became a member. In the 1880s, she began writing articles for such short-lived literary magazines as the *Texas Messenger*, *Ladies' Messenger*, and *Gulf Messenger*. Between April 1887 and October 1888, she contributed no fewer than fourteen articles, signed "Texan," to the *Ladies' Messenger*, published by Mrs. W. H. Foute of Houston. The topics ranged widely, including historical accounts ("The First Anniversary Ball of the Battle of San Jacinto"), gender issues ("Industries for Women"), and education ("The Impolicy of Educating Texas Youth Abroad"). The editors and publishers of these magazines regularly turned to Looscan for advice as well as copy. Sara Hartman, editor of the *Gulf Messenger*, appealed to Looscan in 1894, "It is my purpose to devote some space each month to Texas history or the biographical sketches of prominent Texas heroes, and I would appreciate any suggestions from you in the matter of suitable subjects."[30] Looscan also contributed to the Austin-based *Texas Magazine*, published by Robert E. McCleary in 1896 and edited by Dora Fowler Arthur, Looscan's compatriot in the DRT and in the Texas Woman's Press Association.

Arthur saw both the DRT and the magazine as being of mutual benefit to the women involved as well as to the veterans of the Texas Republic, writing, "How remiss Texas has been in embalming memories of the mothers of Texas for posterity. As ours is a woman's association, now is the golden opportunity to collect and treasure biographical sketches of our mothers who have borne the burden in war and in peace." The *Texas Magazine*, she argued, would provide the DRT with a forum; in exchange, the group would provide a subscription base for the enterprise. Arthur argued that Texas men had written the political and military history of colonial Texas and the republic, but the few women who had made forays into state history had merely rehashed or condensed what the men had already done. Arthur offered the DRT as many pages in each issue of the magazine as the group had subject matter to fill, asking in return only that the sisterhood throughout the state support the publication by subscribing and contributing. Moreover, she argued, the DRT column in the magazine would encourage the donation of pictures, biographical and autobiographical sketches, and other historical items to the DRT. The magazine announced the creation of the TSHA as well as the activities of the DRT and other women's organizations. Arthur served as editor of the DRT section of the magazine, and her correspondence with Looscan clearly reveals that the promotion of Texas history had as much if not more to do with the promotion of Texas women as with the promotion of Texas heroes. "I am an enthusiast in Texas history," she wrote, "and think I see where Texas women can do much with equal grace and ease to enrich our state literature by saving from irrevocable loss the memory of our pioneer women; also the domestic and social history of the colonial and republican periods."[31]

It speaks volumes about the popular interest in Texas heroes that none of these magazines gained much traction. They did, however, disseminate articles written by Looscan. The *Texas Magazine* was purchased from Robert McCleary and published in Dallas in August 1897, with William G. Scarff as editor and publisher and Dudley G. Wooten as editorial supervisor. It covered a wide range of interests, including literature, current events, women's clubs, and poetry. Looscan's contacts and reputation as a Texas historian had prompted Scarff to approach her in 1894 for help securing articles for his planned *New History of Texas*, which he published a few years later as Dudley G. Wooten's *Comprehensive History of Texas*. She not only contributed an article but also provided information to other contributors.[32] In 1897, she contributed to Wooten's *New History of Texas for Schools*. Looscan's writing for newspapers, literary magazines, and historical anthologies such as Wooten's no doubt helped to bring her to the attention of George P. Garrison, a professor of history at the University of Texas, as he began organizing the Texas State Historical Association in 1897.[33]

Michael Looscan's death in September 1897 after a lengthy illness marked another turning point in Adele's life. At age forty-nine, she moved back into her mother's house to become her companion and caregiver: Mary Jane had fallen and had become an invalid. That year also brought an invitation to join yet another organization. In March, Dora Arthur wrote that she had submitted Adele Looscan's name to a TSHA committee and was pleased to see her accept the invitation. Historian Julia Lee Sinks, Arthur pointed out, was a vice president and a fellow, the only woman so honored in the organization.[34]

Within days, Arthur wrote again, requesting a contribution to the DRT section of *Texas Magazine* even though Adele at the time was busy taking care of her husband. Typically, Adele obliged, a tribute to her sense of responsibility regardless of personal inconvenience. A month after her husband's death, she received Garrison's request for an article for the *Quarterly of the Texas State Historical Association*. In December, he wrote again, pleading with her to attend the association's midwinter meeting in San Antonio and to bring with her "as many from Houston as possible." He apologized for pressuring her, explaining that "none of our members in Houston would be more likely to respond favorably to such an appeal." Garrison knew that Looscan's sense of duty, whether to Texas, to education, or to the organizations to which she had committed herself, generally overrode her own comfort. It was simply characteristic of her nature. As her mother observed in her journal, "Adele is more kindhearted and generous than most of us."[35]

At the same time the newly organized TSHA was struggling to establish itself, the DRT was engaged in a monumental struggle of its own, one with lasting importance for Texas, for the DRT, and for Looscan personally. The second Battle of the Alamo was brewing, and Looscan, always at the forefront, found herself caught squarely in the crossfire.

The roots of the trouble stretched back to 1886, when Hugo and Schmeltzer, a wholesale grocery company, purchased the convent portion of the Alamo mission. The old Spanish mission of San Antonio de Valero, which dated to 1718 and had been the site of the fateful 1836 Battle of the Alamo, had fallen into such disrepair that little of it remained.[36] The earliest buildings were of temporary construction and did not survive, but by 1727 work had begun on a stone convent (priest's residence). The two-story, arcaded convent served as the friars' main building, housing offices, kitchens, dining rooms, sleeping quarters, and guest rooms. A portion of this building later became known as the Long Barracks. The mission church was erected in the 1750s, with protective walls erected after the massacre at San Sabá Mission in 1758. These walls, eight feet high and two feet thick, enclosed a main plaza located west of the convent and guarded by small artillery and a fortified gate. During the nineteenth-century struggle for political and military control of Texas, these rudimentary fortifications made the old mission symbolically and strategically important. Between 1810 and 1865, the former mission changed hands at least sixteen times. Private construction during the 1850s obliterated most of the old Indian houses and traces of the outer walls.[37]

The erection of the monument to the heroes of San Jacinto awakened desire on the part of patriotic citizens to see other historic localities honored, but the Texas Legislature displayed little or no enthusiasm for that cause, even for the purchase of the Church of the Alamo. In 1883, the State of Texas finally purchased the chapel from the Catholic Church and turned its care over to the City of San Antonio. When Adina De Zavala became a member of the DRT's executive committee in 1902, she proposed a plan for the preservation of the missions. She was appointed to determine if the missions could be purchased by the state and the Alamo placed in the hands of the DRT. The committee decided to leave the mayor of San Antonio as the site's caretaker with the request that a member of the De Zavala Chapter of the DRT be appointed to help select a custodian for the property. In 1903, the members of the De Zavala Chapter launched a campaign to purchase the Alamo Mission property from Hugo and Schmeltzer. They established an Alamo Mission Fund with the intention of beautifying the surroundings of the Alamo "in keeping with its historical value and sacred significance" and eventually of creating a hall of fame in which would be preserved "the historical relics of the State and busts of its heroes."[38]

The public response to this campaign was less enthusiastic than the DRT anticipated. In 1898, Clara Driscoll, the wealthy granddaughter of a San Jacinto veteran, returned to Texas after spending several years in school in Europe. She joined the De Zavala Chapter in February 1903 and immediately threw herself into the campaign to acquire the Hugo and Schmeltzer property. While fund-raising progressed slowly, an eastern syndicate made Hugo and Schmeltzer an offer to purchase the property for a hotel. Driscoll, asserting her wealth and influence, extracted from Hugo and Schmeltzer a thirty-day option on the property with a five-hundred-dollar cash deposit.[39]

When the option expired without the funds having been raised, Driscoll put up the remaining forty-five hundred dollars to secure the Alamo for Texas. She also made a twenty-thousand-dollar payment in 1904 and guaranteed the payment of all the other notes standing between the DRT and Hugo and Schmeltzer, holding the Alamo as security. Throughout the hectic year of fund-raising, members of Adele Looscan's San Jacinto Chapter of the Daughters, the William B. Travis Chapter in Austin, and the De Zavala Chapter wrote letters; lobbied the legislature; printed circulars, pictures, and poetry; and even ran a restaurant to raise money. Looscan and other members of the DRT also appealed to old friends and business associates for donations. For all their efforts, Driscoll's financial contributions did what all the other Daughters combined could not— preserved the land around the Alamo. When word of her gesture got out, money and sympathy rolled in. In 1905, the Texas Legislature appropriated sixty-five thousand dollars to complete the purchase of the Alamo; the measure also provided that the DRT would serve as the custodian of the property. Somewhere in the process, however, the DRT members split over plans for the Alamo grounds. The dispute seemed to revolve around a misunderstanding about the scene of the battle. By July 1904, Looscan, as historian-general of the DRT, sought to clear up the misconceptions by publishing an article, "The Work of the Daughters of the Republic of Texas in Behalf of the Alamo," in the *Quarterly of the Texas State Historical Association*. She wrote that "an unfortunate and inexcusable ignorance" regarding the Alamo chapel had been "accepted by many who ought to know better as the whole and only theatre of the siege." This detail was significant, because Driscoll was among those who held this belief. She intended that the mission building would come down and that the chapel would be the main feature of the historical site. When Governor Samuel Lanham formally transferred possession of the Alamo and grounds to the DRT, Mary Jones, the organization's president, appointed Driscoll temporary local custodian of the Alamo church and surrounding property.[40]

Members of the DRT divided into two camps, one aligned with the De Zavala Chapter and the other supporting Driscoll. Adina De Zavala remained the Alamo's custodian until the DRT filed a lawsuit to restrain her. Looscan was also named a defendant. De Zavala fought bitterly for two years, dividing and disrupting the DRT's 1907 state convention so thoroughly that it adjourned without accomplishing anything. Driscoll, herself a member of the De Zavala Chapter, resigned from the organization.[41]

The dispute grew more and more acrimonious. Adele Looscan remained loyal to Adina De Zavala despite her increasingly irrational behavior, which culminated with De Zavala barricading herself inside the building for a week in February 1908. While the De Zavala faction may have had history on its side, the Driscoll faction had the money. After all appeals had been exhausted in 1910, the Alamo property was released to the DRT as a whole. The courts ordered the De Zavala Chapter disaffiliated from the DRT, effectively dissolving the chapter, but controversy over the Alamo property raged on. In July 1911, Looscan expressed her dismay in a letter to Governor O. B. Colquitt regarding the two-story convent, which she maintained constituted the most important part of the Alamo still standing: "I have never felt that the building was in danger because I did not believe any Governor of the State of Texas would consent to its destruction. The most thrilling part of the history of Texas is embraced within so brief a period that no citizen of the State should be ignorant of the events comprising it. To me it has seemed simply impossible that a Park, which any city can have, should occupy the space of this most historic barrack, the scene of such heroic conflict as has never been surpassed in the world's history."[42]

The damage to the organization involved more than the dispute over the Alamo. Insults flew from both sides. At a meeting of the San Jacinto Chapter at which Adele and her sister were not present, the chapter president, Mrs. J. J. McKeever, procured from a group of new members, who knew nothing of former proceedings, an endorsement of a statement she had published in the *Houston Post* regarding the truthfulness of ten members of the chapter, including Adele Looscan and Jessie Howe. Looscan expressed deep hurt at the accusations leveled against her and her family and asked that a memorial about her mother that she had presented to the San Jacinto Chapter be returned to her.[43] The *San Antonio Light* reported, "Erstwhile friends have become sworn enemies and those who formerly drank tea and exchanged small talk together are arrayed in a warfare quite as determined as the defense of the Alamo" in 1836.[44] Disagreements persisted regarding the plans not only for the Alamo property but also for the relics that had been donated by veterans and their widows. Some of the items had been personally solicited by Adele Looscan, and she assumed responsibility for them, thereby involving her more deeply in the ongoing feud.

This argument over the historical accuracy of the plans for the Alamo continued for decades, but Adele Looscan did not take part. Former friends had turned on her privately and publicly. She wrote to a donor who had offered historical relics for the Alamo, "I regret very much to feel obliged to tell you of the troubles that prevail in an organization of which for many years I was very proud, but my experience has taught me that a few zealous unscrupulous women can in a short time destroy the prestige of the most worthy organization and their malicious tongues blacken the most spotless reputation."[45] The betrayals, politicization, demagoguery, and cynicism of the DRT, more than the Alamo issue itself, drove Looscan to become a thoroughly disaffected Daughter by 1914, never again to associate with the organization she had helped to found, although her friendships with Adina De Zavala and Hally Bryan endured. Many disaffected members resumed their association with the DRT, including Jessie Howe. Adele never did.

This episode underscored the difference between Adele Looscan and the typical southern clubwoman. Her interest in and focus on Texas history was more compelling than any other motivation for her participation in the DRT. Looscan's club work was motivated less by a desire for status than by her beliefs in the duty to family, the importance of history, and civic responsibility. This was not to say that she had no southern biases. She was a member of the United Daughters of the Confederacy and an admirer of Jefferson Davis. On occasion, she passionately defended the "happy" condition of slaves in Texas. And she resigned from the National Historical Society over its intent to memorialize John Brown by marking the site of his home.[46] Nevertheless, she invested the greatest part of her time and energies in promoting Texas's history and historical sites.

Looscan's departure from the DRT, although a turning point in her life, in no way interrupted the many other activities in which she engaged but merely freed her time and energies for those pursuits. Both Looscan and De Zavala remained in the TSHA, but the schism within the DRT resulted in the loss of a number of female TSHA members. Thus, in 1915, on the recommendation of Judge Zachary T. Fulmore, University of Texas history professor Eugene C. Barker appointed Looscan president of the TSHA.[47] Active as a contributor and committee member since the organization's inception, she did not hesitate to shoulder responsibility for furthering its objectives and addressing its needs and weaknesses.[48]

Looscan's dedication to the mission and goals of the TSHA would have come as no surprise to her mentor, Garrison, who had died of heart failure in 1910. When he, Judge Fulmore, and others decided to try to organize a state historical association in February 1897, Dallas County judge and later U.S. representative Dudley G. Wooten urged them to consider "the importance of enlisting the ladies in this organization and support of" the DRT's members. He continued, "The most intelligent, discriminating and active laborers in the collection and preservation of Texas historical materials have been her noble women, and I can name half a dozen whom I personally know to be peculiarly fitted to take part in this work." Garrison heeded this advice and enlisted the members of the Texas Woman's Press Association who were present at the organizational meeting. All of the women whom Garrison sought to involve in establishing the TSHA were published writers with ties to other historical organizations and to education. Garrison knew that other attempts to organize historical associations in Texas had failed and that success would require him to tap into Texans' desire to preserve their history and combine it with scholarly discipline. He understood that the most zealous promoters of history in Texas at that time were elite women, and he needed a lot of articles relatively quickly for the *Quarterly*. He encouraged and tutored these women in scholarly writing so that they could become reliable contributors, and he appealed to their connections among clubs and other associations such as the Ladies' Reading Club and Texas Veterans to recruit members, raise funds, and collect material.[49]

Adele Looscan tackled all of these responsibilities with her usual intensity. Her correspondence with Garrison and others emphasized her prioritization of Texas history among her many interests. "No subject possesses as much interest for me as Texas History," she wrote in 1897. In March 1898, she assured Garrison, "*The Quarterly* possesses a continued interest for me, and is more thoroughly read than any other periodical, and I am glad to see that the prospects of this Association are so good." In reply to Garrison's request for her help late that year, Looscan wrote, "I will say that any service I can render the Association as member of this Committee, will be cheerfully given." She recruited members, offered information regarding the whereabouts of the personal papers of Texas veterans, and often personally requested that private donors contribute archival material to the association.[50]

Never simply a figurehead, President Looscan was involved in every aspect of the association. In 1916, she personally visited the Rice Institute managers with a view toward placing a complete set of the quarterlies in the school's library. She planned annual meetings, including soliciting papers for sessions and setting the program agenda. She helped popularize the TSHA by holding annual meetings outside of Austin. In promoting Houston as a site, for example, she expected to "work up an audience among the teachers in the schools, Rice Institute, and the Women's Clubs." "How long," she inquired in 1917, "has it been since a meeting has been held elsewhere" than at the University of Texas?[51]

Looscan also stressed the importance of the organization's flagship publication, the *Quarterly of the Texas State Historical Association*, disseminating knowledge of Texas history, increasing membership, and raising money. She believed that an index was key to that effort, and she doggedly sought to persuade other TSHA leaders of the need to prepare one. In 1918, she wrote, "I shall try to attend the meeting at Austin, where I shall recommend the adoption of steps to provide an index for the *Quarterly*." Her contacts in the Daughters of the American Revolution, the United Daughters of the Confederacy, and the General Federation of Women's Clubs aided her on this quest. She received requests for the journal from as far away as the Long Island Historical Society in New York. Both membership and fund-raising campaigns were slowed by World War I, but as the conflict drew to a close, she wrote to TSHA secretary Charles W. Ramsdell, "Do you not think some steps could now be taken to increase our membership? If you will send me a list of present subscribers in Houston, I will see if Mr. Lewis R. Bryan would be willing to assist in getting new ones. But, without an Index," she mourned, "the inestimable articles, the result of so much careful investigation and deep study, are like unvalued jewels scattered through hundreds of pages, and, while preserved, are unavailable to the new student."[52]

Believing the index to the first twenty volumes begun, Looscan took up other concerns, including the creation of the State Library and Archives and a state museum. In 1920, H. Y. Benedict, president of the University of Texas, wrote of his interest in founding a museum to house the state archives as well as artifacts and books.[53] Though the idea had many supporters in the TSHA, such an undertaking was fraught with obstacles. Looscan turned again to written appeals, sending letters to the managing editor of the *Dallas Morning News* asking that he publicize the crowded conditions in the existing state library and the crying need for a new building. To Hally Bryan Perry, Looscan confided that the project needed a good publicity secretary. The first step was to appeal to the legislature; if that failed, the next move was a memorial to Governor James Hogg. Dr. Alex Dienst, who sat with Looscan on the TSHA executive committee, seconded her assessment of the situation: "Until we make an effort with law-makers, I think we do well to not push the matter." The following year, he told her, "Like you, I often think we as a Society are not active enough. But what can we do? Texas is not prosperous—We have no great champion or speaker for us in the House or Senate, and I am satisfied till someone in the House or Senate gets the vision we have of a great State Museum, there will be nothing doing." The creation of a state archives would also require legislation. Over the years, legislators had passed many resolutions favoring the removal of manuscripts from the damp basements where they were currently stored. In the event that a measure were passed ordering the removal of historical manuscripts to the university, Looscan pondered the possibility of having it apply to collections that were not already in the Texas State Library. Moreover, she understood that historical manuscripts were quite inaccessible unless they were systematically calendared and arranged.[54]

Looscan's concern for the preservation and accessibility of state records re-flected her experience with research, in keeping with the intellectual bent she had exhibited since her days as a student at Miss Browne's School. Her expe-rience as a writer and her lessons in historical scholarship under Garrison's tutelage led her, among her other duties as president of the TSHA, to assert an editorial as well as administrative interest in the *Quarterly*. Her correspondence with Ramsdell regularly involved discussions about the solicitation of articles and selection of material for the journal. She even marketed the *Quarterly*, ask-ing him to send her copies to place on sale at book dealers and assuring him that she would be "personally responsible for any numbers not sold."[55]

After 1916, she became worn down by her responsibilities as president of the TSHA, and in 1918 she wrote to Ramsdell and Barker regarding the selection of a new leader for the organization. In what came to be more or less a routine reply, Ramsdell responded that it would not only be difficult to induce someone else to accept the position but more desirable to keep her in it. In 1920, Barker wrote, "We have never had a president who has felt the interest that you feel in the Association, and I am perfectly sincere in saying that I don't know where we should turn if you declined election."[56] Thus, she continued to preside and to remain active, though she traveled less as years went by and relied on cor-respondence to sustain her involvement.

But if Looscan's capacity for travel decreased, her capacity for ideas did not. In 1920, as she prepared to attend the annual meeting in Austin, she wrote to Ramsdell that she believed that if measures could be adopted authorizing the formation of branch societies in places with at least a dozen members, the TSHA could build up interest in Texas history that would greatly help the association. She and other members of the executive committee eventually settled on a plan to encourage county historical societies to affiliate with TSHA with the goals of building membership, raising money, and "correct[ing] many errors current due to the manipulation of the facts of history by newspaper writers."[57]

Looscan's continued value as president was often simply her wisdom and practicality. In 1924, spurred by Ramsdell and Thomas P. Martin, chair of the Committee on Patrons, the TSHA planned for a major capital campaign. Martin, who had been involved with a fund drive for the Texas Memorial Stadium Association, urged a campaign modeled after that one and proposed a goal of at least five hundred thousand dollars. Looscan's immediate response succinctly put the scheme in perspective. "Some of the methods of the Stadium people can be used in a drive for funds for the TSHA," she wrote. "Careful planning and good campaigning certainly must be used. Expert guidance will be needed; time, money and workers will be needed. Can they be found?" She followed with a much more detailed and encouraging letter spelling out what needed to be done and who would need to do it, but she cautioned that unless other officers shared Martin's enthusiasm, she feared the scheme would fail. A year later, Martin resigned as chair of the Committee on Patrons, pointing out that the raising of endowment funds was properly the work not of a university professor "but rather of the publicist and promoter" whether "in the guise of politician or president of an educational institution or statesman or simply as a public spirited citizen."[58] The TSHA then undertook a letter-writing campaign that sought to persuade individual members of local history associations to join the state group.

In 1925, Looscan finally retired as president of the TSHA, but she remained active in efforts to preserve and promote Texas history. In 1922, with Adina De Zavala and others, she had incorporated the Association for the Preservation of the Historical Landmarks in Texas, which sought to work for the repair, restoration, and preservation of the ancient Governor's Palace of Texas at San Antonio and other important landmarks; to preserve the state's cultural heritage in all of its aspects; to inculcate patriotism and love for Texas and its institutions; and to establish or maintain educational, scientific, and charitable institutions such as memorial halls and hospitals. The corporation was to have no capital structure but would be a literary, scientific, social, patriotic, and charitable association—familiar themes of women's clubs in general. However, Texans had come to regard themselves as having a separate identity. Though they may have shared goals with women's organizations in other parts of the country, Adele Looscan and her compatriots differed in their emphasis, as can be seen by comparing her 1890 address to the Ladies' Reading Club of Houston with the address of Adelia A. Dunovant, president of the Oran M. Roberts Chapter of the United Daughters of the Confederacy, "The Study of History," to the Lamar Fontaine Chapter in Alvin, Texas, in 1899. Looscan spoke in broad terms of studying history for personal edification, to bring the individual into "sympathetic relations with the great individual minds that have shaped the form and determined the character of what we call history," to give those who inhabit the present a sense of their place in the great continuum, and to appreciate their position as American women as well as the benefits they derive from that position. Dunovant, conversely, saw history as "a tribute at the feet of our beloved South." It needed to be studied because of its indestructibility, the "regal robe" it draws around the Daughters of the Confederacy, and its utility for inculcating southern principles in a younger generation.[59]

Although ill health rendered Looscan an invalid by 1929, she kept up her remarkable correspondence on behalf of her many causes, as chair of the Historical Committee of the Texas Woman's Press Association, as a member of the Texas History and Landmarks Association, and as supporter of her extended family. Likewise, until her death on November 23, 1935, she continued to correspond with diverse individuals on matters of genealogy, Texas history, education, and historic preservation, never missing an opportunity to promote the sacred memory of the fathers of the republic.

Despite her public activism, Looscan remained very traditional throughout her life. She was a conundrum. She saw herself as espousing and preserving women's sphere of domesticity, yet both she and her mother operated most of their lives outside of that sphere. Both experienced companionate marital relationships if for no other reason than they were unquestionably the intellectual equals (if not superiors) of their spouses and were never timid about it. Then, too, both women lived most of their adult lives as single women, largely responsible for their own economic well-being. Adele represented the third generation of such independent women. Her grandmother, Jane Harris, was a widow for forty years, at least a decade of that time on a very uncertain Texas frontier. Like her mother and many of her peers, Adele's self-identity was closely tied to men—men who sacrificed family for adventure, who were often unsuccessful, and who died before their daughters even knew them. And so they were lionized by their womenfolk, for whose sense of self such hero making was critical. As Adele asserted in her 1890 address to the Ladies' Reading Club of Houston, "It is by pious filial affection, by holy wifely devotion, by sacred motherly love, that we are to earn our worthiest title to respect. So shall we become true women of America, true companions of intellectual men; so shall we be true heirs of our noble ancestry, and worthy of an enlightened posterity."[60] At the same time, she set a rather unorthodox example for women of her class. When she believed that the DRT had abandoned its mission to preserve historical facts, she chose intellectual integrity over loyalty to the organization. She embraced education and scholarly rigor as ends in themselves, not simply as means to other ends. Even as she defended southern "principles," she was unquestionably first and foremost a Texas woman.

Through safe associations with other women, Texas women such as Adele Looscan made a niche for themselves in the public sphere and accomplished three things. They asserted their intellect and used it to influence political and practical outcomes decades before they could engage directly in the political process.[61] They preserved a great many of the physical remnants of Texas history and exalted the men *and women* who participated in it, purposefully crafting a reputation for them and cementing it in memory. They honored their fathers and mothers; they were, indeed, daughters of the Republic of Texas. As Betty Ballinger promised, they kept the memory alive and they fed it. They gave women a public role that unquestionably helped to prepare society and the women themselves for social and political equality.

NOTES

1. Laura Lyons McLemore, "Early Historians and the Shaping of Texas Memory," in *Lone Star Pasts: Memory and History*, ed. Gregg Cantrell and Elizabeth Hayes Turner (College Station: Texas A&M University Press, 2007), 27, 29.

2. Sinclair Moreland, "Adele Lubbock Briscoe Looscan," in *The Texas Women's Hall of Fame* (Austin: Biographical, 1917), 194.

3. Francis R. Lubbock, *Six Decades in Texas: The Memoirs of Francis R. Lubbock, Confederate Governor of Texas*, ed. C. W. Raines (Austin: Pemberton, 1968), 125; Moreland, "Adele Lubbock Briscoe Looscan," 194; Lewis W. Newton, "Briscoe, Andrew," *Handbook of Texas Online*, http://www.tshaonline.org/handbook/online/articles/fbr58 (accessed May 13, 2011).

4. "Early History of Claiborne County Mississippi," in Robert Lowery and William H. McCardle, *A History of Mississippi* (Jackson, Miss.: Henry, 1891), 457–60; *MSGenWeb* (accessed May 27, 2011); Adele Briscoe Looscan, "Harris Family," manuscript, n.d., 8, courtesy of Dorothy Knox Howe Houghton.

5. Mary Jane Briscoe to James M. Briscoe, [after 1851], MC056, box 132, Mary Jane Harris Briscoe Papers, San Jacinto Museum of History, La Porte, Texas (hereafter cited as SJMH).

6. Kate B. Shaifer in Adele Briscoe Looscan, "Mrs. Mary Jane Briscoe," *Southwestern Historical Quarterly* 7 (July 1903): 69; Joseph Thomas and Thomas Baldwin, *A Complete Pronouncing Gazetteer, or Geographical Dictionary of the World* (Philadelphia: Lippincott, 1856), 1907; Adele Briscoe Looscan, "Schools at Harrisburg and Houston," manuscript, n.d., MC041, box 120, Adele Briscoe Looscan Papers, SJMH.

7. Adele Briscoe Looscan, "Miss Mary B. Browne's Young Ladies' School," paper presented at a meeting of the Ladies' Reading Club of Houston, 1916, box 119, Looscan Papers, SJMH.

8. See Christie Anne Farnham, *The Education of the Southern Belle: Higher Education and Student Socialization in the Antebellum South* (New York: New York University Press, 1994), 18, 136; Looscan, "Miss Mary B. Browne's Young Ladies' School."

9. Adele L. Briscoe, Senior's Address, manuscript, July 1864, box 120, Looscan Papers, SJMH.

10. Adele L. Briscoe, Valedictory, Miss Browne's Young Ladies' School, manuscript, July 1866, box 120, Looscan Papers, SJMH.

11. Adele L. Briscoe to Mark Kelley, May 1, 1871, box 108, Looscan Papers, SJMH.

12. Jessie Wade Briscoe to Adele Lubbock Briscoe, June 21, 1870, box 107, ibid.; U.S. Census, 1880; "Michael Looscan," in *The National Cyclopaedia of American Biography* (New York: White, 1900), 8:486.

13. Mary Jane Briscoe, Journal, February 2, 1890, box 135, Briscoe Papers.

14. The Woman's Exchange served as a marketplace where women could earn a livelihood through the sale of their handmade goods, and it became a destination for shoppers seeking high-quality merchandise. The exchange also operated a tearoom serving inexpensive meals and a resource library and offered instruction in cooking, sewing, needlework, chair caning, and other domestic arts.

15. Mary Jane Briscoe, Journal, February 1, 1890, box 135, Briscoe Papers; Barbara Welter, *Dimity Convictions: The American Woman in the Nineteenth Century* (Athens: Ohio University Press, 1976), 4; "Club Women Sponsor Library 29 Years Ago; Federation Is Formed," *Houston Post-Dispatch*, March 25, 1928; Adele B. Looscan, typescript, n.d. (quotation), Mss. 37, box 1, Adele Briscoe Looscan Papers, Houston Metropolitan Research Center, Houston Public Library, Houston.

16. See Elizabeth Hayes Turner, *Women, Culture, and Community: Religion and Reform in Galveston, 1880–1920* (New York: Oxford University Press, 1997), 10. Anne Firor Scott, *The Southern Lady: From Pedestal to Politics, 1830–1930* (Charlottesville: University of Virginia Press, 1970) notes that biographies of hundreds of women show the same progression: missionary society, temperance society, and woman's club. See also Joan Marie Johnson, *Southern Ladies, New Women: Race, Region, and Clubwomen in South Carolina, 1890–1930* (Gainesville: University Press of Florida, 2004), 130; Karen L. Cox, *Dixie's Daughters: The United Daughters of the Confederacy and the Preservation of Confederate Culture* (Gainesville: University Press of Florida, 2003), 1.

17. Scott, *Southern Lady*, 153; *Annual Report of the Ladies' Reading Club of Houston*, 1885–86 (quotations), box 119, Looscan Papers, SJMH. The Ladies Literary Club of Spartanburg, South Carolina, had formed in 1884 for a similar purpose.

18. Betty T. Chapman quoted in Marguerite Johnston, *Houston: The Unknown City, 1836–1946* (College Station: Texas A&M University Press, 1991), 95; Welter, *Dimity Convictions*, 41; Adele Looscan quoted in "The Ladies' Reading Club," *Houston Chronicle*, May 19, 1997.

19. Adele B. Looscan, "Address of the President," speech before the Ladies' Reading Club of Houston, April 2, 1886 (quotation), box 117, Looscan Papers, SJMH; Barbara Welter, "The Cult of True Womanhood: 1820–1860," *American Quarterly* 18 (Summer 1966): 151–74.

20. "The Ladies' Reading Club," *Houston Chronicle*, May 19, 1997; "Club Women Sponsor Library 29 Years Ago; Federation Is Formed," *Houston Post-Dispatch*, March 25, 1928; Johnson, *Southern Ladies, New Women*, 139; "Address of Mrs. M. Looscan to the Ladies' Reading Club on Its 10th Anniversary, April 1895" (quotation), box 120, Looscan Papers, SJMH.

21. Johnson, *Southern Ladies, New Women*, 130.

22. "Club Women Sponsor Library 29 Years Ago; Federation Is Formed," *Houston Post-Dispatch*, March 25, 1928.

23. Nancy Baker Jones, "Perry, Hally Ballinger Bryan," *Handbook of Texas Online*, http://www.tshaonline.org/handbook/online/articles/fpe41 (accessed August 29, 2011); Turner, *Women, Culture, and Community*, 158. A chapter on Betty Ballinger and women's clubs, including the DRT, can be found in Turner, *Women, Culture, and Community*, 169–74.

24. See Birney Mark Fish, "Mary Jones: Last First Lady of the Republic of Texas" (PhD diss., University of North Texas, 2011).

25. Betty Ballinger quoted in Elizabeth Hayes Turner, "Ballinger, Betty Eve," *Handbook of Texas Online*, http://www.tshaonline.org/handbook/online/articles/fba51 (accessed November 7, 2010).

26. Anna Ehinger to Adele B. Looscan, December 1, 1892 (first quotation), box 99, Looscan Papers, SJMH; Nettie Houston Bringhurst to Adele B. Looscan, December 26, 1892 (second quotation), box 97, Looscan Papers, SJMH.

27. Adina De Zavala to Adele B. Looscan, February 6, 1893, box 99, Looscan Papers, SJMH.

28. Andrew Forest Muir, "San Jacinto Battleground State Historical Park," *Handbook of Texas Online*, http://www.tshaonline.org/handbook/online/articles/gks04 (accessed August 29, 2011).

29. Mrs. J. R. Fenn, "Chapter Report," in *Proceedings of the Second Annual Meeting of the Daughters of the Republic of Texas, Held at Houston, Texas, April 20 and 21, 1893*, 5, in Jan DeVault, comp., *The Ladies and the Battlefield: A Partial Chronology of the Efforts of the San Jacinto Chapter, Daughters of the Republic of Texas to Save and Preserve the San Jacinto Battlefield—1891 to 1899* (San Jacinto: San Jacinto Chapter, DRT, 1999), n.p.

30. Sara Hartman to Adele B. Looscan, August 20, 1894, box 100, Looscan Papers, SJMH.

31. Dora Fowler Arthur to Adele Looscan, March 23, 1893 (first quotation), October 27, 1896 (second quotation), box 97, ibid.

32. William G. Scarff to Adele B. Looscan, January 5, 1894–March 14, 1896, Correspondence, box 102, ibid.

33. See Julie Des Jardins, *Women and the Historical Enterprise in America: Gender, Race, and the Politics of Memory, 1880–1945* (Chapel Hill: University of North Carolina Press, 2003), 4, 20.

34. Dora Fowler Arthur to Adele B. Looscan, March 4, 1897, box 97, Looscan Papers, SJMH.

35. Ibid., March 9, 1897 (first quotation); George P. Garrison to Adele B. Looscan, December 21, 1897 (second quotation), box 100, Looscan Papers, SJMH; Mary Jane Briscoe, Journal, February 2, 1890 (third quotation), box 135, Briscoe Papers.

36. L. W. Kemp, "Texas Veterans Association," *Handbook of Texas Online*, http://www.tshaonline.org/handbook/online/articles/vot01 (accessed January 23, 2011); Richard R. Flores, "Private Visions, Public Culture: The Making of the Alamo," *Cultural Anthropology* 10 (February 1995): 99.

37. Susan Prendergast Schoelwer, "San Antonio de Valero Mission," *Handbook of Texas Online*, http://www.tshaonline.org/handbook/online/articles/uqs08 (accessed August 30, 2011).

38. Adele B. Looscan, "A History of the Purchase of the Alamo Mission by the State of Texas," manuscript, n.d., box 119, Looscan Papers, SJMH; L. Robert Ables, "The Second Battle for the Alamo," *Southwestern Historical Quarterly* 70 (January 1967): 378; Adina De Zavala, "An Appeal to the Members of the Senate and House of the Called Session of the 33rd Legislature," quoted in Adele Briscoe Looscan and Jessie Briscoe Howe, "A Correct Statement of the Intention and Purpose of the State in Buying the Alamo Mission Property at San Antonio," pamphlet, 1913 (quotation), box 128, Looscan Papers, SJMH.

39. De Zavala, "Appeal," quoted in Looscan and Howe, "Correct Statement."

40. Charlie Eckhardt, "The Second Battle of the Alamo," *Texas Escapes Online Magazine*, September 4, 2007 (accessed November 16, 2010); Adele B. Looscan quoted in Ables, "Second Battle of the Alamo," 383.

41. Eckhardt, "Second Battle of the Alamo."

42. Adele B. Looscan to O. B. Colquitt, July 3, 1911 (quotation), box 98, Looscan Papers, SJMH. See also Gregg Cantrell, "The Bones of Stephen F. Austin: History and Memory in Progressive-Era Texas," in *Lone Star Pasts*, ed. Cantrell and Turner, 39–68.

43. Adele B. Looscan to Mrs. J. J. McKeever, June 22, 1907, box 101, Looscan Papers, SJMH.

44. *San Antonio Light*, February 11, 1908, quoted in Ables, "Second Battle of the Alamo," 404.

45. Adele B. Looscan to Mrs. Huber, July 22, 1908, box 108, Looscan Papers, SJMH.

46. Adele B. Looscan to Gamaliel Bradford, June 24, 1918, box 108, Looscan Papers, SJMH; Mabel T. R. Washburn to Adele B. Looscan, March 19, 1923, box 1, Looscan Papers, Houston Metropolitan Research Center.

47. Richard B. McCaslin, *At the Heart of Texas: One Hundred Years of the Texas State Historical Association, 1897–1997* (Austin: Texas State Historical Association, 2007), 64–65.

48. Des Jardins, *Women and the Historical Enterprise*, 4.

49. Dudley G. Wooten to George P. Garrison, February 16, 1897 (quotation), General Correspondence, 1897–1926, Texas State Historical Association Records (hereafter cited as TSHA-GC), Dolph Briscoe Center for American History, University of Texas at Austin; McCaslin, *At the Heart of Texas*, 26, 19, 39.

50. Adele B. Looscan to George P. Garrison, December 25, 1897, May 11, December 6, 1898, all in TSHA-GC.

51. Adele B. Looscan to Charles W. Ramsdell, February 11, 1917, in ibid.

52. Emma Toedleberg to Adele L. B. Looscan, February 28, 1917, Adele B. Looscan to Charles W. Ramsdell, November 23, 1918 (quotations), both in ibid.

53. H. Y. Benedict to Adele B. Looscan, August 10, 1920, box 97, Looscan Papers, SJMH.

54. Ibid.; Adele B. Looscan to Hally Ballinger Bryan Perry, November 15, December 13, 1920, Perry (Hally Ballinger Bryan) Papers, Briscoe Center for American History; Alex Dienst to Adele B. Looscan, October 21, 1920 (first quotation), December 6, 1921 (second quotation), box 99, Looscan Papers, SJMH; Adele B. Looscan to Charles W. Ramsdell, February 27, 1918, TSHA-GC.

55. Adele B. Looscan to Charles W. Ramsdell, February 27, March 9, 1918 (quotation), TSHA-GC.

56. Charles W. Ramsdell to Adele B. Looscan, April 16, 1918, in ibid.; Eugene C. Barker to Adele B. Looscan, February 25, 1920 (quotation), box 1, Looscan Papers, Houston Metropolitan Research Center.

57. Adele B. Looscan to Charles W. Ramsdell, June 17, 1923, TSHA-GC.

58. Thomas P. Martin to Adele B. Looscan, October 7, 1924, March 23, 1925 (quotation), Adele B. Looscan to Thomas P. Martin, n.d., November 13, 1924, all in ibid.

59. Andrea Kökény, "The Construction of Anglo-American Identity in the Republic of Texas, as Reflected in the 'Telegraph and Texas Register,'" *Journal of the Southwest* 46 (Summer 2004): 298; Adele B. Looscan, "President's Address," *Annual Reports of the Ladies' Reading Club of Houston, Texas* (Houston: Gray's, 1890), 13–14 (first quotation), box 117, Looscan Papers, SJMH; Adelia A. Dunovant, "Study of History," *Proceedings of the Fourth Annual Convention* (n.p.: United Daughters of the Confederacy, Texas Division, 1900), 1–5 (second quotation), box 118, Looscan Papers, SJMH. Francesca Morgan comments on the differences among southern clubwomen in *Women and Patriotism in Jim Crow America* (Chapel Hill: University of North Carolina Press, 2005), 30–31. See also Cox, *Dixie's Daughters*, 65.

60. Carl N. Degler, *At Odds: Women and the Family in America from the Revolution to the Present* (New York: Oxford University Press, 1980), 28; Looscan, "President's Address," 15 (quotation).

61. Paula Baker, "The Domestication of Politics: Women and American Political Society, 1780–1920," *American Historical Review* 89 (June 1984): 620–47.

Ellen Lawson Dabbs

Waving the Equal Rights Banner

RUTH HOSEY KARBACH

❀ ❀ ❀

On December 1, 1886, a determined Ellen Lawson Dabbs and her four young daughters boarded the train from St. Louis to return to Sulphur Springs, Texas. She knew her intent to divorce Joseph Wilkes Dabbs would significantly change her life and the lives of her daughters. She was aware that her unconventional decision to study medicine as a single parent with four children would alter her life, but she could not have envisioned her own transformation into a political activist, a Populist, and an early leader in the women's rights movement in Texas.[1]

Family, education, religion, and southern culture were powerful shapers of this independent woman born on the Texas frontier in the decade before the Civil War. Her family's liberal interpretation of gender roles empowered her, and new opportunities for educated women during Reconstruction facilitated her entry into the teaching profession. After the failure of her marriage, Methodist churchwomen involved her in the temperance campaign and spurred her earnest fervor for reform. Central to her identity was her heritage as an elite woman descended from generations of southern planters.[2]

When Dabbs eventually became a political editor and speaker for the Farmers' Alliance and People's Party, she advocated in support of women's rights and social reform and served as a delegate to national Populist conventions. By the mid-1890s, she numbered among the founders of the Texas Equal Rights Association and Texas Woman's Press Association and originated and presided over the Woman's Council of Texas. From 1896 to 1901, Dabbs campaigned for the creation of a state vocational college for women. In Texas, she advanced the acceptance of women physicians by integrating the male medical domain, and in 1898, she served in an army hospital during the Spanish-American War.

Mary Ellen Lawson was born April 25, 1853, to Henry Lawson and Amanda Brown Lawson on a plantation in the piney woods of Rusk County, southeast of Dallas between Tyler and Nacogdoches. Her parents, along with her paternal grandparents, had moved from Georgia to Alabama and finally to Texas just before statehood in their quest for fertile, inexpensive cotton land. Within fifteen years, the elite Lawson family owned forty-two slaves and 2,490 acres. Their ancestors included settlers of Virginia and North Carolina. Henry Lawson's able 1852–53 term as a Democrat in the Texas House of Representatives added to the family's prestige.[3]

The only girl in a family of eight children, Ellen was her father's "constant companion." Competition with her brothers motivated the intelligent girl to excel, and her participation in activities usually reserved for males made her venturesome and assertive. Ellen's mother adjusted well to life on a frontier plantation despite her privileged upbringing. She provided moral and religious training to her daughter, supplemented by camp meetings held by Methodist circuit preachers. Amanda Lawson instructed Ellen, along with the three house servants, in nursing and household skills. Ellen's atypical family life in a frontier society with its fluid definition of woman's place blurred the lines between the antebellum separate spheres of women and men.[4]

On March 1, 1862, forty-year-old Henry Lawson enlisted in the Seventeenth Texas Cavalry of the Confederate Army. Amanda Lawson operated the plantation until her husband was discharged because of his age. During wartime, Ellen Lawson attended a country school, where she was educated in southern values along with grammar school subjects. With Confederate defeat in 1865, the traditions and principles of the Lost Cause were passed on to her by her elders; she, in turn, passed them along to her children through her membership in the United Daughters of the Confederacy, organized to preserve and glorify the South's history.[5]

During Reconstruction, fourteen-year-old Ellen was sent to the highly regarded Looney's School in Upshur County. Teachers sat on a platform at the front of the classroom, in which girls and boys were separated by a partition. Ellen was a top student in ancient languages and higher mathematics and soon was teaching other students. For her advanced education, she studied at Furlow Masonic Female College at Americus, Georgia. Art, music, and the natural sciences supplemented the standard academic curriculum. In 1872, Ellen, the class valedictorian, received her mistress of arts degree, the equivalent of an associate degree. With more education than most Texas girls, she matured into an assured "gentlewoman who radiated culture and refinement" in a male-dominated society. She supported herself by teaching science and music at

ELLEN LAWSON DABBS, CA. 1880S

From Frances E. Willard and Mary A. Livermore, eds., *American Women: Fifteen Hundred Biographies* (New York: Mast, Crowell, and Kirkpatrick, 1897).

Melrose Academy, in Nacogdoches County. Her five-year career as a teacher and her mother's appointment as the first postmistress of Lawsonville in 1877 exemplified the expanded role of elite women in the postbellum South.[6]

In 1876, at the seaport of Galveston, the accomplished Ellen Lawson met Joseph Dabbs, an East Texas banker and merchant. Dabbs, a widower with four sons, lived in Sulphur Springs, in Hopkins County. After a one-year courtship, they married on March 17, 1877, with Mordecai Yell, a founder of Methodism in Texas, officiating at the ceremony. Twenty-three-year-old Ellen Dabbs assumed the care of stepsons William, eighteen; Joe, seventeen; Claude, thirteen; and Lee, eleven. The following December, the couple's first daughter, Christmas Ellen Dabbs, was born, but she died nine months later. Three more girls were born in Sulphur Springs: Junia Wilkes in 1879, Mary Malvin in 1881, and Henry Lawson, her grandfather's namesake, in 1884. In addition to her home duties, Ellen Dabbs clerked in the family's mercantile business in Sulphur Springs and helped the family prosper financially. Her three surviving stepsons operated stores in Black Jack and Farmersville. In March 1885, Joseph Dabbs protected the family businesses by placing them in the hands of his sons and moved his second family to St. Louis.[7]

To Ellen, the contrast between Sulphur Springs and St. Louis could not have been greater. The Texas town had twenty-five hundred citizens who were proud of their electric lights, waterworks, and sewer system. St. Louis, an industrial and manufacturing center with a population of five hundred thousand, was a city of culture, with impressive buildings, parks, a public library, and an art museum. In comparison to the Texas town's one academy and no hospital, St. Louis boasted thirty-two colleges and academies and twenty hospitals. The city's religious women promoted and managed homes for dependent women and children and schools for poor children. In her new home, Ellen Dabbs was exposed to woman suffrage advocates, including Virginia Minor, who tested women's right to vote in 1872 in the Missouri courts. Although the Missouri Woman's Christian Temperance Union (WCTU) petitioned for a woman suffrage amendment in 1885, the St. Louis temperance group faced strong opposition from influential owners of breweries and the city's large German population.

Soon after the family arrived in St. Louis, Ellen Dabbs again became pregnant, and Lady Louise was born in February 1886. The urban environment provided new opportunities for the young wife and mother to thrive. The Dabbs family resided in a well-to-do neighborhood, and Ellen, a regular churchgoer, could walk or ride the trolley to the Central Methodist Church, whose minister, Cyrus Felton, championed the cause of woman suffrage. When home and church duties allowed, Ellen enjoyed plays and exhibits and pursued her literary and scientific interests.[8]

By 1886, the field of medicine dominated Ellen's interests. The family physician, Benjamin Hypes, who lectured on modern obstetrics, became a friend, and in the spring, Ellen Dabbs attended events at the St. Louis convention of the American Medical Association. St. Louis's male physicians resisted admitting women to their medical society and banned them from medical schools, even though women had practiced in the city for two decades. Despite these obstacles, thirty-three-year-old Ellen Dabbs resolved to end her unsatisfactory marriage and pursue a medical career.[9]

While Ellen Dabbs's exposure to progressive ideas and pursuit of her interests tested her marriage, the couple's relationship may have been weak from the outset, given the social and cultural divide between them. Joseph Dabbs, a Virginia native two decades older than his wife, adhered to antebellum southern social prescriptions for proper conduct and expected a reserved, compliant spouse devoted to his comfort and welfare. From the second year of their marriage, he questioned Ellen closely about her public excursions without his supervision and suspected her of loose behavior with other men. Ellen Dabbs expected more freedom and challenged her husband's old-fashioned ideas of ladylike conduct. The couple's relationship was further strained by the qualities that made Ellen an excellent choice for a merchant's wife and mother of his sons. A well-educated, articulate woman with a teaching career before marriage was quite different from the idealized antebellum lady confined to the domestic sphere. The couple's different class backgrounds likely fueled her husband's insecurity. While Ellen came from an elite family with large slave- and landholdings, Joseph was from a family with a small farm and no slaves, and he had begun his business career as a traveling tobacco salesman.[10]

Their strained marriage gave way when Ellen Dabbs, who had given birth to five children in seven years, chose not to have more children. Joseph Dabbs strenuously objected to his wife's decision to limit their family through abstinence. The couple's clash reflected an ongoing concern of Victorian women, who faced a significant chance of death during childbirth as well as the emotional and physical stresses of frequent pregnancies. As Ellen undoubtedly knew, voluntary motherhood through abstinence was the only alternative acceptable for a respectable woman. Advocates of birth control included in their ranks suffragists and moral reformers; however, devices to prevent pregnancy remained unpopular because of the fear of female promiscuity. Birth control paraphernalia, labeled as obscene material by the Comstock Law of 1873, could not be distributed through federal mail and were therefore unobtainable for women in rural areas. The majority of physicians adhered to the social values of the period, including the Dabbs family's physician, who stated in a deposition that he had never prescribed a birth control device for any woman.[11]

When Ellen moved into a separate bedroom and refused to have sexual relations with her husband, he responded by physically abusing her. During the couple's divorce case, Joseph denied using violence against his wife and explained one instance away as playful behavior. Testimony by the family's resident sewing woman contradicted his account and described a life-threatening assault, with seven-year-old Junia attempting to intervene. Protection of American women from spousal abuse was in its infancy and faltered for decades because of society's support of supremacy of the patriarch in the family. Ellen Dabbs's maid trivialized the injurious assault by calling it a "tussle," and the family's housekeeper, evasive about the violent incidents, volunteered that her mistress did not show the proper respect toward her husband.[12]

This last assault precipitated Ellen's move to Sulphur Springs. She immediately filed for divorce on the grounds of cruelty. Her two living brothers, an attorney and a medical student, sold their inherited sections of the family farm for a token amount to their sister to produce long-term income for her and her daughters. Though the brothers supported the divorce, they questioned Ellen's plan to become a physician. Undeterred, she pursued her study of medicine with Dr. Edwin Becton, a recent president of the Texas Medical Association.[13]

The divorce proceedings revealed Texas's unusual family code, which combined elements of Spanish law with practices long embedded in southern patriarchal culture. Because of the disputed disposition of the Dabbs family property, Ellen Dabbs's three stepsons as well as her husband were cited in the suit to reverse the sale of the family's East Texas mercantile businesses and landholdings. Unlike southern and eastern states, Texas property amassed during the marriage was designated community property and subject to equal division upon divorce. Under Texas law, a husband managed and controlled community property during marriage, but he could not sell it without his wife's consent or defraud her of her rights. The Dabbs properties in dispute were valued at $55,000 (equivalent to roughly $1.5 million today). Joseph Dabbs claimed that he had sold his interest in the mercantile business to his three sons. Among his extensive landholdings, two properties had been acquired during his marriage to Ellen. The stepsons contended that money given to them by their father and the family stores were inherited through their deceased mother, a questionable legal argument given Ellen's contributions to the business.[14]

Ellen Dabbs sought custody of the couple's four daughters and alimony to support them during the divorce proceedings. Joseph Dabbs countered that she was an unfit mother. Because American courts regarded unproven charges of adultery as a serious attack on the sensibilities of a refined wife, the custody battle in the Dabbs case was based on Ellen's alleged "over familiarity" with men. Without proof, however, the court granted custody of the Dabbs girls to their mother and ordered Joseph to pay fifty dollars per month in child support.[15]

Armed with one year of credit toward a medical degree from her study with Becton, Ellen Dabbs applied for admission to out-of-state medical schools since no Texas medical college admitted women. After several rejections by southern schools because of her gender, she was accepted at the coeducational College for Physicians and Surgeons in Iowa. In the fall of 1888, she moved with her daughters, then aged two through nine, to Keokuk to complete the remaining two years required for a medical degree.[16]

When the College for Physicians and Surgeons temporarily closed in 1889 for reorganization, Ellen Dabbs enrolled at the coeducational Newland School of Midwifery in St. Louis. All of her teachers there were male physicians, but the school's Lying In Institute provided her with practical experience in child delivery. In effect, she arranged an internship to overcome the lack of hospitals open to women doctors. Dabbs graduated from Newland on June 1, 1889, resumed her studies in Keokuk, and received her medical degree on February 26, 1890.[17]

Dabbs chose to establish her first medical practice in Dallas, the most populous city in Texas. In March 1890, she moved there with her daughters and placed a newspaper ad listing her specialty in women's diseases. The male physician-editor of the *Medical Courier*, published in Dallas, described Dabbs as highly intelligent, but the transplanted southern merchants and their wives who comprised the city's large middle class were reluctant to patronize women physicians. One woman doctor left the city after sixteen months, and less than 1 percent of Dallas physicians were women, the lowest rate of any major Texas city.[18]

Just as she faced several lean years while establishing a practice, Ellen Dabbs learned that she would not receive a divorce or any financial settlement. Her husband had manipulated the legal system in Hopkins County to avoid splitting their community property. On the first day of the spring session of district court in Sulphur Springs, Judge Edward Terhune dismissed the Dabbs divorce case because of the nonappearance of the plaintiff, Ellen Dabbs; however, she did not know the hearing had been scheduled. Joseph Dabbs and his sons had essentially bribed the poorly paid Sulphur Springs sheriff and district clerk not to notify her of the hearing.[19]

These machinations did much more than deprive Dabbs of a divorce. She had no legal recourse concerning division of community property, had to pay all court costs for the three-year divorce case, and could not use the funds from the anticipated property division to help secure her new medical practice and benefit her children. If Joseph Dabbs chose not to provide financial support for his daughters, his estranged wife could not petition a Texas court for redress because she had deserted her husband, who continued to live in St. Louis. Without a husband present or a divorce decree in hand, she resorted to representing herself as a widow to conduct business and protect her professional reputation.

By the summer of 1890, Ellen Dabbs was a single working mother, an unusual identity for someone of her class. Rather than retreating from public notice, however, Dabbs returned home to live among friends and family and embraced a radical set of political reform issues. She resumed residence at the Sulphur Springs homestead, hired a housekeeper to care for her daughters, and offered her medical services to people who knew her well. Though the only woman physician in Sulphur Springs, she had a reputation as a leader among Methodist women; was endorsed by her respected mentor, Dr. Becton; and took an active role in the temperance movement. Before her departure for medical school, she had joined local churchwomen in the 1887 campaign for a state Prohibition amendment. She later reflected that the amendment's defeat was "the best education ever accorded Texas women," who had previously been "ignorant, careless, indifferent as to the ballot." Ellen Dabbs and WCTU members across Texas woke up to the fact that Prohibition would never become law in the state unless women received the right to vote.[20]

The inequitable results of the Dabbs divorce case, particularly the disinheritance of her daughters in favor of their brothers, spurred Ellen Dabbs to battle for equality for women. Her evolution as a radical was typical of the small number of women who pursued women's rights in Texas during the 1890s. After her initial political experience in the WCTU, she polished her writing, speaking, and leadership skills through the Farmers' Alliance, graduated into a prominent role in the Texas Populist Party, and emerged as an early leader in the state's women's movement. The energetic Ellen Dabbs participated in political and women's organizations and practiced medicine while caring for her daughters with the help of housekeepers and boarding academies.

Each of her major causes deserves careful investigation, but her partisan political activism required some complex concessions for a woman with a reforming bent. Her first step beyond the WCTU was membership in the Hopkins County Farmers' Alliance. The alliance movement grew out of the economics of the crop lien system, predominant in the financially devastated postbellum South, and the breakup of large plantations. Through the Dabbses' business, Ellen had direct experience with credit extension to farmers based on future crop production, and she saw farm families lose their livelihoods through foreclosures during droughts and financial depression. She observed how sharecroppers and small landholders suffered as a consequence of usurious loan fees, large profit margins for merchants and millers, exorbitant transportation prices, and monetary inflation, and she personally felt the impact of these practices on her Rusk County farm property. Disillusioned and indebted members of the Farmers' Alliance attempted to create cooperatives to lower the cost of supplies and set up gins and mills to cut out the middlemen. By the 1890s, the Farmers' Alliance had moved into the political arena and proposed radical reforms, including public ownership of railroads, bank regulation, a bimetallic standard instead of gold, and a progressive income tax. These proposals struck back at merchants, bankers, and investors who profited from the labor of others but who tightly controlled wealth—in other words, the members of the moneyed class represented by Joseph Dabbs and his sons, who had deprived Ellen Dabbs and her daughters of a share of the family's holdings.[21]

The Texas Farmers' Alliance welcomed ministers and physicians as members and attracted suffragists because women had voting privileges at meetings and held elective offices in the organization. The Texas Alliance opposed gender and class inequities in principle, if not always in fact. Certainly not all members favored woman suffrage, but the alliance offered opportunities to suffragists.[22]

By June 1891, Ellen Dabbs moved into a more active and visible position in the Farmers' Alliance as co-owner and editor of the *Alliance Vindicator*, a Sulphur Springs–based farm and labor reform newspaper with a circulation of fifteen thousand across the South. Her June 13, 1891, article, quoted in the *National Economist*, urged young women readers "to think, to study, to read to keep ready" for suffrage and participation in the alliance. She aimed for an educated electorate of women to reform the political, economic, and social systems.[23]

Once Dabbs advanced into a position of influence in People's Party circles, her life was shaped by the trajectory of those organizations. That is, alliance and Populist events, rather than marriage and childbearing, determined much of the course of her life for the next several years. Indeed, the violent death of *Alliance Vindicator* editor Everett Moore precipitated Dabbs's sale of her interest in the newspaper and relocation with her daughters to Fort Worth in November 1891. Moore and E. M. Tate of the *Hopkins County Echo* had an ongoing argument over the alliance proposal that the government issue paper currency on a per capita basis. A fistfight between the men in downtown Sulphur Springs erupted into a shootout at close range. Tate was charged but never convicted of killing Moore, who suffered five gunshot wounds. Moore's funeral was attended by outraged alliance members from across the state.[24]

The move to Fort Worth placed Dabbs in direct contact with alliance radicals Stump Ashby, William Lamb, and Thomas Gaines, who spearheaded formation of the new Texas People's Party. Shortly after her arrival in the city, Dabbs took over as editor of the *Industrial Educator* and shared a newspaper office with Lamb. When Gaines set up the *Fort Worth Advance*, Dabbs promptly accepted the editorship of that Populist publication. Fort Worth resident Judge Thomas Nugent, who ran for Texas governor twice on the People's Party ticket, encouraged Dabbs in her work to politicize labor union members as bloc voters for the Populist Party.[25]

In February 1892, the Texas People's Party convention elected Dabbs and Bettie Gay, a successful farmer and women's rights activist, as delegates to the National Industrial Conference in St. Louis. An estimated eight hundred delegates from twenty-two organizations, including the Knights of Labor, the wctu, and the Farmers' Alliance, traveled to St. Louis to form a third national political party. Annie Diggs of the National Reform Press Association wrote that Dabbs "could bear her part in public discussion of a controverted question with the most practiced and ready Southern Brethren."[26]

Given her reputation for following difficult points of policy, it is not surprising that Dabbs was appointed to the committee on platforms and resolutions. Here and in later moments in her political career, Dabbs had to prioritize her reform agenda, including the more controversial issue of woman suffrage. Frances Willard, president of the wctu, submitted a platform committee minority report supporting universal suffrage and Prohibition planks, which Dabbs and Everett Fish, a radical Minnesota publisher, endorsed. The Populist leaders, however, tabled the report and thereby prevented the party platform from including planks representing those issues most important to women in the alliance and the wctu—suffrage and Prohibition. Although the two organizations together had membership totaling 410,000 women, few women could vote in national elections. The leaders of the new national third party needed to lure possible voters from the two established parties, and they worried that woman suffrage and Prohibition alienated potential male voters from both the left and the right.[27]

Party leaders' political calculations eventually convinced Dabbs as well. When she took the stage at the Texas People's Party presidential convention in June 1892, she declared it a historic moment—the first time a woman had appeared as a speaker at a Texas political convention. In a turnaround, however, she pledged to support the St. Louis platform at the upcoming national People's Party convention in Omaha and planned to dissuade suffragists from pressing their plank during the convention. Susan B. Anthony, who attended the Omaha convention but was blocked from addressing the platform committee about a suffrage plank, wrote in her diary, "They are quite as oblivious of the underlying principle of justice to women as either of the old parties and, as a convention, still more so."[28]

Dabbs's sacrifice of woman suffrage to party politics reflected party leaders' fears that the issue could split the ranks and doom the fledgling party in its first national outing. Though there was support for votes for women in the Southwest and the West, the issue created strife in the South. Populists vigorously debated suffrage for women in Texas, which contained both southwestern and southern cultural regions. Dabbs may have been influenced by Mary Lease's contention that the economic liberation of women should precede the vote. This argument, supported by many Populists, resonated with Dabbs, who no longer could rely on a "patriarch" for financial support of her and her children.[29]

Despite her 1892 concession to the party majority's views on suffrage, Dabbs often spoke about unequal treatment of women and made a case for woman suffrage. She asserted that the nation's ills evolved from a flawed foundation that reserved political power for men and made women "subservient to unjust laws, obedient to cruelty, voiceless under wrongs," and "controlled by every self-appointed czar." Her marriage and divorce case clearly inspired her rhetoric. Peppered with medical analogies and references to motherhood and the elevated nature of woman, her speeches rang with the conviction that votes in the hands of women would clean up government and ameliorate social problems.[30]

Moreover, Dabbs believed that achieving reform through a voting bloc of African American and white women was more important than confining political power to elite white women. She argued that enfranchisement of African American women was necessary to defeat anti-Prohibition forces. A firm believer in white supremacy, Dabbs expressed outrage at privileges granted to African Americans that were not afforded to white women. She departed from the majority of her southern sisters, however, by advocating votes for African American women, whom she asserted were morally superior to enfranchised African American men. Thus, Dabbs's opinion was more moderate than that of many others in the South, where woman suffrage leaders often maintained that enfranchising white women provided a solution to the "Negro problem" by counteracting votes in the hands of African American men and where some activists advocated giving the franchise only to educated white women.[31]

By the 1896 presidential election, conservatism dominated the country, and perceived threats to established gender roles and public order affected the growth and in some cases survival of liberal organizations. President Grover Cleveland, a Democrat, was blamed for the financial crisis of 1893 and the ensuing deep depression, which featured a staggering 20 percent unemployment rate. In the 1896 presidential race, Republicans fanned public fears by portraying labor unionists and Populist farmers as anarchists, suffragists as shrews, and government regulation of industry and business as tyrannical. Unable to break the two-party system, Populists threw their support to 1896 Democratic presidential candidate William Jennings Bryan. This fusion of Populists and Democrats, the adoption of the free silver plank by the Democratic Party, and a split in the Populist ranks signaled the dying gasp of the People's Party. Republican candidate William McKinley was elected, and though the Populists survived in truncated form in Texas until after the turn of the twentieth century, the political landscape for Dabbs had changed.[32]

During the 1880s and 1890s, when the People's Party rose and fell, activist women considered reform their moral domain. Based on a religious foundation, these reform efforts eventually turned toward secular clubs and to the cause of woman suffrage. Willard's speaking tours in the South in 1881 and 1882 called on Protestant churchwomen to form unions. Unlike the resistance Willard faced in some cities elsewhere in the South, she had a substantial audience at the largest Methodist church in Fort Worth and received praise for her address in the *Daily Democrat*. The Fort Worth WCTU tackled the social ills bred by saloons, gambling dens, and houses of prostitution in Hell's Half Acre, the city's red-light district. With the group's backing, Presbyterians Belle Burchill and Delia Collins established the Benevolent Home for Children in 1887. Four years later, the group lobbied to raise the age of consent for girls from ten years and met success, though limited, with the passage of a state law setting the age limit for statutory rape at twelve. Helen M. Stoddard, a Fort Worth University professor elected the new president of the Texas WCTU in the spring of 1891, quickly achieved prominence in the national organization and secured passage of several laws sponsored by the Texas WCTU. Burchill and Collins were natives of New York, and Stoddard was reared in Wisconsin; all were educated as teachers in New York state. They espoused woman suffrage earlier than their Texas-born sisters. Ellen Dabbs eagerly joined these leaders of the Fort Worth WCTU and served as the physician for the Industrial Home for Women, founded by Collins in February 1892 to reform prostitutes and assist unwed mothers. Stoddard and Dabbs had much in common as single parents, professional women, and Methodists. Just a half year into her membership in the Fort Worth WCTU, Dabbs was chosen as a delegate to the organization's 1892 statewide convention.[33]

On May 10, 1893, Dabbs and a small band of literary women and suffragists founded the Texas Woman's Press Association (TWPA) and the Texas Equal Rights Association (TERA). Both associations helped her widen her network of professional women and establish new relationships among and beyond the WCTU and Farmers' Alliance. Belle Smith, a Dallas literary clubwoman and state fair superintendent of the arts, assumed the presidency of the TWPA and became an important ally. Aurelia Mohl, a veteran journalist, served as a mentor to both TWPA and TERA members. Debate and exchange of ideas at TWPA conventions stimulated its members to publicize women's causes and the work of new women's associations ranging from the United Daughters of the Confederacy to the TERA.[34]

The founding of Texas's first woman suffrage association was initiated by the officers of the National American Woman Suffrage Association (NAWSA), who chose Rebecca Henry Hayes of Galveston to be their representative. Less than a year after Dabbs had endorsed a Populist Party platform that did not include suffrage, she and ten other women issued a call for women to join TERA. Forty-eight women and men signed up at the initial meeting in May 1893 and wrote a comprehensive mission statement in which they explained their goal: "To advance the industrial, educational and equal rights of women and to secure suffrage to them by appropriate State and National legislation." The suffragists elected Hayes president and selected Dabbs as corresponding secretary and a delegate to the NAWSA convention to be held at the Chicago World's Fair (also known as the World's Columbian Exposition).[35]

In May 1893, the TERA delegates, including Dabbs, attended the Congress of Representative Women at the Columbian Exposition. Susan B. Anthony, Lucy Stone, Julia Ward Howe, and Helen Gardner appeared in the midst of a crushing crowd. Anthony read a speech from Elizabeth Cady Stanton before speaking enthusiastically of women's progress during the forty years Anthony had spent working for woman suffrage. The Reverend Anna Howard Shaw, future president of NAWSA, delivered an address on "The Fate of the Republic." Shaw advocated votes for women on the basis of their unique qualities—morality, lawfulness, religiosity, and pacifism—and asserted that women voters would save the nation from decay. Other topics at the Congress included the kindergarten movement, domestic science, and women's careers. Texas women returned home armed with innovative ideas and visions of their public role through their affiliation and confederation with other women. In her address on "Changing Ideals in Southern Womanhood" at the Woman's Congress, Sue Huffman Brady of Fort Worth declared, "The new woman's day has dawned in the South-land."[36]

The establishment of a Fort Worth auxiliary of TERA demonstrated Dabbs's organizational and networking skills. On March 19, 1894, 150 people, half of them men, entered the Fort Worth Chamber of Commerce auditorium, which was lavishly decorated in patriotic red, white, and blue. After TERA's president, Rebecca Henry Hayes, initiated the meeting with an address that characterized men in the image of Satan, state organizer Sarah Trumbull tried to soothe the offended men in the audience by noting that only male politicians and the alcohol lobby opposed woman suffrage. By the time Dabbs passed out membership applications, many people had already left the auditorium.[37]

Hayes's unfortunate speech offended prospective members and antagonized some of Dabbs's labor union and Farmers' Alliance contacts. The TERA officers' support for Prohibition alienated important Fort Worth residents who profited from the sale of alcohol and other vices in Hell's Half Acre. Even Fort Worth officials raised city funds by periodic raids to collect fines paid by madams to keep their girls out of jail. Nevertheless, thirty people, including Judge Nugent and his wife, Catherine, signed up to form the Fort Worth chapter.[38]

In the spring of 1894, Ellen Dabbs was busy sending out flyers and announcements for TERA's second annual state convention, to be held in June in Fort Worth. She also wrote letters and made phone calls for the convention arrangements. She interrupted this flurry of activity in May to speak on "Wanted: Good Government" to two hundred people under the sponsorship of the Dallas TERA. Pointing to the poverty among half of all American citizens and the prevalence of saloons and prostitution, Dabbs asserted that free (unregulated) silver and tariff laws would not solve these social problems. To an appreciative audience, she proclaimed that only the "ballot in the hands of moral, educated, and refined women" could establish ethical government, institute social reform, and provide an environment in which the arts and sciences could flourish. Left unspoken but understood by her listeners was her belief that the female agents of change to whom she referred were white middle-class women. Though she linked cultured women and the vote when lecturing to urban clubwomen, her speeches to Populist audiences did not imply that social reform was the exclusive territory of educated women.[39]

If Dabbs found the politics of Populists difficult when it came to the suffrage question, she found the suffrage movement equally fraught with hard choices, as progressive activists had to decide how to appeal to a conservative public. Dabbs was a featured speaker on a favorite theme of "Municipal Housekeeping" at the June TERA convention in Fort Worth. The organization's officers split, however, over the president's directive not to press for a woman suffrage plank on the platform of any political party. Hayes attempted to keep the Texas suffrage movement out of party politics, while those affiliated with political parties wanted to press forward on gaining the vote for women. When the convention elected new officers, Dabbs was rotated off the executive board, and Hayes was reelected to the presidency. Hayes came out in opposition to Anthony's visit to Texas as part of her tour of southern states, but members of the executive committee disagreed with Hayes's view that Texas women would be unreceptive to the pioneer suffragist from the North. This debate went on publicly and privately for five months and ended when Hayes was deposed and

Elizabeth Austin Turner Fry of San Antonio elected president. The involvement of NAWSA leaders, negative publicity, and internal dissension split Texas suffragists along class and political affiliation lines as well as pitted urban members against rural ones.[40]

Still, Dabbs and the TERA had a number of triumphs. Inspired by the "Woman's Day" at the Columbian Exposition, Dabbs proposed a "Woman's Day" at the Texas State Fair to be held in October 1894. The idea grew into an even grander Woman's Congress at the fair, and Dabbs and Smith arranged a six-day program with topics similar to those featured at the Chicago Woman's Congress. Isadore Miner provided publicity via her "Woman's Century" column in the Dallas Morning News. Fry gave a talk about the role of women in the church, and Hayes lectured on women in politics. Dabbs chose the differences between the sexes as her topic and traced their origins to prevalent child rearing practices. She deplored girls being encased in tight undergarments, confined to the home, and taught to read didactic literature. Asserting that boys led a healthier, more intellectually stimulating life, she advocated a similar lifestyle and education for girls. Essentially, she argued that nurture rather than nature explained the differences between men and women, an enlightened conclusion that was decades ahead of its time.[41]

Attendance at the Woman's Congress was initially low but reached three hundred by the fourth day. The delegates approved affiliation with the National Woman's Council and chartered the Texas Woman's Council, which elected Belle Smith president and a board dominated by suffragists. The Texas Council aimed to develop and support reform and to promote education and professional careers for women. In 1894, Dabbs took over as acting president of the council. For the second congress, Dabbs and her officers focused on representing the umbrella organization as nonsectarian and nonpartisan. Participation by women's clubs and patriotic organizations significantly increased in the second year.[42]

Dabbs urged delegates to circulate petitions and write to legislators to raise the age of consent for girls to eighteen. She pointed out that a seventeen-year-old girl could not consent to marriage or hold title to land, but the law allowed a thirteen-year-old girl to agree to sexual relations. The issue engaged Texas clubwomen, suffragists, journalists, and temperance advocates, who united to protect young girls. Enflamed by exaggerated accounts of white slavery, women reformers believed that their opponents' claim that they would be falsely accused of statutory rape merely proved that men were sexual predators of pure and dispassionate women. Politically, Dabbs's ties to the Texas Farmers' Alliance, People's Party, and Knights of Labor were invaluable in gaining support for an age-of-consent bill. In 1895, Populist legislators sponsored and voted in a bloc to raise the age of consent to fifteen.[43]

Public suspicion that suffragists were using the Woman's Council to promote their cause affected attendance at the 1895 annual meeting. The officers declared that members stood on both sides of the suffrage issue and pointed to the equal voting power of each member organization. Even though fewer women participated that year, Dabbs outlined an ambitious organization of committees to work for civic improvement and educational equality for men and women.[44]

At the 1896 meeting, Dabbs was forced to scale back committee projects to public kindergartens and higher education for women since much organizational work remained incomplete. The Woman's Council was simply too diffuse for this structure to work in a state with 254 counties. The plan to revitalize the Woman's Council as the central organization for Texas women's clubs failed with the founding of the Texas Federation of Literary Clubs and its affiliation with the General Federation of Women's Clubs. The 1897 Woman's Council meeting was canceled after an outbreak of yellow fever in the coastal region of the state, a face-saving measure that marked the organization's demise.[45]

Not one to stay idle for long, Dabbs embarked on a campaign for vocational higher education for Texas women, a cause somewhat less controversial than populism or suffrage. As chair of the Southern Council of Women of Texas, she campaigned for a state-funded industrial college for young women. At the time, it was unconventional to advocate that young women be educated to earn a living rather than reared with marriage as their goal. Dabbs argued that most college graduates would and should marry, and higher education would make them better wives and mothers. Endorsement of marriage and motherhood was essential to win widespread support of vocational education for women. Dabbs's oldest daughter, however, fit the model of the independent career woman. Junia Dabbs attended Oread Institute in Massachusetts on a scholarship, worked as a domestic science teacher and dietitian, married at age thirty, and often lived apart from her husband to pursue her occupation. Practical education for economic self-sufficiency of women was a theme of the populist movement, and as a professional woman who supported her four daughters, Ellen Dabbs served as a model of this New Woman.[46]

Ellen Dabbs advocated coursework in scientific home economics, agriculture, and business skills at the woman's college. Her actions reflected the ways in which the Victorian concept of womanhood persisted and restricted the choices open to young women even as women entered occupations and professions in the twentieth century. Suggestions from Texas women produced a plan reflecting the gender stereotyping of occupations of the period. This era marked the appearance of female typists and store clerks and an increase in women schoolteachers, all low-paying jobs that men were reluctant to continue occupying.[47]

White women did not have access to public higher education in the South until the 1880s, a generation later than their northern sisters. At the turn of the century, American women enrolled in public four-year colleges comprised .2 percent of female students attending institutions of higher education; most female students attended private women's colleges. The University of Texas at Austin had been coeducational since its founding in 1883, but the liberal arts school was regarded as a college for elites. Dabbs protested that Prairie View Agricultural & Mechanical College admitted African American women as well as men, but white women had no state vocational school.[48]

Dabbs promoted Texas Agricultural & Mechanical College, a land-grant institution in Bryan, as the location for a vocational college for girls. Keenly aware of the discrimination against girls, she proclaimed, "Those [public] funds by inheritance belong as much to girls as to boys." The coeducational aspect of the A&M proposal raised controversy among Texas women, but Dabbs insisted that "it is right mentally, morally, and physically to educate the sexes together." Conservative Texas women, however, were not appeased, and though Dabbs claimed that the body of the Woman's Council had endorsed the A&M plan, the vote actually went against her proposal. Former ally Stoddard and the WCTU women proved the strongest opponents of the coeducational plan, decrying the corrupting moral influence of male cadets on innocent young women. Dabbs countered that young ladies would elevate the male students' morals.[49]

In 1899, Dabbs and her associates marshaled strong public support for a bill to create an industrial school, but the measure was referred back to committee. The Democratic Party included a girls' industrial school in its 1900 platform, leading to narrow passage of a 1901 bill. The *Fort Worth Register* backed Dabbs as a representative on the school location commission, but Stoddard was appointed, and the commission chose Denton as the site for the new college.[50]

As Dabbs endeavored to improve the lives of all Texas women, she had to work hard to keep her personal and professional life moving forward. At home, Dabbs closely monitored the progress of her daughters in public schools until their teen years, when they were sent to private female academies and allowed to visit their stepbrothers in Indian Territory and their father in St. Louis. The two older daughters attended Salem Academy in North Carolina, a Moravian school praised in the *Progressive Farmer* for its domestic science and business courses. Her younger daughters were boarding students at Mary Nash College in Sherman, Texas, a Baptist girls' school known for its music academy and innovative physical education program.[51]

Fort Worth proved a relatively congenial environment for a woman physician. Its seven railroads attracted manufacturing concerns, and a variety of businesses sent goods to supply farmers and cattlemen to the West. With the railroads came an influx of people from the northern and eastern United States and Canada, which created a vigorous cultural mix with a western mentality and progressive ideas. In contrast to Dallas, just thirty-three miles away, 8 percent of Fort Worth physicians were women, a higher rate than Chicago, New York, Philadelphia, or Los Angeles. Further, the initial class of the medical department of Fort Worth University included Daisy Emery, who in 1897 became the first woman to graduate from a Texas medical school. Dabbs's medical practice benefited from her labor union connections and her standing in the Farmers' Alliance and Populist Party.[52]

Ellen Dabbs was admitted as the only female physician in the North Texas Medical Society (NTMS), which had a membership of more than three hundred. After Dr. Joseph Fort, who was ailing and not at the convention, poked fun at the "New Woman" in a paper he authored that was read by a board member at an NTMS medical convention, the *Dallas Morning News* reported that Dabbs was "distinctly in favor of the real new woman, a different creature from that drawn by Dr. Fort." Ellen Dabbs served on the committee for obstetrics and gynecology and presented lectures at the group's biennial meetings. Her paper on early childhood diabetes anticipated by more than a century the connection between premature introduction of cereal into infants' diets and early onset of the disease. In 1893, Dabbs declined an offer to become the chair of hygiene at the new Woman's College of Medicine in St. Louis, possibly because the school espoused homeopathy and her estranged husband resided there.[53]

Dabbs's forward-thinking speech on syphilis at an 1895 NTMS convention (later published in the *Texas Courier-Record*) stirred controversy among Texas male physicians. Dabbs blamed the disease on a double standard, noting that some gentlewomen were unhappily wed to men who frequented both "church and saloon, parlor and bawdy house." Curtailing syphilis, she argued, required purity among males as well as females. Well in advance of most male physicians, Dabbs questioned the church's endorsement of the husband's control over his wife's body and asserted that the wife should have that power. Remembering the violence in her marriage, Dabbs felt strongly that a woman should be in charge of her sexuality and have the option to prevent unwanted pregnancies. Two decades later, Margaret Sanger argued that a woman should have the absolute right to birth control, but most physicians still considered any form of contraception taboo. Male medical doctors criticized social advocacy by women physicians such as Dabbs as unprofessional, a damning label in the era of professionalization of the field.[54]

In August 1898, Dabbs volunteered for medical service in the Spanish-American War. As a Populist, Dabbs was probably influenced in this decision by William Jennings Bryan's portrayal of the rebellion of the Cubans against the Spanish as a moral crusade and his criticism of Wall Street bankers who opposed the war. She was proud to continue her family's wartime service, which had begun with the American Revolution and continued through the War of 1812 and the Civil War.[55]

Rampant diseases in the military camps in the South during the summer of 1898 led to a shortage of male medical corpsmen, and Surgeon General George Sternberg appointed Dr. Anita Newcomb McGee to recruit female nurses. Though initially reluctant, male military surgeons accepted trained female nurses but adamantly rejected women serving as physicians. Dabbs and nine other women doctors consequently worked as nurses during the war. The notation "not a graduate nurse" on the records of women physicians reflected the prejudice toward them from the female nurses, who guarded their recent elevation to professional status.[56]

Ellen Dabbs requested that she be sent to care for the Texas soldiers at Camp Cuba Libre in Jacksonville, Florida. When she arrived there, the members of the medical staff were battling a high death rate from typhoid fever and allegations of inadequate medical care. A military investigative commission talked with physicians and nurses during an inspection tour of the camp's hospital on October 17, 1898. The next day, Dabbs's contract was canceled six weeks early. Officials noted in her record, "Lacks professional skills as a nurse." After her dismissal, she testified at commission hearings about the poor hygiene of and diet provided by the camp's military kitchen. Also, she contended that incompetent contract surgeons lacked knowledge of southern diseases. Though her testimony contradicted that of the military surgeons and nurses at Camp Cuba Libre, her report was supported by a military surgeon from another camp and the Jacksonville Red Cross representative. During her work at the Florida military hospital, Dabbs contracted tuberculosis.[57]

In the fall of 1899, a fire destroyed Dabbs's Fort Worth home, but no family members were injured. Dabbs retreated to her Rusk County farm and practiced medicine in the Lawsonville area. Daughter Junia followed in her grandmother's footsteps, by becoming postmistress of Lawsonville. The three younger girls attended the East Texas coeducational Summer Hill Select School, which offered business courses and teacher certification.[58]

In 1903, the family returned to Fort Worth, where Ellen Dabbs renewed her practice. She spoke locally on public school and women's health concerns through the Woman's Department Club, an affiliate of the Texas Federation of Women's Clubs, while Junia Dabbs taught domestic science courses. In 1904,

Henry and Louise Dabbs and their mother visited the St. Louis World's Fair, where the girls performed as singers and dancers. Louise continued her stage career until she married a Los Angeles stage manager in 1912. In 1905, Henry married Hearst newspaper reporter George Sesse in Chicago, and Mary Malvin married Forest Townsley, a ranger at Platt National Park in Oklahoma.[59]

Lee Dabbs provided a personal lien on his stepmother's new Fort Worth house as her finances deteriorated along with her health. In February 1906, Ellen Dabbs traded the Rusk County family farm for a home in Waurika, Indian Territory, where she would be closer to family members. She practiced medicine in Waurika and delivered her first grandchild there in March 1906.[60]

Ellen Dabbs eventually sought a healthful ranch setting on the high plains near Logan in northeastern New Mexico. In an advanced stage of tuberculosis, she faced an agonizing death by massive hemorrhaging. After saying good-bye to each of her daughters, Ellen Lawson Dabbs committed suicide on August 19, 1908, using chloroform, the agent preferred by physicians for euthanasia of terminally ill patients. Because of the fear of contagion through transportation by rail, Dabbs was buried on an unidentified ranch in Quay County, New Mexico, along with other anonymous victims of tuberculosis. No obituary appeared in newspapers, and her estate was financially distressed.[61]

All the surviving Dabbs family members migrated to the Los Angeles area. Joseph Dabbs never remarried; was cared for by his daughter, Henry; and died at age eighty-nine in 1922. His sons, Joe and Lee, a wealthy Los Angeles banker, owned valuable California real estate. Both married much younger women, and Lee's two wives divorced him. Henry and Mary Malvin divorced their husbands, for bigamy and issues concerning family limitation, respectively. Unlike her sisters, Junia had a nontraditional marriage. None of Ellen Dabbs's daughters ever received a share of Joseph Dabbs's wealth.[62]

In retrospect, Ellen Dabbs espoused causes and ideas that were decades ahead of their acceptance by the public, such as woman suffrage and a woman's right to use birth control. The organizers of the Texas Federation of Women's Clubs credited her and the Woman's Council with providing an impetus for the creation of their group. Establishment of free kindergartens accelerated in urban Texas cities with the endorsement by the Woman's Council. In her *History of Woman Suffrage*, Susan B. Anthony recognized Dabbs for establishing the Woman's Council and overseeing its progressive activities. The TWPA continues to this day under the name Press Women of Texas, and the women's vocational college that she championed is now Texas Woman's University.[63]

Ellen Dabbs challenged men to accept professional women and to rethink their assumptions about gender. She advanced the medical service of women in war and stood up for improved health care in military hospitals. Her advocacy of a woman's right to have control over her body and endorsement of nurture as an explanation for the differences between the sexes were far ahead of their time.

Ellen Dabbs displayed naïveté early in her political career, especially when she sacrificed woman suffrage to Populist Party politics and chose a confrontational, sex-laden theme for a presentation to male doctors. Yet she marshaled a coalition of political, union, temperance, and woman suffrage organizations to gain age-of-consent legislation. Though a white supremacist, she advocated giving the vote to African American women as a means of gaining passage of Prohibition. By 1897, her choice of women journalists and wives whose husbands served in the state and national legislatures as executive committee members of the Southern Council of Women of Texas during the campaign for a vocational college for women demonstrated her maturity as a political leader.

Writing a tribute to Judge Nugent, Ellen Lawson Dabbs summed up the last decade of the nineteenth century: "What a spirit of unrest, a changing of ideals, and, associated with this, a new seeking after truth and its relation to man's welfare—mentally, physically, spiritually." Her unrest in marriage, from which she escaped at great financial cost, reflected societal conflict over the proper role of women and led to her emancipation and medical career. It also brought her into the most exciting political movements of the era—the Populist Party and the drive for woman suffrage. As with most turn-of-the-century Progressives, Dabbs based her support of Prohibition on religious principles, and she engaged in the temperance movement for the welfare of all. Her experiences as a doctor reinforced her concern for humanity, but she struggled with societal proscriptions against women and fought to remove the restraints that she had experienced in her life. Thus she provided what may have been her most important contribution to Texas and American women: the model of an intelligent, hardworking woman unwilling to adopt outdated expectations and unrepentant in pursuing her goals.[64]

NOTES

1. Petition, January 13, 1887, *Ellen Dabbs v. W. Dabbs et al.*, Cause 2431, District Court, Hopkins County, Texas; refiled June 29, 1887, Cause 2458 District Clerk's Office, Hopkins County Courthouse, Sulphur Springs, Texas (hereafter cited as Cause 2458); Frances Elizabeth Willard, Mary A. Livermore, and Mary Ashton Rice Livermore, eds., *Great American Women of the Nineteenth Century* (1897; Amherst: Humanity, 2004), 242–43.

2. Drew Gilpin Faust, *Mothers of Invention: Women of the Slaveholding South in the American Civil War* (Chapel Hill: University of North Carolina Press, 1996), 3–4; Jane Turner Censer, *The Reconstruction of White Southern Womanhood, 1865–1895* (Baton Rouge: Louisiana State University Press, 2003), 9.

3. Willard, Livermore, and Livermore, *Great American Women*, 242; Joan Carnegie, great-granddaughter of Ellen Lawson Dabbs, email to author, July 23, 2010; U.S. Census, 1880, Rusk County, Texas, Agriculture Schedule and Slave Schedule, entries for H. M. Lawson and Irvin Lawson; *Nacogdoches Chronicle*, June 14, 1853.

4. *Dallas Morning News*, August 16, 1896 (quotation); Willard, Livermore, and Livermore, *Great American Women*, 242; U.S. Census, 1860, Agricultural Schedule, entry for H. M. Lawson; Elizabeth Silverthorne, *Plantation Life in Texas* (College Station: Texas A&M University Press, 1986), 50; Ann Patton Malone, *Women on the Texas Frontier: A Cross-Cultural Perspective* (El Paso: Texas Western Press, University of Texas at El Paso, 1983), 53; Anne Firor Scott, *The Southern Lady: From Pedestal to Politics, 1830–1930* (Chicago: University of Chicago Press, 1970), 4.

5. H. M. Lawson, Records of the Confederate Army, *American Civil War Records*, www.footnote.com/civilwar_page/109961857_american_civil_war_records 0 (accessed July 8, 2010); Anne Sarah Rubin, *A Shattered Nation: The Rise and Fall of the Confederacy, 1861–1868* (Chapel Hill: University of North Carolina Press, 2005), 28–29; Lloyd A. Hunter, "The Immortal Confederacy," in *The Myth of the Lost Cause and Civil War History*, ed. Gary W. Gallagher and Alan T. Nolan (Bloomington: Indiana University Press, 2000), 185; Julia Jackson Chapter Records, United Daughters of the Confederacy, Fort Worth Public Library, Fort Worth.

6. Doyal T. Loyd, *A History of Upshur County, Texas* (Gilmer: Gilmer Mirror, 1966), 16; Willard, Livermore, and Livermore, *Great American Women*, 243; Beulah Blackwell, "Pioneer Women Teachers of Nacogdoches County," in *Nacogdoches County Families*, ed. Nacogdoches County Genealogical Society (Dallas: Curtis, c. 1985), 1:13 (quotation); *Dallas Morning News*, August 16, 1896; Jim Wheat, "Postmasters and Post Offices of Texas, 1846–1930," http://www.rootsweb.ancestry.com/~txpost/postmasters.html (accessed January 2, 2010); Censer, *Reconstruction of White Southern Womanhood*, 153. Henry M. Lawson was living at the time of his wife's appointment as postmistress, during his daughter's teaching career, and when she married.

7. Willard, Livermore, and Livermore, *Great American Women*, 243; Marriage Certificate, Limestone County, Texas; Christmas Ellen Dabbs Burial, Old City Cemetery, Area 2/D, Lot 218, Sulphur Springs, Texas; Petition, Cause 2458; Dictation from W. A. Dabbs, June 23, 1887, Sulphur Springs, Hopkins County, Texas, Hubert Howe Bancroft Collection, folder 3, box 131, Bancroft Library, University of California at Berkeley; Deposition of J. W. Dabbs, Cause 2458. The masculine name *Henry* for a daughter went against the standard practice of gender-specific given names.

8. Katharine T. Corbett, editor of *In Her Place*, telephone interview by author, November 1, 2010; Petition and Deposition of J. W. Dabbs, Cause 2458.

9. Depositions of J. W. Dabbs and Benjamin Hypes, Cause 2458; Martha R. Clevenger, "From Lay Practitioner to Doctor of Medicine: Women Physicians in St. Louis, 1860–1920," *Gateway Heritage*, Winter 1987–88, 18–20.

10. Petition, Deposition, and Separate Answers of J. W. Dabbs, Cause 2458.

11. Linda Gordon, *The Moral Property of Women: A History of Birth Control Politics in America* (Chicago: University of Illinois Press, 2002), 55; Depositions of Benjamin Hypes and J. W. Dabbs, Cause 2458.

12. Petition, Deposition, and Separate Answers of J. W. Dabbs, Deposition of Bridget Daily, Deposition of Mollie Terrence (quotation), Deposition of Lucinda Ogan, all in Cause 2458; Linda Gordon, *Heroes of Their Own Lives: The Politics and History of Family Violence, Boston, 1880–1960* (New York: Viking, 1988), 3–4.

13. Petition and Application for Continuance, Cause 2458; *Dallas Morning News*, August 16, 1896; Willard, Livermore, and Livermore, *Great American Women*, 243; Pat Ireland Nixon, *A History of the Texas Medical Association, 1859–1953* (Austin: University of Texas Press, 1953), 76.

14. Angela Boswell, *Her Act and Deed: Women's Lives in a Rural Southern County, 1837–1873* (College Station: Texas A&M University Press, 2001), 21. See also Jean A. Stuntz, *Hers, His, and Theirs: Community Property Laws in Spain and Early Texas* (Lubbock: Texas Tech University Press, 2005); Kathleen Elizabeth Lazarou, "Concealed under Petticoats: Married Women's Property and the Law of Texas, 1840–1913" (PhD diss., Rice University, 2007); Stuntz, in this volume.

15. Separate Answers of J. W. Dabbs, Cause 2458 (quotation); Ocie Speer, *A Treatise on the Laws of Marital Rights in Texas* (Rochester, N.Y.: Lawyers Co-Operative, 1929), 734; Order for Alimony and Sustained Motion for Continuance of Alimony, Cause 2458.

16. Willard, Livermore, and Livermore, *Great American Women*, 243; *St. Louis Republic*, September 13, 1904; Regina Markell Morantz-Sanchez, *Sympathy and Science: Women Physicians in American Medicine* (New York: Oxford University Press, 1985), 66–67, 71; John H. Rauch, *Report on Medical Education, Medical Colleges, and the Regulation of the Practice of Medicine in the United States and Canada, 1765–1889* (Springfield, Ill.: Rokker, 1889), 60.

17. *St. Louis Post-Dispatch*, February 26, May 30, 1889; Morantz-Sanchez, *Sympathy and Science*, 164–65; *Keokuk Daily Gate City*, February 27, 1890.

18. Dallas County Physicians Register, 1877–1907, Dallas County Records, Texas and Local History Section, Dallas Public Library, Dallas; *Dallas Morning News*, March 24, 30, 1890; *Texas Courier-Record of Medicine* 7, no. 5 (1890): 256; Elizabeth York Enstam, *Women and the Creation of Urban Life: Dallas, Texas, 1843–1920* (College Station: Texas A&M University Press, 1998), 56–57; Mary Roth Walsh, *"Doctors Wanted, No Women Need Apply": Sexual Barriers in the Medical Profession, 1835–1975* (New Haven: Yale University Press, 1977), 185.

19. Walsh, *"Doctors Wanted,"* 185; Dismissal, April 7, 1890, Cause 2458; W. A. Dabbs et al., grantor, to J. W. Ferguson, grantee, May 12, 1890, 19:201, J. W. Dabbs, grantor, to J. W. Avera, grantee, by Sheriff Sale, April 15, 1890, 19:433, both in Deed Records, Hopkins County, Texas.

20. *Dallas Morning News*, May 17, 1894 (quotation).

21. Lawrence Goodwyn, *Democratic Promise: The Populist Movement in America* (New York: Oxford University Press, 1976), 177–78; Randolph B. Campbell, *Gone to Texas: A History of the Lone Star State* (New York: Oxford University Press, 2003), 324.

22. Melissa Gilbert Wiedenfeld, "Women in the Texas Farmers' Alliance" (master's thesis, Texas Tech University, 1983), 36–39. See also Julie Roy Jeffrey, "Women in the Southern Farmers' Alliance: A Reconsideration of the Role and Status of Women in the Late Nineteenth-Century South," *Feminist Studies* 3 (Autumn 1975): 72–91; Marion K. Barthelme, ed., *Women in the Texas Populist Movement: Letters to the Southern Mercury* (College Station: Texas A&M University Press, 1997).

23. Willard, Livermore, and Livermore, *Great American Women*, 243; *National Economist*, June 13, 1891 (quotation). See also Elna C. Green, *Southern Strategies: Southern Women and the Woman Suffrage Question* (Chapel Hill: University of North Carolina Press, 1997).

24. *Dallas Morning News*, November 8, September 17, October 11, 1891.

25. *Fort Worth City Directory*, 1892–93, 70, 1894–95, 69; *Dallas Morning News*, April 13, 1892; Gregg Cantrell, interview by author, July 29, 2009.

26. *Dallas Morning News*, February 23, 1892; Annie Diggs, "Women in the Alliance Movement," *Arena* 6 (July 1892): 174 (quotation).

27. *New York Times*, February 25, 1892; Goodwyn, *Democratic Promise*, 264–67; Charles Postel, *The Populist Vision* (New York: Oxford University Press, 2007), 94; Barthelme, *Women in the Texas Populist Movement*, 63; *National Economist*, March 5, 1892.

28. *Dallas Morning News*, June 24, 1892; *Omaha World Herald*, July 3, 1892; Ida Husted Harper, *Life and Work of Susan B. Anthony* (Indianapolis: Bowen-Merrill, 1898), 2:727 (quotation).

29. Goodwyn, *Democratic Promise*, 267; Postel, *Populist Vision*, 95.

30. *Galveston Daily News*, March 11, 1894 (quotation).

31. Ibid.; Marjorie Spruill Wheeler, *New Women of the New South: The Leaders of the Woman Suffrage Movement in the Southern States* (New York: Oxford University Press, 1993), 101, 108–9, 112–13.

32. *1896: The Presidential Campaign, Cartoons and Commentary*, 2000, http://projects.vassar .edu/1896/1896home.html(accessed January 19, 2013); Philip S. Foner, *The Spanish-Cuban-American War and the Birth of American Imperialism, 1892–1902* (New York: Monthly Review Press, 1972), 2:392.

33. Judith N. McArthur, *Creating the New Woman: The Rise of Southern Women's Culture in Texas, 1893–1918* (Urbana: University of Illinois Press, 1998), 3–4; *Fort Worth Daily Democrat*, February 18, 1882; Richard F. Selcer, *Hell's Half Acre: The Life and Legend of a Red Light District* (Fort Worth: Texas Christian University Press, 1991), 210; Ruth Karbach, "Duchesses with Hearts of Love and Brains of Fire," in *Grace and Gumption: Stories of Fort Worth Women*, ed. Katie Sherrod (Fort Worth: Texas Christian University Press, 2007), 30–40; *Fort Worth Gazette*, November 16, 1892; "History and Directory of the M.E. Churches, South, Fort Worth, Texas, 1894," First Methodist Church Collection, folder 12, box 1, Archives, Fort Worth Library, Fort Worth; Willard, Livermore, and Livermore, *Great American Women*, 243.

34. Isadore Miner, later Callaway or "Pauline Periwinkle," columnist for the *Dallas Morning News*, and Mary Walton, an editor of the *Fort Worth Gazette* and subsequent owner of *The Scimitar*, wrote forcefully about votes for Texas women. *Dallas Morning News*, April 14, May 11, 1893.

35. *Dallas Morning News*, May 11, 1893; Constitution and By-Laws (quotation), Texas Equal Rights Association Scrapbook, folder 1, box 34, Jane Y. McCallum Papers, Austin History Center, Austin Public Library, Austin.

36. Jeanne Madeline Weimann, *The Fair Women* (Chicago: Academy Chicago, 1981), 537, 539; McArthur, *Creating the New Woman*, 10–12; Sue Huffman Brady, "The Changing Ideals in Southern Womanhood," in *The Congress of Women*, ed. Mary Kavanaugh Oldham (Kansas City, Mo.: Thompson and Hood, 1894), 365, (quotation). See also Megan Seaholm, "Earnest Women: The White Woman's Club Movement in Progressive Era Texas, 1880–1920" (PhD diss., Rice University, 1988).

37. *Fort Worth Gazette*, March 30, 1894.

38. *Woman's Journal*, May 19, 1894; *Fort Worth Gazette*, March 30, 1894.

39. *Dallas Morning News*, March 10, May 10, 27, 1894 (quotation).

40. Jessica S. Brannon-Wranosky, "Southern Promise and Necessity: Texas, Regional Identity, and the National Woman Suffrage Movement, 1868–1920" (PhD diss., University of North Texas, 2010), 111–12, 116–20.

41. *Dallas Morning News*, July 28, 31, October 25, 27, 29, 1893.

42. *Fort Worth Gazette*, October 1, 1894; *Dallas Morning News*, November 3, 1894.

43. *Dallas Morning News*, November 1, 1894; Ellen Lawson Dabbs, "Reform Forces: Can They Unite?" *Union Signal*, Mar 28, 1894; McArthur, *Creating the New Woman*, 84.

44. *Dallas Morning News*, March 9, October 31, 1895.

45. Ibid., October 10, 1897.

46. Willard, Livermore, and Livermore, *Great American Women*, 243; *Dallas Morning News*, February 20, 1899; Jeffrey, "Women in the Southern Farmers' Alliance," 2.

47. *Dallas Morning News*, January 18, March 19, 1897; Sheila M. Rothman, *Woman's Proper Place: A History of Changing Ideals and Practices, 1870 to the Present* (New York: Basic Books, 1978), 42.

48. Lynn D. Gordon, *Gender and Higher Education in the Progressive Era* (New Haven: Yale University Press, 1990), 9, 47; Mabel Newcomer, *A Century of Higher Education for American Women* (New York: Harper, 1959), 49; *Dallas Morning News*, March 21, 1897.

49. *Dallas Morning News*, January 29, 1899 (first quotation), March 21 (second quotation), 16, 1897; Jacqueline Masur McElhaney, *Pauline Periwinkle and Progressive Reform in Dallas* (College Station: Texas A&M University Press, 1998), 133.

50. *Dallas Morning News*, May 23, 1899; *Houston Daily Post*, August 12, 1900.

51. Ellen Lawson Dabbs to R. L. Paschal, April 1, 1897, Chase Livingston Collection, San Francisco; Adelaide Lisetta Fries, *Historical Sketch of Salem Female Academy* (Salem, N.C.: Crest and Eben, 1902), 28–29; Jeffrey, "Women in the Southern Farmers' Alliance," 81.

52. Register of Licensed Physicians, Tarrant County, Texas, District Clerk's Office, Fort Worth; *Fort Worth City Directory, 1892–93* (Dallas: Polk, 1892–93), 354; *Fort Worth City Directory, 1894–95* (Dallas: Polk, 1894–95), 372–73; Walsh, *"Doctors Wanted,"* 185; *Fort Worth University Medical Department Bulletin* 4 (August 1, 1909): 9; Elizabeth Silverthorne and Geneva Fulgham, *Women Pioneers in Texas Medicine* (College Station: Texas A&M University Press, 1997), 83.

53. *Dallas Morning News*, December 12, 1895 (quotation), October 27, 1893; Ellen Lawson Dabbs, "A Frequent Mistake in Diagnosis," *Texas Courier-Record of Medicine* 12 (February 1895): 147–53.

54. Ellen Lawson Dabbs, "A Disease with a History and a Few Thoughts Involved Thereby," *Texas Courier-Record of Medicine* 12 (June 1895): 300 (quotation); Ian Dowbiggin, *A Merciful End: The Euthanasia Movement in Modern America* (New York: Oxford University Press, 2003), 7.

55. Michael Kazin, *A Godly Hero: The Life of William Jennings Bryan* (New York: Knopf, 2006), 87.

56. *Dallas Morning News*, August 14, 1898; Second Report of the National Society of the Daughters of the American Revolution, June 2, 1900, Series 3877, vol. 35, S.Coc. 425, p. 240; Mercedes Graf, *On the Field of Mercy: Women Medical Volunteers from the Civil War to the First World War* (Amherst, N.Y.: Humanity, 2010), 14, 31, 188, 210.

57. Graf, *On the Field of Mercy*, 117; *Charlotte Observer*, October 21, 1898; Personal Data Card of Ellen Dabbs, box 2, Spanish-American War Contract Nurses, 1898–1939, RG 112, Entry 149, Records of the Office of the Surgeon General (Army) Nurses, 1898–99, National Archives and Records Administration, Washington, D.C.; *New Orleans Times-Picayune*, October 20, 1898.

58. *Fort Worth Morning Register*, October 1, 1899; *Rusk County News*, March 6, 1901; Summer Hill Select School Collection Description, Ralph N. Steen Library, Stephen F. Austin State University, Nacogdoches.

59. *Dallas Morning News*, September 21, 1904; *St. Louis Republic*, September 13, 1904.

60. *Waurika News*, February 3, 1906.

61. Joan Carnegie, grèat-granddaughter of Ellen Lawson Dabbs, email to author, July 9, 2010; Dowbiggin, *Merciful End*, 5; "Order for Hearing Petition for Letters of Administration," *Waurika News*, November 17, 1908; Petition to Sell Real Estate, March 17, 1909, County Court, Jefferson County, Oklahoma.

62. Joan Carnegie, great-granddaughter of Ellen Lawson Dabbs, email to author, July 9, 2010.

63. Stella L. Christian, *The History of the Texas Federation of Women's Clubs* (1919; Seagraves, Tex.: Dealey-Adey-Elgin, 1986), 1:5–9; Ida Husted Harper and Susan Brownell Anthony, *History of Woman Suffrage, 1883–1902* (Indianapolis: Hollenbeck, 1902), 4:931.

64. Ellen Lawson Dabbs, "Judge Nugent and the Labor Unions," in *Life Work of Thomas L. Nugent*, ed. Catherine Nugent (n.p.: self-published, 1896), 354 (quotation).

Mariana Thompson Folsom

Laying the Foundation for Women's Rights Activism

JESSICA BRANNON-WRANOSKY

Mariana Thompson Folsom was well known nationally during her life. She was one of the first ordained clergywomen in the United States and an accomplished orator who traveled on behalf of both the Universalist Church and the woman suffrage movement. Among those with whom she corresponded regularly were nineteenth-century national women's rights icons Lucy Stone, Henry Blackwell, and Mary Livermore. Folsom's life was unique for a nineteenth-century woman; it was fashioned out of a mixture of liberalism, Universalism, and Quakerism focused through the lens of first-wave feminism. This ideological cocktail, combined with her sense of adventure, magnetic personality, supportive family and marriage, and connections with like-minded activists, made her investment in social reform both possible and successful.[1]

Much of Folsom's activism was rooted in nineteenth-century reform movements. She at times served as the central contact in Texas for the American Woman Suffrage Association (AWSA) and the National American Woman Suffrage Association (NAWSA) and as a correspondent for a nationally distributed suffrage newspaper, the *Woman's Journal*. She traveled extensively for both organizations, giving hundreds of lectures in cities, towns, and rural communities from the mid-1880s through the 1890s. Folsom was neither wealthy nor a political strategist; instead, she was an educator and a grassroots reformer. Her talent lay in her public oratorical skill and an interest in traveling to spread the messages of reform. By the twentieth century, she was well connected with reformers across Texas and at the national level. She spent her last decade educating a new generation of legislators and the public on woman suffrage and

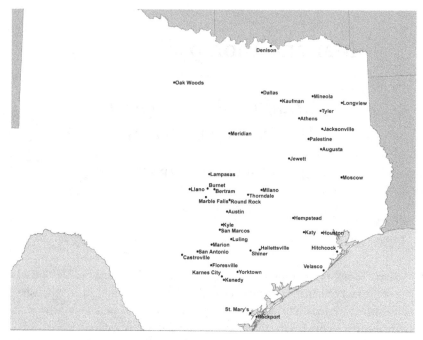

MARIANA THOMPSON FOLSOM'S KNOWN
TEXAS LECTURE TOUR LOCATIONS

Information compiled by author from *Woman's Journal*, December 27, 1884, August 1, 1885, April 24, May 22, June 19, August 7, December 4, 1886, November 12, 1887, July 23, 1892, April 21, 1894, September 7, November 2, 1895, June 13, 20, September 12, November 7, 1896, April 7, 1897, April 23, 1898, July 2, 1898, August 12, September 16, 1899; *Galveston Daily News*, December 21, 1884, February 15, March 24, April 24, 1885, May 9, 1892, August 21, 1896; *Dallas Morning News*, December 3, 1885, November 24, 1893. Cartography by Jeffrey Wells. Courtesy of Texas Christian University.

provided contact between Texas activists and the NAWSA. Nevertheless, since her death in 1909, she has become almost absent from public memory.

The final years of the woman suffrage movement have been well documented by historians. During this time, reformers kept intricate records both to be used in legislative lobbying and to preserve their place in the historic record. Those who planned strategic, widespread, association-oriented political activities were much more likely to leave documented evidence than were their nineteenth-century grassroots predecessors. By nature, nineteenth-century suffragists' activities included independent work that often employed verbal communication but left few records and was often not part of a documented meeting environment. This was certainly the case for Texas woman suffrage organizers before the turn of the century. A look at Folsom's life and times helps provide greater understanding of nineteenth-century grassroots suffragists' unique campaigning style between 1848, the early woman suffrage era marked by the first Seneca Falls Convention, and the years leading up to ratification of the Nineteenth Amendment in 1920. From this perspective emerges a new view of the middle age of the women's rights movement in the United States.

The oldest of ten children, Mariana Thompson was born in Northumberland County, Pennsylvania, on July 30, 1845. Her parents, Samuel Newton Thompson and Susan Drake Thompson, were members of the Religious Society of Friends (known as Quakers). Samuel Thompson was a crockery merchant who specialized in Queen's Ware, produced by the Wedgwood China Company in England. A few years before her sixteenth birthday in 1861, Mariana's father moved the family from Pennsylvania to Mount Pleasant, Henry County, Iowa. At the time, the town was often referred to as the Athens of Iowa because of the community's focus on education. The burgeoning Mount Pleasant promised to provide the Thompsons with a ripe cultural environment in which to raise a growing family and an enterprising place in which to establish themselves economically. Thus, on the eve of the Civil War, the family moved more than thirteen hundred miles westward. At the time, deals between the federal government and railroad corporations made plots of land in Iowa available for very little money. Settlers poured into the state, and Henry County soon had the largest concentration of Quaker communities in Iowa. Samuel and Susan Thompson most likely moved to avoid the growing economic and political strife occasioned by the coming war. Quaker religious beliefs required that their members oppose violence. Sunbury, Pennsylvania, the 1850s residence of the Thompson family, was approximately one hundred miles from the Mason-Dixon Line, potentially placing the family in the midst of growing sectional tensions on the eve of the Civil War.[2]

Even though Mariana came of age during the Civil War, she appeared sheltered from much of it. For the most part, she focused on her family, her friends,
and her preparations to attend the local college. By September 1864, Mariana
started planning to return to Pennsylvania to spend the winter. She closed the
last entry in her diary with the words, "Great changes may [come] over me err
I write in or see this journal again." Her words seemed prophetic.[3]

Sometime between 1864 and 1868, Mariana decided to enroll in the Theological School at St. Lawrence University in Canton, New York. A Universalist
institution founded in 1856, it was the alma mater of the first denominationally
ordained clergywoman in the United States, Olympia Brown, whose ordination
took place in 1863. Ten years earlier, a Universalist congregation had ordained
Antoinette Brown Blackwell, a first in the United States, but her position was
recognized only by the local congregation. In 1863, the Universalist Church also
ordained Augusta Chapin, followed by Phebe Ann Hanaford in 1868, Prudy Le
Clerc in 1869, and Mariana Thompson in 1870.[4]

Thompson enrolled at St. Lawrence University in 1868 and graduated two
years later. During the summer of 1869, she received multiple invitations to take
a pastoral position for twelve hundred dollars a year. Many of the newspapers
reporting this news suggested that she should instead accept marriage if it were
offered. *New York Ledger* columnist Sara Willis Parton (pen name Fanny Fern)
openly objected to the suggestion that Thompson would be better served as a
wife with no pay than as a public leader, writing, "I advise no woman to refuse
twelve hundred independent dollars a year for good, honest labor, to become
such a serf as this."[5]

Even church officials involved with the theological education of these early
clergywomen were often unsure about women's entry into church and public
leadership. Olympia Brown had been denied admission to the Unitarian Theological School in Meadville, Pennsylvania, before she applied to St. Lawrence
University. After receiving Brown's admissions application, the school's president, Ebenezer Fisher, responded that she would be admitted, but he used a
tone and language that he hoped would discourage her from enrolling. It did
not, and Fisher appeared surprised when Brown arrived expecting to attend
the university. Brown later wrote that while at St. Lawrence she received "re-
bukes and sneers or even ridicule. . . . Thus I went on trembling, but undaunted,
through the theological school and passed the ordeal of ordination which was
somewhat bitterly contested."[6]

It is no surprise that women who sought positions in church leadership also
became active in the women's rights movement; they had already become activists by way of their educational and professional choices. In addition, success

in both areas required talent in public speaking and organizational ability. It is unclear when Mariana Thompson became involved with woman suffrage work, but by 1869, she was well enough connected to be invited to give the invocation at the convention organized by Mary Livermore in Chicago to create the Western Woman Suffrage Association. Suffragists Lucy Stone, Henry Blackwell, and Susan B. Anthony attended in an effort to keep the new group from affiliating with either side of the recently split movement. Earlier that year, disagreements among national civil rights leaders had led to a divide that fostered the existence of two national woman suffrage groups—the National Woman Suffrage Association (NWSA), created in May 1869 by Elizabeth Cady Stanton and Anthony, and the AWSA, organized in November 1869 by Stone and Blackwell.[7]

During the spring of 1870, in the midst of increased suffrage activity mounted by the two competing national associations, Thompson graduated from St. Lawrence University. Following her ordination, she took a position at a "large and influential church" in Grand Rapids, Michigan, where she met future women's rights leader Anna Howard Shaw, who credited the young Universalist clergywoman for encouraging Shaw to pursue higher education. According to Shaw,

> Before I had been working a month at my uncongenial trade in Big Rapids, [Michigan, I] was favored by a visit from a Universalist woman minister, the Reverend Marianna [*sic*] Thompson, who came there to preach. Her sermon was delivered on Sunday morning, and I was, I think, almost the earliest arrival of the great congregation which filled the church. It was a wonderful moment when I saw my first woman minister enter her pulpit; and as I listened to her sermon, thrilled to the soul, all my early aspirations to become a minister myself stirred in me with cumulative force. After the services I hung for a time on the fringe of the group that surrounded her, and at last, when she was alone and about to leave, I found courage to introduce myself and pour forth the tale of my ambition. Her advice was as prompt as if she had studied my problem for years. "My child," she said, "You can't do anything until you have an education. Get it, and get it now." Her suggestion was much to my liking, and I paid her the compliment of acting on it promptly, for the next morning I entered the Big Rapids High School, which was also a preparatory school for college.[8]

Shaw eventually earned her doctorate in theology and became the first clergywoman ordained by the Methodist Protestant Church; she also earned her medical degree from Boston University in 1886. She served as the president of NAWSA from 1904 to 1915. Shaw's anecdote not only shows the importance of exposure to examples of success in a field an individual is trying to enter but also provides a good example of the mentorship often present between successful women in both ministerial and suffrage work. These two phenomena were essential to the spread of suffrage support.[9]

In 1871, Mariana Thompson married fellow Universalist minister and St. Lawrence University classmate Allen Perez Folsom. Soon after, the couple combined their ministry, but "the Reverend Mrs. Mariana Thompson Folsom" continued to hold church positions in Universalist congregations. Over the next decade, she and Allen held ministerial appointments in Foxboro, Massachusetts, as well as Fulton and Oswego, New York. Also during these years, the couple had three children. Their daughter, Oriana Thompson Folsom, was born in 1872, with son Allison Thompson Folsom following in 1875, both in Massachusetts. Their youngest daughter, Erminia Thompson Folsom, joined the family in New York three years later. By 1880, the Folsoms had moved to Marshalltown, Iowa, where Allen became a crockery merchant. Mariana continued her ministry, and by 1882, she held simultaneous positions in the Universalist churches of Boone and Eldora.[10]

While it was unusual for American women to work outside the home in such exalted public positions, some of Folsom's contemporaries also split their time as wives, mothers, and clergywomen. In 1889, social activist Frances Willard wrote that the United States had "five hundred women who have already entered the pulpit as evangelists, and at least a score (exclusive of the 350 Quaker preachers) who are pastors, of whom several have been regularly ordained." Quakerism, for example, had upheld from its beginnings the idea that both women and men could be "instruments" of God called to regional or even transatlantic travel as ministers. As far back as the eighteenth century, Quaker women ministers usually married. Furthermore, according to historian Rebecca Larson, even though governmental laws placed the husband in control of his wife's actions, "there were instances when the Quaker meeting clearly supported a minister's religious service over the demands of [her] private relations."[11]

Moreover, new denominations that emerged during the mid-nineteenth century had extended this mix of women's personal and professional opportunity. Historian Barbara Welter argues that American women who wanted more religious responsibility than that of a Sunday school teacher usually had two choices: remain connected to their religious roots through missionary work or join a new religious community that provided women more freedom. Historian Barbara Brown Zikmund adds that since some nineteenth-century Christian denominations—Shakers, Oneidans, Hicksite Quakers, Mormons, and Seventh Day Adventists—were more likely to accept women's expanded religious roles, these communities enjoyed a large portion of their growth during this period from women seeking gender equality. These communities' variants of sectarian liberalism (group belief and practice of the understanding and logical nature of religious ideology) meant that their members rejected some of society's more conservative religious norms and thus opened a door to the redefinition of values and social structures. A growing number of women and men searching for greater freedoms were drawn to the liberalist communities, creating an increased impetus toward gender equality. While it appears that the spread of liberalist religions, including Unitarianism and Universalism, primarily broadened women's clerical opportunities in the Midwest and the Northeast, the phenomenon also appeared in the South. Southern Universalism developed slowly from a number of sources in the eighteenth century, but liberalism began spreading faster in the region following the Civil War in areas including Florida, Oklahoma, and Texas. Between the Civil War and World War I, a number of women in both the Unitarian and Universalist churches were ordained and occupied active ministries in the South.[12]

Universalists' rejection of Calvinist thought in favor of the egalitarian belief in universal salvation meant that no one person had more claim to church membership than any other. The belief of equality in salvation soon translated into some Universalists' expectation of the removal of gendered clerical requirements. As a result, by the second half of the nineteenth century, the Universalist denomination offered a liberal environment for women. Those who joined encouraged further emancipation of women from prescribed nineteenth-century roles. The Folsoms' religious roots and ties to reform communities thus set the stage for the next development in their involvement in women's rights advocacy.[13]

After the family's move to Iowa, Mariana increasingly devoted herself to woman suffrage activities. By 1881, she was a member of the Iowa Equal Suffrage Association finance committee, and she became the association's financial secretary two years later. In that position, she secured pledges, arranged county conventions, and lectured at local suffrage meetings. Folsom then became a woman suffrage lecturer for the Iowa state association, which subsequently sent her into the field to raise money and organize local affiliates. While representing the Iowa organization, Folsom attended a state convention in Minnesota with author, social activist, and women's rights leader Julia Ward Howe.[14]

Considering Folsom's experience as a traveling clergywoman, her public outreach, travel, and education on behalf of woman suffrage closely resembled her Universalist church work. Historian Beverly Ann Zink-Sawyer maintains that the devotion to woman suffrage evidenced by Olympia Brown, Antoinette Brown Blackwell, Susan B. Anthony, and Anna Howard Shaw also represented an "extension" of their religious work and ministries. Zink-Sawyer writes, "The wider social and political worlds of America became their 'parishes.'" In addition, a number of liberal Quaker sects often paired social reform with acts of religious devotion. Anthony, who was raised a Quaker, once responded to an inquiry into her prayer practices by saying, "I pray every second of my life; not on my knees but with my work. My prayer is to lift women to equality with men. Work and worship are one with me." The Folsoms were part of a group of activists who linked secular reform with a belief in a spiritual calling. Mariana and Allen likely transferred their beliefs in their own spiritual callings to the spread and fight for woman suffrage.[15]

In October 1884, the Folsom family left Iowa and headed for Texas. Allen had received an appointment in educational work, and Mariana continued her suffrage activism. By this time, Mariana had worked on suffrage in New York, Massachusetts, and Iowa and had lectured in many other states, including Kansas, Minnesota, and Illinois. She found conditions in Texas to be rustic. She often brought her own candles to light places where she lectured, and once during a storm, she spoke in a room where women sat in the few seats and men stood with their outerwear still on.[16]

Folsom wrote to the editors of the *Woman's Journal* in December 1884 that she had been on a lecture tour in Texas for ten weeks and had given more than sixty lectures. Early on, people had warned her that Texans "will not listen to you on woman suffrage" and that she needed to "handle the subject very tenderly." Folsom, with her professional training as a minister, was an accomplished orator, and newspapers often commented positively on her lectures, describing them as "eloquent" and "interesting," as well as on her personally ("a woman of superior ability and of unbounded energy and enthusiasm," an "educated lady and very pleasant speaker"). Contrary to the warnings, Folsom found her lectures well attended despite "short notices and serious obstacles." She told *Woman's Journal* readers, "Some of the lectures have had few women in the audience, but the men were orderly, and often requested us to stay longer, and promised to get the women out next time." The addition of her knowledge, capabilities, and suffrage connections became central to the successful spread of woman suffrage in Texas.[17]

The Thompson and Folsom families supported Mariana's professional success and saw it as congruent with her duties as wife and mother, largely because of the communities from which Mariana and Allen came. Since Mariana's parents were Quakers, she grew up believing women were equal to men. It was not unusual for Quaker women to become woman suffrage activists: others who did so included Seneca Falls organizer Lucretia Mott, Susan B. Anthony, and twentieth-century National Woman's Party leader Alice Paul. It was often difficult for these women to reconcile the discrepancies between the gender equality practiced in Quaker communities and the absence of such equality in the U.S. legal structure. Furthermore, while in Mount Pleasant, Mariana's parents had encouraged their daughter's pursuit of higher education. When she and Allen first traveled to Texas in 1884, her parents cared for the Folsoms' three children while Mariana lectured across the state and until the couple secured living arrangements. Since Allen had also been educated as a Universalist minister, he, too, was part of this religious community that supported the professional advancement of women. He knowingly married a strong-minded woman who was also a well-known women's rights advocate and religious leader, and with those roles came her social and political commitments.[18]

Mariana and Allen shared an expectation that the wife and mother's abilities outside the home were as important as her roles inside the domestic space. Allen sometimes campaigned with Mariana, writing letters to the *Woman's Journal* and soliciting funds on behalf of the Iowa suffrage association. When his ability to work and earn a living was compromised, she labored to hold the family together and earn an income. Furthermore, it is likely that while she traveled on lecture tours, he took on domestic duties. The Folsoms created a home environment that supported women's equality, complementing their joint advocacy of female political enfranchisement. In turn, their daughter, Erminia, became a suffrage activist in Texas, and the list of supporting members of the Austin Woman Suffrage Association between 1900 and 1920 included their son, Allison.[19]

Folsom stood in contrast to many of the women she encountered during her travels. In May 1887, a *Woman's Journal* reader wrote to its editors about Folsom's lecture in Meridian, Texas, on behalf of women's rights: "Not many men went. Most of the men sneered or growled. The women thought 'she had better have stayed at home and done her housework.' They 'wondered where her children were,' and 'what her husband said.' They pitied the 'poor man.' But some of us had longed to hear something on the subject and attended." Folsom and her family as well as other activists offered living examples of the possibilities brought by women's equality. While not everyone exposed to their examples listened with open minds, nineteenth-century grassroots suffragists' efforts made an important impact. As Folsom was for Shaw, these suffragists were living templates for change.[20]

As she traveled across Texas, Folsom often encountered gender norms that surprised her just as much as her public presence did conservative southerners. In a December 1884 letter to the *Woman's Journal*, she described the behavior of different social classes of men and women and the separation of activity and visibility in public and private spaces. Folsom seemed genuinely surprised by the affluent women whom she described as "timid," living mostly inside and rarely seen in public spaces even in cities. Gender expectations for modesty while living in harsh conditions, she reported, produced a class of women who did not venture onto muddy streets even to shop for their own clothes.[21]

Folsom appeared judgmental. While it was likely that she was aware of criticisms regarding her place as a very public woman, she also seemed somewhat sheltered. She believed that the "timidity" of Texas women was either ridiculous or unusual. Some liberal thinkers in other regions in the United States might have been just as isolated from alternative cultural norms as those living in conservative southern communities. This phenomenon also explains the apparent difficulties woman suffragists from other regions had when approaching southern constituencies, even if the southerners supported woman suffrage.[22]

While initial contact between northern suffragists and southerners sometimes proved challenging, these activities also carved out public space. In hindsight, historians see that women's rights work began altering gender norms in traditionally conservative southern environments, which "emphasized the softness, purity, and spirituality of women while denying them intellectual capacity." For women to request, let alone demand, the right to vote was to claim publicly that southern "gentlemen" were not fulfilling their defined roles. The region's patriarchal ideal commanded that men needed to be trustworthy leaders, with women placing "perfect confidence in [men's] judgment" and believing that they "always knew best." Many southerners took the view that "a difference with your husband ought to be considered the greatest calamity." A vote was a voice, and to declare that women needed to project their own voices was to suggest that women sought the opportunity potentially to differ with the men in their lives.[23]

During this period, however, growing numbers of southern women and men began to take an alternative viewpoint. Some came to support woman suffrage, believing that voting women would provide increased influence for worthwhile causes. Others believed that "if we would be free, let all vote that have an interest in the management of the Government." As these individuals recruited followers for the cause of woman suffrage, a number of different sources facilitated increasing awareness of women's rights in a society taught from childhood to expect women's silence.[24]

The depth to which gender roles defined society often created the line between a person's private interest and public support of women's rights. Many of Folsom's fellow Texas suffragists reported on southerners' hesitation when approached on behalf of the cause. Individuals who privately supported women's rights refused to sign petitions for fear of the stigma attached. In 1885, one Texas suffragist hoped to submit one thousand petition signatures to the next legislature but reported that many "suffragists at heart" refused to sign to avoid losing "prestige." Two years earlier, the same woman noted that teachers shied away from publicly expressing interest in suffrage for fear of "loss of popularity and the stigma of 'strong mindedness.'" Those who professed allegiance to the cause could suffer serious repercussions. One teacher wrote to the *Woman's Journal* to explain that although she supported woman suffrage, she had "never dared to come out and openly advocate the cause, because I am dependent on the public for my work, and could not get a place in the public schools if it were generally known that I am a suffragist." What had been a problem for decades continued to be an issue. Many favorable to the cause did not speak out for fear of social and/or professional rejection.[25]

Even so, Folsom tried to remain optimistic as she corresponded with Lucy Stone and Henry Blackwell of the AWSA urging the creation of a Texas woman suffrage association and asking for financial support in organizing it. They responded hesitatingly, wondering if Texas was ready but agreeing to help if she believed it was. By July 1885, Folsom began to agree with Stone that Texas needed more work before the creation of a state woman suffrage association could occur. She thought that an opening might have existed in Austin during the state legislative session, but many women's rights workers in the state advised her that such efforts needed to wait until the legislature made decisions regarding "the woman's clerkship bill" (requiring the state's treasury, comptroller, and land commission offices to employ female clerks) and Prohibition. The legislators did not take up the latter question but passed the bill regarding women's employment; however, they did not do so until the end of the legislative session, denying Folsom the chance to organize that year.[26]

In a letter to the *Woman's Journal*, Folsom laid out plans to organize a state woman suffrage association before the next legislative session convened in 1887. She informed readers that she had created cooperative committees for future work where possible and that she believed Texas might be the most promising southern state with regard to woman suffrage. Her assessment was correct. The AWSA leadership began to pay more attention to Texas, and at the group's 1885 annual meeting, held in Minneapolis in October, reports were read from twenty-seven other states, with Folsom's described as of "especial interest." Moreover, she was described as having delivered nearly two hundred public addresses by that point.[27]

Personal tragedy put a temporary hold on her work, however. In April 1886, Livermore, an AWSA founder, appealed on Folsom's behalf to the readers of the

Woman's Journal. Folsom had given birth to the couple's fourth child, Clarence, in August 1885; shortly thereafter, her husband had become extremely ill and unable to work, and the family's house burned. The Folsoms had then moved to San Antonio in search of a better situation, but they remained without a house or income. Though Mariana Folsom had not asked for help, Livermore requested that readers of the *Woman's Journal* send donations. They responded, sending money both to the newspaper for the Folsoms and directly to the family. These efforts helped the Folsoms survive and aided Mariana's return to woman suffrage work, which many activists believed was indispensable to the success of the overall movement.[28]

In campaigning for the movement, Mariana Folsom's fame could draw a crowd curious about women's right to vote, and attracting people was essential to educating the public and gaining more support. When she petitioned for the use of public facilities, those in charge sometimes already knew who she was and immediately approved her request and even helped advertise her lectures.[29]

Local pro-suffrage newspapers were important in reaching broader audiences with suffrage arguments and forming a sense of support among those who believed in women's legal equality. Folsom wrote to the *Woman's Journal* that she often saw facts from her speeches quoted anonymously in Texas papers. The editor of the *Hillsboro County Visitor* responded positively to being called a "women's rights man" and provided a long list of reasons why women deserved equal treatment. When Texas newspapers reported positively on woman suffrage, countless Texas residents, some of whom had never before considered the subject, were exposed to it.[30]

Probably the most significant but least measurable way that grassroots suffragists influenced audiences was through speeches, conversations, and the distribution of printed material. Individual stories appeared in newspapers, state and national suffrage records, and family archival collections. In Texas alone, these encounters touched tens of thousands of people—if not more—in the last decades of the nineteenth century. Mariana Folsom traveled across the state regularly for nearly two decades beginning in 1884. In 1886, she reported to AWSA on how she chose locations for her suffrage work. Folsom preferred to begin by focusing on rural towns, which she called "smaller places." While meetings in the cities reported "large and enthusiastic" crowds, she believed that these groups would not support woman suffrage whenever the issue came up for a vote. The smaller "outlying points" had "voters who will take time to think," but she believed that although "such work is less showy, [it lays] the foundation," creating allies so that opponents of suffrage would one day be surprised at the polls. In one such case, a man in West Texas told Folsom that after hearing her speak, he had "talked woman suffrage to his neighbors." After attending another speech, he subscribed to the *Woman's Journal*. After he and his wife read it, they loaned it out; he also related the news from the weekly suffrage paper orally. This personal advocacy by members of close-knit communities was priceless. It often meant that the logic and arguments supporting women's enfranchisement came with a trusted face, possibly adding to the issue's appeal.[31]

During the mid- to late 1880s, Folsom and others toured Texas to spread the word about woman suffrage. She traveled on Texas railroads speaking in towns, educating the public, and becoming increasingly well known across the state. As historian Robert Wiebe and others have pointed out, an extraordinary "revolution in the patterns of distribution" occurred in the United States during the late nineteenth century because of the connectivity railroads provided between small towns and the rest of the nation. While Wiebe referred to the distribution of goods, trains also provided people with increased mobility and thus connectivity. For reformers, this meant that towns and areas connected by railroads were more accessible.[32]

In light of the fact that the majority of southerners lived in rural areas until after World War II and that Texas alone covers 268,581 square miles, ease of travel was essential to successful reform. Many of the towns visited by national temperance and women's rights leader Frances Willard on her first tour of Texas in 1881 were chosen for their accessibility by train. Folsom similarly often traveled by rail, and in 1886, she gave a detailed account that demonstrated the importance of transportation:

> Numerous stage lines run from [San Antonio], besides five railroads. As I went towards Mexico, in all the villages along the way, I found willing listeners, and sometimes gentlemen from other localities who volunteered to arrange a lecture at home on the evening I could be there. . . . In one place I saw the effect of good work [discussed] two hundred miles away. . . . I went a little way toward California. The stations are small, as stock and sheep raising is the main business. There was always a school-house, and I never failed of an audience. . . . On returning [to San Antonio], I went five miles off the railroad to the quaint town of Castroville. . . . Thirty miles out [on another road] I went to Floresville and talked woman suffrage in a neat court-house. The whole village turned out to hear. In all these directions, the question was extremely new.[33]

Transportation that brought woman suffragists to isolated areas of the state had changed since late 1875, when Elizabeth Cady Stanton reported being stuck in Houston and limited in the places she could visit. As Folsom and other reform leaders demonstrated, the ability to reach different areas of the state was essential to create pockets of support. At one point, Folsom suggested that while she had covered a lot of ground by rail, the cause would benefit greatly from a lecturer with a private horse and buggy. Folsom was suggesting that a wealthier suffrage worker with the means to travel more independently would have greater impact. After the mid-1890s, NAWSA leaders began to take social class and wealth into account when choosing state suffrage activists, in large part because of the amount of travel required.[34]

As the 1890s began, a number of transformations were on the horizon for suffrage organizing. Support for woman suffrage was growing in the South, and the decades-old divisions between national woman suffrage leaders ended. At the prompting of Lucy Stone, the AWSA and NWSA began to plan a reunification, and in 1890, they merged into NAWSA, which immediately became the nation's leading suffrage organization, creating a more coherent effort from the grassroots level to the top.[35]

Grassroots, individual, and local suffrage activities had existed for decades across the United States, but state and local work had traditionally been much more the focus of the AWSA than the NWSA. Historian Sally McMillen argues that the newly unified NAWSA accomplished much more locally under the leadership of NWSA officers. Former NWSA leaders Elizabeth Cady Stanton and Susan B. Anthony held the early presidencies, but fellow suffrage icon and central organizer of the AWSA Lucy Stone died in 1893. Stone's absence and Anthony's agenda for directly energizing local groups set the stage for organizing, campaigning, and aligning state association structures to be affiliated with and directed by the national association. At the urging of NAWSA executive member and southerner Laura Clay at the group's 1892 convention, national leaders decided to form a committee to focus on the South.[36]

During the years that Folsom worked to educate Texans about the importance of woman suffrage, no state association existed to help organize suffrage efforts. The call to create a Texas suffrage association came simultaneously from local suffrage activists and the NAWSA. Even so, the Texas Equal Rights Association (TERA) was short-lived, existing from 1893 until 1898, when it crumbled under the pressure of social and political class conflicts. However, successor organizations emerged and began to formalize procedure, hierarchy, and campaigning methods for woman suffrage. In 1903, the Texas Woman Suffrage Association (TWSA) was formed; ten years later, it was reorganized, and in 1916, the group renamed itself the Texas Equal Suffrage Association. NAWSA leaders wielded immense influence in all three of these groups, overseeing their organization and handpicking their first presidents, who were then "elected" by state delegates. While some Texas suffragists rejected such national involvement, most believed in the benefits of being part of the larger reform network and sought to occupy a relatively large portion of national leaders' attention.[37]

One of the changes in the organizational and campaign structure was an end to individual suffragist activity at the grassroots level. Folsom eventually aligned her efforts with those of TERA, a move that both offered benefits and created setbacks. From November 1893 to March 1894, as local TERA auxiliaries formed, Folsom toured the state, giving speeches to audiences of various sizes. She reported to the editors of the *Woman's Journal* in April 1894 that she held eighty-three meetings during her journey. Folsom canvassed along the Gulf of Mexico, through East and Northeast Texas, and down through the center of the state before returning to her home in San Antonio, speaking in Austin, Houston, Denison, Corsicana, and Shiner, among many other cities and towns. The *Dallas Morning News* reported that the question of women's enfranchisement was new to Shiner, but Folsom was well received and spoke to a "fair" sized audience. While she reported to the *Woman's Journal* that people reacted positively to the discussion, she did seem slightly overwhelmed by Texas's size: "There were sixty counties in Colorado to organize, in Texas there are more than two hundred and sixty counties." This statement seems to indicate that Folsom had come to view the state's immense size as an obstacle rather than a potential source of support.[38]

Historians have often discussed what sorts of changes occurred in suffrage campaign strategies and relationships between national leaders and local activists after NAWSA unified, but longtime grassroots suffragists also experienced internal and emotional changes. If they wanted to remain part of their beloved women's rights movement, they would have to modify their campaign methods to align with those of the new generation of national leaders, accepting outside direction. If Folsom had difficulty with this transition, she did not show it, adapting her methods to conform to those of NAWSA.[39]

Folsom attended her first TERA annual convention in 1896. She had been named the association's state lecturer the previous July and again toured the state in August and September, the first time she had spoken on behalf of state and national organizations. The report of her tour published in the *Woman's Journal* discussed conditions and traveling arrangements and how they had improved since she first began work in Texas in the 1880s. Folsom now stayed at times in the large and comfortable homes of suffragists, including those of TERA leaders Elizabeth Austin Turner Fry and Alice McFadin McAnulty. She spoke in large cities just as often as in small towns, a sharp contrast to the rural audiences she had preferred a decade earlier. New groups of people had become interested in suffrage, and Folsom realized it.[40]

But when TERA fractured and faded away, with it went much of the progress made in organizing Texas on behalf of women's rights. Folsom's letters between 1898 and 1900 highlighted the clubwomen's movement in the state and the serious decline in support for woman suffrage. At NAWSA's 1900 annual convention, executives reported that the Texas affiliate had not paid its national dues for the preceding year and concluded that the "Texas [society] ceased to exist two or three years ago."[41]

With TERA gone, Folsom returned in part to her individual style of grassroots reform. This time, though, and for the remainder of her life, she aimed her suffrage work toward association organizing and political and legislative state victories. In 1898, she began to correspond with Texas sculptor Elisabet Ney. The two women discussed strategies for organizing a suffrage association in Austin. Ney gave Folsom a list of people to contact and expressed her desire to address the state legislature on behalf of women's enfranchisement, though she did not do so until 1907, as part of a women's delegation. In 1899, Folsom expressed frustration and annoyance with the current state of women's rights work in Texas:

> The wisdom of the first woman suffragists in asking for equal suffrage with men is confirmed by the experience of those who ask for less and get nothing. During the session of the last Texas Legislature a bill was introduced "To Abolish the Distinction Between Married Women and Other Persons," also a bill making women eligible to the office of County Superintendent of Schools. Both bills were strangled at once. The reason of this is simply because there is no vigorous discussion of woman suffrage in the State.[42]

By 1900, Folsom had moved to Austin, and three of her children—Allison, Erminia, and Clarence—eventually attended the University of Texas. The census that year listed the family as occupying homes in Austin and in Edna, in Jackson County, more than 130 miles away. Mariana was listed with no professional occupation in Edna, but in Austin, she was described as a lecturer, suggesting that this was her true residence. According to family sources, she and Allen separated around this time, but they apparently neither filed for a divorce nor reconciled. Mariana began investing her time in more localized reform. This change coincided with the creation of the TWSA. From 1903 to 1906, the new organization was headed by Houstonian Annette Finnigan, and much of its activity was concentrated in Texas Gulf Coast cities. Folsom had no direct connection with its work. By the turn of the century, a new generation of suffragists had assumed the leadership of NAWSA in New York City, and Carrie Chapman Catt had become the group's president. These new leaders pressed NAWSA-directed state suffrage work, using a strategy that focused on having wealthy and socially prominent women, like Finnigan, use direct political action to win suffrage legislation.[43]

During that time, Folsom was active in the Texas Federation of Women's Clubs (TFWC) and assumed the role of committee chair in charge of trains for its 1905 state convention in Austin. Folsom also corresponded with Susan B. Anthony about getting copies of the existing four volumes of the *History of Woman Suffrage* for the state library. Anthony responded by telling Folsom that the library already had a copy of the most recent volume, published the previous year, and she thought it held the previous three. However, after Folsom had read the copy given to her as a gift by Anthony "to [her] heart's content," she was free to donate it to a local university or high school. Folsom apparently wanted the state library, whose main purpose was to provide state legislators and their staff with information regarding state business, to be able to provide information regarding the background and details of the women's rights movement. Thus, Folsom refocused her original form of grassroots activism, public awareness, toward the legislators' education. Living in the Texas capital provided her with the close proximity to state legislators that she needed for this type of lobbying.[44]

Over the next few years, Folsom continued on this particular path, and on February 1, 1907, Texas representative Jess Alexander Baker of Granbury introduced a measure to grant women the right to vote. After its first reading, the resolution was referred to the Committee on Constitutional Amendments. Baker subsequently arranged for a committee hearing to provide members with more information. He called a number of Texas suffragists to testify regarding woman suffrage. Those questioned by the committee members included Circleville's Alice McAnulty, a former Populist leader and TERA's corresponding secretary; Woman's Christian Temperance Union president Helen M. Stoddard of Fort Worth; Emma J. Mellette of Waco, formerly a resident of Colorado, one of the four states that had granted woman suffrage in the 1890s; Ney; and Helen Jarvis Kenyon and May Jarvis, both of whom were associated with the University of Texas.[45]

The Committee on Constitutional Amendments came back to the House on March 5, 1907, with a majority report opposing Baker's resolution. A small group of legislators also prepared a positive minority report. Though the effort failed, it fostered increased woman suffrage activity inside Texas and revived NAWSA's interest in the state's suffrage potential. Rather than simply dismissing the idea of woman suffrage, a southern legislature had held special committee meetings and hearings to gain information on the subject. This victory, however small, encouraged both Texas and national suffragists, and they decided to reorganize the Texas suffrage association.[46]

During this time, Folsom served as one of Baker's advisers, providing him and other legislators with information on issues involving woman suffrage, including presidential suffrage (the right to vote only for the electors who chose the U.S. president). Some suffrage advocates argued that presidential suffrage and other forms of limited woman suffrage would allow legislators to test the effects of women voting without altering the existing patriarchal power structures at the state and local levels. Such an approach would test not only middle- and upper-class white women's voting loyalty but also whether women who were members of the working classes, who were African American, or who were Mexican American would attempt to vote in significant numbers. Folsom personally believed in universal suffrage, but at some point in the 1880s, she reported speaking on educationally restricted woman suffrage because it was "the wedge" for the topic with southern Texas audiences. By 1907, though, she was adamant that asking for anything short of full woman suffrage would be too "small" and garner too little attention.[47]

In the midst of the increased suffrage activity connected to the proposed Texas suffrage referendum, Folsom corresponded with NAWSA officials, including President Anna Howard Shaw and executive board members Harriet Taylor Upton and Kate Gordon. Shaw was interested in further information about Baker's proposal and promised financial and campaign resources plus a lecture tour if the legislature approved the amendment and submitted it to the state's voters for a referendum.[48]

Shaw arrived in Texas in April 1908 for a brief lecture tour officially hosted by local TFWC affiliates, though the group had not endorsed woman suffrage and would not do so until 1915. She spoke in Dallas, Austin, San Antonio, and Houston, trying to interest the state's clubwomen in the cause and probably seeking to find a leader for the reorganized state suffrage association among the leading cities' socialites. In December 1908, the Austin Woman Suffrage Association was founded, and by the start of 1909, it had paid dues to NAWSA and had twenty-five members, including Mariana Folsom and her daughter, Erminia. Catt, now serving as chair of NAWSA's Congressional Petition Committee, began corresponding with Erminia, encouraging her "little club in Austin." Over the next few years, Texas's woman suffrage activity reached unprecedented heights and became essential to the national campaign.[49]

But Mariana would not be part of that effort. She died on January 31, 1909, at age sixty-three. The *Woman's Tribune* printed a small memorial that stated, "Mariana T. Folsom was widely known at one time as a speaker and writer on the suffrage question. Of late she has been living in Texas, spending much time at the University, until her two sons and her daughter graduated and scattered to do an honorable part in the world's work." With those words, the paper suc-cinctly and precisely marked the changing of the suffrage guard. The following year, Erminia donated money to the NAWSA in memory of her mother, but for the most part, Mariana Folsom quietly slipped from public memory. Preceded in death by most of her longtime companions in the fight for women's rights—Lucy Stone (1893), Elizabeth Cady Stanton (1902), Mary Livermore (1905), and Susan B. Anthony (1906)—her work became part of their legacy.[50]

In the decade after her death, new members of the movement took over the campaign for woman suffrage in Texas. In 1913, the "little club in Austin" helped facilitate efforts to organize what became the largest suffrage association in the state's history, with local affiliates in almost all of Texas's counties. In 1918, the state legislature passed a law providing Texas women with the right to vote in political primaries; the following year, Texas became the first southern state and the ninth in the nation to ratify the Nineteenth Amendment to the U.S. Con-stitution, which made it illegal to deny a citizen the right to vote based on sex.[51]

Mariana and Allen's four children went on to create legacies of their own. At the time of his mother's death, Allison was serving as Terrell County attorney and publishing a small newspaper, the *Trans-Pecos News*. A few years later, Clar-ence became chief counsel in the legal department of the U.S. consul in El Paso. Both eventually moved to California with their father, who died in 1919. Oriana Folsom Measday eventually became an independent businesswoman who ran a successful farm near Alpine, Texas. After a few more years of woman suffrage work, Erminia broadened her endeavors to include such progressive under-takings as prison reform advocacy.[52]

Mariana Folsom was a pioneer in the effort to persuade male voters to see women as full citizens, deserving of equal rights under the law. That the law needed to change was an important component of her message. Her work for national and state suffrage associations laid the base for the state's progress in the direction of equality for women, and Texas led the South in its affirmation of that premise.

NOTES

The author dedicates this essay to her husband, daughter, and parents.

1. Prior to the late nineteenth century, the word *feminism* most often meant having the charac-teristics of being feminine. Yet as early as 1895, the term was used in connection with the advocacy of women's rights. Furthermore, as early as 1852, the term *feminist* was used in connection with advocates of women's rights reforms. Modern scholars studying feminism use the term *first-wave feminism* to describe the reform activities and communities that developed in the eighteenth and

nineteenth centuries and were aimed at creating a discourse and an environment focused on the improvement of women's rights. This essay follows this academic model with the use of *first-wave feminism*. See *Oxford English Dictionary Online*, "feminism," "feminist," http://www.oed.com/ (accessed March 5, 2012); Sarah Gamble, ed., *The Routledge Companion to Feminism and Postfeminism* (New York: Routledge, 2006); Ellen Carol DuBois, *Woman Suffrage and Women's Rights* (New York: New York University Press, 1998), 4.

2. The exact date of the family's removal to Iowa is not known. See Mariana Thompson Diary, January 21, 1862, Texas State Library and Archives, Austin; "Glimpses of Womanhood under Texas's Star and Its Inheritance," folder 15, box 1, Erminia Thompson Folsom Papers, Texas State Library and Archives; U.S. Census, 1880, "Population Schedules," Henry County, Iowa, household of S. N. Thompson; "Iowa Towns," *Des Moines Daily State Register*, January 5, 1869 (quotation); "Letter from Iowa, Burlington, Des Moines Co., Iowa, November 19th, 1855," *Philadelphia Public Ledger*, December 4, 1855; "The Iowa Land Fever," *Philadelphia North American*, July 10, 1856; Nancy A. Hewitt, "Feminist Friends: Agrarian Quakers and the Emergence of Women's Rights in America," *Feminist Studies* 12 (Spring 1986): 27–49; U.S. Census, 1850, Northumberland County, Pa., Population Schedules, entry for S. N. Thompson.

3. Thompson Diary, September 25, 1864 (quotation).

4. Paula D. Nesbitt, *Feminization of the Clergy in America: Occupational and Organizational Perspectives* (New York: Oxford University Press, 1997), 36–37; *The Universalist Register: Containing the Statistics of the Church with an Almanac for 1875* (Boston: Universalists Publishing, 1875), 54, 63, 97, 99; *General Catalogue of the Trustees, Officers, and Graduates and of Students Not Graduates of the St. Lawrence University, Canton, New York, 1856–1910* (Canton: St. Lawrence University Press, 1910), 62.

5. *General Catalogue*, 62; *Galveston Flakes Bulletin*, December 8, 1869; Fanny Fern, "Women on the Platform," in *Ginger-Snaps* (New York: Carleton, 1880), 111–16 (quotation); Terry Novak, "Fanny Fern [Sara Willis Parton] (1811–1872)," in *Writers of the American Renaissance: An A-to-Z Guide*, ed. Denise D. Knight (Westport, Conn.: Greenwood, 2003), 124–26.

6. Olympia Brown, *Acquaintances, Old and New, among Reformers* (Milwaukee: Tate, 1911), 26–31 (quotation).

7. Louise R. Noun, *Strong-Minded Women: The Emergence of the Woman-Suffrage Movement in Iowa* (Ames: Iowa State University Press, 1969), 119n, 119; Elizabeth Cady Stanton, Susan B. Anthony, and Matilda Joslyn Gage, eds., *The History of Woman Suffrage*, vol. 3 (Rochester, N.Y.: Anthony, 1886), 802; Elizabeth Cady Stanton, *Eighty Years and More: Reminiscences, 1815–1897* (New York: Unwin, 1898), 570; Wendy Hamand Venet, *A Strong-Minded Woman: The Life of Mary Livermore* (Amherst: University of Massachusetts Press, 2005), 163–64; "Women's Suffrage Agitation. The Chicago Convention—Speeches, Letters, Resolutions, &c.," *Cincinnati Daily Gazette*, September 11, 1869; Sally G. McMillen, *Seneca Falls and the Origins of the Women's Rights Movement* (New York: Oxford University Press, 2008), 149–75.

8. "Femininity," *Cleveland) Daily Plain Dealer*, October 1, 1870 (first quotation); "Personal Items," *San Francisco Bulletin*, October 3, 1870; Anna Howard Shaw, Elizabeth Garver Jordan, and Rowena Keith Keyes, *The Story of a Pioneer* (New York: Harper, 1920), 55–56 (second quotation); Anna H. Shaw to Mariana T. Folsom, March 6, 1907, Folsom Papers, folder 1, box 1.

9. Shaw, Jordan, and Keyes, *Story of a Pioneer*, 55–56; Anna H. Shaw to Mariana T. Folsom, March 6, 1907, folder 1, box 1, Folsom Papers.

10. *Universalist Register*, 17–110; "Glimpses of Womanhood"; E. R. Hanson, *Our Woman Workers: Biographical Sketches of Women Eminent in the Universalist Church for Literary, Philanthropic, and Christian Work* (Chicago: Star and Covenant, 1882), 496; Phebe Ann Hanaford, *Women of the*

Century (Boston: Russell, 1877), 376 (quotation); U.S. Census, 1880, Marshall County, Iowa, Population Schedules, entry for Allen P. Folsom.

11. Frances Willard, *Woman on the Pulpit* (Chicago: Woman's Temperance Publication Association, 1889), 94 (first quotation); Rebecca Larson, *Daughters of Light: Quaker Women Preaching and Prophesying in the Colonies and Abroad, 1700–1775* (Chapel Hill: University of North Carolina Press, 2000), 93, 135, 143 (second and third quotations).

12. Barbara Welter, "The Feminization of American Religion: 1800–1860," in *Clio's Consciousness Raised: New Perspectives on the History of Women*, ed. Mary Hartman and Lois W. Banner (New York: Harper and Row, 1974), 143; Barbara Brown Zikmund, "The Feminist Thrust of Sectarian Christianity," in *Women of Spirit: Female Leadership in the Jewish and Christian Traditions*, ed. Rosemary Ruether and Eleanor McLaughlin (New York: Simon and Schuster, 1979), 207–22; Samuel S. Hill, Charles H. Lippy, and Charles Reagan Wilson, eds., *Encyclopedia of Religion in the South* (Macon, Ga.: Mercer University Press, 2005), 802.

13. Erwin Fahlbusch and Geoffrey William Bromiley, *The Encyclopedia of Christianity* (Grand Rapids, Mich.: Eerdmans, 2003), 3:775; Brown, *Acquaintances*, 31; Welter, "Feminization of American Religion," 413; Zikmund, "Feminist Thrust, 207–22.

14. NAWSA, *Report of the Sixteenth Annual Washington Convention, March 4th, 5th, 6th, and 7th, 1884: With Reports of the Forty-Eighth Congress* (Rochester, N.Y.: Mann, 1884), 38; Mariana T. Folsom, "Mrs. Folsom in Iowa," *Woman's Journal* (hereafter cited as *WJ*), May 5, 1883; "Mrs. Folsom in Iowa," *WJ*, November 10, 1883; Mariana T. Folsom, "Mrs. Folsom in Minnesota," *WJ*, December 15, 1883; Allen P. Folsom, "The Situation in Iowa," *WJ*, December 8, 1883.

15. Beverly Ann Zink-Sawyer, *From Preachers to Suffragists: Woman's Rights and Religious Conviction in the Lives of Three Nineteenth-Century American Clergywomen* (Louisville, Ky.: Westminster John Knox Press, 2003), 24 (first and second quotations); Margaret Hope Bacon, *Mothers of Feminism: The Story of Quaker Women in America* (New York: Harper and Row, 1986), 151–65; Hugh Barbour, *Quaker Crosscurrents: Three Hundred Years of Friends in the New York Yearly Meetings* (Syracuse, N.Y.: Syracuse University Press, 1995), 182 (third quotation).

16. Mariana T. Folsom, "Mrs. Folsom in Texas (10 Dec. 1884)," *WJ*, December 27, 1884 (quotation); Mariana T. Folsom, "Through the Indian Territory (20 Oct. 1884)," *WJ*, November 1, 1884; Mary A. Livermore, "An Appeal by Mrs. Livermore," *WJ*, April 10, 1886; Elizabeth Cady Stanton, Susan B. Anthony, and Matilda Joslyn Gage, eds., *History of Woman Suffrage*, vol. 2 (Rochester, N.Y.: Mann, 1881), 545.

17. Mariana T. Folsom, "Mrs. Folsom in Texas (10 Dec. 1884)," *WJ*, December 27, 1884 (first, second, seventh, and eighth quotations); *San Francisco Bulletin*, October 3, 1870 (third quotation); *Galveston Daily News*, December 21, 1884 (fourth quotation), February 16, 1885 (sixth quotation), August 21, 1896; *Dallas Morning News*, December 3, 1885 (fifth quotation).

18. "Glimpses of Womanhood"; Larson, *Daughters of Light*, 19–26; Katherine H. Adams and Michael L. Keene, *Alice Paul and the American Suffrage Campaign* (Urbana: University of Illinois Press, 2007), 70; *General Catalogue*, 61, 97, 162; "Friday Morning," *WJ*, December 10, 1881; Iowa Census, 1885, Henry County, Population Schedules, entry for Saml. N. Thompson.

19. Mary A. Livermore, "An Appeal by Mrs. Livermore," *WJ*, April 10, 1886; Allen P. Folsom, "Cornell University," *WJ*, June 14, 1873; Allen P. Folsom, "The Situation in Iowa," *WJ*, December 8, 1883. For evidence of the Folsom children's woman suffrage activism, especially that of Erminia Folsom, see correspondence in folders 4–7, box 1, Folsom Papers; Folsom Membership dues listed in small red account book in folder 11, box 31, Jane Y. McCallum Papers, Austin History Center, Austin Public Library, Austin.

20. M. L. Golden, "A Macedonian Cry from Texas," *WJ*, May 14, 1887 (quotation).

21. Mariana T. Folsom, "Mrs. Folsom in Texas (10 Dec. 1884)," *WJ*, December 27, 1884 (quotation).

22. Ibid. (quotation).

23. Anne Firor Scott, *The Southern Lady: From Pedestal to Politics 1830–1930* (Chicago: University of Chicago Press, 1970), 6, 15 (quotations).

24. Harvey Jirrells, "A Friend in Texas (21 Sept. 1885)," *WJ*, October 3, 1885 (quotation).

25. I. [sic] Michelly, "Suffrage Work in Texas (11 Nov. 1885)," *WJ*, November 28, 1885 (first and second quotations); J. Michelly, "The Cause in Texas (18 July 1883)," *WJ*, July 21, 1883 (third quotation); N. G. P., "From a Texas Subscriber (29 Jan. 1889)," *WJ*, February 16, 1889 (fourth quotation).

26. Lucy Stone and Henry Blackwell to Mariana Folsom, January 22, 1885, folder 1, box 1, Folsom Papers; Mariana T. Folsom, "The Suffrage Campaign in Texas (24 July 1885)," *WJ*, August 1, 1885 (first quotation); Patsy McDonald Spaw, ed., *The Texas Senate: Civil War to the Eve of Reform, 1861–1889* (College Station: Texas A&M University Press, 1999), 2:354; Andrew J. Jutkins, *Hand-Book of Prohibition* (Chicago: Lever, 1885), 156; J. Michelly, "Well Done, Texas! (6 Feb. 1885)," *WJ*, February 14, 1885; Jane Amy McKinney, "Woman's Rights in Texas (15 Feb. 1885)," *WJ*, March 21, 1885 (second quotation).

27. Mariana T. Folsom, "The Suffrage Campaign in Texas (24 July 1885)," *WJ*, August 1, 1885; Susan B. Anthony and Ida Husted Harper, eds., *The History of Woman Suffrage*, vol. 4 (Indianapolis: Hollenbeck, 1902), 411, 416, 432 (quotation).

28. Mary A. Livermore, "An Appeal by Mrs. Livermore," *WJ*, April 10, 1886; Mariana T. Folsom, "Thanks from Mrs. Folsom [Dear Miss Catherine Wilde] (11 May 1886)," *WJ*, May 22, 1886. Listings for contributions found in *WJ*, April 17–May 22, 1886. Additional correspondence regarding financial help for Folsom is in folder 1, box 1, Folsom Papers.

29. Mariana T. Folsom, "Texas Report (10 Oct. 1886)," *WJ*, December 4, 1886.

30. Ibid.; "Good for Texas," *WJ*, August 1, 1885 (quotations).

31. Mariana T. Folsom, "Texas Report (10 Oct. 1886)," *WJ*, December 4, 1886 (quotations). For examples of the discussion of grassroots women's individual suffrage activism in the late nineteenth century, see Jessica S. Brannon-Wranosky, "Southern Promise and Necessity: Texas, Regional Identity, and the National Woman Suffrage Movement, 1868–1920" (PhD diss., University of North Texas, 2010); Stanton, Anthony, and Gage, *History*, vols. 1–3; Anthony and Harper, *History*, vol. 4; *Woman's Journal*, 1870–1900.

32. Robert H. Wiebe, *Search for Order, 1877–1920* (New York: Hill and Wang, 1967), 2, 12, 23, 47, 48 (quotation). For a discussion of transportation in Texas, see John Stricklin Spratt, *The Road to Spindletop* (Austin: University of Texas Press, 1970).

33. Char Miller and David R. Johnson, "The Rise of Urban Texas," *Urban Texas: Politics and Development* (College Station: Texas A&M University Press, 2000), 4; Rupert Bayless Vance and Nicholas J. Demerath, eds., *The Urban South* (Manchester: Ayer, 1971), 4; "Texas' Natural Environment," *Texas Almanac*, http://www.texasalmanac.com/environment/ (accessed July 6, 2009); Judith N. McArthur, *Creating the New Woman: The Rise of Southern Women's Progressive Culture in Texas, 1893–1918* (Urbana: University of Illinois Press, 1998), 7–8; Mariana T. Folsom, "From Southwestern Texas," *WJ*, June 19, 1886 (quotation).

34. Stanton, Anthony, and Gage, *History*, 3:297–98; Geoffrey C. Ward, Ken Burns, Martha Saxon, Ann Dexter Gordon, and Ellen Carol DuBois, *Not for Ourselves Alone: The Story of Elizabeth Cady Stanton and Susan B. Anthony* (New York: Knopf, 1999), 164; Mariana T. Folsom, "From Southwestern Texas," *WJ*, June 19, 1886; Jane Amy McKinney, "Woman's Rights in Texas (15 Feb. 1885)," *WJ*, March 21, 1885.

35. McMillen, *Seneca Falls*, 195–96, 224–29. A number of sources talk about the conflict and duplication of efforts by the AWSA and NWSA. See, for example, Elizabeth Cady Stanton, Susan B. Anthony, and Matilda Joslyn Gage, eds., *History of Woman Suffrage*, vol. 1, 2nd ed. (Rochester, N.Y.: Mann, 1889), vols. 2, 3; Anthony and Harper, *History*, vol. 4; Eleanor Flexner, *Century of Struggle: The Woman's Rights Movement in the United States* (New York: Athenaeum, 1970). For Texas examples, see *WJ*, 1875–88; correspondence in folder 1, box 1, Folsom Papers.

36. McMillen, *Seneca Falls*, 228, 233; Susan B. Anthony to Rachel Foster Avery, April 7, 1895, Anthony (Susan B.)–Avery (Rachel Foster) Papers (quotation), Department of Rare Books, Special Collections, and Preservation, Rush Rhees Library, University of Rochester, Rochester, N.Y.; Paul E. Fuller, *Laura Clay and the Women's Rights Movement* (Lexington: University Press of Kentucky, 1975), 32–33, 51–60; Anthony and Harper, *History*, 4:219; Marjorie Spruill Wheeler, *New Women of the New South: The Leaders of the Woman Suffrage Movement in the Southern States* (New York: Oxford University Press, 1993), 63, 115–16.

37. Brannon-Wranosky, "Southern Promise and Necessity," 86–187.

38. Mariana T. Folsom "Eighty-Three Suffrage Meetings in Texas (4 Apr. 1894)," *WJ*, April 21, 1894 (second quotation); *Dallas Morning News*, January 23, 1894, November 24, 1893 (first quotation). Folsom exaggerated slightly: Texas 234 counties in 1900. See *Texas Almanac*, "Population History of Counties from 1850–2010," http://www.texasalmanac.com/sites/default/files/images/topics/ctypophistweb2010.pdf (accessed February 5, 2014).

39. For examples of histories that discuss the NAWSA unification, see McMillen, *Seneca Falls*; Sara Hunter Graham, *Woman Suffrage and the New Democracy* (New Haven: Yale University Press, 1996); Flexner, *Century of Struggle*; Wheeler, *New Women of the New South*.

40. *Dallas Morning News*, November 24, 1893, January 23, 1894, October 11, 1896; Mariana T. Folsom, "Texas (23 October 1896)," *WJ*, November 7, 1896; Mariana T. Folsom, "Eighty-Three Suffrage Meetings in Texas (4 Apr. 1894)," *WJ*, April 21, 1894.

41. Mariana T. Folsom, "Texas," *WJ*, April 17, 1897; Mariana T. Folsom, "Texas," *WJ*, June 20, 1896; Mariana T. Folsom to Susan B. Anthony (partial copy), July 8, 1898, folder 15, box 1, Folsom Papers; Elisabet Ney to Mariana T. Folsom, [December] 1898, folder 1, box 1, Folsom Papers; *Dallas Morning News*, February 22, 1907; Mariana T. Folsom, "Texas (20 July 1899)," *WJ*, August 12, 1899; Rachel Foster Avery, ed., *Proceedings of the Thirty-Second Annual Convention of the National American Woman Suffrage Association Held at the Church of Our Father . . . Washington, D.C., February 8, 9, 10, 12, 13, and 14, 1900* (Philadelphia: Ferris, 1900), 18 (quotation).

42. Mariana T. Folsom, "Texas," *WJ*, April 17, 1897; Mariana T. Folsom, "Texas," *WJ*, June 20, 1896; Elisabet Ney to Mariana T. Folsom, [December] 1898, folder 1, box 1, Folsom Papers; *Dallas Morning News*, February 22, 1907; Mariana T. Folsom, "Texas (20 July 1899)," *WJ*, August 12, 1899 (quotation).

43. U.S. Census, 1900, Jackson County, Tex., Population Schedules, entry for Allen Folsom; U.S. Census, 1900, Travis, Tex., Population Schedules, entry for Allen P. Folsom; U.S. Census, 1900, Jackson, Tex., Population Schedules, entry for Fred W. Measday; "In Memoriam," *Beatrice Woman's Tribune*, March 6, 1909; "Erminia Thompson Folsom [Bachelor of Science, 1907]," in *Bulletin of the University of Texas: Catalogue 1906–1907* (Austin: University of Texas Press, 1907), 316; "Clarence Stroud Thompson Folsom [Bachelor of Arts, 1907]," *UT Catalogue, 1906–1907*, 388; "Allison T. Folsom," in A. J. Peeler, *Standard Blue Book: Texas Edition, Featuring West Texas and Panhandle Plains Sections* (San Antonio: Standard Blue Book, 1921), 13:166; Susan B. Anthony to Mariana T. Folsom, June 8, 1903, folder 1, box 1, Folsom Papers; Tillie Wier, Mariana Folsom's great-granddaughter, telephone interview by author, July 30, 2009.

44. Mariana T. Folsom to Susan B. Anthony (partial copy), July 8, 1898, folder 15, box 1, Folsom Papers; Susan B. Anthony to Mariana T. Folsom, June 8, 1903 (quotation), folder 1, box 1, Folsom

Papers. A copy of vol. 4 of the *History of Woman Suffrage* exists with a handwritten dedication from Anthony to Folsom. See "The History of Woman Suffrage, Volume IV," Charles Agvent, Rare Books and Manuscripts, http://www.charlesagvent.com/shop/agvent/016097.html (accessed February 5, 2014).

45. *Journal of the House of Representatives of the State of Texas Regular Session Thirtieth Legislature* (Austin: Von Boeckmann–Jones, 1907), 308, 311 (quotation); "Woman Suffrage," *Handbook of Texas Online*, http://www.tshaonline.org/handbook/online/articles/WW/viw1.html (accessed December 18, 2006); *Dallas Morning News*, February 2, 22, 23, 1907; "Woman Suffrage Movement in Texas," *Woman's Tribune*, April 13, 1907; University of Texas, *Catalogue of the University of Texas* (Austin: State Printing Office, 1907), 11, 120–23, 319, 385.

46. *Journal of the House*, 762; "Woman Suffrage Movement in Texas," *Woman's Tribune*, April 13, 1907.

47. Mariana T. Folsom to Henry B. Blackwell, April 2, 1907 (second quotation), Henry B. Blackwell to Mariana T. Folsom, October 8, 1907, both in folder 1, box 1, Folsom Papers; Mariana T. Folsom, "The Suffrage Campaign in Texas (24 July 1885)," *WJ*, August 1, 1885 (first quotation); Carrie Chapman Catt and Nettie Rogers Shuler, *Woman Suffrage and Politics: The Inner Story of the Suffrage Movement* (New York: Scribner's, 1926), 190–91; Wheeler, *New Women of the New South*, 113–25.

48. Anna Howard Shaw to Mariana T. Folsom, March 6, 1907, Harriet Taylor Upton to Mariana T. Folsom, March 25, 1907, Kate M. Gordon to Mariana T. Folsom, February 26, 1908, all in folder 1, box 1, Folsom Papers.

49. Anna Howard Shaw to Mariana T. Folsom, March 6, 1907, folder 1, box 1, Folsom Papers; *Dallas Morning News*, April 12, May 18, 1908; *Austin Statesman*, April 25, 1908; *San Antonio Express*, April 27, 28, 1908; Kate M. Gordon to Mariana T. Folsom, February 26, 1908, folder 1, box 1, Folsom Papers; small red Austin Woman Suffrage Association account book in folder 11, box 31, McCallum Papers; Carrie Chapman Catt to Erminia Folsom, January 18, 1909 (second quotation), folder 4, box 1, Folsom Papers; McArthur, *Creating the New Woman*, 108.

50. "In Memoriam," *Woman's Tribune*, March 6, 1909 (quotation); Anson Titus, ed., *The Universalist Register: The Yearbook of the Universalist Church for 1910* (Boston: Universalist Publishing, 1910), 119; NAWSA, *Forty-Second Annual Report of the National-American Woman Suffrage Association* (Warren, Oh.: Headquarters, 1911), 205.

51. Carrie Chapman Catt to Erminia Folsom, January 18, 1909 (quotation), folder 4, box 1, Folsom Papers; Brannon-Wranosky, "Southern Promise and Necessity."

52. U.S. Census, 1920, Terrell County, Tex., Population Schedules, entry for A. T. Folsom; *Sanderson Trans-Pecos News*, 1903–6, Dolph Briscoe Center for American History, University of Texas at Austin; Ex-Students' Association of the University of Texas, *Alcalde* 3 (1914): 108; California Department of Health Services, Center for Health Statistics, California Death Index, 1940–97; U.S. Census, 1920, Brewster County, Tex., Population Schedules, entry for Oriana Measday.

Jovita Idar

The Ideological Origins of a Transnational Advocate for La Raza

GABRIELA GONZÁLEZ

Ed Idar Jr. remembered what being Mexican meant in early twentieth-century Texas. The rights and protections of U.S. citizenship, while granted to Mexicans by treaty, failed to manifest in social reality. "No Negroes, Mexicans, or Dogs Allowed" signs appeared on the doors, windows, and walls of public accommodations, creating much anxiety for nonwhites. And yet Idar recalled an ironic incident that occurred in the early 1930s when he was a preteen. His family was traveling from San Antonio to Laredo. His father, Eduardo Sr., stopped at a restaurant in Pearsall, Texas. The family stepped inside and took their seats. Amazingly, this family of Mexican Americans received service.[1]

Though Mexicans during this period routinely experienced segregation in certain places, such as movie theaters, and were denied service altogether in others, like restaurants, a dynamic of color, race, and class constructions spared Idar's family from one of the many humiliations Mexicans endured daily. He recalled,

> My mother was very light skinned, and she had light eyes, green eyes. Me and my sisters were medium color. . . . My father always wore a hat, shirt and a tie, and a coat, no matter how hot the weather was. . . . The Anglo used to have a stereotype of the Mexican. We've seen this Mexican . . . the big sombrero, sitting down, humped over. . . . But if you were well-dressed, with a tie and coat and all that, maybe you were okay. . . . That's the only way I can figure why we were not denied service in Pearsall in those years.[2]

Idar seemed convinced that his family had no problems that day because of these factors. But passing for white or gaining marginal acceptance as "Spanish

JOVITA IDAR, CA. 1905

Courtesy of the Woman's Collection, Texas Woman's University, Denton, Texas.

Mexicans" or "Latin Americans" would not be enough for Ed. He became a civil rights lawyer who challenged discriminatory practices and contributed to the transformation of race relations in Texas and the United States.

Ed Idar Jr. hailed from a family of journalists, publishers, teachers, and political activists committed to the struggle for equal rights. One of these activists was Ed's extraordinary aunt, Jovita Idar. Trained as a teacher, she joined the family business of muckraking journalism to address the formidable challenges Mexicans faced in Texas. She later participated in the Primer Congreso Mexicanista (First Mexicanist Congress) organized by the Idars, founded La Liga Femenil Mexicanista (League of Mexican Women), and worked with La Cruz Blanca (White Cross), a medical brigade associated with the Constitutionalist faction of the Mexican Revolution.[3] Jovita Idar's family background and her life and work, analyzed within the context of modernity and specifically the broad historical trends in the United States and Mexico during the nineteenth and early twentieth centuries, can shed light on the nature of her advocacy for *la raza*.[4]

Modernity, liberalism, and Methodism, experienced through a transnationalist political and cultural prism, shaped Jovita Idar's identity and activism. She shared traits with progressive reformers and evangelical Christians in both nations. As teacher, journalist, and activist, Idar used strategies of benevolence and reform to carry out her civil rights work in Jim Crow Texas.[5] Finally, an ethic of social and cultural redemption informed her human rights and social justice sensibilities and efforts.

Jovita Idar, born in Laredo, Texas, on September 7, 1885, lived on the border of two societies experiencing different levels of modernization. Mexico's cultural and intellectual elites, like those of the United States, were influenced by Western European ideas stemming from the eighteenth-century Age of Enlightenment, which privileged rational thought over church dogma as the source of knowledge. Through the development of human reason, humanity could escape feudalistic mentalities and achieve enlightenment, clearing the path to a progressive world where human liberation was possible. Modern society came to be defined by three major elements, capitalism or free enterprise, political liberty, and scientific progress. As the modern mind-set developed in tandem with the rise of nation-states, U.S. and Mexican leaders created institutional structures and sociocultural norms that encouraged economic development, political rights, and progress. Classical liberalism emerged as the political philosophy guiding these two nations during this period.[6] Idar possessed a modernist outlook and held a liberal political perspective, but religion—specifically, Methodism—also formed a part of her ideological makeup. Across the United

States and throughout the nineteenth century, evangelical Christians, inspired by the Social Gospel, participated in myriad reform movements designed to transform society in progressive ways.[7]

In Texas, Methodists made significant inroads among Spanish-speaking people. Beginning in 1874, the West Texas Conference of the Methodist Episcopal Church, South reached out to Mexican Americans by organizing a Spanish-speaking district. These efforts intensified, and by 1885, the Mexican Border Mission Conference, with a team of thirty-one ministers, tended to the spiritual needs of almost 1,400 members. East of the Pecos, Spanish-language churches became organized as the Texas Mexican Mission by 1914 and boasted 1,876 members and sixteen ministers. In 1930, the mission's membership had climbed to 3,837, with twenty-seven ministers. By the end of the decade, it had added churches in New Mexico and changed its name to the Rio Grande Conference.[8]

The Texas missionary effort among Spanish-speaking people served as a precursor to the broader project of proselytizing the Protestant faith in Mexico and the rest of Latin America. What missionaries perceived as an enlightened and progressive enterprise to improve the blighted lives of a Hispanic people imprisoned by ignorance and superstitious "Romanist" dogma comes across as a form of cultural imperialism. Racial stereotypes and gender expectations informed the attitudes and approaches of European American Protestant missionaries seeking to convert and in the process to Americanize Mexican-origin people. Protestantism became conflated with North American civilization and progress.[9]

But could social progress be attained in a racially stratified society? If asked this question, *méxico-texano* activists such as Idar would have answered no, because marginalizations and exclusions based on social constructs of race violated the liberties of entire groups of people. At the turn of the century, social redemption as conceived by these activists involved a struggle to eradicate racism and discrimination from society as well as to deal with problems such as poverty. Like the adherents of the Social Gospel movement, Idar and her associates focused much attention on changing their social and political environment. Cultural redemption, or redeeming *la raza*, represented an intra-ethnic-group effort by middle-class Mexican activists to "uplift" the poor, immigrants, and the working class materially, intellectually, and morally. It involved countless individual conversions to modernity and "respectable society" that would be needed to uplift a colonized people from their subordinate position in the United States.[10]

Jovita Idar's familiarity with the culture and language of modernity, liberalism, and Methodism developed early. Her father shaped her understanding of the world and its possibilities. Nicasio Idar impressed many people who knew him as a consummate professional and civic leader who rose from humble origins in Point Isabel, Texas, to become one of Laredo's most respected citizens. But before he became a community pillar, he sorted his ideas through various experiences. For example, working as a teenage ranch hand at the King Ranch showed him what it meant to be Mexican in nineteenth-century Texas. He later spent time in the border town of Rio Grande City, where he came under the influence of a Mexican Methodist preacher, Clemente Abraham Vivero, whose daughter, Jovita, Nicasio married in 1880. Jovita had acquired from her parents a Protestant religious foundation that was connected to a Social Gospel ethos of service to humanity. Good works and prayer represented Methodist prescriptions for improving society's ills, an approach very much in line with this Mexican family's social outlook and way of life.

Humanity's problems, many liberals believed, could be solved if people lived by certain principles boiled down to three essential priorities for the modern society: develop individual and social group morality, raise the intellectual capital of society through education, and promote material progress through economic development. All persons could contribute to society and improve their individual life chances by mastering the elements of respectability as defined by petit bourgeois values such as thrift, sobriety, patriotism or civic-mindedness, a strong work ethic, discipline of mind and habits, cleanliness, propriety, and refined manners. The Idars in many ways embodied these modern family ideals.

Nicasio and Jovita Vivero de Idar enjoyed a long marriage and parented nine children. To some extent self-educated but also instructed and mentored by Rev. Vivero, Nicasio developed into an extraordinarily intelligent and self-assured man, possessing tremendous drive and energy. After the marriage, he took a job in Nuevo Leon, Mexico, where he found profitable employment in the railroad yards. His wife and children remained in the family's large fifteen-room home in Laredo. Nicasio worked as a yardmaster for twenty years and organized workers in the city of Acambaro. In time, the Idar family enjoyed enough financial stability to allow Nicasio to leave railroad work altogether.[11]

In Laredo, the enterprising Nicasio became involved in various business, civic, and political ventures such as selling real estate, promoting a small cigar company managed by his wife, serving as a justice of the peace and as a U.S. marshal, joining many civic organizations, and becoming a thirty-third degree Freemason. He also began working for and later became the publisher of *La Crónica* (*The Chronicle*), a Spanish-language newspaper. *La Crónica* sought "to educate the people politically, socially, and morally." With the motto, "We work for the progress and the industrial, moral, and intellectual development of the Mexican inhabitants of Texas," *La Crónica* reported on lynchings, segregation, and other violations of natural and inalienable rights.[12]

The three eldest Idar children, Clemente, Jovita, and Eduardo, wrote articles for *La Crónica* until 1914, when the newspaper ceased operations soon after their father's death.[13] Like her brothers, Jovita learned to harness and focus her energies and talents. According to her niece and namesake, Jovita Fuentes de López, her beloved aunt was her grandfather's favorite. Raised in part by Jovita Idar after the death of her mother, Elvira (Jovita's younger sister), Fuentes de López remembered that Nicasio took great pride in his daughter's intelligence and delighted in the fact that she possessed a strong will. Nicasio and Jovita Vivero de Idar sent their eldest children to the Laredo Seminary, a Methodist School founded by missionary Nannie Emory Holding that was well known for its excellence in English-language instruction. Jovita also attended the Domínguez Institute in Laredo, where she was taught and mentored by Professor Simon G. Domínguez, a specialist in foreign languages.[14]

As students at the Methodist Laredo Seminary, Nicasio's older children found reaffirmation for their family's credo of material, intellectual, and moral advancement. The middle-class Methodist messages of industry, study, cleanliness, morality, and discipline heard at the Laredo Seminary would have been familiar to them. They might have also heard the Methodist missionary's language of redemption, but when filtered through a nineteenth-century Anglo-American mind-set, redemption potentially carried ethnocentric undertones.[15]

In her account of her work in Laredo between 1883 and 1893, Holding recalled the joys and challenges of founding a mission home and boarding school on the frontiers of American civilization. The book she produced, *A Decade of Mission Life*, provides a fascinating glimpse of this predominantly Catholic border community from the perspective of a well-intentioned missionary from Kentucky who brought with her the anti-Catholic and racialist thinking common among white Anglo-Saxon Protestants during this period. In describing her pupils, Holding used the racialist language of the period: "Here and there, scattered among these olive buds from the ancient Aztec root, we would sometimes see the pure white flower of Saxon origin. Of these were Lizzie and Flossie, two bright, lovely children, who quite often forgot they were in the minority; but they were made to remember it, when attempting to hold too queenly a sway over their dark-eyed companions." The discourse of hegemony continued even as Holding attempted to present her mission home as a site of harmonious race relations. "As a rule, these two classes—the conquered Aztec and the conquering Saxon—played, sang, and studied harmoniously side by side as though they had sprung from the same race. We, too, knew no difference; each alike found its way to the heart."[16] Holding probably wrote the book for other white Anglo-Saxon Protestants, possibly members of her church, in the hopes that they would continue to support her work if they knew how well Americans and Mexicans under her care were getting along.

Holding also sought to prove that Mexicans could be converted to Protestantism and by extension to modernity and civilization. She proudly recounted a visit during which Methodist bishop Holland Nimmons McTyeire commented on the excellent comportment and dress of her students: "He noticed and spoke of the difference between the appearance of our neatly attired children and the ragged squalor of those who met us at almost every step."[17] For Anglo missionaries, Mexicans could be redeemed if they became Protestants and adopted American traditions and values, habits of the mind, styles, and behaviors.

Over time, however, the much-respected Holding probably developed greater sensitivity regarding the cultural needs and backgrounds of her students. She remained the superintendent at the Laredo Seminary for thirty years, establishing close relationships with many of her students and referring to them as her children and to their children as her grandchildren. Holding described one former student, Lucia, as "a happy wife and mother, and her little boy, Miguel, [is] among my best loved grandchildren."[18] Holding retired at age sixty-eight in 1913, and the school was later renamed the Holding Institute. It enjoyed an excellent reputation, expanding its student body to include young people from Mexico and all over the world.[19]

Jovita earned her teaching credentials at the Laredo Seminary, graduating in 1903. According to her niece, Jovita's time there was a positive experience, though it is not known how she and the other students felt about Holding's language and Anglocentric worldview, if indeed they were aware of it. However, another question arises: How much of Holding's ideology did her students appropriate? With the exception of Holding's racialist perspectives, her ideas might not have seemed terribly offensive or foreign to Idar. Before she enrolled at the Laredo Seminary, Idar had already imbibed from her family the same middle-class social and moral values Holding promoted.[20]

Jovita Idar's articles provide a treasure trove of information about her values and perspectives. Idar not only wrote about her ideals, she lived by them, in the process leaving a record of civil and human rights activism that transcended borders of race, class, gender, and nation within a seemingly socially conventional *gente decente* middle-class culture of respectability.[21]

In an article reviewing the first year of *La Crónica*, Jovita Idar praised the newspaper for being "firm in its purpose of following an honorable path without baseness and without humiliations, defending with enthusiasm and frankness the interests of the *méxico-texano* element."[22] According to this article, Clemente, Eduardo, and Jovita served as the principal writers for *La Crónica*. In this piece, she referred to attacks on the paper, presumably by *La Revista Católica* (*Catholic Magazine*), a New Mexican Catholic paper that she and her colleagues often debated on issues pertaining to doctrinal matters, women, the family, and society. Many articles in *La Crónica* targeted Catholicism or responded to the Catholic positions on freemasonry, liberalism, or something *La Crónica* had printed. Although *La Crónica* writers advanced various arguments for why they thought Catholicism was an antimodern religion causing more harm than good, Jovita Idar encapsulated one of the main areas of discontent when she wrote of Catholics as "those who wish to rule the home and fanaticize women."[23]

Protestant missionaries also saw the Catholic Church in this light and spoke of "Romanism" as a plague on families and society, granting priests too much power and thus undermining liberty. The goal of missionary activity in Mexico and the U.S. Southwest was to convert Catholics into Protestants so that as they assumed leadership roles in institutions, they would bring "Protestant values, moral respectability, and economic progress" to the rest of Mexican and Mexican American societies. In this way, neither the U.S. Southwest nor Mexico as its neighbor to the south would pose a threat to the Anglo-Protestant nation-state as it sought to expand its sphere of influence. Citing Sydney Mead, scholar Paul Barton has identified six characteristics of North American Protestantism that informed missionary work: "the voluntary principle, revivalism, anti-Catholicism, education, social reform, and morality." Barton argues that Protestantes (Mexican Protestants) retained elements of these religious and cultural aspects of Anglo-Protestantism.[24]

The Idar family inherited from Jovita's maternal grandfather, Rev. Vivero, a Mexican Protestantism that appropriated these aspects of North American Protestantism, which happened to coincide with values congenial to the Mexican liberal tradition. For example, the idea of a voluntary relationship between the individual and God suited the priest-averse Idars, who found this principle liberating since it called for individuals to communicate directly with God and actively pursue their own salvation.

As a liberal, Nicasio had good reason to be worried about the Catholic Church. The church had taken some strong positions in reaction to modernist and progressive trends during the nineteenth and twentieth centuries. In 1864, Pope Pius IX issued an encyclical denouncing the separation of church and state, public schools operated by the state, religious freedom, and freedom of the press.[25] While anti-Catholic ideas filled some pages of *La Crónica*, according to Ed Idar Jr., family members were not fanatical in their religious beliefs, nor were they on a quest to persecute Catholics. In fact, Ed's father married a Catholic woman and acceded to his wife's wish to raise their children as Catholics.[26]

The other three characteristics of Protestantism described by Barton—education, social reform, and morality—speak more directly to the strategies of social and cultural redemption. Society's redemption could be achieved through social reform, which would destroy social ailments such as racism. However, to be effective, social reform required that a degraded people be materially, intellectually, and morally lifted up by more advantaged members of society. The Idars, among others, heard the call for the cultural redemption of *la raza* and threw themselves with missionary zeal into the struggle to uplift an oppressed people.

La Crónica focused on this mission of uplift but also expended much energy on a crusade to expose injustice and called for change. In an article on the education of Mexican children in Texas, Jovita Idar called on the *méxico-texano* community to take a proactive approach in this matter because neither the Mexican nor American government had prioritized the preparation and future of these children. "A great part of the scorn with which the foreigners [Americans] around us see us results from the lack of education, and, moreover, because of the gross ignorance of an immense majority of our compatriots and because it is no longer easy to educate those great masses of workers, we can endeavor, even to the point of sacrifice, if necessary, to enlighten our children so that at least we can avert this evil in the future."[27] This paragraph encapsulates the cultural redemption philosophy that tolerance could be achieved through group cultural change. If Mexicans could become more educated, they would no longer be marginalized in the United States. This idea resembles the cultural redemption efforts of Protestant missionaries such as Holding, who, unlike white supremacists calling for strict segregation of Anglos and Mexicans, believed that Mexicans could be converted to Protestantism and assimilated into American society over time.

Missionaries may have shared socialization processes with segregationists but clearly had different priorities. The people of Laredo recognized this difference, and Jovita mentioned a literary piece dedicated to Holding, "El Hada Buena" (The Good Fairy). If people in Laredo saw Holding as a good fairy, it was because they must have seen her in benevolent terms, providing assistance or even guidance and mentoring.[28]

Indeed, the period from the Civil War to 1920 ushered in great changes in Laredo and other modernizing communities in the American Southwest. Immigrants from Mexico, Europe, and other parts of the United States, including missionaries, were often welcomed to Laredo as harbingers of progress who brought ideas, new energies, and sometimes capital to the small bustling border town. The Idars were some of these new arrivals. Jovita proudly listed the many projects her family's newspaper supported, among them the construction of rainwater dams for agricultural irrigation, the establishment of a kindergarten, the founding of a club for businessmen, the creation of a civic league, and the building of a railroad line between Laredo and Rio Grande City. Jovita also reminded readers about La Crónica's commitment to civil and human rights, citing the paper's role in issuing a protest to the Texas Legislature in regard to León Cárdenas Martínez Jr., a fifteen-year-old Mexican boy condemned to death for homicide based on a coerced confession. The commitment to the dissemination of knowledge was highlighted when La Crónica published articles by renowned intellectuals and featured the poetry of local talents such as Sara Estela Ramírez.[29]

While the Idars saw their newspaper as a means of elevating the intellectual capital of adults within the méxico-texano community who had no other recourse for instruction, children represented a different type of challenge. Texas's public school system ostensibly provided education for all of the state's children, but La Crónica readers learned from Clemente Idar's incisive exposé on the Jim Crow school segregation system that méxico-texano children were being left behind, relegated to inferior schools with less qualified and lower-paid teachers. Adding to the problem, the powerful agriculture industry preferred to have young Mexicans working in the fields for low wages rather than in school acquiring the building blocks for a brighter economic future.[30]

Jovita Idar's understanding of the situation with "Mexican" schools came from personal experience. After earning her teaching certificate, she taught in the small town of Los Ojuelos. Appalled by the poor conditions and inadequate equipment as well as the lack of hope in this community, she resigned and turned to political journalism, working alongside her brothers and father and using the media to foment social change.[31]

In her articles, Jovita Idar called on méxico-texanos to take responsibility for their children's education and expressed concerns about assimilation. Idar worried that the drive to assimilate Mexican schoolchildren in U.S.-based schools deprived youngsters of their linguistic and cultural heritage. In an article on the preservation of national identity, Idar agreed that learning English made life in the United States easier and certainly should be encouraged, since méxico-tejanos would need to use the language to defend their rights. Yet losing one's native tongue would lead to the loss of group identity, since language represented the characteristic seal of nationalities and nations.[32]

Idar was particularly disturbed because some Mexican teachers in the United States privileged an assimilationist pedagogy, resulting in a dismal situation whereby the Spanish language "is increasingly forgotten and each day it suffers adulterations and changes that materially hurt the ear of any Mexican as little versed as he might be in the language of Cervantes."[33] Idar proposed that Mexican parents in Texas unite to pay for their children's education by teachers able and willing to teach Spanish. Schools in Monterrey, Saltillo, and other Mexican cities produced young, energetic, knowledgeable teachers who would be only too happy to work in Texas at a reasonable wage.[34]

At the heart of Idar's call for *escuelitas* (private schools for Mexican children in the United States taught by Spanish-dominant or bilingual teachers) and bilingual education lay an understanding of the power of language and culture in the nation-building project. National societies are imagined communities nourished by shared traits whose demise or replacement threatens the integrity of the group's national identity. Idar cited the Aztecs as an example of a people that stopped existing as a nation once their language was lost. Moreover, she decried the lack of instruction on Mexico's national heroes: "If in the American school our children attend, they are taught the biography of Washington and not the one of Hidalgo, and if instead of the glorious deeds of Juárez they are referred to the exploits of Lincoln, as much as these are noble and just, that child will not know the glories of his nation, he will not love her, and he might even see his parents' countrymen with indifference."[35] Idar reminded readers that education could culturally redeem Mexicans in the eyes of the Americans surrounding them and that ignoring this issue would condemn Mexicans to live as a degraded people.[36]

The U.S. emphasis on teaching Mexican children in English-only classrooms troubled Idar, who knew such disregard for the cultural heritage of Mexican children would lead to their further marginalization in American society. Contemporary sociologists Alejandro Portes and Rubén G. Rumbaut describe this process as "dissonant acculturation," arguing that such assimilationist policies deliver the message to the children of immigrants that their linguistic heritage and culture are inferior. As they struggle to fit in, a wedge develops between these young people and their parents, undermining parental authority and ability to protect their children from dangers in school and in the streets.[37]

Concerns about the future of Mexican youth and other critical issues inspired the Idars to mobilize Mexican activists throughout Texas into a civil and human rights congress. The First Mexicanist Congress took place on September 14–22, 1911, in Laredo and resulted in the creation of two organizations, the Great Mexican League for Beneficence and Protection and the League of Mexican Women. These groups' primary concerns included civil rights, cultural retention, and education.[38]

With Jovita Idar as president, the League of Mexican Women framed political participation by *gente decente* women in terms of benevolence, transforming their moral imperatives into a plan of action and focusing on alleviating social ills through charitable projects.[39] Two months after the group's creation, its members—"numerous and very respectable young ladies of Laredo"—began their charitable work in earnest. The league committed itself to providing for the education of two destitute children and found volunteers to provide free instruction. Profesoras María Rentería and Berta Cantú offered the services of their respective *escuelitas*, while the league bought the children new clothes and school supplies.[40]

Some league members were trained educators and professionals, and the education of youth remained the organization's primary focus, though widespread poverty also commanded attention. As a *La Crónica* article probably written by Jovita Idar argued, "One of the ends for which this society shall labor will also be to help the poor of Laredo in some measure. Some who find themselves in the most complete misery and abandonment have had clothes provided by some of the young women and food by the very respectable Señora Doña Tomasita de Mendoza."[41] The article continued, "This association actively works for the general advancement of its members, holds studying and learning sessions, sessions where culture is acquired and talent is developed without orgies and unhealthy ambitions, and dedicates itself to the realization of noble and generous ends. . . ."[42] In addition to informing the community about the group's activities, the article advertised a benefit for the league at the Solorzano Theater. The league needed to raise funds because it did "not count on pecuniary elements, for its members all belonged to the noble working class."[43] Embedded in this text was the message that regardless of financial means, people could still be *gente decente*. However, the educators and others who comprised the group could hardly be considered members of the working class, so another subtext of the message was that despite unequal economic relations, the working poor would be measured by bourgeois moral and cultural standards, which were believed to hold the key to better treatment for Mexicans in Texas. Members of the League of Mexican Women sought to identify with the working poor and to improve their lives as much as possible through a program of social uplift.

But the working poor experienced life on much different terms, meaning that education was a luxury.[44] Elena Medellin de Ramírez, for example, remembered the difficulties encountered by her father, a blacksmith, in providing for his eight children during the Great Depression. Other family members picked cotton, and the Medellins survived on a regular diet of coffee and flour tortillas.[45] Reynaldo García recalled that his father operated an herb stand at the *mercado* (town market) but did not make enough money to support his children, so they went to work as well. Reynaldo left school and got his first wage-earning job at age ten or eleven, running errands for a bakery starting at four or five in the morning. After their father's death, his sister worked at the Singer Sewing Machine factory, where she earned the money for groceries, and he earned the family's rent money by working at a smelter.[46]

The concept of *gente decente* certainly encompassed a broad range of people, from the wealthy to the middle class and even to the working class, provided they met middle-class moral standards. However, for a group of teachers to identify themselves as members of the working class seems like a cultural stretch—unless, of course, such an identification had political significance. By connecting themselves to the poor, the women of the league signaled their identification with another group perceived as weak and in need of protection. Furthermore, at a time when the expansion of capital across South Texas made workers particularly vulnerable and when labor unions began to make inroads into this community, many Mexicans in Texas who were a bit higher on the social scale aligned themselves with workers and unions.[47]

Nevertheless, middle-class privilege, even among low-salaried teachers, made its presence felt. In addition to its work as a political or charitable organization, the league created a social and cultural space for its educated members, meeting in private homes, including that of the Idar family. To generate funds for its charitable projects, it sponsored literary readings and musical and theatrical productions such as the one at the Solorzano Theater.[48] In addition, through Jovita Idar, group members gained access to the media. The league embodied the *gente decente* value system.

Cultural redemption is an important element of transborder political culture that at times seemed like social control but in reality attempted to bring about social transformation by challenging negative stereotypes used to justify the exploitation of Mexican people. But Jovita Idar was as concerned about negative stereotypes of women as she was about the negative images of Mexicans. She believed that sexism, like racism, could be disarmed by calling on women to empower themselves with the shield of education and the robes of respectability. In "Para la Mujer que Lee" (For the Woman Who Reads), which she signed with the pen name Astrea (the Greek goddess of justice), Idar promoted the idea that education elevated women—and by extension men. "The educated woman who has received in the home or school the fundamental principles of a moral education and who follows them, sees herself respected, exalted, and received wherever she goes. . . . The educated woman more often is good, and being good, she spreads an atmosphere of purity that elevates man."[49] This passage contains elements of nineteenth-century Victorian ideas about gender. By this standard, a woman's power rested in her ability to be pure and moral. Her sublime role was to inspire men to find their own moral compass and in this way contribute to civilization.

The article also critiqued women who did not seek an education but instead sought fulfillment in empty and vain pursuits such as "going out into the streets to 'make conquests' and thereby disrespect themselves." She contrasted such a woman with one who was "pure [and] in her own chastity finds defense, for men, no matter how uncultured they might be, always respect the woman who makes herself respected." As in the article on the importance of educating Mexican children, Idar presented the values of the *gente decente* as solutions to social problems plaguing marginalized groups.[50]

In addition to urging people to uplift themselves, Idar critiqued the social structure that encouraged racism and sexism. She highlighted the pernicious manner in which Texas schools threatened the existence of Mexicans as a national group. Long after the battles of the Texas Revolution and U.S.-Mexican War, Idar argued, Anglos continued to think about Mexicans as enemies and to stigmatize them as a social problem.[51] And she followed the feminist line of reasoning when she defined the modern woman as having "broad horizons": "Woman must always seek to acquire useful and beneficial knowledge, for in modern times, she has broad horizons. Science, industry, the workshop, and even the home demand her best aptitudes, her perseverance and consistency in work, and her influence and assistance for all that is progress and advancement for humanity."[52] The modern world needed women who, like Jovita Idar, had prepared themselves educationally to make contributions in different areas. Idar's message of emancipation for women continued in another article, "Debemos Trabajar" (We Should Work), in which she contrasted the lazy, slacker female who idles away precious time shopping and making social calls, "living deceitfully on gossip and lurid tales," to the productive modern woman, who contributed to society regardless of her station. The wealthy modern woman engaged in charity work through her benevolent clubs, while the working woman, recognizing her equality to man—"her natural protector, and not her master and lord"—prepared herself for the struggle.[53]

Idar pointed out that despite opposition from critics of the feminist movement, women were gaining ground. In California, she asserted, women could now serve on juries and in public office. She thought of the naysayers as "those fastidious spirits . . . critics of that woman who, putting aside social conventions, dedicates her energies to working for something beneficial." Idar reprimanded such people for failing to see the positive moral influence wielded by such women, who did not have time for "futile and harmful matters."[54] Idar ended the article with a note about single women who were dignified and hardworking, earning their own keep and helping their families. Useful and productive, such women did not live at the expense of fathers, brothers, and other relatives. As male tramps and loafers were despised by dignified working men, working women did not appreciate useless and do-nothing women.[55]

Thus, the ideal modern woman carved her own path and contributed to social progress. Jovita Idar, like the Progressive New Woman, exemplified a feminist ideal that was not completely divorced from Victorian concepts of womanhood but certainly challenged and stretched the boundaries of a male-dominated society. In Mexico, as a revolutionary movement took shape and finally erupted in 1910, women from all social classes joined the struggle for a new and more democratic country, in the process voicing feminist concerns and claiming political spaces. Scholar Clara Lomas's examination of Leonor Villegas de Magnón's memoirs provides a fascinating picture of how Idar, Teresa and Andrea Villarreal, and many other borderlands women joined in the Mexican struggle for freedom. At the center of Villegas de Magnón's participation in the Mexican Revolution was the La Cruz Blanca, a medical relief organization she founded in 1913.[56]

The work of La Cruz Blanca began on March 17, 1913, when Villegas de Magnón, Idar, and other border residents entered a battle-torn Nuevo Laredo, the community across the border from Laredo, to pick up and care for wounded men. Within two months, the group, predominantly composed of women, became organized as an official medical brigade attached to the Constitutionalist faction of the Mexican Revolution led by General Venustiano Carranza.[57] Following Carranza's troops throughout northern Mexico, La Cruz Blanca established medical brigades in several communities, and on May 20, 1914, Carranza declared La Cruz Blanca a national organization. The following September 14, La Cruz Blanca entered Mexico City with Carranza's triumphant forces.[58]

Border violence subsequently escalated, with a virtual race war erupting. Angered by Mexicans' loss of economic and political power in Texas and by their treatment as social pariahs, a group of borderlands men led by Aniceto Pizaña and Luis de la Rosa formed a seditionist movement, the centerpiece of which was a manifesto known as the Plan de San Diego, a plot to kill all Anglo males over the age of sixteen and return territories to Mexico. *Sediciosos* (seditionists), among whom were both *méxico-texanos* and Mexicans, attacked Anglo-owned and sometimes Tejano-owned ranches, railroad crossings, irrigation systems, and military camps, resulting in significant property damage and some deaths. Anglo-Texan communities responded swiftly, with Rinches (Texas Rangers), other law-enforcement officials, and vigilantes killing hundreds of Mexican-origin people. Most of those killed were not part of the seditionist movement and simply fell victim to the strong anti-Mexican fervor. The Plan de San Diego caused long-standing racist sentiments regarding Mexicans to escalate into lethal levels of vitriol and hatred.[59]

For Villegas de Magnón and other members of the La Cruz Blanca, the violent border situation and tense U.S.-Mexican diplomatic relationship created problems even after the United States recognized Carranza as Mexico's legitimate leader in 1915. Clemente Idar explained the situation to Villegas de Magnón on October 16, 1916, reminding her that although many residents of Laredo had initially favored the Mexican Revolution, much of that support had now morphed into "profound hatred for the revolution and its men. The municipal authorities of Laredo and the county who . . . were ardent fans of Mr. [Francisco] Madero and Mr. Carranza are now dangerously hostile. The [Euro-] American element of this city is antagonistic toward our cause as it has never been before. American journalists scrupulously observe the Mexican press in Texas, and so does the American Justice Department."[60] Clemente went on to list other opponents of Carranza—political refugees, foreign capitalists with property in Mexico, American Catholic clergymen as well as the international Catholic Church, and the more vocal faction of the Republican Party.[61]

By this time, Jovita Idar was working for *El Progreso* (*Progress*), a Spanish-language pro-Carranza newspaper published and partially financed by Leopoldo Villegas, Leonor's brother.[62] On one occasion, Idar risked her life to defend the principle of freedom of the press. In 1914, Mexican revolutionary Manuel García Virgil wrote an editorial for *El Progreso* in which he criticized the Woodrow Wilson administration's military intervention in Veracruz.[63] In retaliation, the Texas Rangers set out to destroy the paper's office and printing presses. But when the Rangers arrived, they found Idar blocking their way and daring them to knock her down. The Rangers backed away but returned early the next morning when Idar was not present and destroyed the building and equipment and arrested the workers.[64]

The incident not only highlights one woman's extraordinary courage but also speaks to the era's societal structures. Idar was a medium- to dark-skinned Mexican American woman challenging the authority of a state police unit known for its intolerance of Mexicans, especially during this period. That she was not knocked down on the spot testifies to the power of gendered class conventions. While the Idars were not rich, their educational privilege; their work as journalists, entrepreneurs, and labor leaders; their involvement in civic life; and their professional and personal networks signaled their solid position as members of Laredo's cultural elite.[65]

In addition to her class and cultural credentials, Idar carried herself with great authority, was highly articulate, and exuded respectability. She and her siblings dressed formally, seeking to combat stereotypes of Mexicans as dirty and unkempt by dressing well and behaving with decorum. She thus constituted a tremendous presence and contrasted sharply to the lower-class Mexicans whom the Rangers regularly encountered, and they did not feel free to attack her.[66]

Undaunted by the challenges they faced, Idar and Villegas de Magnón continued their efforts to help the Constitutionalists. Public support for Carranza needed to be encouraged. Once again, they turned to the media. With the demise of *El Progreso*, the members of the Idar family and Villegas de Magnón planned a new propaganda newspaper, *Evolución* (*Evolution*), to be operated by the Idar family, with Jovita, Eduardo, and Clemente playing principal roles. The Idars provided some capital for this project, as did Carranza, who contributed one thousand dollars, a fifth of the total initial investment.[67]

Jovita Idar took a very active role in the development of *Evolución*. On November 20, 1916, she told Villegas de Magnón, "I bought a press worth more than a thousand dollars and bought plenty of type and everything. I can make a seven-column newspaper and will start soon." Her commitment to *Evolución* ran so deep that she postponed her wedding to start the venture.[68]

In May 1917, Idar married Bartolo Juárez, who came from a respectable Laredo family, but she continued to work for *Evolución*. Idar de Juárez initially handled most of the writing with the exception of the editorials. The newspaper struggled financially, but Clemente secured enough advertising to cover half of the expenses. To increase circulation, Idar de Juárez opened agencies in Monterrey, Saltillo, Torreón, and Tampico in Mexico as well as San Antonio, Corpus Christi, Alice, and elsewhere in Texas.[69]

By April 3, 1918, however, Idar de Juárez was no longer working at *Evolución*, likely because her other commitments left her no time to do so. She and a friend, Maria C. Villarreal, were involved with another benevolent organization, Campamento Amistad (Camp Friendship), and she served as a volunteer nurse with the American Red Cross during World War I.[70]

In 1921, Jovita and Bartolo Juárez moved to San Antonio. In 1928, she ran ads in *La Prensa* (*The Press*), a Spanish-language daily, offering her services as an English-Spanish translator; as an English teacher and tutor for elementary and secondary school students; and as a technician. She listed a printer in Laredo and the county secretary's office as her references.[71]

As in Laredo and in San Antonio, Jovita Idar de Juárez made her presence felt and left her mark as a woman of high principle and deep convictions. Fuentes de López remembered her aunt as a strong, intelligent, serious woman. She was tall and formal but very curious and interested in people.[72]

The most important facets of Jovita Idar de Juárez's life were family, education, church, politics, and community. She spent countless hours helping her nephews and nieces with homework and giving advice. She wanted everyone to get an education, but the type of education mattered. She did not object when her nieces and nephews spoke Spanish but abhorred the use of Spanglish.[73]

Jovita Idar de Juárez was also patriotic and respectful of the histories and traditions of both the United States and Mexico. She took her nieces to events such as the Fiestas Patrias (Patriotic Celebrations) to mark the anniversary of Mexico's independence and introduced them to Justo Sierra's *History of Mexico*, but she was an American citizen with great respect for the United States. She taught her younger family members to sing patriotic songs such as "Columbia, the Gem of the Ocean" and the "Star Spangled Banner." When U.S. presidents visited, Idar de Juárez took her nieces to see them.[74]

Jovita Idar de Juárez's interest in politics and community also found expression in her family life. She often debated political issues with her brothers and took her nieces to community events. She took Fuentes de López and others to the municipal auditorium when labor organizer Emma Tenayuca and other members of the Communist Party met there and a riot broke out. Idar de Juárez might have wanted to teach her nieces about civic life by taking them to see the famous labor leader in action, or perhaps she heard that an anticommunist crowd had surrounded the auditorium and she wanted to teach the girls about differences in political orientation. She also was likely a strong supporter of the Tejana pecan shellers led by Tenayuca who went on strike in 1938 to protest cuts to their already miserably low wages. The Idars were deeply committed to labor organizing and would have understood and sympathized with the plight of this exploited group of women. Whatever her rationale, when the riot broke out, Idar de Juárez regretted having brought her nieces, and they were quite scared to be caught in the middle of a rock-throwing mob. However, they safely escaped.[75]

Idar de Juárez helped the poor by providing for their basic needs, the illiterate by teaching them to read and write, the undocumented by helping them file for naturalization papers, and even young men preparing for the ministry who needed to hone their public speaking skills. She was an excellent teacher and a talented orator. She remained active in the Democratic Party and was a leader in the Trinidad Methodist Church, serving as conference president of the United Methodist Women and as coeditor of the *Heraldo Cristiano* (*Christian Herald*), an organ of the Rio Grande Conference of the Methodist Church. She also held paid employment, working as a physician's assistant at Robert B. Green Hospital. And after the death of her sister Elvira, she and her mother raised Elvira's children.[76]

Jovita Idar de Juárez possessed a tremendous ability to serve, and she often gave far more than she took. Her values mirrored those of her family, especially her father, Nicasio. With her parents' blessing, she grew into an independent and respectable woman, stretching the boundaries of *gente decente* behavior as needed.[77]

Politicized domesticity continued to inform Idar de Juárez's work long after the heady days of the Mexican Revolution and border activism. In October 1940, she published an article that revealed how her perspectives on women and family reflected a nineteenth-century concept of maternal Christian authority. Writing in the *Heraldo Cristiano*, Jovita reminded her female readers about their special responsibility as women and as Christian mothers. The home, the church, and the state were important parts of universal education, but children's education at home by their mothers was the most important factor: "Only the blessed maternal counsel can form Christian and useful characters for society once they have learned that the origin of all wisdom is fear of God." She called on women to be that noble influence, "putting their children on the Christian life path, fulfilling their instincts of kindness and the latent tenderness from the heart of all women, regardless of race and culture."[78]

Jovita Idar de Juárez died in 1946, leaving behind an impressive legacy. Locating her ideological origins, her transnational advocacy for *la raza*, in concepts of modernity, liberalism, and Methodism complicates the story of this intriguing woman. Idar de Juárez combined some ideas that today might be cast as liberating with other ideas that the twenty-first-century political culture would deem conservative. She struggled against racism, promoted education for both men and women, participated in the Mexican Revolution, challenged the Texas Rangers, helped countless people from all backgrounds, and ultimately devoted her entire life in the service of others, whether family or members of the community. Jovita Idar de Juárez lived in the modern world, accepting its freedoms to expand her woman's sphere to the point that its constraints became meaningless. From liberalism she took the intellectual and political framework that structured her activism. But what ultimately drove her missionary spirit was the desire to help others—to transform a racist society and to redeem *la raza*.

NOTES

1. Ed Idar Jr., interview by author, August 31, 2000.

2. Ibid. I translate the self-referent *mexicano* into English as "Mexican." In keeping with the custom of the period, I also use *méxico-texanos*, another self-referent, to refer to Texas-born Mexicans. I do not capitalize it, since the historical actors discussed here did not capitalize it.

3. Jovita Idar vertical file folders, Woman's Collection, Texas Woman's University, Denton.

4. The literal translation of *la raza* is "the race." However, early twentieth-century transborder activists who used this term attached cultural rather than biological meanings and used it to refer to Mexican-origin people regardless of citizenship. Spanish-speaking peoples from the U.S. Southwest to the rest of the Americas might also be referenced using this term.

5. On Progressive reformers in the United States, see Michael McGerr, *A Fierce Discontent: The Rise and Fall of the Progressive Movement in America, 1870–1920* (New York: Oxford University Press, 2003); on reformers in Mexico, see William E. French, *A Peaceful and Working People: Manners, Morals, and Class Formation in Northern Mexico* (Albuquerque: University of New Mexico Press, 1996); on European American and African American evangelical Christians and reform, see Elizabeth Hayes Turner, *Women, Culture, and Community: Religion and Reform in Galveston, 1880–1920* (New York: Oxford University Press, 1997); Evelyn Brooks Higginbotham, *Righteous Discontent: The Women's Movement in the Black Baptist Church, 1880–1920* (Cambridge: Harvard University Press, 1993). On Hispanic evangelical Christians, see Paul Barton, *Hispanic Methodists, Presbyterians, and Baptists in Texas* (Austin: University of Texas Press, 2006); on evangelical Christians in Mexico, see Deborah J. Baldwin, *Protestants and the Mexican Revolution: Missionaries, Ministers, and Social Change* (Urbana: University of Illinois Press, 1990).

6. On classical liberalism, see Paul Schumaker, Dwight C. Kiel, and Thomas Heilke, *Great Ideas/Grand Schemes: Political Ideologies in the Nineteenth and Twentieth Centuries* (New York: McGraw-Hill, 1996), 43–78; Christopher Goto-Jones, "Liberalism," in *The Palgrave Dictionary of Transnational History: From the Mid-Nineteenth Century to the Present Day*, ed. Akira Iriye and Pierre-Yves Saunier (Basingstoke: Palgrave Macmillan, 2009), 656–58. On modernity, see Rana Mitter, "Modernity," in *Palgrave Dictionary of Transnational History*, ed. Iriye and Saunier, 720–23.

7. Jon Butler, Grant Wacker, and Randall Balmer, *Religion in American Life: A Short History* (New York: Oxford University Press, 2008), 185–90, 296–97.

8. Norman W. Spellmann, "Methodist Church," *Handbook of Texas Online*, http://www.tsha online.org/handbook/online/articles/immo1 (accessed January 12, 2013). For more information on the history of Methodists in Texas, see Emory S. Bucke, *History of American Methodism* (New York: Abingdon, 1964); Kennard B. Copeland, *History of the Methodist Protestant Church in Texas* (Commerce, Tex.: *Commerce Journal*, 1938); Olin W. Nail, ed., *History of Texas Methodism, 1900–1960* (Austin: Capital, 1961); Walter N. Vernon, Robert W. Sledge, Robert C. Monk, and Norman W. Spellman, *The Methodist Excitement in Texas* (Dallas: Texas United Methodist Historical Society, 1984).

9. Daisy L. Machado, "Women and Religion in the Borderlands," in *Encyclopedia of Women and Religion in North America*, ed. Rosemary Skinner Keller, Rosemary Radford Ruether, and Marie Cantlon (Bloomington: Indiana University Press, 2006), 1:1137–40.

10. On cultural redemption, see Gabriela González, "Carolina Munguía and Emma Tenayuca: The Politics of Benevolence and Radical Reform, 1930s," in *Gender on the Borderlands: The Frontier Reader*, ed. Antonia Castañeda, Susan H. Armitage, Patricia Hart, and Karen Weatheron (Lincoln: University of Nebraska Press, 2007), 200–229; Gabriela González, "Two Flags Entwined: Transborder Activists and the Politics of Race, Ethnicity, Class, and Gender in South Texas, 1900–1950" (PhD diss., Stanford University, 2005).

11. Elliot Gordon Young, "Deconstructing 'La Raza': Identifying the 'Gente Decente' of Laredo, 1904–1911," *Southwestern Historical Quarterly* 98 (October 1994): 232; Aquilino (Ike) and Guadalupe Idar, interview by Dr. Jerry Poyo and Tom Shelton, October 26, 1984, Institute of Texan Cultures, San Antonio.

12. Ads for Idar's cigar factory and real estate business appear in *La Crónica*; *La Crónica*, February 5, 1910; Teresa Palomo Acosta, "Idar, Nicasio," *Handbook of Texas Online*, http://www.tshaonline .org/handbook/online/articles/fido2 (accessed October 28, 2010).

13. Aquilino and Guadalupe Idar, interview.

14. Jovita Fuentes de López, interview by author, September 11, 2000.

15. Ed Idar Jr., interview; Fuentes de López, interview.

16. Nannie E. Holding, *A Decade of Mission Life* (Nashville: Methodist Episcopal Church Publishing, 1895), 16.

17. Ibid., 25–26.

18. Ibid., 16.

19. Jerry Thompson, *Laredo: A Pictorial History* (Norfolk, Va.: Donning, 1986), 224–25; Nancy Baker Jones, "Idar, Jovita," *Handbook of Texas Online*, http://www.tshaonline.org/handbook/online/ articles/fido3 (accessed November 5, 2010).

20. Fuentes de López, interview.

21. During the late nineteenth century, as Mexico experienced modernization, the developing middle class sought to distinguish itself from the mass of workers through consumption patterns and by claiming the mantle of respectability. The concept *gente decente* ("the decent people" or "the respectable") suited the needs of the members of the middle class, who were unquestionably influenced by modernity and Western culture. See French, *Peaceful and Working People*, 4–6.

22. "El Primer Año de Vida," *La Crónica*, January 8, 1910: "firme en sus propósitos de seguir una carrera honrosa, sin bajezas y sin humillaciones, defendiendo con entusiasmo y con franqueza los intereses del element méxico-texano."

23. Ibid.: "los que quieren dirigir el hogar y fanatizar á la mujer." For a more in-depth analysis of the conflict between the *La Crónica* and the *La Revista Católica*, see González, "Two Flags Entwined," 135–45.

24. Barton, *Hispanic Methodists*, 29–44.

25. Ibid., 35.

26. Ed Idar Jr., interview; Fuentes de López, interview.

27. "Por la Raza: La Niñez Mexicana en Texas," *La Crónica*, August 10, 1911: "Gran parte del desprecio con que nos ven los extranjeros que nos rodean, es debido á la falta de instrucción, y más aun, á la ignorancia crasa de una inmensa mayoría de nuestros compatriotas y puesto que ya no es facil instruir á esas grandes masas de obreros, cuando menos podemos esforzarnos y hasta llegar al sacrificio, si fuero necesario para ilustrar á nuestros hijos, para que cuando menos conjuremos el mal en el future."

28. "El Primer Año de Vida," *La Crónica*, January 8, 1910.

29. Ibid. For Laredo's economic changes after the Civil War, see John A. Adams Jr., *Conflict and Commerce on the Rio Grande: Laredo, 1755–1955* (College Station: Texas A&M University Press, 2008); Emilio Zamora, *The World of the Mexican Worker in Texas* (College Station: Texas A&M University Press, 1995); F. Arturo Rosales, *Testimonio: A Documentary History of the Mexican American Struggle for Civil Rights* (Houston: Arte Público, 2000), 111–12; F. Arturo Rosales, *Pobre Raza!: Violence, Justice, and Mobilization among México Lindo Immigrants, 1900–1936* (Austin: University of Texas Press, 1999), 143.

30. *La Crónica* articles focusing on school segregation included "Los Niños Mexicanos en Texas," November 26, 1910; "La Exclusión de los Niños Mexicanos en la Mayor Parte de las Escuelas Oficiales

de Texas es Positiva," December 17, 1910; "Tanto los Niños Mexicanos como los Mexico-Americanos son excluidos de las Escuelas Oficiales—¿ya se Olvidaron los Tratados de Guadalupe?," December 24, 1910; "La Exclusión en el Condado de Guadalupe," December 31, 1910; "Los Mexicanos de San Angelo Demandan a Los Sindicos de las Escuelas Públicas," December 31, 1910; "La Exclusión de los Niños Mexicanos de la Escuelas Americanas En Algunas Partes de Texas," January 26, 1911.

31. Jones, "Idar, Jovita."

32. "Por la Raza: La Niñez Mexicana en Texas," *La Crónica*, August 10, 1911; "Por la Raza: La Conservación del Nacionalismo," *La Crónica*, August 17, 1911.

33. "Por la Raza: La Niñez Mexicana en Texas," *La Crónica*, August 10, 1911: "que cada día se va olvidando más y cada día va sufriendo adulteraciones y cambios que hieren materialmente el oído de cualquier mexicano, por poco versado que esté en la idioma de Cervantes."

34. Ibid.

35. "Por la Raza: La Conservación del Nacionalismo," *La Crónica*, August 17, 1911: "si en la escuela americana á que concurren nuestros niños se les enseña la Biografía de Washington y no la de Hidalgo y en vez de los hechos gloriosos de Juárez se le refieren las hazañas de Lincoln por más que estas sean nobles y justas, no conocerá ese niño las glorias de su Patria, no la amará y hasta verá con indiferencia á los coterráneos de sus padres."

36. Ibid.

37. Fuentes de López, interview; Alejandro Portes and Rubén G. Rumbaut, "Immigrant America" (2006), in *Thinking through the Past: A Critical Thinking Approach to U.S. History*, vol. 2, *Since 1965*, ed. John Hollitz, 4th ed. (Boston: Wadsworth Cengage Learning, 2010), 348–49.

38. *Primer Congreso Mexicanista, Verificado en Laredo, Texas, EEUU de A. Los Dias 14 al 22 de Septiembre de 1911: Discursos y Conferencias Por la Raza y Para la Raza* (Laredo, Tex.: Tipografía de N. Idar, 1912), 5–6; Acosta, "Idar, Nicasio." For more on the First Mexicanist Congress, see José E. Limón, "El Primer Congreso Mexicanista de 1911: A Precursor to Contemporary Chicanismo," *Aztlán* 5 (Spring–Fall 1974): 85–115; Roberto R. Calderón, "Unión, Paz, y Trabajo: Laredo's Mexican Mutual Aid Societies, 1890s," in *Mexican Americans in Texas History*, ed. Emilio Zamora, Cynthia Orozco, and Rodolfo Rocha (Austin: Texas State Historical Association, 2000), 76–77; Emilio Zamora, "Mutualist and Mexicanist Expressions of a Political Culture in Texas," in *Mexican Americans in Texas History*, ed. Emilio Zamora, Cynthia Orozco, and Rodolfo Rocha (Austin: Texas State Historical Association, 2000), 88–91; Cynthia E. Orozco, *No Mexicans, Women, or Dogs Allowed: The Rise of the Mexican American Civil Rights Movement* (Austin: University of Texas Press, 2009), 70–72.

39. On benevolence, see Lori D. Ginzburg, *Women and the Work of Benevolence: Morality, Politics, and Class in Nineteenth-Century United States* (New Haven: Yale University Press, 1992).

40. "La Liga Femenil Mexicanista," *La Crónica*, December 7, 1911.

41. Ibid.: "Uno de los fines porque trabajará esta sociedad, será tambien por ayudar algo á los pobres de Laredo. Se han visitado algunos que se encuentran en la más completa miseria y abandono, á quienes se ha proveído de ropa por algunas de las señoritas y alimentos por la muy respectable Señora Doña Tomasita de Mendoza."

42. "La Liga Femenil Mexicanista," *La Crónica*, December 7, 1911: "Esta asociación, que trabaja activamente por el adelanto general de sus co-asociados, que verifica sesiones donde se estudia y se aprende, donde se adquiere cultura y se desarrolla el talento sin orgías y sin ambiciones mal sanas, que se dedica á realizar nobles y generosos fines."

43. Ibid.: "no cuenta con elementos pecuniarios, puesto que sus miembros todos pertenecen á la noble clase obrera."

44. Marjorie Coppock, Richard Alaniz, Adriana Craddock, Claudia García, and Sandra P. Thompson, "Changing Cultural Patterns in the Border Community of Laredo, Texas in the Early

1900's," TAMIU Paper Presented at the Southwestern Sociological Association Meetings, San Antonio, March 31, 1994, 4–5, Webb County Heritage Foundation, Laredo.

45. Elena Medellin de Ramírez (b. 1915 in Laredo), interview by Adriana Craddock, spring 1993, in ibid., 10–11.

46. Reynaldo García Sr. (b. in 1909 in Lampazos, Nuevo Leon, Mexico; family moved to Laredo in 1916), interview by Sandra P. Thompson, spring 1993, in ibid., 12–13, 19.

47. Young, "Deconstructing *La Raza*," 229; Zamora, *World of the Mexican Worker*, 61, 162–63; González, "Two Flags Entwined," 69.

48. "Sesion Literaria," *La Crónica*, November 2, 1911.

49. "Para la Mujer que Lee," *La Crónica*, October 26, 1911: "La mujer educada, que ha recibido en el hogar y en la escuela los principios fundamentals de una buena enseñanza moral y que los sigue, se ve respetada, exaltada y atendida en todas partes donde se presente. . . . La mujer, instruida, las más de las veces es buena, y siendo buena esparce un ambiente de pureza que eleva al hombre."

50. Ibid.: "que sale á la calle con deseos de 'hacer conquistas,' faltando aún al respeto que asi misma se deben"; "la mujer que es pura con su misma castidad se ve defendida pues los hombres por incultos que sean siempre respetan á la mujer que se da á respetar." See also Mary K. Vaughan, "Women, Class, and Education in Mexico, 1880–1928," in *Women in Latin America: An Anthology from Latin American Perspectives*, ed. Eleanor Leacock (Riverside, Calif.: Latin American Perspectives, 1979), 64; Christine Stansell, "Women, Children, and the Uses of the Streets: Class and Gender Conflict in New York City, 1850–1860," in *Women's America: Refocusing the Past*, ed. Linda K. Kerber and Jane Sherron De Hart, 3rd ed. (New York: Oxford University Press, 1991), 134; French, *Peaceful and Working People*, 6, 12; on maternalist politics in the United States, see Estelle B. Freedman, *Maternal Justice: Miriam Van Waters and the Female Reform Tradition* (Chicago: University of Chicago Press, 1996); Barbara Welter, "The Cult of True Womanhood, 1820–1860," *American Quarterly* 18 (Summer 1966): 151–57.

51. "Por la Raza: La Conservación del Nacionalismo," *La Crónica*, August 17, 1911.

52. "Para la Mujer que Lee," *La Crónica*, October 26, 1911: "La mujer debe procurer siempre adquirir conocimientos útiles y beneficos, pues en los tiempos modernos tiene amplios horizontes: las ciencias, las industrias, el taller y aún el mismo hogar, exigen sus mejores aptitudes su perseverancia y constancia en el trabajo y su influencia y ayuda para todo lo que sea progreso y adelanto para la humanidad."

53. "Debemos Trabajar," *La Crónica*, November 23, 1911: "viviendo enbudo de chismes ó cuentos vulgares"; "siendo este su protector natural y no su amo y señor."

54. Ibid.: "esos espíritus descontentadizos . . . críticos de aquella mujer, que haciendo á un lado los convencionalismos sociales dedica sus energies á trabajar por algo provechoso"; "cosas futiles ó perjudiciales."

55. Ibid.

56. Clara Lomas, "Transborder Discourse: The Articulation of Gender in the Borderlands in the Early Twentieth Century," in *Gender on the Borderlands*, ed. Castañeda et al., 66.

57. Clara Lomas, ed., *The Rebel: Leonor Villegas de Magnón* (Houston: Arte Público, 1994), xxiii–xxv.

58. Ibid., 237–39.

59. Ibid., 241–42. For an in-depth analysis of the Plan de San Diego, see Benjamin Heber Johnson, *Revolution in Texas: How a Forgotten Rebellion and Its Bloody Suppression Turned Mexicans into Americans* (New Haven: Yale University Press, 2003).

60. C. N. Idar to Leonor Villegas de Magnón, October 16, 1916, folder 10, box 1, Leonor Villegas de Magnón Papers, Special Collections and Archives, University of Houston Libraries, Houston:

". . . odio profundo para la revolución y para sus hombres. Las autoridades de la municipalidad de Laredo y las autoridades del condado que . . . fueron ardientemente adictas al señor Madero y al señor Carranza, hoy son peligrosamente hostiles. El elemento Americano de la comunidad nos es antagónico como nunca lo había sido. Los periodistas americanos observan escrupulosamente a la prensa Mexicana de Texas y lo mismo hace el ministerio de justicia Americano."

61. Ibid.

62. Lomas, *Rebel*, xv.

63. Aquilino and Guadalupe Idar, interview; Michael C. Meyer and William L. Sherman, *The Course of Mexican History*, 4th ed. (New York: Oxford University Press, 1991), 531–33.

64. Aquilino and Guadalupe Idar, interview.

65. Young, "Deconstructing *La Raza*," 229; Beatriz de la Garza, *A Law for the Lion: A Tale of Crime and Injustice in the Borderlands* (Austin: University of Texas Press, 2003), 58–59.

66. Ed Idar Jr., interview; Fuentes de López, interview.

67. Venustiano Carranza to Leonor Villegas de Magnón, October 23, 1916, C. N. Idar to Leonor Villegas de Magnón, October 16, 1916, Venustiano Carranza to Leonor Villegas de Magnón, August 19, 1916, all in Villegas de Magnón Papers.

68. [Jovita Idar] to Leonor Villegas de Magnón, November 20, 1916, folder 10, box 1, Villegas de Magnón Papers: "compre una prensa, de mil y pico dolraes [*sic*], y compre bastante tipos y todo, puedo hacer un periodico de siete columnas y lo voy a principiar muy pronto."

69. Jovita Idar to Leonor Villegas de Magnón, November 16, 1917, folder 11, box 1, Villegas de Magnón Papers. In keeping with Mexican custom, I hereafter refer to Jovita Idar as Jovita Idar de Juárez.

70. "El Enlace Matrimonial de la Srta. Jovita Idar," *Evolución*, May 17, 1917; "Ayudan a la Cruz Roja," *Evolución*, December 26, 1917.

71. "Enseñanzas," *La Prensa*, June 12, 13, July 1, 1928.

72. Fuentes de López, interview.

73. Ibid.

74. Ibid.

75. Ibid. On the pecan shellers' strike, see Zaragosa Vargas, *Labor Rights Are Civil Rights: Mexican American Workers in Twentieth-Century America* (Princeton: Princeton University Press, 2005); Julia K. Blackwelder, *Women of the Depression: Caste and Culture in San Antonio, 1929–1939* (College Station: Texas A&M University Press, 1984); González, "Carolina Munguía and Emma Tenayuca."

76. Fuentes de López, interview; Ed Idar Jr., interview.

77. Fuentes de López, interview; Lomas, *Rebel*.

78. "La Mejor Educación," *El Heraldo Cristiano*, October 1940, Jovita Idar vertical file folders: "Sólo el santo consejo maternal puede formar caractéres cristianos y útiles a la sociedad, cuando hayan aprendido que el principio de toda sabiduría es el temor de Dios"; "pongan sus hijos en el sendero de una vida Cristiana, cumpliendo así con sus instintos de bondad y de ternura latentes en el corazón de toda mujer, sea cual fuere su raza y su cultura."

Maternity Wars

Gender, Race, and the Sheppard-Towner Act in Texas

JUDITH N. MCARTHUR

In February 1916, a worried West Texas woman, Mrs. N.W., wrote twice to the U.S. Children's Bureau for information and advice, unburdening herself of the anxieties of motherhood. In the first letter, she asked for a copy of the bureau's booklet, *Infant Care*, and poured out her concern about her two-year-old son, whom she suspected was anemic. "He is very sallow looking, tongue is always coated, sometimes constipated, although I give him caster oil and castoria, these help temporarily. His ears are yellow looking, no blood seems to be in them." She asked hopefully for "a prescription for a good tonic to build him up and give him an appetite." Two weeks later, Mrs. N.W. wrote again, revealing more problems: the boy also had a recurring eye infection, and she was three months pregnant. Her last pregnancy had ended in grief: she had given birth a month prematurely to a baby girl who lived only a few hours. She requested a copy of the booklet *Prenatal Care*—"I don't want to lose this baby"—and described troubling symptoms. "I have a heavy bearing down feeling, vomit a great deal, and every now and then pains at the mouth of the womb, slight pains in the right side occasionally."[1]

To a twenty-first-century reader, this seems an odd approach to health care—why seek medical advice from a federal agency? But Mrs. N.W. had already exhausted her other options. The local doctor had told her that the two-year-old would outgrow his anemia, which she doubted, since she had never outgrown her own anemic symptoms. She had also taken the boy to an eye doctor, "who prescribed several kinds of eye drops and pastes but his eyes grew worse." Having paid a twelve-dollar consulting fee for nothing, she was trying to cure the condition by bathing the child's eyes in baking soda dissolved in hot water,

MARY EDNA GEARING, CA. 1920S

Prints and Photographs Collection, di_06020.

Courtesy of the Dolph Briscoe Center for American

History, University of Texas at Austin.

all the while worrying about her pregnancy—and with good reason. The baby she had lost the previous year was part of a grim statistic: in 1915, one hundred babies had died for every one thousand live births in the United States. "Any advice you can give me will be so appreciated," she wrote feelingly. "There is no other doctor here who can advise me and I feel so helpless and like a prisoner who can't escape from this hole."[2]

Women like Mrs. N.W. wrote the Children's Bureau 125,000 letters a year, confiding intimate details of their reproductive lives and their children's health problems and laying bare the anxiety and loneliness that often accompanied maternal responsibility. Created in 1912, in response to pressure from social reformers of both sexes, the Children's Bureau was a female beachhead in the federal government, headed and largely staffed by college-educated women who had invented careers for themselves as settlement house workers, child welfare advocates, and public health physicians. Given a broad mandate to investigate and report on any and all matters touching child welfare, director Julia Lathrop began by investigating infant mortality and producing a series of free pamphlets on prenatal and infant care. The booklets were an immediate success, so popular that the U.S. Government Printing Office could not keep up with demand. Women like Mrs. N.W. who accompanied their requests with letters of personal suffering led Lathrop in 1917 to design and propose the Sheppard-Towner Act for the Protection of Maternity and Infancy, the country's first federal social welfare program.[3]

Sheppard-Towner aimed to lower the country's maternal and infant mortality rates, which were among the highest in the industrialized world. Prenatal care was uncommon—the Children's Bureau estimated that 80 percent of women received none at all—and few physicians specialized in pediatrics. (Hence the many letters to the Children's Bureau seeking remedies for babies' digestive problems and bowel irregularities.) Rural women in particular lacked obstetrical services and even basic health care information, and country dwellers often relied on the folk wisdom of their mothers and grandmothers. A farm wife in North Texas with a coughing baby told an appalled observer that the infant would soon be better because her mother had given it medicine—sow bugs mixed with breast milk. "If that don't cure it, you give it mare's milk," she added. "Mare's milk is the best thing there is for whooping cough."[4] The Sheppard-Towner Act was designed to reach such women by providing federal matching grants to the states to set up prenatal and infant care education programs. The funds paid for instruction in nutrition and hygiene, baby and child diagnostic clinics, midwife training, and public health nurses, who visited pregnant women and new mothers. Sponsored by Senator Morris Sheppard of Texas and Representative Horace Towner of Iowa and vigorously backed by women's voluntary associations, it passed Congress in 1921, the first "woman's bill" to succeed in the aftermath of suffrage.[5]

To the network of women who had labored throughout the Progressive era as child welfare and public health advocates, Sheppard-Towner was a triumph of maternalist reform. To its right-wing opponents and the American Medical Association, it was "socialism" in medicine, even though it did not dispense medical services—the public health nurses who examined mothers and babies referred those in need of treatment to private physicians. When Sheppard-Towner came up for renewal in 1927, the opposition prevailed; it was extended for only two more years. Historians point to the demise of Sheppard-Towner as an example of women's declining political power in the postsuffrage years. When no female voting bloc emerged, politicians realized that they could ignore women's legislative requests with impunity. This well-documented, Washington-focused narrative shapes our perception of Sheppard-Towner: in the end, the women lost and the doctors won. But because the act permitted states wide discretion in designing and implementing their maternity and infancy programs, forty-five separate stories emerged (three states refused to participate). Texas offers a case study of potential failure averted. A female political coalition of clubwomen and former suffragists initiated and won a prolonged power struggle with the state board of health and ultimately forced the appointment of a new child hygiene director who was willing to work with a female advisory council drawn from their ranks.

Embedded in this story are several subthemes. One is the extent to which right-wing opposition to Sheppard-Towner reflected not simply small-government conservatism but also hostility to changing gender roles. A second theme is the question of women's political effectiveness after winning the vote. In pursuit of their Sheppard-Towner objectives, organized women combined the pressure-group lobbying traditions of the Progressive era with their newly won voting power for maximum political leverage. Finally, there is the problematic intersection of gender and race. White women challenged the male medical establishment over the implementation and administration of Sheppard-Towner, but they closed ranks with doctors over the "problem" of African American and Hispanic midwives and blamed high maternal and infant mortality rates on the "ignorance" of female birth attendants.

By the time that maternalist women in Texas took up the Sheppard-Towner cause, their voluntary association networks had given them a decade of familiarity with the Children's Bureau and its initiatives. Director Julia Lathrop was a former resident of Chicago's Hull House, the social settlement founded by Jane Addams, and voluntarist women and the settlement movement were well acquainted. To build support for their programs and recruit lobbyists for their legislative proposals, settlement workers volunteered as speakers before clubs and civic groups. Lathrop, Florence Kelley (who, with Lillian Wald of Nurses' Settlement in New York City, originated the idea of the Children's Bureau), and Addams frequently addressed the biennial conventions held by the General Federation of Women's Clubs (GFWC), and the delegates carried those messages home to their state federations. The GFWC and its state affiliates lobbied Congress to create the Children's Bureau, and after the bill finally passed in 1912, Lathrop, in a plenary address at the GFWC Biennial, outlined her vision for the new government agency and what the federation's one million members could do to help make it a reality. Over the next half dozen years, federated clubwomen and other women's organizations lobbied for an increase in the bureau's budget and carried its work into local communities, conducting birth registration initiatives (so that accurate infant mortality studies could be compiled) and well-baby campaigns.[6]

Lathrop formally proposed the concept that became the Sheppard-Towner Act in her 1917 annual report, but clubwomen had already heard the rationale behind it. In an address at the 1916 GFWC Biennial, Lathrop shared the findings of recent Children's Bureau studies that revealed rising maternal mortality and a close connection between maternal ill health and infant deaths. "Neglect and ignorance are the causes," she told the clubwomen. "Federal aid is what is needed."[7] After Lathrop and her associates drafted the bill, Jeannette Rankin, the first woman elected to Congress, introduced it in 1918, and the GFWC formally endorsed and lobbied for it. When the League of Women Voters (LWV) formed the following year, Lathrop, a founding member, persuaded it to create a child welfare committee to help advocate on behalf of the measure. Rankin's bill never came to a vote, and the subsequent version reintroduced by Sheppard and Towner (Rankin having been defeated for reelection) was languishing in 1920 when the Nineteenth Amendment was finally ratified and turned women into voters. At the invitation of the LWV, ten national women's organizations, including the GFWC and the National Congress of Mothers and Parent-Teacher Associations, formed the Women's Joint Congressional Committee (WJCC) to coordinate their lobbying efforts in Washington. The committee immediately got to work by creating a Sheppard-Towner subcommittee headed by Kelley. Under her direction, officers of the WJCC's member organizations testified at hearings and made sure that congressmen and senators were inundated with mail from newly enfranchised female constituents.[8]

Minnie Fisher Cunningham, the former president of the Texas Equal Suffrage Association who was in Washington, D.C., serving as legislative secretary to the president of the LWV, wrote home to a fellow suffragist that the women did not intend to give up while the lives of 250,000 babies and 20,000 mothers were lost every year. "They might just as well let us have these things, because the more they *won't* the more we *will.*" Cunningham subsequently became the LWV's first executive secretary, and in the summer of 1921 she took over as acting chair of the Sheppard-Towner subcommittee while Kelley was out of the country. Cunningham had a private conference with President Warren G. Harding, and other WJCC staffers made the rounds of Capitol Hill offices. By the time the Sheppard-Towner Act finally passed both houses on November 22, 1921, the WJCC was interviewing fifty congressmen a day.[9]

The maternalist lobby then shifted its focus to the states. Grace Abbott, another Hull House alumna, who had a master's degree from the University of Chicago and a long résumé in social service work, had succeeded Lathrop as director of the Children's Bureau, and she continued Lathrop's policy of working closely with voluntarist women. She promptly issued "Steps to Be Taken by Women's Organizations to Secure the Benefits of Sheppard-Towner for a State," and she briefed clubwomen a few months later at the GFWC Biennial. The WJCC told its affiliated organizations to instruct their members to pressure the state legislatures to adopt the act and circulated the Children's Bureau pamphlets explaining its benefits. The LWV, on Cunningham's initiative, dispatched nearly ten thousand of its own Sheppard-Towner leaflets to its state branches for the same purpose.[10] Texas as yet lacked a state lobbying coalition on the WJCC model (although three voluntary associations had made a preliminary effort), and the legislature was not scheduled to meet until 1923. In the interim, however, Governor Pat Neff accepted Sheppard-Towner, as authorized by the act, and designated the state board of health's Bureau of Child Hygiene and Public Health Nursing (BCH) as the administering agency, as also required. Maternalist women in Texas thus had two Sheppard-Towner goals on their agenda in 1922. They had to form a lobbying coalition and to be ready to persuade the legislature to say yes when it convened. At the same time, they needed to monitor the board of health's plans for initiating the maternity and infancy work.

The Sheppard-Towner Act was the crowning achievement of what historian Robyn Muncy has described as a "female dominion" of interconnected agencies and organizations that claimed authority over child welfare policy. The Children's Bureau headed the dominion, while state public welfare agencies and women's voluntary associations constituted its "lower echelons." The School of Social Service Administration at the University of Chicago, where Grace Abbott's sister, Edith, taught, supplied graduates trained in statistics and social research methods to do the dominion's work, and the WJCC served as its lobbying arm.[11] In Texas, which had no female-dominated public welfare agencies, the female dominion assumed a slightly different form. Three voluntary associations—the Texas Federation of Women's Clubs (TFWC), Texas Congress of Mothers and Parent-Teacher Associations (TCM), and Texas League of Women Voters (TLWV)—made child welfare a prominent part of their agendas. Throughout the Progressive era, clubwomen of the TFWC and TCM had spearheaded local and statewide campaigns for pure water, food, and milk as a means of reducing infant and child mortality. At the same time, they had cooperated enthusiastically with Children's Bureau initiatives. Clubwomen investigated the accuracy of birth registrations in their communities (using forms supplied by the Children's Bureau), orchestrated local observances of National Baby Week in 1916, and oversaw the state's data-gathering effort for Children's Year in 1918.[12] When the TLWV formed in 1919 as the successor to the Texas Equal Suffrage Association, the child welfare triumvirate was complete.

In 1922, all three organizations were headed by influential women with abundant experience in public activism. Lily Joseph, president of the TFWC, and Ina Caddell Marrs, president of the TCM, were former teachers. Joseph was a regent of the College of Industrial Arts (now Texas Woman's University) who counted Governor Neff and the president of the University of Texas among her friends. She also initiated and led the TFWC's successful push for a larger legislative appropriation for the public schools. Marrs was an education activist whose husband was running—successfully, it would turn out—for state superintendent of public education in 1922. Later in the decade, she was elected vice president and then president of the national Congress of Mothers and Parent-Teacher Associations. Jessie Daniel Ames, president of the TLWV, was a self-supporting widow with three children who had been part of Cunningham's inner circle in the state suffrage movement, serving as treasurer of the Texas Equal Suffrage Association and as a member of its legislative lobbying corps in Austin. She had direct access to Cunningham at the national LWV headquarters in Washington, and Cunningham had a personal connection to the Children's Bureau—one of her housemates was Dr. Anna Rude, director of the bureau's Division of Hygiene. Described by her biographer as a "blend of ladylike manipulativeness and pugnacity," Ames was a formidable organizer and tenacious advocate who, at the end of the decade, opened a new front in the history of female reform by founding the Association of Southern Women for the Prevention of Lynching.[13]

The educational arm of the child welfare dominion was the University of Texas Bureau of Extension—specifically, its Office of Home Economics, headed by Mary Edna Gearing. Like Julia Lathrop and Grace Abbott, Gearing was part of the cohort of college-educated women who created careers for themselves during the Progressive era by claiming expertise in areas—social work, public health, home economics—where men had no vested interest in excluding them. By making themselves authorities on policies that affected women and children and constructing a foundation of expert knowledge under traditional female responsibilities such as child care and household administration, they created, in Muncy's words, "a new territory they could rule themselves." Gearing grew up in Houston, was educated by private tutors after high school, and began her career by creating and administering a home economics program for the Houston public schools, one of the first such programs in the nation. A founding member of the American Home Economics Association, which grew out of a series of conferences that she and other pioneers in the field held annually at Lake Placid, New York, from 1906 to 1910, Gearing did four summers of coursework at Columbia University and then taught for a year at New York University. In 1912, the president of the University of Texas recruited her to establish the campus's School of Domestic Economy, and she taught there for the rest of her professional life. At a time when gender discrimination severely restricted careers in academia for women, home economics was an open door: Gearing was the first woman to chair a department at the University of Texas and the first to hold the rank of full professor. She was also well connected to the suffrage and voluntary association cultures and closely identified with the women's club movement. Over the years, she held various offices in the TFWC, and in 1922, she was serving a second term as chair of its Committee on Public Welfare.[14]

Through the university's Bureau of Extension (renamed the Division of Extension in 1925), Gearing and her faculty took home economics to the public. Extension pamphlets such as *Suggestions for Infant Feeding* offered advice to mothers in the style of Children's Bureau publications. Others, such as *Instructions for Conducting a Child Health and Nutrition Conference* and *What the Baby Health Conferences Teach*, supplied practical guidance to women's voluntary associations for their community child welfare work. The bureau's Office of Home Economics also prepared exhibits for fairs and community events and dispatched lecturers in nutrition and health to schools, parent-teacher association meetings, and voluntary association conventions. Through the Extension Bureau, Gearing planned and directed an annual "Home Economics Week," which invited clubwomen to campus to hear nationally known speakers, including social reformers such as Kelley, whose topic was child labor in the textile industry. At the request of the TFWC, TCM, and TLWV, Gearing's office sponsored a special conference on citizenship education and home welfare early in 1922 that established a personal link between the Texas child welfare dominion and the Children's Bureau. Grace Abbott was one of the featured speakers, and her topic, "National and State Problems and Their Relation to Health," included a discussion of Sheppard-Towner. Abbott stressed the mortality statistics for children under the age of one, pointing out that Texas would be eligible for $41,530 (based on its population) in federal money for preventive work if the legislature would appropriate a matching amount.[15]

Although only the Texas State Board of Health would have the authority to disburse the appropriation (through the BCH), the women of the state's child welfare dominion naturally expected to have a say in carrying out the mandate of Sheppard-Towner. They had followed its progress since Lathrop first shared her vision at the 1916 GFWC Biennial and had besieged their congressional delegates to vote for it. At the TFWC's 1920 convention, Texas clubwomen had listened to Morris Sheppard (a reliable Progressive in a politically conservative state) describe his efforts to push the bill through the U.S. Senate. The measure was the culmination of decades of infant and child welfare advocacy by voluntarist women, and Grace Abbott emphasized at the 1922 GFWC Biennial that their work was not finished. Women's organizations in every state needed to ensure that the law's objectives were carried out, because "without the cooperation of the women the program must necessarily fail." There was no model plan or blueprint. Each state was free to design its own in accordance with local conditions, but to receive funding, states had to submit working plans and budgets to Washington. Anticipating that state health departments might have their own agendas, Abbott all but told clubwomen to plant a collective foot in the door and stand firm: "In states where no work has previously been undertaken, it may be necessary to make quite clear . . . that the sole interest of women in the Sheppard-Towner Act is that it shall fulfill the purpose for which they urged its passage—reduce the needless and tragic deaths among American mothers and infants."[16]

This was the situation in Texas, as Abbott knew, because Gearing was sending updates. During her trip to Austin to speak at Gearing's conference, Abbott had visited the state health board (although she had not been able to meet with the director) and had helped arrange an informal women's advisory committee on Sheppard-Towner. Its members were drawn from the child welfare dominion, with Gearing as spokesperson.[17] By the summer of 1922, the women of the dominion and the men of the board of health were locked in conflict over the implementation of Sheppard-Towner. Most of the state's medical establishment had opposed the act, contending that it was unwarranted federal interference in state affairs and the entering wedge of socialism. But at the heart of the hostility between the dominion and the doctors lay conflicting definitions of professionalism. In the male view, medicine was a business, and physicians were guardians of expert knowledge that they dispensed for a fee. By contrast, female doctors (who made up only 5 percent of the profession and were far more likely than men to enter public health) and the women of the child welfare corps were service-oriented popularizers of scientific knowledge. Unlike the majority of medical men, they focused not just on the medical aspects of disease but on the social environment of ill health—factors such as nutrition, sanitation, income, and housing.[18]

Consequently, male and female professionals approached maternal and infant mortality from antithetical viewpoints. Medical men defined it narrowly as an obstetrical problem for doctors to solve, while medical women and laywomen regarded it broadly as a complex social problem that required not only a physician's expertise but input from specialists in a variety of other fields, such as social work, public health, and home economics. In a long editorial deploring the passage of Sheppard-Towner, the *Texas State Journal of Medicine* perfectly articulated the gender issue: "There is danger that the social worker, the visiting nurses, et al., will assume control of the situation, to the exclusion of the attending physician, and that the physician will eventually come to feel that the responsibility for the progress of pregnancy and preparation for its termination are not his. He may come to the conclusion that his part in the program is to serve at the time of labor, collect his fee therefor, and fade gracefully away, so as not to interfere with the process of the education of the patient."[19] In other words, Sheppard-Towner authorized women and their expanding professional networks to encroach on territory that the male medical establishment claimed as its own.

Male anxiety over women's high-profile advocacy for expanded social services during the Progressive era and resentment of their new status as voters also underlay some of the hostility to Sheppard-Towner. "The truth of the business is, the bill was passed by the women, gallantly aided by such men, even medical men, as have had their attention directed principally, if not exclusively, to social and welfare problems," the *Texas State Journal of Medicine* complained. Elite women, "who had more time than household cares and more money than children," had convinced their numerous and energetic followers that the law, "in some wonderful manner," would save thousands of mothers and babies, the editor sniped. "The opponents of the bill freely charged that the whole movement soon became one of sex supremacy," he pointed out, stressing that Congress had passed the bill only because it feared women's supposed power at the polls. The sexism here was less overtly scornful than Senator James Reed's when he quipped (to much laughter) on the Senate floor that the bill "proposed to turn the mothers of the land over to a few single ladies holding Government jobs at Washington. I question whether one out of ten of these delightful reformers could make a bowl of buttermilk gruel that would not give a baby the colic in five minutes." But the message was the same: women's claim to expertise and authority was spurious.[20]

Conflicting male and female professionalisms, overlaid with gender antagonism, sparked an extended conflict between the child welfare dominion and the Texas State Board of Health. Dr. John H. Florence, the state health officer, and Dr. H. E. Downs, director of the BCH, had opposed Sheppard-Towner. Once it became law, however, neither had any objection to securing a share of the money for Texas, although their dilatoriness frustrated maternalist women. Since the legislature was not in session in 1922, there was no possibility of a matching appropriation from state funds, but each state that accepted Sheppard-Towner automatically received a grant of five thousand dollars. The state board of health decided to distribute this sum to cities and counties that offered to raise matching funds. When Florence and Downs at last submitted a proposed budget in June 1922, the women were dismayed to learn that only three of Texas's rural counties—Victoria, Orange, and Hays—were represented. Instead, the BCH planned to allocate most of the money to Fort Worth, Dallas, San Antonio, and Houston to support infant and maternity clinics and milk stations administered by city hospitals and private agencies. Ames immediately issued a TLWV bulletin calling the proposal "a moral misuse of funds" and urging the members to protest; as they all knew, the law was intended to benefit small towns and rural districts. She sent a copy to Cunningham in Washington, who passed it on to the Children's Bureau. In an indignant accompanying letter, Ames told Cunningham that "as the Sheppard-Towner Act is going to work out in Texas it really was no triumph for the women at all."[21]

Florence and Downs maintained that the law said nothing about excluding cities, that Downs had understood from a meeting with Grace Abbott in Washington that only 50 percent of the money need be spent on maternity and infancy work, and that the Texas attorney general had ruled that the funds could be spent on any kind of health work. In a summerlong exchange of letters with the Children's Bureau, the two men argued their case, while relations between the board of health and the Texas child welfare dominion grew increasingly tense. Unarticulated gender issues underpinned the debate over funds. If the Sheppard-Towner money were channeled through municipal hospitals and, in the case of Houston, through Baylor College of Medicine, the male medical establishment, rather than traveling nurses, would control the work. When Dr. Ethel Watters, associate director of maternity and infancy at the Children's Bureau, visited Austin during a tour of several states, she informed Abbott that "there is the masculine ego to reckon with here in addition to profound ignorance on the part of the Child Hygiene director who apparently knows no fundamentals of organization or of public health." Florence and Downs were new appointees, in office less than a year, and Downs's predecessor as child hygiene director had been a woman. Bess Ledbetter, the Child Hygiene Bureau's secretary and a member of the TCM, told Watters confidentially that "Dr. Downs was angry with the women of the state because they refuse to recognize him and he stubbornly will do nothing which they want."[22]

In a long talk with Gearing, Watters learned that "all the women's organizations are disgusted with the situation & the leaders," and her assessment of Florence and Downs was unmediated by their shared status as physicians. She found them "wholly political in their attitude and every minute's conversation with them brings out new phases." To the women of the child welfare dominion, *political* was shorthand for shortsightedness, self-aggrandizement, and careerism, the obverse of being service-oriented. Lathrop and Abbott had sedulously protected the Children's Bureau from political turnover with every new presidential administration by enlisting women's organizations to argue the need for a professional at the helm. To both voluntarist and professional women, a "politicized" institution represented a mission defeated. Downs readily admitted that both he and Florence, like most Texas doctors, "are really opposed to the S-T Act & had no patience with it," Watters reported. She suspected the two men of deliberately ignoring rural work so that the legislature could justify refusing to approve the governor's interim acceptance on the grounds that the bill's purpose was not being carried out.[23]

Watters and the Texas child welfare dominion had another concern as well. Bypassing both the local women and the Children's Bureau, the Texas State Board of Health had asked the U.S. Public Health Service (PHS), headed by the surgeon general, to send a representative to Texas. Dr. Joseph Paulonis of the PHS's child hygiene division arrived in early July 1922 to serve as an adviser to Downs's department and to organize child hygiene work in the state. The *Texas State Journal of Medicine* had suggested this course months earlier. The appropriate solution to the maternal-infant mortality problem, it insisted, was better education for physicians rather than for mothers. Failing that, "it would be much better if the United States Public Health Service could be furnished a small part of the appropriation carried by the Maternity Law, with which to extend such information. It could choose its own agency and go about the matter in its own way, which undoubtedly would be along such lines as would conserve the personal element in the practice of medicine"—that is, the doctor-patient relationship and fee-for-service medicine. Since Sheppard-Towner was a reality, the PHS lacked that option, but it could at least compete for territory.[24]

Paulonis told the press that his activities would include "the registration of all births, regulation of midwife practice, correlation of general public health nursing with child welfare nursing, and the establishment of parental and child health centers."[25] While he made no mention of the Sheppard-Towner Act, his agenda was plainly the same, and the women immediately recognized his presence as a strategy for circumventing female control. "The men in charge resent any suggestions from the women and have no intention of working with them," Gearing informed Abbott. "I feel sure that it is one of the reasons for them calling in the U.S. Public Health Service to help." A month later, she sent a dispiriting update on Paulonis: "The man has expressed his frank antagonism to the Children's Bureau administering this fund and said that it was a great mistake and really a blunder that it was not vested in the Public Health Service."[26]

Tensions between the Children's Bureau and the PHS predated Sheppard-Towner. Like the American Medical Association, the PHS defined maternal-infant mortality as a purely medical problem, and as a government agency, the PHS considered the Children's Bureau a rival for funds and influence. When Lathrop initiated the bureau's investigations of the causes of infant mortality in the 1910s, the PHS had protested that her position should be held by a doctor and the studies conducted only by physicians. As the bureau gained recognition and its influence expanded, the surgeon general began a campaign to have the investigations transferred to the PHS, and when Sheppard-Towner was before Congress, PHS officials argued that it, not the Children's Bureau, should direct the program. (Many American Medical Association members had eventually agreed that if the government was going to be involved in health care, the PHS was the best option. Men would be in charge and make sure that social work and home economics did not encroach on the medical monopoly.) Lathrop had tried unsuccessfully to avoid local administration of Sheppard-Towner by state boards of health, fully aware that such authority would bolster the PHS claim. Paulonis's arrival in Texas proved that her reservations were justified: state health departments could offer backdoor entrances to the PHS. Paulonis admitted to Gearing that he was following the Children's Bureau's plan of work and justified his presence on the grounds that the bureau had no doctors. He meant no *male* doctors—the medical establishment considered the bureau's female physicians to be social workers with medical degrees.[27]

By August, relations between the doctors at the state board of health and the child welfare dominion were openly hostile. "The situation is bad," Gearing told Abbott, "and I do not think any improvement can be expected under the present administration." As a state employee, Gearing was sensitive to the possibility that any public criticism she lodged might be construed as territorial rivalry. To avoid any appearance of being "political," she channeled her opposition through the TFWC, where she chaired the Committee on Public Welfare. At her urging, the president, Lily Joseph, and the immediate past president, Florence Floore, whose administration had stressed outreach to rural women, wrote to both Dr. Florence and Governor Neff to protest the diversion of Sheppard-Towner funds to the cities. Gearing was so discouraged that she considered recommending that the TFWC and other voluntary associations refrain from lobbying the legislature to accept Sheppard-Towner in 1923. "It seems to me it is much better not to have it at all than to have it so greatly perverted for personal political aggrandizement," she informed Abbott unhappily.[28]

The Children's Bureau, through its authority to pass judgment on state proposals, had the ability to bring the board of health to heel, and Abbott did so politely but resolutely. Technically, state proposals had to be approved by a three-member Board of Maternity and Infant Hygiene—the director of the Children's Bureau, the surgeon general, and the U.S. commissioner of education—created by the Sheppard-Towner Act. In reality, Abbott made the rulings; the other two members elected her chair and gave their assent to her decisions. In accordance with maternalist women's preference for strengthening public social services, the bureau decided that federal money could not be distributed through voluntary associations or other private organizations. Florence and Downs therefore had to relinquish their proposed collaboration with Baylor College of Medicine, although they tried to argue that voluntary associations that supplied milk and ice were operating under municipal authority and were therefore not private agencies. They conceded when Rude pointed to the section of the act specifying administration by state boards of health.[29]

On the issue of apportioning money to the cities, the men were on firmer ground and defended it stubbornly: "We are unable to find the word 'rural' in the bill; also we are unable to find any intimation whatever as to whether the money shall be spent in cities, counties, towns, or elsewhere."[30] On this point, they were entirely correct. Lathrop's original bill had specified rural assistance, but representatives of urban districts had balked, and Congress deleted the restriction. The Children's Bureau dealt with this setback by acknowledging the letter of the law but administering it according to Lathrop's intent. The impetus for the bill had been women such as the isolated and worried Mrs. N.W. in West Texas. From the moment that the national child welfare dominion began to plan its campaign for the bill in 1917, they had intended its benefits for rural women. As Dr. Dorothy Mendenhall of the Children's Bureau argued, "The rural districts are less able to speak for themselves." The prospect of Sheppard-Towner money being used to buy milk and ice for babies in San Antonio seemed a travesty to women at every level of the dominion, from the Children's Bureau down to local clubs. Abbott simply rejected proposals not aimed primarily at rural constituencies. She told Florence that although the act did not limit funds to rural areas, "cities should, however, be able to take care of their own problem."[31]

With no other recourse, Dr. Florence conceded defeat in early August and returned the matching funds that Dallas, Fort Worth, Houston, and San Antonio had deposited in the state treasury. On August 12, the Board of Maternity and Infant Hygiene in Washington approved the budgets for Victoria, Orange, and Hays Counties, and Sheppard-Towner work began in Texas. The funds paid for a traveling nurse in each county and the upkeep of her car and in Victoria County for the purchase of a car as well. The money also bought supplies for a diagnostic clinic in San Marcos that served all of Hays County.[32] As the child welfare dominion had insisted, no Sheppard-Towner funds went to metropolitan areas.

Vindicated and long past the possibility of reconciliation with Florence and Downs (or Paulonis), the Texas child welfare corps took the battle to the next level. The presidents of the prominent women's voluntary associations, including Joseph (TFWC), Marrs (TCM), and Ames (TLWV), went as a committee to Governor Neff in September and demanded Downs's removal as director of the BCH. With the confidence derived from representing thousands of women who were voting constituents, they also requested that a woman doctor be appointed to the position and that women's organizations be invested with "cooperating" authority on Sheppard-Towner policy. Mindful of the approaching fall election, Neff gave the delegation a sympathetic hearing; he asked the women to suggest a qualified candidate for the child hygiene post, stipulating that she must be a Texas woman and not an outsider. A search committee was quickly formed, with Gearing as chair.[33]

A day later, at the state Democratic convention in San Antonio, the child welfare dominion scored another victory, for which Ames had formulated the strategy weeks earlier. In advance of the July primaries, Ames had sent an action bulletin to local TLWV chapters, instructing the members to attend their precinct conventions after the polls closed and get themselves elected as delegates to their county conventions. At the county conventions, they should make sure that women were elected as delegates to the state convention and try to pass a resolution in favor of Sheppard-Towner. Ames supplied suitable wording: "The —— County Democratic Convention endorses the purpose and object of the Sheppard-Towner Law for the Protection of Mothers and Babies and do hereby ask that the Democratic Convention meeting in San Antonio call upon the 38th Legislature of Texas to take whatever steps are required to make the law available to the mothers and babies of Texas."[34] Following this strategy, the women had sufficient strength at the state convention to get a Sheppard-Towner endorsement written into the Democratic Party platform. Ames especially sa-vored having outmaneuvered Dr. Paulonis, who had attended the convention to work against the endorsement. The women were trying to get him sent back to Washington, she reported to Abbott.[35]

At the same time, Ames and the other presidents of the voluntary associa-tions were engaged in putting together a legislative lobbying coalition modeled on the Women's Joint Congressional Committee and in preparing for the 1923 legislative session. By the end of 1922, the TLWV, TCM, TFWC, Woman's Chris-tian Temperance Union, and the Texas Federation of Business and Professional Women's Clubs had formed the Joint Legislative Committee (JLC), made up of each organization's president and legislative chair. Each organization con-tributed a share of the JLC's operating budget and the salary for an executive secretary, Jane Y. McCallum. Married to the Austin superintendent of schools and the mother of five children, McCallum was a veteran suffrage lobbyist and publicist whose columns had appeared regularly in the Austin press during the campaign for the vote. Having been Cunningham's right-hand woman in the Texas Equal Suffrage Association, she was more than equal to the secretary's job. The JLC members agreed on five measures to put before the legislature, with Sheppard-Towner as the centerpiece of its agenda. It also appointed a Sheppard-Towner subcommittee headed by Ames, who had already, in her capacity as TLWV president, done a legislative canvass on the issue.[36] At their state conven-tions, the member organizations of the JLC devoted a portion of their proceed-ings to Sheppard-Towner, preparing their members to take part in the legis-lative push. When the JLC was assigned office space in the capitol building, the press took note. The *Dallas Morning News* reported that "so quietly have these groups, representing thousands of women from all portions of Texas, united their forces . . . that speculation is rife as to the strength of this new political force henceforth to be reckoned with."[37]

In December 1922, the child welfare dominion won a comprehensive victory over the state board of health. Downs tendered his coerced resignation, and Florence gave notice as well, an unexpected bonus for the women. Thanks to Gearing's advisory committee, Florence's year as state health officer had been frustrating and embarrassing, and the approaching necessity of making the board of health's case for Sheppard-Towner to the legislature could not have pleased him. (He informed the JLC that in view of his impending departure, he saw no point in meeting with the committee members to prepare a Sheppard-Towner budget for 1923, but the women insisted on a consultation.) Dr. W. H. Beazley, the assistant state health officer, became the board's interim head, and Governor Neff invited Gearing's committee to suggest candidates for both vacant positions. Gearing had been unable to find a female physician to take over the BCH. Her group's second choice was Beazley, whom the women considered cooperative, but Gearing correctly suspected that he instead wanted a permanent appointment to the top job. His actions as interim head suggest that he realized that good relations with the dominion would be crucial to this ambition. He certainly gave the women no cause to complain to Neff, and their reception at the board of health changed from cold to cordial. When Gearing's committee "absolutely insisted" that Paulonis be recalled to the PHS, Beazley acquiesced. To Rude at the Children's Bureau, he sent a deferential request for guidance on filling the child hygiene position "in order that I may be in perfect harmony with your Department." Would she recommend seeking a doctor, a nurse, or even a qualified layperson? The Texas dominion had not gotten a woman at the helm, but they had secured a man willing to share the navigation.[38]

Their troubles with the board of health finally settled, the women concentrated on the fate of Sheppard-Towner in the legislative session. They had to secure its reauthorization (Governor Neff's provisional acceptance would expire in 1923) and pry an appropriation out of a legislature reliably parsimonious on social services spending. On the opening day of the session in January 1923, the JLC distributed a carefully prepared leaflet, drafted from literature supplied by the Children's Bureau and the National League of Women Voters, describing the need for and potential benefits of the Sheppard-Towner Act. The document was prefaced by the section of the state Democratic Party platform calling for legislative acceptance, which Ames had taken such pains to secure. Anticipating a chorus of states' rights protests, the pamphlet emphasized that Texas was already accepting federal money to build roads (from the Good Roads Act of 1916) and participating in another "50-50" program, the federal Smith-Lever Act, which matched funds for the Agricultural Extension Service. (Modeling Sheppard-Towner on the popular Smith-Lever Act had been one of Lathrop's most astute decisions.) The act was *not* administered from Washington, the JLC leaflet stressed, nor had the plan of work been designed in Washington. Participation was *not* mandatory: "No mother and no child are compelled to accept the services provided." And knowing the mind-set of the typical southern legislator, the JLC added another disclaimer: "There are no huge salaries paid to people who sit in the office and do nothing."[39]

Despite this careful presentation of the facts, legislators echoed all the arguments that opponents in Congress had voiced in 1921. Right-wingers denounced the act as "an audacious piece of Bolshevism" and "a pernicious Federal snooping bill."[40] One declaimed in classic southern demagogic style that "the Federal government would send 'Nigger' women down here to run over our white women." The Senate Committee on Public Health issued a seventeen-point manifesto recommending rejection, with most of the reasons expressing some iteration of the states' rights/federal interference theme.[41]

The JLC responded with the tactics that maternalist women had polished over the previous two decades of advocacy for social reform. Working in pairs, the Austin lobbyists made the case to each member of the legislature, while a contingent of "key women" (in McCallum's words) throughout the state orchestrated constituent pressure from the JLC's member organizations. The twenty-five members of the TFWC's executive committee (including Gearing) passed and distributed to the press a resolution calling on the Senate to cease "obstructionary" tactics and accept Sheppard-Towner. As always when seeking appropriations for children, the lobbying women were armed with incriminating data to illustrate that (male) agricultural and business interests were generously funded. This time, McCallum could point to the $243,990, part of it federal aid, that Texas had spent on controlling cattle ticks and other livestock diseases in 1921 as evidence that the state put the health of cows and calves above that of mothers and babies. She described the floor fight in the Senate as "vicious," but the bill passed on February 12, 1923, by a substantial margin.[42]

Through the JLC, the child welfare dominion also gained a formal voice at the state board of health. Dr. Beazley, who was granted the state health officer's job in his own right in 1923, created a twelve-member women's advisory council on Sheppard-Towner within the BCH. The council was composed of two representatives chosen by each of the JLC's five member organizations and by the Graduate Nurses' Association, which had been cooperating informally with the JLC and would affiliate in 1925. Marrs was elected president, and Ames was one of the TLWV's representatives. (Gearing, her anxieties about Sheppard-Towner relieved, took a leave of absence from the University of Texas and departed for a year of study in England.) The women's advisory council held its first meeting in Beazley's office in July 1923. Just a year earlier, Beazley's predecessor and the child welfare dominion had been at loggerheads. Now Beazley, in a cordial letter to Dr. Rude, offered to send the Children's Bureau a copy of the minutes and credited the JLC with "putting over" Sheppard-Towner in the legislature. He and the advisory council had discussed a plan to invite every county in the state to participate and had outlined a publicity campaign. The women would divide the state into districts, and each organization would receive one to "work and educate."[43] Amicable relations continued under Beazley's successors, and by 1925, the official report to the Children's Bureau described a working partnership in which "representatives of the bureau of child hygiene attended the State meeting of each of these bodies [in the advisory council] and planned with them the work to be undertaken on behalf of the bureau's maternity and infancy program for the year."[44]

The child welfare dominion had at last achieved the influence it desired, but the new cooperation also benefited the BCH. Based on population, Texas was entitled to $36,450.52 in federal funds. With the matching legislative appropriation, plus the $5,000 automatically granted to each participating state, the total amount available was $77,901.[45] Sheppard-Towner thus gave the bureau its first adequate budget. In addition, the maternalist women constituted a large and enthusiastic free labor force. The JLC continued to do the board of health's lobbying for Sheppard-Towner at each legislative session, securing full appropriations each time, until the act expired in 1929.[46] And only the voluntary associations had the personnel, through their local networks of women's and mothers' clubs, to publicize Sheppard-Towner at the county level and to do the advance preparation that produced good turnouts for the nurses' child health conferences. The TCM alone had thirty thousand members by 1923 and was still growing steadily, with most of the new clubs in rural areas.[47]

Although there is no direct evidence, the outcome of the search for a new director of the BCH suggests that the women of the child welfare dominion had some input or were at least consulted before the appointment was made. The search lasted six and a half months, during which time a supervising nurse ran the bureau and secretary Bess Ledbetter took over the public speaking duties. The successful candidate, Dr. H. Garst, had all the qualifications the dominion desired except being female. There was no "political" taint to Garst; he was an experienced public health physician, working in rural Hidalgo County at the time he was recruited. His arrival in August 1923 to take up Downs's former position initiated a cordial new relationship between the BCH and the dominion. Garst accepted invitations to speak at the fall conventions of the TCM, TFWC, and TLWV, and it is clear from his first biannual report to the Children's Bureau that he had been briefed on the past tensions between the bureau and the women. He praised the JLC for securing the Sheppard-Towner appropriation and reported "working steadily" with the new women's advisory council. McCallum subsequently lauded Garst's "noteworthy enthusiasm" and commended his administration of the BCH as "most satisfactory."[48]

A full Sheppard-Towner appropriation enabled the BCH to hire many more public health nurses and to expand its services. In 1922, when Governor Neff's interim acceptance allowed the maternity work to begin, the state board of health had seven itinerant nurses on staff. Federal funds made it possible to hire three county nurses (assigned full-time to counties that raised matching funds to pay half of a nurse's salary). By early 1924, the first year following a full legislative appropriation, the number of county nurses had risen to twenty-three. Moreover, the number of itinerant minority nurses tripled. Annie Maie Mathis, hired in 1922, was the first African American itinerant nurse, commended by Downs in his first and only report to the Children's Bureau as "doing a very splendid piece of work . . . with the expectant mothers of her race." By the end of 1923, Garst had added a second black nurse and had arranged for a nurse from the Mexican Federal Health Department to work in South Texas. Sheppard-Towner focused on preventive care, and the nurses were teachers, not healers. They provided "education in the hygiene of maternity and infancy," as the Children's Bureau phrased it. They gave instruction in prenatal nutrition and infant care (stressing the importance of breastfeeding) and signed up women to receive a series of ten prenatal letters from the BCH. The African American nurses gave lectures and demonstrations at state and local "Negro" gatherings. Sheppard-Towner nurses worked through home visits, classes, and prenatal and child health conferences, weighing babies and pointing out nutritional deficiencies and physical problems that needed a physician's attention. In 1927–28, BCH nurses conducted 536 health conferences and saw 43,220 infants under one year old; through prenatal conferences and home visits, the bureau reached 7,381 expectant mothers.[49]

Sheppard-Towner funds also paid for a 1924 survey of midwives, with the goal of securing legislation to regulate midwife practice. Doctors had long since displaced midwives among middle- and upper-class urban women, and by the twentieth century, most of the women who followed this traditional female calling were foreign-born or, in the South, African American. Though declining, their numbers were not shrinking fast enough to suit the medical profession, which considered them unqualified to preside at childbirth but a "necessary evil" where doctors were in short supply. Many women, however, preferred female birth attendants. When asked why they had chosen midwives instead of doctors, a sampling of Texas women cited cost, tradition, and availability. "Had a midwife because I can get them so much cheaper than a doctor. They take more pains with you too," one respondent told the midwife-survey nurse. Midwives offered empathy and comfort during labor, using herbal teas and massage to ease the pain: "Granny helps you in your misery." Some did housework and cooking until the mother was on her feet again. As one woman explained, "Molly was closer and doctor higher. Did my washing and charged only $5.00. Really worth more." Minority women overwhelmingly preferred midwives. "Heap of folks thinks midwives more particular. Guess just handed down from slavery time," an African American woman observed. "It is a custom among Mexicans," one emphasized. "Don't like men." One of the most frequently given reasons was simple geographical necessity: "So far from town, had to have a midwife."[50]

Scholars have shown that poverty rather than midwifery accounted for the elevated mortality statistics among African Americans and immigrants. Cultural and racial stereotyping, however, fed a perception that midwives were incompetent and dangerous. Katherine Hagquist, the white registered nurse responsible for midwife education in Texas, described them as "illiterate, usually dirty and in rags, gesticulating, oftentimes not able to talk or understand the English language, superstitious and suspicious."[51] Racial prejudice, however, was not the only driver of the effort to control midwives. Hagquist's African American colleague, Annie Maie Mathis, described "Negro" midwives in identical language: "Ignorant and superstitious, very set in their beliefs and careless as well as filthy."[52] The fundamental issue was professional standing. Midwives were uncredentialed, and public health professionals of both sexes and across racial lines were united in refusing to acknowledge the value of midwives' empirical training, usually learned from female relatives. Abbott and the Children's Bureau staff were convinced that doctors provided better care but realized that midwifery was a necessity in areas that were underserved by physicians. The bureau's solution was training and state licensing for midwives, thereby bringing them into the child welfare dominion. In states that reported a high proportion of midwife-assisted births, Sheppard-Towner funds paid for midwife instructors and supervisors.[53]

Midwife instruction in Texas began after Garst took over at the BCH in the summer of 1923. Since no one had any idea how many midwives were practicing across the state, the first step was to find and identify them. By the end of 1923, the BCH had located 850 and was adding roughly 150 a month to the list; by 1929, the last year of Sheppard-Towner, 4,620 were on record. Each woman was sent a letter directing her to register all births and to put silver nitrate drops (required by state law and supplied free on request) in every newborn's eyes to prevent gonococcal blindness. For statistical as well as monitoring purposes, the BCH furnished a questionnaire on which each midwife was to report monthly the number of cases she delivered, the number of stillbirths, how many times she had called a doctor, and a dozen other questions. When Hagquist was hired in 1924 as "supervisor of midwife control measures," the bureau's efforts to reach midwives shifted into higher gear. In addition to teaching classes for midwives and showing county nurses how to do the same, Hagquist directed a midwife survey in fifteen counties with substantial African American, Mexican American, and European-born (mainly German and Czech) populations.[54]

In six of these counties—Smith, Cameron, Uvalde, Harrison, Bastrop, and Brazoria—Hagquist and her assistants also conducted training classes and reported fairly detailed statistics. The typical midwife was an African American or Mexican-origin woman in her fifties—a "granny." The majority (ranging from

68 to 85 percent) were illiterate, and in most of the counties, the midwives registered fewer than half of the births they oversaw. The use of silver nitrate drops varied wildly, from none at all in Uvalde and Brazoria Counties to more than 50 percent of deliveries elsewhere. In Cameron and Uvalde Counties, where nearly all the midwives were Mexican-born or Mexican American, only one spoke English (or admitted to speaking it). Some of the midwives in each county were tested for syphilis, and a number of positives appeared in the sampled populations. The midwives would certainly have assessed Hagquist as well, noting her disapproval and calculating how to best preserve their livelihoods. Black women, who were skilled at assuming the deferential demeanor that white southerners demanded, earned her condescending commendation as "great imitators [who] take much pride in imitating the methods demonstrated to them by 'white folks.'" Mexican-origin women, who practiced entirely within the Hispanic community, regarded Hagquist as an interloper. She, in turn, found them almost incomprehensibly foreign and "more difficult to manage." Assuming that she meant them no good, the Mexican midwives tried to avoid her.[55]

Dr. Garst transmitted the midwife survey to the state health officer with his own conclusions and recommendations appended. He wanted to see a strict licensing law that would mandate annual recertification and raise the requirements every year. Each midwife would also have to pass a physical examination and test negative for syphilis. His proposal sought to regulate them out of business—doctors and nurses were less stringently monitored—and even if the legislature obliged with a statute, the state lacked the bureaucratic apparatus to enforce it. In the absence of state action, Sheppard-Towner nurses made the only practical effort to "certify" midwives. The Mexican nurse devoted 50 percent of her time to classes for Spanish-speaking midwives. The two African American nurses did midwife instruction in the Black Belt counties. Mathis even organized a midwives association in Beaumont. The Children's Bureau hired an African American physician, Ionia Whipper, to work with southern black midwives, and she spent several months in 1928 teaching in Texas. For the 1928–29 reporting period, the twenty-six county nurses logged 1,633 individual conferences with midwives, in addition to formal classes.[56]

The midwives were taught not obstetrics, since that was physicians' province, but sterile procedure—the necessity of scrubbing themselves and their patients and the proper treatment of the baby's umbilical cord. Eliminating germs most certainly saved lives. Puerperal septicemia was the leading cause of maternal mortality, and Hagquist was told of several cases of infant death from septic infection of the umbilicus in Cameron County. But Sheppard-Towner instructors also made it their mission to transform the midwives' appearance. "In our classes we tried to make them feel that they were absolutely unworthy to go out and wait on a 'brand new baby' without being spotlessly clean," Hagquist emphasized. "If a midwife attended the first class dirty and untidy, I was sure to find her at our next meeting in clean starched dress and face as shiny and clean as if it had been scrubbed with sapolio." Group photos of midwife graduates, black women in immaculate white, accompanied state reports to the Children's Bureau. The instructors' aim may have been to make the midwives look professional (like nurses), but in the process they were, as Molly Ladd-Taylor has pointed out, "symbolically cleansed of their race, their sexuality, and their motherhood."[57]

Far from being passive, midwives made their own decisions, and many seemed to enjoy the training classes. The public health nurse in Colorado County reported good attendance: "Usually after I have a class or two they begin to drift in until finally you are almost swamped with them." Few in any county attended all ten sessions of instruction—for most years, at least three-quarters of participants failed to complete the entire course. Those who persisted sometimes did so at considerable effort, as the nurses gradually came to understand. Hagquist complimented a habitual latecomer for a timely arrival and discovered that to avoid missing the beginning of class, "Aunt Susie" had left home the previous day and stayed overnight with friends, making a journey of fourteen miles on foot.[58]

Some midwives enthusiastically incorporated the new teaching into their practices, administering the free silver nitrate drops, for example, with an explanation of their purpose. "The mothers indorses it to the highest," Amanda Wortham informed the BCH when she wrote for a new supply. But they also exercised their own judgment regarding what was feasible. Patsy Brown interpreted the section on the monthly reporting form asking in how many cases a doctor had been called as a directive, informing the BCH that she did not consider advising patients to consult a physician part of a midwife's duty. "I left it up to the people who I serve, but the ones I serve says they never see any use of calling Doctors."[59]

Even without regulatory legislation, Sheppard-Towner reduced the number of midwives. Although the BCH could not compel them to file monthly reports (and less than half did so) or attend training classes, the new scrutiny was intimidating. "A goodly number of midwives have discontinued practice as a result of our correspondence with them," Garst noted.[60] Those who completed the training, however, enhanced their status as practitioners. In addition to classes taught by public health nurses, Sheppard-Towner funded physician demonstration lectures and classes at county courthouses each spring and fall. Instruction was offered for both new and experienced midwives and included practice sessions with physicians for the novices. A study of six counties in the Brazos River Bottom (Brazos, Burleson, Grimes, Leon, Madison, and Robertson) found that at a time when African Americans were largely excluded from the health care system, these physician-trained midwives transmitted medical knowledge to black families and functioned as "bridging leaders" who could sometimes secure services and assistance from whites for members of the black community.[61]

At no point during the 1920s did Sheppard-Towner reach more than a fraction of Texas mothers and babies. Enthusiasm inevitably bumped up against geography: 254 counties were far more than the child welfare dominion could hope to reach, even with the help of the federal government. The dominion's real achievement was not the number of counties tallied but its success, despite vehement resistance, in pushing the state to participate at all. Appropriating money for social welfare programs and expanding the reach of government were always unpopular with southern politicians, but right-wing opposition to Sheppard-Towner was also linked to antifeminism and resentment of women's public roles. The same "rock-ribbed state's righters," as Jane McCallum called them, who had blocked woman suffrage led the opposition to Sheppard-Towner.[62] Even some reliable male allies from the suffrage campaign withheld support. "The Sheppard-Towner bill belongs to a class of legislation which was conceived in an evil moment for the Nation and State," one wrote to McCallum, declining her invitation to join the JLC's advisory board. "It is laudable to improve the conditions concerning maternity and childhood . . . but I cannot believe that this is a legitimate function of the Federal government."[63]

As scholars such as Robyn Muncy and Theda Skocpol have documented, the partnership between the Children's Bureau and women's voluntary associations in the decade leading up to Sheppard-Towner was crucial to carrying out the bureau's programs. Federations of clubwomen secured state legislation to implement the Children's Bureau's recommendations and supplied the personnel for initiatives such as birth registration and baby-saving campaigns. The events in Texas show this partnership to have been just as important in implementing Sheppard-Towner: local women made it happen. The child welfare dominion was as essential to securing the legislature's reluctant approval as the WJCC was to the act's passage by Congress, and Texas women's dogged determination to have Sheppard-Towner implemented according to their own and the Children's Bureau's intent prevailed against the state board of health's obstructiveness. Grace Abbott acknowledged the essential collaboration between the national child welfare dominion and its state counterparts when she told the General Federation of Women's Clubs that Sheppard-Towner would fail in practice unless women's organizations made certain that its objectives were carried out. In Texas, Mary Gearing, Jessie Daniel Ames, Lily Joseph, Ina Caddell Marrs, and Jane McCallum—backed by a multitude—demonstrated how right she was.

NOTES

1. Quoted in Molly Ladd-Taylor, *Raising a Baby the Government Way: Mothers' Letters to the Children's Bureau, 1915–1932* (New Brunswick, N.J.: Rutgers University Press, 1986), 72, 100–102.

2. Ibid., 101; Molly Ladd-Taylor, "'My Work Came out of Agony and Grief': Mothers and the Making of the Sheppard-Towner Act," in *Mothers of a New World: Maternalist Politics and the Origins of Welfare States*, ed. Seth Koven and Sonya Michel (New York: Routledge, 1993), 323.

3. Robyn Muncy, *Creating a Female Dominion in American Reform, 1890–1935* (New York: Oxford University Press, 1991), 38, 47–56; Ladd-Taylor, "'My Work Came Out,'" 321.

4. J. C. Butts to Jane McCallum, August 6, 1923, box 18, Jane McCallum Family Papers, Austin History Center, Austin Public Library, Austin (hereafter cited as MFP).

5. For overviews of Sheppard-Towner, see J. Stanley Lemons, *The Woman Citizen: Social Feminism in the 1920s* (Urbana: University of Illinois Press, 1973); Sheila M. Rothman, *Woman's Proper Place: A History of Changing Ideals and Practices, 1870 to the Present* (New York: Basic Books, 1978); Muncy, *Creating a Female Dominion*; Theda Skocpol, *Protecting Soldiers and Mothers: The Political Origins of Social Policy in the United States* (Cambridge: Harvard University Press, 1992); Richard Meckel, *Save the Babies: American Public Health Reform and the Prevention of Infant Mortality, 1850–1929* (Baltimore: Johns Hopkins University Press, 1990); Molly Ladd-Taylor, *Mother-Work: Women, Child Welfare, and the State, 1890–1930* (Urbana: University of Illinois Press, 1994); Kriste Lindenmeyer, *"A Right to Childhood": The U.S. Children's Bureau and Child Welfare, 1912–1946* (Urbana: University of Illinois Press, 1997); Kimberly S. Johnson, *Governing the American State: Congress and the New Federalism, 1877–1929* (Princeton: Princeton University Press, 2006); Jan Doolittle Wilson, *The Women's Joint Congressional Committee and the Politics of Maternalism, 1920–1930* (Urbana: University of Illinois Press, 2007).

6. Muncy, *Creating a Female Dominion*, 33, 35, 58–62; Skocpol, *Protecting Soldiers and Mothers*, 482–94, 496–97. See also Kathryn Kish Sklar, *Florence Kelley and the Nation's Work: The Rise of Women's Political Culture, 1830–1900* (New Haven: Yale University Press, 1995).

7. Julia Lathrop, "The Education of Mothers as a Problem of Democracy," in General Federation of Women's Clubs, *Official Report of the Thirteenth Biennial Convention, New York City, May 24–June 2 1916* (Washington, D.C.: General Federation of Women's Clubs, 1916), 601; Skocpol, *Protecting Soldiers and Mothers*, 495.

8. Lindenmeyer, *"Right to Childhood,"* 81–82; Muncy, *Creating a Female Dominion*, 104–5; Wilson, *Women's Joint Congressional Committee*, 19–44, 48.

9. Judith N. McArthur and Harold L. Smith, *Minnie Fisher Cunningham: A Suffragist's Life in Politics* (New York: Oxford University Press, 2003), 97–98.

10. Lindenmeyer, *"Right to Childhood,"* 92; Grace Abbott, "The Responsibility of Clubwomen in Promoting the Welfare of Children," in General Federation of Women's Clubs, *Report of the Sixteenth Biennial Convention, June 20–30, 1922* (Washington, D.C.: General Federation of Women's Clubs, 1922), 509–15; Wilson, *Women's Joint Congressional Committee*, 51; McArthur and Smith, *Minnie Fisher Cunningham*, 98.

11. Muncy, *Creating a Female Dominion*, xii.

12. Judith N. McArthur, *Creating the New Woman: The Rise of Southern Women's Progressive Culture in Texas, 1893–1918* (Urbana: University of Illinois Press, 1998), 33–34, 41–46, 124–27.

13. Fannie C. Potter, *History of the Texas Federation of Women's Clubs, 1918–1938* (Denton: McNitzky, n.d.), 93–95, 101; Debbie Mauldin Cottrell, "Marrs, Ina Caddell," *Handbook of Texas Online*, http://www.tshaonline.org/handbook/online/articles/fmadw (accessed April 17, 2010); Jacquelyn Dowd Hall, *Revolt against Chivalry: Jessie Daniel Ames and the Women's Campaign against Lynching* (New York: Columbia University Press, 1974), 29 (quotation), 32–45.

14. Muncy, *Creating a Female Dominion*, 37; Mary Gearing Biographical File, Dolph Briscoe Center for American History, University of Texas at Austin; Lucy Rathbone, "Mary E. Gearing—Pioneer," *Journal of Home Economics* 39 (January 1947): 6. Mary Gearing left no papers, and biographical information about her is very limited.

15. T. H. Shelby, *Development of Extension Education at the University of Texas, 1909–1952* (Austin: University of Texas Division of Extension, 1966), 14, 99; McArthur, *Creating the New Woman*, 39–41; "Mrs. Marrs Presides at Citizenship Meeting," *Dallas Morning News* (hereafter cited as *DMN*), March 9, 1922.

16. Potter, *History*, 82; Abbott, "Responsibility of Club Women," 511.

17. Anna Rude to Morris Sheppard, April 5, 1922, box 253, Children's Bureau Central File, 1921–24, RG 102 (hereafter cited as CBCF), National Archives and Records Administration, Washington, D.C.

18. Muncy, *Creating a Female Dominion*, 139–43; Rothman, *Woman's Proper Place*, 139–40.

19. "The Passage of the Sheppard-Towner Act," *Texas State Journal of Medicine*, March 1922, 514.

20. Ibid., 515; Ladd-Taylor, *Mother-Work*, 172 (Reed quotation).

21. Texas [Sheppard-Towner Budget], submitted by Bureau of Child Hygiene, State Board of Health, "Bulletin No. 1," attached to Minnie Fisher Cunningham to Children's Bureau, July 11, 1922, both in box 253, CBCF.

22. Anna E. Rude to H. E. Downs, June 27, 1922, H. E. Downs to Grace Abbott, July 6, 18, August 1, 1922, Ethel M. Watters to Grace Abbott, July 24, 1922, all in box 253, CBCF.

23. Ethel M. Watters to Grace Abbott, July 24, 1922, box 253, CBCF.

24. "Passage of the Sheppard-Towner Act," 515.

25. "Expert on Child Welfare in Texas," *DMN*, July 8, 1922.

26. Mary Gearing to Grace Abbott, August 4, September 6, 1922, box 253, CBCF.

27. Muncy, *Creating a Female Dominion*, 139–44; Ethel M. Watters to Grace Abbott, July 24, 1922, box 253, CBCF.

28. Potter, *History*, 77; Mary Gearing to Grace Abbott, August 4, 1922, box 253, CBCF.

29. Anna E. Rude to H. E. Downs, June 27, 1922, H. E. Downs to Grace Abbott, July 6, 1922, both in box 253, CBCF.

30. J. H. Florence to Grace Abbott, August 1, 1922, in ibid.

31. Lindenmeyer, *"Right to Childhood,"* 77 (Mendenhall quotation); Muncy, *Creating a Female Dominion*, 106–8; Grace Abbott to J. H. Florence, August 7, 1922, box 253, CBCF.

32. J. H. Florence to Grace Abbott, August 10, 1922, Texas Bureau of Child Hygiene, State Board of Health, budgets for San Antonio, Victoria County, Fort Worth, Houston, Orange County, Dallas, and San Marcos, [1922], all in box 253, CBCF.

33. Mary Gearing to Grace Abbott, September 6, 1922, box 253, CBCF.

34. "Bulletin #2, County Conventions," attached to Minnie Fisher Cunningham to Children's Bureau, July 11, 1922, in ibid.

35. Jessie Daniel Ames to Grace Abbott, September 13, 1922, in ibid.

36. Emma Louise Moyer Jackson, "Petticoat Politics: Texas Women's Organizations in the 1920's" (PhD diss., University of Texas at Austin, 1980), 92–94; Minutes of the State Board Meeting, November 23, 1922, Texas Parent-Teacher Association Records, box 2.325/U103, Briscoe Center for American History; Minutes of the Joint Legislative Council, October 8, December 13, 1922, box 16, MFP.

37. "Texas Federation Notes," *San Antonio Express*, November 5, 1922; "Women Interested in Maternity Bill," *DMN*, November 5, 1922; "Women to Work at Capitol Jointly," *DMN*, November 23, 1922 (quotation).

38. Minutes of the Joint Legislative Council, November 25, December 4, 13, 1922, box 16, MFP; Mary Gearing to Grace Abbott, January 22, 1923 (first quotation), W. H. Beazley to Anna E. Rude, December 29, 1922 (second quotation), both in box 253, CBCF.

39. "The Sheppard-Towner Act for the Protection of Maternity and Infancy," box 18, MFP.

40. Jane Y. McCallum, "Activities of Women in Texas Politics," in *Citizens at Last: The Woman Suffrage Movement in Texas*, ed. Ruthe Winegarten and Judith N. McArthur (Austin: Temple, 1987), 222–24.

41. Jane Y. McCallum to Mrs. Abe Blum, February 8, 1923 (quotation), box 15, MFP; Senate Public Health Committee Report, box 18, MFP.

42. McCallum, "Activities of Women," 223–25; "Women's Clubs Endorse Sheppard-Towner Bill," *DMN*, January 24, 1923; "Women's Clubs Urge Maternity Bill Passed," *DMN*, February 6, 1923; "Maternity Act Is Passed by Senate," *DMN*, February 13, 1923; Jane Y. McCallum, "Eve in the New Era," *Austin American-Statesman*, October 6, 1946.

43. "Mrs. Marrs Named Council President," *DMN*, July 12, 1923; W. H. Beazley to Anna E. Rude, July 11, 1923, box 253, CBCF.

44. Texas State Board of Health, Bureau of Child Hygiene, Report of Maternity and Infancy Work (hereafter cited as Reports of Work), January 1–June 30, 1925, Children's Bureau Correspondence/Reports, folder 11-47-8, box 30, CBCF.

45. This is the figure specified by the JLC in "The Sheppard-Towner Act for the Protection of Maternity and Infancy," MFP. The *DMN* reported $75,000 ("Maternity Act Is Passed by Senate," February 13, 1923).

46. Johnson, *Governing the American State*, 146.

47. "Mothers' Congress Opens Convention," *DMN*, November 21, 1923.

48. "Director of Child Hygiene Appointed," *DMN*, July 20, 1923; Reports of Work, January 1–June 30, 1923, July 1–December 30, 1923, Children's Bureau Correspondence/Reports, folder 11-47-8, box 30, CBCF; Jane Y. McCallum, statement re. Dr. Garst, n.d., box 15, MFP.

49. Reports of Work, May 1–December 1, 1922, July 1–December 31, 1923, January 1–July 1, 1924, July 1, 1925–June 30, 1926, July 1, 1927–June 30, 1928.

50. Texas State Board of Health, Bureau of Child Hygiene, "Report on the Midwife Survey in Texas, January 2, 1925," in *The American Midwife Debate: A Sourcebook in its Modern Origins*, ed. Judy Barrett Litoff (New York: Greenwood, 1986), 77–79.

51. Ibid., 69.

52. Annie Maie Mathis, "Negro Public Health Nursing in Texas," *Southern Workman* 56 (July 1927): 303.

53. Muncy, *Creating a Female Dominion*, 115–16; Lindenmeyer, "*Right to Childhood*," 96; Molly Ladd-Taylor, "'Grannies' and 'Spinsters': Midwife Education under the Sheppard-Towner Act," *Journal of Social History* 22 (Winter 1988): 255–60.

54. Reports of Work, July 1–December 1, 1923, January 1–June 30, 1924, July 1928–June 1929.

55. Texas State Board of Health, Bureau of Child Hygiene, "Report of the Texas Midwife Survey," 68–76 (quotations at 69, 70).

56. Ibid., 67–68; Reports of Work, January 1–June 30, 1923, July–December 1923, January 1–June 30, 1924, July 1928–June 1929.

57. Texas State Board of Health, Bureau of Child Hygiene, "Report of the Texas Midwife Survey," 71 (first quotation); Ladd-Taylor, "'Grannies' and Spinsters,'" 26 (second quotation).

58. *The Gleaner*, December 1924, 36 (first quotation), box 18, MFP; Texas State Board of Health, Bureau of Child Hygiene, "Report of the Texas Midwife Survey," 75 (second quotation).

59. Amanda Wortham to W. H. Beazley, October 25, 1923, Patsy Brown to H. Garst, January 29, 1924, both in box 18, MFP.

60. Reports of Work, January 1–June 30, 1924.

61. Ruth C. Schaffer, "The Health and Social Functions of Black Midwives in the Texas Brazos Bottom, 1920–1985," *Rural Sociology* 56 (1991): 89–105.

62. McCallum, "Activities of Women," 222.

63. Dudley K. Woodward to Jane Y. McCallum, February 8, 1923, folder 3, box 15, MFP.

Part Three

1925-2000

REBECCA SHARPLESS

In the twentieth century, Texas developed a unique history yet shared much in common with the rest of the United States. The state became increasingly urban and ethnically diverse, with an economic push-pull causing people of all types to head to the cities and creating cultural changes of all descriptions. Events both unique to the state and common to the nation had profound impacts on the lives of women in Texas.

Urbanization was a key theme in Texas history throughout the twentieth century. In 1900, the Texas population was just over three million people, 83 percent of whom lived and worked on farms. At the end of the century, the population reached nearly twenty-one million, and fewer than 3 percent of them worked in agriculture. Fort Worth-Dallas, Houston, and San Antonio developed into huge and sprawling metropolitan areas, and the smaller cities—El Paso, Texarkana, and others—grew significantly. In 1940, Texas became the first state in the South to have a majority of its population living in urban areas. Urbanization both created and reflected shifts in the Texas economy, population, and culture. Women such as Frances Battaile Fisk took advantage of life in the growing cities to promote their love of culture—in Fisk's case, particularly the visual arts.

A second theme for twentieth-century Texas was increasing ethnic diversity. While immigration from Eastern Europe largely stopped after 1914, new arrivals from Mexico continued and increased in number. Rather than remaining a black and white society, much of Texas became triethnic, spreading cultural changes and intensifying racial tensions across the state. All of the cities experienced significant growth in their Mexican populations throughout the century. Immigrant women and their daughters became entrepreneurs, activists, and eventually elected officials. After the Immigration Act of 1965, new arrivals came from all over the world, including Africa, Central America, and Asia. While Houston in particular attracted a highly diverse population, the new arrivals spread across the state, bringing unique customs and lifeways with them.

Despite the state's unusual oil-based wealth, in many ways, the experiences of twentieth-century Texans mirrored those elsewhere in the United States. Rural poverty persisted in Texas just as it did across the rest of the South. The Dust Bowl affected not only Texas but contiguous states. New Deal programs brought employment and relief to many in the Lone Star State.

For Texas women, these major historical shifts provided openings into the worlds outside their homes. World War II brought significant changes to the state, with the establishment of massive military training activity and war industries, internment and prisoner-of-war camps, dramatic rural to urban migration, and a population increase of almost half a million people. Oveta Culp Hobby was the most powerful woman in the American military, but thousands of Texas women entered the military or gained new experiences in the workforce. The changes brought by World War II opened new opportunities for women in sports, including the rodeo. The Cold War manifested itself in many ways throughout Texas, including the expansion of the military-industrial complex, which provided employment for thousands of Texans, male and female. One result of the Cold War was the establishment of the manned spacecraft program in Houston, bringing talented women such as Mae Jemison into the Lone Star State. As elsewhere in the United States, Texas women increasingly worked for wages outside the home.

The civil rights movement had deep roots in Texas, which was the site of several cases that arose from the activities of the National Association for the Advancement for Colored People in Dallas and Houston. These cases—most notably, *Smith v. Allwright* (1944), which struck down the white primary, and *Sweatt v. Painter* (1950), which desegregated the law school at the University of Texas—made their way to the U.S. Supreme Court and became landmarks in the fight for African American equality. In the 1960s, women such as journalist Julia Scott Reed continued the fight for equality. Barbara Jordan was both a beneficiary and an integral part of the movement. She was the first African American woman from the South elected to the U.S. Congress and a tireless worker for expanding civil rights. Young white Texans, including Casey Hayden, found their calling in advocating on behalf of social change, first for African Americans and then for women.

While the feminist movement in Texas had never disappeared, it stirred to life in the 1970s, when Texas women developed a new prominence in electoral politics. Frances Farenthold ran for governor in 1972, the first woman to do so in her own right, and women began appearing on ballots statewide. Thanks to the long-term efforts of Hermine Tobolowsky and her allies, Texas passed its own Equal Legal Rights Amendment in 1972 and hence ratified the national Equal Rights Amendment (ERA). The ERA in Texas withstood a heated rescission effort, and in the end, the Lone Star State remained the only southern state to ratify and stand by the ERA. In 1990, Ann Richards became the first woman elected governor in almost seventy years. With an increasing Republican presence in Texas politics, Kay Bailey Hutchison became the first female senator from the state in 1993.

As the millennium drew to a close, women in Texas defied easy definition beyond diversity. Poor, wealthy, in between; Hispanic, African American, white, or increasingly of mixed ethnicity; all shaped and were shaped by the dramatic demographic, economic, and social shifts of the twentieth century.

Frances Battaile Fisk

Clubwoman and Promoter of
the Visual Arts in Texas

VICTORIA H. CUMMINS AND LIGHT T. CUMMINS

In the first half of the twentieth century, women's voluntary organizations and their members in Texas and throughout the country were in the vanguard of those promoting art appreciation, education, and collecting among the public and in providing venues where American artists could display and sell their work. The decades between the world wars were a lively period of club support for the visual arts in Texas, and one of the people most active in this effort was Frances Battaile Fisk (1881–1946) of Abilene.[1]

The work of Texas clubwomen as advocates for art and artists illustrates a trend identified by historian Karen J. Blair for the United States in general. By the late nineteenth century, men had ceded to women the role of champion of high culture—that is, as long as promoting the fine arts did not clash with women's domestic responsibilities and was conceptualized as a service to home and family. The professional art world was dominated by men and considered outside the proper sphere of female activity. Few women were professional artists, because gender socialization strongly discouraged women from pursuing careers in art. Nevertheless, as members of voluntary organizations, women learned about and promoted fine art as a project of value to their families and communities. Thus, in their support for the arts, clubwomen "labored under the assumption that while they were somehow biologically attuned to beauty, their primary devotion to their families barred them from serious artistic careers. What resulted was a vast network of enthusiastic, organized women, who were less occupied with making art than with the advocacy of art for their loved ones—defined by them quite broadly, to include not only their families but their neighborhoods, social groups, communities and municipalities as well."[2]

MRS. GREENLEAF FISK
Abilene

FRANCES BATTAILE FISK

in *Texas Federation News*, 1927.

Courtesy of the Woman's Collection, Texas Woman's University, Denton, Texas.

Much of the impetus for the promotion of the arts by clubwomen nationwide emanated from the General Federation of Women's Clubs (GFWC), a national organization founded in 1890 and based in Washington, D.C. In 1898, the GFWC's fourth biennial conference adopted a resolution creating a Department of Art with the goal of advancing "the study of art, history, theory and criticism, and the enjoyment of practical methods whereby art interest shall be promoted and supported in America, such as exhibitions of sculpture and painting, and the bringing together of the artists and the people."[3]

In the following decades, this department generated informational materials for state federations and local clubs to use in the study of art, including a pamphlet on how to study art and the *Handbook of Art in Our Country* to disseminate material on American artists. To bring as many people as possible outside of the big cities into contact with high-quality art, the art department followed the lead of the American Federation of Arts and organized a traveling exhibit. This show included not only pictures but also artist biographies and an art lecture presented by a club member. It was available to local clubs for a small rental plus shipping costs. To foster public appreciation of fine art, host clubs were required to make the exhibit open to the general public and to schoolchildren in addition to members. The initiative proved popular, and by 1907, three traveling exhibits had been created; they went to more than two hundred towns in twenty-seven states that year.[4]

In their efforts to promote appreciation for the visual arts, women of the GFWC had to counter public indifference. In 1920, the GFWC's art department chair exhorted her clubs to even greater efforts: "Public opinion still rates art as a non-essential," she wrote, "it is for us to prove it far otherwise, as essential to successful and happy living, for the individual and for the nation." To this end, the GFWC favored organizing local art exhibits where professional, amateur, and public school artists could display their works to the public.[5]

Founded in 1897 and federated with the GFWC in 1899, the Texas Federation of Women's Clubs (TFWC) was the conduit through which the national organization's initiatives were channeled to local Texas clubs. The club movement in Texas grew rapidly in the early twentieth century. In the late 1880s, Texas had only about two dozen women's clubs, but by 1910, the TFWC boasted some ten thousand members. This growth continued until the onset of the Great Depression, making the 1920s the peak of the club movement in Texas. As the TFWC grew, it subdivided the state into numbered geographical districts, each with its own officers and committees reporting to the state organization. By 1926, some seventy-five affiliated clubs with 3,673 members comprised the sixth district of the TFWC alone. That year, in Frances Battaile Fisk's hometown of Abilene, seven clubs with 287 members belonged to the TFWC. The rapidly expanding membership between 1900 and 1930 reflected the clubs' role in the lives of native-born middle-class white women. In addition to providing a social outlet for women afforded leisure time by the household help and labor-saving devices their affluent husbands could provide, club membership allowed women to become activists and insert their concerns into the public sphere in a socially acceptable way. The TFWC and its affiliated clubs participated actively in the broad spectrum of GFWC initiatives, including enthusiastic support for the arts. In Texas, women's clubs encouraged the establishment of art academies and instructional programs, worked to introduce art and art appreciation classes in the public schools, fostered activities to introduce the visual arts into homes across the state, and provided venues where Texas artists could exhibit their work to potential buyers. Municipal art museums in Houston, Dallas, San Antonio, Abilene, El Paso, and elsewhere in the Lone Star State were founded in large part as a result of the work of Texas clubwomen who nurtured the creation of these civic institutions.[6]

Frances Battaile Fisk (who most often publicly called herself Mrs. Greenleaf Fisk) played a significant role in many of these activities during the years between the two world wars. A committed clubwoman, she advocated the visual arts as an important component in defining the quality of life in Texas. She wrote the first critical survey of Texas art and sculpture, the classic *A History of Texas Artists and Sculptors* (1928). In addition, Fisk served in leadership positions in various women's clubs, making significant contributions to furthering appreciation for the arts. She labored to advance appreciation of the visual arts throughout the state in programs such as the Penny Art Fund and National Art Week, helped to establish scholarships for art students, and worked to found an art museum in Abilene. In a 1938 autobiographical sketch, Fisk proudly noted that she "led in cultural and civic activities in local, district, and state offices, serving as district president, state art chairman, and member of the State Club House Building Committee at Austin, for the Texas Federation of Women's Clubs."[7]

In spite of her importance to furthering the visual arts in Texas, however, Fisk's career as a clubwoman and her vital contributions to promoting the appreciation of Texas art have remained unrecognized by and unknown to most Texans, in large part because she left no personal papers. However, women's club records (membership rolls, minutes, newsletters, yearbooks, programs, and scrapbooks) have increasingly become part of archival and library collections. The availability of these records, in addition to the appearance of Internet finding aids and online searching of digitized newspapers, legal records, genealogical data, and other primary materials, permit the historian to recover the public lives of clubwomen such as Fisk. She was typical of white clubwomen of her time. Fisk was a married, middle-class, well-educated, churchgoing Protestant of Northern European descent. She did not challenge traditional values regarding "woman's place," as is evidenced by her withdrawal from the workforce after her marriage and her use of her married name in club documents. Instead she, like her study club colleagues, sought to expand her feminine roles into the civic arena. Because the Fisks did not have children, Frances Fisk was not burdened with child care or household responsibilities, freeing her for intensive club involvement at a younger age than most of her peers.[8]

Frances W. Battaile (pronounced "Battle") was born on December 16, 1881, near Georgetown, Texas. Her family had moved from Virginia in the decade before her birth. The Battailes were churchgoing Methodists who valued hard work and pious living. Known as "Frankie" to her friends and family, young Frances attended public schools in Georgetown and enrolled at Southwestern University in 1895 after her father's death the preceding year. She became a student at the Ladies' Annex, taking a two-year normal school curriculum designed to provide teacher training at the elementary and secondary levels. In addition to education courses, female students at the Ladies' Annex took classes in music and art, interests that shaped the remainder of Frances's life. Rather than bachelor's degrees, Ladies' Annex graduates received diplomas that qualified them to teach and entitled them to call themselves Southwestern University graduates, a practice Frances followed in compiling her credentials. This level of training was consistent with the collegiate education of many Texas women during the 1890s.[9]

At this time, Frances began to show a marked interest in the arts beyond her coursework. She enrolled in the Extension Division of the University of Chicago, an institution with a national commitment to correspondence coursework (known today as distance learning). She took courses in the fine arts and their history, although she never received transcript credit because university rules required that students travel to Chicago to take their final examinations, something she never did. Nonetheless, Frances took pride in this extension work in the fine arts, providing information about her University of Chicago correspondence courses for inclusion in biographical sketches written about her once she became a prominent figure in the women's club movement.[10]

Frances lived with her mother in Georgetown, working as a teacher, for several years after her graduation from Southwestern University. She was active in the local Methodist church, and there she met Greenleaf Fisk, who was visiting from the nearby town of Liberty Hill. Seven years her senior and the editor of the *Liberty Hill Index*, he was active in Democratic Party politics, the Masonic Lodge, and the Methodist church. The two married in the parlor of the Battaile home on May 15, 1902. The Georgetown newspaper noted that "the charming bride, Miss Battaile, has a host of friends who wish her unalloyed happiness" and called Fisk "a young man of sterling integrity [who] deserves the highest measure of success in life."[11]

The Fisks made their home for several years in Liberty Hill, where Greenleaf continued to edit the newspaper and Frances began writing articles for it to occupy her time. As people of ambition, the couple no doubt aspired to greater opportunities than the relatively small town provided them. Over the next fifteen years or so, they moved several times while they sought a place to settle and profitably pursue their interests. Their first chance for advancement came in 1907 when Greenleaf Fisk was offered the editorship of a newspaper in Eastland, a town on the Texas and Pacific Railroad approximately one hundred miles west of Fort Worth. Eastland, the main commercial town of Eastland County, was much larger than Liberty Hill and had several banks, two newspapers, and a stable mercantile economy based on cotton. Greenleaf Fisk enjoyed success there, winning election as the town's mayor in 1908. Both of the Fisks remained active Methodists, and Frances served as a member of the Methodist Missionary Society and attended its statewide meetings.[12]

While living at Eastland, Frances Fisk became involved in women's clubs. As a bustling town, Eastland had two women's clubs that attracted the wives of the town's business and professional leaders, along with single women who were teachers. The Hawthorne Book Club began during Frances's time in Eastland, a weekly meeting of women who gathered to discuss books they had read. Members also donated their personal books as the nucleus of what would become the town's public library. In addition, Eastland also had the Thursday Afternoon Club, whose members pursued a variety of interests and programs. Frances later recalled that these groups began her career in women's club work. Club membership provided her with a social outlet, a chance to continue educating herself, and a protected place to learn organizational and leadership skills such as public speaking that would serve her well during her later career as a leader in the clubwomen's movement.[13]

Her interest in such groups continued when the Fisks moved as Greenleaf advanced his career. While Greenleaf Fisk served as editor of the *Cisco Round-Up* in 1911, Frances joined the town's Twentieth Century Club, which, like its counterpart in Eastland, worked to found a public library. When it was established, the Cisco library operated on the volunteer labor of the women's club members. Frances's active role in women's clubs continued when she and her husband moved to the small Denton County town of Pilot Point in 1914 after Greenleaf purchased part ownership in the *Post-Signal* there. Frances became active in the Nineteenth Century Club, composed of women of social standing and civic influence. Its members "undertook extensive courses of study in history, art, music, and literature," subjects in which Frances had a well-established interest. Members of the Nineteenth Century Club combined study, social, and civic activities. They collected books to donate for public use, giving them to the high school library. The club met weekly in the homes of its members, and Frances Fisk attended regularly. In December 1914, she hosted the group at her home, where she "served delicious refreshments," the club minutes noted, and the women "spent a pleasant hour talking and sewing." Frances also presented programs to the club, including one on the life of Thomas A. Edison. The Fisks maintained an active social life, entertaining in their home and hosting visitors. Frances traveled throughout North Texas, participating in club meetings in neighboring towns, visiting friends, and attending cultural events in White-wright, Sherman, Bonham, Dallas, and Fort Worth.[14]

Greenleaf Fisk, however, did not find the Pilot Point newspaper entirely to his liking, so during World War I, he and Frances moved back to Eastland County, settling again for a time in Cisco, where he again edited the *Round-Up*. A new opportunity arrived in 1920 when Fisk secured the option to purchase a newspaper in nearby Abilene, a thriving town that had emerged as one of the largest in that part of the state. He bought the weekly *Taylor County Times*, which he eventually transformed into a larger paper and renamed the *Abilene Times*. As the courthouse town of Taylor County, Abilene was rapidly becoming the transportation and commercial center for a growing trade zone. The Abilene Chamber of Commerce alternately styled the burgeoning city as the "Athens of the West" because of the colleges located there or as "the future great city of West Texas." The town's population increased 125 percent between 1920 and 1930 and became the largest city between Fort Worth and El Paso. Greenleaf Fisk's newspaper grew steadily over the next several years, eventually publishing both morning and evening editions. He also opened a modern printing plant to further his operations. By the mid-1920s, the *Abilene Times* had become so large that Fisk hired A. Garland Adair, a young newspaperman from Mexia, to serve as editor so that Fisk could concentrate on being the publisher. They styled the *Times* as "Abilene's Greatest Advertising Medium."[15]

The Fisks threw themselves into the life of Abilene. They joined St. Paul's Methodist Church and moved to a house located in the fashionable Parramore neighborhood, northwest of the downtown area. Frances quickly became an active member of several of the most prestigious women's groups in the city. As did many other clubwomen in this period, she chose clubs that engaged civic improvement as well as self-education.[16]

As an Abilene clubwoman, Fisk demonstrated extraordinary levels of commitment. She was an indefatigable participant and founder of clubs. In her peak years of involvement (1923–43), she served in leadership positions in at least seven Abilene clubs as well as the Abilene City Federation of Women's Clubs and at the district and state levels of the TFWC. She also served in numerous leadership capacities in the Art Unit of the Abilene Woman's Forum, a large "department" club subdivided into semiautonomous interest "units," all of which had their own officers and committees, as did the parent club.[17]

Fisk's involvements ranged far beyond the Woman's Forum. She was one of the founders of the Abilene Woman's Club in 1928, serving it over the next fifteen years as vice president, membership chair, chair of the art department, president, director, and member of the advisory board. Fisk also served the Abilene City Federation of Women's Clubs as chair of Art Week, membership chair, auditor, and chair of the arrangements committee for the GFWC Jubilee celebrations in 1940. She held the presidency of the Sixth District of the Texas Federation of Women's Clubs from 1929 to 1931. Later, she was appointed trustee for the TFWC's permanent headquarters fund, tirelessly campaigning to raise money for a permanent club building in Austin. She was the TFWC publicity chair in 1923–24, state chair of Texas artists and sculptors from 1925 to 1927, and later state chair of the TFWC's art division for six years. In addition to her leadership positions, Fisk invariably served as organizer or hostess at one or more club meetings or civic events each year. She also gave programs for her various clubs on art topics such as "Modern German Painters," "What Texas Is Doing for the Development of Art," and "A Century of Collecting in America."[18]

Frances Fisk's most lasting contribution to the promotion of the visual arts was her book, *A History of Texas Artists and Sculptors* (1928). This volume constituted the first attempt to survey systematically the visual arts in the Lone Star State. The book project grew out of Fisk's activities as the state chair for artists and sculptors of the Texas Federation of Women's Clubs, a position she held from 1925 to 1927. She wanted to attract attention to Texas artists and realized that little information was available about art and sculpture in the state. There was no published reference work to which people could turn to find a survey of art history in Texas or to learn about the artists and sculptors working in the state. The lack of such a reference hampered the women's clubs in their attempts to study Texas artists and their work. Fisk therefore decided that she would use her office to create such a reference book and that it should be both comprehensive and readable. As she wrote in the volume's preface, "There was an urgent need for a record in book form dealing exclusively with our painters and sculptors, if our art development was to make progress with our artists." She further observed that the clubwomen "should encourage our young artists who are to carry on the work in our State, and should make it possible for them to interpret the spirit and traditions of Texas, thus bringing our State up to the highest standard in culture."[19]

In the late 1920s, with the TFWC's encouragement, Fisk set out to gather as much information as she could because "there was no material on this subject to be found in any of our libraries, unless it be a few clippings from the daily press or current magazines." In 1928, the TFWC state art division chair, Mrs. W. S. Douglas, reported that Fisk was "compiling a history of Texas talent, which we commend to club women. She has furnished club programs and much information on this subject." Fisk hoped to produce a comprehensive guide to Texas art combining discussion of the periods of art history with biographical vignettes and career sketches of past and present Texas artists. In addition to appealing to individuals interested in art, she especially hoped that the book would be utilized by clubs, schools and libraries.[20]

In compiling material for this book, Fisk relied heavily on the women around the state who reported to her Committee for Artists and Sculptors. Representatives from the various TFWC districts contacted artists and sculptors working in their areas, collected information, wrote drafts about their artistic careers, and furnished these drafts to Fisk. In addition, Fisk contacted many artists and sculptors personally, requesting biographical information, news of their activities, and reports on their artistic accomplishments. Many artists responded with detailed information. Although Fisk realized that her collection methods might produce uneven coverage, she believed her efforts to identify artists in all parts of Texas would guarantee that her book would include the prominent ones as well as emerging artists. Most of this work took place during 1926 and 1927. Fisk used her husband's printing business, the Fisk Publishing Company, to publish a limited edition hardback, with numerous illustrations printed on glossy paper. She marketed it herself for four dollars per copy plus postage.[21]

The book enjoyed a very positive reception, receiving endorsements from the president of the TFWC and Frances Fisk's successor as state chair for Texas artists and sculptors, Dr. Virginia Spates. The director of the Southern States Art League, along with educators Wilber M. Derthick of the University of Wisconsin Extension Division and Ralph Rowntree of the Southern Methodist University art department, praised the book as well. The TFWC was pleased. Josephine Heavenhill, reviewing the book for the *Texas Federation News*, praised its "vast amount of information pleasingly arranged" and declared that Fisk had "accomplished her aim to furnish in comprehensive systematic and illustrated form a volume that may be a valuable reference for library as well as a record of the life and works of the artists." Eleanor Wakefield of the *Houston Chronicle* praised "Mrs. Fisk's pen pictures of the artists" as "particularly deserving of mention, since she is able to bring their personalities into actual being before the reader's eyes." An anonymous reviewer for the *Dallas Morning News* voiced some concerns about the book being "inclusive rather than discriminating" but noted that clubwomen would find a wealth of new information on local artists and applauded the overall accomplishment: "Mrs. Fisk has succeeded in amassing in one volume an astonishing amount of information about the development of art in Texas, about well-known canvasses, about artists of the state." The reviewer also called it a "much-needed volume . . . systematically arranged and carefully indexed."[22]

Despite some limitations, the book proved to be groundbreaking. Fisk began the volume with a brief overview of Texas art history. She divided the state's artistic development into early (1888–1900), middle (1900–1917), and modern (1917–27) periods and then surveyed the artists associated with each period, subdividing them by specialty, medium, and geographical area. The book lacked a table of contents and had a loose organizational scheme, neither consistently chronological nor topical. However, its index identified more than 350 artists who had worked or were currently working in Texas. To help clubs use the book effectively, Fisk prepared a study guide and suggested programs that the book would support. She also was willing to speak to clubs about her research. The book became useful to local clubwomen and art historians. For example, A. M. Carpenter of Abilene, Art Unit leader and longtime head of the Hardin-Simmons University art department, owned a well-marked copy that she used in preparing lectures on Texas artists. More than eighty years after it was published, *A History of Texas Artists and Sculptors* remains a vital reference work on Texas artists active before 1928.[23]

Fisk spent little time resting on her laurels and continued to seek additional ways to promote the visual arts in Texas. When Fisk became chair of the TFWC's Division of Art in 1932, one of her pet projects was the adoption of the GFWC Penny Art Fund in Texas. This art fund had begun with New Jersey clubs in 1917, and in 1930, the GFWC recommended it for all federated clubs. To participate, clubs agreed to pay one cent per member per year into a state fund administrated by a specially appointed officer or the chair of the Division of Art. This officer decided how the state's money would be expended, but all funds collected went to local projects. State federations could win paintings and cash incentives from the GFWC based on the number of clubs participating and the level of art activities supported.[24]

Fisk saw the Penny Art Fund as a way to fund the purchase of works by local artists and implemented the program in Texas. Her plan was to get clubs to join the art fund and then use the money for prizes in a statewide competition to promote art activities. For the inaugural year, 1932, she planned to buy a painting to award to the first- and second-place clubs in two divisions based on membership. She hoped that the contest would stimulate clubs to begin art collections. Winning clubs would be selected based on the number of art-related activities that club members organized, sponsored, or attended during the preceding year. In its first year, the Texas Penny Art Fund took in a mere $15.25, which was supplemented by a $5.00 award from the GFWC "for outstanding work in the promotion of art and adopting the Penny Art Fund." The money was enough to purchase two paintings by Texas artists for the first-place winners. Fisk donated two copies of *A History of Texas Artists and Sculptors* as prizes for the second-place clubs.[25]

The next year, Fisk used the TFWC newsletter to encourage support for the arts when she exhorted clubwomen across the state to "join the plan and be an appreciator—give publicity to your local artists and to the Penny Art Fund Plan.—urge others to join. We may not be able to draw or paint or do sculpture but we can encourage others who are thus gifted." Under her leadership, Texas won a second-place national award in 1934, receiving a painting, *Hydrangea with Hilenium*, by a Seattle artist. One of Fisk's strategies to increase participation levels in the Penny Art Fund and make Texas more competitive for national art prizes was to create incentives for Texas clubs to promote art activities. As part of the Penny Art Fund, Fisk organized an art exhibit for the TFWC state convention. Each district was encouraged to host an exhibit spotlighting local artists at its spring convention and to allow the attending public to choose ten works of art to send to the state convention exhibit. The winning artist chosen there would receive a cash prize of ten dollars. One of Fisk's major objectives for her 1932–33 term as art chair was to circulate inexpensive "loan exhibits" in each of the TFWC's districts. These exhibits would travel to smaller towns and cities, bringing exposure for artists and art to people who lacked the time or funds to travel to larger venues. To host a show, a club needed to pay only the one-way cost of transportation.[26]

Fisk's ambitious plans for the Penny Art Fund grew rapidly in the mid-1930s. By 1935, more than half of the state's seven hundred clubs had joined and were involved in art activities, including sponsoring art programs, exhibits, and contests. Clubwomen visited artists' studios and museums individually and in groups. They purchased works from local artists, both for their own enjoyment and to use as prizes in student competitions. As more clubs joined, Fisk offered additional prizes to reward outstanding art activities. In the spring of 1936, these efforts led the GFWC to recognize the TFWC for "Most Meritorious Art Activities" west of the Mississippi. The prize was an oil painting, *Autumn in Connecticut*, by nationally recognized artist William Patty. The GFWC also recognized Fisk personally for her efforts to promote the Penny Art Fund, awarding her a watercolor, *The Turpentine Pines*, by Myrtle Taylor Bradford, a Florida artist and clubwoman. The painting became part of Fisk's personal art collection.[27]

After Fisk's tenure as state art division chair ended, the TFWC's art-related activities continued to win recognition at the national level, taking third prize in the 1940 Penny Art Fund contest. The Art Unit of the Abilene Woman's Forum, of which Fisk remained an active member even while a state officer, was one of the most successful clubs promoting art activities in Texas. Between 1933 and 1941, it won seven paintings bought with state Penny Art Fund money in recognition of its outstanding work.[28]

As chair of the TFWC's art division and later as art exhibits chair, Fisk also embraced National Art Week. In the late 1920s, a national organization, the American Artists Professional League, started an annual Art Week during which local groups would promote activities that highlighted U.S. artists. With the GFWC's backing, many women's clubs across the country embraced Art Week, sponsoring exhibitions for local artists. The Art Unit of the Abilene Woman's Forum became involved in these efforts under Fisk's leadership. By 1938, a newspaper article reported, "Abilene's observation of American Art Week in November is to be a city-wide event with town and school art groups and merchants cooperating to make it of wide-spread interest." That year, Art Week also featured a special exhibition of paintings owned by Fisk, among them works by Louis Teel, Myra Wiggins, Julius Woeltz, Grace Spaulding John, and other important regionalists.[29]

In the late 1930s, Fisk became chair of Texas's statewide celebration of Art Week, and A. M. Carpenter took Fisk's place as head of the Abilene event. "With Mrs. Greenleaf Fisk, Texas Director, at the helm," reported a news release about the 1940 celebration, "18 chairmen are completing plans today for Texas' participation in the observance of National Art Week. Other towns participating in the observance are Austin, Houston, Bay City, Harlingen, San Antonio, Waco, Fort Worth, Trinidad, Brownwood, Coleman, San Angelo, Winters, Ozona, Del Rio, Alpine, and El Paso." Bolstered by President Franklin D. Roosevelt's 1940 national proclamation urging people to buy "American art for American homes," Fisk's efforts that year enabled a number of Texas artists to sell their work in the program.[30]

The women of the TFWC understood and appreciated the hard work that Fisk had been contributing to promoting the visual arts. When the Sixth District convention met at Midland during 1933, the chair of the scholarship committee recommended that a student loan fund be created and named for her "in recognition of her services to the Federation, not only in the fields of art and her book on Texas art, *A History of Texas Artists and Sculptors*, but as immediate past president of the Sixth District." The fund was to loan money for graduate study in art to female graduates of Texas colleges from the Sixth District, another cause that Fisk had long backed.[31]

In the late 1930s the Art Unit of the Abilene Woman's Forum embarked on an ambitious project that had the potential to transform art appreciation throughout the region: the establishment of a public art museum in the city. Fisk had long argued that Texas needed more art museums and other exhibition venues if the state's artists were to receive necessary exposure. In the late 1920s, she lamented, "Painting and sculpture have been somewhat neglected because there have not yet been found adequate places for exhibitions." Although Fisk's statewide activities prohibited her from taking a major role in this effort, she was involved as much as her busy schedule allowed. At the fall 1937 meeting of the forum's Art Unit, members voted to "sponsor the organization of a civic art and museum association" that would bring national and international exhibitions of art to Abilene. The Art Unit called for a larger meeting to be held the following week at Abilene's Wooten Hotel for both male and female civic leaders. Fisk participated in this meeting. The mayor of Abilene, along with Professor Rupert Richardson of Hardin-Simmons University, spoke, agreeing that an art museum "constituted one of Abilene's greatest civic needs." Those in attendance pledged to become the nucleus of the Abilene Civic Art and Museum Association. They elected the Reverend Willis P. Gerhart as chair and chose other officers and a board of directors for the proposed art museum. Fisk agreed to serve on the board. The Art Unit of the Abilene Woman's Forum proudly became the first club to have 100 percent of its members purchase subscriptions.[32]

The new art museum soon found exhibit space in the West Texas Chamber of Commerce Building and turned to hosting visiting exhibitions while it engaged in a fund-raising campaign. Members of the museum association, including Fisk, also embarked on a campaign to secure works of art for a permanent collection. By the fall of 1939, the Art Unit of the Abilene Woman's Forum had raised funds and selected its first painting for the museum: *The Farmer*, by Marie Hull of Mississippi. As the state federation chair of National Art Week, Fisk formally presented this painting at a special ceremony held in the art museum exhibit room. Abilene's present-day Grace Museum descends from the Abilene Civic Art and Museum Association, and the painting Fisk presented is part of its permanent collection.[33]

Although promoting the visual arts constituted an important part of her club work, Frances Fisk embraced other interests as well. When the GFWC celebrated its fiftieth anniversary in 1940, the City Federation appointed Fisk to chair the Golden Jubilee. She and her committee organized a tea at McMurry College for club members and their friends at which local clubwomen received medals in recognition of their service to individual clubs. Fisk both headed the program and received a medal. In 1928, she organized the Music Unit of the Abilene Woman's Forum to promote the study and performance of good music in Abilene. In addition to the programs presented to its members, the Music Forum organized performance groups for students from kindergarten age to high school and helped organize the Abilene civic orchestra and chorus in 1932.[34]

As president of the Abilene Woman's Forum for eight terms in the 1920s, 1930s, and 1940s, Fisk was responsible for promoting the varied interests of the first art, music, book review, and junior units of the club. As president of the Sixth District of the TFWC from 1929 to 1931, she not only promoted fine arts activities but also was responsible for a broad range of programs, including organizing community cleanup campaigns, running free health clinics, sponsoring lectures on public health, organizing civic beautification and conservation programs, increasing membership through the creation of junior clubs, and encouraging clubs to begin saving to build permanent clubhouses.[35]

In addition, Fisk worked diligently as a member of the building committee during the early to mid-1930s to raise funds for the construction of the TFWC's permanent headquarters in Austin, although with limited results. More than once in her presidential reports, Fisk lamented the low level of support for the permanent headquarters fund. After finishing her term as district president in 1931, she volunteered to serve as one of two Sixth District leaders in the "Penny Bank Campaign in the Interest of Headquarters Permanent," which encouraged each club to fill a bank with 365 pennies each year to help finance the TFWC Austin building. Service on the building committee required her to make monthly trips to various cities to attend meetings, a task that would have required considerable time and effort and may well have been frustrating.[36]

Fisk was active in the Daughters of the American Revolution and United Daughters of the Confederacy. She was active in the Methodist Church, holding state- and district-level offices. In her leisure time, she was a gardener, collected autographed Texana, and assembled a moderate collection of oils, watercolors, and prints, mostly southwestern landscapes. She wrote for her husband's newspapers (mostly unattributed reports on women's club activities) and composed poetry and short plays. She also somehow found time to write a one-act play, *Texas Birthdays in Procession*, that was presented as part of Abilene's celebration of the Texas Centennial in 1936.[37]

Several days before Christmas in 1940, Greenleaf Fisk fell ill with influenza, and he died of cardiac failure on December 29. His funeral at St. Paul's Methodist Church attracted a large crowd of friends, admirers, and family members from across Texas. His pastor lauded him for his loyalty to his friends, his devotion to the church, and his contributions as a citizen. "Among the certainties that are in his life," the minister noted, "his usefulness to the church makes his going a great loss, and his love and devotion to his wife and their home shall not be erased." Frances Fisk took over operating the printing company and remained as involved as possible in her women's club activities.[38]

Running the business was complicated by a series of lawsuits filed against her by an Abilene businessman, J. McAlister Stevenson, a former friend of the family whose wife had been active in many of the same club activities as Frances Fisk. The day after Greenleaf's funeral, Stevenson appeared before the Taylor County Probate Court seeking to replace Frances as executor of Greenleaf's estate. Stevenson contended that he had loaned Greenleaf Fisk more than eight thousand dollars to keep the newspaper and printing business open during the depths of the Depression. (Stevenson had already sued for these funds in 1932 but had lost the case when the court determined that the money was not a loan but an investment in the printing business that had been lost when the company reorganized to avoid bankruptcy.) In early 1941, the probate court rejected Stevenson's request. Stevenson then filed suit against Frances Fisk in state district court, contending that he owned part of the business because of his earlier investment. The court found in his favor, but Frances appealed. After three more years of litigation, the Texas District Court of Appeals reversed the earlier decision, thus confirming Frances's ownership of the company and finally putting an end to the legal battles.[39]

By this time, however, Frances had liquidated the business and moved to Alpine, Texas, where her sister, Willa Morelock, was living. Fisk joined the prestigious Alpine Study Club, which had almost forty members. Not surprisingly, Frances took a very active role in focusing the club on art appreciation activities. In March 1944, for example, the Study Club featured "a program at the College Museum Art Studio on Texas Art and Artists, given by Miltia Hill, Head of the Art Department, and Mrs. Greenleaf Fisk, author of the book *A History of Texas Artists and Sculptors*, as speakers." As part of this program, the club sponsored an exhibit at Sul Ross State Teachers College that featured local works of art.[40]

Fisk's interest in art found a willing audience in the Morelock household. Her brother-in-law, Dr. Horace W. Morelock, had served as president of Sul Ross since 1923 and had long been a friend to the fine arts. He was instrumental in the creation of the college's art department as well as a summer program that brought regional artists to teach and work in Alpine. In 1944, with Morelock's support, Fisk used the Study Club to launch an ambitious project to further the study of Texas art locally. Elected chair of the Alpine Study Club's Fine Arts Committee, she proposed that the college and the club work together to bring a summer lyceum course to Alpine to provide instruction in art and art apprecia- tion. To that end she launched a major fund-raising effort that involved six local civic organizations as well as her club and the college. She headed a committee that planned a fund-raising dinner and worked hard in the late spring of that year to secure additional financial support.[41]

These ambitious plans were abandoned several months later when Fisk be- came ill with throat cancer. Undaunted, Fisk continued her club work as best she could, attending meetings whenever possible. She permitted herself to be elected an officer of the Study Club for 1945–46, even as her physical stamina began to fail. She continued her work as the Fine Arts chair and served as liaison to the Sul Ross art department. But her condition worsened, and she attended her last woman's club meeting in February 1946, at which time she presented the program.[42]

Several weeks later, Fisk signed her will, dividing her modest assets—her personal art collection and several oil leases that had been providing a small monthly income since the Fisks' days at Eastland—among her brother and sis- ters. She also thanked Willa Morelock for her care and love and appointed her as executor. Frances Battaile Fisk died in Alpine on May 30, 1946. Arrangements had already been made for her to be buried in Abilene next to her husband. Notices of her death praised her as one of the founders of the Abilene Woman's Club and noted many of the offices she had held over the years in the TFWC. In addition, she was remembered as the author of *A History of Texas Artists and Sculptors*. The Abilene City Federation of Women's Clubs paid her special tribute in a resolution sent to her siblings: "She was an inspiration to every Club woman, and her knowledge of Club work was invaluable through the years."[43]

As the women who knew and worked with Frances Fisk retired from club activities and died, her name faded from the public consciousness. The Abilene Woman's Club remains vibrant, and at its headquarters can be found a sidewalk brick with Fisk's name, a plaque with a short inscription mentioning her, and a photo of her, along with those of the club's other presidents. Her name also appears on a plaque at the TFWC. These are her memorials. The records of her achievements remain in the archival collections of the many clubs in which Frances Fisk served. And unlike many of the women who worked diligently with her and who are now only names (often married names) in the papers of these clubs, Frances Fisk's historical presence can be recovered today because of the many offices she held and her numerous activities in support of the visual arts. As well, her foundational book, *A History of Texas Artists and Sculptors*, continues to ensure that art historians, collectors, students, and artists interested in early Texas art recognize her name, although most of them probably know little if anything about her life or career. Nearly a decade after Frances's death, her sister, Willa, a clubwoman herself, commented philosophically on the ephemeral recognition of her sister's hard work, even in Texas women's club circles: "Too often, the best and most faithful club women are not appreciated or given the honor and credit due them. A job or good deed well done is, after all, its own reward."[44]

NOTES

1. Published histories of the national and state federations of women's groups as well those of individual clubs offer some insight into art activities. A 1936 article in the General Federation of Women's Clubs magazine addressed Iowa clubs' efforts to promote local art and artists. See "Art Threatens to Supplant Corn as Iowa's Leading Crop," *GFWC Clubwoman* 17 (September 1936): 6, 26–28. Karen J. Blair, *The Torchbearers: Women and Their Amateur Arts Associations in America, 1890–1930* (Bloomington: Indiana University Press, 1994) is the only book-length study of the clubs' broad range of fine arts initiatives. For an excellent article describing many art activities similar to those pursued in Texas, see William M. Tsutsui and Marjorie Swann, "'Light the Beauty Around You': The Art Collection of the Kansas Federation of Women's Clubs," *Kansas History* 26 (Winter 2003–4): 252–63.

2. Blair, *Torchbearers*, 2–3, 5–6, 4 (quotation). See also Karen J. Blair, *Joining In: Exploring the History of Voluntary Organizations* (Malabar, Fla.: Krieger, 2006).

3. Mary I. Wood, *History of the General Federation of Women's Clubs for the First Twenty-Two Years of Its Organization* (New York: GFWC History Department, 1912), 111–12.

4. Ibid., 199, 226, 252–53; *TFWC Yearbook*, 1919–20, 35–36 (quotation), box 7.8, Texas Federation of Women's Clubs Collection (hereafter cited as TFWCC), Woman's Collection, Mary Blagg Hughey Library, Texas Woman's University, Denton.

5. "Appreciation of Art Is Social Necessity Declares Fine Arts Chairman Who Outlines Work for Clubs in Art Music, Literature," *General Federation News* 1 (December 1920): 1, 6, 8.

6. Judith N. McArthur, *Creating the New Woman: The Rise of Southern Women's Progressive Culture in Texas, 1893–1918* (Urbana: University of Illinois Press, 1998), 14–15; *Texas Federation News, Containing the Year Book and Precinct Program, 1925–1926* 4 (July 1926): 137, box 7.9, TFWCC. Writing in 1925, former GFWC president Alice Anne Winter stated that the best clubs combined study and civic work. See Alice Anne Winter, *The Business of Being a Club Woman* (New York: Century, 1925) 3, 8–9. Sources on the white women's club movement in Texas include Megan Seaholm, "Earnest Women: The White Women's Club Movement in Progressive Era Texas, 1880–1920" (PhD diss., Rice University, 1988); Betty Holland Wiesepape, *Lone Star Chapters: The Story of Texas Literary Clubs* (College Station: Texas A&M University Press, 2004); Elizabeth York Enstam, *Women and the Creation of Urban Life: Dallas, Texas, 1843–1920* (College Station: Texas A&M University Press, 1998); Elizabeth Hayes Turner, *Women, Culture, and Community: Religion and Reform in Galveston, 1880–1920* (New York: Oxford University Press, 1997); McArthur, *Creating the New Woman*. There

are also a scattering of master's theses from Texas colleges and universities. For examples of club art activities, see published histories such as *History of the Dallas Federation of Women's Clubs, 1898–1936* (Dallas: Cockrell, n.d.); Mary S. Cunningham, *The Woman's Club of El Paso: Its First Thirty Years* (El Paso: Texas Western Press, University of Texas at El Paso, 1978); Marion Day Mullens, comp., *A History of the Woman's Club of Fort Worth 1923–1973* (n.p., n.d.). On self-education or study clubs in general, see Blair, *Torchbearers*; Theodora Penny Martin, *The Sound of Our Own Voices: Women's Study Clubs, 1860–1910* (Boston: Beacon, 1987); Anne Firor Scott, *Natural Allies: Women's Associations in American History* (Urbana: University of Illinois Press, 1991).

7. Florence Elberta Barns, *Texas Writers of Today* (1936; Ann Arbor, Mich.: Gryphon, 1971), 179–80; "Fisk, Frances Battaile (Mrs. Greenleaf)," in *Notable Women of the Southwest: A Pictorial Biographical Encyclopedia of the Leading Women of Texas, New Mexico, Oklahoma, and Arizona* (Dallas: Tardy, 1938), 124–25 (quotation).

8. Martin, *Sound of Our Own Voices*, 86, 114; Scott, *Natural Allies*, 182; McArthur, *Creating the New Woman*, 15; Seaholm, "Earnest Women," 202–3; Blair, *Torchbearers*, 3.

9. Texas Department of Health, Bureau of Vital Statistics, Standard Certificate of Death for Frances Battaile Fisk, May 30, 1946, Brewster County Clerk's Office, Alpine, Tex.; J. F. Battaile, "The Battaile Family," typescript, n.d., Application for Membership in the National Society of the Daughters of the American Revolution for Janith Dawn Vest Stephenson, Frances Vest, "The Life of My Grandmother," December 12, 1928, manuscript, all in possession of Janith Vest Stephenson, Alpine, Tex.; *Southwestern University Catalogs*, 1895–96, 1896–97, *Southwestern University Alumni Directory, 1840–1920*, http://www.southwestern.edu/cgi-bin/library/special-collections/hist-alum .cgi (accessed October 26, 2010); William B. Jones, *To Survive and Excel: Southwestern University, 1840–2000* (Georgetown, Tex.: Southwestern University, 2006), 88–90, 102–7.

10. "Fisk, Frances Battaile (Mrs. Greenleaf)," 125; *Record of the University of Chicago* 1 (April 3, 1896): 335.

11. U.S. Census, 1900, Precinct 4, Georgetown, Williamson County, Tex.; "Editor Fisk Married," *Bartlett Tribune*, May 16, 1902; "Fisk-Battaile Marriage," *Georgetown Commercial*, May 23, 1902 (quotation).

12. Edwin T. Cox, *History of Eastland County, Texas* (San Antonio: Naylor, 1950), 45–46; Ruby Pearl Ghormley, *Eastland County, Texas: A Historical and Biographical Survey* (Austin: Rupegy, 1969), 68–77; Carolyne Lavinia Langston, *History of Eastland County* (Dallas: Aldridge, 1904), 131; "State News," *Dallas Morning News*, May 5, 1913.

13. Martin, *Sound of Our Own Voices*, 88–97; Scott, *Natural Allies*, 177–78; McArthur, *Creating the New Woman*, 25.

14. "Thursday Afternoon Club," "Publishers for County Considered among 'Giants,'" in Roy Smith, *Gateway to the West: Eastland County History*, (Dallas: Taylor, 1989), n.p.; Pilot Point Club Records and Scrapbook, box 8.55, TFWCC; Minutes of the XIX Century Club, Club Records, Pilot Point Public Library, Pilot Point, Tex. (first and second quotations); "News from Pilot Point," *Denton Record-Chronicle*, October 22, December 11, 1915, December 2, 1916, February 10, March 5, April 19, 1917.

15. Fane Downs, ed., *The Future Great City of West Texas: Abilene, 1881–1981* (Abilene: Richardson, 1981), 21–22; Abilene Chamber of Commerce, *Abilene—The Athens of the West* (promotional magazine), Uncataloged Materials Miscellaneous box, Abilene Public Library, Abilene, Tex.; *Abilene City Directory, 1928*, 67; "A. Garland Adair Buys Abilene Times Interest," *Dallas Morning News*, March 18, 1927.

16. Winter, *Business*, 3, 8–9.

17. Elizabeth Downs, *Let's Make Plans [A Guide for Club Women]* (New York: Knopf, 1942), 12; Martin, *Sound of Our Own Voices*, 108; McArthur, *Creating the New Woman*, 76.

18. Summary compiled by the authors from information in yearbooks, payment cards, minutes, the *Texas Federation News, Texas Federation Yearbooks*, and numerous press clippings at various locations. The records of the Abilene Woman's Club contain much useful information for reconstructing the chronology of Fisk's service. See Abilene Woman's Forum Yearbooks, 1924–25, 1927–28, 1934–35, Art Unit of the Abilene Woman's Forum, Press Books, 1924–25, 1927–28, 1934–35, Rupert Richardson Research Center of the Southwest, Richardson Library, Hardin-Simmons University, Abilene (hereafter cited as Art Unit Press Book). These and other scrapbooks from the Richardson Research Center are available in the West Texas Digital Archive of the Abilene Library Consortium, http://wtda.alc.org/ (accessed December 15, 2012).

19. Frances Battaile Fisk, *A History of Texas Artists and Sculptors* (Abilene, Tex.: Fisk, 1928), 1–2. Mary Q. Burnett, in her capacity as state art chairman for the Indiana Federation of Women's Clubs, published a similar book for her state in 1921. See Mary Q. Burnett, *Art and Artists of Indiana* (New York: Century, 1921). *TFWC Handbook 1925–1926*, 3, box 7.9, TFWCC; *TFWC Handbook, 1926–1927*, 157, box 7.10, TFWCC; Report of the Chair of the Texas Artists and Sculptors Committee, in *TFWC Yearbook, 1926–1927*, 158, box 7.10, TFWCC; Fisk, *History*, 1 (quotations).

20. Fisk, *History*, 1 (quotation); Promotional Flyer for *A History of Texas Artists and Sculptors, 1888–1928*, Coppini-Tauch Collection, 1892–1988, box 3R159, Dolph Briscoe Center for American History, University of Texas at Austin; *TFWC Yearbook, 1927–1928*, 116–17 (quotation), box 7.10, TFWCC.

21. Promotional Flyer for *A History of Texas Artists and Sculptors, 1888–1928*, box 6.5, TFWCC; Fisk, *History*, 1–2. Fisk acknowledged that "valuable assistance has been given by the District chairmen in locating our artists and securing data to be compiled. Special mention should be given to the following chairmen: First District, Mrs. H. I. Kight, Dublin; Second District, Dr. Virginia Spates, Sherman; Sixth District, Mrs. Bob Ware, San Angelo." See *TFWC Yearbook, 1926–1927*, 158–59, box 7.10, TFWCC. See also Mrs. Bob Ware to Waldine Tauch, April 8, 1927, box 3R159, Coppini-Tauch Collection.

22. Promotional Flyer for *A History of Texas Artists and Sculptors, 1888–1928*, box 3R159, Coppini-Tauch Collection; *Texas Federation News* (hereafter cited as *TFN*) 7 (September–October 1929): 71–72 (first and third quotations); Josephine Heavenhill, "A New Book: Texas Artists and Sculptors," *TFN* 7 (July–August 1929): 13 (second quotation); "Week's News among the Bookmen," *Dallas Morning News*, February 3, 1929 (fourth quotation).

23. Mrs. Greenleaf Fisk, "Sixth District Report of the President," *TFWC Yearbook, 1929–1931*, 183–84, box 7.10, TFWCC. Carpenter's annotated personal copy of Fisk, *History*, is in the Reference Collection of the Abilene Public Library. Both Paula Grauer and Michael Grauer, *Dictionary of Texas Artists, 1800–1945* (College Station: Texas A&M University Press, 1999), xvii, and John Powers and Deborah Powers, *Texas Painters, Sculptors, and Graphic Artists: A Biographical Dictionary of Artists in Texas before 1942* (Austin: Woodmont, 2000), vii–viii, acknowledge the importance of Fisk's work to those interested in early Texas art.

24. General Federation of Women's Clubs pamphlet, *The Penny Art Fund at Work*, American Art Week Scrapbook, 1945, box 8.31, TFWCC.

25. "Penny Art Fund Established in Texas in 1932," Abilene Art Forum Miscellaneous Scrapbook, Richardson Research Center; Mrs. Greenleaf Fisk, "Art Division Gets Award," *TFN* 11 (July 1933): 6; Mrs. Greenleaf Fisk, "Texas Wins Painting in P.A.F. Contest," *TFN* 12 (September 1934): 8.

26. Fisk, "Texas Wins Painting," 19 (quotation); Mrs. Greenleaf Fisk, "Start an Art Collection Now," *TFN* 11 (February 1933): 7; Mrs. Greenleaf Fisk, "Prizes to Be Awarded in the Art Division," *TFN* 13 (February 1935): 8.

27. Mrs. Greenleaf Fisk, "Penny Art Fund Growing Fast," *TFN* 14 (January 1936): 5; "Art Information Sought," *TFN* 14 (October 1936): 6.

28. *GFWC Clubwoman* 20 (June 1940): 5; Minutes of Art Unit Meetings, 1936–1937, Art Unit Press Book, 1936–37; "Forum Art Unit Receives Award," December 1, 1941, Art Unit Press Book, 1941–42.

29. Mrs. H. S. Godfrey, "Department of Fine Arts," *GFWC Clubwoman* 17 (October 1936): 18; "City Wide Observance of American Art Week Planned by Forum Unit Members" (quotation), "Loan Collection Added to Unit's Local Artist Exhibition," both in Art Unit Press Book, 1938–39.

30. "Art Week Report Made to Abilene Woman, Chairman," Art Unit Press Book, 1940–41.

31. "The Beginnings of the Frances B. Fisk Art Loan Fund, 6th District, Texas Federation of Women's Clubs" (quotation), Abilene Art Forum Miscellaneous Scrapbook. As a consequence of the Great Depression, organizers had difficulty securing donations for the fund; moreover, few qualified applicants could be found as a consequence of the eligibility restrictions for loan recipients. The fund was used only once and was liquidated in the 1950s, with the proceeds divided among the Sixth District clubs.

32. Fisk, *History*, 4 (first quotation); "Abilene Woman's Forum Moves to Sponsor Museum," Art Unit Press Book, 1947–48; "Civic Art and Museum Ass'n Organized Here," *Abilene Reporter-News*, November 5, 1937; "Woman's Forum, Founded in 1921, Projects Work into Many Places of Community Life," *Abilene Reporter-News*, February 23, 1941 (second quotation).

33. "Thomas Hart Benton Exhibition Program," clipping, n.d., Art Unit Press Book, 1938–39; "Art Unit Donor—First Canvass Presented Local Collection," *Abilene Reporter-News*, November 12, 1939.

34. City Federation of Women's Clubs Minutes, March 16, 1940, City Federation Records, Abilene Public Library, Abilene, Tex.; "Abilene's Pioneer Club Women Receive . . . ," April 14, 1940, Art Unit Press Book, 1938–39; "Woman's Forum, Founded in 1921."

35. Fisk, "Sixth District Report of the President," *TFWC Yearbook, 1929–1931*, 179–84.

36. Mrs. Greenleaf Fisk, "Sixth District: Report of the President," *TFN* 9 (June 1931): 17; "Leaders and Captains of Penny Bank Campaign," *TFN* (June 1932): 4–5; "New Club Home to Be Opened in Late October," *TFN* 10 (July 1932): 8; "A Call for Volunteers on Re-Assembly Day," *TFN* 10 (September 1932): 3.

37. Fisk, "Sixth District," 17; "In Memoriam: Mrs. Greenleaf Fisk," *TFN*, Abilene Art Forum Miscellaneous Scrapbook; "Fisk, Frances Battaile (Mrs. Greenleaf)"; "Loan Collection Added"; Minutes of Art Unit Meeting, March 6, 1936, "Art Unit Host in Guest Fete," March 1936, both in Art Unit Press Book, 1936–37.

38. "At Funeral Service: Publisher Honored for Loyalty to Friends, Devotion to Church," *Abilene Reporter-News*, December 31, 1940.

39. Petition of J. McAlister Stevenson, December 30, 1940, Probate File 2837, Clerk of Courts, Taylor County Courthouse, Abilene, Tex.; *Fisk v. Stevenson*, No. 2334, Court of Civil Appeals, Eastland, Tex., 179 S.QW.2d 432; 1944 Tex. App. LEXIS, 658, January 14, 1944; *Stevenson v. Fisk*, No. 11210, U.S. Circuit Court of Appeals, 151 F.2d 1010; 1945 U.S. LEXIS 3403, December 7, 1945.

40. "Minute Books of the Alpine Study Club," vol. 5, Archives of the Big Bend, Bryan Wildenthal Memorial Library, Sul Ross State University, Alpine, Tex.; Ellen W. Smith, "The Study Club of Alpine: Forty Years of Achievement" (master's thesis, Sul Ross State College, 1949), 154–56; "Annual Spring Report of the Alpine Study Club, Alpine, Texas," March 23, 1946 (quotation) , box 6.83, TFWCC.

41. "Sul Ross Boasts One of the First Museums in the State," Sul Ross Scrapbooks, No. 5, 1939–41, Archives of the Big Bend; Minute Books of the Alpine Study Club, Archives of the Big Bend.

42. Ellen W. Smith, "Study Club of Alpine," 343–46.

43. Last Will and Testament of Frances Battaile Fisk, Probate No. 546, County Clerk's Office, Brewster County Courthouse, Alpine, Tex.; Texas Department of Health, Bureau of Vital Statistics, Standard Certificate of Death for Frances Battaile Fisk, May 30, 1946, Brewster County Clerk's Office, Alpine, Tex.; "Funeral Today for Mrs. Fisk," *Abilene Reporter-News*, May 31, 1946; Resolution, September 11, 1946 (quotation), folder 1945–49, box 3, Abilene City Federation of Women's Clubs Minutes, Abilene Public Library.

44. Willa Morelock to A. M. Carpenter, November 26, 1955, Abilene Art Forum Miscellaneous Scrapbook.

Latinas in Dallas, 1910–2010

Becoming New Women

BIANCA MERCADO

❀ ❀ ❀

Anita Nanez lived in the Little Mexico barrio of Dallas with her husband, José, and their six children. Although José Nanez had a light hauling business during the Great Depression, Anita Nanez wanted to supplement her family's income. Her husband—like most men of that era—was "of the old school" and believed women should not work outside the home. Anita therefore "went around his blind side" and enrolled in a course at Marinello Beauty School. Although she had only a third-grade education, Nanez earned a certificate as a beautician and opened a shop in the front room of her home. By securing for herself an occupation customarily gendered female, Nanez found a way to supplement her family's income and work within the limits of established gender roles and traditional responsibilities for women. Her daughter, Anita Nanez Martínez, remembers her mother's creative and boundary-pushing efforts with pride and affection: "She didn't defy" her husband but rather "found a way to get around" the traditions preventing Mexican women from working to increase the family's income.[1]

Anita Nanez's experience reveals several themes that are common in Latinas' experiences in Dallas. When Nanez enrolled in beauty school, she went against not only the wishes of her husband but also the wider gender expectations of the era. Particularly in Mexican families, custom held that women were full-time wives and mothers. To pursue employment, Nanez, like many other Latinas before and after her, pushed against societal limits, including those espoused by her husband. Her actions influenced her daughter, who learned new ways of being a woman, a wife, and a mother while growing up in a traditional household. Nanez and other Latinas in Dallas in the twentieth century often worked within rather than against prevailing cultural expectations to reshape notions of women's work and womanhood. Anita Nanez Martínez (Anita Nanez's daughter) and others witnessed, were inspired by, and built on new models of womanhood created by preceding generations of Latinas.

Latinos now comprise nearly 40 percent of Dallas's total population. At the turn of the twentieth century, however, Mexicans accounted for less than 1 percent of the city's residents, although immigration laws imposed no restrictions on Mexicans' arrival in the United States. On March 3, 1903, government officials modified an 1885 labor act to prohibit the entry of "unskilled" labor, but for years thereafter, contractors along the Texas-Mexico border still recruited Mexican laborers for U.S. railroad companies by creating their own definitions of "skilled" and "unskilled." Border officials, too, ignored the restrictions.[2] As a result, Dallas's Mexican population mushroomed in the first few decades of the twentieth century.[3]

Census information from these years affirms that even in its nascent stages, Dallas's Mexican community followed the gender rules of the old country. Forty-one of the sixty persons of Mexican descent living in Dallas in 1900 were men, and just nineteen were women. The average age of this population was nearly twenty-nine. Almost two-thirds of the nineteen Mexican women in Dallas were single, a third were married, and the rest were widowed. In accordance with cultural traditions, most of these women did not work for a living—only four of them were employed outside the home, and they worked in fields deemed "appropriate" for women—as domestics, laundresses, seamstresses, and nurses. In contrast, 83 percent of the men worked outside the home, holding positions as food vendors, day laborers, farm laborers, and railroad laborers. The 1910 Census reiterated these cultural and traditional norms. Dallas's 330-person Mexican community was overwhelmingly male, and most of the men worked outside the home, while only a handful of women had paid employment in such fields as washerwomen, cooks, and factory workers. Mexican men often resented women—especially their wives—working or even wanting to work and believed that women's work consisted solely of raising children and keeping house.[4]

Mexican cultural tradition and gendered expectations regarding women's roles dictated women's "proper" place in the home. Families socialized their children along gender lines, training the boys for school and work and the girls for marriage and family. Indeed, "women's assigned role fit neatly into a set of societal expectations of the home." Transplanted Mexicans in Dallas thus adhered to traditional cultural gender norms during the first three decades of their immigration to Dallas.[5]

By 1920, Dallas had more than four thousand Mexicans, and they constituted a majority of the city's new arrivals. These immigrants were even younger than

ADELAIDA CUELLAR WITH GABINA, AMOS, AND JIM CUELLAR

in Lockhart, Texas, ca. 1900.

Courtesy of the Cuellar family and Consolidated Restaurant Operations.

their predecessors, averaging just over twenty years of age. Mexican women for the most part continued their unpaid work in the home. Fewer than two hundred Mexican women worked for pay, but they had begun to shift into jobs typically occupied by men, working on railroads, in factories, and on farms. However, a gendered division of labor within those industries likely existed. And most of the Mexican women who worked for wages were employed as maids, clerks, cooks, dressmakers, laundresses, boardinghouse keepers, nurses, and seamstresses.[6]

With the city's Mexican population growing, Dallas voters fostered the creation of ethnically defined areas. In 1916, the city passed a referendum that imposed residential racial segregation, the first such law in Texas. Although the Texas Supreme Court invalidated the ordinance in 1917, city officials tried to reinstate a modified form of the policy just four years later. The Dallas City Council passed a new law permitting residents to request that their block be designated as black, white, or open. Neighborhoods already exclusively occupied by one race were closed to other races, while open blocks often housed poor and working-class families. Once the city granted this designation, only a written request by three-fourths of the residents on a block could overturn the neighborhood's racial assignment. The isolation of Mexican immigrants in ethnically defined neighborhoods fostered a heightened sense of ethnicity and encouraged immigrants to cling to and uphold Mexican culture.[7]

Areas of Mexican settlement sprang up in three parts of Dallas: Little Mexico (near downtown and the largest such area), East Dallas, and West Dallas. In the 1930s, several graduate students in the sociology department at Southern Methodist University conducted research on the city's Mexican population. According to Ethelyn Davis, "To all appearances Little Mexico forms a city within a city, entirely different from its surroundings." Mexicans lived mostly in homes constructed of scrap wood and tarpaper or in boxcars at the edges of the neighborhood. Streets were unpaved, houses often had no yards, and residents frequently had no privacy.[8]

As they became permanent residents, Mexicans slowly gained access to the city's institutions. The few Mexican children who went to school regularly attended Cumberland Hill School. Located in the heart of Little Mexico, Cumberland Hill was a two-story brick building originally constructed in 1889 on the site of two earlier public schools. From its opening, the new Cumberland Hill School was a "melting pot of nationalities, religions and sects," but by 1925, 95 percent of the school's students were Mexican. Cumberland teachers' primary goal was Americanization, and it was "not . . . at all unusual to see such a program as the following presented at one of the Friday auditorium periods: 'Why

I Love America,' orations by Epimenio Espinosa . . . 'Abraham Lincoln, Savior of His Country,' by Secundia Flores . . . 'The Dallas Spirit,' by Guadalupe Pérez." One of the teachers, Miss Pinkston, commented, "Here we take all of them on the same plan and for one purpose—to make them good, substantial, American citizens. Whether they are American, Swedes, Russian, Mexican, or Chinese they are the same to us—potential Americans."[9]

The Great Depression brought both hardships and opportunities for Texas's Latino families. Widespread unemployment and private charity donations skewed toward Anglo families left many Latino families in severe financial straits. Moreover, their perpetually neglected ethnic neighborhoods declined further, and disease and death rates rose. At the same time, however, some Latinas found new opportunities for work. Women and children earned meager but useful wages producing handiwork in their homes or in small factories. Other women found factory work in nontextile industries, earning similarly inadequate compensation. Federal programs helped some Latinas learn English and acquire the skills to perform clerical work. Although Latinas occupied sales and clerical positions and secured industrial homework during the Great Depression, they often faced cuts to their wages and hours as a result of both economic conditions and racial prejudice. And all the while, they continued their crucial work within the home, caring for children, mending clothing, and cooking meals. Support networks developed among Latinas in similar situations, fostering friendships, survival strategies, and perhaps most important, hope. According to Diana Orozco, her grandmother faced great hardships in Dallas in the 1920s and 1930s but never became bitter or angry. On the contrary, "because they had to live with so little, they learned how important community was. . . . That was the way they survived, by helping each other. They had nothing, but what they did was what they had." Depression-era hardship not only fortified Latinas' connections to other Latinas but also provided them life and work experiences that created postwar opportunities for education and financial stability. Despite the financial and emotional challenges of the 1930s, Latinas learned that they could turn their domestic skills into wage-earning work.[10]

María Luna, a 1923 arrival to Dallas from San Luis Potosí, Mexico, turned her domestic skills into a business venture, thus allowing her a degree of independence not available to most other Mexican women. After working for a few months in Porero's Grocery Store on North Griffin Street, Luna bought a corn grinder from her employer. In February 1924, she opened Luna's Tortilla Factory on Caroline Street in Little Mexico. She had no business training, spoke only Spanish, and refused until her dying day to learn how to pat a tortilla. Instead, Luna ground corn, mixed the *masa* (tortilla dough), and then took dishpans of the dough to the homes of her female employees, returning later in the day to pick up the finished tortillas. In 1926, María Luna married Rudolfo Gonzáles, and by 1927, she had twenty-four employees who produced five hundred dozen tortillas a day. Two years later, she initiated a delivery service to homes in Little Mexico, the West Dallas Mexican barrio, Cement City, and El Rancho Grande. In 1938, Luna moved her tortilla factory to the corner of McKinney Avenue and Caroline Street, and the following year, she turned the business over to her son, Francisco, who mechanized the factory and raised the output of tortillas to one hundred dozen per hour by 1940. In 2001, the Dallas City Council named Luna's Tortilla Factory an official historic landmark. Luna's independence—creating her own business at a time when women generally did not work outside the home—helped redefine the limits of women's work and sphere.[11]

Adelaida Cuellar similarly repurposed her domestic skills and knowledge of Mexican cooking and found independence and success in a business venture that ultimately resulted in the creation of one of the largest Mexican restaurant chains in the United States. Born in 1871 in Nuevo León, Mexico, Cuellar moved to Laredo, Texas, with her soon-to-be husband, Macario Cuellar in 1892. Both spoke only Spanish and took jobs on ranches and as sharecroppers before the turn of the century, when Adelaida decided to open a tamale stand to earn money to support her twelve children. She made and sold homemade tamales at the 1926 and 1927 Kaufman County Fairs, southeast of Dallas, and her sons, Amos and Frank, soon opened a Mexican café in Kaufman with Adelaida as the cook. The Great Depression forced the closure of the café, and Amos and Frank's efforts to open Mexican restaurants in other East Texas towns and in Oklahoma and Louisiana floundered for the next decade.[12]

The Cuellar family's luck changed when two more of Adelaida Cuellar's sons, Macario and Gilbert, opened the El Charro restaurant in Dallas's Oak Lawn neighborhood in 1940. Featuring Mama Cuellar's best recipes, El Charro became a success by 1943, and most of the Cuellar family moved to Dallas to join the family business. The chain expanded to other parts of Dallas as well as to Fort Worth, Waco, and Houston. By 1955, the business had changed its name to El Chico, entered the frozen food business, and expanded across the southwestern United States. Though Adelaida Cuellar's sons created the successful restaurant chain, she had the original idea of using her culinary talent for broader purposes.[13]

Faustina Porras, a native of Chihuahua, Mexico, likewise contributed her invaluable domestic skills to a family business venture that became El Fenix Restaurant. Born on February 22, 1900, Porras moved with her family to Dallas in 1914 as part of one of the first large migrations from Mexico into Dallas. The

Porrases and the other new arrivals settled in what became the Little Mexico barrio, and Porras worked as a field hand and attended school sporadically. At age fifteen, she married Miguel Martínez, also a recent Mexican immigrant, who worked as a hotel dishwasher. By 1918, Faustina and Miguel Martínez had saved enough money to open one of the city's first Mexican restaurants, the Martínez Restaurant on McKinney Street. Faustina Martínez helped her husband run the restaurant, which became known as El Fenix; raised their twelve children; and made tamales at home to serve at the restaurant. During World War II, several of her sons served in the armed forces, and Faustina Martínez became a U.S. citizen. The Martínez children took over the restaurant in 1955, by which time Faustina and Miguel had become prosperous and well-known Texas entrepreneurs. After Miguel's death in 1956, Faustina Martínez took up dancing, earning the nickname "Mama Cha-Cha." She danced well into her eighties and added ceramics and volunteering to her list of activities. She died in Dallas in 1990.[14]

María Luna, Adelaida Cuellar, and Faustina Martínez all broadened the scope of their work beyond the home. They took on new responsibilities in business ventures and stepped just outside Latinas' typical roles. Even though they challenged cultural and societal expectations of women's work, their enterprises were still largely feminine. Luna, Cuellar, and Martínez used the skills and lessons they had learned from the preceding generation of women and gently nudged the limits of gender expectations to earn money outside the home.

Other Latinas in Dallas used more unconventional domestic skills to support their families in the postwar years. Gloria González grew up in the heart of the Little Mexico barrio in Dallas. When she was in the eighth grade, her father became sick and unable to work. González and her brother, who was in the eleventh grade, dropped out of school to find jobs to support their family. In 1944, at the age of sixteen, González found a "wonderful" job wrapping gifts at the Neiman Marcus department store. She soon moved to special orders before becoming a supervisor in the jewelry department. González worked at Neiman Marcus for thirty-six years. Growing up, González no doubt learned from other women in her life that she should do whatever her family needed.[15]

Anita Nanez Martínez followed the barrier-pushing example set by her beautician mother and made the most of wartime and postwar opportunities for women, entering new spheres of leadership and politics. Nanez Martínez was born in the Little Mexico barrio of Dallas on December 8, 1925. Growing up, she often missed school to help her father pick onions or cotton, but she nonetheless completed her education. After graduating from Crozier Technical High School in the early 1940s, Nanez Martínez wanted to attend college, but her family lacked the money to send her, and around that time, her father died and her mother suffered a stroke. She knew that she "was going to have to be the breadwinner of the family," she recalled. She took a job at the Owen Beer Company in downtown Dallas before taking a civil service exam and getting a job at the Aide Service Command. When she could, she took night classes at Southern Methodist University.[16]

After marrying Albert Martínez, son of Faustina Martínez, in 1946, Anita Nanez Martínez assumed the role of homemaker and dedicated volunteer while raising four children, but she also continued her work as an activist for the Dallas Latino community. In 1969, when she was serving as president of Dallas Women's Restaurant Auxiliary and as a member of the board of directors of the YWCA, she was asked to run for the Dallas City Council. Her husband responded, "Are you nuts? Haven't you got enough to do?" To this, Nanez Martínez replied, "Well, that's just it. From up there, I can really effect change." She put her name in the running against twenty-eight other candidates.[17]

Martínez had never before run for an office, but she needed no help campaigning or raising money. Once her name was on the ballot, calls flooded her home from people she had not seen since first grade. Nanez Martínez remembered, "They were calling me to ask me what they could do to help." As the returns came back on Election Day, journalist Ron Calhoun approached Nanez Martínez and asked, "Do you realize what's happening in your race? Well, it's short of a miracle. You have gotten in this . . . contest, and then, gotten it without getting into a runoff." Anita Nanez Martínez was the first Mexican American elected to the Dallas City Council.[18]

After two terms on the city council, Nanez Martínez began what became her most important legacies, the Anita Martínez Recreation Center and the Anita Martínez Ballet Folklórico. The recreation center opened in 1975 and the ballet group, which Nanez Martínez hoped would instill cultural pride in the young people of Dallas, began soon after, and both continue to thrive. In 1973, President Richard Nixon appointed Nanez Martínez to the National Voluntary Service Advisory Council and as an adviser to the Peace Corps. She received a commission from President George H. W. Bush to serve on the Women and Minority Business Administration. Finally, Nanez Martínez has received countless local, state, and national awards for her many years of volunteer work.[19]

Anita Nanez Martínez's time on the Dallas City Council and her subsequent efforts on behalf of Dallas Latinos demonstrate the changes in the United States in the wake of the civil rights and feminist movements. Although men and women had previously engaged in civil rights organizing and activism, the period after World War II saw civil rights efforts evolve into a movement, with activists across the country using many different strategies to achieve their goals. The organizations they created, however, usually reconstituted the gendered divisions of labor present in the public and private spheres, with men taking more formal, public leadership positions and women organizing behind the scenes. But occasionally, Mexican American men and women collaborated, as with the formation of the grassroots Community Service Organization (cso) in California in the 1940s in response to police brutality, discrimination, and lack of educational opportunities. Utilizing citizenship classes, voter registration drives, and lawsuits, the cso worked on behalf of both Mexican Americans and Mexican immigrants. As the civil rights movement evolved in the 1960s and 1970s, so too did the organizations. Later Mexican American activist groups such as the Mexican American Youth Organization organized around issues of Chicano cultural nationalism and social justice.[20]

Women's participation in activist networks in the 1940s and in the civil rights movement of the 1950s and 1960s brought about the feminist movement in the late 1960s. Women activists formed groups such as the National Organization for Women to push for equal rights for women in employment and the law. Younger, more radical activists challenged power relations between men and women and sought to bring about structural change. Chicana feminists later formed groups such as Mujeres por la Raza (Women for the People) to address the needs of Chicanas. The civil rights movement and the feminist movement thus opened new spaces for Latinas to come together, organize, assume leadership roles, and become educated and politicized. These movements also redefined the limits of what was possible for Latinas in both their private and public lives. At the same time, however, many Latinas still drew considerable inspiration and strength from the strong female role models of previous generations.[21]

María Teresa Díaz was among those Mexicans who took advantage of the growing opportunities Dallas offered women in the 1960s. Born in Sabinas, Coahuila, Díaz visited Dallas in 1963, when she was eighteen, and one of her hosts suggested that she could easily find a job and should move there permanently. Later that year, Díaz did so, working first in a shrimp-processing factory and later as a hostess at the El Chico restaurant.[22]

Díaz's time at El Chico reflects the persistence of gender ideals upheld by many Latino families. In 1964, the Cuellar family asked her to be Miss El Chico, a traveling representative of the restaurant. The Cuellars chose Díaz because they liked her quaint Mexican background and the fact that she spoke little English. According to Díaz, she knew only two English phrases: "How many?" and "Follow me, please." Although Miss El Chico's primary role was to create an authentic Mexican image for the restaurant, the Cuellars' notion of a traditional, feminine Mexican woman reflected the ideals still held by many people of Mexican descent in Dallas. Most Latinas negotiated the tensions between this traditional worldview and the growing number of opportunities available for women. Díaz was flattered by the offer to become Miss El Chico but ultimately turned it down because the idea of becoming a spokesperson frightened her. She continued working at El Chico before moving to Neiman Marcus, where she was employed for twenty-eight years.[23]

Many Latinas struggled to push beyond the traditional cultural notions of womanhood. Sylvia Silva grew up in a traditional Latino family wherein her mother taught her to serve her father and nine brothers. She and her three sisters cleaned, prepared meals, waited for the men and boys to eat, drew their baths, and washed their clothes. "It was normal," Silva remembered, "the male was respected." When she was seventeen years old, Silva married and began a family of her own. For twelve years, she served her husband as she had served her father and brothers. Then one day, her husband suffered an accident at work that shattered both his arms. To support her family, Silva enrolled in a Dallas community college and studied real estate. After a short stint as a real estate agent, she bought a temporary employment agency and became a business-woman. Silva, in her words, "became a different person." Indeed, her husband told her she was no longer the girl he married. Silva agreed: "I was like a butter-fly." Diana Flores, conversely, left college to be a wife and mother. Flores attended college at Texas A&I University in Kingsville for one year before marrying and taking a job to support herself and her husband while he attended school. Flores remembered, "When I married and had the children, well, everything comes to a stop, I think, especially if you're a woman, because the emphasis has to be on home and family and, well, work." After her second marriage, Flores went back to school and graduated from Dallas Baptist University. Silva's and Flores's experiences reflect the challenges many Latinas faced while trying both to live up and adjust to the traditional notion of proper activities for Latinas.[24]

Diana Gallego, an accomplished dance instructor, had a different encounter with Mexican tradition. Born on the outskirts of Laredo, Texas, in 1951, Gallego later obtained her bachelor's and master's degrees in dance from Texas Woman's University in Denton. She took over teaching at a dance studio during her senior year at the school and eventually taught more than three hundred students. She married in 1977 and had a daughter five years later. In 1991, Gallego took a job teaching dance in the Dallas Independent School District. The district's human resources department told her that she would be teaching in her area of expertise, classical ballet and modern dance, but two days before the semester started, the school's principal told her that she would be teaching ballet folklórico (traditional Latin American dance). Gallego replied, "Hey, just because I was born on the border and I have Mexican heritage doesn't mean I was born knowing how to do the Jarabe Tapatío [Mexican Hat Dance]! I wasn't born with a pair of folklórico shoes on my feet!" Even though she was not qualified to teach the class, which had been mandated by the federal government, she had already closed her dance studio, so she took private lessons from the Anita Martínez Ballet Folklórico to stay ahead of her students. Two years later, when the school finally offered her a position teaching classical ballet, she turned it down, reasoning, "There are lots of teachers that can teach the classical ballet and modern, but there were very few teachers that can teach the full range of dance, especially the folklórico."[25]

Gallego's experience reveals that Latinas shoulder cultural expectations from many different sources, not just from their own Latino community, thus intensifying the pressure they feel to adhere to those expectations. Gallego chose to use the principal's expectation that she knew ballet folklórico to strengthen her teaching résumé, and in 2013, she became the coordinator for theater and dance programs for the Dallas public schools. She is also the founder of the nonprofit Texas Association for Hispanic Dance and Culture, which sponsors the Texas High School Salsa Championship to encourage the inclusion of Latino culture and the development of high school salsa teams. The association also sponsors the Folklórico Leadership Institute, which brings to Dallas dance professors from Mexico and other parts of the United States. Although Gallego came to ballet folklórico by accident, the experience ultimately enriched her abilities as a dance instructor and changed her perspective.[26]

By the 1980s and 1990s, adhering to Mexican traditions of womanhood and family became less of an issue as more Latinas and other women entered the public sphere. In 1993, Lena Levario became the first Latina judge in Dallas County. Born in 1961 in Pecos, Texas, Levario had wanted to be a carpenter, like her uncle, but when she asked him if she could work with him during the summer, he refused, saying that girls could not do that kind of work. Her father, however, instilled in Levario the belief that she could be anything she wanted to be. He wanted her to be a civil rights attorney to battle injustice, such as the Jim Crow–era abuses he witnessed in West Texas. Levario's mother taught her the importance of getting an education so that she would not have to rely on anyone else. Levario started her activism early. When she was in high school, she tried to join the yearbook staff but discovered that an invitation from a current staff member was required—and all of the staff members were white. She started a petition to change this process and met with the principal, who had circled all the "brown faces" in the yearbook to prove that there was no discrimination on the staff. The policy eventually changed, but Levario did not make the staff. She recalled, "I started learning about politics at a real early age."[27]

After graduating from high school in Pecos, Levario continued on to college and law school at Texas Tech University in Lubbock. In 1986, she moved to Dallas with her husband and took a position as a county public defender. She found Dallas "overwhelming." She faced resistance as a Latina attorney but combated opposition by proving herself. She developed a good reputation and quickly rose to the felony courts. Judges often sent Spanish-speaking clients her way, assuming she spoke fluent Spanish—which she at first did not, although she worked with an interpreter until she was fluent. In 1993, Governor Ann Richards appointed her to fill a vacancy on the district court, making her the first Latina judge in Dallas County.[28]

Levario also participated in organizations geared toward the betterment of Latinos. She was a member of the Hispanic Fifty, which seeks to educate the community about the economic situation of the Hispanic women in the Dallas area. She was also recruited to start a council for the League of United Latin American Citizens (LULAC) in Dallas and later became a legal adviser for the national body and president of the Dallas LULAC council. The strong models provided by both Levario's mother and father facilitated her journey in the law and no doubt inspired her work on behalf of the Hispanic community. Her parents' desire to see Levario obtain an education and pursue her dreams originated from lessons of culture and strength taught by earlier generations.[29]

Diana Orozco had a similarly strong model of womanhood and cultural pride on which to build. Capitalizing on the opportunities available in the wake of the civil rights and feminist movements, Orozco obtained a law degree and ran for justice of the peace in Dallas County. Born in 1960 in Dallas, Orozco received a work-study scholarship to attend Ursuline Academy, where she was one of 5 Mexican American girls in a class of nearly 125. Her father, who moved to Dallas from Laredo in the 1950s, was a teacher and later a principal. Orozco's mother was a homemaker who loved politics and took her young daughter to countless political rallies. At a 1973 rally protesting the shooting of twelve-year-old Santos Rodriguez by a Dallas police officer, Orozco remembered watching various attorneys take the stage and promise to make a difference. Orozco realized that she, too, wanted to be a lawyer. The words of Adelfa Callejo made a particular impression on Orozco—Callejo was the only female lawyer on the stage.[30]

After she graduated from Ursuline Academy, Orozco attended St. Mary's College in South Bend, Indiana, on scholarship. After receiving her bachelor's degree, Orozco entered Southern Methodist University Law School in Dallas on a partial scholarship, graduating in 1985. In 1994, Trini Garza, a trustee of the Dallas school board, ran for justice of the peace in Oak Cliff. He would have been Dallas County's first Latino justice of the peace, but Orozco was unhappy with Garza as a candidate: she wanted not only a Hispanic but "someone that was an attorney and that had better experience and better knowledge than the person that was kind of agreed upon by the powers to be that he was going to take this position." Even though people told her she did not have a chance at winning against the well-known Garza, Orozco entered the race, thinking, "Well, I am going to give it my best shot." She walked the district, visiting nine hundred households in four weeks and ultimately blistering her vocal cords. Such effort, she believes, "made the difference," and Orozco won. Two years later, voters reelected her.[31]

By 2013, according to both Lena Levario and Diana Gallego, Dallas had become a Latino city. In 1980, one in every eight Dallas residents was Hispanic; two decades later, that number was one in three. By 2004, Hispanics had become the largest single ethnic group in Dallas, comprising nearly 42 percent of the entire Dallas population. Nevertheless, the city's Latinos still encounter prejudice. As Levario stated frankly, "It's hard to forget about your race when people keep reminding you about it." According to Orozco, "Sometimes you don't know if [you're having problems] because you are a Hispanic or because you are a woman." Latinas, however, are taking active roles in Dallas communities and pushing for change.[32]

Diana Flores believes that women have already become the leaders of Dallas's Latino community: "I mean anything you go to, Jesus, *es pura mujer* [it's all women]." Levario agreed, citing the organizers of the April 2006 immigration megamarch, which drew nearly half a million participants in Dallas. In a larger sense, she observed, "For whatever reasons, women, minorities got started behind the starting line, ten steps behind the starting line, and it's taken quite a while for us to catch up. . . . I think women are ready to take over this country soon, very soon."[33]

Many of the Latinas discussed here are well-known figures in Dallas history. But the generations of women who preceded them—their mothers, grandmothers, aunts, and others—are less well known despite their profound effect on their successors. The intergenerational exchange of cultural traditions did not perpetuate the belief that the only role for Latinas was that of wife and mother. Instead, this exchange empowered Latinas to take pride in their culture and traditions. They found models of Latina womanhood that celebrated Latino culture while pushing beyond its gender limitations. By learning from the women who came before them, taking advantage of the available opportunities, and finding strength rather than limitation in their cultural traditions, Latinas in Dallas have become new women.

NOTES

1. Anita Nanez Martínez, interview by author, August 5, 2011. Anita Nanez and her daughter, Anita Nanez Martínez, share the same first name and surname. The younger woman married Alfred Martínez and added his surname after hers, thus distinguishing her name from her mother's name.

2. U.S. Census Bureau, "Dallas County, Texas," *State and County QuickFacts*, http://quickfacts. census.gov/qfd/states/48/48113.html (accessed December 6, 2012); Bianca Mercado, "With Their Hearts in Their Hands: Forging a Mexican Community in Dallas, 1900–1925" (master's thesis, University of North Texas, 2008), 15–16; Michael Phillips, *White Metropolis: Race, Ethnicity, and Religion in Dallas, 1841–2001* (Austin: University of Texas Press, 2001), 2, 5, 20–22; William L. Mc-Donald, *Dallas Rediscovered: A Photographic Chronicle of Urban Expansion, 1870–1925* (Dallas: Dallas Historical Society, 1978), 3–4, 10; Darwin Payne, *Big D: Triumphs and Troubles of an American Supercity in the Twentieth Century* (Dallas: Three Forks, 2000), 5–6; Robert Ryer Schermerhorn, "An Occupational History of Mexican Americans in Dallas, 1930–1950" (master's thesis, Southern Methodist University, 1973), 9, 11, 13.

3. In 1900, 60 persons of Mexican descent resided in Dallas, whose total population numbered 42,638. By 1910, the number of Mexicans had risen to 330 and the total population reached 92,104. Ten years later, 4,130 Mexicans lived in Dallas, and the population had swelled to 158,976. See U.S. Bureau of the Census, *Twelfth Census of the United States, 1900: Population* (Washington, D.C.: U.S. Government Printing Office, 1900); U.S. Bureau of the Census, *Thirteenth Census of the United States, 1910: Population* (Washington, D.C.: U.S. Government Printing Office, 1910); U.S. Bureau of the Census, *Fourteenth Census of the United States, 1920: Population* (Washington, D.C.: U.S. Government Printing Office, 1920). The finding of sixty persons of Mexican descent in Dallas comes from a careful examination of the 1900 Census. However, errors in the Census make the precise calculation of the number of Mexicans in Dallas nearly impossible.

4. Vicki Ruíz, *From out of the Shadows: Mexican Women in Twentieth-Century America* (New York: Oxford University Press, 1998).

5. U.S. Bureau of the Census, *Twelfth Census*; Mario T. García, "The Chicana in American History: The Mexican Women of El Paso, 1880–1920—A Case Study," *Pacific Historical Review* 49 (May 1980): 324–25; Alice Kessler-Harris, *Out to Work: A History of Wage-Earning Women in the United States* (New York: Oxford University Press, 1982), vii–xi, viii (quotation), 142–79; U.S. Bureau of the Census, *Thirteenth Census.*

6. U.S. Bureau of the Census, *Fourteenth Census*; Payne, *Big D*, 107; Phillips, *White Metropolis*, 89.

7. Phillips, *White Metropolis*, 63.

8. Ethelyn Clara Davis, "Little Mexico: A Study of Horizontal and Vertical Mobility" (master's thesis, Southern Methodist University, 1936), 1–2; Rick Leal, *Little Mexico: A Barrio* (Documentary, VHS, North Texas Public Broadcasting, 1997); Gwendolyn Rice, "Little Mexico and the Barrios of Dallas," *Legacies: A History Journal for Dallas and North Central Texas* 4 (Fall 1992): 21.

9. Cumberland Hill School File, folder 22, box 1, City of Dallas Landmark Records, Texas/Dallas History and Archives Division, Dallas Public Library, Dallas; "Speaking the League of Nations!," *Dallas Morning News* (hereafter cited as *DMN*), June 7, 1925; Phillips, *White Metropolis*, 69; David Montejano, *Anglos and Mexicans in the Making of Texas, 1836–1986* (Austin: University of Texas

Press, 1987), 165–70, 190–95; Davis, "Little Mexico," 41–44, 46; Carlos Blanton, *The Strange Career of Bilingual Education in Texas, 1836–1981* (College Station: Texas A&M University Press, 2004).

10. Julia Kirk Blackwelder, *Women of the Depression: Caste and Culture in San Antonio, 1929–1939* (College Station: Texas A&M University Press, 1984); Ruth Milkman, *Gender at Work: The Dynamics of Job Segregation by Sex during World War II* (Urbana: University of Illinois Press, 1987); Ruth Milkman, "Women's Work and the Economic Crisis: Some Lessons from the Great Depression," in *A Heritage of Her Own: Toward a New Social History of American Women*, ed. Nancy F. Cott and Elizabeth H. Pleck (New York: Simon and Schuster, 1979), 507–41; Diana Orozco, interview by José Angel Gutiérrez, February 13, 1998, interview 88, transcript, Center for Mexican American Studies.

11. "Woman's Determination Shaped Tortilla Factory," *DMN*, July 7, 1991; "Family-Run Luna's Tortilla Factory Turns 75," *DMN*, February 28, 1999; Francisco Xavier Luna obituary, *DMN*, June 13, 2006; "Iconic Tortilla Factory Finds New Home," *DMN*, August 17, 2007; *DMN*, April 12, 2001.

12. Gerald D. Saxon, "Cuellar, Adelaida," *Handbook of Texas Online*, http://www.tshaonline.org /handbook/online/articles/fcu50 (accessed November 9, 2010).

13. Ibid.

14. Debbie Mauldin Cottrell, "Martínez, Faustina Porras," *Handbook of Texas Online*, http://www .tshaonline.org/handbook/online/articles/fmaja (accessed November 6, 2010).

15. Gloria González, interview by author, August 5, 2011.

16. Anita Nanez Martínez, interview by José Angel Gutiérrez, June 10, 1999, interview 129, transcript, Center for Mexican American Studies, University of Texas at Arlington, Arlington. Nanez Martínez also attended Cumberland Hill School and St. Ann's School.

17. Ibid.

18. Ibid.

19. Ibid.; Collection Description, MA80-1, Anita Martínez Collection, Texas/Dallas History and Archives Division, http://www.lib.utexas.edu/taro/dalpub/08001/dpub-08001.html (accessed February 10, 2014).

20. Francisco A. Rosales, *Chicano!: The History of the Mexican American Civil Rights Movement* (Houston: Arte Público, 1996); Brian Behnken, *Fighting Their Own Battles: Mexican Americans, African Americans, and the Struggle for Civil Rights in Texas* (Chapel Hill: University of North Carolina Press, 2011). Simultaneously, immigration to the United States rose following the enactment of the Immigration and Nationality Act of 1965, which abolished the national origins quota system in favor of a preference system that focused on the skills of immigrants.

21. Joanne Meyerowitz, *Not June Cleaver: Women and Gender in Postwar America, 1945–1960* (Philadelphia: Temple University Press, 1994); Cynthia Orozco, "Mujeres por la Raza," *Handbook of Texas Online*, http://www.tsha.org/handbook/online/articles/vimgh (accessed November 29, 2011).

22. María Teresa Díaz, interview by author, August 5, 2011.

23. Ibid.

24. "Today's Latinas Redefining Gender Roles," *Los Angeles Daily News*, May 2, 1996; Diana Flores, interview by José Angel Gutiérrez, November 3, 2001, interview 148, transcript, Center for Mexican American Studies.

25. Diana Gallego, telephone interview by author, November 14, 2010.

26. Ibid.

27. Lena Levario, telephone interview by author, November 14, 2010.

28. Ibid

29. Ibid. The Dallas LULAC council received a grant in 2010 to establish a mentorship program at R. L. Turner High School in Farmers Branch to help prevent students from dropping out of school.

A suburb of Dallas, Farmers Branch made news in 2006 when its city council approved measures that assessed fines for landlords who rented to illegal immigrants, made English the official language of the city, and allowed local authorities to check the immigration status of suspects in police custody. In 2010, the mayor of Farmers Branch appeared on morning talk shows in Dallas saying that it was wrong for the schools to let LULAC in and alleged that LULAC was trying to indoctrinate the students to become activists. Indeed, his Twitter page features updates he posted from October 20–25, 2010, that read, "It's a sad day when Carrollton–Farmers Branch ISD enters into a partnership with LULAC to mentor our children" and "R. L. Turner High School in Carrollton–Farmers Branch ISD won't allow Young Life to meet on campus but welcomes LULAC to mentor children." Another update contends, "The number of people in Farmers Branch angry about CFBISD's involvement with LULAC continues to grow by the minute." His comments, Levario contends, are thinly veiled racism. Timothy O'Hare, October 2010, http://twitter.com/timothyohare (accessed November 1, 2010); "Texas City OKs Anti-Immigration Measures," *USA Today*, November 14, 2006.

   30. Orozco, interview.

   31. Ibid.

   32. Levario, interview; Gallego, interview; Orozco, interview; Flores, interview; "A New Show of Power," *DMN*, April 30, 2006; "High Hopes, Growth Pains Greet Bishop," *DMN*, April 30, 2007.

   33. Flores, interview; Levario, interview.

Oveta Culp Hobby

*Ability, Perseverance, and Cultural Capital
in a Twentieth-Century Success Story*

KELLI CARDENAS WALSH

In 1931, twenty-six-year-old Oveta Culp married fifty-three-year-old William P. Hobby, the former governor of Texas, in the parlor of her parents' home in Temple, Texas. Friends and members of the press responded skeptically to the unconventional match, but it proved to be a partnership in which the bride would launch a precedent-setting record of public service in the twentieth century. In later years, Oveta Culp Hobby claimed that all she accomplished was the result of her marriage to the Governor, as she called him.[1] Indeed, Will Hobby proved to be a powerful silent partner for his more public, attractive, ambitious wife. But Oveta Hobby's political rise was also aided by an extended network of men, women, and cultural capital. Endowed with ambition, a strong work ethic, and a desire to participate in public service, Hobby became a twentieth-century doyenne in the worlds of politics and media. Using her access to power, she became more powerful and prominent than the men in her political family, but she always returned to her family and chosen city, Houston. Her ascent to political power represented the opportunities available to American women in the twentieth century.

Born January 19, 1905, in Killeen, Texas, Oveta was the second daughter of Isaac "Ike" Culp and Emma Hoover Culp. Later that year, the *Killeen Herald* reported on Isaac Culp's humble origins, noting that he was a self-made man who had little formal education but had nevertheless established a career as a lawyer and jurist.[2] Five more children later joined the family, and while the Culps provided all of them with a sense of civic responsibility and charity, Oveta took those lessons to heart and exceeded the expectations society placed on women.

From an early age, Oveta Culp displayed a serious intellect and interest in learning. Central to developing a desire to succeed was her love of reading. By the time she was ten, she had read the *Congressional Record*; by thirteen, she had read the Bible through at least twice. At fourteen she discovered what would be a lifelong interest in the law and politics.[3] Her friend, Marguerite Johnston Barnes, recalled that Oveta "read voraciously and in wide variety . . . prompted by her lifelong, insatiable appetite for information and ideas."[4] By the time she reached young adulthood, she possessed a library of 750 volumes, impressive for someone of any age. Often described as her father's favorite child, Hobby accompanied him to Austin two of the three times he was elected to the state legislature, and in 1919, she sat with him during legislative sessions. Hobby later recalled that she had a "great interest in the legislative process."[5]

When the Culps were in Austin, a tutor provided lessons for young Oveta, a privilege afforded by her father's position in the legislature and business success at home. In 1919, the family relocated to Temple, Texas, and Oveta enrolled at Temple High School. After graduation, she spent a year at Baylor Female College in Belton, but she soon resumed her lessons in realpolitik. She returned to Austin, attended classes at the University of Texas, and audited law classes, but she never received a postsecondary degree.[6]

When Ike Culp won election to the state House of Representatives in 1923, his eighteen-year-old daughter transitioned from informal learning based on family and community values to formal educational experiences in politics. She initially served as a committee clerk but was soon asked by Speaker of the House James Satterwhite to serve as parliamentarian. She remained in that position for eleven sessions under three different speakers, resigning only when she married in 1931; she then returned briefly at the request of Speaker Emmett Morse in 1939. As parliamentarian, Oveta was responsible for ensuring that proper procedures were followed during the legislative sessions, interpreting bylaws, facilitating meetings, and planning agendas, among other duties. This position enabled her to learn the rules of public policy, and she followed them for the rest of her life.

For women of Culp's generation and social standing, formal education, a career before marriage, and independent travel were increasingly acceptable and available.[7] She became more than a clubwoman, the previous expectation for daughters and wives of politically active men. In the 1920s, Culp was among the 12 percent of women who worked outside the home. As an independent, professional woman, she had opportunities to advance a career based on desire rather than necessity.[8] Influenced by her father, young Oveta Culp became increasingly active in Democratic Party politics. Recognizing his daughter's serious nature and ambition, Ike Culp told her that she was a great comfort to him,

COLONEL OVETA CULP HOBBY

Director of the Women's Army Corps, 1940s.

Courtesy of the Fondren Library at Rice University.

and, he wrote, "I look forward to greater things in the future."[9] Oveta did not disappoint him.

When the legislature was out of session in 1925, Oveta Culp moved to Houston at the urging of her friend, Florence Sterling. Houston was a politically active town, and women were taking a greater role in state and local political events. Moving to the Bayou City was a life-changing decision for Culp, both personally and professionally. There she worked in the circulation department of the *Houston Post*, which was then owned by Ross Sterling, Florence's brother, and honed her political skills under the tutelage of Florence Sterling and Estelle Sharp.[10] Sterling was a generation older than Culp and supported her young friend's independence and political activism. Sterling published a progressive magazine, *A Woman's Viewpoint*, from 1923 to 1927, advocating women's civic and political participation. In 1924, she became president of the Houston-area League of Women Voters. In a nod to Sterling's influence, Hobby became president of the Texas League of Women Voters in 1931.[11]

Oveta Culp also developed a friendship with Estelle Sharp, the widow of Walter B. Sharp, a wealthy oilman and cofounder of Sharp-Hughes Tool Company. After meeting Sharp at a gathering of the Daughters of Jackson, an organization that sought to persuade women to register to vote, Culp became one of several attendees at discussion sessions led by Sharp to teach young women about current events. Reflecting on her mentor, Oveta Culp Hobby later recalled, "Mrs. Sharp opened the world to many of us. . . . She organized a study group and saw to it that we learned about important national and international issues."[12] At the beginning of her professional life, Culp was developing important relationships with women who possessed political clout, influence, and wealth. While for most of her adult life, Culp was the lone woman in a room full of powerful men, she applied the lessons of her female mentors to future success.

The year 1928 offered Culp new access to power, as she worked on several political campaigns, including Tom Connally's U.S. Senate campaign, in the Houston office of Al Smith when he ran against Herbert Hoover for U.S. president, and the Texas gubernatorial campaign of Jim Young. Both Smith and Young lost, but Culp was building her credentials as a political insider and attracting notice from her fellow Texans. When the Democratic National Committee recommended that half of the at-large delegates to the party's national convention should be women, Oveta Culp was an obvious choice. A newspaper article on her selection to represent Harris County gushed that at "only 22 years of age" and having occupied "several positions of distinction that scores of veteran politicians would cherish," she had already "had the most unusual career due to a gift of leadership and very keen ability."[13]

After the convention, a writer for the *Houston Gargoyle*, a local magazine, described Culp's attire—a yellow ensemble that caught lawmakers' attention as well as twenty-seven strings of beads. According to Ruth West of the *Gargoyle*, "She combined ambition, and an immense joy in living, but needed a social secretary."[14] Culp's good looks and professional demeanor made her a press favorite. Unaccustomed to describing a professional woman in terms of public leadership outside the society pages, the press consistently focused on Culp's appearance. The comfort of her upbringing was evident in the way she presented an attractive, modern image of female competence.

In 1930, Oveta Culp made her only bid for elective office, seeking a seat in the state legislature as a representative from Harris County. Her opponent was a member of the Ku Klux Klan who was otherwise unopposed, and the novice candidate felt that a man with his views should at least have opposition. She paid the dollar filing fee and began giving speeches from the back of a truck and printing advertising cards. When a newspaper reporter asked why she was running, she replied, "I think I've always wanted to go to the legislature. Even when I was too young to understand what it meant, when my father used to tell me about it, I thought it would be a wonderful thing to do. And now that I've seen something of the work at first hand, and know what an opportunity it holds for serving Texas, I want more than ever to do it."[15] She lost the election, receiving 4,594 of the 11,620 votes cast, but the defeat did not sour her on politics. In fact, she soon learned that the press would afford her much greater influence on a wide range of issues—women in the military, election-year politics, desegregation, and more. As historian Patrick Cox notes, "The commerce of Texas thrived on political influence and much of this guidance came from influential newspaper publishers."[16] As Hobby became a member of the press, she embraced the increased opportunities available to women of her generation and class.

Culp was part of a generation of women who evolved from suffragists to so-called modern women. She reached adulthood during the Roaring Twenties, when women began expressing themselves with shorter hair and skirts, enrolling in college, and seeking independent personal lives prior to marriage. According to historian Anne Firor Scott, it was not uncommon for middle-class women—or those with some advantages, which is how Hobby identified herself—to continue to work after marriage.[17] Florence Sterling also backed the idea of women's independence outside of marriage, and Culp embraced all of the newfound privileges of public womanhood.

Like others of her generation, Hobby did not identify herself as a feminist; rather, she believed that if she supplied the ability, opportunity would find her. Her son, William Hobby Jr., confirmed that "she never thought of herself as a feminist or pioneer. As she put it, she just did the next thing that came along."[18] In a 1938 speech to female journalists, Hobby said that women had to have a "plus value," but "if you supply the ability and perseverance, success will demand you."[19] While Hobby recognized that her social advantages enhanced her "plus value," her hard work and commitment were also vital to her rise to prominence in state and national politics. She made a personal investment in her education, as evidenced by the number of books she possessed, the law courses she took, and the way she surrounded herself with a network of political insiders who granted her access to power. Like other successful leaders, male and female, she was driven to succeed and believed she had something to contribute.

She also believed that women with "some advantage" had a responsibility to provide leadership and help those who were less fortunate. Years earlier, Emma Culp had instilled a sense of civic responsibility in her daughters, who routinely collected goods and food for Killeen's less fortunate. In Houston, Oveta continued this work by forming a Community Chest to help the needy. She also wrote letters in support of family and friends who she thought might be qualified for particular positions.[20]

Establishing her life in Houston, Oveta Culp audited classes at the South Texas School of Law and worked at the *Houston Post*, which since 1924 had been managed by former governor Will Hobby, a friend of the Culp family. Oveta had known his name since she was a young girl, when her mother participated in Hobby Clubs (political groups dedicated to electing Hobby to the state's highest office). Leaving home to campaign for Hobby in 1918, Emma Culp called out to her teenage daughters, Juanita and Oveta, "Girls, you'll have to look after the peaches. I'm going to campaign for Will Hobby."[21]

In the ensuing decade, Ike Culp had established a friendship with the governor while serving in the legislature, and Oveta became reacquainted with the recently widowed Hobby while working at the *Houston Post*. Despite her claims that she did not realize Hobby was courting her, their relationship developed quickly, and they married in 1931 in a small, private ceremony with only family present. After a reception at the Culp home, the couple honeymooned in Mexico City and returned to their work at the *Houston Post*, where they had adjoining offices and worked together to bring the newspaper back from the brink of bankruptcy.[22]

The placement of their offices offers insight into the Hobby marriage. Though the Hobbys were an odd marital pairing by conventional standards, they bonded over their shared love of politics and Texas. As conservative Texas Democrats, they were nonetheless progressive in their willingness to commit to a modern marriage. Will Hobby, twenty-seven years Oveta's senior, relished watching his wife grow into her role as a national leader. He had confidence in her ability to succeed as a public servant. When asked later about Oveta, the former governor recalled that even in her mid-twenties, "she had a grasp of [politics] that amazed me, and there's nothing I would rather do than talk politics. Beautiful girl, too."[23] For her part, Oveta reflected, "The marriage worked. . . . We liked each other a great deal. I always felt so at ease with him."[24] The age difference worked to Oveta's advantage. Because her husband was older and professionally established, his young, ambitious wife did not threaten his ego, and she was free to work long hours and travel as needed to advance their business and her personal profile.

The Hobbys had two children, William Pettus Hobby Jr., born in 1932, and Jessica, born five years later. Both children had successful careers, beneficiaries of their parents' partnership.[25] When the Governor and Oveta married, he had been out of political office for a decade and the newspaper's financial future was uncertain. But he had political friendships that benefited the Hobbys' business interests. By reorganizing the newspaper and their investments in other media outlets, the Hobbys soon enjoyed the financial comfort to retain household help and child care, freeing Oveta to pursue her career.[26] *Texas Monthly* later profiled the family's fortunes, describing the "Hobby Team" as benefiting from Will's "political clout and money" and Oveta's "social savvy."[27]

As the country plunged into economic depression in the early 1930s, the Hobbys worked to develop the *Post* into a competitive newspaper. Despite her increased professional responsibilities and their young children, Oveta Hobby developed an abiding interest in parliamentary law, a subject she believed was instrumental to her understanding of the law. She wrote a daily column in the *Post*, "How and When in Parliamentary Law," in which she answered questions submitted by readers. In a 1939 speech to the Junior League of Texas, Hobby told her audience that parliamentary law "is recognized as the correct, the polite and the only polite way of doing things in organized groups."[28] Her speeches and the column convinced Hobby that a textbook was the next outlet for promoting her interest in parliamentary law. Although she was sure about writing it, publishers were not certain of a market for such a book. Nonetheless, the southwestern branch manager for Macmillan Publishing, Jack Phillips, assured his boss in New York that "Mrs. Hobby is exceptionally well qualified to write the book." Again, her reputation as a political insider provided her access and advanced her agenda. *Mr. Chairman* was published in 1937, and Texas schools adopted it for teaching parliamentary procedure. In addition, the McClure Newspaper Syndicate picked up her column during the 1940s.[29]

Further influencing what the public read, Hobby "reorganized the [*Post*'s] advertising and circulation departments, hired good editors and writers, and encouraged creative independence in the paper's production."[30] The *Houston Post* was beginning to turn a profit, and Hobby's work was being noticed. As her responsibilities at the newspaper increased, Hobby traveled to Washington, D.C., to attend the American Society of Newspaper Editors convention in 1939. While there, she was selected to participate in an off-the-record luncheon with Major General Harry H. Arnold, chief of the Army Air Corps. Later in the day, she attended another off-the-record meeting, this time with President Franklin D. Roosevelt.[31] The Hobbys had supported FDR in the 1932 and 1936 elections but like many other conservative Democrats had become soured, in part by the president's attempt to increase the number of U.S. Supreme Court justices. Nevertheless, Will and Oveta Hobby maintained a cordial and professional relationship with the president as a consequence of their mutual Texas friend and head of the Reconstruction Finance Corporation, Jesse H. Jones.[32]

In June 1941, Oveta Hobby was again in Washington, this time for talks with the Federal Communications Commission on the Hobbys' recent acquisition of another radio station. While there, Oveta received a call from Brigadier General David Surles of the War Department's Bureau of Public Relations. The department was looking into creating a Women's Interest Section in response to inquiries from women around the country after the draft had been instituted in 1940. Initially reluctant to work in Washington and be separated from her family and the *Post*, she agreed to serve in an advisory capacity. Will Hobby reminded her that everyone had to contribute to the war effort, and a month later, she accepted an appointment as expert consultant to the secretary of war with a salary of a dollar a year. Her skills honed as a parliamentarian, political insider, and newspaper executive were soon on display to the nation. The appointment was an indication of her growing economic, political, and social stature.[33]

Oveta Hobby soon rose from her position as a press agent for the War Department to become the U.S. Army's highest-ranking female officer. Her journey to this precedent-setting position was aided by the army's chief of staff, General George C. Marshall. A few weeks after the bombing of Pearl Harbor, Marshall asked Hobby to testify before the U.S. House of Representatives Committee on Military Affairs in support of the establishment of the Women's Army Auxiliary Corps (WAAC). Hobby prepared remarks to give to Congress, but Marshall threw them away, advising her, "When you go to testify before a congressional committee, you say what you have to say." He also reminded her that he had staff available to answer specific questions regarding military matters. Marshall had full confidence in Hobby's ability to organize and lead the newly formed WAAC: she could cultivate journalists so that they printed positive reports, and she would present a meticulous image of the first women's auxiliaries to the army.[34]

Hobby's reputation preceded her testimony, as Texas representative Robert E. Thompson made a brief statement on her behalf, citing her efficient work as parliamentarian for the Texas statehouse and stating that "most anything she would say would be quite persuasive with me."[35] Congresswoman Edith Nourse Rogers, a Massachusetts Republican, submitted the WAAC bill and named Hobby as the strongest candidate to lead the new corps. Marshall also recommended her. In a confidential memorandum to secretary of war Henry L. Stimson, the general indicated that Hobby, coming from the Women's Interest Section and fresh from observing Allied women in military service, was the only woman who could take over the job without a serious loss of time. With Marshall's support, Hobby was sworn in as the first director of the WAAC on May 16, 1942, and Marshall became an important ally as she set out to recruit, train, and assign women for service in military auxiliaries.[36]

Hobby's network of influential allies also included Rogers; Congresswoman Margaret Chase Smith, a Maine Republican; African American educator Mary McLeod Bethune; and First Lady Eleanor Roosevelt, all of whom wanted women in military service during the war. Hobby presented their goals to a national audience, and as the WAAC's director, she came to embody the substantial role women could play in the political arena.[37] Having reaped the gains of the earlier suffrage movement, these women sought to add wartime military service to women's experiences. Hobby demonstrated her ability to work effectively in the highest echelons of political power, male or female. When she encountered resistance from the military infrastructure, she turned to General Marshall for support. She needed little help in managing the WAAC's one hundred thousand women, however, relying instead primarily on following procedure and established military protocol, skills she had acquired in her years as parliamentarian. She also understood the power of impression management. Intellectually smart and attractive in dress and demeanor, Hobby could hold herself up as an example of the heights women could achieve.[38]

Hobby's appointment was not without its critics. Mainstream newspapers faulted not only her decision to leave her young children at home but also her clothing and her choice of dinner companions. The African American press believed that a white southerner would not give fair treatment and equal opportunity to African American WAACS—the same problems encountered by African American men in the military. Hobby responded in interviews with the *Baltimore Afro-American* and the *Pittsburgh Courier* that she believed that "total war is a total responsibility regardless of sex, race, color or creed."[39] Bethune was a particularly strong ally for Hobby in managing race relations in the first months after the WAAC's formation. Both women understood that all WAACS, black and white, would be under scrutiny as the army's newest recruits, and Bethune knew all too well the additional challenges African American women would face. By mid-1942, the *Pittsburgh Courier* gave Hobby its endorsement: "Mrs. Hobby intends to be liberal and give race women an opportunity to serve in the United States along with white women."[40] Even more telling, the paper's editors acknowledged that segregation in the WAAC reflected a larger governmental policy that could be changed only by Congress.[41]

The program had such success in its first year that Congresswoman Rogers introduced a bill to convert the WAAC to the Women's Army Corps (WAC), removing the unit's auxiliary status and making it a full part of the army. The change was more than symbolic: it would make women eligible for benefits such as life insurance. In addition, women between ages twenty and fifty were now permitted to join. The new WACs were subject to military discipline and committed to serving for the duration of the war plus six months. Hobby received the rank of colonel, though she only received the pay of a major, reflecting salary inequities that extended down through the ranks. Her unwillingness publicly to challenge such discrepancies might have reflected her acceptance of the wartime emergency conditions, or it might have indicated her instinctive conservatism.[42]

The WAAC's early supporters included General Dwight D. Eisenhower. During the North Africa campaign, he became among the first military leaders to have WAACs assigned to his headquarters overseas, and to him, the experience "proved that women can render definite contributions to the winning of the war, and that their capabilities in this regard extend to an actual theater of operations."[43] After first being deployed to Algiers, WACs soon served in Morocco, England, and the Pacific theater. Hobby often traveled to observe their work in the field, spending her thirty-ninth birthday in Algiers while inspecting the WACs stationed there.[44]

In 1944, after four years of nonstop work, Hobby succumbed to the physical strains of the job and was admitted to Walter Reed General Hospital in Washington, D.C., for treatment of anemia, exhaustion, and a throat ailment. Although Marshall chided her for thinking "a minimum of absence is sufficient for the purpose of a complete rehabilitation," she ignored doctors' orders to rest for six weeks and instead recuperated only briefly at her home in Texas.[45] Hobby considered resigning, but her assistant, Lieutenant Colonel Jessie Rice, convinced her that doing so would send a message to other WACs that their job, too, was complete.[46] The WAC's deputy director, Betty Bandel, wrote in a July 15, 1945, letter that Hobby had "fought through the battle wondering whether she should leave, for her own health, six months ago" but had decided to stay on until the end.[47]

In the summer of 1945, both Will and Oveta Hobby were hospitalized, and Colonel Hobby finally drafted her resignation letter. Though she had always viewed her job with the WAC as temporary, she had compiled an impressive record. She had emphasized professionalism and attention to detail, and leading by example, she promoted the idea that femininity and competence were synonymous. She thus exemplified what historian Elizabeth Fox-Genovese has described as a southern lady's training, which emphasized "grace under pressure."[48]

Hobby received congratulations and thanks for her service from the press, from Congress, and at home in Houston. The army recognized her work with the Distinguished Service Medal, and Houston greeted her return with a hero's welcome. General Marshall sent a message to be read at a dinner in her honor at the Rice Hotel: "I take this means of expressing my appreciation and that of the entire Army for the outstanding service rendered by Colonel Hobby. Her mastery of an exceedingly difficult and complex undertaking commands my admiration."[49]

Hobby then resumed her business and social life and the care of her family. Her connections as a professional woman helped her to make the transition back to civilian life without difficulty, but the women she commanded in the WAC had less certain futures. Not until June 1948 did President Harry S. Truman sign into law a measure granting women permanent status in the regular and reserve forces. Nevertheless, their wartime experiences left them better prepared for civilian careers.[50]

Hobby returned to work at the *Houston Post*, modernizing the paper's operations. She was regularly invited to be a guest speaker around the country, often addressing themes such as the genesis of the Cold War and the growing communist threat. At an Advertising Federation of America meeting, she spoke on foreign policy and America's role as a leader in the world, and she admonished her audience, "The time has come for us to take command of our own souls and our own destinies. We have a challenge to high adventure. It is better to live fearlessly for peace than fearfully for war."[51]

In 1952, Eisenhower declared his candidacy for the Republican presidential nomination. Making public his intentions late in the political season, Eisenhower and his campaign staff developed a southern strategy that focused on states' rights issues. Among his supporters were Oveta and Will Hobby, who became leaders in the Democrats for Eisenhower movement. The Hobbys had previously ventured into cross-party politics with their support for Wendell Willkie in the 1940 presidential election and Thomas Dewey in 1944 and 1948. The *Houston Post* declared on its April 13, 1952, front page, "We Like Ike," and consistently supported the former general over the next six months. The paper also printed and distributed four hundred thousand political primers with instructions on how to vote in primaries and the general election. The tutorial was especially helpful to Texas Democrats who wanted to vote in the Republican primary. Oveta Hobby attended Texas's Republican nominating convention in Mineral Wells but did not travel to Chicago to attend the national convention where Eisenhower received the Republican nomination.[52]

After his election, Eisenhower asked Oveta Hobby to serve as the Federal Security Administration executive, with the expectation that the position would become elevated to the cabinet level with the creation of the Department of Health, Education, and Welfare (HEW). Ten years after her WAAC success, she was again asked to build an organization from the ground up. Again she would be a pioneer—just the second woman to serve in a presidential cabinet. And again, the nation was in need, establishing its Cold War policies and defining the role of the federal government in the wake of the New Deal. The appointment would prove a turning point in her career.

Hobby's selection was partial political payback for her role in organizing and leading Democrats for Eisenhower. In addition, according to historian Robert T. Pando, Hobby possessed "a political frame of mind much like" Eisenhower's—more ideologically middle-of-the-road than extremist. As she did with the WAC, Hobby learned standard operating procedures and adjusted them to get work done.[53]

During Hobby's congressional confirmation hearing, Texas representative Lyndon Baines Johnson enthusiastically announced that Hobby was "the type of woman you'd like to have for a daughter or a sister, a wife or a mother, or the trustee of your estate."[54] She won confirmation and set to work, fusing five smaller agencies into the newly created cabinet department, an extension of the role of government that may have provoked ambivalence in Hobby. Nevertheless, she used her considerable skills to do the job as well as possible.[55]

A May 1953 article offered a friendly reintroduction of Hobby to the American public. The author observed that the country's "new godmother from Texas has got off to a very promising start."[56] The most notable achievement of her thirty-one-month tenure was the testing and implementation of the Salk polio vaccine, but it was not without controversy. According to historian David Oshinsky, Hobby was a woman of many talents, with "health administration not being one of them."[57] According to her son, Bill Hobby Jr., "the hardest time of her life came at HEW during the [1954] polio epidemic," when 38,751 cases were reported nationwide."[58]

Hobby and the president were fiscal conservatives who advocated a limited role for government. Distribution of the Salk vaccine coincided with Cold War fears about socialized medicine, and despite the humanitarian need, Hobby favored private rather than federal government distribution of the vaccine. This viewpoint cast Hobby as insensitive and out of touch, a perception that was reinforced when she told a Senate committee investigating vaccine shortages, "I think no one could have foreseen the public demand."[59] Both Hobby and the president failed to understand that a health matter of such magnitude required rethinking their position on the role of the federal government.

Hobby's tenure at HEW also coincided with the U.S. Supreme Court's May 1954 *Brown v. Board of Education* ruling, which eliminated segregation in public schooling. The Court did not rule on the implementation of integration for another year, meaning that Hobby had resigned from the cabinet before significant public school desegregation got under way. Nevertheless, she came in for criticism for the federal government's slow response. As early as 1953, Democratic congressman Adam Clayton Powell Jr., an African American who represented New York City's Harlem, pushed Hobby and the Department of Defense to move on the desegregation of schools on military bases. Hobby was responsive but less proactive than Powell had hoped. She drafted a letter to the congressman in which she wrote that schools operated by the Department of Defense, including one at Fort Benning, Georgia, would be completely integrated at the start of the 1955–56 school year. She noted, however, that matters were more complicated at schools operated by state authorities with state funds on federally owned property.[60]

In June 1954, in the wake of the *Brown* decision, Hobby spoke publicly of the economic and moral costs of discrimination. In her view, U.S. economic growth required all people to be full partners in the economy. Moreover, "no one can measure in dollars the cost to human beings who suffer the stigma of ostracism, the fear of persecution, or the anguish of seeing little children hurt and rejected."[61] In keeping with her middle-of-the-road perspective, she would not spearhead change but would make sure that the law was followed. A profile of "America's Glamorous Godmother" summarized her views: Hobby was a moderate "who believes in free enterprise, but not in freedom to exploit; who sees government as a tool of the people, but not as their master; who realizes that in a country as large and as varied as ours many local problems can be handled most intelligently by local governments, but that others need national support and control."[62] In the words of historian Debra Sutphen, Hobby "left a mixed legacy of accomplishments, controversy and failure," always reflecting a moderate approach to governance.[63]

Hobby submitted her resignation in July 1955, citing the need to return to Houston to take care of her husband, who was in his late seventies and ill. The battle over the testing and distribution of the Salk vaccine had taken its toll; challenges to desegregation and hospital and school funding were on the docket, but they would have to be managed by her successor. At this point in her career, she likely saw no personal or professional need to remain in Washington.[64]

When secretary of the treasury George M. Humphrey heard of Hobby's resignation, he exclaimed, "What? The best man in the Cabinet?" *Time*'s account of her departure noted the "good job" she had done "of gathering a straggle of federal agencies interested in health, education and welfare into one new Cabinet department." For his part, Will Hobby responded to a question about whether Oveta was the smartest member of the cabinet by saying, "Course she is ... but if she weren't, she'd have them thinking she was." Assessments of her career still reflected the era's continuing sexism, however: at the time of her resignation, *Time* noted that she was dressed in a brown-and-white silk dress.[65]

Back home in Texas, Hobby became president and editor of the *Houston Post*. Fresh from her high-profile position in Washington, she was much sought after to serve on various corporate boards. In 1956, she became chair of the board of directors of the newly organized Bank of Texas, and she was the first woman to serve on the board of trustees of the Mutual of New York insurance company. Over the next thirty years, she also served on numerous commissions and foundations and received countless honors. In 1957, Will Hobby underwent surgery to repair a hemorrhaging ulcer, and he never fully recovered. Oveta Hobby set up an office in the Shadyside home they shared and continued to care for him and manage the *Post* until his death in 1964.[66]

In the summer of 1960, inspired by the sit-in movement that had begun in Greensboro, North Carolina, the preceding February, students from Texas Southern University, located in Houston, worked with the school's president, Samuel Nabrit, and a multiracial task force to devise a plan to desegregate the city's public facilities. Hobby and other local media executives agreed not to publicize the students' efforts to stage a sit-in, thereby preventing segregationists from fomenting civic unrest. As Hobby later recalled, by eliminating "undue publicity on the school or hotel or lunchroom desegregation," "the goons" would have no "incentive to come to a school or restaurant." The strategy worked: "As a result of the lack of publicity, the integration plan was carried out smoothly and quietly."[67] According to journalist Thomas Cole, peaceful integration came to Houston "because moderate white Southerners felt compelled to break with diehard segregationists to preserve social peace, a positive media image for their city, and a prosperous economy."[68]

Oveta Hobby continued to guide the *Houston Post* through the 1960s and 1970s. In 1963, the Hobbys purchased the *Galveston News*, the *Galveston Tribune*, and the *Texas City Sun*, selling them profitably four years later.[69] Hobby also supported her longtime friends, Lyndon and Lady Bird Johnson, during Johnson's presidency. In 1969, Hobby told an interviewer that Johnson would be remembered as one of the country's finest presidents, based on the legislation enacted during his time in office and the dignified manner in which he handled the transition from tragedy that began his presidency; she also predicted accurately that the war in Vietnam would mar his record on domestic issues.[70]

By the 1970s, Oveta Hobby helped to launch a new generation of Hobbys: Bill Hobby Jr. was elected Texas's lieutenant governor in 1972 and remained in office for eighteen years. Her political clout remained unchallenged, and in 1976, *Texas Monthly* named her as one of the ten most powerful Texans—the only woman to make the list. When serving as chair of the board of the *Houston Post*, Hobby was "truly a remarkable woman who could exert great influence by the force of her intelligence and personality alone."[71] Her grandson, Paul W. Hobby, narrowly lost a 1998 bid to become the state comptroller.[72]

By 1978, the Hobby family communication interests—primarily the *Houston Post* and television station KPRC—were worth $200 million. Five years later, however, seventy-eight-year-old Oveta Hobby stood by as her son told *Post* executives that the newspaper was for sale as a result of "tax considerations and the changing interest of shareholders."[73] Later in 1983, the *Toronto Sun* purchased the *Post* for a reported $130 million, bringing to an end the Hobby family's association with the paper, which had begun in 1895 when Will Hobby joined the staff as a cub reporter. In 1992, the family sold its five television stations to Young Broadcasting for a reported $600 million.[74] On April 17, 1995, Oveta Culp Hobby suffered a stroke; she died four months later.

Oveta Hobby frequently landed on lists of the richest Americans as well as on lists of the best dressed. In addition, she had what others always described as a presence, but in the twilight of her life, she possessed a dignity developed over nine decades of political experience and public service. In many ways, she had surpassed the highest expectations anyone could have had for a twentieth-century woman—anyone, that is, except for Oveta herself. She began life with some advantage of cultural capital, married well, and worked hard; moreover, she was politically astute. As a child, she watched the political process eagerly from her front-row seat, learning from powerful men. As a professional woman, she was at ease with an approach and pace that brought change without threatening others. She left an impressive record of accomplishment and public service, blazing a trail many other women subsequently followed. Had she been a radical and an agitator, her successes likely would have been overlooked, if she had been able to have them at all. Rather, according to her grandson, Paul Hobby, "she reeked of personal discipline . . . a self-control that seldom lapsed," providing a model of public service that both directly and indirectly empowered others.[75]

To innumerable women, Hobby demonstrated the possibility of balancing work and family while maintaining traditional feminine values. In 1926, Florence Sterling wrote, "It is the exceptional woman who can successfully combine homemaking with a career," and she predicted that "the practice of continuing in business after marriage will become increasingly possible to all women."[76] By Sterling's estimation, therefore, Hobby was an exceptional woman.

When social constructions dictated that women marry and raise families, Hobby spoke out on the virtue of choosing a path that was personally appropriate, even if it meant never marrying. Despite Texas's solid support for the Democratic Party for most of her lifetime, she supported candidates based on their positions. During World War II, she set the standard for women who wanted to serve in the army. As Marguerite Johnston Barnes noted in Hobby's eulogy, "Oveta Culp Hobby leaves a wake for us . . . spreading out across the world, the 100,000 women in uniform, their children, and their friends. The hundreds of millions affected by her work as first secretary of Health, Education and Welfare. The generations who read the *Houston Post*."[77] Hobby showed that women could go as far as their hard work and talent could take them. The measure of her life is the degree to which we now accept and encourage the presence of women in politics and public service.

NOTES

1. Marguerite Johnston (for Hobby) to Ishbel Ross, October 2, 1968, folder 8, box 5, Oveta Culp Hobby Papers, Woodson Research Center, Fondren Library, Rice University, Houston.

2. "Hon. I. W. Culp," *Killeen Herald*, May 26, 1905.

3. Addressing the National Association of Women Lawyers, Hobby claimed that her interest in lawyers and the law was both natural and nostalgic. Oveta Culp Hobby, "Portia in Khaki," *Women Lawyers Journal* 28 (August 1942): 5.

4. Marguerite Johnston Barnes, "The Bookworm," n.d., Marguerite Johnston Barnes Papers, Woodson Research Center.

5. Oveta Culp Hobby to April Mashburn, April 2, 1984, folder 8, box 5, Hobby Papers.

6. Oveta Culp audited law classes at South Texas School of Law in Houston but never took the bar exam according to her son, William Hobby Jr. (email to author, June 17, 2006). The 1925–26, 1927–28, and 1928–29 South Texas School of Law yearbooks list Culp as a freshman in attendance. In all likelihood, she did not attend regularly since she stayed in Austin when the legislature was in session, thus accounting for her continual freshman status. According to "Lady in Command,"

Time, May 4, 1953, Oveta Culp let her mother believe she was studying for a degree at the law school when she was instead at work in Austin. Hobby was featured on the cover of *Time Magazine* on January 17, 1944 ("Wacs Colonel Hobby") and on May 4, 1953 ("Lady in Command").

7. Katherine L. French and Allyson M. Poska, *Women and Gender in the Western Past* (New York: Houghton Mifflin, 2007), 2:450.

8. William H. Chafe, *Women and Equality: Changing Patterns in American Culture* (New York: Oxford University Press, 1978), 30.

9. Isaac Culp to Oveta Culp, January 19, 1926, folder 3, box 7, Hobby Papers.

10. Ross Sterling was also the president of Humble Oil Company, and he later served as Texas governor from 1931 to 1933. Her connection to one of the most powerful oilmen in the country gave Florence Sterling a certain cultural capital with which to expand the confines of tradition.

11. Florence Sterling, "Woman's Hour," *A Woman's Viewpoint*, September 9, 1926, 9; Marguerite Johnston, *Houston: The Unknown City, 1836–1946* (College Station: Texas A&M University Press, 1992), 275. In 1924, Roy Watson sold the *Houston Post* to Ross Sterling, who named W. P. Hobby president of the paper.

12. Johnston, *Houston,* 275. Emma Louis Moyer Jackson, "Petticoat Politics: Political Activism among Texas Women" (PhD diss., University of Texas at Austin, 1981), provides a thorough account of women's political activities by such notables as Florence Sterling, Anna Pennybacker, and Jessie Daniel Ames, among others. Robert T. Pando's "Oveta Culp Hobby: A Study of Power and Control" (PhD diss., Florida State University, 2008) also provides an informative narrative of the politically active women who influenced Culp in the 1920s, including Sterling, Sharp, Ima Hogg, and Minnie Fisher Cunningham. Cunningham led the Texas Equal Suffrage Association and watched with Governor Will Hobby as the Texas Legislature ratified the Nineteenth Amendment, making Texas the first southern state to do so.

13. "Miss Oveta Culp Will Be One of Delegates to Demo Convention," unidentified newspaper clipping, n.d., folder 4, box 4, Hobby Papers.

14. Ruth West, "Thru the Lorgnon," *Houston Gargoyle,* August 14, 1928.

15. Ann Hardy, "Oveta Culp to Carry Family Banner in Race," *Houston-Post Dispatch,* June 24, 1930.

16. "Harris County Vote on Congressional and Legislative Races," *Houston Post-Dispatch,* July 27, 1930; Patrick Cox, *The First Texas News Barons* (Austin: University of Texas Press, 2005), 13.

17. Anne Firor Scott, *The Southern Lady: From Pedestal to Politics, 1830–1930* (Chicago: University of Chicago Press, 1970), 215.

18. Bill Hobby Jr. with Saralee Tiede, *How Things Really Work: Lessons from a Life in Politics* (Austin: Dolph Briscoe Center for American History, University of Texas at Austin, 2010), 16.

19. Oveta Culp Hobby, "Women in Journalism," March 25, 1938, folder 3, box 43, Hobby Papers.

20. Oveta Hobby to Governor Will Hobby, June 14, 1935, Thomas Connally to Oveta Hobby, September 18, 1935, both in folder 5, box 12, Hobby Papers.

21. Liz Carpenter, "A Tribute to Oveta Culp Hobby," January 19, 1986, folder 7, box 5, Hobby Papers.

22. "Oveta Culp Wed to Will Hobby Monday at Parents' Home," unidentified newspaper clipping, folder 8, box 4, Hobby Papers; "Marriage Monday of Wide Interest throughout State," *Temple Daily Telegram,* February 24, 1931.

23. Worth Gatewood, "This Woman's Work Is Never Done," *New York Sunday News,* April 5, 1953.

24. Harry Hurt III, "The Last of the Great Ladies," *Texas Monthly,* October 1978, 148.

25. William P. Hobby Jr. (1932–) graduated from Rice University, served in the U.S. Navy for four years, and returned to Houston, where he held various positions at the *Houston Post*, including serving as president from 1965 until the paper was sold in 1993. He also holds the distinction of being the longest-serving lieutenant governor of Texas. Jessica Hobby Catto (1937–2009) attended Chatham Hall and became notable as a writer, magazine publisher, preservationist, conservationist, and philanthropist. Her husband, Henry Catto (1930–2011), was a San Antonio businessman who held a number of high U.S. diplomatic posts, including the ambassadorship to the United Kingdom (1989–91).

26. Will Hobby bought a controlling interest in the *Houston Post* and radio station KPRC in 1939. The terms of the loan that financed the purchase were very favorable, requiring no down payment and allowing repayment over a long time. The transaction thus paved the way for greater Hobby influence and philanthropy in the years to come.

27. One could argue with this assessment of Will and Oveta's contributions, but they indisputably had more political success and influence and made more money as a team than they did separately. In 1991, the Hobby wealth, in the form of H&C Communications, was estimated at $525 million. See Christine Carroll. "The Texas 100: The Richest People in Texas," *Texas Monthly*, September 1991, 130.

28. Oveta Culp Hobby, "An Introduction to Parliamentary Law" (speech before the Junior League), October 10, 1939, folder 9, box 43, Hobby Papers.

29. Jack Phillips to Mrs. W. P. Hobby, May 22, 1936; Jack Phillips to A. H. Nelson, May 22, 1936; Oveta Hobby to Richard Waldo, May 10, 1939, February 12, 1941, all in folder 1, box 3, Hobby Papers. A discussion of Hobby's book indicated that it was simply written and easy to read. See "Wife of Former Governor Writes Book on Parliamentary Procedure," *Austin-American Statesman*, October 11, 1936.

30. Deborah Sutphen, "Conservative Warrior: Oveta Culp Hobby and the Administration of Americans' Heath, Education, and Welfare, 1953–1955" (PhD diss., Washington State University, 1997), 24–25.

31. "Editors Hear Talks on News by Three Woman Reporters," *Washington Evening News*, April 21, 1939.

32. "William P. Hobby, 86, Is Dead; Governor of Texas, 1917–1921," *New York Times*, June 8, 1964.

33. War Department Order, July 29, 1941, folder 2, box 56, Hobby Papers.

34. Forrest C. Pogue, *George C. Marshall: Organizer of Victory, 1943–1945* (New York: Viking, 1999), 107.

35. U.S. House of Representatives, Committee on Military Affairs, *Congressional Record*, January 21, 1942.

36. Mattie E. Treadwell, *U.S. Army in World War II Special Studies: The Women's Army Corps* (Washington, D.C.: Center of Military History, U.S. Army, 1954), 29.

37. Susan Ware, *Beyond Suffrage: Women in the New Deal* (Cambridge: Harvard University Press, 1981).

38. Jean M. Bartunek, Kate Walsh, and Catherine A. Lacey, "Dynamics and Dilemmas of Women Leading Women," *Organization Science* 11 (November–December 2000): 589–610.

39. "40 Women to Be Sent to WAAC," *Baltimore Afro-American*, May 23, 1942.

40. "Race Women to Be Part of New Army," *Pittsburgh Courier*, May 23, 1942.

41. Kelli Cardenas Walsh, "Oveta Culp Hobby: Transformational Leadership from the Texas Legislature to Washington D.C." (PhD diss., University of South Carolina, 2006), 67.

42. Treadwell, *U.S. Army in World War II*, 220.

43. "Historical Background of the WAAC-WAC," Appendix E, Harriet West Waddy Papers, WAC Museum, Fort Lee, Va.

44. Betty Bandel, *An Officer and a Lady: The World War II Letters of Lt. Col. Betty Bandel, Women's Army Corps*, ed. Sylvia J. Bugbee (Hanover, N.H.: University Press of New England, 2004), 142.

45. George C. Marshall to Oveta Culp Hobby, July 27, 1944, in *The Papers of George Catlett Marshall*, vol. 4, *Aggressive and Determined Leadership, June 1, 1943–December 31, 1944*, edited by Larry I. Bland and Sharon R. Stevens (Baltimore: Johns Hopkins University Press, 1996), 534–35; http://www.marshallfoundation.org/Database.htm (accessed October 30, 2013).

46. Treadwell, *U.S. Army in World War II*, 719.

47. Bandel, *Officer and a Lady*, 183.

48. Elizabeth Fox-Genovese, "Scarlett O'Hara: The Southern Lady as New Woman," *American Quarterly* 33 (Autumn 1981): 399; William H. Gardner, "Mr. and Mrs. Texas," news clipping, Hobby File, box 3, H1, 18, Dolph Briscoe Center for American History, University of Texas at Austin;; "Honoring Oveta Culp Hobby at Mary Hardin-Baylor," *Congressional Record*, March 24, 1994, http://www.gpo.gov/fdsys/pkg/CREC-1994-03-24/html/CREC-1994-03-24-pt2-PgH85.htm (accessed October 30, 2013).

49. "Little Colonel," *Washington Post*, July 14, 1945.

50. Bettie J. Morden, *The Women's Army Corps, 1945–1978* (Washington, D.C.: Center of Military History, U.S. Army, 2000), 35.

51. "Mrs. Hobby Flays Wallace as Ad Parley Opens Here," *Boston Daily Globe*, n.d., folder 12, box 4, Hobby Papers.

52. "We Like Ike," *Houston Post*, April 13, 1952, 1.

53. Pando, "Oveta Culp Hobby," 160.

54. "Lady in Command," *Time*, May 4, 1953, 27.

55. "Secretary Hobby," *A Common Thread of Service: An Historical Guide to HEW*, excerpt from DHEW Publication No. (OS) 73-45 (July 1, 1972), http://aspe.hhs.gov/info/hewhistory.htm#Hobby (accessed January 20, 2014); "Lady in Command," *Time*, May 4, 1953, 26.

56. Clarence Woodbury, "America's Glamorous Godmother," *American Magazine*, May 1953, 19–21, 104–8.

57. David M. Oshinsky, *Polio: An American Story* (New York: Oxford University Press, 2005), 217.

58. Hobby, *How Things Really Work*, 16; Leonard A. Scheele, "Control of Poliomyelitis through Vaccination," *Journal of American Medical Association* 158 (August 6, 1955): 1271–73. For more on the polio epidemic, see Oshinsky, *Polio*.

59. Oshinsky, *Polio*, 218.

60. Charles V. Hamilton, *The Political Biography of an American Dilemma: Adam Clayton Powell, Jr.* (New York: Macmillan, 1991), 201; "Negro Lauds Ike for Race Stand," *Sarasota Herald-Tribune*, June 11, 1953.

61. Oveta Culp Hobby, Howard University Charter Day Speech, March 2, 1954, folder 30, box 45, Hobby Papers; "Bias Called Economic Burden," *New York Times*, June 9, 1954; "Mrs. Hobby Tells Grads Prejudice Will Complicate Lives for Years," *Chicago Defender*, June 20, 1953. As a member of the board of regents at Rice Institute, Hobby supported integration of the school (Pando, "Oveta Culp Hobby," 186).

62. Clarence Woodbury, "America's Glamorous Godmother," *American Magazine*, May 1953, 21.

63. Sutphen, "Conservative Warrior," 349. Despite Sutphen's focus on Hobby's time at HEW, more work is needed to unravel the breadth and complexity of the multiple areas that fell under her management.

64. "Mrs. Hobby Feted by Texas Friends," *Washington Evening Star*, July 25, 1955; Kay Bailey Hutchinson, *American Heroines: Spirited Women Who Shaped Our Country* (New York: HarperCollins, 2004), 250–59.

65. Remarks by the President and Mrs. Oveta Culp Hobby (press release), July 13, 1955, in Robert Branyan and Lawrence Larsen, *The Eisenhower Administration, 1953–1961: A Documentary History* (New York: Random House, 1971), 583–84; Marguerite Johnston (for Hobby) to Ishbel Ross, October 2, 1968, folder 8, box 5, Hobby Papers; "The Administration: 'Farewell with Fanfare,'" *Time*, July 25, 1955, http://content.time.com/time/magazine/article/0,9171,891497,00.html (accessed March 26, 2014); "Lady in Command," *Time*, May 4, 1953, 32.

66. Kay Bailey Hutchison, "Oveta Culp Hobby," in *American Heroines*, available at http://www.humanitiestexas.org/news/articles/womens-history-month-oveta-culp-hobby-senator-kay-bailey-hutchison (accessed March 26, 2014); "Biographical Note," Hobby Papers, http://library.rice.edu/collections/WRC/finding-aids/manuscripts/0459 (accessed March 26, 2014); "William P. Hobby, 86, Is Dead; Governor of Texas, 1917 to 1921," New York Times, June 8, 1964.

67. Oveta Culp Hobby, interview by Marguerite Johnston, n.d., 1, transcript in folder 11, box 11, Barnes Papers; Betty T. Chapman, "Houston Went through Peaceful Segregation Movement in Secret," *Houston Business Journal*, September 21, 2007. For a different perspective on media silence during civil rights protests in Texas, see Dulaney, in this volume.

68. Betty T. Chapman, "Houston Went through Peaceful Segregation Movement in Secret," *Houston Business Journal*, September 21, 2007.

69. Diana J. Kleiner, "Houston Post," *Texas Handbook Online*, http://www.tshaonline.org/handbook/online/articles/eeh04 (accessed January 20, 2014).

70. Oveta Culp Hobby, interview by David G. McComb, July 11, 1969, 34, Lyndon Baines Johnson Library, University of Texas at Austin. Ike Culp and the president's father, Sam Ealy Johnson Jr., had served together in the Texas Legislature.

71. Harry Hurt III, "The Most Powerful Texans: The Power Game in Texas: How It Works and Who Calls the Shots," *Texas Monthly*, April 1976, http://www.texasmonthly.com/story/most-powerful-texans (accessed January 20, 2014). In 1982, the Associated Press gave her the same recognition.

72. "On the Record with Diane Holloway: Hobby Touts Education in the Budget Wars," May 2, 2011, *Travis County Democratic Party*, http://www.traviscountydemocrats.org/2011/05/hobby-touts-education-in-the-budget-wars/ (accessed October 30, 2013).

73. Saralee Tiede, "Post Sale Writes Last Page in an Era of Texas Papers," *Fort Worth Star-Telegram*, July 24, 1983; "Houston Post Publishes Last Edition; Hearst Acquires Operating Assets," April 18, 1995, http://www.hearst.com/press-room/pr-19950418a.php (accessed January 20, 2014); Kleiner, "Houston Post."

74. Kleiner, "Houston Post."

75. William P. Hobby and Jessica Hobby Catto, *Oveta Culp Hobby*, comp. and ed. Al Shire (Houston: privately printed, 1997), x.

76. Sterling, "Woman's Hour," 9.

77. Marguerite Johnston Barnes, "Eulogy at Oveta Culp Hobby Funeral," August 16, 1995, folder 10, box 11, Barnes Papers.

Ranch Women and Rodeo Performers in Post–World War II West Texas

A Cowgirl by Any Other Name—Than Feminist

RENEE M. LAEGREID

Cowgirls hold a strange place in the American conception of the West. In scholarly literature, film, and the popular press, cowgirls are portrayed as icons of feminism. Dressed quite fetchingly in jeans and boots and doing everything their iconic counterparts, the cowboys, can do, they seem the quintessential feminists in action. Yet ranch or rodeo women who came of age prior to or during World War II either appear not to have had a clear understanding of the concept or to have rejected that label outright. Instead, they considered themselves "cowgirls." Despite differences in class and family economy, this moniker identified them as women who could step outside traditional female boundaries among the region's unique environmental, economic, and cultural characteristics but could do so without challenging the established social order.

The community of women who participated in the first all-girl rodeo in Amarillo, Texas, in 1947 is the focal point for exploring this dichotomy of terms. Oral histories from four of the competitors provide insights from which to explore ranch women and rodeo performers' views on gender roles. Their experiences help broaden one's understanding of the complex, multifaceted ways in which gender is constructed in this region. Situating Texas women within the larger, national debate on feminism helps explain the unique regional interplay of feminine and masculine behaviors—attractively dressed and made-up women who rode bulls, for example—and why in this male-dominated society, women could both perform outside the boundaries of traditional female behavior and remain strongly antifeminist.

While the term *feminism* does not have a singular fixed definition, for this essay, *feminism* is defined as a self-conscious attempt by women to change fundamental conditions of gender equality in their society. Rural West Texas is not generally considered a bastion of feminist activity, yet the women who organized, produced, and competed in the 1947 Tri-State Rodeo have been credited as behaving in a feminist manner, or at least as being protofeminists. And not without reason. The story of Nancy Binford and Thena Mae Farr, who produced the rodeo, as well as of the competitors seems a compelling argument for feminist activity. Theirs was the first rodeo organized and produced by women and in which women competed in all the events featured in regular Professional Rodeo Cowboy rodeos: bareback riding, saddle bronc riding, calf roping, team roping, bull dogging (steer wrestling), and bull riding. Although a series of "All Cowgirl" rodeos had been staged in Texas during World War II, they had featured exhibition, or noncompetitive, events and included men on the roster of organizers and even guest performers.[1]

In the context of national feminist activity, Binford and Farr's decision to hold the 1947 rodeo and then continue their production partnership until 1953 seems to illustrate the inroads women had gained during World War II, allowing them to participate in areas outside traditional gendered boundaries. Earlier scholarship on this rodeo generally assumes a feminist perspective, arguing that Binford, Farr, and the women competitors used the Tri-State as a means to fight against the increasingly circumscribed roles for women in the immediate postwar years. Candace Savage, for example, has written that cowgirls had been limited to "sponsor contests or serving as glamour girls in parades and production numbers. The up-and-coming generation of working cowgirls hated these restrictions." In a similar vein, Charlene Walker ascribes the women's drive for equality as their primary motive: the Women's Professional Rodeo Association "includes legendary equestriennes and world champions, and, more so, it was started by a Tech-ex who believed women could rope and ride as good as any man and deserved the chance." Mary Lou LeCompte argues that Farr "dreamed of the chance to compete in real rough stock and roping contests like the cowboys" and had discussed the "frustration at being shut out of rodeo competition" with Binford. Either explicitly or implicitly, changing the rules and/or finding a venue to continue competing in a full slate of rodeo events on par with men's events emerge as the prime motivations for creating the Tri-State Rodeo.[2]

A closer look at the lives of Binford, Farr, and the other riders also suggests that they lived outside the gendered boundaries of the era, implying their status as at least protofeminists. Nancy Binford had grown up on her family's

THENA MAE FARR AND NANCY BINFORD
galloping their horses, 1947.
Courtesy of the National Cowgirl Museum and Hall of Fame, Fort Worth.

ranch outside of Wilderado, Texas. Her parents had settled there in 1911 and encouraged Nancy to enjoy athletics; they also expected her to participate in all the chores necessary in running a large cattle operation—riding, roping, and branding. Binford was thirteen and her older sister, Barbara, was fifteen when their father died in 1934. Despite the large scale of the ranch and farming operation, their mother took over management of the family business, relying on her daughters for help. After high school graduation, Binford attended Texas Technological College, graduating in 1943 with a degree in physical education. She taught high school for one year, but "during the war my mother needed help here on the ranch," so Binford returned to Wilderado in the spring of 1944. The two women subsequently ran the large ranch as a partnership.[3]

Thena Mae Farr, a longtime friend of Binford's, came from a third-generation ranching family located outside of Seymour, Texas. And as with Binford, Farr learned to ride at a very young age and participated in the day-to-day operations of her family's cattle business. She earned the reputation as an accomplished rider and ranch woman, acquiring her own herd in 1944, during her senior year of high school. After graduation, she attended Texas State College for Women (now Texas Woman's University) for one year, returning home in the spring of 1945 to continue in her family's cattle business.[4]

Back on their respective ranches in 1945, the two women had family, ranching, and rodeo connections that placed them in a strong position to organize a rodeo when the opportunity presented itself. As Binford recalled during a 1985 interview, "Amarillo for years had had this regular rodeo and it had become a place where they couldn't even fill the grand stand." Learning that the state fair commissioners for Amarillo's Tri-State Fair would not be holding a rodeo in 1947, according to Binford, "Thena Mae Farr and I decided that we would try to produce an all girl rodeo." They took their idea to the chamber of commerce in Amarillo; "they said if we thought it was possible that they would let us put on an all girl rodeo and see if it would be successful." With approval in hand, the state fair board helped the women advertise their upcoming rodeo. A photo essay appeared in the local paper, telling the story of this novel rodeo and helping generate interest. Captions below the images read, "A Dream in the Making" (Binford and Farr sitting on a fence); "The Girls have reached their decision" (the two sitting on a fence, smiling); "Happy over their decision" (smiling, standing next to a fence); "Girls off to meet Mr. L. B. Herring, Jr., mgr of the Tri-State Fair" (one on horse, other closing corral); "The making of the Tri-State All Girl Rodeo" (Binford and Farr on horseback, Herring standing between the horses and reading the women's proposal); "Happy are the Girls—contract signed" (the two women galloping their horses, waving the contract);

"Not only can they produce a show. . . ." (sitting in house, Binford sewing button on Farr's shirt); "The girls are good cooks, too" (Binford and Farr looking into a pot); "The girls at Miss Binford's 'M' Bar Ranch" (on horseback), concluding with an image of Binford and Farr standing next to a horse trailer that would be awarded to the best all-around cowgirl. Wearing jeans, boots, and simple western shirts, the two women epitomized the image of independent, competent cowgirls.[5]

To draw enough contestants to put on a good show, the two women called on friends, young ranch women like themselves, to help out. Binford recalled, "My last year or two in high school and in college the rodeos around the county would invite different girls to come and ride and they, the girls, were called sponsors or sweethearts. . . . That's how I started rodeo-ing and then meeting some of the girls."[6] The women had developed strong friendships based on their shared experiences as ranch women and the competitive camaraderie that developed during West Texas competitions. Binford and Farr's ranching friends were eager to pitch in.

With the exception of the announcer and pickup men—riders on horseback who picked up rodeo contestants from horses, bulls, or from the ground during bucking events—women filled all the positions as contestants, judges, promoters, and staff supporters at the 1947 Tri-State All-Girl Rodeo. The organizers went to great lengths to fill the slate and make the rodeo a success: twenty-four riders filled up the eighty entries, with the women competing in bareback riding, calf roping, sponsor contest, cutting, team tying, saddle bronc riding, steer riding, and an exhibition bulldogging performance. Dixie Lee Reger Mosley remembered, "Jackie Worthington and myself rode in all seven events, and I was also trick riding and trick roping, and I think I was still riding my horse over the cars at the time. And I was also the rodeo clown. I was a very sore person every morning." Jerry Portwood Taylor was unusual in that she competed in only one event: Farr had pleaded with Taylor's mother to allow Taylor to participate. Taylor was living in Fort Worth at the time but had grown up on a large ranch outside of Seymour, Texas, near where Farr lived, and they were "close as sisters." Taylor's mother finally relented, and Taylor "just flew in. I didn't stay even the whole rodeo. Thena picked me up [from the airport] and took me to the show, [saying], 'She'll kill me if you get hurt.'" Taylor won the cutting competition riding Farr's horse, then returned home.[7]

Since the early 1930s, women had competed in the sponsor contest at regular rodeos, and the Tri-State All-Girl Rodeo also featured this event. The sponsor contests emerged as a rodeo event at the Stamford, Texas, Cowboy Reunion in 1931, where it was the only event for women. The intention was to "add a little charm and glamour to the previously masculine rodeo." To compete, riders had to be "sponsored" by a civic organization or local ranch. To ensure that their "participation would conform to more traditional views of feminine behavior," prizes were awarded based on most attractive riding outfits, best-looking mounts, and best horsemanship (based on subjective and secret criteria). Producers Binford and Farr eliminated the cowgirl costume portion of the contest and ended the practice of having a panel of male judges subjectively evaluate how the women rode around the barrels. At the Tri-State Rodeo, the contest was objectively evaluated—timed—with the woman with the fastest time declared the winner.[8]

Much to the organizers' delight, the rodeo was a huge success. "We had three performances," Binford recalled, "and the last performance in Amarillo they didn't even have standing room only." Newspaper reporters confirmed that "the girls rodeo is a knock-out. . . . The two promoters have a great, great opportunity. No reason why they shouldn't break into Madison Square Garden within the next winter or two." With very few exceptions, such positive stories filled the pages of local newspapers. Support from the state fair board and the riders encouraged Binford and Farr to hold another all-girl rodeo in Amarillo the following year. Once again, the women performed in front of enthusiastic, standing-room-only crowds. With the future for all-girl rodeos looking bright, twenty-three of the cowgirl contestants met immediately after the second Tri-State Rodeo and organized the Girls Rodeo Association (GRA) "to standardize rodeo rules applying to girl contestants, and to eliminate unfair practices." In particular, the association "intended to bar cowgirl sponsor contests from Rodeo Cowboy Association and Girls Rodeo Association–approved rodeos except where it is made a timed event." This insistence on fairness turned the sponsor contest, originally a feminine complement to the cowboys' rodeo events, into the highly competitive, lucrative, and popular event known today as barrel racing.[9]

Although eliminating the costume and equipment judging portions of the sponsor contest, the new GRA rules did not ignore appearance altogether. The bylaws required participants in GRA-sanctioned contests "to ride in the opening parades and always be dressed in colorful attire when they appear in the arena." The following year, the officers updated the GRA rule book to include behavior as well, stipulating that sanctions would be applied to members who swore in the arena, drank publicly on the rodeo grounds, or behaved in an otherwise unladylike manner. The decades between World War I and World War II had witnessed a revolution in manners and morals all across the United States, giving women greater freedom to publicly engage in what had been considered behaviors appropriate only for men—smoking, drinking, and swearing. Although women in urban areas were more likely to engage in this behavior, the rule suggests that the revolution had spread to the rural West. The women who served as elected officials of the nascent GRA did not want to alienate the state fair commissioners or spectators in the increasingly conservative post–World War II era. "Don't ever go to an All-Girl Rodeo and expect to see a bunch of rowdy gals raising the devil," came the word from James Cathey, columnist for *Western Horseman Magazine*. "They are the only professional sportswomen who don't smoke or drink in view of their public. The girls are selling their profession to the public and the public is enthusiastically accepting them." The restrictions demonstrated marketing savvy but applied only to conduct on the rodeo grounds. After the show cowgirls joined cowboys for some fun after a long day at the arena. Dutch Taylor, Jerry Portwood Taylor's husband, a roper from West Texas, recalled, "After the rodeo, well, we'd all go to the street dance, but we still drank and had fun. . . . Jackie Worthington and I—I guess I drank a washtub full of whiskey or more with her." Mary Ellen "Dude" Barton, too, recalled the evenings out: "Most of the time we weren't all that rowdy. We just got into things once in a while." Even so, the freedom and opportunity the cowgirls enjoyed seemed to defy the restrictive norms for post–World War II women.[10]

Binford and Farr accomplished their goal with the 1947 event: the Tri-State All-Girl Rodeo brought their community of amateur cowgirl athletes in a traditional rodeo competition. Between 1947 and 1953, when the two women ceased producing rodeos, interest and acceptance of all-girl rodeos continued to increase among spectators and competitors alike. Cathey was amazed to discover that "the bug bites the fair sex as well as the ruggedest and roughest of the species. Girls love rodeo as well as the boys." And spectators loved watching women compete, too. "The people of the southwest," he continued, "will have over two dozen chances to see one of the All-Girl affairs this summer."[11]

The close-knit group of cowgirls worked hard to keep their all-girl rodeos going. Because of the distances that separated the women and the expense of telephone calls, they gathered after one rodeo to plan the next. Mosley remembered the conversations: "We used to say, okay, our next rodeo is going to be two weeks from now over there. Well now, everybody's got to show up so we've got enough to have a rodeo." The rodeos offered women a time to socialize, a break from the everyday demands of ranch work. "We'd have rodeos Thursday, Friday, and Saturday," recalled Mosley, "and then everybody went back to their ranch and worked hard so they could go to the next rodeo." Ruby Gobble agreed. "We all worked on ranches," she said. "I lived there with Nancy Binford and her mother, worked there. And Katie, her mother, used to work our butts off!

And we'd be so tickled to drive out of there and go to a rodeo so we could rest." Creating a culturally acceptable venue in which women could gather with friends—and get a reprieve from the demands of ranch work—emerged as a motive for continuing the all-girl rodeos.[12]

Friendships aside, the women took competition seriously. Mary Lou LeCompte has written that "the camaraderie and friendship with the group were much stronger than the competition between individuals, since all wanted this sport to succeed," but according to the women interviewed, they took competition seriously. Sitting in the lobby of the Cowgirl Hall of Fame in 2006, Mosley and Gobble joked about competing against one another. When Mosley laughed, "You beat me in the calf roping!" Gobble shot back, "You never will forget that, will you?" And Mosley, responded, "You *always* beat me in the calf roping!" Turning serious, Gobble reflected, "We were all really good friends, but when I roped, rode into the box with the calf, if I could beat Dixie I would. . . . When you're competing, you always want to win." Mosley agreed: "You do want to win, or you shouldn't be competing to begin with. If you don't want to win first, sit out. Don't go." Although they talked about the women riders' willingness to help one another—loaning a rope or piece of tack—everyone played to win, if for no other reason than to earn enough money to go to the next rodeo.[13]

At first glance, protofeminists seems to be an apt description for these women. After all, the renaissance of traditional gender roles that emerged after World War II emphasized a return to more conservative masculine and feminine behaviors. These behaviors, usually defined in opposition to one another, emphasized men as strong and aggressive, women as weak and passive helpmates rather than independent agents. The women who organized and competed in the Tri-State Rodeo hardly seem to fit this description. Then, too, concerns about women crossing the line into "masculine" behaviors appeared in newspaper and journal articles on the all-girl rodeo, either blatantly or obliquely. "Despite the powerful ideology of the happy homemaker, women continued to encroach into the male sphere," wrote one journalist, feeding into social critics' fears that women would rob men of their masculinity by adopting masculine roles. While the cowgirls did not set out to challenge men or masculinity— and had no intention of competing against men—this topic kept resurfacing in newspaper coverage.[14]

Moreover, that initial historical analysis must encounter and explain the antifeminist words of many commentators at the time. Newspapermen's patronizing words contrast with legitimately impressive accomplishments, easily casting for present-day readers a feminist light on actions that the rodeo women themselves may not have understood as such. While guardedly approving of their activities, the language of the articles and essays characterized the women's rodeos as less important than "real" rodeos. An article in the *Quarter Horse Journal* on preparations for the 1948 all-girl rodeo in Amarillo reported, "The female frolic had its inception in Amarillo last fall when a group of girls, most of them reared on ranches in New Mexico, Texas, and Oklahoma and had learned as youngsters the real ups and downs of the cattle business, decided to sponsor a rodeo of their own for a little fun and diversion." This commentary seems dismissive, an example of antifeminist sentiment that allowed women to engage in traditional rodeo events as long as it remained "a diversion," an amateur show, separate from men's "real" competition. Nevertheless, Binford and Farr appeared to have made a significant contribution to women's demands for equality by creating a venue in which women could compete in rodeo on their own terms, thereby paving the way for women to reenter the professional world of rodeo.[15]

Though reading women's actions that flaunted contemporary gender roles as feminist makes sense in a superficial way, emerging oral history theory and new scholarship on rural western women indicate that a more holistic approach is warranted. Given Estelle Freedman's injunction to women's historians to question how multiple identities shaped women's consciousness, we should take seriously the regional context from which rodeo women came and thus must revisit the "protofeminist" characterization of their experience. This admonition prompts different questions, including some about these women's thoughts on feminism. Sixty years later, three surviving members of the Tri-State Rodeo—Dixie Lee Reger Mosley, Dude Barton, and Jerry Portwood Taylor—and Ruby Gobble, who began competing in women's rodeo in 1950, argued against equality as a motivation for their involvement in rodeo and ranching. Indeed, they were a bit surprised, if not disconcerted, to learn that they had been celebrated as feminists.[16]

Since the 1990s, scholarship on women has matured to encompass complicated and often intersecting factors; that same rigor has not been applied to the scholarship on cowgirls in particular. The women connected to the Tri-State Rodeo shared a number of features—their ethnicity, for example. During the 1940s and 1950s in West Texas, non-Anglo ranch women or rodeo contestants were few and far between. Taylor recalled, "There was never a Hispanic girl that rode, or anything, that you know of. One might have been a Spanish girl, [but] she was a rancher, not really a [contestant]." Taylor's comment offers insight into more than just the dearth of Hispanic ranchers: she described a young woman from a ranch family as a rancher herself, and she made class and race assumptions when she characterized a ranch owner as Spanish rather than working-class Mexican.[17]

Yet cowgirls—ranch women and rodeo performers—are not a monolithic group although they lived in the same "country," as Mosley referred to the region, and although all "were ranch women [who] grew up on a ranch." Some, like Taylor, came from old money. Others, like Fern Sawyer, Jackie Worthington, and Judy Hays, "had been longtime ranch families, and they hadn't been doing all that well" until the discovery of oil on their property. Mosley and her sister, Virginia Reger, had spent their entire childhood as part of a family troupe of rodeo performers; the income the girls earned as trick riders helped support their family. Binford and Worthington obtained college degrees, though Barton readily admitted that she only barely graduated from high school: "It wasn't an interest to me at all." While Taylor moved from her family's ranch to Fort Worth at age fifteen and thereafter preferred the glamour of city life, many of the other women remained on their families' remote ranches. The diverse group of participants in the all-girl rodeo also included older women such as Tad Lucas (a champion cowgirl from 1919 to 1929, when opportunities for women in sports blossomed); rank novices; women who married early and often; and "women who don't date men." Dispensing with a monolithic lumping together of the women under the term *cowgirl* demonstrates that the participants defy a simple definition, economic pattern, or even sexual orientation.[18]

In the larger debate on feminism, the idea that Binford, Farr, and other contestants exhibited protofeminist tendencies does not seem outside the realm of possibility, especially considering that Texas women have been both in step with national trends with the feminist movement and outside of it. In her book, *The Cowgirls*, which focuses on women in the West Texas region, Joyce Gibson Roach writes, "The emancipation of women may have begun not with the vote nor in the cities where women marched and carried signs and protested, but rather when they mounted a good cowhorse and realized how different and fine the view. . . . From the back of a horse, the world looked wider."[19] Nevertheless, the culture of West Texas has provided arguments against the feminist movement since before women received the right to vote.

Three unique aspects of the region's social, cultural, and economic environment contributed to the resistance. The feminist movements, supported by white, middle-class urban women, had been predominantly concerned with urban issues that did not necessarily resonate with rural, agriculturally oriented West Texas, especially during the hardscrabble years of the Great Depression and drought. "Ranch and farm women," historian Sandra Schackel notes, were "not a group ready to call themselves feminists." Lingering southern attitudes, too, played a role, with views shaped as much by the concern that involvement in politics would "unsex" white women—a point articulated by a Texas legislator who warned that suffrage would rob women of "those modest charms so dear to us Southern gentlemen"—as by the fear of empowering black women with enfranchisement.[20]

The cowgirls who produced the Tri-State Rodeo and the majority of those who competed in it were born in the 1920s, when attitudes in the region continued to support antifeminist sentiment. On the national scene, the early years after World War II saw the stirrings of a new feminist movement, part of the "increasingly affluent society which was beginning to turn its attention to the question of racial equality." The feminist issues of the time, however, did not resonate in the rural West Texas region: census reports from the 1940s and 1950s indicate at most very small numbers of Hispanics or African Americans in the West Texas counties. Nor did the cowgirls identify with the new feminist emphasis on breaking free of the restrictive parameters of woman's "separate sphere" to engage in society at large. These women had always been engaged. Postwar feminism also became linked to sexual deviance and subversive communist activity, a cause for national alarm as the United States quickly shifted into the Cold War. The few cowgirls described as "women who don't date men," for whom feminism might have provided a community of understanding, would have risked public censure had they admitted to being feminists. Although "the mid-twentieth century was a particularly homophobic time," the cowgirls in the Tri-State Rodeo group did not care about their friends' sexual orientation and encouraged and supported one another.[21]

So why have scholars writing about the Tri-State Rodeo cast the producers and participants as feminists? In part, it is because of their identification as cow- girls. In many ways similar to the male cowboy image, the "cowgirl" has been created, shaped, and marketed by forces outside her world, and those forces may have had agendas that did not resonate with the women themselves. The term *cowgirl* entered the national vernacular through public figures such as Will Rogers and Theodore Roosevelt, who witnessed the skill and daring of female rodeo performers in the late nineteenth century, during the era of the New Woman. And as with her male counterpart, the cowgirl's image carries connotations of the West and of living by virtues that historian Elliot West has cataloged as "an unswerving integrity, a spit-in-your-eye individualism, and a simple and unsullied honesty with others and themselves." In the West, however broadly it was defined, it was possible, sometimes even necessary, for women to step outside of traditional gender boundaries and engage in the same activities as their male counterparts.[22]

Connecting the Tri-State cowgirls with the West is important. The idea of Texas as a western region was still a new concept in the late 1940s. Only a decade earlier, the 1936 Fort Worth Frontier Centennial, held in Fort Worth, consciously sought "a new public view of Texas history that emphasized Texas as both a Western and a quintessentially American state." The city's business leaders capitalized on national trends that had turned to the region "with special enthusiasm during the 1930s and 1940s, years of crisis when Americans were looking for reminders of their abilities and assurances that dangers would be survived." The increasing interaction with Hollywood, the lure of economic growth, and a desire to shift away from the association with its Confederate past encouraged Texas to distance itself from its southern roots and to forge a western identity. Cowboys and cowgirls from Texas became western icons.[23]

When film and media representations of the western woman as cowgirl became widely popular in the post–World War II era, they fit within the contemporary discourse of gender roles: cowgirls as pretty, spunky, very feminine—sexy, even—helpers rather than equals to their counterparts. Dale Evans, a Texas-born singer and actress in western movies, became the quintessential glamour cowgirl, while images of young women in skimpy western costumes appeared as pinups in fashion magazines. "The cowgirl as a subject for the great pin-up artists arrives late in the game—in the 1940s," observes Max Allen Collins, displacing "Indian maidens" as an excuse "for artists to depict pulchritude." The movie industry deserves credit for firmly connecting Texas cowgirls (and cowboys) to the romanticized idea of the West. Indeed, Mosley identified three different categories of cowgirls: movie cowgirls, rodeo cowgirls, and ranch cowgirls. The cowgirls who participated in the Tri-State Rodeo crossed Mosley's categories of ranch and rodeo women; Gobble crossed all three, playing roles in Western movies as well. The term *cowgirl* has expanded to a fourth category—self-definition—as the connection between the West and cowgirls became more firmly fixed in the popular imagination. However, the importance of repudiating the southern past and connecting Texas cowgirls and ranch women to the West is not to be underestimated when casting them as feminists.[24]

During the 1970s and 1980s, women historians began to explore the lives of ranch and rural women of the West. Recalling Frederick Jackson Turner's words that "each age writes the history of the past with reference to the conditions uppermost in its own time," it is not surprising that the Tri-State cowgirls, now western women, found their story interpreted through a lens shaped by emerging feminist scholarship. They seemed likely candidates, enjoying freedoms and adventures that seemed to defy the cultural strictures of urban and suburban women. These cowgirls managed ranches and produced or competed in all of the same rodeo events as men. They trained, loaded, and hauled their own horses and generally traveled alone. And they had great adventures. For example, when her family began to receive oil money, Jackie Worthington bought an airplane and used it to stay connected to friends. Barton remembered, that for one rodeo, "We decided that Jackie would fly to Paducah and pick up a lady that we all knew and we wanted to be with her. So Jackie gets in this plane and flies to Paducah and their airport, and she got there, and they hadn't shredded [mowed] it or nothing. She said sunflowers were higher than that plane when she hit the ground. She said 'I never want to get in that kind of a mess again!' . . . Yep, she picked [the friend] up and took her to the rodeo, and she rode back home with me." Historians during this era tended to view cowgirls' freedom and opportunities through a feminist lens—that is, as evidence that they had gained equality with men in the region.[25]

Returning to the question of how to define the term *cowgirl*, Roach provides a specific definition: "A cowgirl is a female whose life is or was for a significant part influenced by cattle, horses, and men who dealt with either or both, often as dominant figures but not always." Roach recalled that when she asked Jackie Worthington's sister, Ada Worthington Womack if she minded being labeled a cowgirl, she said no: "It's what I was. I don't mind being called one today." Roach suggests that women who could be called cowgirls were the advance guard of the feminist movement: "These women probably never heard of Susan B. Anthony and the rebellious ladies who wished to have the right to do exactly what the cowgirls were doing, but they rode down the same road, some distance in advance of the theoretical feminists." But to consider the cowgirls feminists would be to engage in a type of "linguistic slippage," a misappropriation of causality. For example, an observation such as "environmental and occupational exigencies faced by ranch women and rodeo riders in Texas made it possible, if not necessary, for them to become active in activities prescribed for men" could be simplified into a less accurate assessment such as "cowgirls were feminists or protofeminists because they crossed gender boundaries to participate in men's ranch and rodeo activities." Rather than assuming that activities indicate an acceptance of feminist philosophies or ideals, women may have crossed gender boundaries because their activities supported and were supported by the regional patriarchal culture. In short, there is a distinction between having a feminist agenda and engaging in activities that are culturally acceptable in the region. In this context, place or region plays a significant role.[26]

Indeed, as Freedman points out, "The diversity of female experience [is] best understood at the local or regional level." In his landmark study, based in large part on his observations of West Texas, Walter Prescott Webb concludes that environmental factors created the region's distinctive cowboy ethos—masculine, violent, and fiercely independent. Later scholars studied the infusion of immigrants and the morphing of cultural patterns that "have helped make Texas the special place culturally that it undoubtedly is," thereby drawing attention to gender roles. Gender roles of the ethnic groups that moved from the upland South exhibit striking similarity to attitudes in the West Texas region. Though society remained strictly patriarchal, women were expected to work alongside their husbands or fathers, performing tasks such as working in the fields, tending livestock, and slaughtering cattle that could well have been considered inappropriate in other regions.[27]

Beverly J. Stoeltje also describes the cultural attributes of the "backwoods belles" who moved west into Texas. "The primary distinction between this woman and the refined [southern] lady," she notes, "is in the strength and initiative in coping with the hardships and the demands of the life they led." The defining feature of the Texas women was "their ability to fulfill their duties which enabled their men to succeed, and to handle crises with competence and without complaint." Backcountry culture did not make "womanhood a cult," she argues; rather, it encouraged contempt for "leisure-class standards of femininity." Despite their demanding physical work, women did not become masculinized. Quite the opposite. A great deal of weight was placed on femininity and attention to sensual female dress. Expectations that women would be independent, hardworking, and maintain traditional definitions of beauty shaped the concepts of gender in this region, seamlessly becoming part of the cowgirl culture. The title of the GRA's official albeit short-lived publication, *The Cowgirl Magazine: Powder Puffs and Spurs* (1950), exemplifies the regional attitude toward roles of and expectations for women.[28]

The normative gender behaviors and social patterns seen in post–World War II West Texas were part of the baggage Anglo women who migrated to the Texas frontier brought with them. Not everyone subscribed to or would have been consciously aware of this baggage, but, whether or not people are aware of its role, culture shapes and guides behavior. In particular, these women's concepts of gender and work differed markedly from those of their northern sisters. Historian Ann Patton Malone writes,

> The wives, daughters, and other kin of yeoman farmers, small slaveholders, craftsmen, and tradesmen . . . were probably more comfortable on the frontier than any other groups of Anglo women. Like elite women, they, too, were strongly influenced by the feminine role expectations of the Victorian code . . . but these women also had the advantage of a broader work experience. Because their lives had not been ones of either luxury or abject poverty but of hard work and activity, these yeoman-class frontier women were better prepared to fulfill their expected roles on the frontier. [These women were], in some respects, masculinized by the frontier experience.

Malone is speaking of the first generation "middlin' sort" of Texas frontier women as being more at ease with stepping outside strict gender roles; they moved into the region already familiar with the necessity of fluid gender roles, engaging in whatever chores needed to be done to ensure economic survival. Antifeminist rhetoric in national press and magazines, such as a 1901 essay in which Henry T. Finck argued that women should avoid "all employments which make women bold, fierce, muscular, brawny in body or mind," would have held less weight with Texas frontier women than their urban sisters.[29]

This pragmatic attitude continued, as witnessed by the number of Texas women engaged in the physical, day-to-day activities associated with ranch work, their independence and confidence reflecting regional gender norms that respected if not encouraged women's engagement in activities that in other places would be considered beyond the pale of middle-class acceptability. Photos, interviews, and newspaper clippings depicted the cowgirl athletes as western women challenging the conservative roles blanketing the country: they roped calves and rode bucking broncs; some even rode bulls. But according to the reports, the cowgirls accomplished these feats while looking like ladies. The papers not only described the appearance of Binford, Farr, and the other cowgirl athletes but also reported on their personal lives, describing their after-rodeo hobbies, interests, and family. One paper announced that "after a day in the arena, [cowgirls] went home to cook dinner for the family, work a little needle-point, or maybe on a Friday night, get dressed up for a night on the town" with their husbands. An earlier interpretation considered this emphasis on feminin-ity and domesticity a way to reassure readers that traditional gender distinc-tions and heterosexuality remained intact even as the women competed in the traditionally male sport of rodeo. Such reassurances were especially important for a sport that advertised that women would participate in "all the events that made up the best of male rodeos." But instead of trying to convince the public that cowgirl athletes were indeed feminine women, it seems more likely the cowgirls were celebrated by journalists as embodying the regional norms of feminine and capable women.[30]

The women's acceptance of the existing gender expectations is reflected in how they perceived the importance of rodeo to their careers or futures. None of the women interviewed saw rodeo as a potential career or intended to become a professional rodeo athlete. Binford remembered that when practice began for the 1947 rodeo, "We had eight ropers out the first day and some of them had never thrown a rope in an arena, and there wasn't a calf missed. They were real excited about it, and it turned out real well." According to Mosley, "A lot of it was, like most of the ranch women, they roped calves to work their cattle, and they sort of wanted to have some fun and compete against other women." Mos-ley, like the other women interviewed, "never wanted to compete against . . . men calf ropers," and Gobble recalled wanting "calves small enough that we could rope and throw and make a good show of it and wouldn't make us look like a bunch of idiots out there—which we were, but that's all right. But we wanted to make it look good." Neither woman thought of participating in rodeo as a means of challenging women's role in society or of competing with men. Constructing an organization that encouraged rodeo as a career had not been their goal. Binford remarked, "We did it as a hobby—there wasn't enough money to really say you went to a rodeo to make money—you went because it was a life you liked and a part of a life that you lived."[31]

Ironically, the women who played key roles in establishing the GRA, which later won the right for women to compete in Professional Rodeo Association events, found the focus on individualism and competitiveness disconcerting. Mosley captured the sentiment of her colleagues when she laments that women's rodeo—particularly Professional Rodeo Association barrel racing—has become such big business, part of the shift during the 1970s when "athletics would be turned into a business enterprise [where] winning isn't everything, but striving to win is." Although women had been competing in sports for "over a century, it's only recently that they've been accepted as true athletes—competitive, aggressive, and bold." Mosley said, "I definitely feel confident that all of us . . . had more fun and fellowship than these barrel racers that's making a hundred thousand dollars a year. . . . They gotta stay on the road to make enough money to make a living from it." Similarly, Taylor noted, "All you had was fun, because you didn't make any money." In fact, the women interviewed were troubled by the shift in priorities from competing against one another as a form of socialization to high-stakes individual rivalries. Barton particularly disliked the fact that modern rodeo contestants were not ranch women: "Now most of these women go to school and learn what they do. We learned it by getting out and working at it."[32]

Binford and Farr dissolved their rodeo-producing partnership after the 1953 Colorado Springs All-Girl Rodeo. Binford had already begun to focus more heavily on cutting horse competitions; Farr turned her attention to her family's cattle business. Mosley married after the Colorado Springs rodeo, and as Barton recalled, "When the rodeo was over, she said, 'Well girls, this is it. I'm getting married.'" And that was that. At her wedding just a few weeks later, her white cowboy boots were peeking out from under the hem of her white satin gown. At about the same time, Jackie Worthington became more involved in running the family ranch. Barton could not remember why she quit the rodeo. There was a drought, and she "probably decided it was time to go to work." Though they enjoyed the competitive camaraderie, these women put all-girl rodeos behind them and turned their attentions back to regular life—marriage, family, the demands of running ranches.[33]

Though they had opened the way for cowgirls to become professional rodeo riders, these women did not think of themselves as having done anything special. And they definitely did not see themselves as feminists or protofeminists. Yet when pressed, they recognized that the characteristics that defined them as cowgirls—their independence, assertiveness, and capabilities—are necessary to succeed in the patriarchal culture that permeates the region.[34]

Many of the women who participated in the Tri-State Rodeo needed these characteristics beyond the rodeo arena. In his 1950 essay on the GRA, Cathey wrote, "These girls have an eye for business too. The president, Nancy Binford, manages her mother's ranch near Amarillo. In fact most of the directors manage ranches or some other business, and they certainly manage that rodeo business of theirs." So, too, did many of the contestants. "Ranch girls," Taylor explained, "are independent because they *have* to be independent. They're used to doing things kinda for themselves. And they're used to *thinking*. You know, if you have a business or something like that, like a lot of them, it's been handed down to them . . . well, they've got to *think* about *business*. And men are sometimes hard to do business with. Cause they always will take advantage of you, a lot of the time." She concluded by declaring that independence is "a trait that you have to acquire." Nevertheless, she considered feminism and demanding equality the wrong way to do business. She understood the problems regarding unequal pay and opportunities for women, but she believed that success required working with the region's paternalistic structure.[35]

Fern Sawyer, winner of the all-around award at the 1947 Tri-State Rodeo, well expressed the cowgirls' argument against feminism:

> I don't believe in women's lib. When I started cutting, a woman had to do double good to get the same marking. But I don't believe in preaching women's lib or hollering about it. I believe action proves more than words. . . . The people that are really independent and do things, they don't like women lib. . . . All they're doing is raising hell and putting women in the draft and bunch of crap that they shouldn't be doing. . . . You can't tell me that in America, if you're good at your job, you won't make it. I've seen too many of them make it. And without women's lib.

Sawyer's adamant opposition to feminism was not unique, and most of these women, like her, would probably have seen the feminist movement as unnecessary. They believed that the region's patriarchal system was fluid and diffuse enough to allow women the opportunity to demonstrate their competence and strength of character. Their worldview had been shaped by regional experience—the product of social and historical experiences intersecting with economic and gender systems to "reproduce the socioeconomic and male-dominated structures of [a] particular social order." Overall, the gender system provided an acceptable "set of contingent power relations" that allowed the culture to "reproduce, and reconstruct male dominance." And while it did, the need for young ranch women to help in the family business allowed them to engage in experiences that outsiders perceived as challenging the boundaries of the paternalistic system.[36]

Writing about Texas women and feminism in more recent times, Martha Mitten Allen asserts, "The new rural woman in Texas may not march for 'women's lib,' but she clearly demonstrates the heightened consciousness and feeling of confidence and self-worth that is at the heart of the movement for women's rights. She has been influenced whether or not she knows it, or likes it." Rather than unconsciously benefiting from feminist ideals, the women who participated in the Tri-State Rodeo more likely already had that sense of confidence and self-worth based on a combination of environment, regional culture, and a system of gender relations distinct from those in other parts of the country. The West Texas patriarchy, while circumscribing and limiting women in many respects, also allowed women the latitude to participate in activities that were off-limits to women in other regions of the United States. Whether or not the cowgirls are consciously aware of it, this rationale seems to undergird West Texas women's resistance to feminism.[37]

Taking the long view of regional culture—its origins, persistence, and subtle manifestations—cultural or social patterns that may seem radical from a contemporary perspective instead appear to be perpetuations of long-standing norms. Doreen Massey argues for the importance of focusing on the locality not as static or concrete but as the place where larger social patterns were first expanded. Considering the evidence, it is difficult to ascribe incipient feminism to these ranch women/cowgirls; they had been doing what was expected of them, not pushing the boundaries of gender behavior. Freedman describes feminism as a fundamental revolution in the way men and women thought of one another: by that test, feminism was not present in this context. Cultural heritage and environmental considerations set the stage for gender behaviors in West Texas that varied from other regions.[38]

The participants in the Tri-State Rodeo did not perceive their actions as part of a movement for social change. There was no self-conscious political movement, nor did they consider rodeo a movement for social change. Quite the opposite. For the cowgirls, rodeo reinforced social and political norms. Asked whether she and the other cowgirls were fighting to restate women's place in rodeo, Barton replied, "You know, I hadn't thought anything about it. . . . Some woman was here not too long ago, and she brought up that Gene Autry really . . .

didn't even want [women] to ride in the barrel [races], or anything. I had kind of forgotten, and I said, 'I've been watching him on television—I'm going to quit watching him!'"[39] Perhaps Barton experienced a glimmer of feminist consciousness six decades after the fact.

NOTES

1. The working definition of *feminism* for this essay is compiled from Nancy Cott, *The Grounding of Modern Feminism* (New Haven: Yale University Press, 1987), 4–8; Estelle B. Freedman, *No Turning Back: The History of Feminism and the Future of Women* (New York: Ballantine, 2003), 3–9; Doreen Massey, *Space, Place, and Gender* (1994; Minneapolis: University of Minnesota Press, 2007). For information on all-girl rodeos, see Renee Laegreid, *Riding Pretty: Rodeo Royalty and the American West* (Lincoln: University of Nebraska Press, 2006), 173–95.

2. Candace Savage, *Cowgirls* (London: Bloomsbury, 1996), 95 (first quotation); Joan Burbick, *Rodeo Queens and the American Dream* (New York: Perseus, 2002); Mary Lou LeCompte, *Cowgirls of the Rodeo: Pioneer Professional Athletes* (Urbana: University of Illinois Press, 1993); Beverly J. Stoeltje, "Gender Representations in Performance: The Cowgirl and the Hostess," *Journal of Folklore Research* 25 (September 1988): 219–41; Beverly J. Stoeltje, "Females in Rodeo: Private Motivation and Public Representation," *Kentucky Folklore Record* 32 (January 1986): 42–49; Wayne S. Wooden and Calvin Ehringer, *Rodeo in America: Wranglers, Roughstock, and Paydirt* (Lawrence: University Press of Kansas, 1996); Charlene Walker, "Not for Men Only," *Texas Techsan Magazine*, July–August 1992, 24–25 (second quotation); Mary Lou LeCompte, "Farr, Thena Mae" (third quotation), *Handbook of Texas Online*, http://www.tshaonline.org/handbook/online/articles/ffa28 (accessed February 16, 2013).

3. Nomination Form, Nancy Binford File, National Cowgirl Museum and Hall of Fame Archives, Fort Worth (quotation).

4. Nomination Form, Thena Mae Farr File, ibid.

5. Nancy Binford, interview, Hereford, Tex., 1985, transcript sr20, bbc Cowgirl Interview File (quotations), Nancy Binford Tri-State Scrapbook, both in National Cowgirl Museum and Hall of Fame Archives.

6. Binford, interview (quotations).

7. LeCompte, *Cowgirls of the Rodeo*, 168; Binford Tri-State Scrapbook (each time a rider enters an event, it is considered an entry); Dixie Lee Reger Mosley, interview by author, March 15, 2008 (first quotation); Jerry Portwood Taylor, interview by author, March 16, 2008 (second quotation).

8. Hooper Shelton, *Fifty Years a Living Legend: Texas Cowboy Reunion and Old-Timer Association* (Stamford, Tex.: Shelton, 1979), 94 (quotation); Laegreid, *Riding Pretty*, 77, 80–81.

9. Binford, interview (first quotation); "Seen at the Fairgrounds," unidentified newspaper clipping, n.d., Binford Tri-State Scrapbook (second quotation); Binford Tri-State Scrapbook (third quotation); "Cowgirls Organize Rodeo Group Here," unidentified newspaper clipping, n.d., Binford Tri-State Scrapbook (fourth quotation).

10. LeCompte, *Cowgirls of the Rodeo*, 157 (first quotation); 1949 Girls Rodeo Association Handbook, Binford Tri-State Scrapbook; Estelle B. Freedman, "The New Woman: Changing View of Women in the 1920s," *Journal of American History* 61 (September 1974): 393; James Cathey, "The Girls Rodeo Association," *Western Horseman Magazine*, June 1950, Binford Tri-State Scrapbook (second quotation); Binford Tri-State Scrapbook; Dutch Taylor, interview by author, March 16, 2008 (third quotation); Mary Ellen "Dude" Barton, interview by author, March 15, 2008.

11. Cathey, "Girls Rodeo Association" (quotation).

12. Dixie Lee Reger Mosley and Ruby Gobble, interview by author, October 26, 2006 (quotation).

13. LeCompte, *Cowgirls of the Rodeo*, 169 (first quotation); Mosley and Gobble, interview (second quotation).

14. Laegreid, *Riding Pretty*, 173–95; Renee Laegreid; "'Performers Prove Beauty and Rodeo Can Be Mixed': The Return of the Cowgirl Queen," *Montana, the Magazine of Western History* 54 (Spring 2004): 44–55; Beth Bailey, *From Front Porch to Back Seat: Courtship in Twentieth-Century America* (Baltimore: Johns Hopkins University Press, 1988), 104–5 (quotation).

15. "The Tactless Texan," 1948, Binford Tri-State Scrapbook; "Girls Set to Open Rodeo," 1949, Binford Tri-State Scrapbook; "All Girl Rodeo a 'He-Man' Show," *Quarter Horse Journal*, Binford Tri-State Scrapbook (quotation).

16. See, for example, Katherine Borland, "That's Not What I Said: Interpretive Conflict in Oral Narrative Research," in *Women's Words: The Feminist Practice of Oral History*, ed. Sherna B. Gluck and Daphne Patai (New York: Routledge Press, 1991), 63–75; Judy Long, *Telling Women's Lives: Subject/Narrator/Reader/Text* (New York: New York University Press, 1999); Donald Ritchie, *Doing Oral History: A Practical Guide* (New York: Oxford University Press, 2003); Mosley and Gobble, interview; Mosley, interview; Barton, interview; Jerry Portwood Taylor, interview; Freedman, "New Woman," 393.

17. Jerry Portwood Taylor, interview (quotation).

18. Mosley, interview (first quotation); Jerry Portwood Taylor, interview (second quotation); Barton, interview (third quotation). For information on the "golden era of women's sports," see LeCompte, *Cowgirls of the Rodeo*, 70–99; Leslie Heywood and Shari L. Dworkin, *Built to Win: The Female Athlete as Cultural Icon* (Minneapolis: University of Minnesota Press, 2003), xx.

19. Joyce Gibson Roach, *The Cowgirls* (Denton: University of North Texas Press, 1990), xxi (quotation).

20. Sandra K. Schackel, *Working the Land: The Stories of Ranch and Farm Women in the Modern American West* (Lawrence: University Press of Kansas, 2011), 5 (first quotation); A. Elizabeth Taylor, *Citizens at Last: The Woman Suffrage Movement in Texas* (Austin: Temple, 1987), 36 (second quotation).

21. Freedman, "New Woman," 384 (first quotation); Jerry Portwood Taylor, interview; *University of Virginia Library Historical Census Browser*, http://mapserver.lib.virginia.edu/ (December 4, 2009); Joan Kelly, "The Double Vision of Feminist Theory: A Postscript to the 'Women and Power' Conference," *Feminist Studies* 5 (Spring 1979): 221; Yvonne Keller, "'Was It Right to Love Her Brother's Wife So Passionately?': Lesbian Pulp Novels and U.S. Lesbian Identity, 1950–1965," *American Quarterly* 57 (June 2005): 387 (second quotation). The sources who described the acceptance of lesbian women asked not to be identified.

22. Elliott West, "Selling the Myth: Western Images in Advertising," *Montana: The Magazine of Western History*, 46 (June 1996): 44 (quotation); Ann Terry Hill, "Old-Time Cowgirls," in *Pendleton Round-Up at 100*, ed. Michael Bales and Ann Terry Hill (Portland, Ore.: Graphic Arts), 87.

23. Gregg Cantrell, "The Bones of Stephen F. Austin: History and Memory in Progressive-Era Texas," *Southwestern Historical Quarterly* 58 (October 2004): 148 (first quotation); West, "Selling the Myth," 44 (second quotation).

24. Max Allen Collins, introduction to *Artist Archives: Cowgirl Pinups* (Portland, Ore.: Collectors, 2002), 1 (quotation); Dixie Lee Reger Mosley, telephone interview by Kim Moslander, 1993, National Cowgirl Museum and Hall of Fame Archives; Ruby Gobble File, National Cowgirl Museum and Hall of Fame Archives; Renee Laegreid, "Faux-Lo Pop: Urban Cowboys and the Inversion

of High-Pop," *Metropoli e Nuovi Consumi Culturali: Performance Urbane dell'Identità* 4 (October 2009): 73–88.

25. Frederick Jackson Turner quoted in Patricia Limerick, *The Legacy of Conquest: The Unbroken Past of the American West* (New York: Norton, 1987), 17 (first quotation); Barton, interview (second quotation).

26. Roach, *Cowgirls*, xvi, xxii, xviii; Joan W. Scott, "Gender: A Useful Category of Analysis," *American Historical Review* 91 (December 1986): 1065.

27. Freedman, *No Turning Back*, 2 (first quotation); Walter Prescott Webb, *The Great Plains* (Boston: Ginn, 1931); Wilbur Zelinsky, *The Cultural Geography of the United States*, rev. ed. (Englewood Cliffs, N.J.: Prentice Hall, 1992), 67, 116–18, 124; David Hackett Fischer, *Albion's Seed: Four British Folkways in America* (New York: Oxford University Press, 1989), 676.

28. Beverly J. Stoeltje, "'A Helpmate for Man Indeed': The Image of the Frontier Woman," *Journal of American Folklore* 88 (January–March 1975): 32 (quotation); LeCompte, *Cowgirls of the Rodeo*, 159. Janet Cropper of the Women's Professional Rodeo Association office noted that women in the GRA self-published *Powder Puffs and Spurs* but is not sure who came up with the name (email to author, December 5, 2011).

29. Ann Patton Malone, *Women on the Texas Frontier: A Cross-Cultural Perspective* (El Paso: Texas Western Press, University of Texas at El Paso, 1983), 21–23 (first quotation); Henry T. Finck, "Employments Unsuitable for Women," *Independent* 53 (April 11, 1901): 834–37 (second quotation).

30. Binford Tri-State Scrapbook (first quotation); Joanne Meyerowitz, "Beyond the Feminine Mystique: A Reassessment of Postwar Mass Culture, 1946–1958," in *Not June Cleaver: Women and Gender in Postwar America, 1945–1960*, ed. Joanne Meyerowitz (Philadelphia: Temple University Press, 1994), 234; "All Girl Rodeo Set for Fair," unidentified newspaper clipping, n.d., Binford Tri-State Scrapbook; Mosley and Gobble, interview.

31. Binford, interview (first and fourth quotations); Mosley, interview (second quotation); Mosley and Gobble, interview (third quotation).

32. Joel Nathan Rosen, *The Erosion of the American Sporting Ethos: Shifting Attitudes toward Competition* (Jefferson, N.C.: McFarland, 2007), 78 (first quotation); Mosley and Gobble, interview (second quotation); Jerry Portwood Taylor, interview (third quotation); Barton interview (fourth quotation).

33. Jerry Portwood Taylor, interview; Barton, interview (quotations).

34. Jerry Portwood Taylor, interview.

35. Cathey, "Girls Rodeo Association" (first quotation); Jerry Portwood Taylor, interview (second quotation).

36. Fern Sawyer quoted in Teresa Jordan, *Cowgirls: Women of the American West* (New York: Anchor, 1982), 235 (first quotation); Borland, "'That's Not What I Said,'" 71–72; Kelly, "Double Vision," 224–25 (second quotation); Stephanie J. Smith, *Gender and the Mexican Revolution: Yucatan Women and the Realities of Patriarchy* (Chapel Hill: University of North Carolina Press, 2009), 6.

37. Martha Mitten Allen, "Women on the Land," in *Texas Country: The Changing Rural Scene*, ed. Glen E. Lich and Dona B. Reeves-Marquardt (College Station: Texas A&M University Press, 1986), 129 (quotation).

38. Massey, *Space, Place, and Gender*, 2–5; Freedman, "New Woman," 392.

39. Barton, interview (quotation).

Casey Hayden

Gender and the Origins of SNCC, SDS, and the Women's Liberation Movement

HAROLD L. SMITH

❀ ❀ ❀

"We were the midwives to a great . . . outpouring of the human spirit," Sandra "Casey" Hayden recalled, summing up what she and Mary King accomplished in the 1960s.[1] Hayden (born Sandra Cason) was unique in being a significant early contributor to three of that decade's most important reform movements: the Student Nonviolent Coordinating Committee (SNCC), Students for a Democratic Society (SDS), and the women's liberation movement. Although they were sometimes portrayed as political organizations, Hayden considered them part of a spiritual movement. Before the Beatles made "All You Need Is Love" into an anthem for the era, she perceived these social movements (especially SNCC) as being rooted in love and a desire to create a "beloved community"—a Christian notion of God's earthly kingdom—in a country fractured along class, gender, and racial lines. Although she hoped to achieve this goal through love and nonviolence, Hayden was not a naive idealist. Influenced by Albert Camus, the French existentialist whose writings conveyed the need for constant revolt against the human condition without hope of success, she was a sober realist who recognized that class, gender, and racial barriers would not crumble easily and that the struggle for justice would be ongoing.

Sandra Cason is a fourth-generation Texan who was born in Austin on October 31, 1937, to two recent University of Texas graduates. Her father, William Charles Cason III, was a liberal Democrat who, while a state employee, helped establish the Texas Public Employees Association.[2] Her mother, Eula Weisiger Cason, was from one of Victoria County's "oldest and best known" families.[3] Cason's maternal great-grandfather, Reed N. Weisiger, was a Texas state senator

DORIE LADNER AND CASEY HAYDEN

in Mississippi, 1963.

Photograph by Danny Lyon, Magnum Photos.

from 1891 to 1893. Her maternal grandfather, Robert Sidney Weisiger, had been the Victoria County sheriff for twenty-two years until he had a stroke in 1936.[4]

After Cason's parents divorced when she was six months old, she and her mother returned to Victoria, where they lived with her mother's parents. Robert S. Weisiger was by this time an alcoholic and unable to contribute to the household, so Cason grew up in a matriarchal household that included her grandmother and her mother and her mother's sister, both divorced and working to support the family. Although her mother was a university graduate, employment opportunities for educated women in Victoria were limited, and she worked as executive secretary for Frels' Theaters. Her mother remarried when Cason was eight, and they moved to a barren new subdivision that Cason considered considerably less civilized than her grandmother's home. Cason's stepfather was abusive, and that marriage was also brief.[5]

Sandra Cason led two lives in Victoria. Her public persona was that of a bright, outgoing, popular young woman who seemed to share her community's values. She was her Girl Scout troop's president and at age twelve—at her request—she was baptized into the local Presbyterian church. After enrolling in Victoria Junior College in the fall of 1955, she was a Pirate Belle (one of the most popular women in her class), a member of the honor society Phi Theta Kappa, student council secretary, and president of the college's Westminster Fellowship, a Presbyterian group.[6] One of her classmates came from one of Victoria's oldest and wealthiest families, and Cason's friend invited her to elegant dinner parties and included her as a member of the "house party" when her friend was honored at the Victoria Country Club.[7]

But even in her teens, Cason felt that she was an outsider in her community. Her mother was divorced—twice—at a time when divorce was uncommon and stigmatized. Eula Weisiger Cason was a nonconformist who smoked cigarettes, criticized gendered pay discrimination, and befriended a Mexican American male coworker, behavior considered inappropriate for a white woman in a segregated small town in the 1950s.[8] Raised by her mother to be color-blind, Cason did not realize that segregation was based on law until she read about the Supreme Court's 1954 *Brown* decision in a high school journalism class. She voiced her outrage that Jim Crow laws regulated her associations but then realized that her white classmates were staring at her disapprovingly. She became a Victoria Junior College student the year after the school desegregated and went out of her way to be friendly with the African American woman who integrated it.[9]

This incident contributed to Cason's growing conviction that society "was trapped in a lie" and that something was fundamentally wrong with a social system based on dishonesty. Believing what she had learned in school—that Americans were free and equal—she became disaffected as the disjunction between what she had been taught and how people actually interacted became apparent: whites treated nonwhites as inferior beings, men regarded women as subordinates, and affluent whites considered themselves superior to other social classes.[10]

Although New Left activists have been portrayed as spoiled rich kids, this was not true of Sandra Cason. As a result of her grandfather's illness and her mother's divorces, the family was experiencing downward mobility when she was growing up. Since her mother supported Cason and her stepsister on a secretary's salary, the family lived frugally. Cason wore homemade dresses to church as a child and worked as a teenager and after she enrolled at the University of Texas. When the *Victoria Advocate* reported on the 1956 summer activities of college students from Victoria, Sandra Cason was working in the Sears, Roebuck, and Company credit department, a stark contrast to the leisure activities of the students from wealthy families.[11]

Cason was already critical of her society's racial and gender systems when she enrolled at the University of Texas (UT) in September 1957, but her discontent increased as a result of her involvement in the university YWCA, where she flourished. She became its student vice president and during the 1960–61 term was one of the two student representatives on the board of directors.[12] She became a regional and later a national Y officer and chaired the study group on peace and disarmament at the 1958–59 National Student Assembly of the Ys. Through the Y she was introduced to a nonhierarchical, consensus-building, gender-neutral decision-making system in which all committees had female and male cochairs, a very rare practice at the time.[13]

The Y also strengthened Cason's doubts about racial segregation and was the first institution that led her into radical politics.[14] UT students active in desegregation efforts remembered her as the "driving force in their group," taking the initiative in organizing protests.[15] The Y's southern region's racially integrated meetings provided Cason with her first personal experience with how black students felt about segregation.[16] The 1958–59 national student Y meeting culminated with a civil rights rally in which Cason and the other delegates—black and white—joined hands while singing civil rights songs such as "We Shall Overcome."[17] After returning to Austin, Cason used her positions as cochair of the university Y's Race Relations Committee and chair of the University Religious Council's Social Action Committee to help organize a campaign to desegregate restaurants near the UT campus nearly a year prior to the Greensboro, North Carolina, sit-ins that are credited with starting the 1960s civil rights movement. The UT students tried to secure integration through negotiation, but when that approach failed, an integrated group of students would sit down in a restaurant and request service. They left when asked, but the white students would leave a card stating that they would patronize the restaurant even if it were integrated. They later moved on to picketing some restaurants that refused to serve African American students.[18] This pressure contributed to the desegregation of more than thirty Austin lunch counters and cafes by May 1960.

Unhappy living in an all-white university dormitory, Cason and her roommate, Dorothy Dawson, moved early in 1958 into the Christian Faith and Life Community, an independent Christian lay community a few blocks from campus.[19] This move was a significant statement about their racial views because Christian Faith and Life provided integrated housing at a time when university accommodations remained segregated. (UT allowed black graduate students to enroll in 1955 and admitted undergraduates the following year, but most facilities, including university housing, remained segregated.) Cason remembered her friendships with blacks living in the community as critical to the development of her racial views.[20] Her loyalty to her African American friends made her more aware of the ways in which segregation imposed restrictions on whites as well as blacks since she could not go to movies or eat in restaurants with them.

The Christian Faith and Life Community did more to shape Cason's intellectual development and transform her into an activist than the university's curriculum. She remembered the community as a "Christian existentialist commune."[21] It provided small "intensely confrontational" seminars on liberal theologians such as Rudolf Bultmann that were more challenging than any of her university courses.[22] The clergy there introduced students to a blend of Social Gospel and existentialist theology that insisted that being Christian meant recognizing that all humans—white and nonwhite—were equal in God's eyes and accepting responsibility for helping the disadvantaged.[23]

Albert Camus's life and thought provided a crucial source of inspiration for 1960s New Left activists, and Cason began the serious study of his writings while at the Faith and Life Community.[24] She found Camus relevant because his central concern involved how to lead an authentic life and because he believed that humans give meaning to their lives through action against injustice. But what really caught her attention—and remained integral to her thinking—was his insistence that such action was even more meaningful when undertaken without expectation of success, since doing so acknowledged that action derived its moral value from resisting oppression rather than from eliminating the injustice.[25]

Cason graduated from the University of Texas ampla cum laude in May 1959 with a bachelor's degree in English, but with the YWCA's assistance, she continued her interracial work that summer. She taught vacation Bible school at the East Harlem Protestant Parish in New York City and read works by African American author James Baldwin while living in an African American neighborhood on New York City's worst block. Kept awake at night by rats in the walls, during the day she walked through piles of broken glass that topped her shoes. This encounter with extreme poverty was the second of the two early experiences most important in leading her into radical politics.[26]

Unable to obtain the financial assistance she needed to enroll in Yale Divinity School, Cason returned to UT in the fall of 1959 as a graduate student in English and philosophy with a teaching assistantship in English.[27] In the spring of 1960, when the sit-in movement spread across the South, Cason attended the Austin movement's meetings with her African American friends from the Christian Faith and Life Community and joined them in picketing businesses that refused to serve blacks. Thus, when Constance Curry came to Austin that spring to recruit students for the Southern Student Human Relations seminar run by the National Student Association (NSA), Cason was already a participant in the movement and eager to begin the new life that was opening up to her.[28]

Cason was among fifteen student leaders invited to participate in the NSA's August 1960 seminar at the University of Minnesota. It brought together black and white students from southern colleges for three weeks of studying racial prejudice and methods—such as the recent sit-ins—that could be used to further integration in the South.[29] Through the seminar, Cason became friends with some of the sit-in leaders, including Chuck McDew, who became SNCC's chair later that year.

Cason attended the NSA's national congress in Minneapolis immediately following the seminar and attracted national attention when she persuaded the NSA to endorse the sit-ins. Tom Hayden remembered Cason as a "charismatic" speaker, as she demonstrated in her presentation to the congress. The NSA was forced to confront the sit-in issue when a SNCC delegation asked the group to support the protests. Although initially hostile to the proposal, NSA delegates created a panel of four southern white students, including Cason, to respond to SNCC's request in a special session. The first three panel members opposed it, claiming that the sit-ins violated state law.

Cason—then only twenty-two and speaking with "a southern voice so soft it would not startle a boll weevil"—portrayed the sit-ins as an ethical issue.[30] She noted that while the protests might break state law, these laws had been established to enforce the segregationist beliefs of communities practicing racial discrimination and thus violating the Fourteenth Amendment. The fundamental question, Cason explained, was whether people should continue to give lip service to ending segregation while condemning the nonviolent action that had drawn attention to the wrongness of discrimination. She presented the issue as an opportunity for the students to transform themselves through moral action: "If I had known that not a single lunch counter would open as a result of my action, I could not have done differently than I did."[31]

Cason concluded by reiterating the exchange between Henry David Thoreau, jailed in 1846 for refusing to pay his poll tax to a government that supported slavery, and Ralph Waldo Emerson when he visited Thoreau in jail. When Emerson asked Thoreau what he was doing in there, Thoreau replied, "Ralph Waldo, what are you doing out *there*?" Cason paused and then quietly asked her audience, "What are *you* doing out there?"[32]

When she finished, the delegates remained silent for a moment, and Cason braced for rejection. Instead, she received a standing ovation from the audience, many of whose members were in tears, and the delegates endorsed the sit-ins by a vote of 305 to 37.[33] Cason's speech was a turning point in the NSA's emergence as a significant and continuing supporter of the civil rights movement.[34]

Al Haber, SDS president, and Tom Hayden, a future SDS president, were among those in the audience who were deeply moved by Cason's speech. Haber was eager to recruit new members, and Cason's appeal was obvious: she was intelligent, articulate, enthusiastic, and attractive. Both Cason and Haber were members of NSA's Liberal Study Group (which Haber had created in part to help recruit students into SDS), and Cason remembered being "scooped up" by Haber and through him becoming one of SDS's early members.[35] She loved the excitement and "edginess" of her new friends; the men were "sexier, sharper," and more articulate than those she had known through the Y.[36]

Cason's speech also helped draw Hayden, the editor of the University of Michigan's student newspaper, into the student movement. Hayden, who was not yet an SDS member, noticed that the delegates considered Cason a person of great authority because she had been a leader of the Austin sit-ins and because she had the "ability to think morally [and] express herself poetically."[37] Her stirring appeal to become involved helped him decide to become an activist. Their relationship deepened during the following months as Tom thought about her constantly and realized that he "idolized" her.[38]

After the NSA congress, Cason returned to the University of Texas and became even more deeply involved in the civil rights movement. She was invited to present a workshop on school integration at the October 1960 Atlanta conference at which SNCC was officially established. Cason considered the conference a "transforming experience."[39] She met Ella Baker, the "mother" of sNcc, who became one of Cason's most important mentors, the person to whom she turned years later when she was going through some emotionally rough times.[40] Baker trained several women, including Cason, who helped bring the women's liberation movement into existence, and Cason traced the roots of that movement back to Baker.[41] Baker was responsible for Cason's perception of sNcc as a "womanist" organization: "nurturing, warm, familial, supportive, honest . . . radical and pragmatic."[42] sNcc's original guiding principle was that "through nonviolence, courage displaces fear; love transforms hate."[43] James Lawson's keynote speech, which had everyone "on their feet and in tears," converted Cason to sNcc's philosophy of nonviolence as not just a tactic to undermine segregation but a way of life that freed practitioners from individual ego and gender, class, and racial restrictions so that they became equal members of the beloved community.[44]

Following the sNcc conference, Cason became a catalyst for the movement to desegregate the University of Texas and businesses adjacent to the campus. The other Y activists considered her the group's key leader: she was dynamic and both intellectually and tactically aggressive.[45] She used her position as the chair of the ut student government's Human Relations Committee to meet with ut president Harry Ransom in November to urge that campus housing be desegregated and to encourage faculty groups to become involved.[46] Her commitment to reform energized those around her. According to Ronnie Dugger, the *Texas Observer*'s editor, when Cason joined his group of Texas liberals at Scholz's beer garden, her arrival would transform "a whole group of beer-guzzling louts into a convocation of . . . sturdy Utopians" earnestly debating how best to reform society.[47]

Since the nsa's Minneapolis seminar, Cason had been thinking that ut needed a more effective student organization directing the desegregation effort, and in November 1960 she was primarily responsible for forming Students for Direct Action (sDA).[48] Cason coordinated the meeting of about twenty-five student organizations at which sDA was established and secured sNcc's support for the new group's theater stand-ins.[49] Over the next six months, sDA mobilized from forty to two hundred students two or three nights each week for theater stand-ins: white participants would ask at the ticket window if all citizens were being admitted; when told no, they would reply that they preferred to wait until everyone could attend and would go to the back of the line and repeat the process.[50]

Although the ut Student Assembly endorsed the peaceful protests, some white students were violently opposed. While Cason and other sDA leaders were meeting at the YMCA-YWCA on November 29, a bomb was thrown into the building. The Austin police reported that several students might have been killed if it had blown up in the meeting room, but it went off under a stairwell and did not harm anyone.[51]

Because the theaters were part of national chains, local managers claimed that only the national management could decide to integrate. In response, the SDA leaders began pressuring the theaters' national directors. They started by seeking national backing for their proposal to hold stand-ins in segregated chain theaters all over the country on Lincoln's birthday, February 12. During the Christmas holiday, Cason met with the NSA's executive committee and convinced it to sanction the stand-ins at all U.S. theater chains practicing segregation.[52] Cason also persuaded former NSA president Allard Lowenstein to seek Eleanor Roosevelt's support for the stand-ins. Shortly thereafter, Roosevelt endorsed the UT student efforts in her nationally syndicated "My Day" column and sent a telegram to Cason that read, "I admire so much the stand which the students at The University of Texas have taken."[53] After discovering that the same corporation that owned one of the segregated theaters also owned ABC-TV, Cason (with SNCC's assistance) persuaded SNCC's New York supporters to stage a sit-in at ABC's Manhattan corporate headquarters. Held on June 5, 1961, that protest drew media attention to the corporation's policy, increasing the pressure on its directors to authorize desegregation.[54] The stand-ins and other forms of pressure continued until the movie theaters desegregated later in 1961.

During this period, Cason gained national attention as a student leader; she was included, for example, in a *New York Times* feature story on the national student movement.[55] Civil rights activists Anne and Carl Braden wanted her to direct a project to recruit southern white students to join blacks in the civil rights campaign.[56] Cason thought the Bradens' plan was a wonderful idea, but even though Carl came to Austin to try to persuade her to accept the position, she declined, since she would lose the teaching assistantship that was enabling her to work toward her master's degree.[57]

During the fall of 1960, Tom Hayden's infatuation with Cason intensified, and by the following spring he had begun exploring the possibility of marriage. Having experienced her mother's two unhappy marriages, Cason was originally skeptical, but she withdrew from graduate school during the 1961 spring term— only a few months short of completing her master's degree—and accepted a position as the University of Illinois YWCA's campus program director to be closer to him. She did not abandon her commitment to civil rights, however. She joined a demonstration against hiring discrimination in front of the local

J. C. Penney store and was brought before the YWCA's executive committee, which did not think it dignified for a Y program director to walk a picket line. Cason responded with a discussion of human dignity that caused the committee to decline to reprimand her and instead to recommend that the Y send a delegation to talk to the store's manager about its employment policies.[58]

During the summer of 1961, Cason lived with Hayden in New York City so that they could be closer to the SDS and NSA national offices. The gender divisions in SDS that later became a source of conflict were already apparent. Although Todd Gitlin (SDS president in 1963) remembered Cason as a "revered founding mother of SDS," she spent the summer in SDS's national office typing its entire mailing list onto stencils while the men discussed strategy.[59]

Recent studies of SDS have acknowledged the role of sexism in its decline and in the "terrible waste" of Cason and its other talented female members.[60] This sexism is reflected in several early histories of SDS that identify Cason merely as Hayden's spouse, implying that she derived her importance from him.[61] This viewpoint is misleading for several reasons. Haber had recruited Cason into his small circle of activists before Hayden joined SDS, and they worked together on several projects between August 1960 and December 1961. During this period, Haber was attempting to transform SDS from a tiny student group into one that could provide leadership for the New Left and believed that focusing on civil rights would help accomplish this change.[62] But to have credibility, he needed someone who had participated in the southern civil rights movement and could write movingly about it. Fortunately he had such a person—Sandra Cason—in SDS's New York office. Drawing on Cason's firsthand knowledge, the two of them coauthored working papers on the civil rights movement during the summer of 1961 that Haber's Liberal Study Group used to strengthen NSA support for civil rights at the 1961 NSA congress and to recruit students into SDS.[63] Haber and Cason also coauthored the memorandum requesting financial support for a plan to affiliate SDS with SNCC's Mississippi voter registration project.[64] Thus, by the early fall of 1961—before her marriage to Hayden—Cason had already become a key contributor to Haber's efforts to build SDS into a national organization.

Sandra Cason and Tom Hayden married on October 1, 1961, in the Christian Faith and Life Community's open-air chapel in Austin. The ceremony included a passage from Camus committing the couple to engage in moral action: "I, on the other hand, choose justice in order to remain faithful to the world."[65] The guests constituted a virtual who's who of the Texas and national New Left: Vivien Franklin (an SDA leader), Dorothy Dawson (maid of honor and national SDS member), Robb Burlage (editor of the *Daily Texan*), Ronnie Dugger, Haber (best man), and Michael Harrington (whose book, *The Other America*, placed poverty on the national political agenda).[66] The postwedding celebration included political discussions late into the night that have been portrayed as the origin of the following summer's Port Huron Conference, which marked SDS's real beginning.[67]

Immediately following their wedding, Tom and Sandra (now known as Casey Hayden) drove to Atlanta, where Baker had hired Casey to be a campus traveler for the National Student YWCA Special Project in Human Relations. The job involved traveling to southern college campuses to conduct integrated race relations workshops. Since integrated meetings were illegal, they were organized secretly on white campuses. They undermined segregation on a personal level by facilitating interracial friendships that enabled white students to escape from the "cage of race."[68] Bob Zellner, the first white southerner to become a SNCC field secretary, described Casey during this period as "funny . . . open and loving" and as combining "impeccable manners, gentleness, and a fierce understanding of what was right."[69]

After the Supreme Court reaffirmed that segregated facilities in interstate travel were unconstitutional in the 1960 *Boynton v. Virginia* decision, civil rights groups conducted a series of integrated Freedom Rides to force the federal government to enforce that decision. Casey and Tom participated in the SNCC Freedom Ride from Atlanta to Albany, Georgia, on December 10, 1961. Casey had two roles. She was the mentor for young white women such as Joan Browning who worried because participants in some earlier rides had been brutally beaten. Browning overcame her fears in part because she felt confident that Casey "had the savvy, toughness and caring to do whatever needed to be done" if a crisis arose.[70] Casey's second role was that of the undercover observer (each Freedom Ride had one person who avoided arrest to report what had happened to SNCC, the press, and law enforcement), but Tom was among those arrested. When the trial was held, SNCC leader Charles Sherrod seated himself in the courtroom's white section as a challenge to the segregation system, but the police immediately dragged him from the room. Casey and Tom responded by sitting on the courtroom's African American side. Both were quickly seized by the police and ejected from the courtroom, although Casey hooked her legs under the bench so that the officers had to pry her out sideways to remove her.[71]

After Tom was released from jail, he and Casey went to Ann Arbor, Michigan, for an SDS conference that was a turning point in its emergence as the cornerstone of the New Left. Although SDS had only about six hundred dues-paying members at that point, Haber envisioned a much larger organization. About forty-five activists joined Casey and Tom on December 29–31 to plan the group's transformation. As a step in this direction, Tom was asked to draft the manifesto that became known as the Port Huron Statement. At the conference, SDS also created its first national executive committee, and Sandra Cason Hayden was appointed to it.[72] She was a logical choice because in addition to her previous work with Haber, she was one of the South's leading student activists and was viewed as SNCC's representative on the committee.[73]

The conference concluded with a New Year's Eve party that prefigured the subsequent development of gender relations within SDS. One of the meeting's explicit purposes had been "to extend . . . our personal ties" to create a sense of community within SDS. On New Year's Eve, the men continued their discussion while the women went upstairs and set up food and drink for a party. The women were concerned because the SDS leaders were replicating the traditional gender roles that the women were attempting to eradicate. When the men continued their debate as midnight approached, Casey led the women downstairs and insisted that the men stop and come up for the party. Tom, SDS's president, became angry and insisted that the discussion was more important than a party.[74]

This confrontation was significant on several levels. First, it reflected the women's understanding that social relationships were important in developing a strong organization. In this context, the party was not simply an occasion for fun but was an important step in building the personal ties to which SDS was committed. Second, it suggests that SDS women were developing a gender consciousness. While they were upstairs, the women analyzed the situation in a way that Mickey Flacks, one of the participants, believed "provided the earliest ideology of the women's [liberation] movement."[75] While the women lacked the language to explain why the personal was political, they were beginning to articulate the concept among themselves.

SDS aspired to provide a theoretical basis for the New Left, and its manifesto, the Port Huron Statement, became one of the decade's most important political documents. Although Tom was its official author, Casey read and critiqued all of his drafts.[76] Her assistance in shaping the document is not surprising since she had been an English and philosophy major at UT and had practiced participatory democracy in SNCC. Tom claimed that Camus and C. Wright Mills (professor of sociology at Columbia University and one of the most influential radical social theorists in the post–World War II United States) had the strongest influence on him and Casey while he was writing the Port Huron Statement, but his admission that Casey introduced him to Camus's essays has been overlooked.[77]

In addition to assisting Tom with the conference's manifesto, Casey was also the official convention coordinator. In that role, she and Haber invited Arnold

Kaufman, a University of Michigan political philosopher, to be the meeting's featured speaker. Kaufman was asked to talk on "The Intellectual Foundations of the Left" and—apparently at Casey's request—was urged to include radical Christianity in his presentation as well as Marxist and Enlightenment ideas.[78]

Participants at the June 1962 Port Huron Conference remembered Casey as having played a significant part in the meeting.[79] She contributed to it in several ways. Most of the conference was spent discussing Tom's draft document. Having vetted it before it was presented to the group, Casey endorsed it, with one important exception. Tom's original version proclaimed, "We regard Man as . . . infinitely perfectible."[80] Casey considered this naively optimistic: she saw no arrival of the millennium or any other way to escape the human condition. Rather than viewing humans as inevitably progressing toward greater freedom, she saw the human condition in Camus's terms—"Sisyphus [eternally] pushing the rock up the hill, and [then] it rolls back down."[81] This suggests that Casey not only held a more realistic view of human nature than Tom but also had a deeper understanding of Camus's ideas. After others raised similar objections, the conference revised the document.

Casey was also concerned that the participants develop the sense of community "rooted in love" that the Port Huron Statement urged for American society. Given the acrimonious debates over the manifesto's wording, some form of bonding was needed. Casey encouraged this feeling by leading the participants in singing African American folk songs associated with the civil rights movement, such as "Keep Your Eyes on the Prize," late into the night.[82]

Following the Port Huron conference, Casey and Tom moved to Ann Arbor, where Casey joined the local branch of Women Strike for Peace (WSP). She shared the group's conviction that women had a special interest in peace, and during the October 1962 Cuban Missile Crisis, she and Tom drove to Washington, D.C., to protest the imminent danger of nuclear war.[83] Casey felt at home in the WSP because its "Quaker-like speaking from the heart" reminded her of SNCC and the YWCA and because its members were committed to "speaking truth to power."[84] The Ann Arbor branch's distinctive leadership style was also appealing. Instead of a hierarchical structure, the members viewed themselves as a circle; decision making flowed around the circle but never from the top down, as in most men's organizations. Casey and Mickey Flacks, who belonged to both WSP and SDS, were impressed with the WSP's shared leadership; the disparity between it and SDS's gendered system contributed to their increasing discontent with the latter.[85]

But in other respects, Ann Arbor was not a good fit for Casey. Despite having a college degree and having held several responsible positions elsewhere, the only job she could find to support herself and Tom was a secretarial position at Ann Arbor's Presbyterian church.[86] With Tom now SDS's president, his office in their basement became the SDS headquarters. In contrast to SNCC's action-oriented culture, SDS meetings usually involved intense discussions that too often seemed to Casey like intellectual posturing by young males. Despite her background in philosophy, Casey felt alienated by this style and on at least one occasion withdrew from the meeting after announcing, "I seriously believe y'all are discussing bullshit."[87]

She was also concerned about SDS's pattern of gender relations, which differed significantly from SNCC's. Black women held leadership roles in SNCC, whereas the women in SDS lacked authority. This phenomenon stemmed in part from SDS's internal culture, which disadvantaged women: it was more competitive and based on a debate model. SNCC, in contrast, attached greater value to relationship building.[88] Despite SDS's commitment to participatory democracy, men often ignored women's comments during meetings, as if small children had spoken during a discussion among adults.[89] Casey had less difficulty in being taken seriously than the other women because she was very articulate and because the men granted her special respect as a consequence of her participation in the civil rights movement.[90] Some women viewed Casey as one of the members of SDS's inner circle whose voices mattered; in that respect, she seemed to them "to be one of the boys."[91] But even when Casey did not feel personally disrespected, she empathized with the women who were. She often dealt with this situation by inviting the women upstairs to talk about their lives, thus initiating what later became known as consciousness-raising sessions.[92]

The gender tensions within SDS reflected different views about how to build a movement. Although they lacked the language to explain that "the personal is political" (the idea that personal relationships have political significance), SDS women believed that creating a successful movement started with establishing strong interpersonal relationships among the organization's members.[93] The SDS male members, including Tom Hayden, tended to view personal relationships as separate from and unrelated to building a political movement. This conflicting vision contributed to the end of Casey and Tom's marriage. Casey considered her marriage to have replaced SNCC as her life's "central covenant community."[94] In the early spring of 1963, after Tom had an extramarital affair, a brokenhearted Casey moved back to Atlanta; after an attempted reconciliation failed, their divorce became final in 1965.

While living in Atlanta, Casey Hayden shared an apartment in a black neighborhood with another white woman, Mary King, a Methodist minister's daughter working for SNCC, and the two began reading and discussing prominent feminist authors in addition to Camus.[95] Although Hayden had had serious discussions about gender with Dorothy Dawson in Austin, SDS's treatment of women and the breakdown of her marriage prompted her to resume her reading and reflection on gender issues. Hayden read Betty Friedan's *The Feminine Mystique* but found its preoccupation with suburban white women irrelevant to the problems southern black and working-class women faced.[96] Hayden found the writings of left-wing European women such as Simone de Beauvoir and Doris Lessing especially valuable because they articulated her experience "as a free woman in an enchained culture."[97] Reading de Beauvoir sharpened Hayden's perception that women's roles were not biologically based but socially constructed and that the assumption of male superiority condemned women, regardless of class, to a separate and subordinate caste.[98]

Although impressed by de Beauvoir, Hayden really "loved" Lessing's *The Golden Notebook* because it "mirrored" her own life. Lessing, a white woman, grew up in segregated Rhodesia and joined left-wing groups that fought against apartheid. Hayden found Lessing's book "enormously supportive" for several reasons. It portrayed a woman on the left who demonstrated a "new level of honesty" in relations between women. Lessing also emphasized the personal relationships between men and women that Hayden thought central to building the New Left movement.[99]

When Hayden returned to Atlanta, SNCC was evolving from a small organization requiring little funding to a much larger one that was undertaking expensive voter registration projects in several southern states. Needing someone with contacts among northern liberals who could raise funds and recruit volunteers, James Foreman, SNCC's executive secretary, appointed Hayden to the new position of northern coordinator. Hayden was a perfect fit for the job. She had been trained by the YWCA to organize and administer programs, had personal experience with a northern campus, and through her work with the YWCA, NSA, and SDS had a very wide range of contacts with the kind of students likely to support SNCC.

SNCC had already developed Friends of SNCC organizations on a few northern campuses, but Hayden expanded this effort into a national Friends of SNCC program. Despite being squeezed into a tiny office between Foreman and communications director Julian Bond in SNCC's headquarters, Hayden loved being part of SNCC. She later recalled that she had "never felt so empowered" as she did during these early years in SNCC because the organization was like an egalitarian family whose members shed society's race, class, and gender restrictions when interacting with each other.[100] SNCC was distinctive because "we simply dropped race. [It was] like we'd died and gone to heaven, and it was integrated there."[101] The result was a euphoric sense of being part of the only completely free community in a country in which race, class, and gender identities normally shaped—and restricted—interactions among people.[102]

SNCC's commitment to gender equality was unusual, however, even within the civil rights movement. The male civil rights leaders who planned the August 1963 March on Washington proposed that men and women march separately and that only male speakers address the Lincoln Memorial rally. When the planning committee's sole female member, Anna Hedgeman, initiated a behind-the-scenes women's protest against the sexist arrangements, Hayden joined Pauli Murray and others in objecting to the men's plan. Although the march remained gender segregated—Hayden and the other women proceeded unnoticed on Independence Avenue while the media recorded the men marching down Constitution Avenue, a few women were allowed to sit on the platform, and Daisy Bates, who had been instrumental in the integration of Little Rock's Central High School in 1957, was permitted to speak briefly.[103]

Hayden was one of the first white female SNCC staffers to work in Mississippi. Invited by Bob Moses, SNCC's Mississippi state leader, she began working in October 1963 on a SNCC project in Tougaloo, helping illiterate black adults learn to read. Hayden and her coworkers lived in what became known as the Literacy House, located across from Tougaloo College in an all-black community outside of Jackson. SNCC and other civil rights organizations were initiating a voter registration drive, and it would require a major literacy effort since many African Americans lacked formal education.

Shortly after she arrived, Hayden wrote exuberantly to Howard Zinn, a member of SNCC's national executive committee and one of its senior advisers, "These are beautiful people down here," referring to the black population's courage in rebelling against segregation in one of the South's most repressive states.[104] To Mary King, however, Hayden was frank about the probability of success: "We won't ever really win down here, but a few people are changed and their lives are richer because they see that it's worth fighting to change things." Echoing Camus's conviction that what is important is the personal transformation resulting from the refusal to collaborate with an unjust system, she insisted that this "makes all the difference."[105]

However, Hayden soon developed reservations about her role in the literacy project. Adult African Americans often felt ashamed of being unable to read, and having a white person helping them reinforced images of white superiority that Hayden wished to undermine. When the literacy project moved to Harlem in the spring of 1964, she began working with the SNCC staff who were preparing for the Mississippi Freedom Summer campaign.[106]

Most of SNCC's Mississippi activists originally opposed the Freedom Summer project and agreed to it only when Moses insisted.[107] Hayden shared their concern that a large influx of northern white students would lead to increased violence, and she urged organizers to limit the number of volunteers to at most five hundred.[108] But Moses persuaded SNCC to recruit large numbers of student volunteers, and more than one thousand students, most of them white, came to Mississippi in the summer of 1964 to teach in the Freedom Schools and help with black voter registration.[109]

Hayden and Ella Baker were members of the five-person committee that planned the Freedom Summer project.[110] Hayden and the other committee members, sent out recruiting material to northern universities, established guidelines for recruiting the volunteers, set up a training school for them in Oxford, Ohio, and helped train the first group of volunteers when they arrived in June.[111] She was also one of three women primarily responsible for drafting the Freedom Schools' curriculum.[112]

Hayden was among the SNCC staffers who visited northern college campuses during the winter and spring of 1964 to recruit students. Heather Tobis, a University of Chicago freshman when Hayden spoke there, thought she was an incredibly effective recruiter. Although Hayden was explicit about the danger, she conveyed such a powerful conviction of the cause's moral righteousness and a sense that the volunteers would be helping to make history that according to Tobis, "She just swept us up in her enthusiasm. . . . This is what we had to do."[113]

During the Mississippi Freedom Summer, Hayden worked in the headquarters of the Council of Federated Organizations (COFO) in Jackson. SNCC, the Congress of Racial Equality (CORE), and the National Association for the Advancement of Colored People (NAACP) had jointly formed COFO to coordinate the Mississippi voter registration project. Hayden was among the SNCC staff who went to Oxford in June to train the first student volunteers. It was an emotionally intense experience, since the staff had to tell the students that they would likely be beaten, that they faced the threat of death, and that they could not expect the federal government to protect them. Unsurprisingly, when the staff returned to Jackson, they were "very tired and edgy."[114]

The staff members were even more on edge when three activists disappeared on their second day in Mississippi. Hayden was in COFO's Jackson office on June 21, 1964, when word arrived that Andrew Goodman, a summer volunteer, and two CORE staff members, Michael Schwerner and James Cheney, were missing. Although the activists had anticipated violence, they were stunned at how quickly it happened. Convinced that the young men had been killed, Hayden immediately called Bob Moses at the Ohio training school and warned him, "You have to tell [the volunteers] to be very careful."[115] But even as she spoke, she realized that warnings were futile; the volunteers were in danger no matter how careful they were, and the staff could do nothing to ensure their safety. During the following weeks, the COFO staff stayed by the office's phones twenty-four hours a day, chain-smoking and napping on desks when necessary, hoping for news about their three fellow workers. Their bodies were discovered in August.[116]

Voter registration, the Freedom Summer project's cornerstone, would not be meaningful unless African Americans actually participated in the political process. Once blacks had registered, they would need to attempt to participate in Democratic Party precinct meetings, from which African Americans were generally barred. Hayden spearheaded preparations for this effort.[117] She and others drafted instructions identifying when and where the precinct meetings were scheduled to be held, the rules of parliamentary procedure (in case the African Americans were admitted), how to respond if they encountered violence, and how to conduct separate meetings if access to regular party meetings was denied.[118] As expected, most of the precinct meetings refused to admit African Americans. COFO then organized the Mississippi Freedom Democratic Party (MFDP)—open to blacks and whites—to challenge the segregated party's claim to represent Mississippi at the national Democratic Party convention.

Hayden was one of the program coordinators for the MFDP's convention challenge and considered it her most significant work in Mississippi.[119] Assigned by Moses to find out how to conduct a convention challenge, Hayden prepared recommendations that became the basis for the MFDP's strategy. She reported that gaining the support of the United Auto Workers was crucial not only because the union wielded influence with convention delegates but also because it would likely provide financing for an office to direct the lobbying effort during the convention. Since the issue might end up being decided by the convention delegates in a floor fight, Hayden urged the MFDP to solicit the assistance of Joseph Rauh, the auto workers' lead counsel, who would be the best person to handle floor strategy.[120]

The Democratic convention was held in Atlantic City, New Jersey, and Hayden traveled there ahead of time to help set up the MFDP's lobbying office.[121] When Tom Hayden arrived, he found Casey and other COFO leaders organizing a sophisticated presentation for the convention's credentials committee that offered a slight possibility that the MFDP's delegation might be seated.[122] Workers had gathered thousands of affidavits from Mississippi blacks describing their rejection—often violent—when they attempted to register to vote and to attend Democratic Party precinct meetings; the affidavits had then been placed in file cabinets on the convention floor, where they were accessible to the delegates.[123] While COFO leaders hoped that the credentials committee would seat the MFDP's delegation, they realized that a floor fight was more likely and that the documents describing the brutality against blacks might sway the convention delegates.

Several credentials committee members initially endorsed the MFDP's challenge, which should have ensured a convention floor debate. But fearful that the issue would weaken his election prospects by undermining his support among southern white voters, President Lyndon Baines Johnson exerted intense pressure to prevent the matter from reaching the floor. The committee offered the MFDP two at-large seats, but most of the new party's delegates considered this proposal a betrayal, since it accepted the segregated party's delegates as the legal delegation and thereby implicitly endorsed Jim Crow. Fannie Lou Hamer, who had been beaten for attempting to register to vote and was a cofounder of the MFDP, spoke for the MFDP's delegates in rejecting the offer: "We didn't come all this way for no two seats, 'cause all of us is tired!"[124] Casey Hayden never thought it very likely that the delegation would be seated but felt that a moral person should do the right thing even when there was little chance of success. She was proud of the members of the MFDP delegation for refusing to "buckle" and accept the offer, since, unlike the segregated party, they had been elected legitimately.[125]

The Democratic Party's rejection of the MFDP's challenge marked the end of innocence for those who had risked their lives to send an integrated delegation to the convention. The MFDP's supporters felt betrayed and embittered; Casey Hayden's description of the white liberal Democrats as "finks" was one of the mildest comments.[126]

The MFDP's convention rejection was a watershed in SNCC's development. Many of the group's activists believed that the Democrats' actions had demonstrated that voter registration work and allying with white liberals and the Democratic Party was pointless.[127] Moreover, the failure also undermined support for SNCC's core philosophical beliefs of nonviolence, integration, and reliance on moral suasion. Many black activists perceived it as proof that whites could not be trusted and therefore turned to black separatism. SNCC officially remained integrated for another two years, but the white staff began to feel unwanted: SNCC's beloved community was one of the convention's casualties.[128]

The convention challenge's rejection precipitated a crisis in SNCC. Its Waveland, Mississippi, conference in November 1964 was intended to resolve the issue of what to do next but instead turned into an acrimonious debate about SNCC's structure, its future plans, and the role of whites in the organization.

Since its formation, SNCC had been distinctive in having a decentralized decision-making structure, but at the Waveland conference, James Foreman urged the creation of a strong centralized executive. Casey Hayden was one of the spokespersons for those who resisted this radical change.[129] Although the discussion was couched in ostensibly gender-neutral terms, she realized that Foreman's proposal would shift power from grassroots groups in which women's voices were influential to a male hierarchy; Hayden perceived the underlying issue as feminism versus patriarchy.[130] The matter remained officially unresolved, but over the next few months, SNCC changed to a more hierarchical structure, lost its woman-friendly culture, and evolved from an integrated to a black separatist movement.

Hayden also coauthored the Waveland memo that is considered a watershed in the emergence of a new feminist consciousness that led to the formation of the women's liberation movement.[131] The document, however, was not the initial expression of a feminist consciousness within SNCC. During the spring of 1964, Mary King and other black and white female staff in SNCC's Atlanta headquarters staged a sit-in to protest the growth of sexism in the organization, and a feminist discussion group subsequently began holding meetings.[132] King moved into Literacy House in July, and the other women living there joined in her discussions with Hayden of women's issues.[133] These conversations spilled over into COFO's Jackson office, where they were overheard by a spy for the Mississippi State Sovereignty Commission, a state organization created to maintain racial segregation whose agents played a role in Goodman, Cheney, and Schwerner's deaths. The spy reported that the "strong females" in the office—including Emmie Schrader and Casey Hayden—were promoting a "revolution" involving "the women's fight for equality with men."[134]

But the Waveland memo was not written or even planned prior to the conference. Hayden and several others who had been involved in the Literacy House discussions drafted "The Position of Women in the Movement" spontaneously late one night at Waveland and submitted it for discussion. Both Hayden and King have stressed that they were not responding to personal experiences of gender discrimination in SNCC; rather, they were writing in support of other women who had such experiences.[135] Although they had read de Beauvoir's *The Second Sex*, they consciously avoided using her feminist conceptual framework because the idea of women's rights did not exist in the civil rights movement and terms such as *sexism* were not part of their vocabulary.[136] Instead, their approach—novel at the time—was to suggest an analogy between whites' treatment of blacks and men's treatment of women as a means of demonstrating that both involved discrimination.

The memo began with a list of specific examples of gender bias in SNCC to support the central theme that the subordination of women in SNCC was analogous to the subordination of African Americans in white society: "Assumptions of male superiority are as widespread and deep rooted and every much as crippling to the woman as the assumptions of white supremacy are to the Negro." Just as "Negroes" often endured attitudes of condescension and paternalism from whites, women experienced similar attitudes from SNCC males, and "it needs to be made know[n] that many women in the movement are not 'happy and contented' with their status." The crux of the matter was that women were crucial to the movement's day-to-day operations, but they did not have an equal voice in day-to-day decision making. While recognizing that men would probably feel too threatened by the issue to discuss it seriously, the authors concluded by expressing the hope that the memo would make women more conscious of the "day-to-day discriminations" and thereby begin the transformation of ideas about gender roles "so that all of us gradually come to understand that this is no more a man's world than it is a white world."[137]

Anticipating that the memo would be unwelcome, the authors submitted it anonymously. It was met with "crushing criticism," and the authors were "mocked and taunted" when they were identified.[138] Dona Richards and Jean Smith expressed approval, but most black women were unsympathetic, viewing it either as a diversion from the larger issues that needed to be dealt with or simply a white women's problem.

Although the memo has been portrayed as an angry denunciation of sexism among SNCC's male activists, King and Hayden have rejected that interpretation. Hayden insists that "we really didn't have that anger." Rather than an anti-male manifesto, "it was like we were having an argument with our brothers." The memo was intended to be an "internal education" document to inform SNCC men about the way sexism crept into gender relationships.[139]

Furthermore, the memo was not intended solely as a critique of sexism; it was also an attempt to counter SNCC's growing racial divisions by using gender issues as a means of uniting "the whole of the women in this movement"—that is, both black and white women—during the debate about SNCC's future structure.[140] Hayden and King both felt that SNCC had originally been like an egalitarian gender-neutral family in which women participated on a relatively equal basis but that it had changed and that the proposal for a hierarchical structure symbolized the abandonment of the earlier culture. In raising the question of women, King believed that she and Hayden were "broadening the debate in favor of a decentralized and manifestly democratic SNCC" rather than introducing a new and separate issue.[141] Hayden concurred, claiming that the memo was less about gender in the movement than "maintaining the radical nonviolent core of SNCC, our old womanist, integrationist way, in which leaders and power politics were disarmed."[142] The authors' underlying purpose in criticizing sexism thus was to use it as a means of drawing together SNCC's women in defense of the decentralized structure that had made SNCC a woman-friendly organization.

This attempt to use shared gender issues to strengthen the bonds between black and white women was unsuccessful. During the fall of 1964, white female SNCC activists increasingly felt unwelcome as the ideal of an integrated beloved community gave way to that of a black separatist movement. As racial feelings strengthened, white women were marginalized, but as a consequence of their whiteness rather than their gender. Many black female SNCC activists perceived the memo as a white women's attack on a black organization and responded with "indifference or antagonism."[143] Racial hostility within SNCC increased dramatically during the spring of 1965; white staff were told that they should go organize whites, and the cessation of friendly interracial relationships reinforced this message.

Hayden was emotionally devastated by her expulsion from SNCC. She felt conflicted, depressed, and "very lonely" because she had never perceived it as merely a civil rights organization: it had been "home and family, food and work, and a reason to live."[144] While SDS had shaped her politics, SNCC "had my heart."[145] No longer a part of SNCC's beloved community, Hayden felt adrift: "It was hard to go on."[146]

During the summer of 1965 Hayden, officially on loan from SNCC, worked with SDS's Economic Research and Action Project in Chicago's Uptown district, one of the city's poorest white neighborhoods, on a program called Jobs or Income Now. Since SDS had originally planned to organize unemployed young males, Hayden's proposal that women should organize women was both feminist and innovative. She also originated the strategy of organizing women welfare recipients—mainly Appalachian migrants—into a union to help them understand and defend their rights (anticipating the approach subsequently taken by the National Welfare Rights Organization).[147] She was so successful that the women staged a sit-in at the local welfare office to protest the arbitrary denial of a woman's payment, and Hayden earned the women's respect by joining the protest and then going to jail with them when they were arrested.[148]

Although training the women to handle the welfare bureaucracy was her original focus, Hayden eventually realized that gender conflicts were the project's main obstacle and that they had two dimensions. First, some of the welfare women's boyfriends—most of them unemployed street thugs—battered them and threatened the women with more violence if they associated with Hayden; they also threatened Hayden and her companion.[149] Second, the Economic Research and Action Project's women organizers had been discussing the sds men's sexist attitudes since the spring of 1965, and the discussions intensified after Hayden arrived.[150] The sds male organizers shared some of the street thugs' sexist assumptions and were trying to organize these men; activists did not want to jeopardize their efforts by objecting to how the thugs behaved toward women. By the end of the summer, Hayden had concluded that the Left would have to develop a feminist consciousness before projects such as the one in Chicago could succeed.[151]

The gender conflicts that Hayden witnessed in Chicago thus led directly to the second feminist essay that she and King coauthored, "Sex and Caste: A Kind of Memo." The Chicago experience sharpened Hayden's awareness of the difficulty of organizing women in a setting without a feminist consciousness and led her to resume thinking about recruiting other women for a collective effort to create that consciousness. At the end of the summer, she briefly went to Berkeley, writing the first draft of "Sex and Caste" on the train from Berkeley to a labor organizing workshop at the Highlander Folk School in Tennessee.[152] She and King wrote the final version in Virginia in November 1965. It differed from their previous memo in that it was written solely for women, critiqued women's subordinate position throughout society rather than in just one organization, insisted that personal relationships were political, and attempted to create a women's network to address women's issues.[153]

"Sex and Caste" was a watershed in women's history in part because it challenged the widespread assumptions that female subordination was the natural order of things and that personal relationships lacked political significance. The document began by noting that women have subordinate status both in public roles and in personal relationships with men and by insisting that the latter was no less important than the former. Since the term *gender system* was not available to them, the authors portrayed women as suffering from a sex caste system analogous to the racial caste system that subordinated blacks. These caste systems were similar in that both were socially constructed, although their defenders claimed that they were the inevitable result of biological differences. Efforts to explain this idea to men usually made them defensive, however, to the point that they sounded like "white segregationist[s] confronted with integration." The authors concluded that "the problems between men and women" and the difficulties women experienced in functioning in society as equal human beings were "among the most basic that people face," and they raised the possibility of a women's movement to address these concerns while accepting that most women would probably prefer to continue working on the problems of war, poverty, and race.[154]

They mailed the memo to forty-four women—black and white—in SNCC, SDS, the NSA, the Student Peace Union, and the Northern Student Movement.[155] It was not intended to provoke a rebellion; it was an attempt to sustain a sense of sisterhood among women activists, many of whom shared Hayden's feeling of floundering about, unsure of what to do next.[156] Hayden and King hoped that the memo would initiate conversations among movement women about issues that really mattered to them as women and thus maintain a sense of community "so we could all keep going together," but it was not intended to start a new organization.[157] It was sent to several African American women because the authors were deeply concerned about the rift that had developed between black and white movement women, and one of the memo's explicit objectives was to try to heal those divisions.[158]

Although black women generally ignored it, the memo triggered an immediate reaction among white women activists. Stunned at how clearly it articulated their grievances, women read and reread it until their original copies were almost illegible, and women's groups began forming to talk about it.[159] Many of the issues about which women felt deeply involved personal relationships with men, matters that had been considered private and therefore inappropriate for reform movements to consider. Readers found the memo radical and exciting because it challenged these fundamental gender assumptions. At SDS's December 1965 national conference, gender tensions escalated when the women insisted on holding a workshop—in effect, the first SDS women's caucus—to discuss the memo.[160] Women at the workshop were so shocked by the memo's perceptiveness that they read it aloud; it precipitated a three-day discussion about women in SDS and the personal humiliations many of them had experienced.[161] The SDS men's unwillingness to take gender issues seriously led to a full-scale rebellion by SDS women and to the emergence of the women's liberation movement in 1967.[162]

The "Sex and Caste" memo also contributed to a fundamental shift in the women's movement's ideology. Prior to the 1960s, most women's organizations believed that fairness for women meant treating them differently than men. But women in SNCC were convinced by their experience with the civil rights movement that fairness for all people, regardless of race or gender, required equal treatment. The "Sex and Caste" memo was not unique in the mid-1960s in urging equality for women, but it was distinctive in insisting that equal legal rights were insufficient; equality in personal relationships was also necessary to overcome women's traditional subordination in marriage and elsewhere.

The intellectual ferment generated by "Sex and Caste" and other sources transformed the women's movement's ideology from being difference-based to being rooted in the idea of equality.

After moving to New York City late in 1965, Hayden embraced the counterculture (which she considered a new form of the movement). She worked for the New York Department of Welfare for a couple of years before moving to a rural Vermont commune with other Mississippi movement veterans. She resumed reading Gandhi and other Eastern thinkers, became a Buddhist, taught yoga, and had two children with Donald Campbell Boyce III, a "yogi-carpenter" who helped Hayden and others establish the Integral Yoga Institute in San Francisco in 1970. Despite these efforts to find inner peace, the memory of her separation from SNCC remained so painful that not until 1988, when SNCC held a reunion at Trinity College in Connecticut (during which she cried all the way through her speech), did the "great healing" begin.[163] Since 1989, Hayden has lived in Tucson, Arizona. She is married to Paul Buckwalter, an Episcopal priest and community organizer; belongs to a Zen community; and remains active in the fight against racial and other forms of injustice.[164]

NOTES

1. Casey Hayden, preface to Mary King, *Freedom Song* (New York: Morrow, 1987), 9.

2. Casey Hayden, emails to author, September 7, 2009, June 15, 2010.

3. "Sheriff Weisiger Resigns Due to Failing Health," *Victoria Advocate*, May 14, 1936, 1.

4. R. S. Weisiger to Commissioners Court of Victoria, May 10, 1936, in *Victoria Advocate*, May 14, 1936; Sandra Cason, "Women's Consciousness and the Nonviolent Movement against Segregation, 1960–1965" (1989), 2, folder 10, box 26, Sally Belfrage Papers, Tamiment Library, New York University, New York.

5. Casey Hayden, "Fields of Blue," in *Deep in Our Hearts: Nine White Women in the Freedom Movement* (Athens: University of Georgia Press, 2000), 337; Tom Hayden, *Reunion: A Memoir* (New York: Random House, 1988), 48.

6. *The Pirate* (Victoria College Yearbook), 1956, 1957, Victoria Regional History Center, Victoria College Library, Victoria, Tex.

7. "Parties Held During Week in Honor of Miss Sue Lander," *Victoria Advocate*, December 25, 1955; "Afternoon Senior Tea Held for Miss Welder at Club," *Victoria Advocate*, February 14, 1955.

8. Casey Hayden, interview, 1988, in Margaret M. Braungart and R. G. Braungart, "The Life-Course Development of Left- and Right-Wing Youth Activist Leaders from the 1960s," *Political Psychology* 11 (1990): 259; Casey Hayden, "Doing the Work Up and Down" (manuscript), 14, in possession of the author.

9. Casey Hayden, email to author, September 4, 2009.

10. Casey Hayden, preface, 8.

11. Cason, "Women's Consciousness," 2; "College Set Returns for Summer Courses at University," *Victoria Advocate*, June 17, 1956.

12. Amanda Baxter, "Women Activists in the Civil Rights Movement at the University of Texas at Austin, 1954–1964" (senior honors paper, University of Texas at Austin, 1997), 23, Dolph Briscoe Center for American History, University of Texas at Austin.

13. Casey Hayden, "Fields of Blue," 338; Doug Rossinow, *The Politics of Authenticity* (New York: Columbia University Press, 1998), 102.

14. Casey Hayden, email to author, September 4, 2010.

15. Doug Rossinow, "'The Break-Through to New Life': Christianity and the Emergence of the New Left in Austin, Texas, 1956–1964," *American Quarterly* 46 (September 1994): 319.

16. Cason, "Women's Consciousness," 3.

17. Rossinow, "'Break-Through to New Life,'" 316.

18. Casey Hayden, email to author, February 25, 2010; Casey Hayden, interview, in Lynne Olson, *Freedom's Daughters: The Unsung Heroines of the Civil Rights Movement from 1830 to 1970* (New York: Simon and Schuster, 2001), 170.

19. Casey Hayden, email to author, July 12, 2010.

20. Casey Hayden, "Fields of Blue," 340.

21. Casey Hayden, interview, in *The Sixties at Forty: Leaders and Activists Remember and Look Forward*, ed. Ben Agger (Boulder, Colo.: Paradigm, 2009), 82.

22. Casey Hayden, interview, 1996, in Wesley C. Hogan, *Many Minds, One Heart: SNCC's Dream for a New America* (Chapel Hill: University of North Carolina Press, 2007), 97.

23. Casey Hayden, email to author, September 7, 2009; Rossinow, *Politics of Authenticity*, 75–76.

24. George Cotkin, *Existential America* (Baltimore: Johns Hopkins University Press, 2006), 226; Cason, "Women's Consciousness," 3.

25. Casey Hayden, interview, 1993, in Rossinow, *Politics of Authenticity*, 77.

26. Casey Hayden, "Fields of Blue," 338–39.

27. Casey Hayden, email to author, September 15, 2009.

28. Casey Hayden, "Fields of Blue," 340.

29. U.S. National Student Association, *Steps toward Equality: A Report on Desegregation in the United States* (Philadelphia: U.S. National Student Association, 1961), 31.

30. Don Morrison, "White Coed Backs Sit-Ins, Gets Ovation," *Minneapolis Morning Tribune*, August 26, 1960.

31. Sandra Cason, NSA speech, 1960, in *Women and the Civil Rights Movement, 1954–1965*, ed. Davis W. Houck and David E. Dixon (Jackson: University Press of Mississippi, 2009), 138.

32. Ibid.

33. U.S. National Student Association, *Steps toward Equality*, 32.

34. Don Morrison, "White Coed Backs Sit-Ins, Gets Ovation," *Minneapolis Morning Tribune*, August 26, 1960; Constance Curry, "Wild Geese to the Past," in *Deep in Our Hearts*, 18–19.

35. Casey Hayden, interview, in *Sixties*, ed. Agger, 82.

36. Casey Hayden, "Fields of Blue," 340.

37. Tom Hayden, *Rebel: A Personal History of the 1960s* (Los Angeles: Red Hen, 2003), 36.

38. Tom Hayden, *Reunion*, 42.

39. Casey Hayden, "Doing the Work," 4.

40. Casey Hayden, "Fields of Blue," 345.

41. Casey Hayden, "Ella Baker as I Knew Her: She Trusted Youth!," *Social Policy* 34 (Winter 2003–Spring 2004): 103; Carol Giardina, *Freedom for Women: Forging the Women's Liberation Movement, 1953–1970* (Gainesville: University Press of Florida, 2010), 29.

42. Casey Hayden, "Ella Baker," 101.

43. SNCC credo in James Miller, *Democracy Is in the Streets* (Cambridge: Harvard University Press, 1987), 50.

44. Casey Hayden, "Fields of Blue," 341–42; Casey Hayden, "SNCC Women and the Stirrings of Feminism," in *A Circle of Trust: Remembering SNCC*, ed. Cheryl L. Greenberg (New Brunswick, N.J.: Rutgers University Press, 1998), 133.

45. Rossinow, *Politics of Authenticity*, 102.

46. Casey Hayden, "Fields of Blue," 341; Baxter, "Women Activists," 36.

47. Ronnie Dugger, *Our Invaded Universities* (New York: Norton, 1974), 75.

48. Casey Hayden, emails to author, September 4, 2009, February 23, 2010.

49. Students for Direct Action to [SNCC Executive Committee], [December 1960], in Students for Direct Action, *The Student Nonviolent Coordinating Committee Papers, 1959–1972* (Sanford, N.C.: Microfilming Corporation of America, 1982), reel 44.

50. "Students Demonstrate against Texas Theater," *Texas Observer*, December 9, 1960.

51. "Integration Group Escapes 'Y' Bombing," *Daily Texan*, November 30, 1960; Dwonna N. Goldstone, *Integrating the Forty Acres: The Fifty-Year Struggle for Racial Equality at the University of Texas* (Athens: University of Georgia Press, 2006), 77.

52. "Stand-In Leaders Plan to Continue Demonstrations," *Daily Texan*, January 5, 1961; Martin Kuhlman, "Direct Action at the University of Texas during the Civil Rights Movement," in *The African American Experience in Texas*, ed. Bruce A. Glasrud and James Smallwood (Lubbock: Texas Tech University Press, 2007), 323.

53. Sandra Cason to Al Lowenstein, January 12, 1960, Allard K. Lowenstein Papers, box 6, Southern Historical Collection, University of North Carolina, Chapel Hill; "Stand-In Leaders Plan to Continue Demonstrations," *Daily Texan*, January 5, 1961.

54. Jack Newfield, *Somebody's Gotta Tell It: A Journalist's Life on the Lines* (New York: St. Martin's, 2003), 56; Gay Talese, "Sit-In Is Staged at A.B.C. Office," *New York Times*, June 6, 1961.

55. Nan Robertson, "Campuses Show New Interest in Political and Social Issues," *New York Times*, May 14, 1962.

56. Catherine Fosl, *Subversive Southerner: Anne Braden and the Struggle for Racial Justice in the Cold War South* (New York: Palgrave Macmillan, 2002), 254.

57. Anne Braden to Ella Baker, December 8, 1960, Carl and Anne Braden Papers, box 34, Wisconsin State Historical Society, Madison.

58. Casey, "Fields of Blue," 343.

59. Todd Gitlin, *The Sixties: Years of Hope, Days of Rage* (New York: Bantam, 1987), 369; Casey Hayden, interview, in *Sixties*, ed. Agger, 212.

60. David Barber, *A Hard Rain Fell: SDS and Why It Failed* (Jackson: University Press of Mississippi, 2008), 230.

61. Sara Evans, *Personal Politics: The Roots of Women's Liberation in the Civil Rights Movement and the New Left* (New York: Knopf, 1979), 112.

62. Kirkpatrick Sale, *SDS* (New York: Random House, 1973), 36.

63. See, for example, Al Haber and Sandra Cason, "Civil Rights in the North," [summer 1961], in *Americans for Democratic Action Papers, 1932–1965* (Sanford, N.C.: Microfilming Corporation of America, 1978), reel 139.

64. Al Haber and Sandra Cason, "Memo Re: Proposed Student Project in Voter Registration," August 3, 1961, cited in Miller, *Democracy Is in the Streets*, 70.

65. Sandra Cason and Tom Hayden wedding program, in possession of Casey Hayden.

66. "Miss Sandra Cason Weds Thomas Hayden in Austin," *Victoria Advocate*, October 8, 1961; Tom Hayden, *Reunion*, 52; Michael Harrington, *Fragments of the Century* (New York: Simon and Schuster, 1977), 142.

67. Rossinow, *Politics of Authenticity*, 136.

68. Casey Hayden, "Fields of Blue," 344–45.

69. Bob Zellner, *The Wrong Side of Murder Creek: A White Southerner in the Freedom Movement* (Montgomery, Ala.: New South, 2008), 142.

70. Joan C. Browning, "Shiloh Witness," in *Deep in Our Hearts*, 68.

71. Casey Hayden, "Fields of Blue," 347.

72. Sale, *SDS*, 40; SDS National Executive Committee Minutes, May 6–7, 1962, *Students for a Democratic Society Records, 1958–1970* (Sanford, N.C.: Microfilming Corporation of America, 1977), series 5, reel 1.

73. Casey Hayden, email to author, October 15, 2009.

74. Casey Hayden, interview, Mickey Flacks, interview, both in *Sixties*, ed. Agger, 169–71; Mickey Flacks, interview, in Hogan, *Many Minds*, 111–12.

75. Flacks, interview, in Hogan, *Many Minds*, 112.

76. Casey Hayden, email to author, October 15, 2009.

77. Tom Hayden, *Reunion*, 76.

78. Robert A. Haber and Sandra C. Hayden to Dr. Arnold Kaufman, May 12, 1962, Arnold S. Kaufman Papers, box 4, Bentley Library, University of Michigan, Ann Arbor.

79. Gitlin, *Sixties*, 367; Paul Booth cited in Evans, *Personal Politics*, 111.

80. Miller, *Democracy Is in the Streets*, 122.

81. Casey Hayden, interview, in Hogan, *Many Minds*, 109.

82. Bob Ross cited in Jack Newfield, *A Prophetic Minority* (New York: New American Library, 1966), 131.

83. Tom Hayden, *Reunion*, 104.

84. Cason, "Women's Consciousness," 5.

85. Amy Swerdlow, *Women Strike for Peace: Traditional Motherhood and Radical Politics in the 1960s* (Chicago: University of Chicago Press, 1993), 241.

86. Tom Hayden, *Rebel*, 94.

87. Tom Hayden, *Reunion*, 107.

88. Casey Hayden, interview, in *Sixties*, ed. Agger, 212.

89. Casey Hayden, email to author, October 15, 2009; Rebecca E. Klatch, *A Generation Divided: The New Left, the New Right, and the 1960s* (Berkeley: University of California Press, 1999), 157.

90. Casey Hayden, email to author, October 15, 2009.

91. Klatch, *Generation Divided*, 170.

92. Casey Hayden, "Fields of Blue," 348.

93. Hogan, *Many Minds*, 112.

94. Casey Hayden, "Fields of Blue," 349.

95. King, *Freedom Song*, 162.

96. Ibid., 78.

97. Casey Hayden, "A Nurturing Movement: Nonviolence, SNCC, and Feminism," *Southern Exposure* 16 (Summer 1988): 51.

98. King, *Freedom Song*, 76, 444.

99. Casey Hayden, "Fields of Blue," 351–52; Casey Hayden, interview, in Olson, *Freedom's Daughters*, 270; King, *Freedom Song*, 76–77.

100. Cason, "Women's Consciousness," 11.

101. Casey Hayden, "Sermonette on the Movement," *Southern Changes* 9 (December 1987): 28.

102. Cason, "Women's Consciousness," 8.

103. Charles Euchner, *Nobody Turn Me Around: A People's History of the 1963 March on Washington* (Boston: Beacon, 2010), 142, 157.

104. Howard Zinn, *SNCC: The New Abolitionists* (Boston: Beacon, 1965), 12.

105. Casey Hayden to Mary King, October 29, 1963, in King, *Freedom Song*, 122.

106. Casey Hayden, "Fields of Blue," 355.

107. John Dittmer, *Local People: The Struggle for Civil Rights in Mississippi* (Urbana: University of Illinois Press, 1994), 207–9; Hogan, *Many Minds*, 160.

108. Casey Hayden, "Fields of Blue," 355.

109. Doug McAdam, *Freedom Summer* (New York: Oxford University Press, 1988), 4.

110. Casey Hayden, "Fields of Blue," 355.

111. Hogan, *Many Minds*, 349; Casey Hayden, "Fields of Blue," 357.

112. Dan Schechter, "Freedom Schools and Community Centers" (memorandum based on author's recent trip to Mississippi), [fall 1964], 6, *SDS Records*, series 2.a, reel 9.

113. Heather Tobis, interview, in Olson, *Freedom's Daughters*, 296.

114. "Report of Operator #79" (the Mississippi Sovereignty Commission's spy in the Jackson COFO office), June 22, 1964, SCR ID 9-32-0-16-1-1-1, Mississippi State Sovereignty Commission Records, 1994–2006, series 2515, Mississippi Department of Archives and History, Jackson.

115. Sandra Cason, interview, in Henry Hampton, Steve Fayer, and Sarah Flynn, *Voices of Freedom: An Oral History of the Civil Rights Movement from the 1950s through the 1980s* (New York: Bantam, 1990), 189.

116. Casey Hayden, "Doing the Work," 9.

117. King, *Freedom Song*, 337.

118. Casey Hayden, "Fields of Blue," 356.

119. Casey Hayden, "Doing the Work," 7.

120. Casey Hayden to Bob Moses et al., April 15, 1964, in Students for Direct Action, *The Student Nonviolent Coordinating Committee Papers*, subgroup A, series 16, file 29, reel 41.

121. Theresa Del Pozzo, "The Feel of a Blue Note," in *Deep in Our Hearts*, 184.

122. Tom Hayden, *Reunion*, 118.

123. Hogan, *Many Minds*, 190.

124. Kay Mills and Marian Wright Edelman, *This Little Light of Mine: The Life of Fannie Lou Hamer* (Lexington: University Press of Kentucky, 2007), 5.

125. Tom Hayden, *Reunion*, 118; King, *Freedom Song*, 347.

126. Tom Hayden, *Reunion*, 119.

127. William Chafe, *Never Stop Running: Allard Lowenstein and the Struggle to Save American Liberalism* (Princeton: Princeton University Press, 1998), 200; Hogan, *Many Minds*, 196.

128. McAdam, *Freedom Summer*, 124.

129. Hogan, *Many Minds*, 217.

130. Cason, "Women's Consciousness," 14.

131. Hogan, *Many Minds*, 232.

132. Giardina, *Freedom for Women*, 31, 83.

133. Casey Hayden, interview, in *Rebels with a Cause*, ed. Helen Garvey (Los Gatos, Calif.: Shire, 2007), 98.

134. "Report of Operator #79," July 3, 1964, SCR ID #9-32-0-19-1-1-1, Mississippi State Sovereignty Commission Records.

135. King, *Freedom Song*, 459; Casey Hayden, interview, 1990, in Belinda Robnett, *How Long? How Long?: African American Women in the Struggle for Civil Rights* (New York: Oxford University Press, 1997), 119.

136. King, *Freedom Song*, 458; Casey Hayden, "Fields of Blue," 365.

137. "SNCC Position Paper: Women in the Movement," in Students for Direct Action, *The Student Nonviolent Coordinating Committee Papers*, frames 784–85, reel 12.

138. King, *Freedom Song*, 450.

139. Casey Hayden, interview, in Olson, *Freedom's Daughters*, 338.

140. "Women in the Movement," in Students for Direct Action, *The Student Nonviolent Coordinating Committee Papers*, frame 785, reel 12.

141. King, *Freedom Song*, 448.

142. Casey Hayden, "Fields of Blue," 365.

143. King, *Freedom Song*, 462.

144. Casey Hayden, "Fields of Blue," 368; Casey Hayden, preface, 7.

145. Evans, *Personal Politics*, 119.

146. Casey Hayden, preface, 7.

147. Evans, *Personal Politics*, 144.

148. Casey Hayden, "Fields of Blue," 369; "JOIN Press Release," [June] 1965, in Todd Gitlin and Nanci Hollander, *Uptown: Poor Whites in Chicago* (New York: Harper and Row, 1970), 237; Richard Rothstein, "Chicago: JOIN Project," *Studies on the Left* 5 (Summer 1965): 121.

149. Casey Hayden, "Fields of Blue," 370.

150. Evans, *Personal Politics*, 148.

151. Casey Hayden, personal communication, in Jennifer Frost, *"An Interracial Movement of the Poor": Community Organizing and the New Left in the 1960s* (New York: New York University Press, 2001), 154.

152. Casey Hayden, "Fields of Blue," 370; Casey Hayden, "In the Attics of My Mind," in *Hands on the Freedom Plow: Personal Accounts by Women in SNCC*, ed. Faith S. Holsaert, Martha Prescod Norman Noonan, Judy Richardson, Betty Garman Robinson, Jean Smith Young, and Dorothy M. Zellner (Urbana: University of Illinois Press, 2010), 384.

153. King, *Freedom Song*, 458.

154. Casey Hayden and Mary King, "Sex and Caste: A Kind of Memo," *Liberation* 10 (April 1966): 35, 36.

155. Mary King, interview, in Elizabeth Jacobs, "Revisiting the Second Wave: In Conversation with Mary King," *Meridians: Feminism, Race, Transnationalism* 7 (2007): 109.

156. Cason, "Women's Consciousness," 17.

157. Casey Hayden, "Doing the Work," 15; King, interview, in Jacobs, "Revisiting," 110.

158. King, *Freedom Song*, 462.

159. Ruth Rosen, *The World Split Open: How the Modern Women's Movement Changed America*, 2nd ed. (London: Penguin, 2006), 114; Giardina, *Freedom for Women*, 92.

160. Gitlin, *Sixties*, 369.

161. Ibid., 370; Susan Brownmiller, *In Our Time: Memoir of a Revolution* (New York: Dial, 1999), 14.

162. Giardina, *Freedom for Women*, 161.

163. Casey Hayden, "Fields of Blue," 373.

164. Ibid., 373–74.

Julia Scott Reed

Presenting the Truth about African Americans in Dallas

W. MARVIN DULANEY

In 1967, the *Dallas Morning News* hired Julia Scott Reed as its first African American columnist. Reed became a pioneer for the city's African Americans, covering the African American community in a way that was unprecedented. Having worked as a reporter for two African American newspapers, she brought an extraordinary level of professionalism and race consciousness to the job that allowed her to address issues that most U.S. daily newspapers usually ignored. She was hired to write her column at a critical juncture in the civil rights era, when the Black Power movement had emerged and civil disorders and social unrest plagued the American landscape. In the middle of this national turmoil, she wrote a column that not only addressed race relations but also presented and told the truth about African Americans in Dallas.

Though popular perception of the civil rights movement has not yet fully acknowledged women's importance, Julia Scott Reed and many other women had a significant impact. Early scholarship on the civil rights movement tended to focus on the roles of heroic leaders such as Dr. Martin Luther King Jr. and male-dominated organizations such as the National Association for the Advancement of Colored People (NAACP) and the Southern Christian Leadership Conference (SCLC), but more recent works have revealed women's active participation in the movement. Scholarly monographs, biographies, autobiographies, and several compilations of essays on women in the civil rights movement have helped to describe more accurately the diversity of participants. Recent historiography has also expanded the overall understanding of the movement. Historians and scholars in other disciplines have moved from defining the movement as a series of legal challenges to segregation laws and direct action tactics

JULIA SCOTT REED, CA. 1960

Photograph by Marion Butts. From the collections of the Texas/Dallas
History and Archives Division, Dallas Public Library, Dallas.

to overturn discriminatory practices to analyses of the organizing tactics and behind-the-scenes efforts to improve the lives of African American citizens. This expansion of the understanding of the breadth, complexity, and diversity of the civil rights movement also led scholars to examine how local people contributed to the movement beyond the lawsuits and the marches and demonstrations. In Dallas, Julia Scott Reed was one of the many persons who participated in the movement behind the scenes, yet she played a major role in promoting its results.[1]

Reed's background did not mark her as significantly different from other African American women of her era. Julia McGee was born in Dallas in 1917 to Johnnie and Nina Bell McGee. Her father died when she was very young, and for the first eight years of her life, she lived in a fashionable white neighborhood where her mother was employed as a maid. After moving with her mother to one of Dallas's African American communities, she attended Booker T. Washington High School, graduating in 1935. Like many of her contemporaries at Washington High School, Julia McGee was a part of the "shortchanged generation." Overcrowding at the high school meant that she attended classes for only four hours per day. The school had been built to accommodate six hundred students, but with nineteen hundred enrolled, they had to attend in two shifts. Despite these educational restrictions, McGee moved on to Wiley College Extension for two years and then graduated from Phillips Business College with training in journalism and communications. She later stated that the death of her father and her mother's poor health had prevented her from leaving Dallas to attend college elsewhere.[2]

Sometime between her graduation from high school and 1940, McGee married Jack Scott. No official record documents her marriage, but the 1940 Dallas city directories listed Jack Scott, a porter, as her husband and her occupation as a maid. Jack Scott was thirteen years her senior. According to her adopted daughter, Gayle Eubanks Coleman, Julia divorced Scott in 1957 and then lived with her mother and adopted daughter until she remarried in 1966.[3]

Even if her personal history was less than remarkable, she certainly lived in remarkable times. While she was attending Booker T. Washington High School in the 1930s, A. Maceo Smith, executive secretary of the Dallas Negro Chamber of Commerce, and the Reverend Maynard H. Jackson, pastor of New Hope Baptist Church and spokesperson for the Interdenominational Ministerial Alliance, started the Progressive Voters League (PVL) and revived the local branch of the NAACP. From 1935 to 1956, Smith and Jackson used poll tax payment campaigns, bloc voting, and lawsuits to gain concessions from Dallas's white leadership. Through their efforts, as well as those of other ministers and members of the

NAACP and the PVL, such as the Reverend E. C. Estell and Juanita Craft, African Americans in Dallas obtained a new high school, two new public housing projects, the right to serve as jurors in Dallas County, jobs in the postal service, and the appointment of the city's first African American police officers.[4]

When Julia Scott became active in the civil rights movement in the 1950s and the 1960s, it had reached a crossroads. After the *Brown* decision, white political leaders in Texas decided to resist the U.S. Supreme Court's decision and refused to desegregate the state's public schools. Instead, the state legislature and the state attorney general attacked the NAACP, charging the organization with barratry and operating in the state without a license. The state legislature also passed a law making it illegal for public employees to be members of the NAACP. These repressive actions had a chilling effect on the organization's Dallas branch: membership declined, and it became ineffective for several years. Despite these challenges, Julia Scott, Minnie Flanagan, and Juanita Craft remained steadfast members. While Flanagan became the branch's president and Craft led the NAACP Youth Council, Scott conducted yearly membership drives at her church.[5]

As the Dallas NAACP regained some of its membership, its leaders began to demand the full integration of the city's schools, equal access to all public facilities, and the right to participate in the city's political arena. In March 1960, two ministers, one black and one white, attending Perkins Theological School at Southern Methodist University, carried out the city's first sit-in. Subsequent direct action protests downtown challenged segregated lunch counters and service in department stores. After a visit to Dallas by NAACP executive secretary Roy Wilkins, who advocated the immediate desegregation of public schools as well as public facilities, black representatives of the Dallas NAACP and the Negro Chamber of Commerce and white representatives from the Dallas Citizens Council, a group of white businessmen that had dominated and controlled city politics and economic development since 1937, formed the Committee of Fourteen. Consisting of seven blacks and seven whites, the committee began negotiations to desegregate all of Dallas's public life. While the Committee of Fourteen negotiated the desegregation of public schools and public accommodations, African Americans formed the Dallas Community Committee and began to test whether Dallas's institutions were desegregating in practice. Among the testers was Julia Scott, a reporter for the *Dallas Express*, an African American newspaper.[6]

Given the important events that were to dominate her young adult years, Julia Scott's decision to begin a career in the black press was ideal. She started as the office secretary for the Texas edition of the *Kansas City Call*, a black weekly. By

1951, she had joined the *Dallas Express* as a "rewrite and telephone reporter." She also started hosting "The News and Views," a talk show on Fort Worth radio station KNOK. Scott developed her career as a journalist at the *Express*, and the two served each other well.[7]

Like many black weekly newspapers, the *Dallas Express* required its staff to work across occupational lines, and out of necessity Julia Scott became more than just a "rewrite and telephone reporter." At first, she wrote "soft news" stories for the *Express* about events sponsored by African American social clubs. Eventually, she began writing stories about politics, civil rights, and other issues that affected the city's African Americans. In 1954, for example, she reported on the NAACP's national convention, which was held in Dallas. She also covered the desegregation of the city's buses, and in 1963 she was present when Jack Ruby shot Lee Harvey Oswald, who had assassinated President John F. Kennedy.[8]

Many African American newspaper reporters and writers participated in the events that they covered, and Scott was no exception. In 1953, she took part in the boycott of Dallas department stores that refused to allow black women to try on clothes before purchasing them. In addition to reporting on the NAACP's 1954 national convention, she served on its publicity committee. In 1958, she won election as a Democratic Party precinct chair, a position she held for twenty-three years. She was also active in the PVL, the Dallas Council of Voters, and the Dallas NAACP. After a 1960s incident at the Sanger Tea Room in which she and other testers were refused service, her activism and career again coincided: she published a report that the establishment was not integrated and that further direct action would be necessary to force the tea room to comply with the "voluntary desegregation" endorsed by the Committee of Fourteen.[9]

Scott was also active in community affairs beyond civil rights, but the intersection with the movement was never far away. In 1954, she served on the board of the Roundup Community Theater, an organization started by African Americans to promote theater productions by and for the local community. In 1957, she worked with the Dallas Negro Chamber of Commerce to study and report on the effects of narcotics on the African American community. As an indication of her ongoing concern for young people, she participated in a 1963 "dramatization" of the findings of the Dallas County Youth Study. For several years, she also served as the chair for the female division of the annual March of Dimes campaign in Dallas's African American community. In 1965, she was elected to the board of directors of the League for Educational Advancement, an educational association formed by African Americans and whites who wanted to break the stranglehold the Dallas Citizens Council and the Citizens Charter

Association held on the Dallas school board and to promote the full integration of the city's public schools.[10]

The Committee of Fourteen led those efforts. But the years between its formation in 1960 and the social unrest of 1967 and 1968 were marked by only limited success in achieving integration. The failures of these years were precisely what opened up a more enduring and ultimately important role for Scott. The committee succeeded in its efforts to carry out desegregation without the demonstrations and civil disorder that had plagued the process in some other cities, yet the two factors that ensured this success were distinctly conservative: the influence of the Dallas Citizens Council and the cooperation of the Dallas media. The Dallas Citizens Council used its influence to force uncooperative stores and facilities to accept desegregation. The Dallas media, dominated by the A. H. Belo Company, which controlled the city's major newspaper, the *Dallas Morning News*, and one of its three major television stations, cooperated with the Dallas Citizens Council to promote an atmosphere of peaceful negotiation and to suppress coverage of dissenters and others who wanted to disrupt the process and hurt the city's image. When the Committee of Fourteen decided that token integration of the city's schools should occur in 1961, for example, the local media used their influence to bring in Walter Cronkite, the national anchor for CBS News, to narrate a film, *Dallas at the Crossroads*, that depicted the disorder and violence that had accompanied the desegregation of schools in Little Rock in 1957 and New Orleans in 1960. The film carried the message that such incidents would not be tolerated in Dallas. All of the local television stations aired the film, which was also shown to various community groups, and a brochure with the same title and message was distributed to more than one hundred thousand Dallas residents.[11]

For the most part, thanks to the Committee of Fourteen's efforts, Dallas whites did not create incidents as the city's public schools and public facilities were desegregated. Indeed, the *Dallas Morning News* and the city's black and white leaders congratulated themselves on achieving desegregation with no instances of violence and only a handful of demonstrations by African Americans and their white supporters. On the floor of the U.S. Senate, Texas's John Tower even praised the city's leaders for their desegregation efforts. Several African Americans and whites, however, also criticized the *News* for deliberately suppressing information about the sit-ins that had occurred in the city in 1960 and 1961 and for the absence of coverage on issues relevant to African Americans. Moreover, some African Americans and whites disagreed with the process of "managed desegregation," believing that African Americans had to win their rights through the ballot box and through public protests.[12]

By the mid-1960s, proponents of more forceful desegregation determined that the efforts led by the Committee of Fourteen were no longer tenable. Though the school system was officially integrated, the public schools largely remained segregated, and African Americans still could not purchase homes in most areas of Dallas. The at-large election of seats on the city council and the school board meant that no African American had ever won election to either body. Thus, while the Committee of Fourteen had made much progress in ending the most visible signs of segregation, it still existed and still dominated the lives of African Americans.[13]

For these reasons, in the late 1960s, two new groups emerged to challenge the "Dallas Way" of achieving desegregation: the Student Nonviolent Coordinating Committee (SNCC) and the Southern Christian Leadership Conference (SCLC). In doing so, they helped to create the conditions in which African Americans could secure media access to communicate more widely their community's plight. Both organizations began to stage street demonstrations in Dallas and to threaten violence and other direct action tactics to end segregation and achieve full equality for African Americans. In 1968, SNCC activists led a demonstration at a South Dallas supermarket, protesting the inferior quality of food sold there and demanding that the store owners sell the store to them. After causing some damage to the store, three protesters were arrested and subsequently sentenced to ten years in jail. One year later, the SCLC's Peter Johnson visited Dallas to promote a film on the life of Dr. Martin Luther King Jr. Johnson observed the way the city government was treating African American homeowners in the South Dallas neighborhood that bordered Fair Park. The city needed the property adjacent to Fair Park and the Cotton Bowl to expand parking for visitors and sought to use eminent domain to buy out the homeowners without paying a fair price. Johnson decided to stay in Dallas to advocate for the fair treatment of the homeowners. In an effort to get the attention of Mayor Erik Jonsson and the city council, Johnson led a series of boycotts, protests, and demonstrations to expose what he considered to be the unfair displacement of African Americans from their homes. Thus, Dallas began to experience many of the same types of urban protests that were occurring in other U.S. cities.[14]

New pressures arose. From 1965 to 1968, racial violence occurred in more than 150 American cities. After the 1967 riots, President Lyndon Baines Johnson created the National Advisory Commission on Civil Disorders to study and develop ways to prevent urban conflict. In its 1968 report, the commission concluded that "white racism"—individual and institutional—was the root cause of America's urban racial violence. The report singled out the police for its role in creating and fostering the atmosphere that led to the disorder, a finding that did not surprise most Americans. However, the report also cited the news media's coverage of the civil unrest and their historic, biased coverage of the nation's African American communities as contributing to the violence.[15]

The *Dallas Morning News*'s coverage of the African American community exemplified the advisory commission's criticism. The *News* covered only desegregation efforts that supported the policies dictated by the Committee of Fourteen and the Dallas Citizens Council. It ignored dissent and suppressed coverage of protests and demonstrations. Moreover, the paper failed to report adequately on racial problems or to employ minorities: its editors made no attempt to achieve the minuscule 5 percent average minority representation that the advisory commission found on most of the nation's major newspaper staffs. Before 1967, the *Dallas Morning News* employed no African American staff members. As was typical of major newspapers, the *News* had stopped using such derogatory terms as *coons* and *darkies* to ridicule African Americans by the early 1950s, but a decade and a half later, its coverage of the African American community remained unbalanced. Between January 1966 and the end of June 1967, the paper printed only 224 stories about the activities of Dallas's African Americans, and more than half of those pieces focused on crimes committed by African Americans or in which they were suspects.[16]

Only when the conservative approach to desegregation had been discredited and African American activists had forcefully claimed a public voice did the editors of the *Dallas Morning News* decide to do something to improve the paper's coverage of the city's black community. Julia Scott had married Ewell "Jimmy" Reed on December 3, 1966, and taken his name, and in June 1967, the *News* offered Julia Scott Reed the opportunity to write a column on the African American community. Reed believed that she had been hired to counter charges that white newspapers promoted racial stereotypes by covering only crime and other sensational stories about African Americans. In addition, the powder keg that was U.S. race relations was about to explode into widespread urban rioting in the summer of 1967, creating a climate in which the *News*'s editors finally recognized their long-term failure to report fairly and accurately on the city's blacks and sought to improve the paper's coverage. By the time Reed's first column was published on July 2, violence had already broken out in Tampa, Cincinnati, Atlanta, and other cities.[17]

When Reed received the job offer from the *Dallas Morning News*, she was serving as the *Dallas Express*'s city editor. She was at the pinnacle of her journalistic career, and the *News* clearly recognized both her talents and her central place in the African American community. She was a member of Golden Gate Baptist Church and Zeta Phi Beta Sorority. She drove a Cadillac and was known for her refined mannerisms, excellent grooming, and stylish clothing. People called her the "red-haired lady editor."[18]

The choice of Reed as the *News*'s first African American staffer was ironic. Although she was more than qualified and was clearly the best person for the position, an April 1967 *News* article had demonstrated contempt for the city's black newspapers and predicted their demise. Reporter David Dunnigan had ridiculed the sensationalism, lack of advertising, and poor news coverage in the city's three African American weeklies, the *Post Tribune*, *In Sepia Dallas*, and the *Dallas Express*. He singled out the *Express* as the worst offender because of its frequent crime-related headlines that focused on African Americans. Dunnigan had interviewed Reed for the piece, and she admitted to using sensationalism to sell newspapers. But she also noted that the *Express* was seventy-five years old, and she vowed that it would not stop covering the African American community just because white-owned newspapers had started to pay attention to some of the news there.[19]

Reed's column, "The Open Line," appeared in the *News* three times each week from July 1967 to December 1978 and provided more thorough coverage of people, events, and issues in the local African American community than most of the nation's major newspapers had previously provided. Perhaps her most important accomplishment was that she presented African Americans' diversity and achievements and their awareness of and attitudes toward issues that affected their lives. In short, she presented a view of Dallas's African American community of which most whites had no awareness or understanding.

Reed already had won much public recognition for her community service. In 1958, the Golden Gate Baptist Church presented her with a letter of commendation for organizing its annual religious drama program. One year later, the Dallas Branch of the NAACP recognized her role in its Golden Anniversary membership campaign. In 1965, she became the first African American member of the Dallas Press Club. Although her invitation to join the club had split the organization and she was embarrassed by the racist reaction of some of its members, she was flattered that the organization would consider her for membership. Her initial July 1965 application for membership was rejected, but one month later, the Press Club's members voted unanimously to admit her. In April 1966, the Dallas Red Cross recognized her support of its annual fund-raising campaign, and in May, she was elected to the Dallas chapter of Theta Sigma Phi, the national professional society for women in journalism.[20]

In her first "Open Line" column, Reed wrote about the fund-raising campaign for the Moorland YMCA, which African Americans had created in 1930. She related the history of this example of African American self-help, citing the four community leaders who had conceived the idea. She described the build-ing's importance to the African American community: for thirty-seven years, it had not only provided youth programs but also hosted meetings, forums, and seminars. She reported on the plans to expand the YMCA, and announced that Mayor Jonsson had received pledges from white donors to match up to fifty thousand dollars raised by the African American community.[21]

This inaugural column established the style and methodology that Reed used in many of her subsequent columns: she informed both black and white read-ers of positive and constructive activities occurring in the African American community; she provided background and historical context for those activi-ties; and she provided white readers with positive examples of interracial co-operation. The vast majority of Reed's columns concerned successful African Americans who were making positive contributions to the community, and the underlying message was always that African Americans were hardworking citi-zens who deserved to be treated fairly.

In other instances, though, Reed did not shy away from directly addressing racial issues. As the race riots continued across the United States during the summer of 1967, Reed wrote three columns in which she assured white readers that African Americans would not riot in Dallas. In "Riots Appear Unlikely Here" (July 30), "Calm Prevails among Negroes" (August 6), and "Dallas Enjoys Racial Peace" (December 24), she described efforts by the NAACP, the Dallas police department, and black and white community leaders to maintain calm and to defuse potentially explosive issues. She cited the community's establish-ment of a chapter of the Urban League and of the Opportunities Industrial Center, which provided training and jobs for African American youth; the end of the demeaning "Negro Achievement Day" that had restricted black atten-dance at the Texas State Fair to a single day; and the November election of Dr. Emmett Conrad as the first African American member of the school board. She concluded that all of these achievements and events had helped to promote goodwill and to improve race relations.[22]

In October 1967, Reed contributed to an unprecedented three-part series of articles that presented insights into the city's African American community. "The Negroes of Dallas" reiterated much of the information that Reed was pub-lishing in her columns, but it also noted African Americans' discontent with their lack of representation in city government and the dearth of available economic opportunities. Reed showed that the seven African Americans on the Committee of Fourteen did not represent the diversity of the community's viewpoints and that the city needed to do more to address the problems affect-ing African Americans in South and West Dallas. The tone of the series, the

TABLE 1. Number of "Open Line" Columns
Written by Julia Scott Reed, 1967–1978

Year	Number of Columns
1967	44
1968	134
1969	158
1970	158
1971	119
1972	139
1973	137
1974	137
1975	129
1976	134
1977	108
1978	92
Total	1,489

multiple opinions presented, and the focus on the strength of the black middle class and on the services provided by black fraternal and social organizations reflected Reed's knowledge and ability to find people who could accurately speak about African Americans' concerns.[23]

In her first six months at the *News*, Reed wrote 44 "Open Line" columns. Over the next eleven years, she wrote 1,445 more columns, for an average of 131 per year. In 1969 and 1970, she produced 158 columns each year; in 1978, when a stroke ended her career, only 92 "Open Line" columns appeared (see table 1). In addition to the "Open Line" columns, she wrote hard news stories about politics and other events that related to African American or women's issues. However, her strongest voice appears in her columns, as she provided a steady flow of information on subjects as wide ranging as politics, women's issues, current events, charitable events, awards programs, notable African American residents and visitors, local black history, civil rights issues, and national events such as the assassination of Dr. Martin Luther King Jr., the National Women's Conference in 1970, and the annual Urban League and NAACP conventions (see table 2).

The diversity of topics and the positions that she took indicate that she had carte blanche to address whatever subject she wanted and to write whatever she felt appropriate. Although she sought to promote good race relations, she

TABLE 2. Topics of "Open Line" Columns in Three Sample Years

Topics	1970	1973	1976
Individual Profiles	65 (41%)	55 (40%)	43 (32%)
Community Events/Visiting Speakers	27	24	31
Churches/Ministers	15	9	10
Community Development/			
Career Opportunities	14	12	10
Civil Rights and Race Relations	3	3	10
Politics	7	5	6
NAACP/Urban League/			
Negro Chamber of Commerce	3	6	7
Social/Fraternal Organizations	4	7	3
History (Local and State)	1	3	5
Women's Issues	4	0	6
Miscellaneous (Firsts, Travel,			
Bishop College)	15	13	3
Total Number of Columns	158	137	134

also challenged policies that she thought were wrong, biased, or insensitive. In 1968, after the city council passed an antiriot ordinance that many African American community organizations and leaders thought was "aimed directly at the Negro community," Reed reported their concerns and categorized the city as boxing itself in with an unnecessary action. She also noted that, once again, an all-white city council had passed an objectionable ordinance that African Americans could not challenge legitimately because they had no representation in city government.[24]

Reed's most common subject was members of Dallas's African American community. In 1970, for example, she profiled artist Arthello Beck; the city's first black police captain, Donald Stafford; airline mechanic Freddie Sims; community leader R. A. Hester; and podiatrist Larry Lundy. In 1973, she introduced the community to the president of the National Council of Negro Women, Minnie Page; Bishop College campus queen Jo Walker; newscaster Iola Johnson; and philanthropist Pearl C. Anderson. Her 1976 profiles included park center director Ella Mae Warner; retired nurse Alvernon Tripp; community leader and civil rights pioneer A. Maceo Smith; and E. C. Ransom, a participant in a "Big Brother" program where he mentored a child. By sharing these individuals' life stories and accomplishments, Reed held them up as role models for African Americans and as lessons in black humanity for whites.[25]

"The Open Line" also served as a clearinghouse for the many events that took place in Dallas's African American community. She announced and often reported on major community events and interviewed visiting speakers, including major national celebrities. She introduced readers to and analyzed the opinions of noted African American leaders such as former SNCC member and Georgia state legislator Julian Bond, boxer Archie Moore, Dallas native and Syracuse University sociologist Charles V. Willie, baseball Hall of Famer Joe Black, theologian Howard Thurman, writer Margaret Walker Alexander, band leader Cab Calloway, *Ebony* magazine publisher John H. Johnson, actress Pam Grier, opera singer Marian Anderson, magazine editor Marcia Gillespie, and dozens of others.[26]

Reed did more than merely publicize the arrival of these notables; she also told their stories and educated the entire community about their significance. For example, she provided her readers a biography of Bond and explained that the U.S. Supreme Court had ordered the Georgia legislature to seat him after he was denied his position because he opposed the Vietnam War. Reed described how the Daughters of the American Revolution had denied Anderson the use of Constitution Hall for a free public concert in 1939 and pointed out that Smith and the Negro Chamber of Commerce had welcomed Anderson to perform in Dallas in 1938 but had been forced to house her in a private home because no Dallas hotel would offer her accommodations. Reed explained that Moore had come to Dallas to encourage young people to join the Boys and Girls Clubs and thus avoid the mistakes that he had made. And in addition to providing readers with a synopsis of Alexander's life and long literary career (citing her award-winning poem, "For My People," published in 1942), Reed interviewed the author about her book, *Jubilee*, and discussed the book's history of the enslavement of Alexander's family.[27]

Reed's contribution to an understanding of politics was critical to the black community, although the topic did not rank among her most frequent subjects. She addressed the history of African American participation in Dallas politics as well as reasons why people should participate in the political process on all levels, including registering to vote and the importance of casting ballots, both of which reflected her experience in the struggle to win the vote unfettered by poll taxes and white primaries. She also highlighted African American political firsts and sought to combat what she saw as African Americans' emerging political apathy. She remained active in local politics. Indeed, in 1965, when the Citizens Charter Association (CCA) began to allow African Americans to participate in its meetings to select candidates for Dallas political offices, Reed was the first African American woman to attend the group's meetings. Recognizing her political skills gained as precinct chair and demonstrated in her

columns, the cca's president appointed Reed to its most powerful committee, the Endorsement Committee, in 1972. The following year, Reed's presence
caused the committee to back its first Mexican American and African American
candidates. When the cca threatened not to endorse George Allen, the first
African American elected to the city council, for a third term, Reed argued on
his behalf, telling cca members, "You white folks are all the same. Just as soon
as we get a leader in our community that we can follow and that can get the job
done for us, you want to kick him out and give us another leader. Well, we're
not going for that."[28]

In December 1967, Reed wrote that the naacp had started a statewide drive
to add ninety-five thousand names to the voting rolls. One month later, she
recounted the importance of local efforts to register African Americans in the
election of attorney Joseph Lockridge as the first African American state legislator from Dallas County and Dr. Emmett Conrad as the first African American
member of the Dallas school board. Ten years later, she informed her readers
about a voter registration drive and political rally sponsored by the Interdenominational Ministerial Alliance. The rally's keynote speaker was Walter Fauntroy,
the District of Columbia's delegate to the U.S. House of Representatives.[29]

Reed interviewed Allen both before and after his 1969 election to the Dallas
city council. In 1972, she reported on the elections of Barbara Jordan as the first
African American from Texas to serve in the U.S. House of Representatives
and of Eddie Bernice Johnson as the first African American woman from Dallas County to serve in the Texas Legislature; she later relished covering their
lectures and other appearances in Dallas. Reed also reported on the elections of
the first two African American women, Lucy Patterson and Juanita Craft, to the
Dallas city council and of Kathlyn Gilliam as the first African American woman
on the Dallas school board.[30]

Reed saw participation in city politics as one way for African Americans to
improve their lives and communities, and she repeatedly used the stories of
Smith, Craft, and Emmett Whitman, the pvl's president, to make the point that
African Americans had to vote as a bloc to achieve progress. When John Wiley
Price, who later became Dallas County's first African American commissioner,
assumed the leadership of the pvl in 1978, Reed wrote a special column introducing him to the community and informing her readers that he was reviving
an organization that had once "affected political decisions in city, county and
state politics." She also acknowledged that Price was "controversial," having already attracted attention for his "flamboyant dress" and lifestyle. Nevertheless,
she seemed to endorse his plan to return the pvl to exclusive control by African
Americans, to eliminate political illiteracy among blacks, and to hold elected
officials accountable to their constituency.[31]

Despite Reed's emphasis on the importance of voting and political participation, she lamented the growing political apathy in the African American
community. In April 1968, shortly after his assassination, she observed that "the
late Dr. Martin Luther King Jr. emphasized the ways to achieve freedom and
equality . . . through the ballot not bullets, through voting not rioting. Negroes
in Dallas underscored this idea last April 6 when they went to the polls and
voted 20 percent of their political strength, while riots were going on all over
the country." She thus both commended Dallas' African Americans for voting
in the school board election and avoiding violence and criticized the low turnout among black voters. Civic responsibility, Reed believed, required African
Americans to participate in all elections.[32]

This theme recurred frequently in Reed's writings. She devoted multiple columns to African Americans' failure to register and failure to vote for every office
on the ballot. She decried the black community's low 20 percent turnout for the
1972 presidential election between George McGovern and Richard Nixon. In
1974 and 1975, Reed reported that only 13 percent of registered African Americans had voted and continued to urge African Americans to take advantage of
their hard-won right to cast ballots.[33]

As the most prominent voice in the Dallas African American community,
Reed received abundant praise for her work from both the black and white
communities. In 1968, Reed's sorority, Zeta Phi Beta, honored her as its Woman
of the Year. The following year, Theta Sigma Phi made her one of two recipients
of its Matrix Award, presented to outstanding women in the fields of writing
and broadcasting. Other accolades followed, including an Extra Mile Award
from the Business and Professional Women's Club of Dallas. By the end of 1970,
she had received nine awards for her column, and in 1975, the National Association of Media Women honored her along with Rosa Parks and Motown
Records's Esther Gordy Edwards.[34]

In December 1978, Reed suffered a stroke that put an end to her career. The
stroke affected her speech and her ability to walk and left her largely home-
bound. Although she went out on occasion with assistance from her adopted
daughter, she was no longer active in community affairs. In 1984, when a short
article in the *Dallas Morning News* asked, "Whatever happened to Julia Scott
Reed?," she replied, "I'm coming along." She died on October 19, 2004.[35]

One way of measuring the importance of Reed's columns is the large number of "letters to the editor" they generated as well as the personal letters of
congratulations and encouragement she received. These letters praised her for
informing the community about issues relevant to all citizens regardless of race.
Several commended her for improving race relations by providing evenhanded
coverage of the city's racial issues. In December 1967, her former principal at

Booker T. Washington High School, Dr. John Leslie Patton, wrote, "Please accept this belated congratulations on your affiliation with the Dallas Morning News. To be a columnist for a newspaper such as this is, indeed, the zenith in news reporting and self fulfillment! . . . Your column is scholarly, informative, and inspirational. The Dallas Morning News is to be congratulated for utilizing your tremendous talent as a writer!"[36]

Such praise, however, masked the fact that Reed was writing for a very conservative newspaper. During her twelve years as a columnist, the *Dallas Morning News* never modified its conservative positions on civil rights for African Americans, its opposition to school desegregation, or its resistance to the inclusion of more African American and Latino citizens in city government. According to one of Reed's contemporaries at the paper, editor and columnist Robert Miller, her hiring appears to have constituted a sincere attempt to provide fair and objective coverage of the African American community, and it certainly provided good public relations. (Reed was given a desk in a highly visible area of the newsroom.) But the presence of Reed and other African American reporters had no effect on the newspaper's editorial positions.[37]

Reed's tenure at the *News* occurred during a transitional period of leadership among African Americans in Dallas. She, A. Maceo Smith, George Allen, and Juanita Craft represented an older generation of activists who were in the process of being replaced by younger leaders such as Peter Johnson, Al Lipscomb, Diane Ragsdale, and John Wiley Price. Unlike Reed, they were not willing to negotiate for citizenship rights and political power. They took the struggle to the streets, disrupted city council and school board meetings, and even advocated armed violence. Reed's column represented the declining voice of black conservative leadership.

Nevertheless, Reed made a difference. Her columns constituted a valuable source of information for Dallas's African American community and provided that community with a voice. In addition, her columns are an invaluable historical resource for students of the African American experience and race relations in Dallas during a critical time. She presented the truth about the Dallas African American community and made the entire city take notice.[38]

NOTES

1. See, for example, Stephen B. Oates, *Let the Trumpet Sound: A Life of Martin Luther King Jr.* (New York: Harper and Row, 1982); David Garrow, *Bearing the Cross: Martin Luther King Jr. and the Southern Christian Leadership Conference* (New York: Morrow, 1986); Taylor Branch, *Parting the Waters: America in the King Years, 1954–1963* (New York: Simon and Schuster, 1988); Patricia

Sullivan, *Lift Every Voice: The NAACP and the Making of the Civil Rights Movement* (New York: New Press, 2010); Charles Payne, *I've Got the Light of Freedom: The Organizing Tradition and the Mississippi Freedom Struggle* (Berkeley: University of California Press, 1995); Aldon Morris, *The Origins of the Civil Rights Movement: Black Communities Organizing for Change* (New York: Free Press, 1986); J. Todd Moye, *Let the People Decide: Black Freedom and White Resistance Movements in Sunflower County, Mississippi, 1945–1986* (Chapel Hill: University of North Carolina Press, 2004); Mary King, *Freedom Song: A Personal Story of the 1960s Civil Rights Movement* (New York: Morrow, 1987); Septima Poinsette Clark, *Ready from Within: Septima Clark and the Civil Rights Movement, a First Person Narrative* (Navarro, Calif.: Wild Trees, 1986); Vicki L. Crawford, Jacqueline A. Rouse, and Barbara Woods, eds., *Women in the Civil Rights Movement: Trailblazers and Torchbearers, 1941–1965* (Brooklyn, N.Y.: Carlson, 1990); Belinda Robnett, *How Long? How Long?: African American Women in the Struggle for Civil Rights* (New York: Oxford University Press, 1997); Bettye Collier-Thomas and V. P. Franklin, eds., *Sisters in the Struggle: Women in the Civil Rights–Black Power Movements* (New York: New York University Press, 2001); Lynne Olson, *Freedom's Daughters: The Unsung Heroines of the Civil Rights Movement from 1830 to 1970* (New York: Scribner, 2002); John Dittmer, *Local People: The Struggle for Civil Rights in Mississippi* (Urbana: University of Illinois Press, 1995); Jo Ann Gibson Robinson, *The Montgomery Bus Boycott and the Women Who Started It: The Memoir of Jo Ann Gibson Robinson,* ed. David J. Garrow (Knoxville: University of Tennessee Press, 1978); Elizabeth Jacoway and David R. Colburn, eds., *Southern Businessmen and Desegregation* (Baton Rouge: Louisiana State University Press, 1982).

2. Mary Brinkerhoff, "Club Honors Columnist for Extra Mile," *Dallas Morning News* (hereafter cited as *DMN*), October 24, 1970; Joe Simnacher, "Influential Black Journalist Played Pivotal Role in Dallas," *DMN*, October 21, 2004; "A Celebration of the Life of Julia Scott Reed, July 17, 1917–October 19, 2004" (Funeral Program), folder 1, box 1, Julia Scott Reed Collection, DeGolyer Library, Southern Methodist University, Dallas; "Poll Tax Drive," *Dallas Express* (hereafter cited as *DE*), December 26, 1936; Julia Scott Reed, "Special Time at Booker T.," *DMN*, May 28, 1969; Darwin Payne, *Quest for Justice: Louis A. Bedford and the Struggle for Civil Rights in Texas* (Dallas: Southern Methodist University Press, 2009), 38–39; "Biography of Julia Scott Reed," Julia Scott Reed Biography Folder, Texas-Dallas Collection, Dallas Public Library, Dallas. Bedford, who attended Washington High School after Reed, describes how students at the school were "shortchanged" in their education.

3. *Worley's Greater Dallas City Directory, 1940* (Dallas: Worley, 1940), 828; Jack Scott obituary, *DMN*, October 27, 1977; "Feted by Family on Her Birthday," *DE*, July 24, 1965; Gayle Eubanks Coleman, telephone interview by author, September 19, 2011. See also *Worley's Greater Dallas City Directory,* 1951, 1952, 1953–54, pp. 837, 861, and 910, respectively.

4. W. Marvin Dulaney, "The Progressive Voters League: A Political Voice for African Americans in Dallas," *Legacies* 3 (Spring 1991): 27–35; W. Marvin Dulaney, "Whatever Happened to the Civil Rights Movement in Dallas, Texas?," in *Essays on the American Civil Rights Movement,* ed. W. Marvin Dulaney and Kathleen Underwood (College Station: Texas A&M University Press, 1993), 72–76.

5. "Court Order Closes NAACP," *DMN*, September 23, 1956; "NAACP Halted in Texas," *DE*, October 27, 1956; "Raps Passage of Anti-NAACP Bill as Misuse of Power," *DE*, February 1, 1958; "Texas Bluffed Out of NAACP Says Wilkins," *DE*, March 21, 1959; "Dallas NAACP to Begin Membership Drive," *DE*, April 25, 1959; "Local NAACP to Back Sit In Project," *DE*, March 12, 1960; Dallas Branch NAACP, Certificate of Award to the Aeschylus Club of Religious Drama in Recognition of Membership in the Golden Anniversary Club, February 15, 1959, folder 1, box 1, Reed Collection; Dulaney, "Whatever Happened?," 76–77; W. Marvin Dulaney, "The Rise, Fall, and Rise Again of the Dallas NAACP," in *Lone Star Legacy: African American History in Texas* (Detroit: Aquarius, 2011), 41–42.

6. Dulaney, "Whatever Happened?," 78–79; Jim Schutze, *The Accommodation: The Politics of Race in an American City* (Secaucus, N.J.: Citadel, 1986), 116–19. For a complete list of the members of the Committee of Fourteen, see Dulaney, "Whatever Happened?," 79.

7. "Mrs. Julia Scott Elected to Dallas Press Club," *Dallas Post Tribune*, August 28, 1965; "A Celebration of the Life of Julia Scott Reed, July 17, 1917–October 19, 2004" (Funeral Program), folder 1, box 1, Reed Collection; Joe Simnacher, "Influential Black Journalist Played Pivotal Role in Dallas," *DMN*, October 21, 2004.

8. "A Celebration of the Life of Julia Scott Reed, July 17, 1917–October 19, 2004" (Funeral Program), folder 1, box 1, Reed Collection; Joe Simnacher, "Influential Black Journalist Played Pivotal Role in Dallas," *DMN*, October 21, 2004; "I Have Known Dallas for Sixty Years or More . . . Julia Scott Reed," *Dallas Post Tribune*, March 2, 1994. For examples of Reed's early news articles, see Julia Scott, "Nat'l Meet Opens with Big Parade," *DE*, June 1, 1954; Julia Scott, "City Council Refuses to Return Signs on Buses," *DE*, August 4, 1956; Julia Scott, histories of Dallas's African American social clubs in the Centennial Emancipation Proclamation Edition of the *DE*, August 3, 1963, folder 6, box 1, Reed Collection.

9. "Citizens Organize to Stop Discrimination against Negro Women in Dept. Stores," *DE*, July 18, 1953; "Urges Negroes to Close Accounts at Biased Department Stores," *DE*, August 29, 1953; Ernest C. Estell to Roy Wilkins, May 28, 1954, folder 5, box 11A52, Papers of the National Association for the Advancement of Colored People, Library of Congress, Washington, D.C.; "Mrs. Julia Scott Elected Chairman of Precinct 306," *DE*, August 2, 1958; "Mrs. Julia Scott in Campaign for Precinct Head," *DE*, April 30, 1960; "Porchlight Paraders Push Poll Tax Sale," *DMN*, January 29, 1964; "Dallas County Democrats Elect Precinct Chairmen," *DMN*, May 4, 1964; Norma Adams Wade, "Pioneering Journalist's Papers Donated to SMU," *DMN*, January 17, 2007; "Sit-In Demonstrators to Tell 'Marshall' Story," *DE*, April 30, 1960; "'Sorry—Tea Room Not Integrated,' Sees No Immediate Change in Policy," *DE*, May 7, 1960.

10. Rual Askew, "New Faces in 'Shrike' Production," *DMN*, January 31, 1954; "Television Headliners," *DMN*, April 5, 1957; "Program to Dramatize Youth Study Findings," *DMN*, September 7, 1963; "Scott-Lockridge Head March of Dimes Campaign," *DE*, December 24, 1966; Carlos Conde, "School Group Picks Officers," *DMN*, February 4, 1965.

11. Richard Austin Smith, "How Business Failed Dallas," *Fortune*, July 1964, 156–57; William Brophy, "Active Acceptance—Active Containment: The Dallas Story," in *Southern Businessmen and Desegregation*, ed. Jacoway and Colburn, 137–50; Darwin Payne, *Dallas Citizens Council: An Obligation of Leadership* (Dallas: Three Forks, 2008); "Dallas Citizens' Preparation for School Integration on TV Program August 13," *DE*, August 12, 1961; Dulaney, "Whatever Happened?," 81–82; Schutze, *Accommodation*, 129–33; Glenn M. Linden, *Desegregating Schools in Dallas: Four Decades in the Federal Courts* (Dallas: Three Forks, 1995), 41–45; *Dallas at the Crossroads* (Brochure), folder 5, box 1, A. Maceo Smith Papers, African American Museum, Dallas.

12. "Senator Tower Lauds Dallas," *DE*, August 19, 1961; "Integration: Leaders, Newspapers Get Praises," *DMN*, September 22, 1963; Ruby Clayton McKee, "Federation Chairman Blasts Blackout of News on Sit-Ins," *DMN*, August 30, 1961; Rhett James, "Dallas 2nd Year Token Desegregation," *DE*, September 22, 1962; Schutze, *Accommodation*, 105–7, 116–17.

13. "Total Integration of Dallas Schools Not until 1967," *Dallas Post Tribune*, July 31, 1965; Linden, *Desegregating Schools in Dallas*, 51–57; "Is Dallas Really a Model City?," *DE*, July 13, 1968; "Don Perkins Wants Home in Dallas," *DE*, July 27, 1968. The latter article reported that even one of the beloved Dallas Cowboys could not rent an apartment in a white Dallas neighborhood because he was the wrong color.

14. "SNCC Leader Jailed," *DE*, July 20, 1968; "SNCC Pickets OK Supermarket," *DE*, July 27, 1968; "SCLC Visitor Assumes Role of Observer," *DMN*, December 2, 1969; "Six Organizations Voice Downtown Boycott Support," *DMN*, December 14, 1969; "Mayor to Look into Fair Park Issue," *DMN*, January 2, 1970; Brian D. Behnken, "The 'Dallas Way': Protest, Response, and the Civil Rights Experience in Big D and Beyond," *Southwestern Historical Quarterly* 111 (July 2007): 23–26.

15. U.S. Riot Commission, *Report of the National Advisory Commission on Civil Disorders*, Otto Kerner, chair (New York: Bantam, 1968), 3–7, chap. 15, "The News Media and the Disorders."

16. Ibid., 383–86. However, as late as 1957, the editors of the *News* objected to the NAACP's campaign to eliminate the use of such words. See "Removing Words," *DMN*, July 26, 1957; Ray Tucker, "Negro Gains in South Inspire National Drive," *DMN*, November 7, 1957.

17. County of Dallas Marriage License 963 1783, December 8, 1966; Robert Miller, telephone interview by author, January 29, 2013; Norma Adams Wade, email to author, February 3, 2011. Julia Scott Reed divorced Ewell "Jimmy" Reed in 1971. See "Rites Planned for Ewell Reed," *DMN*, March 19, 1971.

18. "Mrs. Julia Scott Reed Resigns as Express Editor," *DE*, September 9, 1967; Coleman, interview.

19. David Dunnigan, "Negro Newspapers Face Threat of Extinction," *DMN*, April 2, 1967.

20. "Problems at the Dallas Press Club," *Dallas Post Tribune*, July 3, 1965; "Mrs. Julia Scott Elected to Dallas Press Club," *Dallas Post Tribune*, August 28, 1965; "Scores a First; Joins Press Club," *DE*, August 28, 1965; "Awards and Certificates," folder 1, box 1, Reed Collection; "Red Cross Re-Elects Its Officers," *DMN*," April 27, 1966; "Journalism Fraternity to Install," *DMN*, May 10, 1966.

21. "Lay Cornerstone for YMCA at Dallas," *Philadelphia Tribune*, May 1, 1930; Julia Scott Reed, "Moorland Y to Get Help," *DMN*, July 2, 1967.

22. "Riots Appear Unlikely Here," *DMN*, July 30, 1967; "Calm Prevails among Negroes," *DMN*, August 6, 1967; "Dallas Enjoys Racial Peace," *DMN*, December 24, 1967.

23. "The Negroes of Dallas: Religion, Clubs Knit Together Upper, Middle Class," *DMN*, October 1, 1967; "The Negroes of Dallas: Ballot Box Channels 'Power,'" *DMN*, October 2, 1967; "The Negroes of Dallas: Service Organizations Find Volunteers Scarce," *DMN*, October 3, 1967.

24. "Dallas Riot Ordinance," *DMN*, August 14, 1968; Julia Scott Reed, "City Boxes Itself In with Riot Ordinance," *DMN*, August 21, 1968; "Dallas Mayor Promises Rioters 'Full Justice,'" *DMN*, August 27, 1968; "Clergymen Attack Riot Ordinance," *DMN*, August 27, 1968; Carolyn Barta, "Anti Riot Ordinance Defended," *DMN*, October 31, 1968.

25. "Black Artist, Self Taught," *DMN*, February 4, 1970; "First Negro Police Captain," *DMN*, January 11, 1970; "Freddie Sims Job Honor at Braniff No Accident," *DMN*, May 7, 1970; "Event Honors R. A. Hester," *DMN*, May 20, 1970; "Negro Doctors Show Increase," *DMN*, October 14, 1970; "Project Honors Noted Woman," *DMN*, June 7, 1973; "Jo Walker to End Reign," *DMN*, April 26, 1973; "Newscaster Enjoys Job," *DMN*, June 13, 1973; "Work Cut by Leader," *DMN*, September 26, 1973; "Hard Work Pays Off for Park Pioneer," *DMN*, February 18, 1976; "Mrs. Tripp Elected Woman of Year," *DMN*, February 25, 1976; "Mayor Proclaims 'Maceo Smith Day,'" *DMN*, March 25, 1976; "E. C. Ransom a Big Brother," *DMN*, June 25, 1976.

26. "Willie Story One of Success," *DMN*, November 9, 1967; "Ministers' Institute Offers Noted Preacher," *DMN*, April 9, 1969; "Julian Bond Coming Here," *DMN*, March 19, 1969; "Boxing King Tells ABCs," *DMN*, September 10, 1969; "Joe Black to Host Event," *DMN*, June 22, 1972; "Pamela Grier Riding Crest," *DMN*, December 21, 1972; "Cab Calloway Has Old Touch," *DMN*, November 28, 1975; "Poet-Novelist Concerned," *DMN*, April 9, 1975; "'Committee of 100' Slates Black Publisher," *DMN*, July 29, 1976; "Marian Anderson Due at Fair Park," *DMN*, March 13, 1977; "Essence Editor Due at UFA Observance," *DMN*, June 5, 1977.

27. "Julian Bond Coming Here," *DMN*, March 19, 1969; "Boxing King Tells ABCS," *DMN*, September 10, 1969; "Poet-Novelist Concerned," *DMN*, April 9, 1975; "Marian Anderson Due at Fair Park," *DMN*, March 13, 1977.

28. Julia Scott Reed, "Negro Suffrage under 30 Years Old," *DMN*, August 30, 1970; Dulaney, "Progressive Voters League," 27–28. For Reed's participation in the meetings of the Citizens Charter Association, see "Citizens Charter Ass'n Meet," *DE*, January 23, 1965; "CCA Forms Committees for Action in City Election," *DMN*, December 9, 1972; Carolyn Barta, "CCA More 'People Oriented' Now," *DMN*, March 5, 1973. See also John L. Schoellkopf, CCA President, to All Citizen's Charter Association Members, December 5, 1972, folder 26, box 1, Smith Papers; George Allen, interview by Gerald Saxon, April 23, 1981, 36–37, Texas-Dallas Collection; Darwin Payne, *Big D: Triumphs and Troubles of an American Supercity in the Twentieth Century* (Dallas: Three Forks, 2000), 410; "The New CCA," Luncheon Program, February 23, 1973, Lucy Patterson Papers, Special Collections Library, University of Texas at Arlington.

29. "NAACP Drive Seeks 95,000 on Voter Rolls," *DMN*, December 11, 1967; "Voter Crusade Unites Groups," *DMN*, January 11, 1968; "Texas Negroes Schedule Voter Push," *DMN*, October 16, 1968; "Negro Voter Drive Set," *DMN*, December 30, 1970; "Clark Optimistic on Voter Drive," *DMN*, January 27, 1971; "Organizations Slate Meetings to Register Voters," *DMN*, January 1, 1975; "Baptists Urged to Get Out Vote," *DMN*, September 17, 1976; "Beauticians Push for More Votes," *DMN*, September 19, 1976; "Fauntroy to Speak at Rally," *DMN*, November 6, 1977.

30. "Widow Faced Tough Decision," *DMN*, May 16, 1968; "Negroes Backed Their Choice," *DMN*, June 26, 1968; "City Elects First Negro," *DMN*, April 4, 1969; "Senator Jordan to Give Talk," *DMN*, November 13, 1969; "Group to Hear Jordan," *DMN*, April 16, 1972; "Win Pleases Mrs. Johnson," *DMN*, June 7, 1972; "Jordan Urges Unity Theme," *DMN*, August 3, 1972; "Rep. Jordan Begins Work," *DMN*, January 14, 1973; "New Trustee Tells Plans," *DMN*, April 18, 1974; "Rep. Jordan at Workshop," *DMN*, October 16, 1975; "1975 Good Year for Area Blacks," *DMN*, January 1, 1976; "Rep. Johnson to 'Take Notes,'" *DMN*, July 11, 1976.

31. "200 Leaders Talk Politics," *DMN*, October 12, 1967; "Three Issues Concern Negroes," *DMN*, October 26, 1967; "Dallas Negroes Recall History," *DMN*, February 29, 1968; "Honor Slated for Whitman," *DMN*, September 24, 1969; "League Head Steps Down," *DMN*, November 15, 1973; "Negro Suffrage under 30 Years Old," *DMN*, August 30, 1970; "Call Issued for Voters," *DMN*, April 13, 1975; "Black History from a Leader," *DMN*, November 13, 1975; "Mayor Proclaims 'Maceo Smith Day,'" *DMN*, May 25, 1976; "Voters Group Drives for Clout in Dallas," *DMN*, January 8, 1978; Kelvin Bass, "Love Him or Hate Him: John Wiley Price Is Still Standing," *Eclipse*, April–May 2004, 60–62.

32. Julia Scott Reed, "Participation Looking Better," *DMN*, April 25, 1968.

33. "Negro Voters Slow to Act," *DMN*, March 26, 1972; "Black Vote Fragmented," *DMN*, May 14, 1972; "Voter Apathy Examined," *DMN*, November 15, 1972; "Which Way Black Voter?," *DMN*, November 3, 1974; "Black Voter Apathy Cited," *DMN*, March 30, 1975; "Are You Eligible to Vote This Year?," *DMN*, February 12, 1976.

34. "Mrs. Reed Selected by Society," *DMN*, February 19, 1968; "Mrs. Dillard, Mrs. Reed among Matrix Award Winners," *DMN*, March 9, 1969; "Dallas B & P W to Recognize News Staffer," *DMN*, October 11, 1970; Mary Brinkerhoff, "Club Honors Columnist for Extra Mile," *DMN*, October 24, 1970; "Media Women to Honor Rosa Parks," *Chicago Defender*, September 16, 1975.

35. "Whatever Happened to . . . ," *DMN*, August 12, 1984; Daniel J. Nabors and W. Marvin Dulaney, "Reed, Julia Scott," *Handbook of Texas Online*, http://www.tshaonline.org/handbook/online /articles/fre78 (accessed February 15, 2014).

36. J. L. Patton Jr. to Julia Scott, December 11, 1967, Reed Collection, Correspondence. Letters about Reed's column include Mr. and Mrs. Zedrick Moore, "The Open Line," *DMN*, August 16, 1967;

Ernest Seale, "Informative," *DMN*, October 16, 1967; J. Howard Payne, "Valuable Feature," *DMN*, January 11, 1968; Caesar Clark, "Julia Reed," *DMN*, January 25, 1968.

37. Miller, interview. For examples of the newspaper's ongoing conservatism, see "Rights for Whom," *DMN*, May 31, 1967; "Integration and Law," *DMN*, September 3, 1968; Mike Kingston, "Dallas Schools: After the Sound and Fury," *DMN*, July 26, 1975; "Backward Ho?," *DMN*, January 31, 1975.

38. "Reception to Honor Mrs. Reed," *DMN*, March 4, 1979; Norma Adams Wade, "She Blazed a Trail in Journalism," *DMN*, October 27, 2004.

Barbara Jordan

The Paradox of Black Female Ambition

MARY ELLEN CURTIN

❀ ❀ ❀

In 1962, Barbara Jordan, a young African American lawyer and civil rights activist in Houston, decided to make her first run for the state legislature. She lost that race and another two years later, but persevered to gain her first electoral win in 1966. In 1969, just as she was beginning her second term as a Texas state senator, a reporter from the *Houston Chronicle* posed a delicate question. If the next census led to the creation of a new congressional seat in Houston, would Jordan run, even if it meant competing with Curtis Graves, another young black politician who also was starting his second term in the Texas Legislature? Jordan did not hesitate: "If there's a collision course between Mr. Graves and me, I shall not defer. I shall not defer to him or anyone else if I think I can win."[1]

Jordan's determination to seek congressional office set off a chain of events that led to her emergence as one of the most important African American politicians of the twentieth century. In 1972, Jordan defeated Graves to become one of the first two African Americans from the South to serve in Congress since Reconstruction. She displayed superb oratorical and political skills throughout the Watergate crisis in the summer of 1974, led the fight to renew and expand the Voting Rights Act in 1975, and played a starring role in the Democratic National Convention in 1976. Her ascendancy to even higher ranks, such as the Supreme Court or the vice presidency or a cabinet position, seemed possible. But multiple sclerosis forced Jordan to retire from politics. She left Washington and became a professor at the Lyndon B. Johnson School of Public Affairs at the University of Texas. Over the next two decades, Jordan spoke at Democratic National Conventions, testified against the nomination of archconservative Robert Bork to the Supreme Court, and participated in a presidential blue-ribbon commission on immigration. For her service to the country, Bill Clinton awarded her a Presidential Medal of Freedom. When her failing health allowed, Jordan traveled widely. She spoke at West Point just three months before her death on January 17, 1996, at the age of fifty-nine.[2]

Throughout her astounding career, Jordan remained true to her roots in the civil rights movement, telling an interviewer in the mid-1970s, "I entered politics because it was the most effective manner in which to help the residents of Houston."[3] But personal ambition also contributed to Jordan's decision to run for office. "In my *other* life, I was in the spiral to get ahead. . . . I didn't ask myself, 'what are you ambitious to do?' I wanted to be all that I could be. I was propelled by a driving force and was leading what I now consider to be an unbalanced life."[4] Jordan's desire to succeed is typical of officeholders. As political scientist Joseph A. Schlesinger has noted, "Ambition is the heart of politics," and representative government depends on "a supply of individuals with strong office drives."[5] But Jordan faced a paradox. Her ambition, a necessary quality to compete in politics, was cited as evidence of personal failure. In the October 1976 edition of *Texas Monthly*, for example, an unnamed critic said, "I have watched Barbara Jordan for almost ten years . . . and I have yet to see any evidence she is interested in anything beyond the advancement of Barbara Jordan."[6] The stigma of self-aggrandizement haunted Jordan during her last years in Congress.

Jordan's quest for higher office and the criticism she faced are part of a bigger story about how the political ambition of black women made American democracy more inclusive. This essay reexamines Jordan's activism in the Texas civil rights movement and explores the political context of her drive to reach higher office. It also contrasts the way that Jordan's black constituents viewed her ambition with the opinions of some in the press who covered her career. They did not always perceive Jordan's leadership positively, but Jordan's ambition galvanized her community and inspired black voters to push back against white supremacy.

Jordan's experiences as an early elected leader confirm but add nuance to the work of political scientists R. Darcy and Joseph Hadley, who suggest that despite the "double disadvantage" of race and sex, black women who sought political office after the passage of the 1965 Voting Rights Act were more likely to succeed than white women. Black female candidates expressed "greater ambition for elected public office" than did their white female counterparts and were more likely to have a background in political activism. Darcy and Hadley conclude that this combination of ambition and experience explains the "puzzle" of black women's success.[7] In Jordan's case, civil rights activism indeed laid the foundation for her electoral achievements. Darcy and Hadley, however, overlook the significance of personal ambition in explaining the success of black female

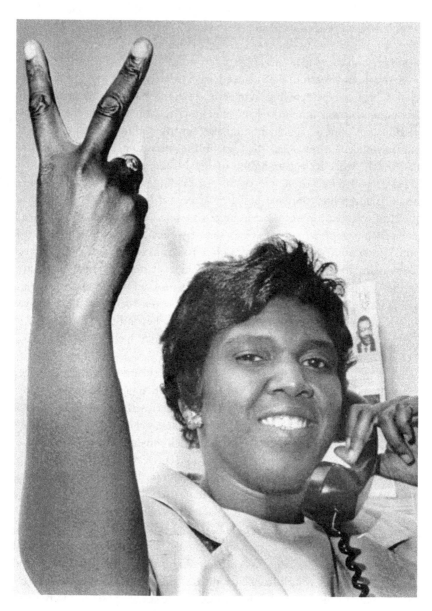

BARBARA JORDAN

celebrates after winning the Democratic nomination

for the Texas Senate race, May 7, 1966.

Courtesy of Bettmann/Corbis.

politicians such as Jordan. Furthermore, she was frequently perceived through the lens of "mammy" and depicted as cold and ungenerous. Contrary to what Darcy and Hadley suggest, race and sex stereotypes negatively affected Jordan.

In recent years, political scientists and feminist authors have questioned the assumption that personal ambition is simply an unhealthy desire to dominate. Psychiatrist Anna Fels interviewed women who "hated the word ambition. . . . For these women ambition necessarily implied egotism, selfishness, self-aggrandizement, or the manipulative use of others for one's own ends." Fels sought to break the dichotomy between ambition and selflessness and to remove the negative connotations many women associated with the word *ambition*. She argues that all healthy human ambition contains two components, mastery of a skill and expectation of recognition: "Without an element of mastery, we have little control over our destiny. Without recognition, we feel isolated and, ultimately, demoralized." Individual drive is not enough; a person needs a supportive environment as well as the capacity to forge skills that will garner recognition. Without such a supportive environment, Fels concludes, it is difficult for many women of achievement, education, and experience to admit to possessing ambition, let alone to act on that ambition. Fels believes that many contemporary women experience a conflict between an internal drive to do well and the fear that their ambitions will be dishonored or used against them.[8]

In a similar vein, political scientists Richard L. Fox and Jennifer L. Lawless suggest that skewed perceptions of their leadership qualifications hold back qualified women from running for office. These authors have found that experienced women are more likely than similarly qualified men to refrain from expressing ambitions. In other words, women who have qualifications equal to those of men think themselves less qualified to run for office. Furthermore, women are less likely to be asked to run. For Fox and Lawless, the lack of female officeholders cannot be explained solely by sexism in the electorate or by structural deficiencies in the American party system. Without a pool of female candidates who are willing to run or who have been asked to run, the number of women officeholders cannot rise. Unlike Darcy and Hadley, Fox and Lawless do not see a significant difference in the experiences of black and white women in politics. Instead, their evidence from the 1980s forward points to a general pattern in which qualified women are less likely to put themselves forward for political office or to be asked to run.[9]

Jordan's early career suggests a different pattern. Historians can shed light on the question of race and female political ambition by investigating the circumstances under which black women put themselves forward or were asked to run during the civil rights/Black Power era. Broader narratives that trace

race, voting, elections, and political parties in the aftermath of the 1965 Voting Rights Act have tended to ignore the personal aspect of individual ambition and competitiveness inherent in such races.[10] And though feminist scholars agree that during the late 1960s, popular ideas concerning women's capacity to lead and run for office changed, the exact relationship between second-wave feminism and individual decisions to run for political office remains unclear.[11] As the political behavior of African American women emerges as a field in its own right, the story of Jordan, who ran against both white men and black men and who struggled to maintain her base of black support, provides an early example of both the power and the limits of black female ambition.[12] Black women such as Jordan acted on their political ambitions because of a complex combination of social, political, and personal circumstances. What led them to office and how they were perceived by the general public illuminates how African Americans mobilized coalitions to elect black representatives and gain formal political power.

Jordan's interest in formal politics was an extension of her activism, to be sure, but it also reflected a personal and feminist desire to achieve independence and recognition. Houston's black community seems to have delighted in her competitive nature and her singular drive to succeed. Democratic Party officials in Houston initially asked her to run for office, but Jordan subsequently asserted her personal determination to go higher. The voices of criticism that came later in her career show the difficulty that black women encountered in making the transition from selfless activists to politicians, especially when they had to work closely with white men. Racial and sexual stereotypes continuously placed Jordan in a paradoxical place where her ambition was perceived contrarily by different groups.

Family and community expectations formed Jordan's competitive personality and were always central to shaping her ambitions. Born in 1936 and educated in the 1950s, Jordan grew up within the core institutions—church, school, and family—that defined the black working-class experience in segregated Houston.[13] As a girl, Jordan competed in school speech contests and church recitations, and her family provided praise and support. In high school, Jordan mastered debate, oratory, and academics, winning the annual Girl of the Year prize awarded to the senior with the best overall academic and extracurricular performances. At sixteen, Jordan traveled with her mother to Chicago to participate in the finals of a national speech tournament sponsored by a Baptist church organization. She continued winning plaudits and national recognition in black newspapers while on the debate team at Texas Southern University.[14] At the age of twenty, Jordan gained admittance to Boston University's law school, the first white-majority school she had ever attended. Although moments of insecurity crept in during this period, Jordan persevered and gained her law degree.[15] The stereotype of the 1950s was that girls were set on marrying young, but Jordan's family, friends, and wider circle of relations supported her professional ambitions.

After she graduated from law school in 1959, Jordan returned to Houston, where she encountered a grim reality: unemployment. After she took the state bar exam, Jordan could not find a job. She was overqualified for work available to black women and excluded from law firms because of her race and gender. Since emancipation, black women had been looking up from the bottom rung of the employment ladder, and little had changed by the mid-twentieth century. In 1940, more than 80 percent of Houston's black working women were employed as domestics, and during the 1960s, black women still found themselves in dire economic straits.[16] African American women in Houston's black neighborhoods also worked as beauticians, ran small restaurants, and sold cosmetics and hair care products; a minority earned an income as teachers. In the early 1960s, Houston was a booming city; petrochemicals, oil, and steel were just a few of the growing industries, but according to an American Friends Service Committee report, even with college degrees, "many Negroes find they must accept jobs far below their training." Such exclusion affected all African Americans, regardless of their professional aspirations: the Houston Bar Association did not accept blacks, and neither did San Jacinto High, the city's only vocational high school.[17] Employment barriers erected by sex and race discrimination in education, business, and government stood firm.[18] Because she was female and African American with a degree from a school outside of Texas, Jordan had difficulty finding legal work in Houston. She recalled that in 1960, "I had passed two bar exams, but I did not have that much to do really," so she decided to work for John F. Kennedy's presidential campaign.[19]

In Texas, civil rights work and political work were often contiguous. From 1960 to 1961, a series of student-led nonviolent direct actions targeted segregated restaurants and department stores.[20] Yet working for voting rights and political candidates had formed the core of black activism in Texas for much of the twentieth century. *Smith v. Allwright* (1944), which ended the white primary, had its roots in Houston. The plaintiff, Lonnie E. Smith, was from Jordan's church, and she knew the minister involved in raising money and gaining support for the case.[21] After the *Smith* decision, more Texas blacks began to vote, and they worked on numerous political campaigns, but as a group, they remained stymied. Overall registration was low, and few candidates appealed directly to African American voters. In fact, until the 1960s, Texas politicians such as Governor Allan Shivers had explicitly sought votes on the basis of maintaining the racial status quo and school segregation. Legal gains for blacks were matched not by greater political power but only by minor promises for advancement; poll taxes and other "antidemocratic contrivances" remained in effect.[22]

In 1960, a newly energized group of liberal Texas Democrats and leaders in the organized labor movement sought to mobilize black voters behind Kennedy. They wanted to undermine the conservative leadership that had rejected President Harry S. Truman in 1948 and endorsed Dwight Eisenhower in 1952. Liberal organizers wanted to register enough new black voters to strengthen the liberal wing of the overwhelmingly conservative, segregationist Texas Democratic Party. Kennedy's campaign staff in Houston concurred that voter registration was necessary and pronounced that the young Massachusetts senator could "win in Harris County (and in Texas) by concentrating on Democratic voters who didn't go to the polls in the last two presidential elections."[23] A moribund wing of the Texas Democratic Party was suddenly transformed into a movement of black, white, and Latino activists who had a revived strategy for sweeping the conservatives out of power: register minorities to vote, and they would vote for Kennedy.

But convincing black Texans to vote for Kennedy initially proved difficult. Many black voters were suspicious of the unknown northern senator and his endorsements by southern Democrats. "We are beginning to wonder just what commitment Kennedy has made to make him so strong in the South," opined the editors of the *Houston Informer*, an African American paper.[24] Texas Democrats had to dispel those suspicions and fears, and Jordan, who had no such misgivings, perhaps because of her years as a law student in Boston, went to work for Kennedy. She helped to nurture mutual respect and trust between the Democratic Party and black voters. She read out the party's national platform on civil rights before a gathering of 150 black precinct judges and precinct chairs during a luncheon at Pleasant Hill Baptist Church. Her endorsement of the campaign was a part of the party's efforts to woo black voters.[25]

Jordan made her political reputation in the churches and meeting places where blacks gathered to hear her urge them to register to vote.[26] Labor organizer Eddie Ball remembered, "Where she really was great was recruitment. She would go to a church, and make one of those speeches, and we'd have volunteers running out of there . . . people volunteering to be registration clerks." The results were phenomenal, according to Ball: "We wound up with over sixty thousand registered to vote" in the 1960 election. The coalition was important not just because of its numbers but also because it raised the average black voter's political leverage. Increased black voting, as activist Larry Goodwyn pointed out in the *Texas Observer*, was key to attacking segregation and the state's de facto one-party system. After Kennedy's victory, politicians had to be more careful about alienating black voters: "The tremendous rise in the voting power of Negroes and Latin Americans . . . gives an ever broadening base to the liberal labor minorities coalition. Leaders of these minorities will play increasingly powerful parts in the political decision making of the liberal wing of the party."[27] Organized labor also recognized the importance of black voting and civil rights. After meeting with Kennedy, Houston labor leader Hank Brown brought the message of integration home to the rank and file in the electrical trade: "I know this is unpopular with many of you, but there is going to have to be room for Negroes in the labor movement."[28] Because of the Kennedy campaign, white union leaders and liberal Texans began to pay more attention to black activists, leaders, and voters.

The Kennedy campaign began Jordan's dual career in activism and politics. Jordan developed and led the block worker program for Harris County's forty black or largely black voting precincts. Voter registration was labor-intensive and neighborhood-based. Block workers went door to door to urge registration, payment of the poll tax, and appearance at the polls for the primary and then again on Election Day. Speaking and touring in Houston's neighborhoods introduced Jordan to local party activists and gave her leadership experience although she was only twenty-four. She recalled that "in those precincts we worked, there was a turnout of some 80 percent of the vote. It was the most successful get out the vote that anybody could recall in Harris County."[29] Jordan had proved her worth as a speaker and as an organizer, and although there was no doubt which she enjoyed more, both skills proved crucial to her future success. Encouraging blacks to register became her new vocation, a direction taken by many other southern black activists.[30] The Kennedy battle marked the beginning of Jordan's relationship with the Texas Democratic Party as well as with the movement to end segregation. In Texas, the two were linked.

For the next six years, Jordan engaged in politics, broadly defined. Every two years, she ran for political office, but she also worked on civil rights issues such as school integration, economic development, and voter registration. Between 1962 and 1963, Jordan became an important part of the Democratic Coalition, a statewide campaign to repeal the poll tax. The Coalition's newsletter singled out her leadership in organizing the Houston drive: "The biggest job in Texas is being handled by the headquarters in Houston. Barbara Jordan is doing an around the clock job of directing her staff on the distribution of kits and the recruiting of blockworkers." Although the drive failed to repeal the poll tax in Texas, the campaign registered thousands of new black voters, raised Jordan's profile among black Houstonians, and further increased her knowledge of door-to-door organizing in black communities.[31]

By 1963, Jordan was a member of the executive committee of the National Association for the Advancement of Colored People (NAACP), a platform she used to speak out against resistance to school integration in Houston. She joined one hundred picketers at a school board meeting and read a statement denouncing the appointment of a black board member known to oppose integration: "It is clear that such a position and the selection of the person to fill this position would be designed not to elevate the status of Negroes but to further degrade them." One of the placards held by a protester read, "Down with Uncle Toms."[32] For the next three years, Jordan remained on the NAACP board and participated in the efforts of People for the Upgrading of Schools in Houston (PUSH), led by the Reverend William Lawson, to force the school board to integrate.

Furthering her activism, Jordan joined national and state efforts to confront injustice. African Americans had experienced inferior schooling, poor job prospects, and discrimination in hiring. According to the 1960 census, the median income of black Texans was less than half that of whites, while the black unemployment rate remained twice that for whites. In the spring of 1963, according to the *Texas Observer*, "the issue of jobs for Negroes has come to the surface with the fierceness of a pent up cause."[33] Thus, when a quarter of a million Americans gathered in Washington to march for jobs and justice and to hear Martin Luther King Jr. and other black leaders make the national case for an end to segregation, a few thousand Texans staged their own march down the main streets of the state's capital. They pressed their case for greater economic opportunity with Governor John Connally. It was a tense time. "Austin Seeking to Avert Clash by Racists," read one headline. The police stopped the "Indignant White Citizens Council" from marching down Congress Avenue to confront the civil rights crowd. Still, on August 29, 1963, in what was probably "the largest civil rights march Texas has yet had," approximately one thousand marchers took to Austin's streets. The crowd included delegations from all of Texas's major cities, an AFL-CIO delegation from Houston, Larry Goodwyn of the Democratic Coalition, the elderly, and the youth of Austin. All were singing freedom songs and carrying signs: "Segregation is a New Form of Slavery," "We Are Tired of Gradualism," "No More 50 Cents per Hour," and "Freedom Now."[34] Among the speakers at Rosewood Park after the march to the capital were Dallas attorney W. J. Durham, Dr. Ruth Bellinger McCoy, and "Barbara Jordan, Houston lawyer."[35] After the March on Washington and the demonstrations in Austin, Jordan became even more involved in activism and continued her drive to become the first African American elected to the Texas House of Representatives since Reconstruction.

In the midst of this stage of her activism, Jordan ran twice for elective office. In 1962, Jordan agreed to run for the state legislature and was the only black candidate among the twelve supported by the liberal coalition of the Harris County Democrats.[36] Jordan felt optimistic about her chances, and party organizer Chris Dixie encouraged her to think she could win: "You're going to get ninety per cent of the black vote, thirty per cent of the white vote. There's no way you can lose." But there was. She received thirty-six thousand votes, while her conservative opponent, Willis Whatley, received sixty-five thousand, "and that was that." Jordan doubted the process. How could other liberals win when she could not? "The feeling I had was that I had been used to get black people to vote. . . . The votes were just not there from these fine white people. That was very puzzling to me, and disturbing."[37] Jordan was further astonished when a white professor, a member of the Democratic Party coalition, spelled out the prejudice she faced: "A professor at Rice University who came into my campaign headquarters during that first race had said to me: 'You know it's going to be hard for you to win a seat in the Texas Legislature. You've got too much going against you: You're black, you're a woman, and you're large. People don't really like that image.'"[38] The professor's statement perhaps indicates how little alleged political experts understood about black voters. Nevertheless, he pinpointed a problem Jordan faced: how to gain white votes. Within her community, Jordan had always been a star, her booming voice and large presence an attribute while she spoke on the podium and on the stage. How could these things now be a disadvantage?

Despite this initial setback, Jordan's ambition to succeed in politics had been stoked; the fire would not die. Anger at segregation in general became righteous indignation in particular when she saw those less qualified sitting in positions of power. "One day I went to Austin to testify, and when I sat up in the House gallery and looked down at Willis Whatley at his desk, I thought, 'I ought to be in his place, I deserve it.'"[39] By 1964, Jordan had been involved in voter registration drives for more than four years. She had marched with the NAACP and become a known advocate for immediate compliance with school integration. She firmly situated herself on the progressive side of issues and took risks by taking more militant civil rights stands. In 1964, Jordan ran again as the only black candidate in the liberal coalition for the state House of Representatives, but although the black turnout surpassed previous records, she again lost to

Whatley. One of her friends and political advisers, Dr. Wilhelmina Perry, an African American sociologist, blamed party headquarters for the "chaos" of Jordan's 1964 campaign: "The liberal Democrats were calling all the shots. . . . Somebody said, 'We made you. We expect you to follow our agenda. If you don't, we'll withhold the money.'"[40] After her loss, Jordan remembered eschewing her crowds of supporters, driving around alone in her car, and thinking, "Is a seat in the state legislature worth continuing to try for? . . . [W]hy are you doing this?"[41] She felt frustrated and angry. When she received a call telling her that the election analysis was ready, she snapped, "I've got the analysis for you: I didn't win."[42] Once again, Jordan's defeat symbolized blacks' continued exclusion from political power and her own failure to garner white votes.

Jordan's second defeat forced her to look at her campaigns in a new light. She began to see herself more as a black candidate and less as part of a liberal-labor coalition. The civil rights movement was gaining momentum and attention, and her activism and running for office in the face of great odds brought her recognition, especially in Chicago, where her old friend and fellow attorney, Ernestine Washington, now lived. When Jordan spoke there at a banquet honoring a prominent black Illinois legislator, she received top billing in the *Chicago Defender*. More than eight hundred guests attended the banquet, among them prominent attorneys, school board members, Cook County superintendents, and members of civil rights organizations and political groups, including Daisy Bates, the NAACP director from Little Rock. The *Defender* described Jordan as a "pioneer in the voter registration drive in the Southwest and runner up in the race for the Texas legislature" and reported that Jordan "brought down the house, with the line: 'Negroes today reject Uncle Toms and Uncle Thomases— Uncle Toms with PhD degrees.'"[43]

Jordan's political candidacies did not slow her civil rights activism. In 1965, as a member of PUSH, she supported a walkout of nine thousand students from five of Houston's black high schools to protest the slow pace of integration. To show the level of community discontent, PUSH planned a "house to house drive" to defeat a scheduled $58.9 million school bond election.[44] Jordan favored a mix of marching and voting to achieve total integration of the Houston schools. "The barriers against us will fall if we push, and we will push. . . . No one can squelch this movement," she said at a Houston rally. Jordan charged that the members of the Houston school board were not complying with the Civil Rights Act of 1964, "and they know it."[45] Later in the year, Jordan's speeches questioned the sincerity not just of Texas but also of the nation as a whole. In August 1965, she gave a "stimulated" and "provocative" address to a large audience at Valparaiso University in Indiana, where she spoke alongside Illinois state senator (and later U.S. senator) Paul Simon. Jordan told the audience, "No nation state has excelled America in the nobility of her pronouncements. The time honored words of the Declaration of Independence continue to excite and inspire the spirit of this country. Yet we continue to struggle for their meaning. We are still trying to define America; to affirm and actualize its promise." She contrasted the "pious traditionalism of the law" with the reality of the black experience, emphasizing that although blacks had always been inwardly hostile, they had rarely been able to show their dissatisfaction and anger. But times had changed. Paraphrasing Frederick Douglass, she announced that power could not "be received as a gift; it must be taken, for it is in the process of striving for power that people become powerful; it is in the process of fighting for freedom that they become free."[46] Between her political campaigns, Jordan continued to focus on the struggles of the civil rights movement.

Jordan's defeats in 1962 and 1964 led her to work even harder for black equality and made her rethink the public's perception of her as a leader. Being black and female made her stand out; so did being unmarried.[47] Jordan had told her family that she was too busy with politics to consider marriage, and now she wrestled with how to convey her independent, unmarried status to the electorate. "The public believed that a woman had to have, over and above and beyond other aspirations, a home and family. That was what every normal woman was supposed to want. And any woman who didn't want that was considered something a little abnormal." Pressure from family members to marry and adopt a more conventional life struck her as unjust and unfair. "Where a man was concerned, the public perception was that he was supposed to get out there and lead and do and make decisions and the rest of it; and no one said to him that he needed to care for the babies, or iron the curtains, or clean the johns. That was not expected of him. What was expected was that he'd marry a woman to do it for him. And why not?" After her second disheartening defeat, Jordan was tempted to simply withdraw from the fray. But she resolved to push herself and to convey her passion to win as a positive trait. "The question you have to decide, Barbara Jordan, is whether you're going to fly in the face of what everybody expects out there because you've got your eye someplace else, or whether you can bring the public along to understand that there are some women for whom other expectations are possible."[48] Jordan had fixed her "eye" on winning political office, and she threw all of her energies into the next race.

By 1966, political circumstances had changed in Jordan's favor. A combination of Supreme Court and local court decisions had forced the Texas Senate to redistrict itself based on population. Jordan could now run for the state Senate in a district with a small black majority and no incumbent.[49] She declared her-

self a candidate, but she had an opponent, Charles Whitfield, a liberal white labor lawyer and an experienced politician. Whitfield had previously represented
the largely black Fifth Ward neighborhood in the Texas House, and he believed
that his progressive voting record on civil rights made him the natural heir to
the new Senate seat. He fought Jordan in the primary, questioning her inexperi-
ence and arguing that black voters should not support her just because she was
African American.

Jordan responded to Whitfield with a highly organized campaign. Her headquarters was located on Lyons Avenue, the main street in the Fifth Ward. She
drew on the local black women who had been her block workers since 1960,
a strategy that she later described as "the primary factor" in the election. She
had lists of all the precinct judges and the names of all those willing to work
in each neighborhood. Each worker was "furnished with a block worker kit,
a letter of instructions and campaign material."[50] When Jordan responded to
Whitfield's charge that a vote for her was a racist vote, her campaign theme
emerged: "Our time has come," she said at a rally. For twenty years, black voters
had sent whites to office. Now Jordan urged those voters to seize the day: "Can
a white man win? I say to you NO. Not this time. Not . . . this . . . time!"[51] Black
voters were frustrated at the slow pace of change, and according to a Houston
sociologist, "The whole community is a bomb. Negroes are repressed and there
is this latent anxiety."[52] When the 1966 May Democratic primary came, Jordan
beat Whitfield by more than five thousand votes and received 98 percent of the
black vote in her district.[53] Jordan's win sent the message that African Americans needed to see their own become political leaders. "We needed a victory,"
Jordan stated. "This is the only way. We've been talking a long time, but they
always come back and say, 'We don't see anything.' They don't win. A victory in
a body like the statehouse will do more to help the Negro recognize his voting
strength than anything I can think of."[54] Her election provided tangible evidence
of black voting power and unity.

Jordan's victory also represented an important achievement for black women.
As she noted, the black community and her family held many traditional expectations about women's place in the home. To promote her campaign, Jordan
had to raise money, make speeches, be a leader, and make the case for why she
was the better candidate. Running for office differed dramatically from being an
influential behind-the-scenes organizer, requiring unabashed confidence that
she would win. Black voters, who had long cast ballots but had never elected a
black person to the legislature, appreciated Jordan's honest satisfaction in de-
feating her opponent. Her victory was theirs. On election night, joyful supporters caused pandemonium in Houston's streets, and Jordan was the focus:

"Cars were jammed in the street, with people spilling out onto the sidewalk and leaning out of upstairs windows. When they saw her, the scream went up: HERE SHE COMES!"[55]

In 1966, the Black Power movement was making an impact in the South, and Jordan explicitly portrayed herself as the black candidate for change. Black Houstonians saw Jordan not as the coalition candidate but as the black candidate, representing the race with dignity. They took pride in her law degree, her elegant oratory, her attacks on segregation, and her victory. When it was time for her to take the oath of office, ten busloads of black Houstonians traveled to Austin to watch. James Stanley, a retired black teacher from Houston, wept and recalled the memory of his paternal grandmother, who "carried with her to her grave, on both her soul and her body, the ineffable scars of human slavery." As he watched Jordan's swearing-in ceremony, Stanley thought of his grandmother and of the pain of black Texans who were "beaten with axe handles at the polls." Overcome with emotion, Stanley looked at Jordan and thought of the struggle of the entire black race in America. He praised the new state senator as "the most beautiful woman in the world" and "a symbol of all Negro womanhood in the world." To Stanley, Jordan's sex did not impede her claim to race leadership. Instead, Jordan represented old-fashioned race pride as well as the new movement focused on Black Power. "Grandmother, your prayers are answered. We have the right now, not only to die for our country but to live for her. We have the right not only to obey the law but to help make the law. . . . [N]ot only do we vote, we hold office."[56] Historian Elsa Barkley Brown has argued that since emancipation, "collective autonomy"—the idea that individual freedom was tied up with the progress of the group—was central to African American political life.[57] To Stanley and other black Houstonians, Jordan's success was not merely a lesson in individual achievement; her ambition to run for office and to win fulfilled a collective historical demand for justice and social change.

While in office, Jordan continued to promote African American participation in politics. She worked with organized labor, white liberals, and local blacks to register black voters and encourage them to pay their poll taxes. On October 6–8, 1967, she sponsored a workshop on electoral politics that attracted three hundred black activists to Wimberley, a rural retreat just outside of Austin. The underlying messages were self-reliance and independence. "Negroes for too long—for reasons of survival—have practiced the art of 'followship,'" she observed. Jordan advocated a different strategy. At the 1967 Texas Leadership Conference, Jordan urged black candidates to build up their own organizations as she had: "If NEGROES are going to lead, the leaders must talk to each other. . . . YOU must get the voters registered; YOU must get your registered voters to the polls." Jordan was fired up. Her campaign had been a success, as had her block workers program. "WE ARE HERE TO EXCHANGE IDEAS TO TAKE BACK TO OUR HOME COMMUNITIES WHICH WILL CHANGE THE FACE OF TEXAS AND THE NATION."[58] Coalition politics and alliances with whites were essential for black success, but Jordan was also telling black candidates that to be respected, they needed to bring their own organizations and committed voters to the table. Even within the context of a biracial coalition, blacks needed to increase racial solidarity to promote their interests.

Throughout her career in the Texas Senate, Jordan continued to have her differences with white liberals yet remained an important part of the coalition opposing Democratic Party conservatives.[59] After she was reelected to the Senate in 1968 and became a viable candidate for Congress, however, Jordan's image changed. To African Americans in Houston, she remained a respected racial leader who brought benefits and pride to her constituents. By 1972, the *Forward Times* was speculating that Jordan could become the first African American president.[60] But white liberals had begun to view her more cautiously in the second half of the 1960s, especially as she developed closer ties with President Lyndon Baines Johnson, whose blunders in Vietnam enraged the Left. For Jordan, Johnson's commitment to civil rights always outweighed his foreign policy debacles. In October 1971, he endorsed her bid for Congress and attended a fund-raiser in her honor. And after she won a seat in the U.S. House in 1972, Johnson remained her adviser and mentor until his death the following year.[61]

As Jordan's political career progressed, she was lauded by the press, audiences, and her constituents. The congresswoman's speaking prowess and national popularity took her far from the working-class, black Houston neighborhood of her youth. Rumors had Jordan as a candidate for a U.S. Supreme Court vacancy, and in 1975, *Redbook* magazine found that 44 percent of Americans polled chose Jordan as the first female president.[62] The avalanche of popularity emphasized Jordan as a charismatic orator and pragmatic politician rather than an activist with strong community ties. Some detractors explained her popularity and seeming influence on her appeal as a "mammy" figure: in slavery, the story went, female house slaves garnered favor with white elites while selling out their fellow blacks. Jordan was now doing the same. Genuine political differences could explain some of this criticism, but ultimately what reduced Jordan in the eyes of her Democratic critics was not her politics but the perception she was ambitious, cold, and selfish and sold out principles for advancement.[63] Jordan's black constituents and her critics perceived her relationships with powerful whites very differently. That difference helps to explain some of the simmering tensions in the political alliances between African Americans and white Democratic Party liberals.

Jordan initially gained the national spotlight with a televised speech during the summer 1974 Watergate hearings; two years later, her address to the Democratic National Convention resulted in immense media coverage and scrutiny. Jordan campaigned hard for the party's nominee, Jimmy Carter, and her convention performance was widely credited with reviving the party's fighting spirit. In Texas, however, her status within the party came under increasing criticism, culminating in two articles that appeared in the October 1976 edition of *Texas Monthly* magazine, "What Does This Woman Want?," by journalist Walter Shapiro, and William Broyles's lengthy biographical piece, "The Making of Barbara Jordan."[64] The tone of this pair of pieces differed greatly from more positive earlier coverage. Both authors credited Jordan as a liberal who had worked on behalf of an increase in the minimum wage, fair labor practices, and antidiscrimination laws and who had won an expanded Voting Rights Act in 1975. Yet both authors also suggested that her ambition had led to a lack of a moral center. As Broyles put it, "The central dilemma about Barbara Jordan is that while almost everyone believes she has this central core beyond politics, this ultimate devotion to long-standing principles, no one really knows what it is. No one can point to many long-standing principles that she has made the establishment recognize." Broyles then recited a barrage of criticisms against Jordan from liberal whites who felt that Jordan shut them out: "Her friends say she is really only comfortable with Southerners, including blacks like Georgia's Andrew Young but also some of the most reactionary members of Congress."[65] Was Jordan guilty of becoming friendly with white conservatives only to promote her career? The implied answer was yes.

It is true that Jordan was wary of white liberals as well as open to cordial relations with selected conservatives. Memories of her early losses and the difficulty of getting white votes stayed with her, but perhaps Jordan had reason to be skeptical of her white liberal allies. In a 1972 article in the *Texas Observer*, Molly Ivins, a well-known liberal journalist in Austin, reported that one of Jordan's fellow senators had referred to her as "that nigger bitch" and that another, eager to praise her to an audience of black voters, remarked, "Why that nigger girl is the smartest member of the Senate." Ivins was lampooning the racism of Texas legislators, but Jordan could hardly have appreciated reading such things in print, especially in such a glib manner. Ivins could not free herself from atrocious stereotypes, writing that when white audiences first encountered Jordan, they saw her as a joke. "They tend to snigger and assume that anyone who looks that much like a mammy is going to be pretty funny to hear." Clearly, Ivins was perplexed: "You can't prove how liberal you are by showing that you're buddies with her—that's like trying to pal it up with Charles de Gaulle."[66] Such images must have stuck in Jordan's heart and mind. Jordan knew she could never escape the mammy image, but she could maintain her dignity and her distance.

In his 1976 article, Broyles took the mammy stereotype even further:

> She has been called Aunt Jemima by both her friends and her enemies, and although she doesn't like it, the metaphor is apt. In appearance she conjures up the common memories of a culture—she is every black maid, black cook, black mammy. She comes to us direct from Gone with the Wind or Uncle Tom's Cabin, an enduring stereotype of the black women who lived closest with whites, who sustained the web of mutuality. The awesomeness of her presence is rooted in her explicit destruction of that image, as if every black mammy and Aunt Jemima had risen up with their rolling pins to take over the world.[67]

Broyles was referring to the perception of the mammy as the original sellout. She lived in the big house; she took care of the master's children, allegedly loving them more than her own; she was trusted enough that whites asked her about what was happening down in the quarters. In short, the mammy was more than a symbol of jest or trust; in this context, she was a race traitor and a sellout to those in power. Broyles's image of the mammy in revolt sought to rob Jordan of her achievements; it erased her years of anger against segregation and negated her hard work to end it. Despite her education, intelligence, activism, and manners, the white journalists looking at Jordan could see only mammy. That image haunted Jordan throughout her political career, as disgruntled liberals used it as a prism through which to view her alliances with those in power.

The Democratic Party establishment also did not know how to handle Jordan's ambitions. After Carter's 1976 victory, she was one of only a few African Americans and women considered for a cabinet spot. She met with the new president but was wary. She had heard reports that the only cabinet position open to an African American was that of United Nations ambassador, but Jordan let it be known that she was interested in being attorney general. Observers perceived her actions as presumptuous, leading to a critical *Washington Post* article in which journalist Walter Pincus suggested that Jordan was not qualified for a cabinet post. More damningly, he used an unnamed source to assert that Jordan wanted the cabinet position only to keep her in the limelight until she was ready to run against John Tower for the U.S. Senate in 1978. The specter of personal ambition haunted her. Pincus mentioned that Jordan supported Texas oil and gas interests, and he used disparaging quotes, all from unnamed sources: "'She's a Texan first, a black second and a woman third,' an unnamed 'leader' of the women's political movement said yesterday." Furthermore, Pincus observed, Jordan was "not friendly" and had emerged from her meeting with Carter wearing a "cold, fixed expression, according to a reporter on the scene." The title of the article was "Barbara Jordan Caught Up in Hardball Politics," but the politics entrapping her were not necessarily the politics of Washington but rather the refusal of the press and liberals to accept a black woman who wanted to rise.[68]

Black journalists also contributed to Jordan's growing negative image. A similarly critical tone appeared in a 1977 article in the black magazine *Encore*. In "Will the Real Barbara Jordan Please Stand?," Paula Giddings noted that after the attorney general debacle, Jordan's "once rapidly ascending political star seemed to have been braked, at least temporarily. Within twenty-four hours the politician who had seemed above critics was being criticized by both colleagues and the press." Giddings depicted Jordan as an unprincipled politician out only for herself. "'Don't quote me,' said a black politician, 'she is the most vindictive person I know, and she holds our political futures in her hands.'" "She's not a champion of the black cause," said Chris Dixie, one of the liberal leaders of the Harris County Democrats and the man who had first convinced Jordan to run. Giddings also invoked the mammy image to explain why white politicians liked Jordan.

> To some whites, [Jordan's] visual appearance also symbolized the kind of solace that [*Gone With the Wind* actress] Hattie McDaniel provided on the screen; after [U.S. Representative] Wayne Hays gave his first speech in the House defending his [sexual] relationship with Elizabeth Ray [his assistant], it seemed natural that he would immediately come over and sit next to Jordan. To others it serves as an exculpation of their guilt; after all, to like and support a Barbara Jordan is proof that one is not racist or sexist. And to some she provides the satisfaction of a McDaniel snatching off that kerchief and demanding to be given the respect that her wisdom deserved (she really ran the house anyway). Among Houston's blacks Jordan is the home town child who made it big. . . . She is the less than rich, less than attractive studious lady from the 5th ward who hobnobbed with the powerful and emerged intact.

Giddings made no mention of Jordan's activism and her years of struggle as a black candidate or member of the NAACP. Instead, Giddings criticized Jordan for allegedly showing no sympathy to civil rights protesters in Houston, being mean to her political opponents, making alliances with the powerful, and wanting to keep other blacks out of office.[69]

Other journalists looked beyond the personal. Writing in March 1975, Meg Greenfield of *Newsweek* magazine seemed to understand the various forces pulling at Jordan as she sought to establish a political identity: "Which duty, which aspect of what a person is comes first? And how much independence and individuality must be yielded up to meet their various claims?" Jordan was "determined to build her national reputation in a way that transcends the issues of her race and gender—while still pressing what she regards as the legitimate public claims of both." Jordan, Greenfield believed, sought to "enlarge the context of the civil rights and poverty battles she was fighting and to make her own experience of hardship and injustice the basis of a more inclusionary, generous politics."[70] Jordan never apologized for her ambition or for seeking personal relations with those in power. But many white allies in the Democratic Party as well as some party leaders could not see her ambition in terms larger than personal aggrandizement.

Barbara Jordan's early political career illuminates how ambitious women leaders galvanized black voters and American democracy in the 1960s. Until recently, the ambition of black women politicians has been used to explain only a singular anomaly: the "puzzle" of the success of black women politicians in light of their "double disadvantage." But in retrospect, it makes little sense to compare black and white women politicians in the 1960s because they worked in such different contexts. Jordan was a product of a segregated black community that needed educated, ambitious individuals willing to risk defeat in the political arena. She took that risk because of her anger about segregation and her desire to develop a career in politics. For all African Americans, leadership in formal electoral politics posed new tests and opportunities distinctive from the challenges of organizing. As a single black woman, however, Jordan faced additional obstacles because she challenged traditional views concerning female dependency and appearance.

Jordan's ambition was also an expression of community will. During the 1960s, she inspired a core of community activists to register voters for school integration, the Kennedy campaign, and to end the poll tax. Those workers then became loyal to her. Black Houstonians felt an intense identity with the congresswoman. They had supported the liberal-labor coalition with their votes and campaign work, yet African Americans were also keen to elect a black candidate who symbolized the end of slavery and segregation. They expected Jordan to aim higher and identified strongly with black leaders not as "role models" but as representatives of the popular will. Frustrated in their political aspirations for generations, black Houstonians treasured winning candidates such as Jordan whose victories tempered cynicism toward the political process. As long as Jordan was perceived as serving her race and her constituents, African American voters in Houston applauded her ambition. They identified strongly with her success; her ambition uplifted them. Blacks had been excluded from the ballot for decades and had suffered extreme economic and political marginalization. In that context, then, it made sense to celebrate Jordan's achievements as symbolic of the rise of the race. And, indeed, with her success came greater minority representation in city and state government.

White liberals, conversely, saw black voting in a practical light—it enlarged liberalism's influence in the party. White liberals were essential to Jordan's career: without their support, Jordan would not have been able to launch her initial forays for the Texas House of Representatives. But because white liberals had not lived under the thumb of white power, they had difficulty understanding Jordan's temperament, why she formed her own organization for the 1966 Texas Senate campaign, or why she became friendly with certain conservatives. All of these aspects of her personality and strategy were interpreted as evidence solely of personal ambition. Ironically, whites often believed that Jordan's singular ambition threatened the coalition they had so proudly forged. The bigger picture, however, is that Jordan resented the racial and sexual stereotypes foisted on her. More significantly, she disagreed with the strategy of alienating powerful people. Finally, her experience of defeat had taught her, rightly or wrongly, that black strength in the labor-liberal coalition would be honored only if black voters were powerful as a group, and her rise proved their collective power. She understood that the members of her community were pushing her to rise high because she had the opportunity to do individually what they collectively could not. Rarely has a politician so perfectly represented the outsized ambitions of her community as Barbara Jordan did.

NOTES

1. "Senator Jordan: Even as Little Girl She Was One of the Rare Ones," *Houston Chronicle*, November 30, 1969.

2. Mary Beth Rogers, *Barbara Jordan: American Hero* (New York: Bantam, 1998), 324–56; "Jordan, Barbara Charline (1936–1996)," *Biographical Directory of the United States Congress, 1774–Present*, http://bioguide.congress.gov/scripts/biodisplay.pl?index=J000266 (accessed February 18, 2014).

3. Questionnaire, "Biography" folder, "Miscellaneous 1974–75" box, Barbara Jordan Archives, Texas Southern University, Houston. All references to the Jordan Archives use the terminology of the first finding aid.

4. Malcolm Boyd, "Where Is Barbara Jordan Today?," *Parade Magazine*, February 16, 1986, 12.

5. Joseph A. Schlesinger, *Political Parties and the Winning of Office* (Ann Arbor: University of Michigan Press, 1991), 34–35; Joseph A. Schlesinger, *Ambition and Politics: Political Careers in the United States* (Chicago: Rand McNally, 1966). For a summary of the literature on ambition, see Richard L. Fox and Jennifer L. Lawless, "Explaining Nascent Political Ambition," *American Journal of Political Science* 49 (July 2005): 642–59. See also Pauline Terrelongue Stone, "Ambition Theory and the Black Politician," *Western Political Quarterly* 33 (March 1980): 94–107.

6. William Broyles, "The Making of Barbara Jordan," *Texas Monthly*, October 1976, http://www .texasmonthly.com/story/making-barbara-jordan (accessed February 16, 2014).

7. R. Darcy and Charles D. Hadley, "Black Women in Politics: The Puzzle of Success," *Social Science Quarterly* 69 (September 1988): 29–45. See also Linda Faye Williams, "The Civil Rights–Black Power Legacy: Black Women Elected Officials at the Local, State, and National Levels," in *Sisters in the Struggle: African American Women in the Civil Rights–Black Power Movement*, ed. Bettye Collier-Thomas and V. P. Franklin (New York: New York University Press, 2001), 306–31; Katherine Tate, *Black Faces in the Mirror: African Americans and Their Representatives in the U.S. Congress* (Princeton: Princeton University Press, 2003), 40–50.

8. Anna Fels, *Necessary Dreams: Ambition in Women's Changing Lives* (New York: Random House, 2004), 5, 8–9.

9. Jennifer L. Lawless and Richard L. Fox, *It Takes a Candidate: Why Women Don't Run for Office* (Cambridge: Cambridge University Press, 2005). See also Richard L. Fox and Jennifer L. Lawless, "Entering the Arena: Gender and the Decision to Run for Office," *American Journal of Political Science* 48 (April 2004): 264–80; Richard L. Fox and Jennifer L. Lawless, "If Only They'd Ask: Gender, Recruitment, and Political Ambition," *Journal of Politics* 72 (April 2010): 310–26; Richard L. Fox and Jennifer L. Lawless, "Gendered Perceptions of Political Candidates: A Central Barrier to Women's Equality in Electoral Politics," *American Journal of Political Science* 55 (January 2011): 59–73.

10. A few basic texts on the Voting Rights Act include J. Morgan Kousser, *Colorblind Injustice: Minority Voting Rights and the Undoing of the Second Reconstruction* (Chapel Hill: University of North Carolina Press, 1999); Richard Valelly, *The Two Reconstructions: The Struggle for Black Enfranchisement* (Chicago: University of Chicago Press, 1994); Chandler Davidson and Bernard Grofman, eds., *Quiet Revolution in the South: The Impact of the Voting Rights Act, 1965–1990* (Princeton: Princeton University Press, 1994); Chandler Davidson, ed., *Minority Vote Dilution* (Washington, D.C.: Howard University Press, 1989); Bernard Grofman, ed., *Minority Representation and the Quest for Voting Equality* (Cambridge: Cambridge University Press, 1992); Jack Bass and Walter DeVries, *The Transformation of Southern Politics: Social Change and Political Compromise since 1945* (New York: Basic Books, 1976); Richard C. Cortner, *The Apportionment Cases* (Knoxville: University of Tennessee Press, 1970). A sample of the most important books on African American politicians includes Tate, *Black Faces in the Mirror*; Richard Fenno, *Going Home: Black Representatives and Their Constituents* (Chicago: University of Chicago Press, 2003); David T. Canon, *Race, Redistricting, and Representation: The Unintended Consequences of Black Majority Districts* (Chicago: University of Chicago Press, 1999); Carol M. Swain, *Black Faces, Black Interests: The Representation of African Americans in Congress* (Cambridge: Harvard University Press, 1993); Steven F. Lawson, *Running for Freedom: Civil Rights and Black Politics in America since 1941* (New York: Wiley, Blackwell, 2008); Michael B. Preston, Lenneal J. Henderson Jr., and Paul Puryear, eds., *The New Black Politics: The Search for Political Power* (New York: Longman, 1982); Mervyn M. Dymally, ed., *The Black Politician: His Struggle for Power* (Belmont, Calif.: Duxbury, 1971); Lani Guinier, *Tyranny of the Majority: Fundamental Fairness in Representative Democracy* (New York: Free Press, 1994). There is a large literature on black mayors not mentioned here. For an influential approach to popular African American understandings of politics, see Melissa Harris-Lacewell, *Barbershops, Bibles, and BET: Everyday Talk and Black Political Thought* (Princeton: Princeton University Press, 2004).

11. A few basic texts on the modern history of gender and politics include Myra Marx Feree, "A Woman for President?: Changing Responses, 1958–1972," *Public Opinion Quarterly* 38 (Autumn 1974): 395; Lawless and Fox, *It Takes a Candidate*; Susan J. Carroll and Richard L. Fox, eds., *Gender and Elections: Shaping the Future of American Politics*, 2nd ed. (Cambridge: Cambridge University

Press, 2009); Anne Kornblut, *Notes from the Cracked Ceiling: Hillary Clinton, Sarah Palin, and What It Will Take for a Woman to Win* (New York: Crown, 2009).

12. Jewel L. Prestage, "In Quest of the African American Political Woman," *Annals of the American Academy of Political and Social Science* 515 (May 1991): 88–103; Cathy J. Cohen, "A Portrait of Continuing Marginality: The Study of Women of Color in American Politics," in *Women and American Politics: New Questions, New Directions*, ed. Susan J. Carroll (New York: Oxford University Press, 2003), 190–213; Williams, "Civil Rights–Black Power Legacy"; Sharon Wright, "Black Women in Congress during the Post–Civil Rights Movement Era," in *Still Lifting, Still Climbing: African American Women's Contemporary Activism*, ed. Kimberly Springer (New York: New York University Press, 1999), 149–65; Darcy and Hadley, "Black Women in Politics," 629–45; Lisa Garcia Bedalia, Katherine Tate, and Janelle Wong, "Indelible Effects: The Impact of Women of Color in the U.S. Congress," in *Women and Elective Office: Past, Present, and Future*, ed. Sue Thomas and Clyde Wilcox (New York: Oxford University Press, 2005), 152–75; Wendy G. Smooth, "African American Women and Electoral Politics: Journeying from the Shadows to the Spotlight," in *Gender and Elections*, ed. Carroll and Fox, 117–42; Marjorie Lansing, "The Voting Patterns of American Black Women," in *A Portrait of Marginality: The Political Behavior of the American Woman*, ed. Marianne Githens and Jewel L. Prestage (New York: McKay, 1977), 379–94; Duchess Harris, *Black Feminist Politics from Kennedy to Clinton* (New York: Palgrave Macmillan, 2009); Melissa Harris, *Sister Citizen: Shame, Stereotypes, and Black Women in America* (Cambridge: Harvard University Press, 2011).

13. Jordan came from a working-class family where both parents contributed to the family income but her father was the dominant breadwinner. He worked in a warehouse; her paternal grandfather drove a delivery truck. Both were deacons in the Baptist Church. For more on Jordan's family background, see Barbara Jordan and Shelby Hearon, *Barbara Jordan: A Self-Portrait* (New York: Doubleday, 1977); Rogers, *Barbara Jordan*.

14. Jordan participated in numerous national debate tournaments and traveled as far away as Iowa to compete against students from schools such as Northwestern University and the University of Chicago. See *Chicago Defender*, March 24, 1956.

15. Jordan and Hearon, *Barbara Jordan*, 75–98.

16. James M. Sorelle, "'An de Po Cullud Man Is in de Wuss Fix uv Awl': Black Occupational Status in Houston, Texas, 1920–1940," *Houston Review* 1 (Spring 1979): 15–26.

17. Steve Wilson, Speech before the Human Relations Forum, November 18, 1960, in Employment on Merit Report, Houston, Southern Regional Council, Archives of the American Friends Service Committee, Philadelphia.

18. Chandler Davidson, *Biracial Politics: Conflict and Coalition in the Metropolitan South* (Baton Rouge: Louisiana State University Press, 1972), 106–25. Jordan's friend from Texas Southern University and coeditor of the yearbook, Andrew Jefferson, was admitted to University of Texas Law School the same year Jordan left for Boston. When he graduated, he joined a law office run by his brother-in-law and was soon hired by the district attorney's office in San Antonio (Andrew Jefferson, interview by author, March 27, 2001). For a white woman's account of discrimination in legal education and in practice in Texas during the 1950s, see Louise Ballerstedt Raggio, *Texas Tornado: The Life of a Crusader for Women's Rights and Family Justice* (New York: Citadel, 2003), 111–12. See also Karen Berger Morello, *The Invisible Bar: The Woman Lawyer in America: 1638 to the Present* (Boston: Beacon, 1986).

19. Jordan and Hearon, *Barbara Jordan*, 109–10.

20. For the story of the student sit-ins in Houston, see Thomas Cole, *No Color Is My Kind: The Life of Eldrewey Stearns and the Integration of Houston* (Austin: University of Texas Press, 1997).

21. For an overview of *Smith v. Allwright* and the role of the Reverend Albert A. Lucas of the Good Hope Missionary Baptist Church, see Merline Pitre, *In Struggle against Jim Crow: Lulu B. White and the NAACP, 1900–1957* (College Station: Texas A&M University Press, 1999).

22. Davidson, *Biracial Politics*, 55–56, 84–85.

23. *Houston Post*, September 6, 1960.

24. *Houston Informer*, July 30, 1960 (after Kennedy had gained endorsements from the Democratic Party in Virginia and Alabama).

25. Ibid., October 15, 1960.

26. Jordan and Hearon, *Barbara Jordan*, 110.

27. Eddie Ball, interview by author, April 14, 2004; *Texas Observer*, December 13, 1962.

28. "Texas Is Integrating: A Special Report," *Texas Observer*, June 28, 1963: "The weapons Negroes are using today to seek rights are the same weapons used by organized labor 30 years ago to bring us to the position we hold today. I think the Negro, the one who is qualified, ought to have the same chance that such tactics brought to the labor movement 30 years ago."

29. Jordan and Hearon, *Barbara Jordan*, 110.

30. After the 1960 Freedom Rides, one strand of civil rights workers, along with the Kennedy administration, focused on voter registration in the South (Valelly, *Two Reconstructions*, 175).

31. *Texas Democratic Coalition Newsletter* 1, no. 6 (1963), Texas AFL-CIO Papers, vol. 110-26, folder 5, box 9, Texas Labor Archives, University of Texas at Arlington.

32. *Dallas Morning News*, July 7, 1963.

33. *Texas Observer*, June 28, 1963. Annual income in 1960 was $1,150 for blacks and $2,573 for whites.

34. "The Austin March," *Texas Observer*, September 6, 1963.

35. *Dallas Morning News*, August 27, 1963.

36. Jordan and Hearon, *Barbara Jordan*, 113.

37. Ibid., 114–15.

38. Ibid., 115.

39. Ibid., 116.

40. Wilhelmina Perry, telephone interview by author, July 23, 2009.

41. Jordan and Hearon, *Barbara Jordan*, 117.

42. Ibid.

43. *Chicago Defender*, March 2, 4, 12, 16, 1964.

44. Ibid., May 18, 1965.

45. *Dallas Morning News*, May 16, 1965.

46. *Chicago Defender*, August 7, 1965.

47. Hattie Mae White, an outspoken opponent of segregation, was elected to the Houston school board in 1958. Married to a physician, she was often referred to by her husband's name, Mrs. Charles White (Davidson, *Biracial Politics*, 194–95). Houston NAACP leader Lulu White was also married (Pitre, *In Struggle against Jim Crow*, 14).

48. Jordan and Hearon, *Barbara Jordan*, 118.

49. The U.S. Supreme Court's decision in *Reynolds v. Sims* (1965) paved the way for challenges to the malapportionment of the Texas Senate. Because of malapportionment, urban Houston, with a population of nearly one million, had one Senate seat, the same as a sparsely populated rural

county. Thanks to another Supreme Court decision, *Kilgarlin v. Martin* (1966), the Texas Senate was compelled to redistrict its single-member seats according to population, and Houston received three more seats, one of which included all of the precincts that Jordan had won in her previous races. For an account of the 1966 election in Houston, see Rogers, *Barbara Jordan*, 103–6; Mary Ellen Curtin, "Reaching for Power: Barbara C. Jordan and Liberals in the Texas Legislature, 1966–1972," *Southwestern Historical Quarterly* 108 (October 2004): 213–15.

50. "Southern Regional Council Interview with Barbara Jordan," Texas State Senate CSR series, Organizations, General, 1967–72, Jordan Archives.

51. Jordan and Hearon, *Barbara Jordan*, 134.

52. "Black Houston," *Texas Observer*, May 13, 1966, emphasizes the economic deprivation of black Houston. For descriptions of daily life in Houston's black neighborhoods, see Saul Friedman, "Life in Black Houston," *Texas Observer*, June 9–23, 1967. For an explicit comparison with Watts, the Los Angeles neighborhood that experienced rioting in 1965, see Blair Justice, "An Inquiry into Negro Identity and a Methodology for Investigating Potential Racial Violence" (PhD diss., Rice University, 1966).

53. Chandler Davidson, "Negro Politics and the Rise of the Civil Rights Movement in Houston, Texas" (PhD diss., Princeton University, 1968), 170–73; Davidson, *Biracial Politics*, 101–2.

54. Molly Ivins, "A Conversation with Miss Jordan," *Texas Observer*, May 27, 1966.

55. Jordan and Hearon, *Barbara Jordan*, 134.

56. James Stanley, "Man's View of Barbara Jordan," *Forward Times*, January 21, 1967.

57. Elsa Barkley Brown, "To Catch the Vision of Freedom: Reconstructing Southern Black Women's Political History, 1865–1880," in *Unequal Sisters: A Multicultural Reader in U.S. Women's History*, ed. Vicki L. Ruiz and Ellen Carol DuBois (New York: Routledge, 2000), 125–26.

58. Texas Leadership Conference, Political Files series, Campaign Activities, 1967–72, Jordan Archives.

59. Curtin, "Reaching for Power," 211–31.

60. "Barbara Jordan Could Be President," *Forward Times*, June 17, 1972.

61. Rogers, *Barbara Jordan*, 158–59, 174–75.

62. Liz Carpenter, "Women Who Could Be President," *Redbook*, July 1975.

63. Rogers, *Barbara Jordan*, 230–32.

64. Walter Shapiro, "What Does This Woman Want?" *Texas Monthly*, October 1976, 134.

65. Broyles, "Making of Barbara Jordan."

66. Molly Ivins, "A Profile of Barbara Jordan," *Texas Observer*, November 3, 1972.

67. Broyles, "Making of Barbara Jordan."

68. Walter Pincus, "Barbara Jordan Caught Up in Hardball Politics," *Washington Post*, December 16, 1976.

69. Paula Giddings, "Will the Real Barbara Jordan Please Stand?," *Encore American and Worldwide News*, May 9, 1977, 16.

70. Meg Greenfield, "The New Lone Star of Texas," *Newsweek*, March 3, 1975.

Hermine Tobolowsky

A Feminist's Fight for Equal Rights

NANCY E. BAKER

Ann Richards, former Texas governor, once said, "Hermine Tobolowsky was one of the great Texas heroes. . . . [H]er fight for legal justice is unparalleled." Hermine Dalkowitz Tobolowsky (1921–95) was known during her lifetime as the mother of the Equal Rights Amendment in Texas. So synonymous with sexual equality did Tobolowsky become that state legislators referred to such proposed legislation as "Hermine's bills." One of the most important activists for women's rights in twentieth-century Texas, Tobolowsky's carefully crafted public image was that of a conservative who valued time-honored institutions such as marriage, the family, religion, and patriotism. Tobolowsky's brand of feminism relied on moderation and embraced certain aspects of women's traditional roles of wife and mother, though her own life often defied tradition. Her conservative approach to feminist reform involved using regional appeals (through states' rights rhetoric) and developing arguments aimed specifically at persuading men that sexual equality would benefit them, too. Given that Tobolowsky's feminist activism succeeded in a southern state that was widely recognized in the 1950s as one of the most hostile to women's rights, her story offers significant lessons regarding feminism, reform, and the history of the South.[1]

Little has been written about Tobolowsky. A few brief essays offer biographical sketches of her background and focus on her role in securing legal equality for women in Texas. The larger questions of what Tobolowsky represents, what can be learned from her legacy, and how her story relates to a national women's rights movement are not addressed. This may be, in part, because historians have only recently begun to consider how Texas history relates to U.S. history more broadly. In opening this field of inquiry, Texas historiography has grappled with the questions of when and how Texas entered the modern age and left the nineteenth century behind and consequently has started to include works on women in the twentieth century.[2]

Judith McArthur and Harold Smith's survey of twentieth-century Texas women's history is a notable achievement, not only as the first such survey but also for identifying areas of historiographical neglect. McArthur and Smith point out that historians have done little with the history of second-wave feminism in Texas, particularly during the 1970s. However, as historian Jessica R. Pliley observes, McArthur and Smith's use of the "wave metaphor" when discussing feminism is problematic.[3] (The "wave metaphor" refers to the periodization of women's rights movements in the United States into two waves; typically, historians define first-wave feminism as focused on woman suffrage and running from 1848 to 1920, with decades of inactivity following until second-wave feminism burst forth in the early to mid-1960s.)

Since the 1990s, a plethora of studies have argued that feminism was not dormant between the 1920s and the 1960s, as had previously been thought; instead, organized feminist activism was occurring in many contexts and with varying agendas that historians had overlooked. Recent edited collections of essays further contribute to this deemphasis of the focus on waves in favor of a more complicated understanding of the continuities of women's rights activism during the twentieth century. In this historiographical context, Tobolowsky and the Texas Federation of Business and Professional Women's Clubs (TX-BPW) can be seen as further evidence of feminist activism occurring in a period that previously appeared devoid of such activism. Women's clubs of the 1950s laid the groundwork for the later feminist organizations, and "civic engagement in the 1940s and 1950s was an important precondition for grassroots feminism."[4] The TX-BPW's campaign for a state Equal Legal Rights Amendment (ELRA) provided continuity between the first and second waves of feminism and served as a bridge between a local feminism of the 1950s and 1960s and the national campaign during the 1970s for a federal Equal Rights Amendment (ERA). At the heart of the TX-BPW's campaign was Hermine Dalkowitz Tobolowsky.

Born in San Antonio in 1921, Hermine Dalkowitz learned from her parents and religious community the values that she spent her life championing. Dalkowitz's father, Maurice Dalkowitz, had emigrated alone at age fourteen from Lithuania. Jews fleeing Eastern Europe in the late nineteenth century left behind intense anti-Semitism. The world they had known was undergoing wrenching changes. Capitalism was replacing feudalism, and "the new ideas of Socialism, Zionism, Russian revolutionary populism, and Yiddish cultural nationalism [were] being debated all over Eastern Europe." Maurice arrived in

HERMINE TOBOLOWSKY

giving a speech, ca. 1960.

Courtesy of the Woman's Collection, Texas Woman's University, Denton, Texas.

Texas with no resources, but he worked hard and started a successful business in San Antonio. His lack of formal education did not prevent him from being a voracious reader and mastering several languages.[5]

Hermine Dalkowitz's mother, Nora Brown Dalkowitz, had been a rebellious young woman. Seeking an education against her parents' wishes, Nora worked her way through business school. Maurice and Nora married and together built a successful retail business. The Dalkowitzes had two children, Hermine and Marcus. A natural defender of the underdog, Hermine "fought [Marcus's] battles in school if he needed her help," and the two were close. The Dalkowitz home included seven other people, all of whom worked in Dalkowitz's chain of twenty-eight South Texas general stores. Maurice Dalkowitz respected his daughter's intellectual gifts, bringing her to "political rallies, introduc[ing] her to judges, and talk[ing] about the law with her." In this fashion, he inculcated Hermine with an interest in politics and the law from an early age. Even as a young woman, Hermine was more interested in domestic and foreign political developments than in typical teenage pastimes. Her family's active involvement in Temple Beth-El, which had the "controversial Rabbi Ephraim Frisch" urging his congregation to engage in political activism, further directed her attentions toward politics.[6]

The Dalkowitz family instilled in Hermine the importance of education and of independence. Jews had traditionally considered education a strictly male endeavor, but by the late nineteenth century, this stricture was being challenged by young women eager to engage in the life of the mind. For some well-to-do merchant families, having an educated daughter was a status symbol. Maurice Dalkowitz was more pragmatic in his encouragement, telling Hermine, "A woman who can earn her own living won't have to stand for any nonsense." The determined Hermine earned her undergraduate degree at Incarnate Word College and Trinity College and her law degree at the University of Texas Law School in a mere five years.[7]

While in law school in Austin, Hermine Dalkowitz experienced overt sexual discrimination. On one occasion, an assistant dean met with the first-year female students to discourage them from their studies. He advised, "Girls, there is no need for you to study law. I know that you are here just to find husbands, so I'm giving you a list of all of the eligible men right now. We don't want you to waste your time here." This educator's attitude was not unusual for the era. Ignoring the pervasive bias, Dalkowitz was one of two women in her class to complete her law degree; nine others had dropped out. Dalkowitz was ranked among the top ten students in her class, and she earned the honor of serving on the *Texas Law Review* board.[8]

Once Dalkowitz had finished her law degree in 1943, she found that she had sufficiently impressed Dean Charles McCormick that he arranged for her to interview for the prestigious position of law clerk with the Texas Supreme Court. Dalkowitz arrived for the interview in a "very quiet, dignified" fashion and was shocked when she entered the room and the chief justice brusquely insulted her:

> Without looking up at me, the Chief Justice said, "I don't know why the dean is bothering me with this damn fool interview. There isn't a woman born who has sense enough to be a clerk in the Supreme Court." . . . This was the wrong thing to say to me. So I said, "Well I think this is just about the time that you learn something about your duties as a public servant. Your salary is paid by the people of Texas, over one half of whom are women." And I gave him quite a lecture. . . . So I had a little circle of Supreme Court justices standing outside the door before I finished. And as I walked out and Judge [J. E.] Hickman . . . said, "Young lady, I want you to know that graduating law students don't usually lecture chief justices of the Supreme Court, but he had it coming."[9]

Soon thereafter, the San Antonio law firm of Lang, Byrd, Cross, and Labon aggressively recruited her, ignoring her repeated rejections of their offer of employment. Dalkowitz was won over when the firm promised to allow her to do a brief for a case before the Texas Supreme Court, an unheard-of honor for a newly minted lawyer.[10]

Dalkowitz soon learned why her new employers were offering her the honor of a Supreme Court case. The case involved racial discrimination against a Hispanic man who had been barred from using a San Antonio swimming pool. The firm's other lawyers assumed the case could not be won and thus were reluctant to accept it. Years later, Tobolowsky explained, "It was a civil rights case before we had any civil rights laws. . . . Today, he'd win his case. But in 1943, the case was lost, of course." After four more years with that firm, Dalkowitz opened her own private practice.[11]

In 1950, Dalkowitz's aunt introduced the young lawyer to Hyman Tobolowsky. A conservative, cautious Dallas business executive, Hyman astonished Hermine when he proposed to her on their second date. He told her that he had never met another woman who discussed the law, politics, and foreign policy at length, and he knew if he married her, "he'd never be bored." Perhaps Hermine saw in Hyman a man who, like her father, valued her intellect and her independence. In August 1951, Hermine and Hyman married, and Hermine moved to Dallas. The couple joined the reform Jewish congregation of Temple Emanu-El. Demonstrating that her interests lay with her work rather than with homemaking, Tobolowsky "furnished the entire house in a two-hour shopping spree and set up her law practice in the back office." Hyman and Hermine never had children, and Hyman fully supported his wife's political activism, while she marveled at his encouragement and considered him essential to her success.[12] Hyman must have known what he was agreeing to when he married Hermine, since she had joined the TX-BPW in 1945.

The National Federation of Business and Professional Women's Clubs (BPW) had its origins in 1919, when the YWCA backed the development of a new organization "as an outgrowth of the Women's War Work Council and the National Business Women's Committee." The new BPW stipulated that all members must be employed full-time, and it attracted "clerical and other white-collar workers as well as teachers and attorneys" and a smaller number of business owners. By the 1950s, the BPW had grown into one of the largest national women's groups in the United States, encompassing more than three thousand clubs and a total of 165,000 individual members. During the Cold War era, women's clubs were racially homogeneous, and most leaders of white groups were "prosperous, professional, . . . urban women." For five decades, the BPW "fought long and hard for equal legal rights and equal opportunities for women," starting with campaigns to educate women voters and proceeding by 1946 to fight for legal sexual equality.[13] Passage of the federal ERA became an important part of the BPW's agenda.

The federal ERA was born out of the success of the woman suffrage movement. After the ratification of the Nineteenth Amendment in 1920 gave women the right to vote, woman suffrage organizations were in transition. The National American Woman Suffrage Association, led by Carrie Chapman Catt, became the League of Women Voters, devoted to nonpartisan political engagement and education. Alice Paul's National Woman's Party (NWP) decided after some internal debate to continue as a single-issue lobbying group, now with "complete legal equality between men and women" as its cause. Paul wrote the initial version of the ERA and persuaded sympathetic legislators to introduce the amendment in Congress in 1923. For nearly fifty years, the NWP remained unshakably committed to the ERA. Other women's rights activists and groups generally aligned against the proposed amendment, believing that it would erase protective labor legislation and hurt working-class women. By the 1940s, a handful of groups, including the BPW, had changed their positions. Hoping to build on the greater participation of women in the workforce necessitated by World War II, the BPW launched a national pro-ERA campaign beginning in 1946. Despite the group's efforts and those of the NWP and the handful of other organizations working to advance the ERA, the amendment made little progress until the 1970s. From 1970 to 1972, both houses of Congress held hearings and votes on the ERA, and it finally passed on March 22, 1972.[14]

If thirty-eight states ratified the amendment by 1979, the ERA would become part of the U.S. Constitution. At first, the ERA did well, with thirty states ratifying it in the first year. However, momentum subsequently slowed, and by January 1977, only thirty-five states had ratified. Congress then extended the ratification deadline to 1982, but no more ratifications were forthcoming, and the ERA died. In fact, five states rescinded their ratifications, while many other states, including Texas, had rescission movements that failed.[15] The story of the ERA in Texas is unique, however.

Unlike the majority of states that ratified the federal ERA, Texas had a vigorous pro-ERA movement dating back to the late 1950s thanks in large part to Hermine Tobolowsky and the TX-BPW's efforts to obtain a state equal rights amendment. Other organizations and clubs participated in the campaign for sexual equality in Texas, but none were more dedicated than the TX-BPW.[16] And no one within the TX-BPW worked harder for sexual equality than Hermine Tobolowsky.

Tobolowsky avoided the appearance of radicalism at all times. Tobolowsky's traditional personal style and moderate feminist views reflected a deliberate choice. Images of Tobolowsky in the media from the 1950s to the 1980s reveal an eminently respectable matron. She wore hats and gloves when they were still part of the well-dressed woman's wardrobe and in later decades favored demure professional attire. Cultivating a ladylike demeanor, Tobolowsky was described by more than one reporter as "soft-spoken." Tobolowsky concurred: "I speak quietly and I never get excited and raise my voice." Despite her professional identity as a lawyer, Tobolowsky emphasized her married status and her husband's importance in her life. In one interview, she said she was "delighted to use Mrs. (instead of the fashionable Ms.) because I think one of the smartest things I did was marry my husband." The interviewer concluded that Tobolowsky was "no women's libber," a description he intended as a compliment. On another occasion, Tobolowsky told a reporter, "Most men want equal rights for everyone too. Many are confusing this with Women's Liberation. But I've been trying to get this passed for the last 15 years. We have no quarrel with men." Although not a radical feminist, Tobolowsky kept clippings on the women's liberation movement and annotated them in ways that suggest her views. She seems to have abhorred the use of violence and to have found problematic the tactic of boycotting states that had not ratified the amendment.[17]

Tobolowsky's attempts to cultivate an image as a moderate feminist entailed emphasizing that sexual equality in Texas would benefit men as much as it would benefit women. Indeed, her focus on improving married women's status generated criticism that she was concerned not with the rights of women but with the rights of women like herself.[18] Given that for more than seventy years, critics had portrayed feminism and women's rights as a threat to marriage and the family, Tobolowsky's emphasis on married women's rights, on her own marriage, and on wanting an amendment that would benefit both sexes seems to have been a calculated attempt to render moot assumptions that feminism was antimale or antifamily.

Other feminists in the late 1960s expressed similar concerns about feminism being perceived as too extreme. National Organization for Women (NOW) founder Betty Friedan was horrified by radical feminists' "'bra-burning' image and hate rhetoric," which she felt would drive away large numbers of women from the feminist movement, and she claimed that "NOW members in the 'media'" had helped to protect "the movement from its own excesses in their coverage." Tobolowsky, however, went further than most feminists in distancing herself from radicalism by openly describing herself as a "conservative." In her words, "I believe in the greatest individual freedom for everyone, as long as the rights of others are respected."[19]

Tobolowsky seized every opportunity to emphasize that legal sexual equality would benefit both men and women. Well before Tobolowsky led the ELRA campaign, she was using the argument of equality benefiting both sexes to support proposed legislation to grant married women the right to control their own separate property (an issue on which Texas lagged far behind most other states). As early as 1956, Tobolowsky contended that "passage of the legislation . . . will aid the businessmen as well as married women, for the men will be able to make contract[s] and hold the women to the contract[s]." After the TX-BPW focused on its proposed state equal rights amendment, Tobolowsky ensured that men's interests were a key part of the campaign. One brochure "For Men Only" used humorous cartoon illustrations to make the case that legal sexual discrimination against women also hurt men and that sexual equality was beneficial for all. In 1960, the TX-BPW referred to the ELRA as "Equal Legal Rights for Men and Women" and, more stirringly, "the Crusade for Freedom of Texas men and women." Tobolowsky crafted a standard pro-ELRA speech to be delivered to male audiences, explaining the various benefits the ELRA would offer them. Even after others took over the helm of the TX-BPW, Tobolowsky's argument that equality benefited men remained standard. In 1965, while lobbying the state legislature to pass the ELRA, the TX-BPW president, Modell Scruggs (known generally as Mrs. Jack Scruggs), echoed Tobolowsky when she told reporters, "This is not just an equal rights for women bill[,] but also for men."[20]

Unlike many later feminists fighting for sexual equality, Tobolowsky took seriously the attacks of her opponents who claimed that women's rights contradicted the Bible, and she used her religious knowledge to respond. For example, in 1961, Tobolowsky wrote a letter to the TX-BPW membership in which she acknowledged that some state legislators were using biblical arguments against the ELRA. In response to these attacks, Tobolowsky argued that "secular laws of the State of Texas . . . do not and never have followed the dictates of the spiritual law of the Bible." To support this position, Tobolowsky referred to the biblical passage "Render unto Caesar the things that are of Caesar, and unto God the things that are of God." The proposed ELRA, which was expected to affect laws relating to "property, contract, employment, divorce and criminal laws," dealt only with "'Caesar's' things." Tobolowsky then offered a list of examples of other areas of the law that contradicted biblical precepts, among them judging others, punishing criminals, charging interest, and holding borrowers responsible for their debts beyond seven years. Tobolowsky pointed out that the Bible explicitly demanded that believers do justice, and she seized the biblical high ground when she declared, "We are asking the legislators of the State of Texas to do JUSTICE; to free Texas women from laws that have caused them untold hardships because they are discriminatory. This, too, is the Lord's command."[21]

The BPW was one of many Cold War–era national women's groups to adopt rhetoric linking women's rights with national security. "Professional and working class women's groups found a fairly hospitable environment in the Cold War years for their activism. . . . [C]lubwomen [and others] used a range of arguments to nudge their way into debates about citizen obligation in a nuclearized Cold War" that included anticommunism, maternalism, and feminism. During the 1950s, the BPW actively promoted civil defense programs, and the organization's leaders were concerned enough about the threat of communist subversion to go to the trouble of reprinting and distributing to members a detailed article on how to spot and resist such subversion. The TX-BPW also distributed literature reminding members that patriotic citizens paid their poll taxes so that they were prepared to vote in all elections. The idea that voting was a patriotic duty became a cudgel, as in one pamphlet devoted to the subject: "Freedom to Vote in Accordance with One's Own Conscience Is a Priceless American Heritage. Failure to Vote Is a Betrayal of That Precious Privilege."[22]

Tobolowsky must have found congenial the BPW's emphasis on patriotism and civil defense. She had strong anticommunist credentials, useful in an era when Texas was home to one of the nation's most vicious Red Scares. As the media mentioned more than once, Tobolowsky was a former speaker for the Freedom Forum and had given "many lectures on Americanism in South Texas."

During an interview just after she assumed the TX-BPW presidency, Tobolowsky steered the discussion toward her interest in Americanism, stating her goal for the organization as educating "the general public to strengthen their faith in American heritage." Tobolowsky's work on legal equality for women received only the briefest mention, and the larger theme of her patriotism completely overshadowed her feminism. By 1959, the national BPW had modified its agenda from nonpartisan voter education to actively fighting for women's rights, so Tobolowsky's decision to downplay feminism seemed deliberate. Her decision to use patriotic, almost conservative rhetoric, however, mirrored the national BPW's use of national security and the Cold War as support for women's rights. Tobolowsky and the TX-BPW further cemented their patriotic, conservative image in their response to the antifeminist claim that sexual equality would lead to women being drafted into the military. Tobolowsky and the TX-BPW retorted to such criticisms by asking, "Do opponents . . . really believe women are less patriotic than men? Do they really believe women are unwilling to serve their country?"[23]

Aside from women's rights, Tobolowsky held fairly conservative political views. She and her husband were supporters and friends of Texas state senator George Parkhouse, and in correspondence with him, Hyman Tobolowsky wrote, "Those of us who follow the conservative philosophy of government need and depend on you." In 1974, Hermine Tobolowsky told a reporter, "I've always been so conservative and so identified with conservative politics that it is ridiculous to think I'd be involved with anything radical." But despite her best efforts, she could not prevent the media or her opponents from seeing her as a radical, simply because she was questioning the status quo and seeking reform. In an article hostile to women's rights activists, the *Wall Street Journal* referred to Tobolowsky as "militant" because she claimed that labor laws ought to be extended to protect men as well as women. (Tobolowsky no doubt thought she was once again promoting the moderate idea that sexual equality benefits both sexes.)[24]

In addition to striking a patriotic, conservative tone, Tobolowsky and the TX-BPW adopted a regionally specific strategy. In an era when "states' rights" had become a term fraught with potentially negative meaning in the rest of the nation, the TX-BPW chose to use that term in a conspicuous fashion. In one of the organization's earliest pamphlets on the need for sexual equality under the law, the TX-BPW wrote, "Many groups turn to the Federal government to correct abuses in State law, but because we believe in States Rights we want our own State Legislature to give the women of Texas all of the legal rights of citizenship—we ask no special privileges—only the legal benefits to which we are entitled as citizens of Texas and the United States. Let's all get busy and correct these inequities in the law so that WE CAN BRAG ABOUT TEXAS!"[25] This argument appeared to pit women's rights activists against civil rights activists.

During and after World War II, the civil rights movement had made gains whenever the federal government took the lead in dismantling racial discrimination. In 1947, Harry S. Truman became the first president ever publicly to address the National Association for the Advancement of Colored People, and he laid out precisely the approach that the TX-BPW later seemed to deride. Truman said, "We must make the Federal government a friendly, vigilant defender of the rights and equalities of all Americans. And again I mean all Americans." Truman created a committee to study the problem of racial discrimination, and the committee's report, To Secure These Rights (1947), set an agenda for extensive federal intervention to ensure racial equality.[26]

Federal intervention in what many whites in the South considered local issues led to tremendous resentment and the use of the phrase states' rights as code for "pro-segregation." The TX-BPW never indicated any racially discriminatory attitudes; however, its use of states' rights as an argument for women's rights and its advocacy of paying the poll tax suggests a degree of opportunism and a desire to establish itself as anything but radical.[27]

Despite her carefully crafted public image of patriotism and political moderation, Tobolowsky may have privately harbored more intense feelings about women's equality than she ever indicated to legislators or the media. Her personal sentiments are suggested by ephemera such as a handwritten comment on a news clipping she had saved concerning the state legislature's failure to pass the ELRA in 1965. Near an unflattering photo of anti-ELRA senator Dorsey Hardeman, Tobolowsky wrote, "der Fuhrer (sp) doesn't look very happy," a comparison to Hitler that suggests Tobolowsky's antipathy if not outright hostility toward Hardeman. Yet Tobolowsky's public comment on that occasion was much more circumspect, "The members of the House . . . who defeated the legislation have done a disservice to the women of Texas."[28] The depth of Tobolowsky's personal feelings and her strenuous efforts to modulate how she represented her position in public reflect the difficult position women occupied in Texas law at the time.

In the 1950s, Texas law required women to shoulder the same responsibilities as men but did not grant women the same rights, and this discrepancy made Texas among the worst places in the nation for women's rights. Texas women were required to pay taxes and could be sued. If a husband became physically unable to work, his wife was required to support him; further, both parents bore responsibility for their children's financial needs. Finally, thanks to a 1957 state law most likely passed in a moment of anticommunist hysteria, Texas could draft women as well as men into the state militia. Yet according to the TX-BPW's count, at least forty-four statutes and a significant number of court decisions imposed "legal hardships and indignities" on women in Texas. Many of these inequities concerned women's ability to dispose of property or to manage business affairs, but others were more lurid: a man's killing of his wife's boyfriend was "justifiable homicide," while a wife's killing of her husband's girlfriend was murder.[29]

In 1957, Tobolowsky and the TX-BPW attempted to persuade state legislators to reform property laws so that married women could control their own property separately from their husbands. Some state legislators were rudely dismissive. According to Tobolowsky, "Sen. Dorsey Hardeman and Sen. Wardlow Lane called women 'stupid.' . . . That didn't set well with me." Another legislator exclaimed, "Why, when a woman marries, her husband becomes her master—the least he can expect is her property." Lane attached amendments to the proposed bill that caused confusion and ensured additional sexual discrimination against married women. In effect, by asking for reform, women had been punished. In response, Tobolowsky "got her dander up and swore she would fight until women were recognized equal where their rights were concerned in the same way they were judged equal when it came to taxes and other responsibilities."[30]

As a result of this failed attempt at piecemeal legal reform, Tobolowsky became convinced that only a constitutional amendment could secure legal equality for Texas women. At the TX-BPW's 1957 annual convention, she suggested that the organization compile a list of all the state laws that were sexually discriminatory and then compose a single constitutional amendment to eradicate all of them. The convention delegates agreed, and Tobolowsky undertook the laborious task of doing the legal research and writing the amendment. The end result was the Texas Equal Legal Rights Amendment, which stated, "Equality under the law shall not be denied nor abridged because of sex, race, creed, or color." In 1958, she and the TX-BPW began lobbying for passage of the amendment. Beginning the following year, the TX-BPW ensured that the ELRA was introduced into every session of the legislature, but the measure did not pass until 1971. Tobolowsky's role in the fight earned her the description "the general of the Texas women's battle."[31]

Initially, Tobolowsky's staunchest foes were state legislators who claimed that the ELRA would remove existing legal protections of women. Legislators at first tried to keep the bill bottled up in committee; when all else failed, they resorted to amendments that undermined its intent. Some legislators who promised to support the ELRA reneged when it came time to vote. Tobolowsky and the BPW responded by campaigning to unseat the most hostile legislators, registering a notable success with Lane's 1962 defeat. While his departure ended public displays of contempt toward Tobolowsky and other ELRA supporters, opposition legislators resorted to underhanded tactics such as questioning Tobolowsky's character: some legislators gossiped that she was a foul-mouthed drunk and a prostitute and that she had even attacked a legislator with an umbrella. Ever the lady, Tobolowsky once remarked cheerfully, "I'm more encouraged than ever. . . . [O]ur opponents are starting to attack me personally. That means they're running out of even flimsy excuses to beat us down!"[32]

Beginning in 1963, the most organized, sustained opposition to the ELRA emerged from the Texas State Bar Association, which recycled the arguments it had used in the 1950s to try to thwart Tobolowsky's campaign to have women permitted to serve on juries. The bar association's main theme was that the change was too sweeping and would result in legal chaos, with women left unprotected. Instead, the bar association advocated piecemeal legislative reform—precisely the path Tobolowsky had tried and found a dead end. In place of the ELRA, the bar association proposed an overhaul of matrimonial property laws. The TX-BPW and the Texas Bar Association briefly attempted to work out a compromise, but no common ground could be found. The bar association attacked the ELRA and worked to pass the competing bill until the legislature passed the Marital Property Act in 1967. The measure "gives women control over their separate property and over that part of the community property which the wife earns. Married women with their own income are allowed to contract and are responsible for their debts." Three years after the act's passage, Tobolowsky thought that it had not effected significant change, since private businesses as well as the state government continued to require husbands' signatures when wives sought to manage property or obtain credit.[33] Tobolowsky remained convinced that only the ELRA would end legal sexual discrimination in Texas.

Tobolowsky traveled all over the state to give speeches in support of the ELRA. She and other supporters held "press conferences, appear[ed] on local talk shows to explain the Amendment, and distribut[ed] literature at county fairs. Weekly newspapers in Texas printed a series of articles on the impact of the proposed state Equal Legal Rights Amendment," blanketing the state with their message.[34]

National political developments may have helped the drive for sexual equality in Texas. In 1970, the U.S. Congress began to give more serious consideration to the ERA than had been the case in years. This federal attention may have given either legitimacy or urgency (from a states' rights viewpoint) to the issue of sexual equality. The Texas Legislature finally passed the state ELRA in April 1971, sending the amendment on to the voters to decide at the polls in November 1972. In March 1972, Congress passed the federal ERA, and the Texas Legislature quickly ratified it. That November, Texas voters approved the ELRA by an overwhelming four-to-one margin. The TX-BPW rejoiced, holding victory celebrations in members' homes across the state on Thanksgiving Day, crediting the ELRA's success to "the loyalty and support of many BPW members for many years" and to the efforts of "many co-workers (many non-BPW friends) in each county of the State!"[35] Though the chain of events is complex, the legislature's approval of the ELRA before the ratification of the ERA suggests that Tobolowsky and the TX-BPW had smoothed the way for the federal amendment.

Mere months later, in 1973, conservative Texas women mobilized an anti-ERA movement, which consisted of several state-level organizations, some affiliated with national anti-ERA and conservative organizations, conservative religious denominations, and businesses headquartered in Texas. The Committee to Restore Women's Rights, founded and led by Dianne Edmondson, was linked to STOP ERA and the John Birch Society. Women Who Want to Be Women (WWWW) was heavily populated by Church of Christ members as well as indebted to the Mary Kay Cosmetics Company and the Parker Chiropractic Research Foundation for support. The WWWW also coordinated with STOP ERA. John Birch Society member Wanda Schultz led the Texas chapter of Happiness of Womanhood. In addition, anti-ERA organizations such as the Committee to Rescind the ERA, Women Activated to Rescind, Daughters Already Well Endowed, and the Texas Farm Bureau lobbied the legislature.[36]

In 1975, the Texas House of Representatives considered a rescission bill, HCR 57, and the House Committee on Constitutional Revision held a public hearing on the matter on April 14. Proponents of rescission focused their arguments on three key themes: the ERA was "unnecessary, undesirable, and uncertain."[37]

According to anti-ERA arguments, the ERA was unnecessary because piecemeal legal reforms were more specific and therefore preferable. Recent laws were touted as proof that this approach worked. Taking the argument one step further, Phyllis Schlafly, organizer of the STOP ERA campaign, claimed there was no need for further legislation, as "All the machinery is there to help any woman who has been discriminated against."[38]

Anti-ERA witnesses insisted that the amendment lacked the support of most women, ignoring the results of the referendum on the ELRA. Edmondson painted the ERA as part of a radical feminist minority's conspiracy to force change on all: "It is apparent to anyone researching the [feminist] movement that certain radical elements who hold most of the decision-making positions are seeking a change in our society's structure and morals. . . . [T]he ERA is the primary legislative goal of these radical feminists."[39]

Finally, anti-ERA witnesses portrayed the ERA as uncertain because they did not trust either the U.S. Supreme Court or the federal government. Looking at controversial contemporary issues such as school busing and abortion, conservatives derided the idea that the Supreme Court could be relied on to make reasonable decisions. Some anti-ERA witnesses used the ERA as a proxy for their discomfiture with specific areas of social change; for example, STOP ERA circulated a flyer that included the graphic and supposedly true story of a white woman who was jailed with white and black men for a nonviolent offense. A black man attempted to rape the woman, who was saved only by the timely intervention of the guards. The implicit fear that sexual equality would result in race mixing (whether via busing or rape) suggests that uneasiness with federally enforced racial integration was a subtext in the ERA debate.[40]

Although supporters saw the ERA as a simple statement of equal rights for all, anti-ERA witnesses predicted a cascade of potential disasters: single-sex schools and sports teams would be declared illegal; all public facilities, including restrooms, prisons, and hospitals, would be unisex; rape would no longer be a crime; churches would be forced to ordain women; same-sex marriage and homosexual adoption of children would be legalized; abortion would be rampant; traditional gender roles would no longer be allowed; women would be forced to work outside the home to earn at least 50 percent of their families' income, requiring them to place their children in vast government-run day care centers; women who divorced their husbands might find themselves losing custody of their children and forced to pay child support and alimony; women would be drafted and sent into combat; state legislators would stand by, helpless, as the federal government stripped them of states' rights in the matter of sex discrimination; and the Supreme Court would force unwanted, threatening novelties on the public with impunity.[41] And, according to these conservative witnesses, the amendment offered not a single compelling benefit. The Texas House of Representatives was unmoved, and HCR 57 died in committee.[42]

Three southern states—Tennessee, Kentucky, and Texas—ratified the ERA, but only Texas did not rescind its ratification. Three factors explain this striking outcome. First, Texas lacked a compelling argument that rescission would correct a legislative error. In other states, rescissionists argued that the legislature had sneaked the ERA past them by rushing to ratify and dispensing with the usual procedures, debates, and hearings.[43] However, neither argument had any traction in Texas. Thanks to Tobolowsky's leadership and the efforts of the TX-BPW and other women's organizations, the state had had a pro-ERA movement since the 1950s. And between 1970 and 1972, the fates of the state amendment and the federal amendment had become entwined; the referendum on the ELRA had given voters the last word. Opponents had difficulty arguing that the ERA's ratification had been out of step with public sentiment.

Second, the Texas Legislature had been dismissive of nearly all piecemeal legal reforms until the ERA became a live issue in Congress in 1970; state legislators then passed the ELRA. As Tobolowsky testified at the 1975 hearing, "Very frankly, the Texas Legislature showed no interest in changing discriminatory laws until we got that amendment into our Texas constitution." The legislators' refusal to act undermined the anti-ERA argument that a constitutional amendment was not needed when piecemeal reforms could address specific problems. Moreover, supporters of the ERA could point out that the ELRA had been in place for more than two years without Texas experiencing any of the dire consequences opponents had predicted.

Third, pro-rescission witnesses at the 1975 public hearing had included people from other states, among them legislators from Tennessee and Louisiana, a female member of the United Rubber Workers from Ohio, and Phyllis Schlafly from Illinois. The use of non-Texan witnesses may have tainted the cause as part of an out-of-state agenda, and some legislators certainly resented the presence of "outside agitators." In contrast, Texas representative Sarah Weddington, who coordinated the pro-ERA testimony, emphasized that all of her witnesses were Texans.[44]

Although the anti-ERA activists had not succeeded in 1975, they vowed to continue the fight. In January 1977, Democratic representative Clay Smothers and Republican senator Walter Mengden introduced a bill seeking to recall the state's ratification of the ERA. If the bill had passed, the Texas government would have sought to repossess the ratification documents from the federal agency that collected such documentation, pursuing legal action against the federal government if necessary. At an April 1977 rally in Austin, three hundred people, most of them reportedly women, listened as Smothers, a conservative African American from Dallas, argued that the federal amendment would cause "more decisions like they gave us on busing. It's all about states' rights. You have to admit the federal judiciary is irresponsible."[45] But like the attempt at rescission, the recall effort failed.

Undaunted, ERA opponents persisted, abandoning the single-issue strategy in favor of establishing themselves as profamily conservative groups with a broader agenda. In the summer of 1975, WWWW became the National Association of the Ws, led by President Lottie Beth Hobbs, choosing its new name to encourage male membership. The Ws opposed a slew of "moral threats"—

feminism, pornography, and abortion, among others—and encouraged parents to demand that their children's school textbooks reflect conservative family values. The Ws declared that their agenda covered "all issues that involve the family" with the goal of "turn[ing] this country around."[46]

With the ERA's 1982 demise, Hermine Tobolowsky reflected on feminism, legislative battles, and the amendment's fate. It had failed, she argued, because proponents had handled the national campaign poorly:

> For starters, they should have explained the issue to men. They should have told them that equal rights is good for business, that the ERA was not designed to destroy the American family, that the ERA was not just a women's movement. . . . In Texas, . . . we let it be known very fast that we weren't taking anything away from the men. We were becoming their partners. . . . [N]ational ERA backers made the mistake of assuming that people understood the ERA.[47]

Tobolowsky's concerns sprang from the reality of how opponents perceived feminists. Schlafly frequently alleged that feminists were "destructive of the family, of values that I think are important. All of them hate men and children, you know." As one Houston ally wrote to Tobolowsky, "Despite what anyone says, I do believe that the N.O.W. organization has done us a great deal of harm here in Texas, as their more militant members have really received adverse publicity, at least here in Houston." Similar perceptions of NOW's radicalism plagued the ERA ratification effort elsewhere in the South, including in Memphis, Tennessee.[48] The amendment might well have had more success if, as Tobolowsky suggested, its proponents had developed regional strategies that took local norms into account. Tobolowsky was convinced that only a feminism that scrupulously avoided an antimale, antifamily tone could succeed. Despite her passionate commitment to sexual equality, she accepted the argument of sexual difference when it was prudent to do so. Above all, she embraced moderation and rejected radicalism.

For the remainder of her life, Tobolowsky continued her involvement in the TX-BPW as well as in numerous other organizations—the National Council of Jewish Women, Hadassah, the Women's Foundation of Texas, the American Bar Association, the National Association of Women Lawyers, the Dallas Women's Political Caucus, and Temple Emanu-El. She also continued her fight for women's rights nationwide, participating in a variety of battles, among them the unsuccessful 1992 campaign to pass a state ERA in Iowa, until her death in 1995. To the end, she remained a moderate voice for sexual equality.[49]

Anti-ERA leader Lottie Beth Hobbs echoed Tobolowsky's assessment that the perceived radicalism of supporters was responsible for the ERA's defeat, citing activists' use of "hunger strikes, chaining themselves together in capitols, [and] staging sit-ins in legislative chambers. . . . Those tactics weren't on the level of reason, discussion, and response—the levels of the people of this country." Similarly, Illinois state senator Forest Etheredge, a Dallas native, said that he initially backed the ERA but became disgusted by supporters' "emotionalism," which "alienated a number of moderates." In his view, "radical proponents . . . adopted the ERA as their own cause and . . . drove the moderates away." In light of anti-ERA activists' success in repackaging themselves as profamily and in wielding considerable influence in later decades, feminist reformers might have done well to pay greater attention to Tobolowsky's words: "We have no quarrel with men."[50]

NOTES

1. "Hermine Tobolowsky: The Passing of a Legend," *Texas Woman* 63 (September–October 1995): 1 (first quotation); "Hermine Tobolowsky to Be Honored in Conjunction with Texas ERA Anniversary," *Texas Jewish Post*, November 11, 1982 (second quotation); Carolyn Patrick, "Women's Rights Legislation: The Next Session May Prove Better," *Dallas Morning News* (hereafter cited as *DMN*), June 16, 1965 (third quotation).

2. For essays on Tobolowsky, see Gladys R. Leff, "Opening Legal Doors for Women: Hermine Tobolowsky," in *Lone Stars of David: The Jews of Texas*, ed. Hollace Ava Weiner and Kenneth D. Roseman (Waltham, Mass.: Brandeis University Press, 2007), 233–38; Rob Fink, "Hermine Tobolowsky, the Texas ELRA, and the Political Struggle for Women's Rights," *Journal of the West* 42 (Summer 2003): 52–57; Tai Kreidler, "Hermine Tobolowsky: Mother of Texas's Equal Legal Rights Amendment," in *The Human Tradition in Texas*, ed. Ty Cashion and Jesús F. de la Teja (Lanham, Md.: Rowman and Littlefield, 2001), 209–20. For more on modernization and Texas, see Nancy Beck Young, "Beyond Parochialism: Modernization and Texas Historiography," in *Beyond Texas through Time: Breaking away from Past Interpretations*, ed. Walter L. Buenger and Arnold De Leon (College Station: Texas A&M University Press, 2011), 221–69. For examples of historiography on Texas that includes women's history, see Judith N. McArthur and Harold L. Smith, *Texas through Women's Eyes: The Twentieth-Century Experience* (Austin: University of Texas Press, 2010); Judith N. McArthur and Harold L. Smith, "Not Whistling Dixie: Women's Movements and Feminist Politics," in *The Texas Left: The Radical Roots of Lone Star Liberalism*, ed. David O'Donald Cullen and Kyle G. Wilkison (College Station: Texas A&M University Press, 2010); Rebecca Sharpless, *Fertile Ground, Narrow Choices: Women on Texas Cotton Farms, 1900–1940* (Chapel Hill: University of North Carolina Press, 1999).

3. Jessica R. Pliley, review of *Texas through Women's Eyes: The Twentieth-Century Experience*, by Judith N. McArthur and Harold L. Smith, *Southwestern Historical Quarterly* 115 (October 2011): 226–27.

4. For examples of works deemphasizing the wave metaphor, see Kathleen A. Laughlin and Jacqueline L. Castledine, eds., *Breaking the Wave: Women, Their Organizations, and Feminism, 1945–1985* (New York: Routledge, 2011), 13 (quotation); Nancy A. Hewitt, ed., *No Permanent Waves: Recasting Histories of U.S. Feminism* (New Brunswick, N.J.: Rutgers University Press, 2010).

5. Hermine Tobolowsky, interview by Ellen Peyton, January 12, 1983, Hermine Tobolowsky Papers, Woman's Collection, Texas Woman's University, Denton, Tex. (hereafter cited as HTP-TWU); Annelise Orleck, *Common Sense and a Little Fire: Women and Working-Class Politics in the United States, 1900–1965* (Chapel Hill: University of North Carolina Press, 1995), 17 (quotation).

6. Tobolowsky, interview (all quotations); Leff, "Opening Legal Doors for Women," 233–34.

7. Orleck, *Common Sense*, 19, 22; Ruby Jones, "Hermine Tobolowsky," *Texas Jewish Post*, undated clipping (quotation), HTP-TWU; Joel Simnacher, "Women's Rights Advocate Hermine Tobolowky Dies," *DMN*, July 27, 1995.

8. "Dallas Attorney Speaks on Equal Legal Rights," *Plano Star-Courier*, October 22, 1972 (quotation); Betty Friedan, *The Feminine Mystique* (1963; New York: Dell, 1983), chap. 7; Leff, "Opening Legal Doors for Women," 234.

9. Thom Marshall, "A Look at Dallas' Past by Four Who Were There," *Dallas Times Herald*, February 26, 1984.

10. Ibid.; Leff, "Opening Legal Doors for Women," 234. Marshall's article highlighted four oral history interviews in the Dallas Public Library Oral History Collection; the interview with Tobolowsky was conducted in 1980.

11. "Anybody Who Wants to Take Her on Is Welcome To . . . ," unidentified newspaper clipping, HTP-TWU.

12. Ibid. (all quotations). Temple Emanu-El was known first as Jewish Congregation Emanu-El and then as Congregation Emanu-El before taking its current name in 1974. For more information, see Gerry Cristol, "Temple Emanu-El, Dallas," *Handbook of Texas Online*, http://www.tshaonline .org/handbook/online/articles/ijt01) (accessed January 16, 2012). Hyman Tobolowsky died suddenly in 1968, leaving Hermine Tobolowky grief-stricken.

13. Kathleen A. Laughlin, "Civic Feminists: The Politics of the Minnesota Federation of Business and Professional Women's Clubs, 1942–1965," in *Breaking the Wave*, ed. Laughlin and Castledine, 17 (first quotation); Laura McEnaney, *Civil Defense Begins at Home: Militarization Meets Everyday Life in the Fifties* (Princeton: Princeton University Press, 2000), 90–91 (second quotation), 91–92 (third quotation); Barbara Richardson, "The Women Fight On," *Dallas Times Herald*, July 13, 1969 (fourth quotation). See also Laughlin, "Civic Feminists," 13, 17–18. This essay uses variations on the phrase *legal sexual equality*, which is how Tobolowsky and her contemporaries referred to the reforms they sought; today, scholars might instead use the phrase *gender equality*.

14. Susan Ware, *Beyond Suffrage: Women in the New Deal* (Cambridge: Harvard University Press, 1981), 5; Susan D. Becker, *The Origins of the Equal Rights Amendment: American Feminism between the Wars* (Westport, Conn.: Greenwood, 1981), 15 (quotation), 16–23; Cynthia Harrison, *On Account of Sex: The Politics of Women's Issues, 1945–1968* (Berkeley: University of California Press, 1988), 7–11; Laughlin, "Civic Feminists," 13; Donald G. Mathews and Jane Sherron De Hart, *Sex, Gender and the Politics of ERA* (New York: Oxford University Press, 1990), 35–49.

15. Rescission movements succeeded in Nebraska, Tennessee, Idaho, Kentucky, and South Dakota. However, whether a state legally could rescind the ratification of an amendment has never been determined. For more on rescission, see Nancy Elizabeth Baker, *Unequaled: Rescission and the Equal Rights Amendment* (Waco: Baylor University Press, forthcoming).

16. A partial list of other organizations that worked to obtain the ELRA includes Democratic women's clubs; Republican women's clubs; the League of Women Voters; the National Council of Jewish Women; the Parent-Teacher Association; Pilot Clubs; the University of Texas Women; the Veterans of Foreign Wars Women's Auxiliary; and the Texas Women's Political Caucus (which

began after the ELRA had passed the legislature). See Texas Federation of Business and Professional Women's Clubs, "Equal Legal Rights Amendment Public Forum" (flyer), October 26, 1972, HTP-TWU. See also Mary Lu Zuber, "Lady, You're Not at All Equal under Texas Law," *Houston Chronicle*, October 8, 1972.

17. See the file of photos of Tobolowsky in HTP-TWU. For one anecdote in which she recalls that she always wore a hat and gloves and behaved respectably, Thom Marshall, "A Look at Dallas' Past by Four Who Were There," *Dallas Times Herald*, February 26, 1984. See also Carolyn Lesh, "High Profile: Hermine Tobolowsky," *DMN*, October 19, 1986. In Lesh's article, Tobolowsky remembers "wearing white gloves and a large hat" while testifying at a 1957 hearing at the State Capitol. Debbie K. Solomon, "'Mother of ERA': Backers Put Wrong Foot First," *Dallas Times Herald Extra—East*, July 7, 1982 (first quotation). See also Karen Klinefelter, "Leading Lady: Her Brand of 3 R's Is Aimed at Adults," *Dallas Times Herald*, July 22, 1959; Thom Marshall, "A Look at Dallas' Past by Four Who Were There," *Dallas Times Herald*, February 26, 1984 (second quotation); "Woman Lawyer Gives Talk on Equal Rights Amendment," *El Paso Times*, October 27, 1972 (third quotation). See also Richard E. Farson, "The Rage of Women," *Look*, December 16, 1969, 21 (a friend sent this article to Tobolowsky with an note indicating that she assumed Tobolowsky would share her discomfiture at the violent tactics described in the article); Patrick J. Buchanan, "Punishing Saints, Sinners," *San Antonio Express*, January 10, 1978 (Tobolowsky had marked off the section of the article where Buchanan argued that the boycott was so underhanded, "the libbers . . . don't deserve to win"), both in HTP-TWU.

18. Hermine D. Tobolowsky, "Referendum: For Equal Rights Amendment," *Texas Bar Journal*, December 1963, 1074.

19. Veronica Geng, "Requiem for the Women's Movement," *Harper's*, November 1976, 54 (first and second quotations); Erika Sanchez, "She Has Struggled for Every 'Extra Mile,'" *Dallas Morning News*, October 8, 1978 (third and fourth quotations).

20. Ruby Clayton McKee, "The Woman's Angle," *DMN*, September 20, 1956 (first quotation); Texas Federation of Business and Professional Women's Clubs, *For Men Only*, n.d., HTP-TWU. According to a later newspaper account, Tobolowsky authored *For Men Only* (as well as several other pamphlets). See "Discuss Amendment 7 Tonight at Cameo Meet," *Plano Star-Courier*, October 25, 1972. Ruth Fox, Constance Stathakos Condos, and Hermine Tobolowsky to Mrs. Odell Bailey, November 29, 1960 ("Equal Legal Rights for Men and Women"), Hermine Tobolowsky to BPW members, November 28, 1960, folder 3, box 8, HTP-TWU. The second letter is a form letter to BPW members, addressed to "Dear" with no name following this salutation. Hermine D. Tobolowsky, "ELR in '72, speech #4—MEN," folder 27, box 12, Hermine Tobolowsky Papers, Southwest Collection/Special Collections Library, Texas Tech University, Lubbock (hereafter cited as HTP-TT); "All Agree Women Need More Rights," *San Antonio Light*, February 10, 1965, 12 (second quotation). Opening this speech, Tobolowsky referred to November 7, 1972 (when the state's voters would cast their ballots on the ELRA), as a day that "will probably become known as 'male emancipation day.'"

21. Hermine D. Tobolowsky to BPW members, March 28, 1961, HTP-TWU.

22. Laura McEnaney, "Cold War Mobilization and Domestic Politics: The United States," in *The Cambridge History of the Cold War*, vol. 1, *Origins*, ed. Melvyn P. Leffler and Odd Arne Westad (Cambridge: Cambridge University Press, 2010), 106–7, 436 (first quotation); "Our Own Communists Can Cripple Us," reprinted from "Changing Times," *Kiplinger Magazine*, February 1951, folder 5, box 12, HTP-TT; *Pay Your Poll Tax* (Fort Worth: Texas Federation of Business and Professional Women's Clubs, n.d.), HTP-TWU (second quotation).

23. Houston experienced a particularly vicious Red Scare in the 1950s. See Don E. Carleton, *Red Scare!: Right-Wing Hysteria, Fifties Fanaticism, and Their Legacy in Texas* (Austin: Texas Monthly Press, 1985). Ruby Clayton McKee, "The Woman's Angle," *DMN*, September 20, 1956 (first quotation). Tobolowsky's involvement in the Freedom Forum was mentioned repeatedly in newspaper articles about her in the 1950s. See, for example, "B&PW to Hear Woman Attorney," *San Angelo Standard-Times*, April 20, 1958; Karen Klinefelter, "Leading Lady: Her Brand of 3 R's Is Aimed at Adults," *Dallas Times Herald*, July 22, 1959 (second quotation). The BPW suggested that communists used sexual inequality against the United States in propaganda campaigns, that women who experienced discrimination might prove more receptive to communist subversion, and that national security required continual, full employment so that no state of emergency would result from another wartime labor shortage. Laughlin, "Civic Feminists," 15, 18, 21 (third quotation). *Are Women People?* (Fort Worth: Texas Federation of Business and Professional Women's Clubs, n.d.), HTP-TWU (fourth quotation). Tobolowsky and the TX-BPW used this retort repeatedly, usually after pointing out that as of 1957, Texas already had the power to draft women.

24. Hyman Tobolowsky to George Parkhouse, March 23, 1957, HTP-TWU (first quotation); Barbara Richardson, "Hermine Tobolowsky—Protecting Women's Rights," *Dallas Times Herald*, undated clipping, HTP-TWU (second quotation); Wayne E. Green, "Sex and Civil Rights: Women's Groups Fight Last Vestiges of Bias on Job, before the Law," *Wall Street Journal*, May 22, 1967 (third quotation).

25. *Legal Discrimination against Women in Texas* (Fort Worth: Texas Federation of Business and Professional Women's Clubs, 1958), HTP-TWU.

26. For examples of the success of this approach, see Terry H. Anderson, *The Pursuit of Fairness: A History of Affirmative Action* (New York: Oxford University Press, 2004), 22, 38–39, 40 (quotation), 41–46, 51–52.

27. Ibid., 42 (first and second quotations). The TX-BPW's implied criticism of the civil rights movement eventually gave way to a more overtly inclusive approach, as evidenced in a 1972 TX-BPW bumper sticker (folder 24, box 12, HTP-TT):

> Happiness is . . . EQUALITY.
> Whether
> Black, White, Brown
> Protestant, Catholic or Jew
> Amendment 7
> applies to YOU!

There is some evidence that, during the campaign for legal sexual equality in Texas, Tobolowsky and the TX-BPW attempted outreach efforts to Latina women via the Spanish-language press and pamphlets printed in Spanish, but it is difficult to measure the timing, the extent of these efforts, or the results. See, for example, Oscar Salas, "Conozca sus Derechos," *El Sol de Texas*, n.d., clipping in HTP-TWU. See also Tobolowsky, interview.

28. Gayle McNutt, "Misses by 9 Votes in House: Equal Rights Measure Fails," *Houston Post*, March 3, 1965.

29. *Legal Discrimination against Women*; Kay Holmquist, "Women's Elusive Goal: Full Legal Rights for All," *Fort Worth Star-Telegram*, February 28, 1971 (quotations).

30. Ernest Stromberger, "15-Year Struggle: Dallas Attorney Sees Win in Long Proposition 7 War," *Dallas Times Herald*, October 31, 1972 (first quotation); Kay Holmquist, "Women's Elusive Goal:

Full Legal Rights for All," *Fort Worth Star-Telegram*, February 28, 1971; *Legal Discrimination against Women* (second quotation).

31. Leff, "Opening Legal Doors for Women," 235 (first quotation). In newspaper coverage, Tobolowsky and the TX-BPW received the vast majority of the credit for the amendment's passage. Though other groups were involved for at least part of the decade prior to passage, they received few mentions by name in newspaper accounts or in the files of the TX-BPW. Mary Lu Zuber, "Lady, You're Not at All Equal under Texas Law," *Houston Chronicle*, October 8, 1972 (second quotation).

32. Ann E. Margolin, "A History of the Texas Equal Legal Rights Amendment," (graduate seminar paper, Southern Methodist University, 1983), folder 1, box 12, HTP-TT; Sylvia Porter, "Laws of Texas Long Geared to Policy of 'For Men Only,'" *Boston Herald*, November 24, 1961 (quotation).

33. For a summary of the anti-ELRA arguments, see Margaret H. Amsler, "Referendum: Against Equal Rights Amendment," *Texas Bar Journal*, December 1963, 1005, 1076, 1078, 1079. Amsler was a professor of law at Baylor University and former member of the Texas House of Representatives. Louise B. Raggio, interview by Sheree Scarborough, March 25, 27, 2003, 33–36, University of Texas Law Library, Austin; Carolyn Patrick, "Women's Rights Legislation: The Next Session May Prove Better," *DMN*, June 16, 1965; Kay Holmquist, "Women's Elusive Goal: Full Legal Rights for All," *Fort Worth Star-Telegram*, February 28, 1971 (quotation).

34. Letter and attached packet of material on the ERA, addressed to Texas state legislators (Senator/Representative) from Barbara Vackar, State Coordinator of Texans for Equal Rights Amendment, [1975], HTP-TWU.

35. Leff, "Opening Legal Doors for Women," 236. The tally was 2,066,307 votes in favor of the ELRA, and 534,037 votes against. See Robert E. Ford, "Texas Vote Analyzed," *DMN*, November 12, 1972; Texas Federation of Business and Professional Women, "Victory Celebration in Honor of Hermine D. Tobolowsky: Oh, Thank Heaven for Amendment Seven!," November 1972, folder 23, box 7, HTP-TT (quotation).

36. Public hearing on HCR 57, House Communications, Video/Audio Services Office, John H. Reagan Building, Austin. The written records of the Texas House of Representatives Video/Audio Services for HCR 57 include a list of proponents and opponents of HCR 57 who were prepared to testify at the April 1975 hearing. "Political Intelligence: Mary Kay and the ERA," *Texas Observer*, March 28, 1975; Betty Barnes, interview by Louis Marchiafava, May 12, 1975, transcript, Oral History Collection, Houston Metropolitan Research Center, Houston Public Library Digital Archives, Houston; Nancy E. Baker, "Focus on the Family: Twentieth-Century Conservative Texas Women and the Lone Star Right," in *The Texas Right: The Radical Roots of Lone Star Conservatism*, ed. David O'Donald Cullen and Kyle G. Wilkison (College Station: Texas A&M University Press, 2014), 140–42.

37. Public hearing, HCR 57.

38. Ibid.

39. Ibid.

40. "Women Debate ERA," *Dallas Times Herald*, February 12, 1975. The jail incident (which had allegedly occurred in Tennessee) was a popular anti-ERA argument nationwide. New York state senator Karen Burstein took the time to research the story and concluded it was a myth. For the flyer, see "STOP Equal Rights Amendment," n.d., folder 18, box 7, HTP-TT. For more on how the ERA could be used to discuss racial integration, see Mathews and De Hart, *Sex, Gender, and the Politics*, 174, chap. 6.

41. Public hearing, HCR 57.

42. Carolyn Barta, "ERA Vote Appears Likely," unidentified newspaper clipping, folder 18, box 7, HTP-TT. The article describes the rescission bill as "bottled up in committee."

43. Baker, *Unequaled*, chap. 2.

44. Public hearing, HCR 57.

45. Norma Cude, "Sniping at ERA," *Texas Observer*, March 11, 1977; Patti Kilday, "ERA Would Give Court More Power, Rally Told," *DMN*, April 14, 1977 (quotation). The organizations in attendance included the WWWW, Texans United for Families, and Texans against the ERA.

46. Nene Foxhall, "W's Probe Moral Decay," *DMN*, August 29, 1975; Sharon Cobler, "Anti-ERA Movement Goes National," *DMN*, November 27, 1975; Nene Foxhall, "Faction Broadens Attack," *DMN*, July 3, 1975 (first quotation); "Ideals Forum Topic," *DMN*, August 22, 1975 (second quotation).

47. Debbie K. Solomon, "'Mother of ERA': Backers Put Wrong Foot First," *Dallas Times Herald Extra—East*, July 7, 1982.

48. Dale Wittner, "One Mother Is Fighting to Remain a 'Woman,'" *Houston Chronicle Texas Magazine*, May 6, 1973; [Virginia O. Voelker] to Hermine Tobolowsky, October 31, 1974 (second quotation), folder 34, box 7, HTP-TT; Stephanie Gilmore, "The Dynamics of Second-Wave Feminist Activism in Memphis, 1971–1982: Rethinking the Liberal/Radical Divide," *NWSA Journal* 15 (Spring 2003): 94–117.

49. "Hermine Tobolowsky: The Passing of a Legend," 1; Leff, "Opening Legal Doors for Women," 237.

50. Leslie Pound, "Supporters Mulling Theories for Failure to Win Ratification," *DMN*, June 30, 1982 (first and second quotations). For more on the rise of the Christian Right based on a " profamily" agenda, see Daniel K. Williams, *God's Own Party: The Making of the Christian Right* (New York: Oxford University Press, 2010).

Mae C. Jemison

The Right Stuff

JENNIFER ROSS-NAZZAL

In June 1987, when the National Aeronautics and Space Administration (NASA) named its first class of new astronauts since the *Challenger* accident, the media focused primarily on Dr. Mae C. Jemison, the first female astronaut of color, not the other fourteen members of the class. Although NASA had been selecting astronauts since 1959, more than twenty-five years passed before an African American woman joined the corps. Jemison, NASA determined, had the "right stuff," and she quickly became the face of the newest group of space explorers.

News coverage of her selection was so extensive that strangers recognized her on the streets of Los Angeles, where she lived at the time. National and regional news organizations eagerly scheduled interviews with her. The *CBS Evening News* featured the cat-loving doctor on a brief segment, while the *Houston Chronicle* and *USA Today* published articles about her. Jemison's employer, CIGNA Health Plans, eventually relieved her of her physician duties so that she could devote her attention to the numerous interviews and even offered her the assistance of its public relations person.[1]

Jemison had always dreamed of becoming an astronaut, but she knew she faced daunting odds. From 1959 to 1987, the space agency had named 172 astronauts, only a small fraction of them women and minorities. NASA had started considering women and minorities for the Astronaut Office less than a decade before Jemison's selection, and, before she joined the ranks, only four African American men and thirteen white women had worked in the office as astronauts. To achieve her goal, Jemison overcame numerous obstacles, including gender and racial biases. With perseverance and dedication, she earned degrees in engineering and medicine—both nontraditional fields for women and minorities. Before she turned thirty, she worked as a physician in Los Angeles

MAE C. JEMISON

in her launch entry suit of 1992. Official portrait.

Courtesy of NASA.

and Africa. After she became an astronaut, Jemison was surprised to encounter gender issues, and after less than six years as an astronaut, during which time she flew in space only once, she resigned from the space agency. She continued blazing new trails, however, forming businesses inspired in part by her passion for space. Her adopted state of Texas became home to the Jemison Group, a technology consulting firm; the Earth We Share science camps; and BioSentient, a medical devices company. She continues to live in Houston today.

Jemison's experiences as a student, a physician, an astronaut, and a businesswoman exemplify how the threads of gender and race are intertwined in the fields of science, engineering, and space exploration. As her life illustrates, science and technology shape ideas about the sexual and racial divisions of labor as well as educational opportunities for women and minorities.[2] Jemison's story in particular emphasizes the biases often experienced by women and minorities from elementary school through higher education. Becoming an astronaut meant challenging the profession's hypermasculine image, and her experience helps to explain how human spaceflight expanded to include women of color. Her story also highlights the challenges civilian scientists faced in the astronaut corps nearly a decade after the Astronaut Office began accepting them in greater numbers.

Throughout her life, Jemison has challenged biases against women and minorities, and she has pushed for opportunities for others to participate in the human spaceflight program and the world of science and engineering. Much of Jemison's drive for equality came out of the feminist and civil rights movements as well as her interest in her cultural heritage. In the 1980s, these movements opened doors for women in fields typically filled by men and in positions of power.[3] Jemison, along with her female and black colleagues in the Astronaut Office, became some of the most visible examples of the changes wrought by these movements.

Mae Jemison was born on October 17, 1956—just before the dawn of the space age—to Charlie and Dorothy Jemison in Decatur, Alabama. About two weeks before Jemison's first birthday, the Soviet Union launched Sputnik, the satellite that started the space race with the United States, and in 1958, when Jemison was still a toddler, President Dwight D. Eisenhower established NASA. Soon thereafter, NASA announced a manned satellite project, known later as Project Mercury.

The term *manned* literally reflected the status of women's participation in the U.S. space program at the time. To be an astronaut was men's work, not women's, and the Mercury Project truly was a man's project. NASA's female employees in the 1960s included nurse Dee O'Hara, assigned to the astronaut corps, and a handful of female scientists and engineers; the vast majority of the agency's female employees were support staff—that is, secretaries.[4]

When it came time to select candidates for NASA's new program, the selection committee discussed the possibility of picking astronauts from a host of dangerous occupations: mountain climbers, race car drivers, scuba divers, and test pilots. They agreed on the benefits of selecting military test pilots, a group that excluded women. Robert R. Gilruth, head of the Space Task Group, which included the astronauts, explained that the selection of test pilots "made it quite simple and logical to delegate flight control and command functions to the pilot" in the space capsule. In short, the success of the early spaceflight programs depended on the pilot's in-flight performance. Also, recruiting military men was more convenient, since they already held secret clearances, and NASA could avoid an unnecessarily public process to field potential candidates.[5]

The first astronaut class, selected in 1959, consisted of seven white male military test pilots. Known as the Mercury 7, the men came to NASA from the U.S. Air Force, the U.S. Navy, and the U.S. Marine Corps.[6] The decision to select test pilots shaped the Astronaut Office well into the Space Shuttle Program, even as civilian scientists, women, and minorities joined the astronaut corps in ever-increasing numbers.

While the decision makers agreed that male test pilots were the best choice for astronauts, researchers and physicians who studied men's and women's space fitness in the late 1950s and early 1960s believed that women were better suited than men to serve as astronauts, and studies proved it. In tests involving tight spaces and isolation, women tended to score better than men. Plus, women were smaller and lighter and consumed less water, food, and air than did men, making it cheaper and easier to launch them into space. Other reasons abounded. Dr. William K. Douglas, the personal physician for the Mercury 7, believed that because women's reproductive organs are located internally, they were better protected from the radiation of space than men's. In 1960 and 1961, female aviators participated in the same medical tests the Mercury 7 underwent, and thirteen passed the rigorous examination. Others went on to complete the second and third rounds of tests. Nevertheless, none of these women flew in space because of societal "expectations about what women could and *should* do with their lives."[7]

While women wanted to join the astronaut corps in the 1960s and serve their country, none were granted access into the male-dominated world of military jet test piloting from which all the astronauts except two classes of scientist-astronauts were chosen. (NASA did, however, send the scientist-astronauts to flight school, and they, too, became pilots.) Prior to the 1978 selection, the general requirement for astronauts included a minimum of one thousand hours of piloting jet aircraft. Thus until 1978, all astronauts were pilots, and without jet piloting experience, women could not meet NASA's basic requirements for becoming an astronaut. Until the military began accepting women to train as jet pilots, no woman could gain that experience. The navy began training women as pilots in 1973, and shortly thereafter, the army opened helicopter training to women, although they remained barred from jet training. Women finally began to enter the military test pilot schools in the 1980s—first the navy in 1982, then the air force six years later.

In contrast, the Soviet Union trained five women as cosmonauts in 1962. Soviet society was more egalitarian than American society, and men there agreed that women should participate in spaceflight. Supporters of this idea included many top-level leaders of the Soviet space program, prominent scientists, and Communist Party officials, who saw the flight of a Soviet woman in space as part of the U.S.-Soviet space race. The Soviets believed that sending a woman into space would be a propaganda coup, shaming Americans with another Soviet first. In 1961, Soviet cosmonaut Yuri Gagarin had been the first man to orbit the Earth, beating astronaut Alan Shepard into space, and in June 1963, Valentina Tereshkova, called "Gagarin in a skirt," became the first woman in space.[8]

Space exploration and the heroes of the program—the astronauts—interested Jemison as a child. She told historian Henry Louis Gates Jr. that she knew "song, line, and verse" about the spaceflights of the 1960s, and that she believed that some day she would fly in space. Like several other female astronauts who became interested in space at a young age, Jemison was not deterred by the fact that the astronauts were all white, male test pilots. Her parents raised her to believe she was equal to men. When she told one acquaintance that she wanted to become an astronaut, he responded, "You mean like the guys who go to the moon? Give me a break."[9] Rather than deterring Jemison, such episodes drove her to continue toward her goals. Whatever others might think, the stubborn Jemison refused to believe that these goals seemed too lofty for a black girl.

Even at the age of five, Jemison had a rebellious side and rejected societal expectations for girls and people of color. When her kindergarten teacher asked, "What do you want to be when you grow up?," Jemison answered, "I want to be a scientist." "Don't you mean a nurse?" the teacher asked. That response made the little girl "plain indignant": she placed her hands on her hips and insisted, "No, I mean a scientist." At the time, of course, it was unusual for a black girl to think she could become a scientist. According to society, science was a man's domain, not a woman's; women were nurses, teachers, or secretaries. The public, including teachers, knew only of Marie Curie and a few other well-known female scientists. Jemison, however, refused to be limited, and her dreams reflected the cultural changes and movements occurring around her.[10]

Cultural ideas about the role of women and minorities in the workplace were shifting, and the Jemisons recognized these changes and emphasized the importance of education to their three children. In 1960, when Mae was three, her parents chose to move to Chicago because despite having finished two years of college, Dorothy Jemison could only find work as a domestic in Alabama. In Chicago, Dorothy completed her bachelor's degree, became a teacher, and went on to earn a master's degree. Dorothy and Mae's uncle talked regularly about "how as a black person you better be twice as good as a white person to get anywhere." When Mae would ask her mother how to spell a word, she would be told to use the dictionary. Dorothy encouraged the girl to rely on her herself, not her parents, and in so doing stimulated her younger daughter's passion and interest in exploring, the study of science, and the development of analytical skills. When Jemison wanted to do a high school science project on sickle-cell anemia, a common ailment affecting African Americans, her mother had her not only research the topic but also contact the Hektoen Hematology Labs at the Cook County Hospital. She ended up conducting research there and called the experience "one of the most positive and enabling" of her life.[11]

Jemison's family had lengthy conversations about the political and social issues then facing the United States. The Jemisons believed that any topic was worthy of discussion in their home and saw the importance of analyzing questions and providing evidence for their conclusions—excellent training for a scientist. As activists in the South fought for integration, voting rights, and full equality for African Americans, the Jemisons sat down to dinner and discussed Black Power, civil rights, and the Nation of Islam; the children also learned about African American history. Before the phrase "Black Is Beautiful" became commonplace and the Afro hairstyle became a fashionable part of black culture, Jemison's parents believed that their culture, heritage, and skin color were beautiful and frequently told their children so. After listening to South African singer Miriam Makeba, Dorothy Jemison and her daughters cut their hair short and wore it natural, which "was anathema to beauty" at the time. They proudly used the term *black* and subscribed to the *Liberator* magazine, known as the voice of the African American protest movement, as well as to the *Chicago Defender* and *Muhammad Speaks*.[12] During this same time, feminism witnessed a rebirth with the publication of Betty Friedan's *Feminist Mystique*.

Popular culture reflected the revolution under way in American society and helped to promote a rebellion of women, although the media sent "mixed messages about what women should and should not do, what women could and could not be."[13] Popular television shows in the 1960s on space exploration and science fiction reflected conventional gender roles about women's place in society, the family, and the workforce even as their characters moved beyond the bounds of domesticity. Onboard the *Starship Enterprise* on the television show *Star Trek*, which began appearing in 1966, the token female characters were subordinates to the men. From 1965 to 1970, *I Dream of Jeannie* depicted the experiences of astronaut Tony Nelson and the female genie he released from a bottle. The show portrayed Jeannie as a "dumb, shapely, ditzy blonde with too much power" who called astronaut Nelson "Master." By contrast, he was brilliant, working in a field that "women allegedly *couldn't* master." The same themes appeared in science fiction novels. Jemison, a fan of the genre, devoured Isaac Asimov and Arthur C. Clarke novels. Although both authors featured white men as heroes, she came to identify with them. While she enjoyed these books, their portrayal of women and people of color as merely sidekicks or supporting characters, not protagonists, "pissed" Jemison off because "only one side of the story was being told."[14]

Jemison also failed to understand why women were not flying the Mercury and Gemini spacecraft, and no adult could explain to her the gender barriers that excluded women from the ranks of the American astronaut corps. After all, Tereshkova had flown in space. *Star Trek*, which featured a diverse group of space fliers, including a black female character, Lieutenant Uhura, appealed to Jemison's feminist sensibilities and reaffirmed her belief that women could and should be astronauts. Moreover, *Star Trek* proved that someone else—Gene Roddenberry, the show's creator—agreed that the idea of women astronauts was not crazy.[15]

In the early 1970s, more women began to attend technical schools and earn undergraduate degrees in engineering and science, but college majors still remained highly segregated by sex. Few females considered earning degrees in the male-dominated fields of engineering, the life sciences, mathematics, or the physical sciences. Most pursued degrees in education or the health professions. Those who majored in engineering were often influenced by good pay, the women's movement, and affirmative action programs.[16]

Jemison was one of a small handful of women who decided to pursue engineering degrees. She received a four-year National Achievement Scholarship and gained admission and scholarship offers to some of America's leading technical and engineering schools, among them the Massachusetts Institute of Technology (MIT), Rensselaer Polytechnic Institute, and Stanford University. Her interest in MIT may have stemmed from a program sponsored by its Association of Women Students to encourage high school girls to apply.[17] She ultimately accepted an offer from Stanford, leaving the Midwest for Silicon Valley in 1973, when she was sixteen, and completing her degree in chemical engineering while also fulfilling the requirements for a bachelor's degree in African and Afro-American studies.

Jemison followed a path blazed by America's first woman in space, Sally K. Ride. A California native, Ride had attended Stanford, earning dual degrees in physics and English. The two women had many other similarities: both were feminists and were renaissance women, maintaining strong interests in fields outside of science. Jemison spoke Russian and Swahili, while Ride enjoyed reading Shakespeare. Both were athletes—Jemison a dancer and Ride a tennis player.

Pursuing an engineering degree at Stanford proved to be challenging for Jemison, in part because of racial and gender biases in her science and engineering courses. Jemison often felt invisible, as if professors were "look[ing] through" her. In her freshman chemistry course, she sat in the front row and asked questions, which her professor ignored. If he answered, he insinuated that she was stupid for not knowing the answer. But "when a white boy down the row asked the exact same questions," the faculty member praised the young man for his insight.[18]

Jemison's experiences were not unusual. Women who majored in engineering at American universities in the 1970s found that discrimination was rampant, even after the 1972 passage of Title IX, which ended admission quotas for women who attended professional programs like engineering or law schools. Female students at MIT and other major universities often felt isolated and had few role models in their academic fields of study, but MIT—unlike Stanford—engaged with the feminist movement and pushed for equal opportunities for female students. While MIT did not eliminate the barriers women faced, women there found some benefits from this effort. Similar programs appeared at other universities, among them the University of Washington, where Professor Irene C. Peden and the Society of Women Engineers mentored several female engineering students.[19]

Looking back over her time at Stanford, Jemison noted that her determination to complete an engineering degree in four years left her "bruised and bloodied." Her Stanford experience taught her that people could judge her and doubt her "intelligence and aptitude on sight," based on the color of her skin and her gender. "It was a harsh blow," she lamented.[20]

Following graduation, Jemison chose to attend Cornell University Medical College, though she did not intend to practice medicine but rather had the unusual goal of becoming a biomedical engineer. Jemison was one of a growing number of women choosing to attend medical school in the 1970s as a consequence of changing attitudes about women's place in society, a civil rights case filed against medical schools, equal opportunity legislation, and the feminist movement, among other factors. Women had attended Cornell since 1898, when the university established its medical school. Only a small number of the school's medical students were minorities. The 105 students in Jemison's class included only 10 blacks and 30 women.[21]

When Jemison entered medical school, she had been influenced by the feminist movement and supported its basic tenets. She sought equal treatment by her male counterparts and refused "to be belittled as" a lady. Jemison was never afraid to assert herself. On the eve of her first class, a man approached a group of students playing cards and asked, "Are the girls losing?" Jemison, who had grown tired of the term *girl*, objected: "Black men would not tolerate being called anything with 'boy' in it at all, so why should I?" She replied that the women were, in fact, winning, "and the boys are losing." Her father had taught her that assertiveness was a perfectly acceptable trait for a girl or woman, "so when I'd run into guys later on who had a problem with me, it didn't matter because my dad was the manliest man I knew. And he thought I was fine, so that was that." And when she worked with surgeons, whom she called "the most egotistical, difficult people to deal with," she held her own.[22]

Several of the most influential events of Jemison's life occurred when she traveled abroad as a medical student. After completing her second year of medical school, Jemison worked in Kenya with the African Medical Education and Research Foundation (AMREF), which provided surgical and health services to East Africans living in remote areas often inaccessible to automobiles. Most Kenyan doctors practiced in Nairobi, the capital, leaving the rest of the country to the AMREF. Jemison knew a great deal about African culture, history, and politics and was thrilled to visit the continent. She worked on a health survey, assisted during surgeries, and participated in community medicine projects.[23]

Her experience in Kenya, an earlier trip to Cuba, and time in a Cambodian refugee camp pointed Jemison in a new direction. She decided not to apply for a residency program but to explore primary health care for people in developing countries. The deans at Cornell objected strenuously to her plan, emphasizing the importance of completing a residency program. Nonetheless, like many other female medical students of the time, Jemison fashioned "a new kind of professional identity," rejecting the traditional path for recent medical school graduates in favor of a position that reflected her values and interest in Africa.[24]

Many of her African American colleagues shared her belief in the importance of "making a difference" in their communities. Yet as Jemison later told poet

Nikki Giovanni, she did not "believe in altruism. I've gotten much more out of what I have done than the people I was supposed to be helping." Her time at the Cambodian refugee camp was an invaluable experience: "I learned much more about medicine . . . than I could have in a lifetime somewhere else. I refuse to think those people owe me any thanks. I got a lot out of it."[25]

In the summer of 1976, before Jemison's senior year of college, NASA announced that applications would be accepted for the first class of space shuttle astronauts and encouraged qualified women and minorities to apply. In addition, NASA dropped the requirement that all astronauts have jet piloting experience. The agency anticipated hiring fifteen pilots and fifteen mission specialists (scientist-astronauts who would conduct research in space) but instead selected fifteen pilots and twenty mission specialists for the class of 1978, which included the first female and minority astronauts. Samuel E. Denard, a graduate student in engineering at Stanford, a close friend of Jemison's, and an enthusiastic supporter of the space program, encouraged her: "You need to apply to NASA to be an astronaut *right now*! They're bringing in mission specialists. You don't have to be an air force pilot or in the military. They really want to refocus." The changes in the space agency were stimulated by the civil rights and feminist movements. The Civil Rights Act of 1964 had prohibited sex and racial discrimination in employment and created the Equal Employment Opportunity Commission. As of 1972, NASA and other federal agencies had to implement affirmative action plans, resulting in a more diverse and inclusive workforce.[26]

The decision to include women and minorities challenged not only the image of astronauts but also the traditions in an astronaut corps composed primarily of test pilots. Alan L. Bean, who was in charge of astronaut candidate training for the 1978 class, had not previously worked with professional women before. Prior to his selection as an astronaut in 1963, he had been a navy test pilot, and he initially believed that being an astronaut was "a man job." Because "a lot of things that you do as an astronaut aren't that genteel," he thought that only men should fill those slots (although he eventually realized that women could be just as qualified as men). He had no objections to minority astronauts—as long as they were men. In his view, "We could turn minority astronauts into 'real' astronauts faster than women into 'real' astronauts."[27] Such viewpoints may have reflected the military's integration three decades earlier.

Some observers have argued that NASA had more difficulty integrating civilian scientists into the Astronaut Office than accepting African Americans or women, primarily because test pilots tended to be politically conservative, while the scientists tended to be liberals. As astronaut and air force flight test engineer Richard M. Mullane explained, 1978 represented "the first time in history [that] the astronaut title was being bestowed on tree-huggers, dolphin-friendly fish eaters, vegetarians, and subscribers to the *New York Times.*" He believed that the civilian candidates who were offered jobs were innocent, soft, and inexperienced, especially when compared to men who had flown combat missions in Vietnam.[28] Although the office became more diverse, test pilots remained in charge until 2009, just prior to the end of the Space Shuttle Program, when Peggy A. Whitson, a biochemist, took the helm. For years, the office tended to reflect the hierarchical command structure present in the military, and the status differences between test pilots and mission specialists did not begin to change until the International Space Station era.

When the first six female astronauts arrived in 1978, NASA faced some technical challenges, from making spacesuits that fit women to creating a waste collection system (a toilet) that worked for both sexes. But the biggest challenge was entrenched cultural attitudes about women in the workforce and in the Astronaut Office. Dr. Carolyn L. Huntoon, who had worked at the Johnson Space Center (JSC) since 1970, often acted as the "mother hen" for the six women astronauts. She ran interference for them, especially with older men who were unaccustomed to working with younger women in positions of power. When a man complained to Huntoon that a female astronaut said his idea was incorrect, she replied, "Now, which male astronaut hasn't spoken up in a meeting and told you something?" To herself, Huntoon thought, "What were other people expecting of women astronauts?"[29]

Jemison did not apply to the astronaut corps until 1985 and did not join the office until two years later. After graduating from medical school in 1981, she spent a year at the Los Angeles County–University of Southern California Medical Center, where she learned more about primary care and medicine and searched for a way to work overseas in a developing country. Her approach reflected that pursued by many African American female physicians, who sought careers in community service and chose primary care specialties over other fields. Although her choice was not "glamorous," she believed that working at the Los Angeles center had helped to round out the training she received in New York.[30]

Jemison eventually took a position with the Peace Corps, serving as the area medical officer for Sierra Leone and Liberia from 1983 to 1985. Life in these countries was harsh, and conditions were often crude. Some of the doctors with whom Jemison worked had "little or no equipment, medication, or supplies" as a consequence of a lack of funds. Electricity was unreliable, and she regularly witnessed the effects of tropical diseases such as Lassa fever, an endemic viral illness that she had only read about in her textbooks. While far from an ideal place to practice medicine, Jemison gained vast knowledge of tropical and infectious diseases and conducted a series of research projects for the National Institutes of Health and the Centers for Disease Control, working on a hepatitis B vaccine and treatments for schistosomiasis (a disease caused by a parasite that lives in water) and rabies. She learned the value of flexibility in trying situations and gained "an appreciation of the challenges life poses to so many people." The skills she mastered in Africa would be important to the selection committee at NASA.[31]

In the summer of 1985, Jemison came back to the United States after two and a half years in Africa. With NASA increasing the number of missions it expected to fly, the agency announced that it would begin accepting applications from civilians on an ongoing basis. Jemison decided to apply to be part of the next class of shuttle astronauts, to be named in the spring of 1986. She contacted her old friend, Sam Denard, who was working in Houston and invited her to visit the space center. He introduced her to African American astronaut Ron Mc-Nair and some key supporters of minority and female astronauts, including Joseph D. Atkinson, head of JSC's Equal Opportunity Programs Office. Atkinson met regularly with promising minority candidates for the Astronaut Office and took credit for recruiting McNair for the corps. Atkinson showed great interest in Jemison's engineering and medical background. Huntoon, who served on the 1978 selection board, also encouraged her to apply.[32]

She did, but astronaut selection was put on hold when the *Challenger* space shuttle was torn apart by aerodynamic forces it was not designed to withstand shortly after liftoff in January 1986. Later that year, NASA reopened the selection process, and Jemison updated her application. To reach women and minorities, the space agency sent flyers to historically black colleges and universities, the Society of Women Engineers and other professional groups for women and minorities, graduate schools, and scientific and technical government agencies. Only 117 of the almost 2,000 applicants, including Jemison, were invited to participate in interviews and physicals at the JSC. Jemison worried that her "slightly hip-hop Afro style" would be too outlandish for NASA's conservative astronaut corps, but she realized that there was nothing she could do and decided not to spike or tease her bangs.[33]

The weeklong process consisted of a thorough medical and psychological exam and an interview with the selection board, chaired by George W. S. Abbey. The board included Atkinson and Huntoon as well as a handful of astronauts from the 1978 class, among them Anna L. Fisher, and veteran astronaut John W. Young, who had walked on the moon. Jemison was thrilled: "I remember thinking, 'There's John Young!'"[34]

Jemison was at ease during her interview. The format was familiar to her; medical schools and the Peace Corps tended to meet and talk with candidates by panel. Furthermore, she believed she could "go anywhere" and "do anything," given her experience in medical school, as a doctor in developing nations and in Los Angeles, and at Stanford University. With her background in fields that had few women, the idea of working in an office composed mainly of men "was no big issue."[35]

After the final round of interviews, the board ranked interviewees within their disciplines, looking for people with a "good mix of education, experience, and outside activities." Those with advanced degrees had an edge, although a graduate degree was not mandatory. The panel also considered other achievements or skills, such as pilot's licenses, athletic ability, and scuba training. They looked for committed team players, people with a sense of humor, people who were levelheaded. They asked themselves two big questions: "Is this a person you'd feel comfortable sending out to your hometown to talk to the public and talking to Congress and talking to the press?" and "Is this somebody I would feel comfortable flying with?"[36] Jemison was exactly the type of candidate they wanted.

But Jemison heard nothing until June 4, 1987, when Abbey called to ask if she still wanted to work as an astronaut. Her answer was unequivocal: "Yes. Absolutely!" Abbey asked her not to tell anyone until the media was notified the following day. She continued to see patients all day but called her parents that night and told them, swearing them to secrecy. When she woke up the next morning, her life had changed dramatically. The news had leaked, and everyone wanted to interview one of the new astronaut candidates.[37]

Her early days as an astronaut witnessed the development of an important network of support. On August 24, NASA welcomed its newest fifteen astronauts, seven pilots and eight mission specialists. Jemison and Jan D. Davis were the only two women, and Jemison was the only nonwhite.[38] African American astronaut Charlie Bolden and his wife, Jackie, hosted a special get-together for Jemison and invited all the other African American astronauts and several top African Americans employed at the Houston center. Bolden, an aviator with the U.S. Marines, had worked at NASA since 1980, and had piloted the last successful space shuttle mission prior to the *Challenger* accident. He wanted to introduce Jemison to the people on whom she could call if she needed advice. Jemison appreciated Bolden's help and the people she met through him.[39]

Cultural attitudes about women in professional positions at NASA had changed somewhat over the preceding decade. The agency had more female engineers and scientists, but observers still believed that "customs and social attitudes" had a long way to go to "allow real equality between the sexes in the workplace." Female professionals totaled nearly 13 percent of the women employed at the JSC in 1984, but some fields remained primarily closed to them.[40] The Flight Director's Office selected Michele Brekke as its first female flight director in 1985, but she never commanded a flight control team, and not until 1992 did Linda Ham become the first woman to direct a mission.[41]

What most surprised Jemison was the pecking order in the Astronaut Office. Looking back, she believes that she was "a little naive," thinking that her experience and education would put her on equal footing with others in the office. "I didn't realize that I wasn't supposed to think that I was as equal as everyone else. I didn't realize that there was this pilot military hierarchy" in the astronaut corps, and that she and the other mission specialists were lower down the ladder.[42] Although NASA had selected more mission specialists than pilots since 1978, test pilots continued to head the office and serve as mission commanders. Daniel C. Brandenstein, a naval test pilot, headed the office during most of Jemison's tenure, with mission specialist Steven A. Hawley, an astronomer, as his deputy until June 1990. The attitudes Jemison witnessed may have reflected the persistence of the tensions that astronaut and air force flight test engineer Mullane described when he came in 1978.

Jemison questioned why the commander was always a pilot. The commander traditionally managed the flight crew and landed the shuttle with assistance from the pilot, while one of the flight crew's mission specialists served as the flight engineer and assisted the commander and pilot during launch and landing. Mission specialists never flew the orbiter. But, Jemison argued, there was no reason why a mission specialist could not be in charge. During a medical emergency, she explained to her new colleagues, the doctor in charge commanded the situation, managed the team, and made all the decisions but did not administer medicine or work on the patient. This command structure could be replicated in the shuttle. Some pilots agreed, though others were less open to change. The skills Jemison had developed while handling surgeons and their "God complex" did not work as well with test pilots, and Jemison believes that her ideas frequently were cast aside.[43] The problem may have also stemmed in part from the fact that all of the pilots and commanders were men. NASA's first female pilot, Eileen M. Collins, did not arrive until the summer of 1990. She flew her first mission five years later, and commanded a 1999 space shuttle flight.

In keeping with NASA policy, Jemison and the other members of her class spent a year in the astronaut training program before officially being designated astronauts. The candidates regularly flew in high-performance T-38 jets to NASA centers and contractor facilities, so they participated in survival training. They had to learn what to do if they bailed out of a T-38 in a remote area or over a body of water, and they completed air force wilderness and water survival training classes. They visited all ten NASA centers and familiarized themselves with their various functions. Although NASA no longer required astronauts to be test pilots, the agency expected mission specialists to fly at least fifteen hours each month in the backseat of a T-38. Astronauts also occasionally flew in the KC-135 aircraft, which gave them an opportunity to experience a few moments of weightlessness. And the candidates attended classes in meteorology, mathematics, astronomy, navigation, physics, and computers.[44]

While in the T-38s, astronauts wore blue flight suits. When Jemison went for her fitting, she found that the standard flight suit was sized for men and did not properly fit women's breasts, small waists, and hips—even though women had been in the office for nearly a decade. When Jemison asked the other female astronauts why no one had pressed for a women's flight suit, they said that accepting the status quo was easier and that they did not want to make a fuss. Jemison found such attitudes strange, asking whether men would be content to make do with ill-fitting suits and insisting that NASA provide women astronauts with suits and other gear that was tailored to them. Contrary to feminists who argue that men and women are no different from one another, Jemison believed that biological differences between the sexes were important, and some of the women who subsequently joined the Astronaut Office shared her views. Air force test pilot Pamela A. Melroy, for one, took pride in the term *woman astronaut*, and she became the third woman to pilot an orbiter and the second to command a space shuttle mission.[45]

The first six women NASA chose to fly in space saw themselves primarily as astronauts, not women astronauts. On her first spacewalk, Kathryn D. Sullivan's spacesuit fit poorly, but she "reckoned the wrong thing to do was to turn the first evolution of a woman doing a spacewalk into controversy over, 'We need different flight rules and oh, see, now she's asking for more equipment.'" Other female astronauts took the same attitude. In 1984, when Judith A. Resnik became the second American woman in space and the media emphasized the historic nature of her flight, she preferred to focus on the fact that she was "the 40th or 45th, or whatever the number is, American astronaut to go on the Space Shuttle in a period of a couple of years, and how far we've come in a few years."[46]

Ever since Project Mercury, astronauts had been assigned specialist tasks to enable them to learn more about their spacecraft and the equipment they would use in space. Jemison became a Cape Crusader, working at the Kennedy Space Center in Florida with engineers and technicians preparing the orbiters for launch and integrating payloads (satellites or experiments, for example) into the shuttle's cargo bay. The assignment was one of the coveted jobs in the Astronaut Office. Cape Crusaders worked inside the orbiter as it sat on the launch pad; they set up the flight deck to make sure that the switches were properly configured for liftoff and loaded the vehicle with the crew equipment. A prime crusader had the honor of strapping the crew into their seats prior to launch. The crusaders also watched launch and landing, two of the most exciting parts of the shuttle missions. After the vehicle landed, they helped the crew exit and carried some of their flight equipment out of the orbiter. According to astronaut Jerry L. Ross, the only assignment "that beats [being a Cape Crusader] is to actually do the flight yourself!"[47]

Bolden was Jemison's boss during this assignment. Given the loss of a vehicle and crew in 1986, the efforts of the Cape Crusaders were considered vital to the nation's return to spaceflight. Bolden directed the newest member of his team to be "very, very thorough" when walking through the Orbiter Processing Facility, "looking under things in the nooks and crannies."[48] The first flight after the accident included a tracking and data relay satellite in its cargo bay to replace the one NASA lost during *Challenger*'s final launch. The return-to-flight mission finally launched on September 29, 1988, restoring confidence in the agency and marking a new beginning for NASA.

Exactly one year later, NASA named Jemison to a Spacelab flight sponsored by Japan and the United States. NASA announced crews for five shuttle missions, but Jemison was the lead story—she would become the first African American female astronaut to fly. Jan Davis and Mark C. Lee were also selected for the mission, with a commander and pilot to be named at a later date. NASA Public Affairs announced that Jemison would be serving as a payload specialist.[49]

Payload specialists were not trained astronauts; they had their own separate office. They were from foreign countries, Congress, and industry, and each one monitored a specific experiment onboard the space shuttle. Being a payload specialist sometimes meant being treated like a third-class citizen, and the announcement must have been a slap in the face to Jemison. According to Commander Brewster Shaw, when Mexico's first payload specialist flew, Shaw felt that he needed to padlock the shuttle's airlock to prevent the specialist, who had limited training, from accidentally opening the door. Ultimately, Japanese astronaut Mamoru Mohri became the payload specialist on Jemison's mission, and press releases started referring to her as "science mission specialist." NASA had just created this position as part of the preparations for building a space station; the science mission specialist would advocate on behalf of researchers with scientific experiments onboard the shuttle and would concentrate on science operations. The remainder of the crew included commander Robert L. "Hoot" Gibson, pilot Curtis L. Brown Jr., and mission specialist Jay Apt.[50]

The expansion of spaceflight to women of color thrilled other black women. When Sharon Caples McDougle, then working as a suit technician for Boeing Aerospace, heard that NASA had named its first "sister," she wrote her name next to Jemison's on the assignment sheet to alert everyone that she, the only black woman in her area, would work with the first female African American astronaut. "I didn't want anybody else assigned to her," McDougle later explained. She had never met Jemison or demanded to be assigned to a mission or astronaut before, but she was excited by the historical significance of this assignment and wanted to make the flight memorable for Jemison. "I wanted to make sure she was taken care of, she was comfortable, and I wanted to be the one to do that," McDougle said. McDougle was awed by Jemison's accomplishments, joking "What haven't you done? Can you cook?" After meeting Jemison, McDougle concurred with Jemison's college roommate, who called the future space flier modest, sincere, and "down-to-earth." McDougle described her as "a normal person" who "in the next moment . . . can be super doctor scientist."[51] They spent the next year working closely together as the crew trained for the flight, and during this time Jemison learned the importance of the NASA saying, "Fly as you train."

Astronauts needed to learn as much as they could about the spacecraft, hardware, and experiments before they flew. Crews and flight control teams trained regularly, so when NASA declared go for launch, the on-orbit tasks the crew completed were rote. Crews constantly worked different scenarios—the what-ifs—in case something went wrong, and astronauts had to complete a catalog of courses at the space center before flight. For every hour of flight, a crew spent about six hours training on the ground. At JSC, the crew members practiced their scheduled activities, launch, and landing in the shuttle simulators. Because this was a Spacelab flight, the crew also trained at the Marshall Space Flight Center Payload Crew Training Complex in Huntsville, Alabama, and in Japan.

In addition, mission specialists spent hours with scientists, known as the principal investigators, on the various experiments that would be flown onboard their flight. Jemison and Patricia S. Cowings of the NASA Ames Research Center worked together on the autogenic feedback training experiment. Cowings had trained as a backup payload specialist before any women had been selected as astronauts, and, she recalled, "they didn't even have a uniform [fitted] for me," a similar problem that Jemison experienced more than a decade later. Officials even asked her "what size jockey shorts [she] wore." (The underwear issue, at least, had been resolved by Jemison's time: according to Bean, one of the first six women astronauts told him, "The women don't like boxer shorts. We want panties.") Cowings, like Jemison, also had trouble getting the flight suit to fit properly. A man who had never worked with women crew members complained, "I don't understand it. If it fits in the chest, it's too big at the waist and the sleeves are too long. If it fits on your waist, the hips are too small." To which she sarcastically replied, "Go home and look at [your] wife. Women are shaped differently than men!"[52]

Cowings was now working on a series of experimental techniques that she believed could help astronauts learn to control motion sickness (which affected about 70 percent of those onboard the space shuttle) without the use of prescription drugs. Jemison would be a guinea pig. Cowings trained her in the techniques so that if she began to feel sick, she could consciously control her body's response. Jemison also became the coinvestigator for a bone cell research experiment and worked with the Japanese on their experiments.[53]

During her training, Jemison did not hesitate to share her opinions. She believed that her presence on the flight meant nothing if she did not weigh in on key issues: "What difference [does it make] if you have a place at the table and you act just like everybody else and you mind your table manners?" NASA, however, emphasized teamwork, and some colleagues saw her as less than a team player. When the crew traveled to Japan, the other members stayed at a U.S. military hotel, but Jemison had always been interested in other cultures, and she preferred to stay at a Japanese inn. Her decision caused some friction, and relations among crew members grew increasingly strained.[54]

Media coverage before the flight was extensive. Jemison was humble about her role as the first African American woman in space, describing herself as just having happened "to be the first one that NASA selected," though many others had the necessary skills. Moreover, she emphasized, her selection was proof that the United States was moving forward, "but we can't just stop with one person." And, astronomers and scientists from across the globe had the skills and talents necessary for spaceflight and deserved to be included.[55]

On September 12, 1992, McDougle helped dress Jemison in her Launch Entry Suit (sized for men) and wished her well. *Endeavour* lifted off the pad at 10:23 a.m., and Jemison, sitting on the middeck, grinned as the crew rode into space. Hers was the fiftieth shuttle mission, and it marked a number of firsts: the first African American female astronaut, the first astronaut from Japan, and the first and only married couple in space. (Jan Davis and Mark Lee had married about a year and half earlier, leading the press to speculate about whether they would have sex in space.)

Jemison spent most of her time in the Spacelab, where she conducted research for the scientists with whom she had worked so closely on the ground. At the beginning of each shift, she paid homage to Nichelle Nichols's Lieutenant Uhura with a slight variation of her radio call: "Huntsville, Endeavour. All hailing frequencies are open." The young girl who had rejected the belief that women could not be astronauts had finally achieved her lifelong goal: as Jemison put it, "The circle was complete." The lab ran twenty-four hours a day, with the crew split into two teams. Davis and Jemison worked on the blue team in the lab, while Apt monitored the vehicle. Jemison devoted her time to the motion sickness study and an experiment to learn how zero gravity affected frogs from embryos to adulthood.[56]

Recognizing the historical significance of her flight and wanting to democratize spaceflight for everyone, Jemison carefully selected items to take onboard that reflected her pride in her African heritage. She took "things for people who would not have been represented on the shuttle otherwise, things that other folks wouldn't take up, or people who would not have felt like they were a part of it": a flag for the Organization of African Unity; a banner for Alpha Kappa Alpha, an African American sorority; and an African Bundu statue from the Women's Society in Sierra Leone. She also carried an Alvin Ailey American Dance poster, a certificate for Chicago public school students, and a banner for a school named after her. Jemison wanted Americans to know that spaceflight was open to everyone. While in space, she listened to music by Stevie Wonder and Shirley Bassey as well as Nigerian drummer Babatunde Olatunji.[57]

When the shuttle landed at Kennedy Space Center after an eight-day flight, McDougle was there, ready to lend a hand to Jemison. Astronauts' muscles sometimes atrophy in space, and the suit techs provide wheelchairs and assistance to those who feel weak. Not Jemison. As McDougle recalled, Jemison strode off of *Endeavour* and said, "Hey, Sharon! How you doing?"[58]

Jemison's accomplishment meant a great deal to the African American community. To McDougle, it meant that African American women had "finally made it." *Jet* magazine featured Jemison on its cover, while *Ebony*'s cover trumpeted the "Year of the Black Woman" and featured Jemison as well as Olympic gold medalist Jackie Joyner-Kersee, Senator Carol Moseley Braun, Congresswoman Maxine Waters, and actress Halle Berry.[59]

Back on Earth, Jemison began a whirlwind public relations tour of the United States. She visited schools and impressed on students the importance of studying math and science. So many communities wanted to hear Jemison speak that NASA extended her tour. She visited Atlanta, Los Angeles, and her hometown of Chicago, where she celebrated her thirty-sixth birthday. For Nichols, the highlight of Jemison's week in Chicago was seeing her join cheerleaders in her high school fight song "in her astronaut jumpsuit, no less."[60]

Following her media tour, Jemison returned to JSC and waited to be selected for another flight. She was selected for a Montgomery Fellowship at Dartmouth

University, taking a three-month sabbatical from NASA to teach a course, "Space Age Technology and Developing Countries," an issue in which she had been interested for years.[61]

Jemison grew increasingly frustrated with NASA because she believed that the agency was not using her abilities or creativity, and she resigned about six months after her flight. She had weighed the issue carefully, seeking the advice of Julian M. Earls, another prominent African American who had worked at the NASA Lewis Research Center since 1968 and had applied to the astronaut corps a decade later. Jemison eventually realized that if she left the agency, her "world wouldn't fall apart," and she decided to work on "teaching, mentoring, health care issues, and increasing participation in science and technology of those who have traditionally been left out." Many observers questioned her decision, but she was simply following her own path, just as she had when she graduated from medical school. Still excited about space, she wanted to find new ways of pursuing her passion.[62]

Homer Hickam, the author of *Rocket Boys*, on which the movie *October Sky* was based, served as her training manager for the space shuttle flight. He told *Stanford Today* that the Astronaut Office was too limiting for Jemison's personality and interest: "I see Mae as sort of an all-around ambassador. She just really wanted to make a connection with the world."[63]

Jemison taught environmental studies at Dartmouth and founded the Jemison Institute for Advancing Technology in Developing Countries there. The institute sought to identify, assess, and implement "advanced technologies that may be employed advantageously to the development of less industrialized nations." Space technology, she argued, would greatly benefit the Third World, allowing Africa "to jump over the Industrial Age into the Space Age." In 1993, she founded the Houston-based Jemison Group, which combined her interests in technology and social issues by seeking to use advanced technology to help solve problems in underdeveloped nations, to promote science and technology education, and to help people with a passion for space exploration become involved with the program. One of the group's projects involved improving health care in remote areas of West Africa through the use of a satellite telecommunication system called Alafiya (meaning "good health" in Yoruba). The group also offered advice on the design and use of solar electrical cells for developing countries, where it is often difficult to access fossil fuel.[64]

Jemison also established the Earth We Share, an international space camp to improve scientific literacy among twelve- to sixteen-year-olds, and BioSentient, which won a license to market the anti-motion-sickness techniques on which she had worked in space. She realized that the techniques could also be used to combat migraine headaches and anxiety as well as other ailments.[65]

Throughout her life, Dr. Mae C. Jemison has challenged gender and racial stereotypes. She rejected the biases that traditionally plagued the fields of science, engineering, and space exploration and helped to diversify the Astronaut Office. But Jemison sees her legacy in broader terms, her status as the first African American female astronaut provided her with "a stronger, more visible platform from which to discuss the importance of individuals taking responsibility not only for themselves, but also for how they treat others and this planet."[66] She fulfilled her dream of spaceflight twenty years ago, and she now spends her time pushing others to go boldly where they have never been.

NOTES

1. "Space Is Her Destination," *Ebony*, October 1987, 93; Mae Jemison, interview by author, May 6, 2010.

2. Studies of gender and technology and race and technology include Bruce Sinclair, ed., *Technology and the African American Experience* (Cambridge: MIT Press, 2004); Nina E. Lerman, Ruth Oldenziel, and Arwen P. Mohun, eds., *Gender and Technology: A Reader* (Baltimore: Johns Hopkins University Press, 2003).

3. Sara M. Evans, *Born for Liberty: A History of Women in America* (New York: Free Press, 1997), 313.

4. Roger D. Launius, "'We Can Lick Gravity, but Sometimes the Paperwork Is Overwhelming': NASA, Oral History, and the Contemporary Past," *Oral History Review* 30 (Summer–Autumn 2003): 123.

5. Robert R. Gilruth, "From Wallops Island to Project Mercury, 1945–1958: A Memoir," presented at the Sixth History Symposium of the International Academy of Astronautics, Vienna, Austria, October 1972, box 50, Manned Spacecraft Center/Johnson Space Center series, Johnson Space Center History Collection, University of Houston–Clear Lake, Houston (hereafter cited as JSCHC) (quotation); Joseph D. Atkinson Jr. and Jay M. Shafritz, *The Real Stuff: A History of NASA's Astronaut Recruitment Program* (New York: Praeger, 1985), 35–37.

6. Loyd S. Swenson Jr., James M. Grimwood, and Charles C. Alexander, *This New Ocean: A History of Project Mercury* (Washington, D.C.: NASA, 1966), 164.

7. Margaret A. Weitekamp, *Right Stuff, Wrong Sex: America's First Women in Space Program* (Baltimore: Johns Hopkins University Press, 2004), 64–65, 106–10; Betty Skelton Frankman, interview by Carol L. Butler, July 19, 1999, JSCHC; Amy Foster, "The Gendered Anniversary: The Story of America's Women Astronauts," *Florida Historical Quarterly* 87 (Fall 2008): 173 (quotation).

8. Bettyann Holtzmann Kevles, *Almost Heaven: The Story of Women in Space* (New York: Basic Books, 2003), 19–38; David J. Shayler and Ian Moule, *Women in Space—Following Valentina* (Chichester, U.K.: Praxis, 2005), 43–67.

9. Henry Louis Gates Jr., *In Search of Our Roots: How Nineteen Extraordinary African Americans Reclaimed Their Past* (New York: Crown, 2009), 244 (first quotation); Mae Jemison, *Find Where the Wind Goes: Moments from My Life* (New York: Scholastic, 2001), ix (second quotation). For an example of another female astronaut who did not let gender deter her passion for space, see Bonnie J. Dunbar, interview by author, December 22, 2004, JSCHC.

10. Jemison, *Find Where the Wind Goes*, vii–viii.

11. Ibid., 52, 78.

12. Ibid., 50–52 (quotation); Gates, *In Search of Our Roots*, 244–46.

13. Susan J. Douglas, *Where the Girls Are: Growing Up Female with the Mass Media* (New York: Times Books, 1995), 9.

14. Douglas, *Where the Girls Are*, 134–35 (first and second quotations); Jemison, *Find Where the Wind Goes*, 47–48 (third quotation); Amy E. Foster, *Integrating Women into the Astronaut Corps: Politics and Logistics at NASA, 1972–2004* (Baltimore: Johns Hopkins University Press, 2011), 38–39. A survey of *Star Trek* can be found in two books: Micheal C. Pounds, *Race in Space: The Representation of Ethnicity in Star Trek and Star Trek: The Next Generation* (Lanham, Md.: Scarecrow, 1999); Daniel Leonard Bernardi, *Star Trek and History: Race-ing toward a White Future* (New Brunswick, N.J.: Rutgers University Press, 1998).

15. Jemison, *Find Where the Wind Goes*, 171; Jemison, interview.

16. National Center for Education Statistics, *Findings from the Condition of Education, 1997*, no. 11, *Women in Mathematics and Science* (Washington, D.C.: U.S. Department of Education, 1997), 16; Martha Moore Trescott, "Women in the Intellectual Development of Engineering: A Study in Persistence and Systems Thought," in *Women in Engineering: Pioneers and Trailblazers*, ed. Margaret E. Layne (Reston, Va.: ASCE Press, 2009), 100.

17. Amy Sue Bix, "From 'Engineeresses' to 'Girl Engineers' to 'Good Engineers': A History of Women's U.S. Engineering Education," *NWSA Journal* 16 (Spring 2004): 40.

18. J. Alfred Phelps, *They Had a Dream: The Story of African American Astronauts* (Novato, Calif.: Presidio, 1994), 208 (first quotation); Jemison, *Find Where the Wind Goes*, 118 (second quotation).

19. Bix, "From 'Engineeresses,'" 39–41; Dunbar, interview. For an example of isolation and bias, see Judith S. McIlwee and J. Gregg Robinson, *Women in Engineering: Gender, Power, and Workplace Culture* (Albany: State University of New York Press, 1992), 53.

20. Jemison, *Find Where the Wind Goes*, 124–25.

21. Ellen S. More, Elizabeth Fee, and Manon Parry, eds., *Women Physicians and the Cultures of Medicine* (Baltimore: Johns Hopkins University Press, 2009), 6; Ellen S. More, *Restoring the Balance: Women Physicians and the Profession of Medicine, 1850–1995* (Cambridge: Harvard University Press, 1999), 216–19; Weill Cornell Medical College, http://www.med.cornell.edu/archives/history/medical_college.html?name1=Cornell+University+Medical+College&type1=2Active (accessed October 1, 2010); Jemison, *Find Where the Wind Goes*, 136.

22. Naomi Rogers, "Feminists Fight the Culture of Exclusion in Medical Education, 1970–1990," in *Women Physicians and the Cultures of Medicine*, ed. More, Fee, and Parry, 206 (first quotation), 220; Jemison, *Find Where the Wind Goes*, 139 (second, third, and fourth quotations); Gates, *In Search of Our Roots*, 244 (fifth quotation); Jemison, interview (sixth quotation).

23. Arturo F. Gonzalez Jr. "Flying Doctors," *Canadian Doctor* 44 (February 1978): 14–16, 19–20.

24. Jemison, *Find Where the Wind Goes*, 165–66; Rogers, "Feminists Fight," 221 (quotation).

25. Joyce Tang, "African Americans in Medical Professions," *Humboldt Journal of Social Relations* 21 (September 1995): 25 (first quotation); Nikki Giovanni, "Shooting for the Moon," *Essence*, April 1993, 60 (second and third quotations).

26. "NASA to Recruit Space Shuttle Astronauts," NASA Lyndon B. Johnson Space Center News Release 76-44, July 8, 1976, Public Affairs Office, NASA Lyndon B. Johnson Space Center, Houston; Phelps, *They Had a Dream*, 209 (first quotation). Affirmative action proved to be a particularly contentious issue at NASA. See Kim McQuaid, "'Racism, Sexism, and Space Ventures': Civil Rights at NASA in the Nixon Era and Beyond," in *Societal Impact of Spaceflight*, ed. Steven J. Dick and Roger D. Launius (Washington, D.C.: NASA, 2007), 421–49.

27. Alan Bean, interview by author, February 23, 2010, JSCHC.

28. Mike Mullane, *Riding Rockets: The Outrageous Tales of a Space Shuttle Astronaut* (New York: Scribner, 2006), 29–30.

29. Foster, "Gendered Anniversary," 160, 169–70 (first quotation); Carolyn L. Huntoon, interview by author, April 21, 2008, JSCHC (second and third quotations).

30. More, *Restoring the Balance*, 236–37, 242; Grady Wells, "Dreaming of Space: A Conversation with Dr. Mae Jemison," *U.S. Black Engineer*, Fall 1987 (first quotation), Mae C. Jemison Biographical File, NASA Historical Reference Collection, NASA Headquarters, Washington, D.C.

31. Jemison, *Find Where the Wind Goes*, 168.

32. "NASA Alters Astronaut Selection Process," NASA Lyndon B. Johnson Center News Release 85-024, June 7, 1985, Public Affairs Office, NASA Lyndon B. Johnson Space Center, Houston; Fred Dalton and David Chambers, "Diversity and EO at NASA . . .: We've Come a Long Way," *Endeavor*, Fall–Winter 2008, http://odeo.hq.nasa.gov/documents/Endeavor_Fall-Winter_08.pdf (accessed October 10, 2010); Jemison interview.

33. Jemison, *Find Where the Wind Goes*, 186.

34. Jemison, interview.

35. Ibid.

36. Duane Ross, presentation to summer interns, June 29, 2001, NASA Johnson Space Center History Office, Houston.

37. Jemison, *Find Where the Wind Goes*, 189–90; Jemison, interview; "Space Is Her Destination," 93.

38. Steve Nesbitt, "Rigorous Training Ahead: Astronaut Candidates Are Here," *Space News Roundup*, August 28, 1987, 1.

39. Jemison, interview.

40. Federal Women's Program, *Network* 5 (May 1985): 3 (quotation), NASA Lyndon B. Johnson Space Center History Office; Historical Progress of Women at JSC, March 21, 1990, NASA Lyndon B. Johnson Space Center History Office.

41. University of Minnesota, "M, Fall 2001, http://www1.umn.edu/urelate/m/fall2001/david kapell.html (accessed February 26, 2014); Michael Cabbage, "Still Haunted by Columbia's End," *Baltimore Sun*, February 1, 2004, http://articles.baltimoresun.com/2004-02-01/news/0402010042_1 _linda-ham-shuttle-columbia-accident (accessed February 25, 2014).

42. Jemison, interview.

43. Ibid.

44. "Astronaut Selection and Training," January 1984, box 3, Flight Crew Operations subseries, Center series, JSCHC.

45. Jemison, interview; Kevles, *Almost Heaven*, 181.

46. Jemison, interview; Kevles, *Almost Heaven*, 132; Kathryn D. Sullivan, interview by author, May 28, 2009, JSCHC (first quotation); "Judith A. Resnik," http://www.challenger.org/about/history /resnik.cfm (accessed April 22, 2011) (second quotation).

47. "Cape Crusaders Are Shuttle Crew's Eyes and Ears," December 19, 2003, http://www.nasa .gov/missions/shuttle/f_crusaders.html (accessed December 10, 2010); Jerry L. Ross, email to author, April 25, 2011 (quotation).

48. Jemison, interview.

49. See, for example, *Florida Today*, September 30, 1989, NASA News, "Astronauts Named for Five Space Shuttle Missions," September 29, 1989, both in Jemison Biographical File.

50. Brewster H. Shaw, interview by Kevin Rusnak, April 19, 2002, JSCHC; Jemison, interview; Shayler and Moule, *Women in Space*, 261–62; "NASA Announces Crew Members for Future Shuttle Flights," NASA News, August 23, 1991, Jemison Biographical File.

51. Sharon Caples McDougle, interview by author, July 9, 2010, JSCHC (first, second, third, fourth, and sixth quotations); Marilyn Marshall, "Close-Up: A New Star in the Galaxy," *Ebony*, December 1992, 122 (fifth quotation).

52. "Patricia S. Cowings, Ph.D.," *NASA Quest: Women of NASA*, http://quest.arc.nasa.gov/people /bios/women/pc.html (accessed August 2, 2010) (first quotation); *Oakland Tribune*, February 7, 1977 (second quotation); Bean, interview (third quotation); "Virtual Take Our Daughters to Work Day QuestChat Archive," *NASA Quest: Women of NASA*, April 22, 1999, http://quest.nasa.gov/women /archive/4-22-99pc.html (accessed August 2, 2010).

53. For details on the type of training Jemison received from Cowings, see Ron Eglash, "An Interview with Patricia Cowings," in *The Cyborg Handbook*, ed. Ron Eglash (New York: Routledge, 1995), 93–99; Jemison, interview.

54. Jemison, interview.

55. *Washington Times*, September 8, 1992, Jemison Biographical File (first quotation); *Houston Chronicle*, September 10, 1992 (second quotation); James Hartsfield, "Spacelab-J Worldwide in Character," *Space News Roundup*, August 14, 1992, 1, 4.

56. Jemison, *Find Where the Wind Goes*, 177, 179, 181; Jemison, interview; Warren E. Leary, "U.S.-Japan Mission Is a Shuttle First," *New York Times*, September 13, 1992.

57. Jemison, interview.

58. McDougle, interview.

59. Ibid.; "Dr. Mae Jemison Becomes First Black Woman in Space," *Jet*, September 14, 1992, 34–38, Jemison Biographical File; *Ebony*, October 1992.

60. Nichelle Nichols, *Beyond Uhura: Star Trek and Other Memories* (New York: Putnam's, 1994), 297.

61. Jemison, interview.

62. Ibid. (first quotation); "Astronaut Jemison to Teach, Be Mentor," *Space News Roundup*, March 15, 1993, 1 (second quotation); Simeon Booker, "Ticker Tape U.S.A." *Jet*, April 12, 1993, 11.

63. *Stanford Today*, July–August 1996, http://www.stanford.edu/dept/news/stanfordtoday /ed/9607/pdf/ST9607mjemison.pdf (accessed December 20, 2010) (third quotation).

64. "Dr. Mae Jemison," *NASA Quest: Women of NASA*, http://quest.nasa.gov/women/TOD TWD/jemison.bio.html (accessed August 8, 2010) (first quotation); Giovanni, "Shooting for the Moon," 60 (second quotation); Jendayi Frazer, "Advancing African Health Care through Space Technology: An Interview with Dr. Mae C. Jemison," *Africa Today* 40 (September 1993): 70–74 (third quotation); "Dr. Mae C. Jemison," Dorothy Jemison Foundation, http://www.jemisonfounda tion.org/drmae.htm (accessed November 12, 2010).

65. Jemison, interview.

66. Jemison, *Find Where the Wind Goes*, 195.

Epilogue

Exploring Women's Stories: A Personal Perspective

PAULA MITCHELL MARKS

❀ ❀ ❀

Where are the women's stories? How can we locate them? How can we examine and interpret them? How can we share the stories and insights and make them an integral part of U.S. historical understanding and heritage? These are some of the questions that inspired this collection of essays. In the 1970s and 1980s—the early years of the new field of women's history—a growing number of historians asked these questions and many others. Decades later, we can see in the essays in this volume how rich and varied are the responses. To appreciate such responses more fully, though, it is helpful to remember why the questions entered the study of history when they did, to note some of the exploratory paths that have developed from them, and to consider the development of Texas women's history in particular. What follows is a personal, perhaps idiosyncratic, accounting of that journey by one who was fortunate to enter women's history—and Texas history—in the early 1980s. Though my interests in frontier histories and material culture color the following observations, I hope this narrative resonates with others who have engaged with the questions of women's history over the years and offers some illumination for those who have not.

For many of us educated in the U.S. school system in the 1950s and 1960s, history at the national level seemed to be primarily the story of politicians, presidents, and generals; of the men who helped or opposed their rise to and exercise of power; and of the men who followed and advised them. Western history was bound up with the popular culture images on television shows, in movies, and in novels, focusing primarily on the "taming" and settling of "the" U.S. frontier of the nineteenth century. This fixed mythology centered on the image of the strong individual Anglo male entering and mastering the wilderness, in one way or another as an agent of "civilization." Southern history carried the imprint of the Old South, as the Lost Cause of the Civil War still exerted its influence almost a century after the war's end and even as African Americans, weary of waiting and asking for equal rights, moved the civil rights movement into its most active phase to date.

In all of this, most women were simply invisible, as historians as well as historical actors. For example, in the "standard text" for college history courses in the 1940s and 1950s, Ralph Henry Gabriel's *The Course of American Democratic Thought*, works such as Elizabeth Cady Stanton and Susan B. Anthony's *History of Woman Suffrage* were ignored; in fact, no work by a woman was cited.[1] In historical narratives, women, if mentioned at all, were often seen only as appendages or even baggage—the pioneer loading his wife and children into the Conestoga wagon for the trip west. Or they were seen as "helpmates" to successful white men. One stunning example of this perspective is the "standard" biography of Margaret Fuller by Mason Wade, which I read for a biography class in the early 1980s. A prominent Transcendentalist, journalist, and editor, Fuller authored a powerful feminist study, *Woman in the Nineteenth Century* (1845). Yet the title of Wade's 1940 volume sets the tone: *Margaret Fuller, Whetstone of Genius*.[2] Everything Fuller did is presented in the biography as a means to highlight the genius of the Transcendentalist men such as Ralph Waldo Emerson and Henry David Thoreau.[3]

In the mid-twentieth century, the messages about women's presence and women's roles were always at best mixed. Dee Brown's popular history, *The Gentle Tamers: Women of the Old Wild West* (1958), was identified as late as 1980 as "the most widely read book on women in the West."[4] It at least sought to include women in the western mythology, but it did so within the dominant story: the women were depicted as trivializing stereotypes who joined their men in "taming" the West, as reflected in such chapter titles as "The Army Girls," "Some Ladies of Easy Virtue," "Pink Tights and Red Velvet Skirts," and "Schoolmarms and Maternal Forces."

Cultural perspectives regarding women's roles and women's agency did start changing noticeably in the 1960s, both in U.S. culture and politics and in historical studies. Minority Americans, women as well as men, were making their voices heard; Dolores Huerta, for example, gained attention as a labor organizer, and civil rights advocate Maya Angelou published a best-selling autobiographical account of her early life in racially segregated Arkansas.[5] Betty Friedan spoke for a large number of women in the dominant culture by questioning the constricting role assigned educated women in *The Feminine Mystique* (1963), and a "second wave" of feminism began (the first was the late nineteenth/early twentieth century "wave" culminating in the enactment of woman suffrage in

1920).[6] Although women's rights issues remained obscured by national attention to other matters—largely racial tensions and the Vietnam War—federal legislation such as Title VII of the 1964 Civil Rights Act started addressing discriminatory treatment toward women as well as other groups.

In the historical field, researchers started resurrecting the work of previous women's historians and searching out primary sources on and by women.[7] About the same time, a wonderfully nurturing development for the claiming, reclaiming, and interpreting of women's stories was the rise of social history, with its emphasis on the textured lives of "ordinary" people. Through it would come an increasing awareness of the limits of "contribution" history—the addition to the record of a woman who "contributed" to some male-dominated enterprise—in doing justice to women's lives. As it did for other new and reviving fields, the "new social history" also helped turn the lens on differences in women's experiences based on race, class, gender, and region.[8]

Changes in the 1960s, then, led in the 1970s not only to more significant political, economic, and legal advances for women but also to more focused attention on women's history, made manifest in the establishment of women's studies programs and the field of women's history. Throughout the decade, historians made use of limited resources and battled traditional understandings of what was historically significant to create opportunities for women's history scholarship.[9]

One welcome development of this period was a recognition of the previously unacknowledged artistry women had brought to their daily activities. The stories of quilters and of their lovingly handmade quilts over various generations were particularly valuable for understanding gendered experiences of the past. In the late 1970s, many young women responded with deep appreciation to *The Quilters: Women and Domestic Art, an Oral History* (1978), by Patricia Cooper and Norma Bradley Allen.[10] The two had collected accounts from older rural women in West Texas and New Mexico, providing photos of the women and their quilts; through the reminiscences, we listened with these women to the windmills creaking in the night and shared the excitement they felt as they worked out patterns and colors, bringing beauty to often stark surroundings.[11]

Much of the 1970s scholarship centered on white middle- and upper-class urban women—those who had been able to push in some way into the public sphere, if not into recorded history. It was important work, but these historians were also laying the groundwork for broader studies and creating a vocabulary for talking about women's experience. "Public sphere," for example, took on new meanings after Nancy Cott's *The Bonds of Womanhood: "Women's Sphere" in New England, 1780–1835* (1977) introduced the concept of separate men's (public) and women's (private) spheres taking form in the early republic era and a resulting "cult of domesticity."[12] The result of such groundwork, as Gerda Lerner wrote in 2004, was that "an explosion of feminist scholarship" occurred between 1981 and 1987, with the field of women's history generally synonymous with this scholarship.[13]

I entered the American studies doctoral program at the University of Texas at Austin in 1980 and graduated in 1987—grand timing for anyone drawn to U.S. women's history. Did I know or appreciate my good fortune? Yes, but not as much as I do now, looking back. From my current perspective, I realize just how remarkable were the number of field-shifting publications that first saw light in my early graduate school years. The breadth of topics they represented meant we would no longer be mired in an agenda set by mainstream male history. Take, for example, new questions about the experiences of large groups of pioneering women in the Midwest. Joanna Stratton's *Pioneer Women: Voices from the Kansas Frontier* (1982) included hundreds of first-person accounts collected by Lilla Day Monroe in the 1920s and edited and published by her great-granddaughter, Stratton. What were southern plantation mistresses' lives really like? Catherine Clinton's *The Plantation Mistress: Woman's World in the Old South* (1983) showed these elite women as both harassed and harassing, some of them nipping down to the basement to take opium to make it through another day. How did minority women's experience differ from that of more privileged women? Gloria T. Hull, Patricia Bell Scott, and Barbara Smith opened our eyes more fully to some of the challenges African American women faced with *All the Women Are White, All the Blacks Are Men, But Some of Us Are Brave: Black Women's Studies* (1982).[14]

By 1990, women's history had evolved into a field in which scholars pieced together, interpreted, and shared women's stories in increasingly complex and satisfying ways. This process was evidenced in part by the publication of a book that made an impression on many women's historians and won the Pulitzer Prize in history, became a PBS *American Experience* presentation, and became a curriculum component for many a U.S. history course: Laurel Thatcher Ulrich's *A Midwife's Tale: The Life of Martha Ballard, Based on Her Diary, 1785–1812* (1991).[15] Ulrich took seemingly mundane source material—Ballard's diary of her herbal expeditions into the woods, her work delivering babies, and her family and community relationships on a frontier of the early republic—and fashioned an account that illuminated the complex ways in which Ballard operated as a midwife, herbalist, doctor's assistant, wife, mother, and frontier community member in a preindustrial world.

Ballard's Maine is a long way from the Texas of these essays. But the method and larger lesson—that women's history had much to tell us—landed firmly in the Lone Star State. Indeed, Texas women's scholarship has developed in strong and vibrant ways along with U.S. women's history. Just as Texas suffragists were among the most active in organizing and gaining the vote for women in the early twentieth century, Texas women's historians from the 1970s to the present represent well the growth in the field's scope and depth.

Historians have extended and deepened the field despite the lingering presence of a frontier myth echoing the national one and particularly deep-rooted in Texas: the idea that rugged, individualistic Anglo males went to Mexico's northern frontier and forged a separate nation, then a state, all the while maintaining a unique sense of independence and pride.[16] Within this mythology, much is made of Alamo survivor Susannah Dickinson and of captured servant Emily West, who entered the revolutionary mythology as Emily Morgan, "the Yellow Rose of Texas." These women have been used in historical accounts to further the old "triumphalist" male-dominated narrative, and sometimes to examine it, but such focus on solitary figures in the service of myth does little or nothing to advance women's history.

How, then, has women's history transformed our understanding of Texas history, and how does it reflect and demonstrate the degree to which U.S. women's history has developed?[17] First, earlier published historical accounts by and about women were rediscovered and acknowledged—works such as Anna Pennybacker's late-nineteenth-century history of the state and Annie Doom Pickrell's *Pioneer Women in Texas* (1919).[18] Much emphasis in the 1970s was on collecting women's stories, best illustrated by Evelyn Carrington's *Women in Early Texas* (1975) and a wonderful set of accounts by German women who migrated to nineteenth-century Texas that was edited by Crystal Sasse Ragsdale the following year.[19]

But Texas women's history has also benefited from a particularly engaged interest in women's history outside of academia. Two decades before her term as governor, Ann Richards helped to initiate the Texas Women's History Project. In 1975, Richards visited a multimedia "What Is a Texan?" exhibit at the Institute for Texan Cultures in San Antonio and left asking, "Where are the women?"[20] With Mary Beth Rogers as director and Ruthe Winegarten as research director, and with the fund-raising efforts of Lady Bird Johnson's former social secretary, Liz Carpenter, and the support of Ellen Temple and others, the project produced a bibliography in 1980 and a traveling exhibit, *Texas Women: A Celebration of History*, the next year. In the same period, Ann Fears Crawford and Crystal Sasse Ragsdale published *Women in Texas: Their Lives, Their Experiences, Their Accomplishments* (1982).[21] All of these efforts spurred others of us to follow their trailblazing in locating and working with women's stories.

My primary-source research efforts began with a treasure trove of diaries and correspondence between nineteenth-century pioneers Mary and Samuel Maverick; using these sources as the basis for my dissertation, I wrote a dual biography of the couple.[22] I faced the challenge of any biographer: how to accurately, honestly, and sensitively represent those lives in relation to their times and secondarily to our own. And at a time before feminist academics discussed theoretical questions about women's biography so extensively, I and others working with the stories of individual women also faced the challenge of feminist biography: how to represent those lives in a way that demonstrated the choices women had and did not have, how they perceived those choices, and how they navigated the world they inhabited as a result.[23] By wrestling with these questions, we gained a clearer understanding of significant aspects of women's experience that did not fit into standard male-centered narratives.

In the 1980s, Texas women's scholarship was developing around certain themes also emerging in the national forum—themes such as frontier life, the suffrage movement, and the effects of race, class, and gender on women's experience. The offerings included the publication of valuable primary sources in edited volumes, including Jo Ella Powell Exley's *Texas Tears and Texas Sunshine: Voices of Frontier Women* (1986); A. Elizabeth Taylor's *Citizens at Last: The Woman Suffrage Movement in Texas* (1987), including documents edited by Ruthe Winegarten and Judith N. McArthur; and Janet G. Humphrey's *A Texas Suffragist: Diaries and Writings of Jane Y. McCallum* (1988).[24] New works also included more extensive analysis, such as that found in Julia Kirk Blackwelder's examination of caste and culture in depression-era San Antonio.[25] Women's homemade artistry continued to be studied and celebrated through such works as Suzanne Yabsley's *Texas Quilts, Texas Women* (1984) and Karoline Patterson Bresenhan and Nancy O'Bryant Puentes's *Lone Stars: A Legacy of Texas Quilts, 1836–1936* (1986).[26]

In the 1990s, Texas women's scholarship expanded its focus on women's activities of the late nineteenth and early twentieth centuries with sophisticated studies of individual women leaders, including educator Annie Webb Blanton and Dallas journalist and reformer Isadore Sutherland Miner Callaway (also known as Pauline Periwinkle), as well as in-depth analyses of women's movements. So important were these studies that their authors are now familiar to all Texas historians and include most prominently Debbie Mauldin Cottrell, Elizabeth Hayes Turner, Jacquelyn Masur McElhaney, Judith N. McArthur, and Elizabeth York Enstam.[27] These historians were exploring the identities of civically engaged women—white, black, and occasionally Latina—and how they worked and networked for political, economic, and societal reform.

While this exploration led to a focus primarily on urbanizing and urbanized Texas women, women's history continued to expand in regard to frontier and rural Texas as well. As my research led into neglected areas of frontier women's experience, I approached Texas A&M University Press with the idea of a small volume on home textile production in nineteenth-century Texas and was delighted to find the folks there considered the topic worthwhile. After the publication of the resulting book, *Hands to the Spindle: Women and Home Textile Production, 1822–1880* (1996), another frontier historian mentioned that he had in response included "spinning" and "weaving" in the index of his latest book—a tiny example of writing women's work into history, but a satisfying one nonetheless.[28] A notable rural history book of the 1990s was Rebecca Sharpless's excellent study of farm women, which aided in a gradual movement to serious scholarly treatment of more twentieth-century topics.[29] The overall scholarship had grown enough that Nancy Baker Jones and Debbie Mauldin Cottrell edited and published *Women and Texas History: An Archival Bibliography* (1998).[30]

In the first decade of the twenty-first century, Texas women's history expanded again, with further twentieth-century study but also with more attention to Latina experiences and creative approaches to revisiting earlier eras. Women in public leadership has remained a popular topic, with biographies of Anna Pennybacker and suffragist and gubernatorial candidate Minnie Fisher Cunningham and surveys of women in politics building on the previous studies of women in public life.[31] Historical research on and by Latinas has yielded publications ranging from Teresa Palomo Acosta and Ruthe Winegarten's *Las Tejanas: Three Hundred Years of History* (2003) to *Chicanas in Charge: Texas Women in the Public Arena*, by José Angel Gutierrez, Michelle Melendez, and Sonia A. Noyola (2007). Cynthia Orozco's study of the Mexican American civil rights movement carefully examines the participation of women in the movement in Texas, while *Recovering the Hispanic History of Texas* (2010), a set of essays exploring gender and sexuality and other themes, gives some sense of the opportunities ahead in Latina scholarship.[32] Meanwhile, African American women continue to enter the historical record through such works as Bruce A. Glasrud and Merline Pitre's *Black Women in Texas History* (2008).[33] Tireless NAACP leaders Lulu B. White and Juanita Craft in particular have also received scholarly attention.[34]

For those of us who prefer to range indefinitely in pre-twentieth-century history, some of the recent scholarship has mined the eighteenth and nineteenth centuries in ways that open up new research and intellectual possibilities for these time periods. I am thinking here of two books from 2001: Angela Boswell's *Her Act and Deed: Women's Lives in a Rural Southern County, 1837–1873* and Mark Carroll's *Homesteads Ungovernable: Families, Sex, Race and the Law in Frontier Texas, 1823–1860.*[35] Both made extensive use of public records to answer intimate questions about women's lives and circumstances, sometimes with intriguing results: for example, Boswell discovered the power a common culturally idealized female identity wielded among German, African American, and Anglo women in nineteenth-century Colorado County. Jean A. Stuntz also used legal documents to great effect in *Hers, His, and Theirs: Community Property Law in Spain and Early Texas* (2005).[36]

One feature of any good historical work—a feature that the books mentioned here share to one degree or another—is the ability to surprise us, to challenge what we thought we understood. For example, I remember being unable to go to sleep after reading William Cronon's *Changes in the Land: Indians, Colonists, and the Ecology of New England* (1983) shortly after it appeared; he had told the story of colonial New England in a way completely new and exciting to me. A similar recent Texas history work is Juliana Barr's study of Native American interaction with Spaniards from the 1680s to the 1780s.[37] While other recent authors had challenged the idea that Native Americans were always victims in interactions with Europeans and Euro-Americans (just as historians have challenged this idea in regard to women and patriarchal culture), Barr fully articulated this challenge to old assumptions in her study of Texas Indians and Spanish would-be colonizers, and she skillfully showed the roles that Indian women played in maintaining Indian power, forcing the Spaniards to adapt. Works such as these revise our widely accepted narratives in ways that all historians can appreciate.

The story of women's history in Texas since the 1970s, then, has been one of continual evolution in topics, approaches, and scholarly perspectives. The practice of writing women into the record and thereby expanding and deepening it has also been a key corrective to the old, tired mythologies of Texas history mentioned earlier.[38] As we move further into the twenty-first century, no doubt technology will play a larger role; already, many of us look for information and sources to websites such as the *Handbook of Texas Online*, produced by the Texas State Historical Association; the Women in Texas History website of the Ruthe Winegarten Memorial Foundation for Texas Women's History; and the Texas Woman's University online women's history collection site.[39] But however we go about it, the basic questions continue to guide us: Where are the women's stories? How can we locate them? How can we examine and interpret them? How can we share them and the insights they offer and make them an integral part of U.S. historical understanding and heritage? These essays have offered some answers as well as further questions, a reminder of how dynamic women's history remains and how many possibilities for research and interpretation continue to unfold.

NOTES

1. This observation is made by Linda K. Kerber, Jane Sherron De Hart, and Cornelia Hughes Dayton in the introduction to *Women's America: Refocusing the Past*, 7th ed. (New York: Oxford University Press, 2011).

2. Mason Wade, *Margaret Fuller, Whetstone of Genius* (New York: Viking, 1940).

3. Wade was following in the footsteps of Emerson, William H. Channing, and James Freeman Clarke, who heavily edited Fuller's memoirs and failed to give her her intellectual due.

4. Dee Brown, *The Gentle Tamers: Women of the Old Wild West* (New York: Bantam, 1958). See Joan M. Jensen and Darlis A. Miller, "The Gentle Tamers Revisited: New Approaches to the History of Women in the American West," *Pacific Historical Review* 49 (May 1980): 173.

5. Maya Angelou, *I Know Why the Caged Bird Sings* (New York: Random House, 1969).

6. Betty Friedan, *The Feminine Mystique* (New York: Norton, 1963). For a recent analysis, see Stephanie Coontz, *A Strange Stirring: The Feminine Mystique and American Women at the Dawn of the 1960s* (New York: Basic Books, 2011).

7. See, for example, Julia Spruill, *Women's Life and Work in the Southern Colonies* (New York: Norton, 1998), which was first published in 1938. A number of anthologies contain profuse sources from the 1960s and 1970s; a good one is Miriam Schneir, *Feminism in Our Time: The Essential Writings, World War II to the Present* (New York: Vintage, 1994).

8. Prominent women's historian Gerda Lerner introduced the term *contribution history* in her "Placing Women in History: Definitions and Challenges," *Feminist Studies* 3 (Autumn 1975): 5. While contribution history can include an examination of women within male-dominated society, at its most basic, it simply inserts a few women into a traditional narrative without necessarily challenging the terms of that narrative.

9. For context, see Ruth Rosen, *The World Split Open: How the Modern Women's Movement Changed America* (New York: Viking Penguin, 2000).

10. Patricia Cooper and Norma Bradley Allen, *The Quilters: Women and Domestic Art, an Oral History* (New York: Anchor/Doubleday, 1978). This book was originally published by Doubleday in 1977, with the Anchor edition appearing in 1978 and Texas Tech University Press republishing it in 1999; references to this work often fail to take into account the earlier publishing dates and the volume's early popularity.

11. *The Quilters* became the basis for a stage play that enjoyed great popularity in the early 1980s; the play is described at *Dramatists Play Service*, http://www.dramatists.com/cgi-bin/db/single .asp?key=1891 (accessed January 12, 2012).

12. Nancy F. Cott, *The Bonds of Womanhood: "Woman's Sphere" in New England, 1780–1835* (New Haven: Yale University Press, 1977). Another key text is Barbara Welter, "The Cult of True Womanhood, 1820–1860," *American Quarterly* 18 (Summer 1966): 151–74.

13. See Gerda Lerner, "U.S. Women's History Past, Present, and Future," *Journal of Women's History* 16 (Winter 2004): 12.

14. Joanna L. Stratton, *Pioneer Women: Voices from the Kansas Frontier* (New York: Simon and Schuster, 1982); Catherine Clinton, *The Plantation Mistress: Woman's World in the Old South* (New York: Pantheon, 1983); Gloria T. Hull, Patricia Bell Scott, and Barbara Smith, eds., *All the Women Are White, All the Blacks Are Men, but Some of Us Are Brave: Black Women's Studies* (New York: Feminist, 1982). The Hull book is sometimes referenced as *But Some of Us Are Brave: All the Women Are White, All the Blacks Are Men: Black Women's Studies.*

15. Laurel Thatcher Ulrich, *A Midwife's Tale: The Life of Martha Ballard, Based on Her Diary, 1785–1812* (New York: Knopf, 1991).

16. This story is intertwined with the concept of Manifest Destiny. For an exploration of how women in Texas might have related to this idea of divinely sanctioned expansionism in the decades before the Civil War, see Adrienne Caughfield's *True Women and Westward Expansion* (College Station: Texas A&M University Press, 2005).

17. The titles that follow are not meant to represent a full bibliography but are offered to give a sense of the field and its development.

18. See Anna J. Hardwicke Pennybacker, *A New History of Texas for Schools* (Austin: Pennybacker, 1888); Annie Doom Pickrell, *Pioneer Women in Texas* (Austin: Steck, 1929). Pickrell's book, reissued by State House Press in 1991, is more useful for its dated reflection of the romanticized upper-middle-class perspectives of its author than for its information. A good discussion of the development of Texas women's history can be found in "A Short History of Texas Women's History" *Women in Texas History*, www.womenintexashistory.org (accessed January 8, 2012).

19. Evelyn M. Carrington, ed., *Women Early in Texas* (1975; Austin: Texas State Historical Association, 1994); Crystal Sasse Ragsdale, *The Golden Free Land: The Reminiscences and Letters of Women on an American Frontier* (n.p.: Landmark, 1976).

20. See Ellen C. Temple, "The Texas Women's History Project and the Liz Carpenter Award" (speech), March 3, 2011, http://www.humanitiestexas.org/newsroom/spotlights/April11/carpenter/index.php (accessed January 8, 2012).

21. Ann Fears Crawford and Crystal Sasse Ragsdale, *Women in Texas: Their Lives, Their Experiences, Their Accomplishments* (Burnet, Tex.: Eakin, 1982).

22. The diaries and letters were located among the papers of the Maverick family of San Antonio at the Barker Texas History Center in Austin (now part of the Dolph Briscoe Center for American History at the University of Texas at Austin).

23. I later came across and appreciated the insights of Sara Alpern, Joyce Antler, Elisabeth Israels Perry, and Ingrid Winther Scobie, *The Challenge of Feminist Biography: Writing the Lives of Modern American Women* (Urbana: University of Illinois Press, 1992). My dissertation became Paula Mitchell Marks, *Turn Your Eyes toward Texas: Pioneers Sam and Mary Maverick* (College Station: Texas A&M University Press, 1989).

24. Jo Ella Powell Exley, *Texas Tears and Texas Sunshine: Voices of Frontier Women* (College Station: Texas A&M University Press, 1986); A. Elizabeth Taylor, *Citizens at Last: The Woman Suffrage Movement in Texas* (Austin: Temple, 1987); Janet G. Humphrey, *A Texas Suffragist: Diaries and Writings of Jane Y. McCallum* (Austin: Temple, 1988).

25. Julia Kirk Blackwelder, *Women of the Depression: Caste and Culture in San Antonio, 1929–1939* (College Station: Texas A&M University Press, 1998). An earlier book, Jacquelyn Dowd Hall's *Revolt against Chivalry: Jessie Daniel Ames and the Women's Campaign against Lynching* (New York: Columbia University Press, 1979), is also worthy of note for its relatively early treatment of race and class issues.

26. Suzanne Yabsley, *Texas Quilts, Texas Women* (College Station: Texas A&M University Press, 1984); Karoline Patterson Bresenhan and Nancy O'Bryant Puentes, *Lone Stars: A Legacy of Texas Quilts, 1836–1936* (Austin: University of Texas Press, 1986).

27. See Debbie Mauldin Cottrell, *Pioneer Woman Educator: The Progressive Spirit of Annie Webb Blanton* (College Station: Texas A&M University Press, 1993); Elizabeth Hayes Turner, *Women, Culture, and Community: Religion and Reform in Galveston, 1880–1920* (New York: Oxford University Press, 1997); Jacquelyn Masur McElhaney, *Pauline Periwinkle and Progressive Reform in Dallas* (College Station: Texas A&M University Press, 1998); Judith N. McArthur, *Creating the New Woman: The Rise of Southern Women's Progressive Culture in Texas, 1893–1918* (Urbana: University of Illinois Press, 1998); Elizabeth York Enstam, *Women and the Creation of Urban Life: Dallas, Texas, 1843–*

1920 (College Station: Texas A&M University Press, 1998). Also of interest is Marion K. Barthelme, ed., *Women in the Texas Populist Movement: Letters to the Southern Mercury* (College Station: Texas A&M University Press, 1997).

28. Paula Mitchell Marks, *Hands to the Spindle: Women and Home Textile Production, 1822–1880* (College Station: Texas A&M University Press, 1996).

29. Rebecca Sharpless, *Fertile Ground, Narrow Choices: Women on Texas Cotton Farms, 1900–1940* (Chapel Hill: University of North Carolina Press, 1999).

30. Nancy Baker Jones and Debbie Mauldin Cottrell, *Women and Texas History: An Archival Bibliography* (Austin: Texas State Historical Association, 1998).

31. See Kelley M. King, *Call Her a Citizen: Progressive-Era Activist and Educator Anna Pennybacker* (College Station: Texas A&M University Press, 2010); Judith N. McArthur and Harold L. Smith, *Minnie Fisher Cunningham: A Suffragist's Life in Politics* (New York: Oxford University Press, 2005); Nancy Baker Jones and Ruthe Winegarten, *Capitol Women: Texas Female Legislators, 1923–1999* (Austin: University of Texas Press, 2000); Sonia R. Garcia, Valerie Martinez-Ebers, Irasema Coronado, Sharon A. Navarro, and Patricia A. Jaramillo, *Politicas: Latina Public Officials in Texas* (Austin: University of Texas Press, 2008).

32. Teresa Palomo Acosta and Ruthe Winegarten, *Las Tejanas: Three Hundred Years of History* (Austin: University of Texas Press, 2003); José Angel Gutierrez, Michelle Melendez, and Sonia A. Noyola, *Chicanas in Charge: Texas Women in the Public Arena* (Lanham, Md.: AltaMira, 2007); Cynthia Orozco, *No Mexicans, Women, or Dogs Allowed: The Rise of the Mexican American Civil Rights Movement* (Austin: University of Texas Press, 2009); Monica Perales and Raul A. Ramos, eds., *Recovering the Hispanic History of Texas* (Houston: Arte Público, 2010). For a study of an earlier Latina, see Jane Clements Monday and Fran Vick, *Petra's Legacy: The South Texas Ranching Empire of Petra Vela and Mifflin Kenedy* (College Station: Texas A&M University Press, 2007).

33. Bruce A. Glasrud and Merline Pitre, eds., *Black Women in Texas History* (College Station: Texas A&M University Press, 2008).

34. See Merline Pitre, *In Struggle against Jim Crow: Lulu B. White and the NAACP, 1900–1957* (College Station: Texas A&M University Press, 2010); Brian D. Behnken, "The 'Dallas Way': Protest, Response, and the Civil Rights Experience in Big D and Beyond," *Southwestern Historical Quarterly* 111 (July 2007): 1–29; Stefanie Decker, "Women in the Civil Rights Movement: Juanita Craft versus the Dallas Elite," *East Texas Historical Journal* 39 (Spring 2001): 33–42.

35. Angela Boswell, *Her Act and Deed: Women's Lives in a Rural Southern County, 1837–1873* (College Station: Texas A&M University Press, 2001); Mark Carroll, *Homesteads Ungovernable: Families, Sex, Race, and the Law in Frontier Texas, 1823–1860* (Austin: University of Texas Press, 2001).

36. Jean A. Stuntz, *Hers, His, and Theirs: Community Property Law in Spain and Early Texas* (Lubbock: Texas Tech University Press, 2005).

37. William Cronon, *Changes in the Land: Indians, Colonists, and the Ecology of New England* (New York: Hill and Wang, 1983); Juliana Barr, *Peace Came in the Form of a Woman: Indians and Spaniards in the Texas Borderlands* (Chapel Hill: University of North Carolina Press, 2007).

38. For the ways in which Texas historical perspectives have changed, see Walter L. Buenger, "Three Truths in Texas," in *Beyond Texas through Time: Breaking away from Past Interpretations*, ed. Walter L. Buenger and Arnoldo DeLeón (College Station: Texas A&M University Press, 2011): 1–49.

39. See *Handbook of Texas Online*, http://www.tshaonline.org/handbook/online (accessed January 21, 2014); *Women in Texas History*, http://www.womenintexashistory.org/ (accessed January 21, 2014); "About the Woman's Collection," *Texas Woman's University*, http://www.twu.edu/library/about-womans-collection.asp (accessed January 21, 2014).

Writing Texas Women's History

Looking Back, Looking Forward

REBECCA SHARPLESS, ELIZABETH HAYES TURNER,

AND STEPHANIE COLE

The body of writing on Texas women's history is unusually deep and long. Many of its twists and turns mirror those that have shaped women's history in the nation as a whole, but some are the product of a diverse state population that has long been fascinated with its own past. The historiography that follows here aids readers in placing the essays in this volume within the larger narrative of American women's history. Despite (or perhaps given) the state's long-standing appetite for history and the many publications in Texas women's history, its size, its diversity, and the ever-changing developments in national interpretations of women's experiences have left plenty for scholars to do, and those suggestions for further research are perhaps the most important part of this analysis.[1]

Unlike many southern states, Texas's women's history begins well before the 1970s. Yet in those years, writing on that history consisted almost completely of autobiographies, reminiscences, and edited primary sources. Notable exceptions to these trends were Annie Doom Pickrell, *Pioneer Women of Texas* (1929), which contained biographical sketches of almost eighty white women in nineteenth-century Texas, and Kate Adele Hill, *Home Builders of West Texas* (1937), describing the lives of eleven women.[2] In the 1930s and 1940s, biographies of atypical women such as Belle Starr and Bonnie Parker appeared, and studies of women such as Margaret Lea Houston, who gained public notice as the wife of a famous man, also cropped up. These early publications testify to how Texas's interest in its own lively past helped to drive a somewhat precocious production of "compensatory" and "contribution" history as it would later be practiced elsewhere in the United States.[3]

In the 1970s, second-wave feminism transformed the field of women's history nationally at the same time that the "new social history" pushed scholars toward greater inclusivity. Nationwide, many archivists made it their mission to acquire manuscript collections pertaining to women and organized archival holdings to feature women's history. As universities in the late 1970s and 1980s began to develop training in women's history and offered programs in women's studies, scholarship on women in such fields as sociology, anthropology, and psychology inspired historians to take in a broad array of social science techniques to uncover the nearly hidden world of women's history. As a body of published scholarship began to emerge, the field followed a trajectory of discovery, analysis, and reinterpretation that was replicated in the subfield of Texas women's history. Scholars have identified these interpretive frameworks as "compensatory history," or the discovery of important women and their activities, and "contribution history," which followed as historians began to weigh the importance of women's organizations and their impact on their communities and on national politics.

Nationally, women's history quickly matured beyond these frameworks, adding to its complexity. The overarching questions now include the social construction of gender, the ongoing challenges to the notion that all women maintained separate spheres from men, and the explanation of women's multiple identities based on race, class, and other variables; these questions slowly appeared in the subfield of Texas women's history. The new scholarship has generally placed women on a continuum, with women having less power than men but some women having far greater access to society's traditionally construed rewards than others. The history of women of all social classes and of African American, Asian American, Mexican American, and Native American women has blossomed as scholars are intent on discovering new material and on removing barriers. The move toward a more theoretical evaluation of women's history led to discussions of gender and society's constructs of what constitutes masculinity and femininity. Without understanding the roots of societal prescriptions for women and men, the history of women was in danger of remaining a descriptive venture of lives lived, obstacles overcome (or not), and full equality between the sexes unrealized. Gender analysis studies included a better understanding of the relationship between society and women and between men and women in historical context, which not only added to the growing accumulation of published works in women's history but also brought yet another layer of complexity to the field.

As the field of women's history took root throughout the United States in the 1970s and 1980s, Texas historians tentatively followed the lead. A series of early works were of the "recovery" variety, pointing out that women have existed in various aspects of life in the Lone Star State, telling their stories with little context or analysis. Indeed, a number of the books were collections of biographical essays of prominent women and thus were not much different from the "famous women" biographies of the pre-second-wave feminism years.[4]

Alongside national developments were local ones. Perhaps the most significant was the creation of the Texas Women's History Project of the Texas Foundation for Women's Resources. The project included a 1981 exhibit, *Texas Women: A Celebration of History*, with an accompanying book of the same title and a bibliography.[5] Another indication of the field's growth was a bibliographic essay, "Women in Texas History," by Ann Patton Malone. The twelve-page essay, the eleventh and last in *A Guide to the History of Texas* (1988), presented titles of hundreds of articles, autobiographies, and nonscholarly books published as early as 1838. The Texas State Historical Association also gave women's history a boost with a short-lived emphasis for the revised edition of the *Handbook of Texas*, sponsoring a 1990 conference, Women and Texas History. The conference, with thirty-two paper sessions and a keynote by historian Elizabeth Fox-Genovese, resulted in *Women and Texas History: Selected Essays* (1993). The thirteen essays, clustered around the general themes of reform, work, and literature, comprised the first collection written by a group of professionally trained historians.[6]

In 1991, more than a decade before the University of Georgia Press began its influential series Southern Women: Their Lives and Times, Fane Downs wrote a historiographical essay, "Texas Women: History at the Edges," optimistically observing that "the academic exile of women's history is ending."[7] In 1992, the Texas State Historical Association, with funding from Ellen Clarke Temple, created the Liz Carpenter Award for the best scholarly book on Texas women's history, testifying to the growing interest and vibrancy of the field.

The influence of both local history and national trends has meant that as Texas women's history expanded after 1990, it followed predictable lines. The periods that we know the most for Texas women have mirrored the interests of Texas historians and women's historians in general. From the former, the field has gained new perspectives on those pioneering women of the antebellum and Civil War eras; the latter group has focused heavily on a period in which women gained influence through the reform movements of the turn of the twentieth century. Investigations of Texas women have reshaped the understanding of those eras, however, and have often had an impact on the study of topics outside them.

Spanish colonial and borderlands studies have thrived in Texas in recent years, and women's history is an integral part of that intellectual vibrancy. Perhaps the best example of Texas women's historians breaking new ground and consequently helping to transform the narrative of Texas's past is Juliana Barr's much-heralded *Peace Came in the Form of a Woman: Indians and Spaniards in the Texas Borderlands* (2007). Barr argues that "Native American constructions of social order and of political and economic relationships—defined by gendered terms of kinship—were at the crux of Spanish-Indian politics in eighteenth-century Texas."[8] She looks at the interactions among the Caddos, Spanish, French, and Apaches and the role that gender played in that diplomacy.

In *Hers, His, and Theirs: Community Property Law in Spain and Early Texas* (2005), Jean A. Stuntz uses her legal training to illuminate the influence of Spanish law on the legal rights of women in Spanish Texas and through statehood, in contrast to the limited rights under English common law. Patricia Garza de León and three generations of her family are the focus of Ana Carolina Castillo Crimm's *De León: A Tejano Family History* (2004). Patricia de León played an active role in the family's immigration from Mexico and settlement of the town of Victoria.[9]

The transitional period between Mexican independence and the end of the Civil War has also received good scholarly attention. Mary Scheer edited *Women and the Texas Revolution* (2012), eight essays that examine women's roles both in groups and as individuals during Texas's war with Mexico. Mark Carroll's *Homesteads Ungovernable: Families, Sex, Race, and the Law in Frontier Texas, 1826–1860* (2001), uses the body of law evolving in the rich Texas culture to examine power in families and between households and the states. Adrienne Caughfield, *True Women and Westward Expansion* (2005), examines the transmission of domesticity to Texas as women immigrated; Anglo women benefited from Manifest Destiny, while Indians, Tejanas and African American women almost always suffered from it. Biographies such as Paula Mitchell Marks's *Turn Your Eyes toward Texas: Texas Pioneers Sam and Mary Maverick* (2001), and Light Cummins's study of Emily Austin add excellent personal dimensions to the antebellum period. Angela Boswell considers the roles of women in Colorado County in the middle of the nineteenth century in *Her Act and Deed: Women's Lives in a Rural Southern County, 1837–1873* (2001), finding that "southern ideals regarding women took root in and pervaded Colorado County's society and laws" for both slave and free women, largely unchanged by the Civil War.[10]

In the second half of the nineteenth century, Texas became more diverse with immigrants from Eastern Europe and from other parts of the United States. Several writers have investigated the significance of ethnicity on the lives of Texas women. Charles H. Russell, *Undaunted: A Norwegian Woman in Frontier Texas* (2006), writes of Elise Waerenskjold, who immigrated to Texas from

Norway in 1847, eventually settling in Van Zandt County. Waerenskjold advocated immigration and maintained a lively correspondence until her death in
1895. Family life in South Texas is the focus of *Petra's Legacy: The South Texas
Ranching Empire of Petra Vela and Mifflin Kenedy* (2007), by Jane Clements
Monday and Frances Brannen Vick. Petra Vela de Vidal married into one of
Texas's premier ranching families and raised eight children in a sprawling, multicultural home.[11] Ruthe Winegarten, Janet G. Humphrey, and Frieda Weirden
provided a broad overview of African American women's lives in *Black Texas
Women: 150 Years of Trial and Triumph* (1995), while Winegarten and Marc
Sanders narrowed the focus to one location in *The Lives and Times of Black
Dallas Women* (2002). Merline Pitre and Bruce Glasrud edited *Black Women
and Texas History* (2008), a collection of nine chronological essays from slavery
to the year 2000. Winegarten and Teresa Palomo Acosta provided a similar
overview for Hispanic women across the state in *Las Tejanas: 300 Years of History* (2003).[12]

In the field of American women's history, reform during the Progressive
period has been an excellent topic for study, and Texas is no exception, with
several sophisticated volumes. In *Women, Culture, and Community: Religion
and Reform in Galveston, 1880–1920* (1997), Elizabeth Hayes Turner documents
how women became committed to founding public organizations, focusing on
the role of religion, class, and race on women's activities and the consequences
of women's civic activism. Judith N. McArthur's *Creating the New Woman: The
Rise of Southern Women's Progressive Culture in Texas, 1893–1918* (1998) traces
female-inspired efforts to restrict child labor, reform juvenile justice, protect
the labor supply, secure minimum wage and maximum hour legislation for employed women, establish settlement houses, and abolish red-light districts. In
Pauline Periwinkle and Progressive Reform in Dallas (1998), Jacquelyn Masur
McElhaney depicts the life of *Dallas Morning News* journalist Isadore Miner
Callaway (aka Pauline Periwinkle), editor of the "Woman's Century" pages.
Callaway encouraged club work and crusaded for libraries, playgrounds, juve-
nile courts, and food purity.[13]

Studies of woman suffrage and politics followed the significant work on the
Progressive era. The earliest example came from A. Elizabeth Taylor, who pub-
lished a pathbreaking article in the *Journal of Southern History*, "The Woman
Suffrage Movement in Texas" (1951). The suffrage movement opened the doors
for Texas women officeholders, and Debbie Mauldin Cottrell documented the
reform career of the first woman elected to the Texas legislature in *Pioneer
Woman Educator: The Progressive Spirit of Annie Webb Blanton* (1993). No other
Progressive era woman held more esteem than Minnie Fisher Cunningham,

president of the Texas Equal Suffrage Association, and Judith N. McArthur and Harold L. Smith take a sophisticated look at this woman in politics in *Minnie Fisher Cunningham: A Suffragist's Life in Politics* (2003), which examines the career of the Democratic activist and candidate. Kelley M. King explores the life of a similar figure and rival, Anna Pennybacker, in *Call Her a Citizen: Progressive-Era Activist and Educator Anna Pennybacker* (2010).[14] In *Capitol Women: Texas Female Legislators, 1923–1999* (2000), Ruthe Winegarten and Nancy Baker Jones recount the progress of women officeholders through eighty-six short biographies of women in the Texas legislature before 2000. No serious study of Miriam Ferguson exists, but two biographies have been devoted to Ann Richards: *Claytie and the Lady: Ann Richards, Gender, and Politics in Texas* (1994), written by Sue Tolleson-Rinehart and Jeanie Ricketts Stanley three years after Richards's gubernatorial election; and Jan Reid, *Let the People In: The Life and Times of Ann Richards* (2012).[15] The turbulent period of the 1970s also remains underdocumented, save for the work of Nancy Baker excerpted in this volume.

Women also entered the public life of Texas in a variety of other ways. In *Women and the Creation of Urban Life: Dallas, Texas, 1843–1920* (1998), Elizabeth York Enstam traces women's roles in establishing the social and cultural infrastructure, economy, and public institutions of Dallas. The Woman's Commonwealth, a celibate woman's religious order in Belton, is the topic of Sally L. Kitch's *This Strange Society of Women: Reading the Letters and Lives of the Woman's Commonwealth* (1992). She argues that the Sanctificationists, as the group was also called, achieved identities as independent and self-reliant women because their religious motivations were unassailable and because their prosperity promoted the town's interests." Betty Holland Wiesepape found that women had been meeting to read, discuss, and write literature in Texas since the 1850s, and in *Lone Star Chapters: The Story of Texas Literary Clubs* (2004), she argues that literary clubs played a more important role in developing regional writing than had previously been acknowledged.[16]

Women and work have long been among the subjects of great interest to women's historians, and Paula Mitchell Marks's *Hands to the Spindle: Texas Women and Home Textile Production, 1822–1880* (1996) investigates women's hardworking roles as subsistence farmers in the nineteenth century. In *Fertile Ground, Narrow Choices: Women on Texas Cotton Farms, 1900–1940* (1999), Rebecca Sharpless details the work of twentieth-century sharecropping and landowning women in the Blackland Prairie region. Women in the ranching and cattle industry after the Civil War are the subject of the sixteen essays in *Texas Women on the Cattle Trails* (2006), edited by Sara R. Massey. The experiences of the women varied, as some women merely accompanied family members, while others actually trailed their own cattle. Julia Kirk Blackwelder redeveloped the study of women in the public workforce with *Women of the Depression: Caste and Culture in San Antonio, 1929–1939* (1984), which focuses on Mexican, black, and Anglo women, particularly in the pecan industry, where Mexican American women comprised the bulk of the shellers in the Alamo City. Blackwelder followed up with a study of Houston beauty operators in *Styling Jim Crow: African American Beauty Training during Segregation* (2004).[17]

While the civil rights movement in Texas has received healthy scholarly interest, only two monographs explain in greater detail the roles of women. Merline Pitre's *Struggle against Jim Crow: Lulu B. White and the NAACP, 1900–1957* (1999), analyzes the life of Houston activist Lulu B. White, the head of the Houston NAACP who was instrumental in two key U.S. Supreme Court cases. In *No Mexicans, Women, or Dogs Allowed: The Rise of the Mexican American Civil Rights Movement* (2009), Cynthia Orozco uses gender as one of the topics for examining the leaders and members of the movement in Texas.[18]

Clearly, *Texas Women: Their Histories, Their Lives* could not possibly fill all the gaps that need filling in Texas women's history, and a host of topics remain to be researched. A growing number of articles, master's theses, and doctoral dissertations attest to the continued interest in Texas women's history. Barr's work on Apache, Caddo, and Comanche women represents simply the tip of the iceberg of Native American women's history. Yet to be written are full-length studies of women in each of Texas's major Native economic groups—hunters, horticulturalists, and pastoralists. Such studies would be particularly valuable if they took a community or regional perspective, examining Indian women as a part of multicultural communities and conflicts. Research on antebellum local communities and networks of women could help shed light on slaveholding women, an area in which much work remains to be done. Light Cummins's biography of Emily Austin provides a glimpse into the refined planter world supported on the backs of enslaved men and women, but nonbiographical approaches, perhaps focusing on life-cycle periods of childhood, marriage, spinsterhood, and widowhood, would add much to our knowledge of Texas history and southern women's history. Eric Walther's essay in this volume suggests the future of work on those in bondage and presents a tantalizing entrée into the world of female slaves, but further Texas-based studies would benefit from a transnational or comparative perspective.

Another field open to investigation is that of Texas women's experiences during the Civil War. Men, women, and their families on the frontier, particularly in northern counties, found themselves torn between supporting the Confederacy and protecting their own farms, a concern played out across the South by yeoman farm families. For North Texans, however, wives faced the very real danger of protecting the homestead against Indian raids. Some female-headed families moved to the outlying forts for safety, becoming refugees and burdens on the overtaxed Texas militia. Likewise, Indian women also sought refuge in the forts. There is little information about how these women fared. Those families without male protection who were attacked by Comanche or Kiowa tribes encountered the very real possibility of capture and enslavement. Researching the lives of women living on the margins of the state, supporting one war while fighting another at home, is a rich vein for scholars to pursue.

In the aftermath of the war, as "Gone to Texas" became a mantra among migrants from other states, especially in the South, Texas drew the land-hungry to its rich prairies. Ranching empires, already developed out of the bountiful early colonies, symbolized for newcomers the possibilities of prosperity. Mary Ann (Molly) Dyer Goodnight and Cornelia Adair have been the subject of various articles and sketches, but they merit full-length biographies as ranching/trail-riding women, and other women in the ranching culture also await fuller treatment.[19] More studies of postwar rural women await scholars' full integration into the Texas landscape. Along the same lines, a history of women émigrés and their experience in migrating and assimilating to Texas climes also stands out as a potential subject to complement Barbara J. Rozek's *Come to Texas: Enticing Immigrants, 1865–1915* (2003).[20]

Twentieth-century Texas women provide the subject for a recent book of documents and analysis by Judith N. McArthur and Harold L. Smith, *Texas Through Women's Eyes: The Twentieth-Century Experience* (2010). Here one can find the richest of treasures on women's lives in modern times, yet many of these topics await further exploration. Issues involving women's education, politics, labor (including sex occupations), civil and ethnic rights, race and gender equality, second-wave feminism, and reproductive rights are clearly explained, with documents filling in the greater details—a guide of sorts to future research projects.[21] The time period of research perhaps most in need of exploration is the Great Depression and the effects of the New Deal on women's lives. Sharpless's *Fertile Ground, Narrow Choices* covers 1900 through the 1930s and begs for a companion piece on women in cities or in New Deal agencies such as the Works Progress Administration or the National Youth Administration. Blackwelder's *Women of the Depression* provides a model for interpretation of women's conditions in urban areas according to ethnicity, class, and occupation.

Other topics that need expanding include histories of conservative women in the Democratic Party such as Miriam A. Ferguson, who served as governor twice between 1924 and 1936. In the 1950s, when Republicans began gaining ground in Texas, women initiated party gatherings, held fund-raisers, and organized supporters. There is work to be done to discover what motivated conservative women to bring two-party politics to Texas, especially given the ascendancy of conservative women in grassroots state and national political causes after 1980.[22]

Likewise, businesswomen such as Mary Kay Ash, founder of Mary Kay, one of the nation's largest cosmetic companies, are also waiting to be discovered and have their histories written. Other notables in this arena include Bette Graham, the inventor of Liquid Paper, and real estate agents Ebby Halliday in Dallas and Martha Turner in Houston. Just as Bianca Mercado's essay in this volume explores Mexican American women in Dallas who built businesses based on food preparation, other scholars have the opportunity to explore the history of enterprising women such as Ninnie Baird, who used her domestic skills to found Mrs Baird's Breads in Fort Worth in 1908. She expanded her business first to bakeries in Dallas and Houston and after World War II to other major cities in the state.

Texas's women mayors have included Kathy Whitmire and Annise Parker (Houston), Annette Strauss and Laura Miller (Dallas), Lila Cockrell (San Antonio), and Carole Keeton Strayhorn (Austin). These women and others who have been politically active at the state level merit fuller biographies, and the scholarship would benefit from a larger history of women's entry into politics during the turbulent late 1960s and early 1970s. One woman legislator in special need of attention in this period is Frances Farenthold, elected to the Texas House of Representatives in 1968 and a champion of the Texas Equal Legal Rights Amendment, which was ultimately ratified in 1972. Then she mounted an unsuccessful challenge to Dolph Briscoe for the governorship in 1972 and 1974. Another notable figure, Senfronia Thompson, has served longer in the Texas House than any other woman and longer than any African American. She has sponsored and overseen the passage of more than three hundred bills, most of them supporting women, children, and the elderly and or prohibiting racial profiling. Alongside these and other women state and national legislators, another Texas icon, political pundit Molly Ivins, author of hundreds of articles and seven books, deserves a scholarly biography written by a historian. The same is true for Sarah Weddington, who took abortion rights to the U.S. Supreme Court in *Roe v. Wade* (1973), and for Lady Bird Johnson, who was very much a public persona. Students of history also might well ask about the impact of the Voting Rights Act of 1965 and the implementation of Title VII of the 1964 Civil Rights Act on female entry into male-dominated businesses and political landscapes.

Much work remains to be done in understanding the history of working women. Viewed through the lens of historical change over time, professional women, including those who have worked in the oil patch as engineers and scientists as well as professors, doctors, dentists, attorneys, and public or private schoolteachers, would provide a template for understanding the advancement of women into professional roles as well as challenge the strictures of the still-extant glass ceiling. Histories of laboring women and their unions provide another open field for investigation, particularly when combined with ethnicity. Emma Tenayuca, who inspired workers during the 1938 pecan shellers' strike in San Antonio, is only one such notable labor leader. Researchers should also consider Mary Salinas's life and her leadership role in desegregating the meat-packing industry in Fort Worth as president of the local branch of the United Packinghouse Workers of America in 1954. Contextualizing the activities of working women within the era of civil rights initiatives of the 1950s and 1960s is another promising avenue of investigation. Students of history should question the impact of the civil rights laws on unionism, the *Brown v. Board of Education* decision on women teachers in public schools, or the women's liberation movement on working musicians such as Janis Joplin and others whose countercultural lyrics echoed the refrains of a liberation-seeking generation.

Finally, given that Texas has swung back and forth between progressive and conservative forces, scholars should inquire further about the women's movement's adherents and their reactionary opponents. The National Women's Conference in Houston in 1977 epitomized the conflict between left-leaning women and conservative objectors to the conference's stated goals. Three presidents' wives, including Lady Bird Johnson, and thousands of delegates endorsed a fairly liberal agenda for advancing women's rights, and they prevailed but were opposed by busloads of women from evangelical churches whose male pastors insisted they attend the meeting. These women and others brought into question the legitimacy of the Equal Rights Amendment (ERA), acceptance of homosexuality, reproductive rights, abortion, and funding for Planned Parenthood, which opened its first clinic in Dallas in 1935. The conference played a critical role in the conservative resurgence in U.S. politics, and Texas women such as Dianne Thompson, who later became president of the National Federation of Republican Women, helped to spearhead the (unsuccessful) movement to rescind Texas's ratification of the ERA. Another conservative woman with both state and national influence is Susan Weddington, who was the first woman to chair a state Republican Party when she led the Texas GOP from 1997 to 2004. Weddington, Thompson, and others led the party to adopt what was among the nation's most conservative party platforms, one that questions many of the causes with which women activists have long been associated—birth control, public education, and civil rights.

Indeed, the rise of the Religious Right and women's roles in its ascendancy are topics that need a scholarly hand, as is the question of why the Parent-Teacher Association, which originated as the National Congress of Mothers at the turn of the twentieth century, became hostile to the women's movement. Moreover, there is the question of the role of religion in motivating change. In the Progressive era, evangelical women and women from nonfundamentalist denominations promoted Prohibition, seen today as a conservative movement but considered progressive at the time, and took on such problems as municipal housekeeping, age-of-consent laws for girls, child labor reform, and women's right to vote. Yet by the 1970s and 1980s, evangelical women lined up to create such organizations as Women Who Want to Be Women, the Committee to Restore Women's Rights, and Happiness of Womanhood and to urge that Texas rescind its 1972 ratification of the ERA. Why this change? And why did other Texas women's groups, such as the American Association of University Women, the National Organization for Women, and Texas Women's Political Caucus, support the ERA and other progressive women's goals?

This particular debate between progressive and conservative women had— and still has—important implications for the progress of equal rights for gays and lesbians in Texas, an area of scholarship that is beginning to be researched. Before the AIDS crisis of the 1980s, gay men and lesbian women often did not find common cause, and in fact male discrimination against lesbians was as apparent in the "gayborhood" as it was in heterosexual society. When the AIDS epidemic struck, gay men, already ostracized from polite society, became demonized as dangerous to the public, and because little was known about how to stop the advance of the disease, health care was inadequate and sometimes refused. To ameliorate the crisis in Dallas and other cities, lesbian women mounted campaigns to help the very ill, nursed those who were not admitted to hospitals, and provided a caring environment for the dying. As medical treatments improved, the men did not forget those charitable acts and united in common cause as a lesbian/gay/bisexual/transgender community, seeking equality in the workplace, the right to marry, and other legal protections denied gays and lesbians.[23]

Texas's early advantage in women's history no longer holds, as both southern and western history have proven enormously productive in recent years. The scholarly histories of Texas women now continue to evolve alongside the fields of southern, western, and U.S. women's history. The picture of a vibrant field, now more than forty years old, is reflected on every page of this volume.

NOTES

1. This essay focuses on monographs, though it occasionally refers to recent dissertations. Readers interested in a particular topic are encouraged to consult guides to journals and to theses and dissertations to uncover further works.

2. Annie Doom Pickrell, *Pioneer Women of Texas* (Buffalo Gap, Tex.: Statehouse, 1991); Kate Adele Hill, *Home Builders of West Texas* (San Antonio: Naylor, 1970). Bibliographic essays on Texas women include Ann Patton Malone, "Women in Texas History," in *A Guide to Texas History*, ed. Light Townsend Cummins and Alvin R. Bailey Jr. (New York: Greenwood, 1988), 123–36; Fane Downs, "Texas Women: History at the Edges," in *Texas through Time: Evolving Interpretations*, ed. Walter L. Buenger and Robert A. Calvert (College Station: Texas A&M University Press, 1991), 81–101.

3. Vance Randolph, *Wildcats in Petticoats: A Garland of Female Desperadoes, Lizzie Merton, Zoe Wilkins, Flora Quick Mundis, Bonnie Parker, Kate Bender, and Belle Star* (Gerard, Kans.: Haldeman-Julius, 1945); Theresa Moore Hunter, *Romantic Interludes: Love Stories of Texas Heroes* (San Antonio: Naylor, 1936).

4. Notable early examples include Evelyn Carrington, *Women in Early Texas* (Austin: Jenkins, 1975); Mary D. Farrell and Elizabeth Silverthorne, *First Ladies of Texas: The First One Hundred Years, 1836–1936, a History* (Belton, Tex.: Stillhouse Hollow, 1976); Francis Abernethy, *Legendary Ladies of Texas* (Dallas: E-Heart, 1981); Ann Fears Crawford and Crystal Sasse Ragsdale, *Women in Texas: Their Lives, Their Experiences, Their Accomplishments* (Burnet, Tex.: Eakin, 1982).

5. Nancy Baker Jones, foreword to *Women and Texas History: Selected Essays*, ed. Fane Downs and Nancy Baker Jones (Austin: Texas State Historical Association, 1993), viii; Ruthe Winegarten and Mary Beth Rogers, *Texas Women's History Project Bibliography* (Austin: Texas Foundation for Women's Resources, 1980); Mary Beth Rogers, *Texas Women: A Celebration of History* (Austin: Texas Foundation for Women's Resources, 1981). The project also published a biographical anthology: Mary Beth Rogers, Sherrie A. Smith, and Janelle D. Scott, *We Can Fly: Stories of Katherine Stinson and Other Gutsy Texas Women* (Austin: Temple and Texas Foundation for Women's Resources, 1983).

6. Malone, "Women in Texas History," 123–36; Downs and Jones, *Women and Texas History*.

7. Downs, "Texas Women," 100.

8. Juliana Barr, *Peace Came in the Form of a Woman: Indians and Spaniards in the Texas Borderlands* (Chapel Hill: University of North Carolina Press, 2007), 2.

9. Jean A. Stuntz, *Hers, His, and Theirs: Community Property Law in Spain and Early Texas* (Lubbock: Texas Tech University Press, 2005); Ana Carolina Castillo Crimm, *De León: A Tejano Family History* (Austin: University of Texas Press, 2004).

10. Mary L. Scheer, ed., *Women and the Texas Revolution* (Denton: University of North Texas Press, 2012); Mark Carroll, *Homesteads Ungovernable: Families, Sex, Race, and the Law in Frontier Texas, 1826–1860* (Austin: University of Texas Press, 2001); Adrienne Caughfield, *True Women and Westward Expansion* (College Station: Texas A&M University Press, 2005); Paula Mitchell Marks, *Turn Your Eyes toward Texas: Texas Pioneers Sam and Mary Maverick* (Austin: University of Texas Press, 2001); Light Townsend Cummins, *Emily Austin of Texas, 1795–1851* (Fort Worth: Texas Christian University Press, 2009); Angela Boswell, *Her Act and Deed: Women's Lives in a Rural Southern County, 1837–1873* (College Station: Texas A&M University Press, 2001), 10.

11. Charles H. Russell, *Undaunted: A Norwegian Woman in Frontier Texas* (College Station: Texas A&M University Press, 2006); Jane Clements Monday and Francs Brannen Vick, *Petra's Legacy:*

The South Texas Ranching Empire of Petra Vela and Mifflin Kenedy (College Station: Texas A&M University Press, 2007).

12. Ruthe Winegarten, Janet G. Humphrey, and Frieda Weirden, *Black Texas Women: 150 Years of Trial and Triumph* (Austin: University of Texas Press, 1995); Ruthe Winegarten and Marc Sanders, *The Lives and Times of Black Dallas Women* (Austin: Eakin, 2002); Merline Pitre and Bruce Glasrud, eds., *Black Women and Texas History* (College Station: Texas A&M University Press, 2008); Ruthe Winegarten and Teresa Palomo Acosta, *Las Tejanas: Three Hundred Years of History* (Austin: University of Texas Press, 2003).

13. Elizabeth Hayes Turner, *Women, Culture, and Community: Religion and Reform in Galveston, 1880–1920* (New York: Oxford University Press, 1997); Judith N. McArthur, *Creating the New Woman: The Rise of Southern Women's Progressive Culture in Texas, 1893–1918* (Urbana: University of Illinois Press, 1998); Jacquelyn Masur McElhaney, *Pauline Periwinkle and Progressive Reform in Dallas* (College Station: Texas A&M University Press, 1998). For another study of women in religious organizations, see Pat Martin, "Hidden Work: Baptist Women in Texas, 1880–1920" (PhD diss. Rice University, 1982). http://alexandria.rice.edu/uhtbin/cgisirsi/YM4NltMkCl/FON DREN/227860056/9.

14. A. Elizabeth Taylor, "The Woman Suffrage Movement in Texas," *Journal of Southern History* 17 (May 1951): 194–215, reprinted with documents as *Citizens at Last: The Woman Suffrage Movement in Texas* (Austin: Temple, 1987); Debbie Mauldin Cottrell, *Pioneer Woman Educator: The Progressive Spirit of Annie Webb Blanton* (College Station: Texas A&M University Press, 1993); Judith N. McArthur and Harold L. Smith, *Minnie Fisher Cunningham: A Suffragist's Life in Politics* (New York: Oxford University Press, 2003); Kelley M. King, *Call Her a Citizen: Progressive-Era Activist and Educator Anna Pennybacker* (College Station: Texas A&M University Press, 2010).

15. Ruthe Winegarten and Nancy Baker Jones, *Capitol Women: Texas Female Legislators, 1923–1999* (Austin: University of Texas Press, 2000); Sue Tolleson-Rinehart and Jeanie Ricketts Stanley, *Claytie and the Lady: Ann Richards, Gender, and Politics in Texas* (Austin: University of Texas Press, 1994); Jan Reid, *Let the People In: The Life and Times of Ann Richards* (Austin: University of Texas Press, 2012).

16. Elizabeth York Enstam, *Women and the Creation of Urban Life: Dallas, Texas, 1843–1920* (College Station: Texas A&M University Press, 1998); Sally L. Kitch, *This Strange Society of Women: Reading the Letters and Lives of the Woman's Commonwealth* (Columbus: Ohio State University Press, 1992), 18; Betty Holland Wiesepape, *Lone Star Chapters: The Story of Texas Literary Clubs* (College Station: Texas A&M University Press, 2004).

17. Paula Mitchell Marks, *Hands to the Spindle: Texas Women and Home Textile Production, 1822–1880* (College Station: Texas A&M University Press, 1996). Rebecca Sharpless, *Fertile Ground, Narrow Choices: Women on Texas Cotton Farms, 1900–1940* (Chapel Hill: University of North Carolina Press, 1999); Sara R. Massey, ed., *Texas Women on the Cattle Trails* (College Station: Texas A&M University Press, 2006); Julia Kirk Blackwelder, *Women of the Depression: Caste and Culture in San Antonio, 1929–1939* (College Station: Texas A&M University Press, 1984); Julia Kirk Blackwelder, *Styling Jim Crow: African American Beauty Training during Segregation* (College Station: Texas A&M University Press, 2004).

18. Merline Pitre, *Struggle against Jim Crow: Lulu B. White and the NAACP, 1900–1957* (College Station: Texas A&M University Press, 1999); Cynthia Orozco, *No Mexicans, Women, or Dogs Allowed: The Rise of the Mexican American Civil Rights Movement* (Austin: University of Texas Press, 2009).

19. Massey, *Texas Women*.

20. Barbara J. Rozek, *Come to Texas: Enticing Immigrants, 1865–1915* (College Station: Texas A&M University Press, 2003).

21. Judith N. McArthur and Harold L. Smith, *Texas through Women's Eyes: The Twentieth-Century Experience* (Austin: University of Texas Press, 2010).

22. See Meg McKain Grier, *Grassroots Women: A Memoir of the Texas Republican Party* (Boerne, Tex.: Wingscape, 2001).

23. Karen S. Wisely, "The Dallas Way in the Gayborhood: The Beginnings of a Gay and Lesbian Community in Dallas, 1965–1986" (master's thesis, University of North Texas, 2011).

Contributors

NANCY E. BAKER is assistant professor of history at Sam Houston State University. She is the author of *Unequaled: Rescission and the Equal Rights Amendment* (forthcoming), *Texas Feminism between and beyond the Waves* (forthcoming), and "Focus on the Family: Twentieth-Century Conservative Texas Women and the Lone Star Right," in *The Texas Right: The Radical Roots of Lone Star Conservatism* (2014). Baker received her PhD in U.S. history from Harvard University in 2003.

JULIANA BARR is associate professor of history at the University of Florida. She is the author of *Peace Came in the Form of a Woman: Indians and Spaniards in the Texas Borderlands* (2007), which won awards from the Southern Historical Association, the Berkshire Conference of Women Historians, and the Texas State Historical Association. She received her PhD from the Program in the History of Women at the University of Wisconsin at Madison in 1999.

ANGELA BOSWELL is professor of history at Henderson State University in Arkadelphia, Arkansas. She is the author of *Her Act and Deed: Women's Lives in a Rural Southern County, 1837–1873* (2001), which won the Liz Carpenter Award from the Texas State Historical Association, and coeditor of *Women Shaping the South: Creating and Confronting Change* (2006). Boswell earned her PhD in U.S. history from Rice University in 1998.

JESSICA BRANNON-WRANOSKY is assistant professor of history at Texas A&M University–Commerce. She is the author of "Investing in Urban: The Connected Growth of the Woman's Monday Club and the Entrepreneurial Elite of Corpus Christi, Texas," in *This Corner of Canaan: Essays on Texas in Honor of Randolph B. Campbell* (2013), and of "Reformers, Populists, and Progressives: Texas between Reconstruction and the Roaring Twenties, 1875–1920," in *Discovering Texas History* (forthcoming). She is the digital media author for *Give Me Liberty: An American History* (2013, 2014). She received her PhD in U.S. history from the University of North Texas in 2010.

STEPHANIE COLE is associate professor of history at the University of Texas at Arlington. She is the author of "Finding Race in Turn-of-the-Century Dallas," in *Beyond Black and White: Race, Ethnicity, and Gender in the U.S. South and Southwest* (2001), which she co-edited, and "'Neither Matron nor Maid': Gender, Race, Class, and Marriage in Jim Crow

Texas," in *Honoring a Master: Essays in Honor of Bertram Wyatt-Brown* (2011). She is the coeditor of *The Folly of Jim Crow: Rethinking the Segregated South* (2012). Cole received her PhD in U.S. history from the University of Florida in 1994.

LIGHT T. CUMMINS is the Guy M. Bryan Jr. Professor of History at Austin College and was the official state historian of Texas from 2009 to 2012. He is the author of *Spanish Observers and the American Revolution, 1775–1783* (1992), *Louisiana: A History* (7th ed., 2014), and *Emily Austin of Texas 1795–1851* (2009), which won the Liz Carpenter Award from the Texas State Historical Association. He received his PhD in U.S. history from Tulane University in 1977.

VICTORIA H. CUMMINS is professor of history at Austin College. She is the coauthor of "Building on Bolton: *The Spanish Borderlands* Seventy-Five Years Later," *Latin American Research Review* (2000). She received her PhD in Latin American history from Tulane University in 1979.

MARY ELLEN CURTIN is assistant professor of history at American University in Washington, D.C. She is the author of *Black Prisoners and Their World, Alabama, 1865–1900* (2000) and of a forthcoming biography of Barbara Jordan. Curtin received her PhD in U.S. history from Duke University in 1992.

W. MARVIN DULANEY is associate professor of history and chair of the Department of History at the University of Texas at Arlington. He is the author of *Black Police in America* (1996); "Women in the South Carolina Civil Rights Movement," in *Southern Black Women in the Modern Civil Rights Movement* (2013); "'We Still Love Lucy': Lucy Patterson, Dallas's First African American Councilwoman," *Legacies* (2013); and "Documenting the Life and Legacy of Malcolm X," *Journal of African American History* (2013). He received his PhD in U.S. history from Ohio State University in 1984.

GABRIELA GONZÁLEZ is associate professor of history at the University of Texas at San Antonio. She is the author of *Redeeming La Raza: Transborder Modernity, Race, Respectability, and Rights* (forthcoming) and "Carolina Munguía and Emma Tenayuca: The Politics of Benevolence and Radical Reform, 1930s," *Frontiers* (2004). She received her PhD in U.S. history from Stanford University in 2005.

RUTH HOSEY KARBACH is an independent scholar living in Fort Worth. She contributed two chapters to *Grace and Gumption: Stories of Fort Worth Women* (2007), "Duchesses with Hearts of Love and Brains of Fire" and "The Modern Woman," as well as one chapter, "Dining, Decorating, and Dieting with the Modern Woman," to *Grace and Gumption: The Cookbook* (2007). A graduate of the University of Texas at Arlington in 1968 with a bachelor's degree in sociology, she pursued graduate studies in criminology at Sam Houston State University.

RENEE M. LAEGREID is associate professor of history at the University of Wyoming. She is the author of *Riding Pretty: Rodeo Royalty in the American West* (2006) and is coeditor of *Women on the North American Plains* (2006). She received her PhD in U.S. history from the University of Nebraska in 2002.

PAULA MITCHELL MARKS is professor of American studies in the New College and Master of Liberal Arts Programs at St. Edward's University. She is the author of *Turn Your Eyes toward Texas: Pioneers Sam and Mary Maverick* (1989), which received the T. R. Fehrenbach Award from the Texas Historical Commission and the Kate Broocks Bates Award from the Texas State Historical Association; and *Hands to the Spindle: Texas Frontier Women and Home Textile Production* (1996), which won the Liz Carpenter Award from the Texas State Historical Association. She received her PhD in American civilization from the University of Texas at Austin in 1978.

JUDITH N. MCARTHUR is lecturer in history at the University of Houston–Victoria. She is the author of *Creating the New Woman: The Rise of Southern Woman's Progressive Culture in Texas, 1893–1918* (1998); coauthor of *Minnie Fisher Cunningham: A Suffragist's Life in Politics* (2003), winner of the Liz Carpenter Award from the Texas State Historical Association and the T. R. Fehrenbach Award from the Texas Historical Commission; and coauthor of *Texas through Women's Eyes: The Twentieth-Century Experience* (2010), also winner of the Liz Carpenter Award. She received her PhD in U.S. history from the University of Texas at Austin in 1992.

LAURA LYONS MCLEMORE is head archivist at Louisiana State University at Shreveport. She is the author of *Inventing Texas: Early Historians of the Lone Star State* (2004) and "Early Historians and the Shaping of Texas Memory," in *Lone Star Pasts: Memory and History in Texas* (2007), and she is currently working on a biography of Adele Briscoe Looscan. She received her PhD in U.S. history from the University of North Texas in 1998.

BIANCA MERCADO is a PhD candidate at Yale University, completing a dissertation on Mexican communities and urban redevelopment in Dallas. She received her master's degree from the University of North Texas in 2008.

JENNIFER ROSS-NAZZAL is the historian for the NASA Johnson Space Center in Houston. She is the author of *Winning the West for Women: The Life of Emma Smith DeVoe* (2011) and has published numerous articles. She is the author of "You've Come a Long Way, Maybe: The First Six Women Astronauts and the Media," in *Spacefarers: Images of Astronauts and Cosmonauts in the Heroic Era of Spaceflight* (2013). She earned her PhD in U.S. history from Washington State University in 2004.

ROBIN C. SAGER is assistant professor of history at the University of Evansville. She is the coauthor of "Beyond National Borders: Researching and Teaching Jovita González," in *Teaching and Studying the Americas: Engaging Cultural Influences from Colonialism to the Present* (2010). She received her PhD in U.S. history from Rice University in 2012.

REBECCA SHARPLESS is associate professor of history at Texas Christian University. She is the author of *Fertile Ground, Narrow Choices: Women on Texas Cotton Farms, 1900–1940* (1999), which won the Coral Horton Tullis Memorial Prize and the Liz Carpenter Award, both from the Texas State Historical Association, and the T. R. Fehrenbach Award from the Texas Historical Commission; and *Cooking in Other Women's Kitchens: Domestic Workers in the South, 1865–1960* (2010), winner of the Bennett H. Wall Award from the Southern Historical Association. She earned her PhD in American studies from Emory University in 1993.

HAROLD L. SMITH is professor of history at the University of Houston–Victoria, a fellow of the Royal Historical Society of Great Britain, and winner of the Texas State Historical Association's H. Bailey Carroll Award for "'All Good Things Start with the Women': The Origins of the Texas Birth Control Movement, 1933–1945," *Southwestern Historical Quarterly* (2011). He is coauthor of *Texas through Women's Eyes: The Twentieth-Century Experience* (2010), winner of the Liz Carpenter Award from the Texas State Historical Association; and *Minnie Fisher Cunningham: A Suffragist's Life in Politics* (2003), which won the Carpenter Award and the T. R. Fehrenbach Award from the Texas Historical Commission. He is the author of *The British Women's Suffrage Campaign, 1866–1928* (2nd ed., 2007). He received his PhD in British history from the University of Iowa in 1971.

JEAN A. STUNTZ is professor of history at West Texas A&M University. She is the author of *Hers, His, and Theirs: Community Property Law in Spain and Early Texas* (2005), which won the Presidio La Bahia Award from the Sons of the Republic of Texas and the Texas Old Missions and Forts Award from the Texas Catholic Historical Society. She received a law degree from Baylor Law School in 1979 and a PhD in U.S. history from the University of North Texas in 2000.

ELIZABETH HAYES TURNER is University Distinguished Teaching Professor and professor of history at the University of North Texas. She is the author of *Women and Gender in the New South, 1865–1945* (2009) and *Women, Culture, and Community: Religion and Reform in Galveston, 1880–1920* (1997), which won the Coral Horton Tullis Memorial Prize from the Texas State Historical Association; coauthor of *Galveston and the 1900 Storm: Catastrophe and Catalyst* (2000); and coeditor of *Lone Star Pasts: Memory and History in Texas* (2007), winner of the T. R. Fehrenbach Award from the Texas Historical Commission. She received her PhD in U.S. history from Rice University in 1990.

KELLI CARDENAS WALSH is assistant professor of history at Fayetteville State University. She is the author of articles in *African American National Biography* and *Black Women in America: An Historical Encyclopedia*. She received her PhD in U.S. history from the University of South Carolina in 2006.

ERIC WALTHER is professor of history at the University of Houston. He is the author of *The Fire-Eaters* (1992), *Shattering of the Union: America in the 1850s* (2003), and *William Lowndes Yancey and the Coming of the Civil War* (2006), which won the James A. Rawley Award from the Southern Historical Association. He received his PhD in U.S. history from Louisiana State University in 1988.

Index